Business Intelligence Applications and the Web:

Models, Systems and Technologies

Marta E. Zorrilla
University of Cantabria, Spain

Jose-Norberto Mazón
University of Alicante, Spain

Óscar Ferrández
University of Alicante, Spain

Irene Garrigós
University of Alicante, Spain

Florian Daniel
University of Trento, Italy

Juan Trujillo
University of Alicante, Spain

A volume in the Advances in Business
Information Systems and Analytics
(ABISA) Book Series

Senior Editorial Director:	Kristin Klinger
Director of Book Publications:	Julia Mosemann
Editorial Director:	Lindsay Johnston
Acquisitions Editor:	Erika Carter
Development Editor:	Myla Harty
Production Editor:	Sean Woznicki
Typesetters:	Chris Shearer, Milan Vracarich, Jr.
Print Coordinator:	Jamie Snavely
Cover Design:	Nick Newcomer

Published in the United States of America by
Business Science Reference (an imprint of IGI Global)
701 E. Chocolate Avenue
Hershey PA 17033
Tel: 717-533-8845
Fax: 717-533-8661
E-mail: cust@igi-global.com
Web site: http://www.igi-global.com

Library of Congress Cataloging-in-Publication Data

Business intelligence applications and the web: models, systems and technologies / Marta E. Zorrilla ... [et al.] editors.
    p. cm.
  Includes bibliographical references and index.
  ISBN 978-1-61350-038-5 (hardcover) -- ISBN 978-1-61350-039-2 (ebook) -- ISBN 978-1-61350-040-8 (print & perpetual access) 1. Business intelligence. 2. World Wide Web. I. Zorrilla, Marta E., 1971-
  HD38.7.B8716 2011
  658.4'7202854678--dc23
                            2011021833

This book is published in the IGI Global book series Advances in Business Information Systems and Analytics (ABISA) Book Series (ISSN: 2327-3275; eISSN: 2327-3283)

British Cataloguing in Publication Data
A Cataloguing in Publication record for this book is available from the British Library.

Advances in Business Information Systems and Analytics (ABISA) Book Series

Madjid Tavana
La Salle University, USA

ISSN: 2327-3275
EISSN: 2327-3283

MISSION

The successful development and management of information systems and business analytics is crucial to the success of an organization. New technological developments and methods for data analysis have allowed organizations to not only improve their processes and allow for greater productivity, but have also provided businesses with a venue through which to cut costs, plan for the future, and maintain competitive advantage in the information age.

The **Advances in Business Information Systems and Analytics (ABISA) Book Series** aims to present diverse and timely research in the development, deployment, and management of business information systems and business analytics for continued organizational development and improved business value.

COVERAGE

- Big Data
- Business Decision Making
- Business Information Security
- Business Process Management
- Business Systems Engineering
- Data Analytics
- Data Management
- Decision Support Systems
- Management Information Systems
- Performance Metrics

IGI Global is currently accepting manuscripts for publication within this series. To submit a proposal for a volume in this series, please contact our Acquisition Editors at Acquisitions@igi-global.com or visit: http://www.igi-global.com/publish/.

Titles in this Series

For a list of additional titles in this series, please visit: www.igi-global.com

Managing Enterprise Information Technology Acquisitions Assessing Organizational Preparedness
Harekrishna Misra (Institute of Rural Management Anand, India) and Hakikur Rahman (University of Minho, Portugal)
Business Science Reference • copyright 2013 • 345pp • H/C (ISBN: 9781466642010) • US $185.00 (our price)

Information Systems and Technology for Organizations in a Networked Society
Tomayess Issa (Curtin University, Australia) Pedro Isaías (Universidade Aberta, Portugal) and Piet Kommers (University of Twente, The Netherlands)
Business Science Reference • copyright 2013 • 432pp • H/C (ISBN: 9781466640627) • US $185.00 (our price)

Cases on Enterprise Information Systems and Implementation Stages Learning from the Gulf Region
Fayez Albadri (ADMO-OPCO, UAE)
Information Science Reference • copyright 2013 • 370pp • H/C (ISBN: 9781466622203) • US $185.00 (our price)

Business Intelligence and Agile Methodologies for Knowledge-Based Organizations Cross-Disciplinary Applications
Asim Abdel Rahman El Sheikh (The Arab Academy for Banking and Financial Sciences, Jordan) and Mouhib Alnoukari (Arab International University, Syria)
Business Science Reference • copyright 2012 • 370pp • H/C (ISBN: 9781613500507) • US $185.00 (our price)

Business Intelligence Applications and the Web Models, Systems and Technologies
Marta E. Zorrilla (University of Cantabria, Spain) Jose-Norberto Mazón (University of Alicante, Spain) Óscar Ferrández (University of Alicante, Spain) Irene Garrigós (University of Alicante, Spain) Florian Daniel (University of Trento, Italy) and Juan Trujillo (University of Alicante, Spain)
Business Science Reference • copyright 2012 • 374pp • H/C (ISBN: 9781613500385) • US $185.00 (our price)

Electronic Supply Network Coordination in Intelligent and Dynamic Environments Modeling and Implementation
Iraj Mahdavi (Mazandaran University of Science and Technology, Iran) Shima Mohebbi (University of Tehran, Iran) and Namjae Cho (Hanyang University, Korea)
Business Science Reference • copyright 2011 • 434pp • H/C (ISBN: 9781605668086) • US $180.00 (our price)

Enterprise Information Systems Design, Implementation and Management Organizational Applications
Maria Manuela Cruz-Cunha (Polytechnic Institute of Cavado and Ave, Portugal) and Joao Varajao (University of Tras-os-Montes e Alto Duoro, Portugal)
Information Science Reference • copyright 2011 • 622pp • H/C (ISBN: 9781616920203) • US $180.00 (our price)

www.igi-global.com

701 E. Chocolate Ave., Hershey, PA 17033
Order online at www.igi-global.com or call 717-533-8845 x100
To place a standing order for titles released in this series, contact: cust@igi-global.com
Mon-Fri 8:00 am - 5:00 pm (est) or fax 24 hours a day 717-533-8661

Table of Contents

Section 1
BI with Web Data

Adriana Marotta, Universidad de la República, Uruguay
Laura González, Universidad de la República, Uruguay
Lorena Etcheverry, Universidad de la República, Uruguay
Bruno Rienzi, Universidad de la República, Uruguay
Raúl Ruggia, Universidad de la República, Uruguay
Flavia Serra, Universidad de la República, Uruguay
Elena Martirena, Universidad de la República, Uruguay

Fadila Bentayeb, University of Lyon, France
Nora Maïz, University of Lyon, France
Hadj Mahboubi, CEMAGREF Centre Clermont-Ferrand, France
Cécile Favre, University of Lyon, France
Sabine Loudcher, University of Lyon, France
Nouria Harbi, University of Lyon, France
Omar Boussaïd, University of Lyon, France
Jérôme Darmont, University of Lyon, France

Ramón A. Carrasco, University of Granada, Spain
Miguel J. Hornos, University of Granada, Spain
Pedro Villar, University of Granada, Spain
María A. Aguilar, University of Granada, Spain

Section 2
Engineering Web-Enabled BI

Foreword

It was an afternoon in the early November of 2010 when I sat in front of my laptop thinking on ways to highlight the topic of this book you have in hand. Having been involved in the area of business intelligence for quite some time, I knew that business intelligence over the Web has been a rather neglected topic by the largest part of the research community and not frequently appearing in the mainstream research venues. For me this was a reason good enough for a reference book on the topic, however, I felt I needed a little bit more breadth in my knowledge of the area. As typically happens with people involved in similar tasks, I resorted to the Web (and if you think better about it, this is already an argument by itself) and browsed to Wikipedia's entry for "business intelligence" (in fact, there is an entire category of articles for business intelligence in Wikipedia, but I went right to the homonymous, "main" page). There, I did a simple text search for the word "Web." Surprise: the term was not used in the page at all. A month later, there are a couple of low-key appearances of the term in the same page...

The whole situation is actually mind-provoking, since we do know for sure that the world is rapidly changing towards publishing both data and functionality over the Web. Tim Berners-Lee, in his speech in TED 2009, gave the tone for the future of Internet's usage, by asking the audience to "demand raw data!!" The main idea is that more and more, individuals and government agencies will post data on the Web; analysts can then retrieve the data they deem relevant and work with them. Yet, people in the Information Systems engineering world know that for data to be used by business intelligence tools, we need them to have structure, integrity, compliance to the reference values of the underlying databases, and in general, conformance to the principles regulating the structure and integrity of an Information System (and in particular, a data warehouse). On top of that, even if we can indeed obtain the structure for these Web data, are they trustworthy? Relevant? Available when needed?

At the same time, the Web has already transformed from an "announcement board" where people would post and retrieve information to an environment with two characteristics: (a) a collaboration platform where people share and reuse data in order to work together, and, (b) an automated processing environment where enterprises export functionalities in an automated way in order to conduct business. So, on the one hand, there is a move towards working with collaborative tools and the Semantic Web, and on the other hand, we observe the spread of mashups and software facilities exported as services as the means to speed up and automate business processes.

And where does Business Intelligence fit in such a new and versatile environment? Well... you have to read through the book to find out...

Zorrilla, Mazón, Ferrández, Garrigós, Daniel, and Trujillo have done a great job in compiling a book that fills the gap in the related bibliography with an interesting and comprehensive coverage of the challenges that we face for linking business intelligence and the Web. The book contains a mixture of research insights, system architectures, discussion of tools, and real-world cases and organizes the discussion of these issues in two areas of coverage. First, the book covers the area of exploitation of data that are already present in the Web for the purposes of business intelligence. The book discusses topics like the management of unstructured text and its combination with super-structured environments like data warehouses and OLAP tools, as well as the management of relevance, freshness, and in general, quality of the Web data with a view to its exploitation via business intelligence tools. The second area involves the automation of data processing and the usage of the Web as a platform for business intelligence including topics like BI-as-a-service, mashups and the Semantic Web for business intelligence, and, collaborative business intelligence.

The book mainly acts as a reference for the state of the art in several areas, including problems and challenges that are not straightforward to be addressed as well as suggestions for paths to follow. The book's primary target is breadth of coverage, with suggestions of the relevant readings for further probing and initial insights for solutions, rather than an in-depth investigation of technical problems in the typical research-oriented fashion. In this sense, the text is easy to follow without losing its interest or significance. In my opinion, the book's primary audience is the interested researcher or practitioner who wants to get a broader view of the environment around the combination of Web and business intelligence, with pointers to the state of the art, as well as the broader challenges that remain open.

Panos Vassiliadis
December 2010, Ioannina

Preface

Over the last decade, we have witnessed an increasing use of **Business Intelligence (BI)** solutions that allow business people to query, understand, and analyze their business data in order to make better decisions. Traditionally, BI applications allow management and decision makers to acquire useful knowledge about the performance and problems of business from the data of their organization by means of a variety of technologies, such as data warehousing, data mining, business performance management, OLAP, periodical business reports, and the like. Research in these areas has produced consolidated solutions, techniques, and methodologies, and there is a variety of commercial products available that are based on these results.

More recently, a new trend in BI applications has emerged: BI applications no longer limit their analysis to the data of just one organization or company. Increasingly, they also **source their data from the outside**, thus complementing internal company data with value-adding information from the Web (e.g., retail prices of products sold by competitors), in order to provide richer insights into the dynamics of today's business and to better support decision-making processes. As a result, BI applications aim to assist the dynamics of modern management practices, where decision-making requires a comprehensive view of the market and the business ecosystem as a whole, and hence, BI using just internal company data no longer suffices.

Interestingly, in parallel to the movement of data from the Web into BI applications, we are now also experiencing the movement of BI applications from internal company information systems to the Web: Business Intelligence as a service (e.g., hosted BI platforms for small- and medium-sized companies) or software support to manage business outsourcing or crowd sourcing is the target of huge investments and the focus of enormous research efforts by both industry and academia. The underlying idea is moving the processing and analysis of large bodies of data into the cloud and consuming BI via the Web.

In light of these trends, conciliation of Business Intelligence and the Web is of paramount importance for further progress in the area. Specifically, this book presents a selection of chapters falling into two main topics:

- **Data from the Web feeding BI applications**. In the last decade, the amount and complexity of data available on the Web has been growing rapidly. As a consequence, designers of BI applications making use of data from the Web have to deal with several issues. Many interesting research challenges arise when the Web is seen as a data repository: Web warehousing models, data quality issues, integration of Semantic Web technologies, Web mining technologies, BI with unstructured or semi-structured data, Web intelligence methodologies, or the application of natural language processing (NLP) techniques to the BI field.

- **BI applications moving to the Web**. The movement of BI applications from internal company Information Systems to applications that are accessible over the Web implies the need for Web-specific design competencies. In this context, research is focused on using Web engineering methodologies and technologies in BI: real-time BI and business performance management applications, Web mashups and RIA for BI development, usability and accessibility for BI applications, security issues in BI, and so on.

In short, the **aim of this book** is to provide an overview of the two main current research lines about (i) how to fully exploit the huge amount of data available on the Web with BI applications, and (ii) how to apply Web engineering methods and techniques to the design of BI applications. This book aims to share theoretical or applied models and systems regarding decision making with data from the Web, showing emerging technologies and tendencies regarding BI systems and the Web and their applications in different fields, and provide the academic community with a base text that could serve as a reference in business and computer science undergraduate and graduate courses.

The **target audience** of this book is varied and spans researchers and academics working on both BI and the Web, practitioners and software developers, managers and executives of companies operating in the BI market, and lecturers and students of related courses. *Researchers and academics* will find an analysis of the state of the art and an outline of current and future research challenges. *Practitioners and software developers* will find hints to cutting-edge implementation solutions and technologies. *Managers and executives* will find a comprehensive spectrum of current trends and market needs. Finally, *lecturers and students* will gain an interesting insight into the relationship between BI and the Web.

The book is structured into **two sections** that group chapters into thematically related areas:

BI with Web Data

This section comprises 8 chapters that specifically focus on the problem of processing and analyzing data that are sourced from the Web. The first five chapters describe how BI systems deal with these issues from different points of view: quality, storing complex data, semantic integration, and text OLAP analysis, among others. The following three chapters discuss the importance of NLP in BI.

Marotta et al. explain in Chapter 1, "Quality Management in Web Warehouses," a reference architecture for quality-aware Web Warehouses, which is useful for evaluating and managing quality aspects through all the life cycle of a Web Warehouse. The challenging task of designing a Web Warehouse requires the management of quality aspects to (i) properly select Web sources with which to populate the Web Warehouse, and to (ii) measure and offer quality attributes to final users of the Web Warehouse to improve their decision making.

Next, in Chapter 2 "Innovative Approaches for Efficiently Warehousing Complex Data from the Web," Bentayeb et al. propose extracting information from the Web, and transforming and loading it to a Web Warehouse, which provides uniform access methods for automatic processing of the data. Specifically, the authors present three research lines (i) the use of XML as a logical and physical model for complex data warehouses, (ii) associating data mining to OLAP to allow elaborated analysis tasks for complex data, and (iii) schema evolution in complex data warehouses for personalized analyses.

In Chapter 3, "An Extraction, Transformation and Loading Tool Applied to a Fuzzy Data Mining System," by Carrasco et al., the authors present a tool with which to semantically integrate heterogeneous data from various websites into a BI system to empower the decision making process. They also present a real case study from the Business School at the University of Granada (Spain).

As unstructured documents including text data from the Web constitute the majority of business data, in Chapter 4, "Incorporating Text OLAP in Business Intelligence," Park and Song present a Text OLAP solution to perform multidimensional analysis of text documents in the same way structured relational data is analyzed. The aim of their approach is to seamlessly analyze structured and unstructured data, thus realizing the total BI.

In Chapter 5, "A Semantic Approach for News Recommendation," Frasincar et al. describe the importance of news items in the business decision process. Moreover, they present the problem of traditional news recommenders, and how this problem is overcome by using semantic similarity measures. Existing semantic similarities as well as new proposals for semantic similarity are discussed and evaluated in this chapter. The results point out that the application of semantics successfully improves traditional recommenders.

Pallotta et al., in Chapter 6 "Interaction Business Analytics: Making Business Sense of Customers Conversations through Semantic and Pragmatic Analysis," propose an interaction business analytics perspective focused on unstructured customers' interactions. Such a perspective extends the understanding of business data achieved by statistical methods through deriving valuable information from unstructured data. They present a new approach for interaction business analytics based on argumentative analysis obtained by a deep linguistic processing of conversations. Examples from three different scenarios are presented, showing the benefits of the proposed approach.

Chapter 7, "OpAL: A System for Mining Opinion from Text for Business Applications," presents the need for computational approaches capable of dealing with subjective data on the Web. A feature-based opinion mining system is described and evaluated in several scenarios. Different natural language processing techniques applied to opinion mining are discussed throughout the chapter. Furthermore, the authors also describe a robust and multilingual method for opinion retrieval. The results reported by this system are very encouraging, demonstrating the business potential behind the processing of subjective information.

Lastly, Henschel et al., in Chapter 8, "A Unified Approach for Taxonomy-Based Technology Forecasting," propose a technique using bibliometric indicators that allows decision makers and researchers alike to understand the state of the art of their area of interest. As a concrete example, the authors discuss a case study in the field of renewable energy.

Engineering Web-Enabled BI

This section collects 6 contributions that concentrate on the problem of engineering advanced BI applications that leverage on Web technologies. Chapters 9 and 10 focus on service-oriented technologies. Chapters 11 and 12 deal with collaborative BI. And the remaining chapters survey two relevant topics within engineering Web-enabled BI: Semantic Web and real-time BI and situational analysis.

In Chapter 9, "Business Intelligence-as-a-Service: Studying the Functional and the Technical Architectures," by Essaidi et al., the authors provide a study on the benefits of the SaaS model for the design of business intelligence architectures and propose a functional architecture to support common on-demand business intelligence services. Next, they describe and discuss the utility of a service, which helps developers to design data warehouses based on MDA and 2TUP. Finally, they offer an open-source solution for the implementation of their approach.

Zorrilla and García, in Chapter 10, "A Data Mining Service to Assist Instructors Involved in Virtual Education," describe an on-demand data mining service developed in their university, which aims to help instructors involved in distance education to discover their students' behavior profiles and obtain models about how they navigate and work in their virtual courses. In the chapter, the authors justify its necessity and utility for both professors and students and describe its architecture based on SOA and standard Web technologies.

Chapter 11, "BIN: Business Intelligence Networks," proposes a framework, called Business Intelligence Network, for sharing BI functionalities over complex networks of companies that are pursuing mutual advantages through the sharing of strategic information. After proposing their architecture, they outline the main research issues involved in its building and operating, and focus on the definition of an ad-hoc language for expressing semantic mappings between the multidimensional schemata owned by the different peers, aimed at enabling query reformulation over the network.

Berthold et al. envision in Chapter 12, "Towards Ad-Hoc and Collaborative Business Intelligence," a highly scalable and flexible BI platform that is able to perform ad-hoc analyses in a collaborative manner. The authors describe the main blocks of their proposal which aim to complement traditional BI environments in order to overcome these challenges and empower the business users.

In Chapter 13, "Real-Time BI and Situational Analysis," the authors provide an elaborated and forward-looking survey of current data warehousing trends from the perspective of both the applications and the database systems and review state-of-the-art techniques that may help addressing the typical problems that emerge when building a real-time data warehouse. The chapter further nicely connects to the domain of the Web by extending the typical architecture of real-time data warehouses toward mashup situational data analysis.

Berlanga et al. in Chapter 14, "Semantic Web Technologies for Business Intelligence," describe in detail the convergence of BI with one of the most influential technologies in the last decade: the Semantic Web. They make a survey about the use of Semantic Web technologies in the different stages of the development of BI applications: data integration, multidimensional modeling, intelligent BI querying, scalability issues, and so on.

As the above summary shows, this book summarizes current research advances in BI and the Web, emphasizing research solutions, techniques, and methodologies which combine both areas in the interest of building better BI solutions. Novel proposals are presented throughout the two sections in which the book is structured, giving the reader a general view as well as detailed descriptions of approaches addressing the main issues posed in this book.

To contribute to the sharing of knowledge, the book stresses the use of technologies capable of dealing with data obtained from the Web, i.e., semistructured or unstructured information, with the aim to achieve better understanding and analysis of business data, and likewise, Web engineering methods and techniques, which can be applied to the design of BI applications hosted in the Web.

To the best of our knowledge, this is the first book that puts together topics about BI and the Web, and as such, aims to emphasize the interconnections that exist among the two research areas and to highlight the benefits of a joint use of BI and Web practices, which so far have acted rather independently, often in cases where their joint application would have been sensible.

Acknowledgment

We are indebted to all the authors who submitted their chapters and made a great effort in their improvement after all the review rounds that were carried out. Furthermore, we would also like to express our gratitude to the Editorial Advisory Board and to all the reviewers for their effort and work in carefully reviewing all the chapters. Special thanks to Panos Vassiliadis for his willingness in writing such a nice foreword. We owe part of the success of this book to them. Finally, we would also like to express our sincere gratitude to IGI Global for giving us the opportunity to publish this book.

Section 1
BI with Web Data

Chapter 1
Quality Management in Web Warehouses

Adriana Marotta
Universidad de la República, Uruguay

Raúl Ruggia
Universidad de la República, Uruguay

Laura González
Universidad de la República, Uruguay

Flavia Serra
Universidad de la República, Uruguay

Lorena Etcheverry
Universidad de la República, Uruguay

Elena Martirena
Universidad de la República, Uruguay

Bruno Rienzi
Universidad de la República, Uruguay

ABSTRACT

Web Warehouses (WW) are data warehouses that consolidate data from the Web. The process of building them presents several challenges, most of them related to the autonomy and dynamicity of Web sources. In this context, managing quality aspects becomes a fundamental issue since information about quality is needed to properly select Web sources to populate the WW. Additionally, measuring and propagating quality values to the WW might provide final users with valuable information to improve decision-making processes. In this chapter, we present a reference architecture for quality aware Web Warehouses, which specifies the main components to evaluate and manage quality aspects through all the life cycle of a WW and considers quality regarding data and services.

DOI: 10.4018/978-1-61350-038-5.ch001

INTRODUCTION

Supported by new technology trends, like Web 2.0, Cloud Computing and Web Services, information available on the Web is increasing every day. Consequently, Web Warehouses (WW), Data Warehouses (DW) which consolidate data from the Web (Cheng et al., 2000; Marotta et al., 2002; Soper, 2005), have become a valuable tool for decision making in many areas.

However, given the dynamic and autonomous nature of Web Data Sources (WDSs) (Bhowmick et al., 2004), the process of building a WW presents major challenges. First, web data can be delivered through many heterogeneous formats and protocols, including among others HTML pages, XML documents, RSS or ATOM feeds, SOAP Web Services and Restful Web Services. Second, WDSs are usually managed by third-parties, leading to uncertainty in terms of availability, cost and unexpected changes in the format or protocols they use to deliver data.

In this context, managing quality aspects becomes a fundamental issue. On the one hand, quality information is needed to properly select the WDSs to populate the WW. Additionally, measuring and propagating quality values to the WW might provide end users with valuable information to improve decision-making processes.

This chapter presents a Reference Architecture for Quality Aware Web Warehouses, which specifies the main components to evaluate and manage quality aspects through all the lifecycle of a WW. In this reference architecture, quality is considered regarding data and services. Data Quality (DQ) deals, on one hand, with all the quality aspects related with web data, like completeness, freshness and accuracy, and on the other hand, with quality aspects that are of particular interest in the context of Data Warehouses, like hierarchy completeness and measure precision. Quality of Service (QoS) deals with the aspects concerning the services that provide or manipulate the data, like availability, response time and reputation. Based on this quality information, it is possible

to perform a quality aware discovery of WDSs, and to provide a quality driven runtime adaptation mechanism, during the extraction stage, to deal with the highly dynamic nature of the Web. As well, the platform addresses the measurement, propagation, aggregation and management of quality metadata, through all the stages needed to populate a WW. This provides the end user valuable quality information, which can be leveraged to take more accurate and confident decisions.

In order to manage quality information we take the approach followed in (Etcheverry et al., 2008), where quality is characterized via multiple dimensions, each of which captures a high-level aspect of quality. Each quality dimension consists of a set of quality factors, where each factor represents a particular aspect of a quality dimension. Finally, quality metrics are instruments to measure a particular quality factor. Several metrics might exist for the same quality factor.

Our proposal mainly focuses on three aspects: (i) a reference architecture for managing quality in a WW, (ii) management of data and service quality in web data sources, and (iii) management of data quality in the DW component of the WW. These three aspects are closely related. While the last two items deal with the management of data and service quality, the reference architecture provides the global environment to connect the components that perform the different involved tasks, including quality management.

This chapter is organized as follows. Next section presents existing works covering some of the topics we address within this chapter and how our solution is positioned with respect to them. Then, we present and describe a reference architecture for quality aware WW, focusing on how quality is managed throughout the architecture. After that, we present in detail a proposal for managing web-data quality and a proposal for managing DW quality, describing the development of a case study in which we exemplify the main stages in a WW implementation following our approach. Finally, we identify future research directions and we present the conclusions of the chapter.

BACKGROUND

In this section, we present existing works regarding some of the topics addressed within this chapter and we describe how our work is positioned with respect to them. First, we analyze various works concerning data quality in DWs and Data Integration Systems. Then, we present existing knowledge on quality in WDSs; we survey works regarding quality in Web applications, Web Services and Mashups. Finally, we review works that propose WW platforms that deal with different implementation issues.

Data Quality in Data Warehouses and Data Integration Systems

Data Quality is an active research area in which significant progress has been made in the last two decades. Nevertheless, as stated in (Madnick et al., 2009) and (Batini et al., 2009), several research problems remain open. Most of these problems are related to new types of information systems, such as Web-related information systems, where DQ assessment methodologies must deal with the quality of semi-structured or unstructured data and new types of quality dimensions need to be explored, such as accessibility. Within Data Warehousing systems, DQ issues may compromise their usability and, as stated in (Ballou and Tayi, 1999) lack of concern for the quality of data is the most probable cause of failure in Data Warehousing projects. Even though a lot of research has been done, there are still open research problems in Data Warehouse DQ, in particular methods must be devised to guide data retrieval by quality requirements expressed by users and to propagate data quality metrics to query results (Rizzi et al., 2006).

Several aspects related to DW quality have been studied in the literature. Some works, basically based on case studies, analyze sources of poor quality and types of errors (Hinrichs and Aden,

2001; Rudra and Yeo, 1999). Other authors focus on the specification of DQ dimensions relevant to DW, such as (Ballou and Tayi, 1999, Helfert and Herrmann, 2002). There are also some proposals that focus on the quality of the DW design (Calero et al., 2001). Other works deal with source selection problem in DW in order to satisfy DQ requirements (Vaisman, 2007) and with the propagation of quality values when aggregating data in OLAP (Marotta et al., 2006). Another quality aspect concerning OLAP, the correctness of data summary, has been addressed in (Horner et al., 2004, Horner and Song, 2005) by implementing a catalog of summary constraints, which aims to guide the accurate design and usage of summarized data. Finally, the influence of non-functional requirements in DW design has been analyzed in (Batini et al., 2009).

A more general approach is followed by the DWQ Project (Jarke and Vassiliou, 1997; Jarke, 1999; Vassiliadis et al., 2000), which proposes a Goal Question Metric based methodology for the elicitation of quality requirements and its assessment in the context of DW systems. According to DWQ approach quality can be defined as an aggregated view of the metadata and data of the warehouse and depends on the quality of the sources, the quality of the extraction process and the quality of the DW components itself. This project does not propose a specific set of DQ dimensions and metrics specific for DW systems.

Most recently, in (Daniel et al., 2008), the authors propose a mechanism to trace DQ from the sources to users view, enhancing reports with data quality information. However, this approach proposes to define and assess DW data quality based on its relational implementation, and not over DW domain components such as cubes, dimensions and measures.

Our proposal contributes in the definition of DW data quality in terms of DW domain concepts, releasing DQ specification from DW logical design decisions.

In turn, Data Integration Systems (DIS) are information systems that integrate data from different independent data sources and provide users with a uniform access to the data by means of a global model. WWs are a particular case of DIS. Quality management in DIS involves computing the quality values of the integrated data by taking as input the quality of the sources, and has been addressed in (Akoka et al., 2007; Bouzeghoub and Peralta, 2004; Peralta et al., 2004).

Most techniques for quality management in DIS will be applied in the context of WW, especially the propagation of quality values through the data integration operations.

Quality of Web Data Sources

Quality of WDSs is a crucial issue in various contexts given the amount, heterogeneity, dynamicity and autonomy of Web sites.

Data quality in Web sites has been analyzed in different works. (Caro et al., 2005)the authors present a state of the art of data quality in Web applications, identifying accuracy, completeness and timeliness as the most widely regarded quality aspects in the works they analyzed. Additionally, in (Zhu and Buchmann, 2002) the authors propose twelve criteria for evaluating and selecting Web resources as external data sources of a DW. The criteria are grouped into three categories (stability of a Web Source, quality of the Web Data and application specific) and include, among others, availability, objectivity and relevance. Additionally, various works have also analyzed Data Quality in a more general way (Batini et al., 2009), identifying quality factors which might also be applied on a Web context.

With the advent of the Web Services technology and the Service Oriented Computing paradigm, current Web sites are not only providing data but also functionalities. This gave rise to various works which analyze and indentify Quality of Service aspects. The OASIS organization, for example, is developing a Web Services Quality Model in which various quality factors for Web

Services (Kim et al., 2010) are identified. The factors are grouped in six categories: Business Value, Service Level Measurement, Interoperability, Business Processing, Manageability and Security. Additionally, in (Cappiello et al., 2008) a quality model for service monitoring and adaptation is presented. The model was the result of a wide literature survey and identifies more than seventy quality attributes which are grouped in ten categories.

Additionally, Web users have started combining components (data, functionalities and presentation) from different Web sites giving rise to the Mashup concept and the subsequent requirement to handle components quality. In (Cappiello et al., 2009) the authors analyze quality properties of Mashup components and define a quality model for them. The model is organized in three main quality dimensions (API Quality, Data Quality and Presentation Quality) and includes quality attributes like learnability, accuracy, security and reputation.

Most of these works identify quality factors without focusing on a WW context and some of them only consider quality factors for specific WDS types. Our work focuses, on the contrary, in a WW context and takes a broader approach considering quality factors regarding various types of WDSs and identifying which of them are pertinent in a WW scenario. We also analyze for which stages, during the WW life cycle, these quality factors are relevant, analyzing which of them might be propagated to the WW to provide value added information to the WW end user.

Web Warehouse Platforms

Various Web Warehouse platforms have been proposed in the literature dealing with specific problems of WW development. For example, in (Bhowmick et al., 2003) and (Bhowmick et al., 2004) the authors describe the project Whoweda (Warehouse of Web Data) whose objective is to design and implement a WW that materializes and manages useful information from the Web. The authors focus on a Web data model and algebra for web information access, manipulation and visualization, as well as a Metadata representation model. Besides, in (Zhu, 1999) the author presents a framework for warehousing selected Web content, using a partially materialized approach and an extended ontology to achieve data integration. Finally, in (Marotta et al., 2002) the authors propose a wrapper - mediator architecture in order to minimize the impact of Web sources changes on the DW schema.

None of these works consider quality as an integral issue during the whole life cycle of a WW. The reference architecture proposed in this chapter considers quality management aspects starting from the WDSs and all through the different stages until the end user interacts with the WW.

A REFERENCE ARCHITECTURE FOR QUALITY AWARE WEB WAREHOUSES

We present a reference architecture, over which a WW with service and data quality management can be implemented. We describe the general design, then we comment the main issues in web data and service quality management, and finally we briefly explain how all the collected quality metadata is combined and becomes valuable quality information for the end user of the WW.

General Architecture

The proposed architecture comprises three main stages in the WW lifecycle: (i) data extraction, (ii) data integration and (iii) data transformation and loading to the DW. At the same time, it includes Quality Metadata, which guides quality management at the different stages. The architecture is shown in Figure 1.

The Data Service Infrastructure (DSI) module provides the execution environment to implement, host and execute Data Services (DSs), which ac-

cess and extract data from WDSs. The DSI module has three main responsibilities. First, it has to provide the mechanisms to extract data from different types of WDS and expose them as homogeneous DSs using standard technologies, like XML and HTTP. To perform this task, it includes specialized components which have the knowledge to deal with specific protocols (HTTP, SOAP, etc) and to transform different data formats to a common one. Second, the DSI module has the responsibility to monitor the DSs and periodically measure quality (QoS&DQ_M module) to allow a quality driven discovery of them. This involved quality information is stored as DQ and QoS metadata. Finally, the DSI provides runtime adaptation mechanisms, in the extraction process, to react to possible degradation in DSs' quality.

The Integrator module, which invokes the DSs, carries out data integration and provides data in a normalized format (e.g., XML), generating the Integrated Database (IDB). Its main responsibilities are quality-oriented selection of DSs, data integration, and generation of quality metadata associated to the integrated data. The Integrator interacts with expert users, who perform the main data integration decisions, such as object identification and conflict resolution. This interaction is achieved through a rich user interface.

The ETL and OLAP modules carry out the classic functions of DW context. In addition they have to perform quality metadata propagation. In order to do this, they have to capture QoS and DQ metadata associated to the processed data.

In turn, DWQ_M module implements a data quality measurement process, which receives data quality metadata as input and combines it with new measurements performed over the DW.

As can be seen in Figure 1, there is a specialized user that interacts with the system at the source selection and integration stage, while final users interact with the OLAP interface receiving the quality information additional value.

Figure 1. Web warehouse reference architecture

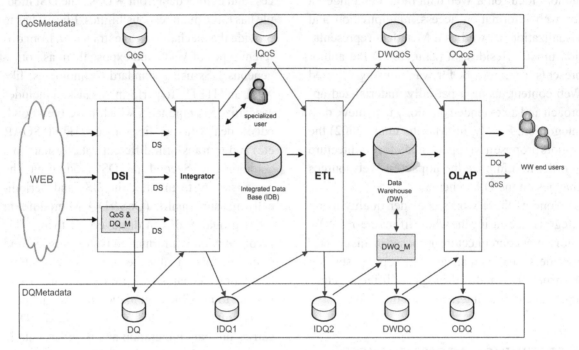

Quality Management in the WW Platform

Quality management in the proposed architecture starts in the DSI module, which allows specifying a set of candidate WDSs for the WW. After selecting the candidate WDSs, a specialized user can specify the set of quality properties to measure. These quality properties refer to data quality related dimensions (Batini and Scannapieco, 2006; Strong et al., 1997), like completeness, consistency, freshness, accuracy and uniqueness, and Quality of Service related dimensions (Cappiello et al., 2008; Kim et al., 2010), like performance, dependability, security, reputation, cost and usability. Quality information, which is automatically acquired and/or calculated by this module, is used by the specialized user to perform a quality aware discovery of DSs (which encapsulate the access to the WDSs). In addition, the runtime adaptation mechanism leverages this information to perform quality driven adaptations.

The Integrator module uses the quality values of the data provided by the DSs to guide the integration operations and then computes the corresponding quality values. The Integrator has the responsibility to manage the graph of transformation and integration operations that generates the data according to the IDB schema, and to generate the quality metadata associated to IDB data. As stated in the Background, techniques to achieve this are presented in the works for Data Integration Systems (Akoka et al., 2007; Bouzeghoub and Peralta, 2004; Peralta et al., 2004).

When data arrives to the DW, a considerable amount of quality information about these data is available in the Metadata. However, several aspects of data quality, which are specific to DW and OLAP information, are still to be addressed. Such aspects concern, not only the relevance of the different kind of information for the DW users (e.g. DW-measures accuracy might be more relevant than other attributes' accuracy), but also the transformation suffered by data in this context (e.g. aggregations of DW-measures). These issues are addressed through data quality dimensions that are specialized in DW and OLAP. In addition, this WW architecture includes a module for measuring DW quality. Then, quality information is propagated through the different transformations to the final state of the data (see a propagation strategy for OLAP systems in (Marotta et al., 2006).

In all cases, quality evaluation could be performed through external services, as shown in (González et al., 2009).

Quality Metadata

Quality information is registered independently from data items, but it always maintains a link to the corresponding data. Each quality value has a reference to a table, an attribute or a cell, according to the quality measurement granularity.

Each process module queries quality metadata and generates new metadata (see Figure 1). First, the DSI module interacts with the WDSs to acquire quality data (e.g. response time, data completeness) which is stored by the module (DQ and QoS). In the Integrator module, integration decisions are made based on this quality information and, when data integration is achieved, new quality metadata corresponding to the integrated data (IDQ1 and IQoS) is generated. The ETL module also takes in consideration the received quality metadata and updates it (generating IDQ2) in the cases where cleaning tasks are applied or quality is modified for some other reason. DWQ_M module is in charge of measuring data quality in the DW and it also takes as input already existing quality metadata. It generates new quality metadata that corresponds to DW data (DWDQ). Similarly, QoS metadata is propagated generating DWQoS. OLAP module updates the corresponding quality metadata referencing to the new objects it generates (producing ODQ and OQoS).

WEB DATA SOURCES QUALITY MANAGEMENT

Traditionally, data extraction from the Web involves developing specialized programs, usually called wrappers, which have the knowledge to acquire the relevant data from a WDS. Wrappers generally transform the extracted data to another format, for example XML, to deliver them to other programs or to place them in a persistent storage (Laender et al., 2002).

Developing wrappers can be a time consuming task, so it becomes necessary evaluating WDSs quality in order to decide if it is worth building them. Wrappers may be developed because WDSs have been chosen to populate the WW or because the quality of a WDS requires further evaluation. Additionally, once wrappers are developed WDSs quality information can change. Consequently, the continuous monitoring of WDSs quality and the possibility to dynamically change the WDSs from which data are extracted is a must.

In order to face these issues, we propose a quality driven process to select and extract data from the Web, which is based on the previously defined Reference Architecture. In addition, we identify a set of quality factors for WDSs.

Web Data Selection and Extraction Process

The Web data selection and extraction process involves four main steps: (i) candidate WDSs selection, (ii) Data Services (DS) development (which encapsulate wrappers extraction logic), (iii) DSs selection to populate the WW and (iv) DS invocation by the integrator module. Most of these steps leverage quality information to accomplish their tasks. For example, candidate WDSs selection is based on quality information regarding cost and standards support, among others. Additionally, we consider that WDSs quality might be propagated to the WW to make this information available to end users.

As shown in Figure 2, the selection and extraction process is mainly supported by the DSI module, which provides an execution environment to host DSs and mechanisms that aid in describing, publishing, discovering and invoking DSs, following a service oriented approach. The DSI module manages DSs quality to support a quality aware discovery of DSs, and provides a runtime adaptation mechanism aiming to maintain the DSs quality level. Furthermore, it provides quality information that can be propagated to the WW.

Following, we describe each of the steps of the quality driven process, and analyze how the different DSI components support it.

Step One: Candidate Web Data Sources Selection

Given that developing wrappers could be a tedious and costly task, analyzing WDSs in order to evaluate if wrappers should be built becomes essential.

The outcome of this step is a set of candidate WDSs for which wrappers will be developed.

Wrappers can be built just because a WDS have been found appropriate to populate the WW, or because a more detailed analysis of the WDS quality is needed.

The selection of candidate WDSs is performed taking into account various quality factors (e.g. reputation, dependability, etc.). In the section "Quality Factors for Web Data Sources" we analyze which quality factors might be relevant for this task.

Step Two: Data Services Development and Deployment

After selecting the set of candidate WDSs, wrappers have to be developed to extract the data and to perform the required transformations.

Data extraction can be implemented from scratch or various tools can be used, like the

Figure 2. Quality driven data extraction process

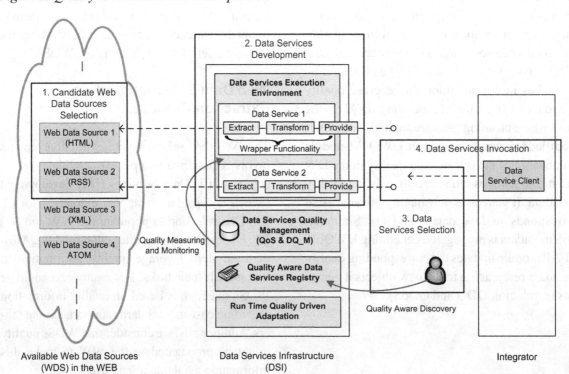

Yahoo Query Language (YQL) (Yahoo Developer-Network, 2010), Web Harvest (Nikic and Wajda, 2010), HTML Unit (Bowler, 2010) or the ones presented in (Laender et al., 2002).

In order to provide a homogeneous access to various types of WDSs, we propose implementing Data Services (DSs) to encapsulate the extraction logic that wrappers might implement. DSs also perform the required data transformations to deliver data using XML. DSs can also be composed to create new DSs. We propose leveraging Web Services technologies (e.g. WSDL and SOAP) to describe and invoke DSs. This is due to the fact that the DSI module might be provided by a third party, requiring the use of Web protocols like HTTP.

To support the development of DSs, the DSI module offers an execution environment which provides a set of transformation and communication facilities. Additionally, DSs could be externally implemented, hosted and executed, as long as they can be accessed through the specified standards (SOAP, XML and HTTP). In this case, a proxy service is deployed in the DSI module to mediate between the integrator and the external DS. This mediation is required in order to measure DS quality and eventually take corrective actions in case of DSs unavailability or quality degradation.

Step Three: Data Services Selection

Once DSs have been developed, some of them have to be selected to populate the WW. This selection is aided by two DSIs components: the Data Service Registry (DSR) and the Data Service Quality Management (QoS&DQ_M) component.

The DSR component provides functionalities to search and discover the deployed DSs according to functional and non-functional (QoS) characteristics. The QoS&DQ_M component continuously monitors DSs quality through various quality measurement facilities. These facilities use different mechanisms to evaluate quality factors. On the one hand, they can use the information that goes through the DSI module when a client application (e.g. the Integrator module) invokes the DSs. Additionally, the facilities can directly interact with a specific WDS to perform quality measurement tasks. Finally, there may be more general utilities which provide measurement functionalities for a specific type of WDS (e.g. SOAP Web Services).

The quality information computed by the QoS&DQ_M module is then made available to the DSR component and the Integrator module, so it can be propagated to the WW.

Step Four: Data Services Invocation

Once the DSs have been selected, the extraction process might be scheduled to run periodically.

Given that quality information can change over time, the DSI module supports a quality driven adaptation mechanism aiming to maintain a certain quality level.

The DSI module also supports an event-driven updating mechanism in which new data are pushed to the Integrator module as soon as they are available in the WDS.

Quality Factors for Web Data Sources

In this section we present a set of quality factors for WDSs, that even though it might be further extended or adjusted to a specific domain, we believe that it covers various common WW quality requirements. An example of such requirements is the need to have information regarding the stability of WDSs or regarding the completeness of the data they provide (Zhu and Buchmann, 2002)

After reviewing the literature, we notice that Web data quality factors can be organized in two broad categories: service related factors and data related factors. After presenting the factors within these two categories, we analyze their relevance for selecting candidate WDSs, for selecting DSs and for propagating their values to the WW.

Service Related Quality Factors

The quality factors belonging to this category are selected from quality related literature regarding Web Services (Cappiello et al., 2008; Kim et al., 2010) Web Applications (Caro et al., 2005) and Mashups (Cappiello et al., 2009). The factors are organized in six quality dimensions: Service Level, Interoperability, Security, Business Value, Usability and Stability.

Table 1 presents factors for the Service Level dimension. Some metrics found in the literature for the Performance factor are response time, throughput and transaction time. Table 2 presents factors for the Interoperability dimension. Standards Support can refer, for example, to the Data Format (XML, RSS, GData, etc) or to the Communication Protocol (HTTP, REST, SOAP, etc). Table 3 presents factors for the Security dimension. Security metrics can be considered on two technical perspectives: Transport Level and Message / Data Level. Other factors that might be included within the Security dimension are authorization and non-repudiation, among others. Table 4 presents factors for the Business Value dimension. Table 5 presents factors for the Usability dimension. Finally, Table 6 presents factors for the Stability dimension.

Web Data Quality Factors

The set of quality factors proposed for this category is the result of a deep analysis of data quality dimensions literature (Batini et al., 2009; Cappiello et al., 2008; Fitzpatrick, 2000; Lee et al., 2002; Mecella et al., 2002; Naumann et al., 2004; Peralta et al. 2004; Zhu and Buchmann, 2002), combined with our own experience in data quality models definition. We organize data quality factors in six quality dimensions: Accuracy, Completeness, Freshness, Uniqueness, Consistency and Reliability.

Table 7 presents factors for the Accuracy dimension. Table 8 presents factors for the Com-

pleteness dimension. Table 9 presents factors for the Freshness dimension. Table 10 presents factors for the Consistency dimension. Table 11 presents the factor for the Uniqueness dimension. Table 12 presents factors for the Reliability dimension.

Quality Factors in the WW lifecycle stages

Throughout the selection and extraction process, not all quality factors might be relevant for a specific task. In this section, we analyze whether the identified quality factors are relevant for the following tasks:

- **Selecting Candidate WDS:** The relevant factors for this task are the ones used to decide whether it is worth building a wrapper for a WDS.
- **Selecting DSs to Populate the WW:** Once wrappers are built and encapsulated in DSs, the specialized user has to select the DSs to use, among many that might provide the same data. The relevant quality factors for this task are the ones which are used to make this selection.
- **Propagating Quality Values to the WW:** The relevant quality factors to propagate to the WW are the ones which might be useful for WW end users.

It is important to note that this analysis considers a very general scenario. It is expected that the relevance of a quality factor might vary according to a specific context or domain.

As shown in Table 13, we found that all the identified factors are relevant for the WDS candidate selection given that they can affect the decision of developing a wrapper or not. For the DS Selection, the Interoperability and Usability factors are not important anymore given that during this stage wrappers have already been developed. However, the rest of the factors remain relevant. Finally, we consider that the identified security

Table 1. Service level dimension

Dimension	Factors
Service Level represents how quickly and soundly services can respond.	**Performance** characterizes how well a service performs.
	Dependability is the ability to deliver services that can justifiably be trusted.

Table 2. Interoperability dimension

Dimension	Factors
Interoperability refers to the capability of a WDS to be used in different and heterogeneous environments.	**Standards Support** is a measure of whether the WDS complies with standards.

Table 3. Security dimension

Dimension	Factors
Security refers to the ability that can protect a WDS from various threats like unauthorized access, exposure, forgery and destruction.	**Confidentiality** is the property that sensitive information is not disclosed to unauthorized individuals, entities or processes (Kissel, 2006).
	Integrity is the property that data has not been altered in an unauthorized manner (Kissel, 2006).
	Authentication consists in verifying the identity of a user, process, or device (Kissel, 2006)

Table 4. Business value dimension

Dimension	Factors
Business Value of a WDS means the economic worth delivered by applying the WDS on a business.	**Cost** is the level of payment for the value generated by using a WDS.
	Reputation is the collective reputation formed explicitly or implicitly by WDS consumers.

Table 5. Usability dimension

Dimension	Factors
Usability refers to the ease with which a user can learn to operate, prepare input for, and interpret the output of the WDS	**Learnability** is the capability of the WDS to enable the user to learn how to consume it.
	Extraction complexity refers to how complex is to develop the extraction process for a WDS.
	Content accessibility is the capability that the content provided for the WDS can be read by everyone, regardless of location, experience, or the type of computer technology used.

Table 6. Stability dimension

Dimension	Factors
Stability is a measure of the frequency of change related to the WDS.	**Location stability** refers to how stable is the location of a WDS.
	Structure / Interface Stability refers to how stable is the structure / interface of a WDS.

Table 7. Accuracy dimension

Dimension	Factors
Accuracy is the distance between v and v', being v' the value considered as correct.	**Syntactic Correctness** is the closeness of a value v to the elements of the corresponding definition domain D.
	Semantic Correctness is the closeness of the value v to the true value v'.
	Precision concerns the level of detail of data representation. It captures the gap between the level of detail of data in the system and its expected level of detail.

Table 8. Completeness dimension

Dimension	Factors
Completeness is the extent to which data are of sufficient breadth, depth, and scope for the task at hand.	**Density** is the proportion of non-null-values provided by sources in the attributes.
	Coverage is the percentage of the real world the source covers.

Table 9. Freshness dimension

Dimension	Factors
Freshness refers to the idea of how old is the data.	**Currency** captures the gap between the extraction of data from the sources and its delivery to the users.
	Timeliness captures how often data changes or how often new data are created in a source.

Table 10. Consistency dimension

Dimension	Factors
Consistency captures the violation of semantic rules defined over (a set of) data items.	**Domain Integrity** measures the satisfaction of rules over an attribute content.
	Relation Integrity measures the satisfaction of rules between attributes of the same table.
	Reference Integrity measures the satisfaction of rules between attributes of different tables.

Table 11. Uniqueness dimension

Dimension	Factors
Uniqueness captures the level of duplication of data	**Duplication** measures the quantity of data that represent the same real world entity or fact as other data.

Table 12. Reliability dimension

Dimension	Factors
Reliability is the trustworthiness of data; this depends mainly on the reputation of the provider.	**Credibility** is the level of user confidence in the WDS.
	Objectivity refers to the lack of bias in the data.

Table 13. Relevance of quality factors

Dimension	Factor	WDS Candidate Selection	DS Selection	WW Propagation
Service Level	Performance	X	X	
	Dependability	X	X	
Interoperability	Standards Support	X		
Security	Confidentiality	X	X	X
	Integrity	X	X	X
	Authentication	X	X	X
Business Value	Cost	X	X	
	Reputation	X	X	X
Usability	Learnability	X		
	Extraction Complexity	X		
	Content Accessibility	X		
Stability	Location Stability	X	X	
	Structure / Interface Stability	X	X	

factors are important to propagate to the WW. For example, integrity can guarantee end users that the data they are considering for taking decisions have not been altered in an unauthorized manner.

Finally, we consider that all data related quality factors are relevant for the three tasks. First, these quality data can be useful for deciding whether or not to develop a wrapper and it can also provide valuable information for selecting one DS instead of other. Additionally, we understand that the availability of this information can be an important resource for the end user.

Case Study: Hotels Web Warehouse

In this section, we present a case study that was implemented in the context of our research work, which is used throughout the chapter in order to show the application of the different proposed mechanisms.

The case study consists in a WW, whose final users are people interested in doing a market research for the building of new hotels. Information for this research is obtained from several WDSs in order to perform a comprehensive analysis of different obtained data. The WW allows its users to analyze, through time, hotels information, such as rooms' availability and costs, tourists' evaluations of the hotels, and existence of events of different types (cultural, sportive, etc.) near the hotels.

Following the quality-driven selection and extraction process, we carried out a sequence of tasks which are described in the next sections.

Candidate Web Data Sources Selection

We started with a list of WDSs that could potentially fulfill our requirements (i.e., that were related to the hotel business). Although those WDSs could be provided through heterogeneous protocols and formats, after an extensive search on the Web, the options were narrowed down to HTML pages (online booking sites) and Web Services.

Based on this preliminary list of candidate WDSs, a basic business value analysis was conducted, according to the cost factor. We notice that all candidate SOAP/REST Web Services charge for using them, whereas the online booking sites were free to perform searches. Since it was a prerequisite to use freely available Web data, we decide using the free data extraction from HTML pages.

A further analysis of well-known booking sites from the end-user point of view allowed us to choose three sites based on the following quality factors: the reputation and learnability of the site, and the coverage and density of the data it provides. To evaluate the latter, some partial, empirical observations were carried out, taking into account the requirements that were specified in the case study (e.g. a booking site must provide information about users, evaluations, etc.).

After this analysis, extraction complexity and content accessibility were evaluated for those three WDSs. We found that one of those sites imposes severe restrictions on the content that is available to Web robots, disallowing access to the search page. Since we are using the YQL API to implement the DSs, and since YQL robots honor the Robots Exclusion Protocol, we discarded all WDSs with this accessibility restriction, which leaves us two websites to be used as suitable WDSs. Those sites will be referred to as WebSite1 and WebSite2 hereinafter, due to confidentiality reasons.

Data Services Development and Selection

For WebSite1 and WebSite2, we implemented DS1 and DS2, respectively, to extract the data they provide. Since both WDSs provide HTML pages, it was fit to implement the extraction process using Web scraping techniques and tools. We leaned towards YQL for its easy-to-understand SQL-like syntax.

The extraction module of a DS not only acquires data from the WDS, but it feeds a relational database with the acquired data as well. This database acts as the intermediate storage where the QoS&DQ_M can measure some quality factors offline. This can be particularly interesting for some metrics that cannot be conveniently ex-

ecuted on the fly when the DS is invoked, due to performance restrictions. The results are stored in a second relational database, the quality metadata database (in Figure 1, QoS and DQ databases). This quality database allows storing measures according to the DS (e.g. DS1), the quality factor (e.g. precision), the granularity (e.g. tuple, attribute, etc.) and the specific object (e.g. the hotels table). We present some partial results of such measurements in Table 14, using the quality factors and metrics previously discussed.

As explained before, this quality metadata is made available to the DSR component, allowing a quality-driven DS discovery.

Data Service Infrastructure Implementation

In order to implement the DSI module we leverage an Enterprise Service Bus (ESB) product, given that the capabilities it provides (Chappell, 2004) facilitate the implementation of the DSI functionalities. Concretely, its communication, transformation (e.g. XSLT) and event-driven capabilities can be used to implement DSs.

In addition, ESB products usually provide various out-of-the-box monitoring capabilities. Therefore, besides the Data Quality information we present in Table 14, we also have QoS information (e.g. response time).

As well, the ESB capabilities can be leveraged to implement corrective actions in case of quality degradation. In this sense, various works have used these facilities (Batini et al., 2009) to implement self-adaptive behaviors in an ESB. As an example, we implemented a cache service (Fang et al., 2006) to which requests can be routed when, for example, the response time is too high.

Table 14. Partial quality factors measurements

DS	Quality Factor	Granularity	Object	Quality Value
DS1	Syntactic Correctness	Value	User.country_name	0.463
DS2	Syntactic Correctness	Value	User.country_name	0.619
DS1	Density	Attribute	Hotel.chain_name	0.462
DS2	Density	Attribute	Hotel.chain_name	0.365
DS1	Precision	Value	Costs.price	0.389
DS2	Precision	Value	Costs.price	0.393
DS1	Relation Integrity	Value	Rooms.total_hotel	0.686
DS2	Relation Integrity	Value	Rooms.total_hotel	0.603
DS1	Domain Integrity	Attribute	Hotels.category	0.925
DS2	Domain Integrity	Attribute	Hotels.category	1

DATA WAREHOUSE QUALITY MANAGEMENT

The approach of defining data quality in terms of its fitness for use (Pipino et al., 2002; Strong et al., 1997; Wand and Wang, 1996; Wang and Strong, 1996) is widely accepted in the literature. From this viewpoint it is difficult to define the concept of data quality, since it depends on the intended use of the data, on the context where they will be used and on the user's notion of quality. For each application domain quality models represent specific quality definitions and criteria, which are associated to domain objects and related to the way data are obtained and to the operations applied to these data.

DWs may be considered as a particular application domain. They are systems that have a specific purpose, which is to allow decision making oriented data analysis. They have a set of domain objects, such as dimensions, hierarchies and measures. In addition, they have a specific kind of users, who are business managers and decisions makers. Considering DWs as a particular domain allows us to define a data quality model for it, taking into account different importance degrees of quality properties over DW objects.

DW Domain

We consider a domain model for DWs, over which we will define the quality dimensions and factors. MultiDim (Malinowski and Zimanyi, 2008) is a conceptual multidimensional model that allows representing at the conceptual level all elements required in DW and OLAP applications.

Figure 3 shows the simplified MultiDim metamodel. It represents: (1) dimensions, which are composed of one or more hierarchies, or of one level, (2) hierarchies, which are composed of levels, (3) levels, which are composed of attributes, (4) fact relationships, which include measure attributes and are related to a set of levels. A level is identified by a key, which is composed by a set of attributes.

Terminology: A *member* of a level is an instance of the level. We use the term *cube* as a synonym of *fact relationship*. We call *level-identifier* to the *key* represented in the metamodel.

Case Study: DW Requirements and Design

In this section we continue with the case study previously presented. The following are some of the elicited WW user requirements:

Figure 3. Metamodel of the MultiDim model (Malinowski and Zimanyi, 2008)

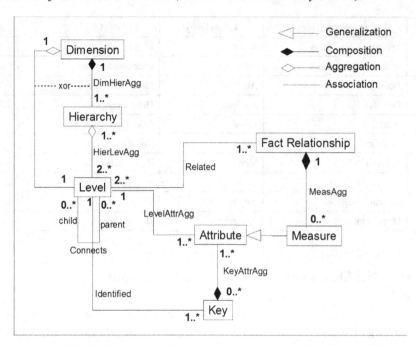

REQ1: Available and occupied rooms by season.

Users want to analyze the number of available and occupied rooms in different hotels according to seasons in the year, and according to dates. Additionally, they want to discriminate the number of occupied rooms by room type and also by cities, countries and region.

REQ2: Hotels with available rooms.

The number of hotels with available rooms, grouped by hotel chain, is also required. This measure will also be considered by cities, countries and regions, by events and by time.

REQ3: Hotel rooms' prices.

It must be possible to obtain the average prices of the hotels' rooms, considering room and hotel types, grouping hotels by category and chain. This measure should also be considered by seasons and dates of the year.

A multidimensional model was constructed from the requirements presented above. Some of its fact relationships, dimensions and hierarchies are shown in Figure 4 and Figure 5, following MultiDim notation, previously introduced.

In Figure 4 the fact relationship Availability is represented with its measures: number of available and occupied rooms, total number of rooms and number of hotels with available rooms. Figure 5 shows the fact relationship Offer with the measure price, which is an average of the prices of the rooms in the different hotels, taking into account seasons, room type, hotels and dates.

DW-Specific Data Quality Factors

In order to define a data quality model for DW systems we consider a set of problematic scenarios. These scenarios are error-prone situations that frequently exist in a DW system, mainly caused by the DW logical design, data loading processes, source data quality, and certain OLAP operations applied to DW data. In the context

Figure 4. Fact relationship availability

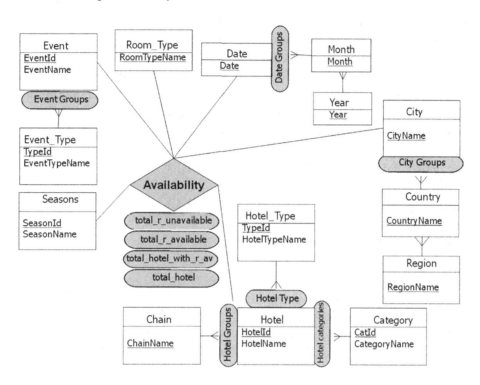

Figure 5. Fact relationship offer

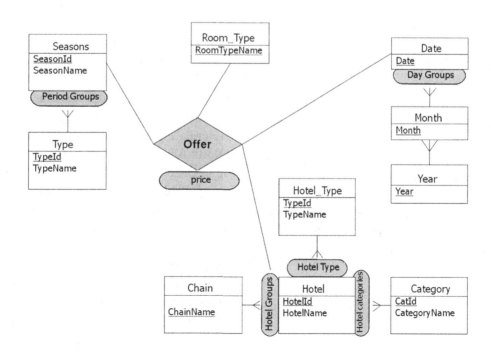

of these scenarios, data quality problems often arise, constituting a set of typical errors that can be found in this kind of systems. DW data quality dimensions and factors can be defined from the consideration of these typical errors, resulting in a data quality model for this kind of systems.

In the following we present some problematic scenarios and the data quality factors derived from these contexts, classifying these factors in quality dimensions previously defined for data quality. We also specify the domain object to which each data quality factor applies.

The presented scenarios were defined taking into account typical DW problems that are shown in the literature (Kimball and Ross, 2002; Malinowski and Zimanyi, 2008) and found in our own experience in DW systems development. In general, the mentioned literature problems are presented in order to motivate good design guidelines, but at the same time, they show data quality problems that may arise in complex contexts. Therefore, the defined set of quality factors for DWs is not intended to cover all the possible DW-specific quality problems; it is only one possible set.

Examples shown in each scenario correspond to the Case Study presented before.

Scenario 1: Denormalized Hierarchies

Star schemas are often used in DW logical design (Kimball and Ross, 2002). In this kind of schema, for each DW dimension, conceptual hierarchies are represented in a de-normalized table (dimension table). Therefore, all the levels of a hierarchy coexist in the same table, where the primary key is the identifier of the lowest level of the hierarchy, while the other level-identifiers can be repeated through the table.

Let $D(\underline{X}1, Y_1, X_2, Y_2, ..., X_n, Y_n)$ be a dimension table.

For each hierarchy level i, X_i, is the set of attributes that identify each member of level i and Y_i is the set of descriptive attributes of level i. There exists functional dependencies (fds) (1) between level-identifier attributes and descriptive attributes for each level, and also (2) between level-identifier attributes from consecutive levels, that should be satisfied:

$$X_1 \rightarrow Y_1, X_2$$

$$X_2 \rightarrow Y_2, X_3$$

$$\cdots$$

$$X_n \rightarrow Y_n$$

Due to the de-normalization of the dimension table, these fds may not be satisfied and inconsistencies may appear. This is a serious problem in DW context, since aggregations according to the hierarchy levels (*roll-up* operations) would give erroneous results.

Example: Suppose the hierarchy *City-Country-Region* (see Figure 4) is implemented, in the relational DW, as a dimension table *Location (city-name, country-name, region-name)* with *city-name* as the primary key. Fd *country-name → region-name* should be satisfied by all instances, but it is not enforced by the relational system. Due to an error in the loading process, the country value 'Mexico' appears with the region value 'Central America' in some tuples and with the region value 'North America' in other tuples. When data are aggregated in the OLAP environment, in order to see available rooms per *Region*, some rooms from 'Mexico' will be counted for 'Central America' and not for 'North America.'

Quality Dimension: Consistency
Quality Factor: Hierarchy-levels Consistency
Domain Object: hierarchy
Metric: Verification of satisfaction of fds between level-identifiers and between level-

identifiers and descriptive attributes, on the relational DW.

Scenario 2: Heterogeneity in Level-Identifier Domains

When a level-identifier is an attribute whose values should belong to certain discrete domain, but the attribute values come from different sources, these values may belong to different discrete domains not being detected during DW loading.

Summarizing information at this level will result in confusing groups of data.

Example: Consider the level-identifier attribute *country-name*, whose values should belong to a discrete domain. Suppose that in the web sources different domains are used so that value 'USA' is used in WebSite1, while value 'United States' is used in WebSite2, corresponding to the same country in real-world. When data is summarized by country, two different groups will be generated for the same real-world country.

Quality Dimension: Accuracy
Quality Factor: Level-identifiers Syntactic Correctness
Domain Object: level-identifier
Metric: Given a selected attribute domain for the level-identifier attribute, verify that the values of the attribute belong to the domain.

Scenario 3: Null and Dummy Values in Level-Identifiers

Frequently, caused by incompleteness in sources data, many DW attributes have NULL values. These cases are particularly important when the attributes are (or compose) level-identifiers. When NULL values exist in level-identifiers, OLAP analysis is seriously affected, since some groups of information are not shown and also measure aggregations do not consider the measure values of all detailed *fact table* information.

A common strategy to avoid the described NULL values is to generate *dummy values* that act as placeholders in the level-identifiers. This strategy allows OLAP tools to show and consider in aggregations all the measure values that are found in detailed data, but there may be problems when filtering data according to conditions over the level-identifiers (*slice* or *dice* operations) where *dummy values* fall outside.

Example: Consider the level-identifier attribute *chain-name* in the *hotel* dimension. Suppose in web source WebSite1 the chain of the hotel does not appear. In the DW, there will be problems when grouping hotels by chain, since some of them will have a NULL value.

In this scenario the following two quality factors may be defined.

Quality Dimension: Completeness
Quality Factor: Level-identifiers Completeness
Domain Object: level
Metric: Percentage of NULL values found in the identifier of the level.
Quality Dimension: Completeness
Quality Factor: Level-identifiers Fictitious Values
Domain Object: level
Metric: Percentage of dummy values found in the identifier of the level.

Scenario 4: Heterogeneity in Measures Precision

When the values of a measure attribute come from different sources or are the results of calculations made during the DW loading process, they may lose precision.

When aggregations over the measures are applied, the lost precision can impact very hardly, resulting in erroneous measure values.

Example: Suppose the measure *price* (see Figure 5), which is stored as an integer number in the DW, is populated with some values that come from WebSite1 with a precision of one decimal

Table 15. DW-specific data quality factors

Dimension	Factor	Domain Object
Accuracy	Level-identifiers Syntactic Correctness	level identifier
	Measure Precision	measure
Consistency	Hierarchy-levels Consistency	hierarchy
	Inter-cube Consistency	pair of cubes
Completeness	Level-identifiers Completeness	level
	Level-identifiers Fictitious Values	level

digit, and other values that come from Website2 with a precision of two decimal digits. When prices are averaged in the context of OLAP operations, they may give results that are not the same as if they were averaged using the original precision.

Quality Dimension: Accuracy
Quality Factor: Measure Precision
Domain Object: measure
Metric: Trace measure value through loading process maintaining original precisions.

Scenario 5: Same Real World Activity Feeding Different Data Cubes

Sometimes two data cubes contain information about the same entities and activities of real world, allowing analyses from different perspectives, but they are fed by data coming from different sources. In these cases, a numeric relation that can be verified may exist between measures of the cubes.

In this scenario, consistency between the measure values of the cubes should be controlled (Horner et al., 2004).

Example: Consider the cubes represented in Figures 4 and 5. Consistency between the measures *total_r_available* of one cube and *price* of the other cube may be controlled. A consistency rule may be that the *price* of a room in high season cannot be lower than the average *price* of the room if *total_r_available* is less than certain number.

Quality Dimension: Consistency
Quality Factor: Inter-cube Consistency
Domain Object: pair of cubes
Metric: Application of consistency rules between corresponding measures of the two cubes.

Table 15 summarizes the DW data quality factors.

Quality Measurement in the DW

Quality assessment in DW and OLAP data is achieved through the combination of: (a) data and service quality metadata propagated from previous stages in the system (see Figure 1), and (b) new quality measurements applied to the DW (DW-specific quality factors). In addition, in some cases, the propagated data quality values are used as input for the new data quality measurements over the DW. For example, *precision* is one of the data quality factors that are measured immediately after data extraction, at DSI module (see Figure 1). This factor could have been measured over attributes that later (after integration, transformation and loading into the DW) become DW measures. In these cases, the values of *Measure Precision* factor may be deduced from these previous measurements, which are registered in the quality metadata.

The quality information that is provided to the final user of the WW consists of a set of quality values associated to DW objects. These values correspond to the quality factors shown in Table

Table 16. Data warehouse quality factors

Dimension	Factor	Domain Object
Data Quality		
Accuracy	Level-identifiers Syntactic Correctness	level identifier
	Measure Precision	measure
	Syntactic Correctness	descriptive attribute
	Semantic Correctness	descriptive attribute
Consistency	Hierarchy-levels Consistency	hierarchy
	Inter-cube Consistency	pair of cubes
Completeness	Level-identifiers Completeness	level
	Level-identifiers Fictitious Values	level
	Coverage	dimension
Freshness	Currency	cube
	Timeliness	cube
Service Quality		
Security	Confidentiality	attribute value
	Integrity	attribute value
	Authentication	attribute value
Business Value	Reputation	attribute value

16. As can be observed, some data quality factors are associated only to certain DW objects, which are considered relevant to these factors due to their role in the DW. Some other quality factors, like service ones, are associated to each data value, because they were propagated from the sources as metadata of each data value.

Note that coverage, currency and timeliness quality factors are measured at the DSI module and propagated towards the DW, with a reference to the corresponding data. In Table 16, we associate these factors to the DW domain objects that correspond to each factor according to the semantic of the factor. Coverage is measured with respect to real-world entities, concept that corresponds to the dimensions in the DW. Freshness dimension factors are measured on facts that vary over time, concept that correspond to cube instances in the DW.

Case Study: WW Quality

Following the examples presented in the scenarios of DW quality problems, quality values for factors: Level-identifiers Syntactic Correctness in *country-name*, Level-identifiers Completeness in *chain-name*, and Measure Precision in *price*, are obtained from the quality values measured in the DSI module (see Table 14), propagated and contained in the data quality metadata. The values of rest of the factors defined for DW are calculated in the DW measurement module (DWQ_M) and the rest of the quality values are the ones that are propagated from DSI module.

FUTURE RESEARCH DIRECTIONS

In spite of the advances in the field, several issues on quality management in Web Warehouses remain open. The application of service oriented architectures and middleware technologies in

Web Warehouse and DW systems would enable to improve data processing in large distributed and loosely-coupled systems. The present work is a step forward in this direction as shows an interesting and promising approach.

In turn, DW-specific quality factors may be further studied, achieving a set of basic but complete quality aspects applicable and useful for any DW.

Using quality values to guide data processing operations appears to be highly promising, but still lacks of underlying formalization. On the other hand, user quality requirements should be considered in the data processing. Models for query preferences (DeAmo and Giacometti, 2008) may provide a useful background for addressing these problems.

One of the critical topics is to deal with the volatile nature of information in the Web, which gives rise to changes in the quality of data sources and, consequently, impacts on the overall system quality. In this regards, a probabilistic-based approach proposed in (Marotta and Ruggia, 2008), which addresses such changes on freshness and accuracy data quality factors, constitutes a step forward to tackling these issues.

CONCLUSION

Data quality has always been recognized as a key issue in Data and Web Warehouses as it concerns the reliability of information to be used in decision-making. In recent years, the growth of information sources in the Web has given rise to new challenges in the area. On the one hand, new technologies like Web Services, XML and middleware platforms facilitate accessing data sources distributed in the Web as well as processing the extracted data. On the other hand, the proliferation of data sources in Internet requires assessing, not only data quality, but also the quality of the service corresponding to such sources.

In order to deal with these matters, this chapter proposes a reference architecture for WW, which combines a comprehensive quality management approach with distributed service-oriented computing capabilities.

The presented quality management approach takes into account not only data quality, but also quality of services, which provides key information about the practical usability of external sources. In addition, quality information is used to filter undesirable items and also to guide the processes of source selection, as well as data extraction and integration. Finally, the framework structuring factors and metrics, which enables to represent the quality aspects that are specific to the different parts of the Web Warehouse, provides the means to state what factors have to be propagated to the different stages of the WW. In this regards, a relevant contribution of this work is the definition of a group of specialized quality dimensions for web data services, as well as for DW systems' data.

Distributed and service oriented information processing enable to strengthen the WW quality management in different ways. Service orientation provides the means to encapsulate Data Services and to execute them regardless their physical location, enabling to take advantage of large-scale distributed processing facilities, like Cloud Computing ones, as well as to deal with regulations restricting detailed data transfer (e.g. data protection and privacy). In addition, this approach promotes the application of event-based, message-based and asynchronous data processing mechanisms, which are implemented by middleware products associated to service oriented architectures (e.g. Enterprise Service Bus).

A concrete view of the addressed topics is provided through an application example from Tourism, especially Hotels domain, where information about hotels characteristics, location, prices, etc. is managed.

REFERENCES

Akoka, J., Berti-Equille, L., Boucelma, O., Bouzeghoub, M., Comyn-Wattiau, I., & Cosquer, M. … Cherfi, S. S.-S. (2007). A framework for quality evaluation in data integration systems. In J. Cardoso, J. Cordeiro, & J. Filipe (Eds.), International Conference on Enterprise Information Systems, 3, (pp. 170–175).

Ballou, D. P., & Tayi, G. K. (1999). Enhancing data quality in data warehouse environments. *Communications of the ACM, 42*(1), 73–78. doi:10.1145/291469.291471

Batini, C., & Scannapieco, M. (2006). *Data quality: Concepts, methodologies and techniques.* New York, NY: Springer-Verlag Inc, Series on Data-Centric Systems and Applications.

Batini, C., Cappiello, C., Francalanci, C., & Maurino, A. (2009). Methodologies for data quality assessment and improvement. ACM Computer Surveys, 41(3), 16:1–16:52.

Bhowmick, S. S., Madria, S. K., & Ng, W. K. (2003). Representation of Web data in a Web warehouse. *The Computer Journal, 46*(3), 229–262. doi:10.1093/comjnl/46.3.229

Bhowmick, S. S., Madria, S. K., & Ng, W. K. (2004). *Web data management: A warehouse approach.* New York, NY: Springer-Verlag Inc.

Bouzeghoub, M., & Peralta, V. (2004). A framework for analysis of data freshness. In F. Naumann, & M. Scannapieco, (Eds.), MIT Information Quality Industry Symposium, (pp. 59–67). ACM.

Bowler, M. (2010). HtmlUnit. Retrieved June 21, 2010 from http://sourceforge.net/projects/htmlunit

Calero, C., Piattini, M., Pascual, C., & Serrano, M. (2001). Towards data warehouse quality metrics. In D. Theodoratos, J. Hammer, M. A. Jeusfeld, & M. Staudt (Eds.), Design and Management of Data Warehouses, CEUR Workshop Proceedings, vol. 39. Retrieved from CEUR-WS.org

Cappiello, C., Daniel, F., & Matera, M. (2009). A quality model for mashup components. In M. Gaedke, M. Grossniklaus, & O. Dáz (Eds.), International Conference on Web Engineering (LNCS 5648, pp. 236–250). Springer.

Cappiello, C., Kritikos, K., Metzger, A., Parking, M., Pernici, B., Plebani, P., & Treiber, M. (2008). A quality model for service monitoring and adaptation. In D. Karastoyanova, R. Kazhamiakin, A. Metzger, & M. Pistore (Eds.), Workshop on Monitoring, Adaptation and Beyond at Service Wave Conference, (pp. 29–42).

Caro, A., Calero, C., Caballero, I., & Piattini, M. (2005). Data quality in Web applications: A state of the art. In IADIS International Conference WWW/Internet, v. 2, (pp. 364–368).

Chappell, D. (2004). *Enterprise service bus: Theory in practice.* O'Reilly Media.

Cheng, K., Kambayashi, Y., Lee, S., & Mohania, M. (2000). Functions of a Web warehouse. In Kyoto International Conference on Digital Libraries: Research and Practice, (pp. 160 –167). Los Alamitos, CA: IEEE Computer Society.

Daniel, F., Casati, F., Palpanas, T., Chayka, O., & Cappiello, C. (2008). Enabling better decisions through quality-aware reports in business intelligence applications. In M. P. Neely, L. Pipino & J. P. Slone (Eds.), MIT International Conference on Information Quality, (pp. 310–324).

DeAmo, S., & Giacometti, A. (2008). Preferences over objects, sets and sequences. In Fritzsche, P. (Ed.), *Tools in artificial intelligence* (pp. 49–76). InTech.

Etcheverry, L., Peralta, V., & Bouzeghoub, M. (2008). Qbox-Foundation: A metadata platform for quality measurement. In 4th Data and Knowledge Quality Workshop (DKQ) at QDB.

Fang, Y., Fang, R., Tian, Z., Lane, E., Srinivasan, H., & Banks, T. (2006). Cache mediation pattern specification: An overview. Retrieved June 21, 2010, from http://www.ibm.com/developerworks/webservices/ library/ws-soa-cachemed/

Fitzpatrick, R. (2000). Additional quality factors for the World Wide Web. In Proceedings of the Second World Congress for Software Quality. Citeseer.

González, L., Peralta, V., Bouzeghoub, M., & Ruggia, R. (2009). Qbox-services: Towards a service-oriented quality platform. In C. A. Heuser & G. Pernul (Eds.), ER Workshops, (LNCS 5833, pp. 232–242). Springer.

Helfert, M., & Herrmann, C. (2002). Proactive data quality management for data warehouse systems. In L. V. S. Lakshmanan (Ed.), DMDW, CEUR Workshop Proceedings, vol. 58, (pp. 97–106). Retrieved from CEUR-WS.org.

Hinrichs, H., & Aden, T. (2001). An ISO 9001: 2000 compliant quality management system for data integration in data warehouse systems. In D. Theodoratos, J. Hammer, M. A. Jeusfeld, & M. Staudt (Eds.), DMDW, CEUR Workshop Proceedings, vol. 39. Retrieved from CEUR-WS.org

Horner, J., & Song, I.-Y. (2005). A taxonomy of inaccurate summaries and their management in olap systems. In L. M. L. Delcambre, C. Kop, H. C. Mayr, J. Mylopoulos & O. Pastor (Eds.), Lecture Notes in Computer Science, 3716, 433–448. Springer.

Horner, J., Song, I.-Y., & Chen, P. P. (2004). An analysis of additivity in olap systems. In I.-Y. Song & K. C. Davis (Eds.), ACM Sixth International Workshop on Data Warehousing and OLAP, (pp. 83–91).

Jarke, M., & Vassiliou, Y. (1997). Foundations of data warehouse quality. In Proceedings of the 2nd Conference on Information Quality, Massachusetts Institute of Technology, Cambridge.

Jarke, M. (1999). Architecture and quality in data warehouses: An extended repository approach. *Information Systems*, *24*(3), 229–253. doi:10.1016/S0306-4379(99)00017-4

Kim, E., Lee, Y., Kim, Y., Park, H., Kim, J., Moon, B., et al. Kang, G. (2010). OASIS Web services quality factors. Retrieved June 21, 2010 fro: http://www.oasis-open.org/committees/ download. php/38503/ WS-Quality_Factors_ v1.0-r10.doc

Kimball, R., & Ross, M. (2002). *The data warehouse toolkit: The complete guide to dimensional modeling*. Wiley.

Kissel, R. (2006). Glossary of key information security terms. Retrieved June 21, 2010, from http://csrc.nist.gov/publications/ drafts/nistir-7298/ draft-nistir-7298 -rev1_glossary-key-security-terms.pdf

Laender, A. H. F., Ribeiro-Neto, B. A., da Silva, A. S., & Teixeira, J. S. (2002). A brief survey of Web data extraction tools. *SIGMOD Record*, *31*, 84–93. doi:10.1145/565117.565137

Lee, Y. W., Strong, D. M., Kahn, B. K., & Wang, R. Y. (2002). AIMQ: A methodology for information quality assessment. *Information & Management*, *40*, 133–146. doi:10.1016/S0378-7206(02)00043-5

Madnick, S. E., Wang, R. Y., Lee, Y. W., & Zhu, H. (2009). Overview and framework for data and information quality research. *Journal of Data and Information Quality*, *1*(1), 1–22. doi:10.1145/1515693.1516680

Malinowski, E., & Zimanyi, E. (2008). *Advanced data warehouse design: From conventional to spatial and temporal applications*. Springer-Verlag.

Marotta, A., & Ruggia, R. (2008). Applying probabilistic models to data quality change management. In J. Cordeiro, B. Shishkov, A. Ranchordas, & M. Helfert (Eds.), International Conference on Software and Data Technologies (ISDM/ABF), (pp. 296–299). INSTICC Press.

Marotta, A., Motz, R., & Ruggia, R. (2002). Managing source schema evolution in Web warehouse. *Journal of the Brazilian Computer Society*, *8*(2), 20–31. doi:10.1590/S0104-65002002000200003

Marotta, A., Piedrabuena, F., & Abelló, A. (2006). Managing quality properties in a rolap environment. In E. Dubois & K. Pohl (Eds.), Lecture Notes in Computer Science, 4001, 127–141. Springer.

Mecella, M., Scannapieco, M., Virgillito, A., Baldoni, R., Catarci, T., & Batini, C. (2002). Managing data quality in cooperative Information Systems. In R. Meersman, & Z. Tari (Eds.), Lecture Notes in Computer Science, 2519, 486–502. Springer.

Naumann, F., Freytag, J. C., & Leser, U. (2004). Completeness of integrated information sources. *Information Systems Journal*, *29*(7), 583–615. doi:10.1016/j.is.2003.12.005

Nikic, V., & Wajda, A. (2010). Web-harvest. Retrieved June 21, 2010, from http://web-harvest.sourceforge.net/

Peralta, V., Ruggia, R., & Bouzeghoub, M. (2004). Analyzing and evaluating data freshness in data integration systems. *Ingénierie des Systèmes d'Information*, *9*(5-6), 145–162. doi:10.3166/isi.9.5-6.145-162

Pipino, L. L., Lee, Y. W., & Wang, R. Y. (2002). Data quality assessment. *Communications of the ACM*, *45*(4), 211. doi:10.1145/505248.506010

Rizzi, S., Abelló, A., Lechtenbörger, J., & Trujillo, J. (2006). Research in data warehouse modeling and design: Dead or alive? In I.-Y. Song & P. Vassiliadis (Eds.), ACM Sixth International Workshop on Data Warehousing and OLAP, (pp. 3–10).

Rudra, A., & Yeo, E. (1999). Key issues in achieving data quality and consistency in data warehousing among large organizations in Australia. In Hawaii International Conference on System Sciences.

Soper, D. S. (2005). A framework for automated Web business intelligence systems. In Hawaii International Conference on System Sciences.

Strong, D. M., Lee, Y. W., & Wang, R. Y. (1997). Data quality in context. *Communications of the ACM*, *40*(5), 103–110. doi:10.1145/253769.253804

Vaisman, A. (2007). Data quality-based requirements elicitation for decision support systems. In Wrembel, R., & Koncilia, C. (Eds.), *Data warehouses and OLAP: Concepts, architectures and solutions*. Hershey, PA: Idea Group.

Vassiliadis, P., Bouzeghoub, M., & Quix, C. (2000). Towards quality-oriented data warehouse usage and evolution. *Information Systems Journal*, *25*(2), 89–115. doi:10.1016/S0306-4379(00)00011-9

Wand, Y., & Wang, R. Y. (1996). Anchoring data quality dimensions in ontological foundations. *Communications of the ACM*, *39*(11), 86–95. doi:10.1145/240455.240479

Wang, R., & Strong, D. (1996). Beyond accuracy: What data quality means to data consumers. *Journal of Management Information Systems*, *12*(4), 5–33.

Yahoo Developer Network. (2010). Yahoo! query language - YDN. Retrieved June 21, 2010 from http://developer.yahoo.com/yql/

Zhu, Y., & Buchmann, A. P. (2002). Evaluating and selecting Web sources as external information resources of a data warehouse. In T. W. Ling, U. Dayal, E. Bertino, W. K. Ng, & A. Goh (Eds.), Web Information Systems Engineering Conference, (pp. 149–160). IEEE Computer Society.

Zhu, Y. (1999). A framework for warehousing the Web contents. In L. C. K. Hui & D. L. Lee (Eds.), Lecture Notes in Computer Science, 1749, 83–92. Springer.

Chapter 2
Innovative Approaches for Efficiently Warehousing Complex Data from the Web

Fadila Bentayeb
University of Lyon, France

Sabine Loudcher
University of Lyon, France

Nora Maïz
University of Lyon, France

Nouria Harbi
University of Lyon, France

Hadj Mahboubi
CEMAGREF Centre Clermont-Ferrand, France

Omar Boussaïd
University of Lyon, France

Cécile Favre
University of Lyon, France

Jérôme Darmont
University of Lyon, France

ABSTRACT

Research in data warehousing and OLAP has produced important technologies for the design, management, and use of Information Systems for decision support. With the development of Internet, the availability of various types of data has increased. Thus, users require applications to help them obtaining knowledge from the Web. One possible solution to facilitate this task is to extract information from the Web, transform and load it to a Web Warehouse, which provides uniform access methods for automatic processing of the data. In this chapter, we present three innovative researches recently introduced to extend the capabilities of decision support systems, namely (1) the use of XML as a logical and physical model for complex data warehouses, (2) associating data mining to OLAP to allow elaborated analysis tasks for complex data and (3) schema evolution in complex data warehouses for personalized analyses. Our contributions cover the main phases of the data warehouse design process: data integration and modeling, and user driven-OLAP analysis.

DOI: 10.4018/978-1-61350-038-5.ch002

INTRODUCTION

Traditional databases aim at data management (i.e., they help organize, structure, and query data). They are transaction processing-oriented and are often qualified as production databases. In opposition, data warehouses have a very different vocation: analyzing data (Kimball & Ross, 2002; Inmon, 2005) by exploiting specific models (star, snowflake and constellation schemas). They are termed as On-Line Analytical Processing (OLAP) databases. Data are then organized around indicators called measures, and analysis axes called dimensions. Dimension attributes either form a hierarchy or are just descriptive. Dimension hierarchies allow for obtaining views of data at different granularities (i.e., summarized or detailed through roll-up and drill-down operations, respectively).

Research in data warehousing and OLAP has produced important technologies for the design, management and use of information systems for decision support. To achieve the value of a data warehouse, incoming data must be transformed into an analysis-ready format. In the case of numerical data, data warehousing systems often provide tools to assist in this process. Unfortunately, standard tools are inadequate for producing relevant analysis when data are complex. Indeed, with the development of Internet, the availability of various types of data (Web data, multimedia data, biomedical data, etc.) has increased. Thus, users require applications to help them obtaining knowledge from the Web. For example, in the context of e-commerce, analyzing the behavior of a customer, a product, or a company consists of monitoring one or several activities (commercial or medical pursuits, patents deposits, etc.). The Web then becomes a real data source with which decision support applications should deal.

Furthermore, many Business Intelligence (BI) applications necessitate external data sources. For instance, performing competitive monitoring for a given company requires the analysis of data available only from its competitors. In this context, the Web is a tremendous source of data, and may be considered as a farming system.

However, the specific characteristics of Web data make it difficult to create such applications. One possible solution to facilitate this task is to extract information from the Web, transform and load it to a Web Warehouse, which provides uniform access methods for automatic processing of the data. Web Warehousing extends the lifetime of Web contents and its reuse by different applications across time.

Moreover, the special nature of complex data poses different and new requirements to data warehousing technologies, over those posed by conventional data warehouse applications. In this case, the data warehousing process should be adapted in response to evolving complex data and information requirements. Tools must be developed to provide the needed analysis. Therefore, the issue that may arise "Can we OLAP complex data?" To address this issue, we need a new generation of data warehousing models that can organize complex data in a multidimensional way and new OLAP operators that can analyze them.

The XML formalism has emerged as a dominant W3C standard for describing and exchanging semistructured data among heterogeneous data sources. Its self-describing hierarchical structure enables a manipulative power to accommodate complex, disconnected and heterogeneous data. It allows describing the structure of a document and constraining its contents. With its vocation for semistructured data exchange, the XML language offers great flexibility for representing heterogeneous data, and great possibilities for structuring, modeling and storing them.

Furthermore, a data cube structure can provide a suitable context for applying data mining methods. More generally, the association of OLAP and data mining allows elaborated analysis tasks exceeding the simple exploration of a data cube. The aim is to take advantage of OLAP, as well as data mining techniques, and to integrate them into the same analysis framework in order to provide an enhanced analysis process for complex data by extending OLAP analysis capabilities.

In this chapter, we present three innovative researches recently introduced to extend the capabilities of decision support systems, namely (1) the use of XML as a logical and physical model for complex data warehouses, (2) the association of data mining with OLAP to allow elaborated analysis tasks for complex data and (3) the schema evolution in complex data warehouses for personalized analyses. Our contributions cover the main phases of the data warehouse design process: data integration and modeling and user driven-OLAP analysis.

Our first contribution consists of using XML to model complex data warehouses (Boussaïd et al., 2006; Boussaïd et al., 2008). XML is suitable for structuring complex data coming from different Web sources and bearing heterogeneous formats (Mahboubi, 2009). XML indeed embeds both data and schema, either implicitly or explicitly through schema definitions (DTD or XML Schema). This type of metadata suits data warehouses very well. Moreover, XML query languages such XQuery help formulate analytical queries that would be difficult to express in a relational, SQL-based system (Beyer et al., 2005).

Our second contribution deals with complex data analyzing based on data mining technologies. Classical OLAP tools are indeed ill-adapted to analyze Web data directly. OLAP facts representing complex objects need appropriate tools and new ways to be analyzed. Combining data mining methods with OLAP tools is an interesting solution to enrich OLAP capabilities and to analyze complex data from the Web. We propose to extend OLAP to describe, cluster and explain of complex data (Ben Messaoud et al., 2006, 2007a, 2007b).

Our third contribution studies the problem of specifying changes in multidimensional databases. These changes may be motivated by evolutions of user requirements, as well as changes in Web sources (Hurtado et al., 1999b; Espil & Vaisman,

2001). The rule-based multidimensional model we provide supports both data and structure changes. The approach consists of creating new hierarchy levels in OLAP dimensions for data warehouse schema evolution according to relevant personalized analysis needs (Bentayeb et al., 2008; Favre et al., 2007).

Throughout this chapter, we use a running example to illustrate our contributions. It is extracted from a project we jointly carried out with linguist colleagues. This project (named CLAPI) dealt with the on-line integration, storage, management and analysis of spoken language interaction corpora (Aouiche et al., 2003). Funded by the French Ministry of Higher Education and Research, it provides Web access1 to the CLAPI corpus database through user-friendly query and quantitative analysis tools (a new feature in spoken language research) that allow researchers in linguistics to elaborate hypotheses and validate results on a significant volume of data.

A conceptual schema of our excerpt from CLAPI is provided in Figure 1. A corpus is made of audio and/or video recordings of real-life interactions (e.g., classrooms, divorce conciliations, conflicts in queues…). Each speaker in a recording is identified (with a pseudo; the database is anonymous) and may appear in several interactions. To be exploited by linguists, recordings are textually transcribed. These transcriptions are actually structured in XML and feature both tokens (i.e., oral forms of words, such as "h'llo" for "hello") and interactional phenomena (e.g., pauses, laughs, speech overlaps…). Finally, scientific studies produced by researchers in linguistics are attached to the corresponding recordings, which may be several when the study is transversal. All this information is available on the Web and stored with the help of standard Web technologies such as XML and its derivatives (e.g., RDF for metadata).

In this context, OLAP is able to provide linguist users statistical information regarding analysis dimensions such as speakers, tokens, phenomena

Figure 1.CLAPI excerpt UML class diagram

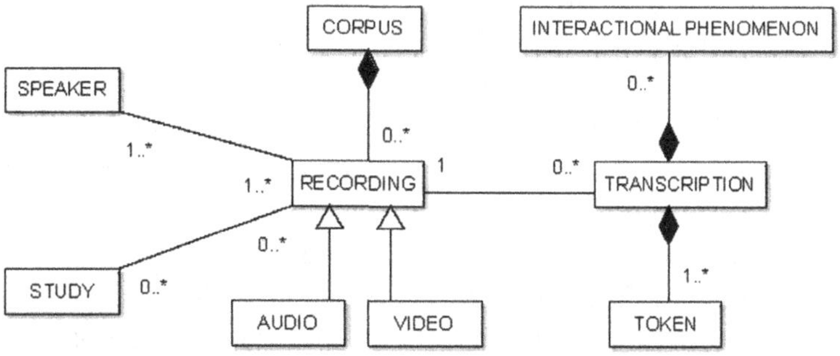

or time elapsed within a single interaction. It also helps compare several similar interactions (e.g., classrooms, conflicting situations…). For instance, simple analysis scenarios include:

- count the frequency of a given token over a determined period of time;
- count the frequency and evolution of speech overlaps over a determined period of time;
- number identified phenomena (such as laughs) over a determined period of time;
- compute the total, average, maximum and/or minimum pause time spent by speakers over a determined period of time.

Answering such queries requires fetching and integrating source data from the Web, dealing with data complexity and building suitable (XML) data cubes onto which suitable OLAP operations must be applied.

The remainder of this chapter is organized as follows. First, we discuss the related work regarding complex Web data warehousing. Then, we detail our three contributions regarding XML data warehousing, combining OLAP and data mining techniques for complex data analysis, and analysis personalization in complex data warehouses. We finally conclude this chapter and provide future research issues.

GENERAL LITERATURE REVIEW

Complex Data Integration

In data warehousing, the prime objective of storing data is to facilitate the decision process. To achieve the value of a data warehouse, input data must be transformed into an analysis-ready format. In the case of numerical data, data warehousing systems often provide tools to assist in this process. Unfortunately, standard tools are inadequate for producing a relevant analysis axis when data are complex. In such cases, the data warehousing process should be adapted in response to evolving data and information requirements. In a data warehousing process, the data integration phase is crucial. Data integration is a hard task that involves reconciliation at various levels: data models, data schema, data instances, and semantics.

Two main and opposing approaches are used to perform data integration over heterogeneous data sources. In the mediator-based approach (Rousset, 2002), data remain located at their original sources. User queries are executed through a mediator-wrapper system (Goasdoué et al., 2000). A mediator reformulates queries according to the content of the various accessible data sources, while the wrapper extracts the selected data from the target source. The major advantage of this approach especially in a Web context is its flexibility, since mediators are able to reformulate and/or approximate queries to better satisfy the user. However, when data sources are updated, modified data are lost, which is not pertinent in a decision-support context where data historicity is important.

In opposition, in the data warehouse approach, selected data from various sources are centralized in a new multidimensional database, the data warehouse (Inmon, 2005; Kimball, 2002). In a data warehouse context, data integration corresponds to the Extract, Transform, and Load (ETL) process that accesses, cleans and transforms heterogeneous data before they are loaded into the data warehouse. This approach supports data dating and is tailored for analysis. Some studies combine the mediation-based integration and data warehousing (Rousset, 2002). Other authors propose a logic description framework or a language (e.g., CARIN) for information integration (Goasdoué et al., 2000; Calvanese et al., 1998).

The special nature of complex data poses different and new requirements to data warehousing technologies, over those posed by conventional data warehousing applications. Hence, to integrate complex data sources, we need more than a tool for organizing data into a common syntax. The integration of complex data in a database is an issue that has been little studied. Jensen et al. (2001) propose a general system architecture for integrating XML and relational data sources at the conceptual level in a Web-based OLAP database. A "UML snowflake diagram" is built by choosing the desired UML classes from any source. The process is deployed through a graphical interface that deals only with UML classes and makes data sources transparent to the designer. Other approaches for an easier integration of complex data semantics have also been published. A framework for video content understanding, consisting of an expert system that uses a rule-based engine, domain knowledge, visual detectors and metadata to enhance video detection results and presenting

the semi-automatic construction of multimedia ontologies, is presented in (Jaimes et al., 2003). Semantic indexing techniques for complex data also exist (Stoffel et al., 1997). These techniques are based on domain knowledge made available in the form of ontologies. This research overcomes the difficulty of efficiently integrating semantic knowledge stored as ontologies in ways that support the efficient indexing of large databases. Finally, Baumgartner et al. (2005) describe how public information can be extracted automatically from Web sites, transformed into structured data formats, and used for data analysis in Business Intelligence systems. Authors design an architecture, called Lixto, for processing Web data in an efficient manner. They also exploit the XML formalism to manage extracted data and make them exploitable into an SAP business information warehouse.

To process complex data, it is also important to consider their metadata. To take this information into account, it is necessary to use appropriate management tools. An integrative and uniform model for metadata management in data warehousing environments uses a uniform representation approach based on UML to integrate technical and semantic metadata and their interdependencies (Stohr et al., 2002). Standards for describing resources that we consider as complex data already exist. The Resource Description Framework (Lassila & Swick, 1999) is a W3C-approved standard that uses metadata to describe Web contents. It is possible to describe all kind of resources using RDF. Another important standard is MPEG-7 (Manjunath et al., 2002). Its most important goal is to provide a set of methods and tools for the different aspects of multimedia content description. MPEG-7 focuses on the standardization of a common interface for describing multimedia materials (representing information about contents and metadata).

Data Warehouse Modeling

Multidimensional modeling aims at representing data according to user requirements. It represents information to be analyzed as a set of points in a space with several dimensions that are analysis axes.

Currently, although no model is recognized as standard, three concepts are admitted by the data warehousing community as the bases of multidimensional modeling: the concept of "data cube" and those of "dimension" and "fact." The first suggested models are based on structures (cubes) that do not represent all the concepts expressed by users, but the characteristics of their implementation. To define a multidimensional model that represents the concepts of the real world independently from any physical aspect, other concepts must be added. Multidimensional analyses require concepts that are close to the vision of decision makers, and to the semantics of decision. The introduced concepts are: hierarchies, various types of star, snowflake and constellation schemas (Kimball 2002), parameters, and weak attributes (Golfarelli et al., 1998).

However, dimensional modeling must be adapted to take into account the specificities of complex data. Some proposals regard multidimensional modeling by using XML as a base language for describing data warehouses. Krill affirms that vendors such as Microsoft, IBM, and Oracle largely employ XML in their database systems for interoperability between data warehouses and tool repositories (Krill, 1998). Nevertheless, we distinguish two separate approaches in this field.

The first approach focuses on the physical storage of XML documents in data warehouses. XML populates warehouses since it is considered an efficient technology to support data within well suited structures for interoperability and information exchange. Baril and Bellahsène introduce the View Model (Baril, & Bellahsène, 2003), which is a method capable of querying XML databases. A data model is defined for each view to organize

semi-structured data. An XML warehouse, named DAWAX (DAta WArehouse for XML), based on the View Model is also proposed. Hümmer et al. (2003) propose an approach, named XCube, to model classical data cubes with XML. Nevertheless, this approach focuses on the exchange and the transportation of classical data cubes over networks rather than on multidimensional modeling with XML.

The second approach aims at using XML to design data warehouses according to classical multidimensional models such as star and snowflake schemas. XML-star schema (Pokorný, 2001) uses Document Type Definitions (DTDs) to explicit dimension hierarchies. A dimension is modeled as a sequence of DTDs that are logically associated similarly as referential integrity does in relational databases. Golfarelli et al. (1998) introduce a Dimensional Fact Model represented via Attribute Trees. They also use XML Schemas to express multidimensional models by including relationships with sub-elements (Golfarelli et al. 2001).

However, Trujillo et al. (2004) think that this approach focuses on the presentation of multidimensional XML rather than on the presentation of the structure of the Multidimensional Conceptual Modeling (MCM) itself. They claim that an Object Oriented (OO) standard model is rather needed to cope with all multidimensional modeling properties at both structural and dynamic levels. Trujillo et al. (2004) provide a DTD model from which valid XML documents are generated to represent multidimensional models at a conceptual level. Nassis et al. (2004) propose a similar approach where OO is used to develop a conceptual model for XML Document Warehouses (XDW). An XML repository, called xFACT, is built by integrating OO concepts with XML Schemas. Nassis et al. (2004) also define Virtual dimensions by using XML and UML package diagrams in order to help the construction of hierarchical conceptual views. The X-Warehousing process is entirely based on XML: it designs warehouses with XML Schemas at a logical level, and then populates them with valid XML documents at a physical level (Boussaïd et al., 2006). Further, since it uses XML, our approach can also be considered a real solution for warehousing heterogeneous and complex data in order to prepare them for future OLAP analysis.

OLAP

Online Analytical Processing (OLAP) is an efficient technique for explorative data analysis. This trend is obvious, given the popularity of many OLAP systems (Codd, 1993), such as Essbase (Arbor Software) or Express (Oracle Corporation) for instance. Based on a multidimensional conceptual view of the data, these systems are especially well-suited to data analysis, and their characteristics are significantly different from those of relational databases. The analysis process concerns basic or aggregated data containing relevant information. OLAP allows to model data in a dimensional way and to observe data from different perspectives. This approach consists of building data cubes (or hypercubes) on which OLAP operations are performed. A data cube is a set of facts described by measures to be observed along analysis axes (dimensions) (Kimball, 2002; Inmon, 2005; Chaudhuri & Dayal, 1997). A dimension may be expressed through several hierarchies. Many aggregation levels for measures can be achieved to obtain either summarized or detailed information using OLAP operators. Thus, hierarchies allow sophisticated analyses and data visualization in a multidimensional database (Jagadish et al., 1999). However, the classical OLAP operators are only well-suited to numerical data, whereas, in recent years, more and more data sources beyond conventional alphanumerical data have come into being. This phenomenon especially appears when we wish to analyze and aggregate such objects as chemical compounds or protein networks (chem/bio-informatics), 2D/3D objects (spatial/geographic data and pattern recognition), circuits (computer-aided design, simulation), XML data (with loose schemas) and Web activi-

ties (human/computer networks and interactions). Such data are not only individual entities. Interacting relationships among them are also important and interesting. These relationships carry more semantics than entities themselves. Exploiting the semantics of complex data can then build decision-making information that is more relevant than OLAP classical approach allows.

In this context, several efforts have made done to define adequate complex data analysis. Some are spatially dedicated to define adequate operators for multimedia and spatial data analysis. For instance, Bimonte et al. (2007) propose a Web-based GIS-OLAP integrated solution supporting geographical dimensions and measures, and providing interactive and synchronized maps, pivot tables and diagrams displays in order to effectively support decision makers. Arigon et al. (2007) help user select the best representation of medical data according to various functional versions of the dimension numbers. Others studies aim at performing OLAP analyses over XML data (XOLAP) representing complex data. Such research work proposes to extend the XQuery with near OLAP capabilities such as advanced grouping and aggregation features. For instance, Hachicha et al. (2008) propose to express a broad set of OLAP operators with the TAX XML algebra.

All these contributions have a common point. They are based on their specific areas to adapt existing tools to make them suitable for the analysis of their requirements.

However, the limitations of traditional OLAP remain. It is the use of other techniques, such as data mining or information retrieval, combined with on-line analysis, that help obtain new analytical capabilities to process complex data.

The most recent proposals are especially interested in the OLAP analysis of social networks, interactions, or the Web 2.0 (Sifer, 2005; Aouiche et al., 2009). For example, Sifer (2005) propose to explore Web logs using a specific representation rather than data cubes. OLAP operations are based on coordinated dimension views and correspond to selection operations. Aouiche et al. (2009) give more attention at analyzing tag-clouds. Such data are becoming usual in so-called Social Web applications. For this sake, the authors define a set of rules to formally recognize an OLAP application and define a set of adequate OLAP computation of tag clouds as top-k queries.

XML DATA WAREHOUSING

Already standard on the Web, the XML language has also become a standard for representing business data (Beyer et al., 2005). It is particularly adapted for modeling complex data originating from heterogeneous sources, particularly from the Web. Moreover, XML query languages such as XQuery help formulate analytical queries that would be difficult to express in a relational system (Beyer et al., 2005). In consequence, there has been a clear trend toward XML warehousing for a couple of years. In this trend, we propose to represent complex data from the Web as XML documents. Then, a multidimensional model is designed to obtain an XML data warehouse. Finally, on-line analysis (OLAP) can take place.

Related Work: XML Data Warehousing and OLAP

Research in XML warehousing may be subdivided into three families. The first focuses on Web data integration for decision-support purposes. Web data sources are described by XML Schemas that are transformed into graphs used for selecting facts and creating a logical schema that validates the data warehouse (Golfarelli et al., 2001; Vrdoljak et al., 2003). In addition, the Xyleme system also supports query evaluation and change control (Xyleme, 2001). In these approaches, no particular warehouse model is proposed. All these proposals are reviewed by Pérez and al. (2008). Here, authors mainly focus on studies considering XML and its extensions as canonical

formalisms for Web application interoperability: meta-data representation, data interchange and heterogeneous and distributed Web data analysis (OLAP). They survey works dealing with the integration of XML data from heterogeneous and distributed sources (data warehouses), XML multidimensional design (semi-automatic ways) and XML-compatible OLAP systems. Authors also discuss approaches addressing how OLAP and Information Retrieval (IR) can be combined to explore text-rich document collections and to analyze acts and documents together in so-called contextualized warehouses.

By contrast, the second family of XML warehousing approaches explicitly bases on classical warehouse logical models (star-like schemas) and supports end-user analytical tools. An XML warehouse is then composed of documents representing facts and dimensions (Pokorný, 2001; Hümmer et al., 2003; Park et al., 2005). A methodological effort has also been made to cover processes such as data cleaning, summarization, intermediating XML documents, updating/linking existing documents and creating fact tables (Rusu et al., 2005), or to represent user analysis needs and match them with source data (Boussaïd et al., 2006). All these approaches more or less converge toward a unified XML warehouse model. They mostly differ in the way dimensions are handled and the number of XML documents used to store facts and dimensions.

Finally, the third XML warehouse family relates to document warehouses. Here, an XML data warehouse is a collection of either materialized or virtual XML views, which provide a mediated schema that constitutes a uniform query interface (Baril and Bellahsène, 2003; Rajugan et al., 2005; Nassis et al., 2005; Zhang et al., 2005).

Though XML data warehousing issues are quite broadly addressed, fewer authors actually push through the whole decision-support process and address the multidimensional analysis of XML data, which is termed XML-OLAP or XOLAP. This is mainly achieved by extending existing languages such as Microsoft MDX or XQuery with XML-specific operators (Park et al., 2005) or grouping, numbering, aggregation and cube operators (Beyer et al., 2005; Wang et al., 2005; Wiwatwattana et al. 2007), respectively. In the same frame of mind, some proposals extend existing OLAP clients to incorporate dimensions and measures extracted from external XML sources (such as Web pages) into a data cube (Pedersen et al., 2006). Such extensions are exploited as ordinary dimensions and measures, and allow handling unexpected or short time data requirements. They involve novel multi-granular data models and query languages that formalize and extend the existing system (Pedersen et al., 2006).

XML Warehousing and Analysis Methodology

Though feeding data warehouses with XML documents from the Web is getting increasingly common, methodological issues arise. The multidimensional organization of data warehouses is indeed quite different from the semi-structured organization of XML documents. Their architecture is subject-oriented, integrated, consistent, and data are regularly refreshed to represent temporal evolutions. An XML formalism can definitely be used to describe the various elements of a multidimensional model (Boussaïd et al., 2006), but XML can only be considered as a logical and physical description tool for future analysis tasks. The reference conceptual model remains the star schema and its derivatives.

Hence, we propose an XML multidimensional (and thus analysis-oriented) model to derive a physical organization of XML documents. To support this choice, we propose a modeling process that achieves complex data integration. We first design a conceptual UML model for a complex object. This UML model is then directly translated into an XML Schema, which we view as a logical model. At the physical level, XML documents that are valid against this logical model may be mapped

into a relational, object-relational or XML-native database. After representing complex data as XML documents, we physically integrate them into an Operational Data Store (ODS), which is a buffer ahead of the actual warehouse.

At this stage, it is already possible to mine the stored XML documents directly (e.g., with XML structure mining techniques). In addition, to further analyze these documents' contents efficiently, it is interesting to warehouse them (i.e., devise a multidimensional model that allows OLAP analyses). However, classical OLAP operators cannot handle XML's complexity and XOLAP operators are still few. Thus, we also propose a solution at this level.

XML Data Warehouse Model

Existing XML warehouse models mostly differ at the logical and physical levels in the number of XML documents used to store facts and dimensions. A performance evaluation study of these alternatives shows that representing facts in one single XML document and each dimension in one XML document allows the best performance in a snowflake schema (Boukraa et al., 2006). Moreover, this representation also allows to model constellation schemas without duplicating dimension information. Several fact documents can indeed share the same dimensions. Furthermore, since each dimension and its hierarchy levels are stored in one XML document, dimension updates are more easily and efficiently performed than if dimensions were either embedded with the facts or all stored in one single document.

Hence, we propose to adopt this architecture to represent XML data warehouses (Mahboubi et al., 2009). It is actually the translation of a classical constellation schema into XML. More precisely, as XCube (Hümmer et al., 2003), our reference data warehouse model is composed of the three types of XML documents: dw-model.xml represents warehouse metadata (schema, including dimension hierarchies); a set of facts$_f$.xml docu-

Figure 2. Dw-model.xml graph structure

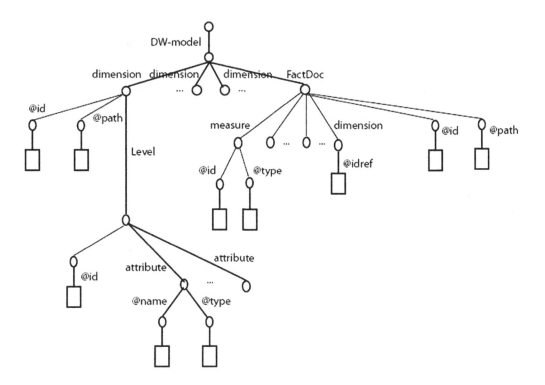

ments help store facts (i.e., dimension references and measure values); and a set of dimension$_d$.xml documents help store dimension member values.

Figure 2 represents dw-model.xml's graph structure. Its root node, DW-model, is composed of dimension and FactDoc nodes. A dimension node defines one dimension, its possible hierarchical levels (Level elements) and attributes (including their types), as well as the path to the corresponding dimensiond.xml document. A FactDoc element defines a fact (i.e., its measures, internal references to the corresponding dimensions, and the path to the corresponding factsf.xml document). Figure 3(a) represents the factsf.xml documents' graph structure. It is composed of fact nodes defining measures and dimension references. The document root node, FactDoc, is composed of fact subelements, each of whose instantiates a fact (i.e., measure values and dimension references). These identifier-based references support the fact-

to-dimension relationship. Finally, Figure 3(b) represents the dimensiond.xml documents' graph structure. Its root node, dimension, is composed of Level nodes. Each defines a hierarchy level composed of instance nodes that in turn define the level's member attribute values. In addition, an instance element contains Roll-up and Drill-Down attributes that define the hierarchical relationship within the dimension.

An example of instantiated dw-model.xml document is provided in Figure 4. It refers to a CLAPI-based study we made with our linguist colleagues to observe token (term in a transcription) frequencies, with respect to location in the transcription (begin, middle, end) and speaker sex. Due to space constraints, we cannot provide all dimensions and fact instances in this chapter, but the reader can extrapolate from Figure 4 the contents of dim-time.xml, dim-speaker.xml, dim-transcript.xml and facts.xml, respectively.

Figure 3. Factsf.xml (a) and dimensiond.xml (b) graph structures

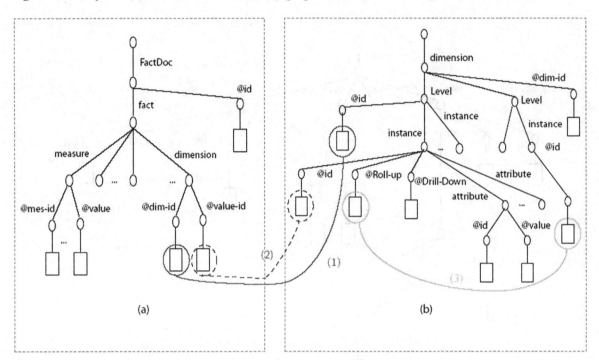

Figure 4. Sample dw-model.xml document

```
<?xml version="1.0" encoding="utf-8">
<DW-model>
    <dimension id="time-d" path="dim-time.xml">
        <Level id="location-in-transcription">
            <attribute name="location" type="string" />
        </Level>
    </dimension>
    <dimension id="speaker-d" path="dim-speaker.xml">
        <Level id="speaker">
            <attribute name="sex" type="boolean" />
        </Level>
    </dimension>
    <dimension id="transcription-d" path="dim-transcript.xml">
        <Level id="token">
            <attribute name="term" type="string" />
        </Level>
        <Level id="transcription">
            <attribute name="transcription-name" type="string" />
        </Level>
    </dimension>
    <FactDoc id="facts" path="facts.xml">
        <measure id="frequency" type="real" />
        <dimension idref="time-d" />
        <dimension idref="speaker-d" />
        <dimension idref="transcription-d" />
    </FactDoc>
</DW-model>
```

Algebraic Expression of XOLAP Operators

This last decade's efforts for formalizing OLAP algebras have helped design a formal framework and well-identified operators. Existing OLAP operators, previously defined in either a relational or multidimensional context, are now being adapted to the data model of XML documents (i.e., graphs) and enriched with XML-specific operators. However, most existing approaches that aim at XOLAP do not fully satisfy these objectives. Some favor the translation of XML data cubes in relational, and query them with extensions of SQL. Others tend toward multidimensional solutions that exploit XML query languages such as XQuery. However, in terms of algebra, this work only proposes a fairly limited number of operators.

As Wiwatwattana et al. (2007), we aim at an XML-native solution that exploits XQuery. For this sake, we use the rich TAX Tree Algebra for XML (Jagadish et al., 2001) to support OLAP operators. We can express in TAX the main usual OLAP operators: cube, rotate, switch, roll-up, drill-down, slice, dice, pull and push (Hachicha et al., 2008). By doing so, we significantly expand the number of available XOLAP operators since, up to now, related papers only proposed at most three operators each (always including cube). We have also implemented these XOLAP operators into a software prototype that helps generate the corresponding XQuery code. This querying interface is currently coupled to TIMBER XML-native DBMS, but it is actually independent and could operate onto any other DBMS supporting XQuery.

In the next step of our work, we are taking inspiration from the principle of X^3 (Wiwatwattana et al., 2007) to enhance our XOLAP operators and truly make them XML-specific. For instance, we are currently working on performing roll-up and drill-down operations onto ragged hierarchies (Beyer et al., 2005).

COMBINING OLAP AND DATA MINING FOR COMPLEX DATA ANALYSIS

We address in this section the issue of Web data analysis. Among decision-support technologies, OLAP offers techniques to visualize, summarize, and explore data. However, classical OLAP tools are unsuitable and unable to deal with complex data originating from heterogeneous sources, particularly from the Web. For example, when processing images, sounds, videos, texts or even XML documents, aggregating information with classical OLAP does not make any sense. We are

not able to compute a sum or an average operation over such data. Hence we think that OLAP facts representing complex objects need appropriate tools and new ways to be analyzed. Besides, OLAP does not provide automatic tools to investigate interesting patterns from multidimensional data. In order to enrich its traditional capabilities and to analyze complex data from the Web, we propose to associate the OLAP technology with data mining techniques. Our general approach states that OLAP and data mining should be fully merged and considered an integral part of a unified analysis process. We propose three main approaches based on coupling OLAP and data mining. These approaches aim at extending OLAP to description, clustering, and explanation. In this part of the article, we briefly present these approaches: their objectives, their principles, and their results.

Related Work: Coupling OLAP and Data Mining

The major difficulty when combining OLAP and data mining is that traditional data mining algorithms are mostly designed for tabular datasets organized in individual-variable form. Therefore, multidimensional data are not suited for these algorithms. Nevertheless, a lot of previous studies motivated and proved an interest for coupling OLAP with data mining methods. Ramakrishnan et al. (2007) discuss a class of new problems and techniques that show great promise for exploratory mining in cube spaces. We distinguish three major approaches in this field.

The first approach tries to extend the query language of decision support systems to achieve data mining tasks. The DBMiner system, proposed by Han (1998), summarizes this approach. Some extended OLAP operators feature data mining methods such as association, classification, prediction, clustering and sequencing. Han defines OLAP Mining as a new concept that integrates OLAP technology with data mining techniques and allows performing analyses on different portions and levels of abstraction in a data cube. He also introduces OLAM (On-Line Analytical Mining) as a process for extracting knowledge from multidimensional databases. He expects that, in the future, OLAM will be a natural addition to OLAP technology that enhances the power of multidimensional data analysis. Chen et al. (2000) discover behavior patterns by mining association rules about customers from transactional e-commerce data. They extend OLAP functions and use a distributed OLAP server with a data mining infrastructure. The resulting association rules are represented in particular cubes called Association Rule Cubes. Goil & Choudhary (1998) think that dimension hierarchies can be used to provide interesting information at multiple concept levels. Their approach summarizes information in a data cube, extends OLAP operators and mines association rules. Some other researches consist of integrating mining functions in the database system using SQL. Chaudhuri et al. (1999) propose a data mining system based on extending SQL and develop a client-server middleware that performs a decision tree classifier in MS SQL Server 7.0.

The second approach consists of adapting multidimensional data inside or outside the database system and applies classical data mining algorithms on the resulting datasets. This approach can be viewed with respect to two strategies. The first one consists of taking advantage from multidimensional database management systems (MDBMS) to help construct learning models. The second strategy transforms multidimensional data and makes them usable by data mining methods. For instance, Pinto et al. (2001) integrate multidimensional information in data sequences and apply on them frequent pattern discovery. In order to apply decision trees on multidimensional data, Goil & Choudhary (1998) flatten data cubes and extract a contingency matrix for each dimension at each construction step of the tree. Chen et al. (2001) think that OLAP should be adopted as a pre-processing step in the knowledge discovery process. In the same context, Maedche et al. (2000)

combine databases with classical data mining systems by using OLAP engine as interface to process telecommunication data. In this interface, OLAP tools create a target data set to generate new hypotheses by applying data mining methods. Tjioe & Taniar (2005) propose a method for mining association rules in data warehouses. Based on the multidimensional data organization, this method is capable of extracting associations from multiple dimensions at multiple levels of abstraction by focusing on measurements of summarized data. In order to do this, the authors propose to prepare multidimensional data for the mining process according to four algorithms: VAvg, HAvg, WMAvg, and ModusFilter. Fu (2005) proposes an algorithm, called CubeDT, for constructing decision tree classifiers based on data cubes. This algorithm works on statistic trees which are representations of multidimensional data especially suitable for the construction of decision trees.

The third approach is based on adapting data mining methods and applying them directly on multidimensional data. Palpanas (2000) thinks that adapting data mining algorithms is an interesting solution to provide elaborated analysis and precious knowledge. Parsaye (1997) claims that decision-support applications must consider data mining within multiple dimensions. He proposes a theoretical OLAP Data Mining System that integrates a multidimensional discovery engine in order to perform discovery along multiple dimensions. Sarawagi et al. (1998) propose to integrate a multidimensional regression module, called Discovery-driven, in OLAP servers. This module guides the user to detect relevant areas at various hierarchical levels of a cube. Imielinski et al. (2002) propose a generalized version of association rules called Cubegrades. The authors claim that association rules can be viewed as the change of an aggregate's measure due to a change in the cube's structure. Dong et al. (2001) enhance Cubegrades and introduce constrained gradient analysis. Their proposition focuses on extracting pairs of cube cells that are quite different in aggregates and similar in dimensions. Instead of dealing with the whole cube, constraints on significance, probability, and gradient are added to limit the search range. Finally, Chen et al. (2005) introduce *Prediction Cube*. In contrast to standard cubes, in which each cell value is computed by an aggregate function (e.g., SUM or AVG), each cell value in a prediction cube summarizes a predictive model trained on the data corresponding to that cell, and characterizes its decision behavior, or predictiveness.

This previous work has proved that associating data mining to OLAP is a promising way to allow the power of elaborated analysis tasks. This affirms that data mining methods are able to extend OLAP analyze. In addition to this work, we have proposed three main contributions to this field.

OLAP Aggregation by Clustering

When users analyze complex data from the Web, they need more expressive aggregates than those created from the elementary computation of additive measures. We think that OLAP facts representing complex objects need appropriate tools and new ways of aggregation since to be analyzed. To summarize information about complex data, we should gather similar facts into a single group and separate dissimilar facts into different groups. In this case, it is necessary to consider an aggregation by computing both descriptors and measures. Instead of grouping facts only by computing their measures, we also take their descriptors into account to obtain aggregates expressing semantic similarities. Facts can be aggregated with a sum or average function but it is not interesting in the Web data context. However, it would be more interesting if facts seeming similar could be aggregated.

In order to do so, we couple OLAP with data mining to create a new type of online complex data aggregation. We have already proposed a new OLAP operator, called OpAC (Operator for Aggregation by Clustering), that combines OLAP with an automatic clustering technique (Ben Messaoud et al., 2006). We use the Agglomerative Hierarchical Clustering (AHC) as an aggregation strategy for complex data. We proved the interest of this new operator and its efficiency in creating semantic aggregates. More generally, the aggregates provided by OpAC give interesting knowledge about the analyzed domain. Our operator deals with all types of data by handling a data cube modeled by XML. For example, the new operator enables to note that some tokens like "Hello," "Hi," and "Good morning" form a significant aggregate since they have the same location in the transcription (they are at the beginning).

Furthermore, we also propose some evaluation criteria that help validate our operator. These criteria aim at assisting the user and helping him/her to choose the best partition of aggregates that fits with his/her analysis requirements.

Multiple Correspondence Analysis to Organize Data Cubes

OLAP provides the user with visual tools to summarize, explore and navigate into data cubes in order to detect interesting and relevant information. However, exploring a data cube is not always an easy task. Obviously, in large cubes containing sparse data, the whole analysis process becomes tedious and complex. In such a case, an intuitive exploration based on the user's experience does not quickly lead to efficient results. Current OLAP provides query-driven and visual tools to browse data cubes, but does not deeply assist the user and help him/her to investigate interesting patterns.

We propose to provide the user with an automatic assistance to identify interesting facts and arrange them in a suitable visual representation. We suggest an approach that allows the user to get relevant facts expressing relationships and displays them in an appropriate way that enhances the exploration process independently from cube size (Ben Messaoud et al., 2007b). Thus, we carry out a Multiple Correspondence Analysis (MCA)

Figure 5. Two representations of a cube

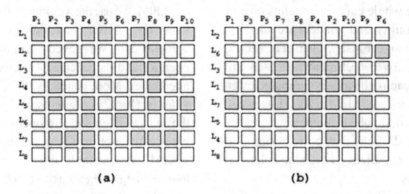

on a data cube as a preprocessing step. Basically, MCA is a powerful describing method even for huge volumes of data. It factors categorical variables and displays data in a factorial space constructed by an orthogonal system of axes that provides relevant views of data. These elements motivate us to exploit the results of MCA in order to better explore large data cubes by identifying and arranging interesting facts. The first constructed factorial axis summarizes the maximum of information contained in the cube. We focus on relevant OLAP facts associated with characteristic attributes (variables) given by the factorial axes. These facts are interesting since they reflect relationships and concentrate significant information. For a better visualization of these facts, we highlight them and arrange their attributes in the data space representation by using test-values. For example, consider the cube of Figure 5.

On the one hand, representation 5(a) displays frequencies of tokens (P1, . . ., P10) crossed by locations in the transcription (L1, . . ., L8). In this representation, full cells (gray cells) are displayed randomly according to lexical order of tokens and of locations. On the other hand, Figure 5(b) contains the same information as Figure 5(a) but it displays a data representation visually easier to analyze. Figure 5(b) expresses important relationships by providing a visual representation that

gathers full cells together and separates them from empty cells.

To evaluate the visual relevance of multidimensional data representations, we also propose a new criterion to measure the homogeneity of cell distribution in the representation space of a data cube. This criterion is based on geometric neighborhood of data cube cells, and also takes the similarity of cell measures into account and provides a scalar quantification for the homogeneity of a given data cube representation. It also allows evaluating the performance of our approach by comparing the quality of the initial data representation and the arranged one.

Association Rules for Explanation in Data Cubes

OLAP techniques do not allow the identification of relationships, groupings or exceptions that could hold in a data cube. To that end, we propose to extend OLAP tools to explanation capabilities by mining association rules in multidimensional data. This new approach is capable of automatically explaining relationships and associations that could exist in data cubes. In the study we made with our linguist colleagues, the frequency of a token can be particularly high at the end of transcriptions. This frequency can be explained by an association between the token, the location in the transcription and the speaker sex. For example, this token is often use by women to finish a talk.

Frequent itemset, sequential itemset and association rule mining help achieve this goal. We propose an on-line environment for mining association rules in data cubes (Ben Messaoud et al., 2007a). We use the concept of inter-dimensional meta-rule that allows users to guide the mining process and focus on a specific context from which rules can be extracted. Our framework also allows a redefinition of the support and confidence measures based on aggregate functions (SUM and COUNT) used as cube indicators (measures). Therefore, the computation of support and confidence according to the COUNT measure becomes a particular case in our proposal. In addition to support and confidence, we use two other descriptive criteria (Lift and Loevinger) to evaluate the interestingness of mined associations. These criteria are computed according to a sum-based aggregate measure in the data cube and reflect interestingness of associations in a more relevant way than what is offered by support and confidence. We develop our proposal according to a bottom-up algorithm for searching association rules. Our algorithm consists of an adaptation of the traditional Apriori algorithm to multidimensional data. In addition, in order to focus on the discovered associations and validate them, we provide a visual representation based on the graphic semiology principles. Such a representation consists of a graphic encoding of frequent patterns and association rules in the same multidimensional space as the one associated with the mined data cube.

To improve decision support systems and to give more and more relevant information to the user, the need to integrate new user's needs into the data warehouse process becomes obvious. This challenge arises in applications such as analyzing online store transactions, summarizing dynamic document collections, and profiling Web traffic. In the following section, we address the problem of personalized OLAP analysis end present our

solution to help users to get relevant analyzes from the data warehouse.

ANALYSIS PERSONALIZATION IN COMPLEX DATA WAREHOUSES

Because of the role of data warehouses in the daily business work of a company, the requirements for design and implementation are often dynamic and subjective. In such a context, it is very helpful to provide users with the most relevant data warehouse model for personalized decision queries. The obtained model must be in continuous evolution with respect to new analysis needs and/or data source changes. In the context of personalized OLAP queries in data warehouses, we thus develop the Rule-based Data Warehouse (R-DW) approach (Bentayeb et al., 2008), in which user aggregation rules help integrate and share user knowledge and allow the warehouse model to evolve by generating new dimension hierarchies. Our approach is based on an extension of the concept of personalization applied to data warehouses, since we deal not only with user preferences but also with new analysis needs. The main consequence of our approach then consists of considering schema evolution in data warehouse models. In this chapter, we particularly focus on XML data warehouse evolution, since XML data warehouses allow for analyzing complex data from the Web.

Related Work: Personalization and Schema Evolution in Data Warehouses

Personalization

Personalization has been mentioned for many years in various domains such as information retrieval and databases. In these domains, personalization usually consists of exploiting user preferences to provide pertinent answers to users. More precisely, in the context of databases, personalization mainly takes the form of adding predicates to queries (Kießling, 2002). In the context of information retrieval, the idea consists of representing user profile with keywords (Domshlak & Joachims, 2007) in order to define a restricted research area. In these domains, personalization then consists of finding pertinent answers within a profusion of data.

Research studies about personalization in data warehouses are recent and constitute an emerging trend. The first work is inspired from the concept of restriction, particularly focused on data visualization and user preference-driven navigation. Bellatrèche et al. (2005) define a dedicated profile that allows refining queries to show only a part of data, which meets the user's preferences. Ravat & Teste (2008) propose a solution to personalize OLAP navigation by exploiting the definition of preferences through weights. In this case, the user assigns weights to the multidimensional concepts to directly get the desired analysis, avoiding a lot of navigation operations. Garrigós et al. (2009) proposed the personalization in data warehouses according to a conceptual point of view with UML.

Through several research studies exist in data warehouse personalization, we note a lack in integrating user knowledge into warehouse models to take new user analysis needs into account. This constitutes an important issue since only few analysis possibilities are known in the design step of a data warehouse. In this context, we propose to create new analysis axes to meet new user analysis needs.

Data Warehouse Model Evolution

We can distinguish in the literature two types of approaches that take data warehouse model evolution into account: model updating and temporal modeling. The first approach consists of enriching the data warehouse schema (Blaschka et al., 1999; Hurtado et al., 1999a, 1999b) with adapted evolution operators that allow an evolution of the schema. In this case, only one schema is supported and evolution history is not preserved.

In opposition, the second approach keeps track of schema evolution, by using temporal validity labels. These labels are affixed on dimension instances (Bliujute et al., 1998), on aggregation links (Mendelzon & Vaisman, 2000), or on schema versions (Bebel et al., 2004; Body et al., 2002; Morzy & Wrembel, 2004). In such a data warehouse, each version describes a schema and data at certain periods of time. In order to appropriately analyze multiversion data, an extension to a traditional SQL language is required.

Both approaches do not directly involve users in the data warehouse evolution process, and thus rather constitute a solution for data source evolution than for user analysis need evolution. A personalization process then constitutes a promising research issue to provide relevant analysis for new user needs.

Data Warehouse Model Evolution for User Personalized Analysis

In a decision-support context, the system must be user-centered to cope with users' analysis needs. However, in classical decision-support systems based on a data warehouse, user role is limited to data navigation with OLAP. Based on a fixed data warehouse model, navigation allows for answering expected decision queries but offers a limited capacity to take new analysis objectives into account. We propose to personalize the OLAP process to ensure the integration and the exploitation of new analysis needs defined by users.

In this context, we introduce a data warehouse model evolution (i.e. structure and data) in which personalized analysis possibilities can be shared by different users. The personalization process is based on the user knowledge about data aggregation, which is the basis of data organization in multidimensional models. Then, our key idea consists of generating new analysis axes by dynamically creating new dimension hierarchies

Figure 6. Architecture for OLAP personalization

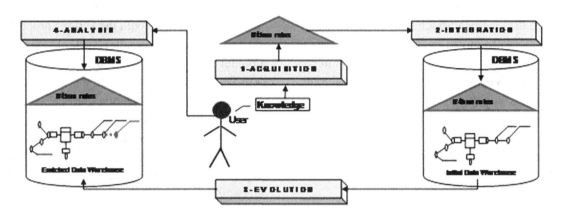

or extending existing old ones. More precisely, we define new granularity levels inside the data warehouse schema. This provides a real time evolution of dimension hierarchies to cope with personalized analysis needs.

To support our proposed data warehouse model evolution, we define an evolving data warehouse formal model based on aggregation rules, R-DW (Rule-based Data Warehouse), which is independent of any implementation considerations. We first introduced this model in (Bentayeb et al., 2008). Aggregation rules of R-DW allow defining new user needs and consequently creating new granularity levels in the current data warehouse. The R-DW model is composed of a "fixed" part, corresponding to fact tables and the dimensions directly linked to fact tables; and an "evolving" part, defined by aggregation rules. Aggregation rules define aggregation links between two successive levels in a dimension hierarchy and are under the form of "if-then" rules, where an "if" clause defines conditions on the first level and a "then" clause defines the desired (second) level to be created.

We define in the following our global architecture for data warehouse evolution for analysis personalization in which the R-DW model takes place. In this architecture, the user not only navigates within data, but he/she also expresses his/her knowledge to generate new analysis possibilities. Our architecture is composed of four parts corresponding to four phases of our personalized decision support system (Figure 6): (1) users' knowledge acquisition, (2) knowledge integration, (3) data warehouse model update, and (4) OLAP.

In our approach, we consider a specific user's knowledge, which provides new aggregate data. The acquisition phase aims at collecting user knowledge under the form of "if-then" aggregation rules. Aggregation rules are divided into two types of rules: structure rules and data rules. Structure rules help define the structure of aggregation links, meaning that they allow defining the level to be created, the attributes defining the new level, on what level the new one is based, on what attributes of this lower lever conditions are expressed. Data rules instantiate structure rules, meaning that they define the aggregation link on data themselves. To build a new level, the user defines one structure rule, and various data rules. Data rules define the various instances to be created in the new level and the condition that defines the link with the instances of the lower level. Each data rule corresponds to one instance of the level to be created.

Rules are then integrated within the data warehouse model (integration phase) and used to create new levels in the dimension hierarchy (evolution phase). The last phase, namely on-line analysis, consists of applying decision queries onto the updated data warehouse schema. To validate our data warehouse model evolution, we propose a prototype implemented in the relational context through the WEDriK (data Warehouse Evolution Driven by Knowledge) platform (Favre et al, 2007) under Oracle 10g.

A User-Driven Approach for Complex Data Analysis

Since our R-DW model is independent from any implementation, we propose to exploit R-DW to deal with complex data. More precisely, we propose to adapt and apply our approach to complex data warehouses represented in XML format. Thus, we consider the XML data warehouse model presented in a previous section. Because of the specificities of XML storing, XML data warehouse evolution is not an easy task. Indeed, we have to consider that structure and data are mixed in documents, even if the data warehouse schema is represented in dw-model.xml. Moreover, we have to take the organization of information as a tree into account.

The personalization process consists of creating a new level within a given hierarchy. It implies not only creating this level with required data, but also the links with (an)other level(s). Moreover, we have to deal with both structure and data. To achieve this evolution in the XML data warehouse, we have to consider the evolution of two documents: the document representing the data warehouse model (dw-model.xml) and the document of the dimension that is concerned by level creation (dimensiond.xml).

The evolution process is based on the use of "if-then" rules defined by the user. For a given structure rule and the set of corresponding data-rules, we are building one granularity level. The interest of the structure-rule is to determine the structure of the level. Thus, we can modify the dw-model.xml document by adding a Level node.

The dimensiond.xml document concerned by the evolution of the hierarchy is also modified to include the new level with the various properties and the links with the existing level @Drill-Down if the level is added at the end of a hierarchy, @ Drill-Down and @Roll-Up if the new level is inserted between two existing ones.

The implementation requires updates of XML documents. First, a Web interface allows user interaction. The interface helps user define graphically its structure rule and data rules. This interaction is developed using PHP scripts. The evolution of the XML data warehouse requires updates within XML documents that are used to store the data warehouse. Xupdate is a lightweight XML query language for modifying XML data. It is specified by the XML:DBInitiative. It is a simple XML update language used to modify XML content by simply declaring what changes should be made in XML syntax. Various operations can be combined to achieve our evolution, such as inserting an element after, inserting an attribute, updating attribute, etc. Another possibility is to consider the use of DOM (Document Object Model) to achieve the evolution. Indeed, DOM is a platform and language-independent standard object model for representing HTML or XML documents. Thus, it is possible to use PHP scripts with DOM.

As an example, let us consider the study we made with our linguist colleagues. The token frequencies were observed with respect to location in the transcription and speaker sex. The initial data warehouse has been designed according to the CLAPI database and the identified analysis needs. Now, let us suppose that a linguist needs to aggregate frequencies by grouping some locations together. For instance, he wants to know where some tokens appear in the transcription (beginning, middle, and end). Even if this need has not been initially expressed, our personalization process allows for evolving the data warehouse to provide an answer. The linguist is then able to formulate the following aggregation rules (structure rule and

Figure 7. Updated sample dw-model.xml document

```
<?xml version="1.0" encoding="utf-8">
<DW-model>
    <dimension id="time-d" path="dim-time.xml">
        <Level id="location-in-transcription">
            <attribute name="location" type="string" />
        </Level>
        <Level id="group-of-location-in-transcription">
            <attribute name="location-group" type="string" />
        </Level>
    </dimension>
    <dimension id="speaker-d" path="dim-speaker.xml">
        <Level id="speaker">
            <attribute name="sex" type="boolean" />
        </Level>
    </dimension>
    <dimension id="transcription-d" path="dim-transcript.xml">
        <Level id="token">
            <attribute name="term" type="string" />
        </Level>
        <Level id="transcription">
            <attribute name="transcription-name" type="string" />
        </Level>
    </dimension>
    <FactDoc id="facts" path="facts.xml">
        <measure id="frequency" type="real" />
        <dimension idref="time-d" />
        <dimension idref="speaker-d" />
        <dimension idref="transcription-d" />
    </FactDoc>
</DW-model>
```

Figure 8. Updated sample dim-time.xml document

```
<?xml version="1.0" encoding="utf-8">
<dimension dim-id="time-d">
    <Level id="location-in-transcription">
        <Instance id="begin" Roll-up="extreme">
            <attribute id="location" value="begin">
        </Instance>
        <Instance id="middle" Roll-up="middle">
            <attribute id="location" value="middle">
        </Instance>
        <Instance id="end" Roll-up="extreme">
            <attribute id="location" value="end">
        </Instance>
    </Level>
    <Level id="group-of-location-in-transcription">
        <Instance id="extreme" Drill-Down=("begin","end")>
            <attribute id="location-group" value="extreme">
        </Instance>
        <Instance id="middle" Roll-up="middle">
            <attribute id="location-group" value="middle">
        </Instance>
    </Level>
</dimension>
```

the corresponding data rules) through an interface, to express how to aggregate data.

- **Structure Rule:** If ConditionOn(location-in-transcription, {location} then Generate (group-of-location, {group-location}
- **Data Rules:**
  ○ 1. If location in {'begin,' 'end'} then group-location={extreme}
  ○ 2. If location not in {'begin,' 'end'} then group-location={middle}

With these rules, the XML data warehouse can be modified: the dw-model.xml document and the dim-time.xml document that corresponds to the dimension that is enriched by a new level. In practice, the dw-model.xml presented in the Figure 4 is modified to include the new level (Figure 7).

The dim-time.xml document is also updated to take into account the new level and its instances since the new level concerns the time dimension (Figure 8).

Thus, the linguist is able to compute frequencies with respect to the group of locations and other dimensions, getting an answer to his own analysis needs.

CONCLUSION

We presented in this chapter a complete solution to warehouse complex data from the Web. Even if much recent research has focused on the design of multidimensional models (Luján-Mora et al., 2006), only few research work addresses the issues of managing and analyzing complex data.

First, we defined a reference XML data warehouse model that unifies and generalizes existing, similar schemas from the literature. This model explicitly takes into account complex features that are possible in XML, but would be intricate to implement in a relational system, such as complex hierarchies and irregular facts.

To provide semantics to OLAP operators, we extend the capabilities of OLAP to description, clustering and explanation by coupling OLAP with data mining techniques. The AHC method is used to define a new OLAP aggregation operator to analyze complex data. To improve navigation into data cubes, we also used the MCA method to reorganize facts inside the data cube by identifying interesting facts. Finally, to help explanation from multidimensional data, we used frequent association rule mining to extract relationships and associations between facts.

To design and build data warehouses, traditional data and goal-driven approaches bear the latent risk of not meeting user requirements. Therefore, user-driven developing approaches seem promising for successful completion of data warehouse projects. In this chapter, we proposed an advanced data warehouse architecture that serves as a modeling framework for user oriented OLAP analyses that take new analysis needs into account. Our main idea is to define a user-oriented evolution of dimension hierarchies in the XML data warehouse. To this end, we proposed a rule-based data warehouse model that presents the

advantage of evolving incrementally according to the user's needs.

The perspectives opened by this work are numerous. Let us summarize them. First, we will take inspiration from the principle of X^3, Wiwatwattana et al. (2007)'s XML cube operator, to enhance our XOLAP operators and truly make them XML-specific. For instance, we are actually currently working on performing roll-up and drill-down operations onto the ragged hierarchies defined by Beyer et al. (2005). Moreover, to improve personalization and decision query processes, we will also investigate the joint evolution of data sources and analysis needs. Finally, we intend validate our approach experimentally by studying its performance in terms of storage space, response time and algorithms complexity.

FUTURE RESEARCH ISSUES

The specific characteristics of Web data make the design of BI applications difficult. Such applications help users obtain knowledge from the Web. Content acquisition from the Web can be broken into two phases: information retrieval and information extraction. Web information retrieval is the process of gathering potentially relevant content. Knowledge creation starts from information collected from various sources, then information is normalized and structural and semantic integration must be achieved.

One possible solution to facilitate this task is to extract information from the Web, transform and load it into a Web warehouse, which provides uniform access methods for automatic data processing. Web warehousing is conceptually similar to data warehousing approaches used to integrate relational information from databases. However, the structure of the Web is very dynamic and cannot be controlled by warehouse designers. Web models do not frequently reflect the current state of Web data sources. Thus, Web warehouses must be redesigned at a late stage of development. From this point of view, two promising research issues can be studied to achieve Web data warehousing:

First, information retrieval and data mining techniques may be used to collect relevant information from the Web and extract knowledge from them. These techniques are not only useful as analysis support tools, but also as modeling support tools. The semantics extracted from Web data can indeed help build relevant multidimensional models and data cubes. Therefore, relevant analyses can be performed and then presented in a form suitable for use by various individuals playing different roles in an organization. Hence, combining information retrieval, data mining techniques and OLAP can help build relevant Web data cubes.

Second, semantic Web technologies may be employed to collect semantically appropriate data from the Web. More specifically, the Resource Description Framework (RDF) may be used for describing Web data, and the Web Ontology Language (OWL) for creating an ontology that restricts the semantics of RDF descriptions. We think that, using this approach, we can implement a piece of software that assists users in designing a suitable OLAP schema and performing data extraction, transformation and loading (ETL).

REFERENCES

Aouiche, K., Bentayeb, F., Boussaïd, O., & Darmont, J. (2003). *Conception informatique d'une base de données multimédia de corpus linguistiques oraux: l'exemple de CLAPI 2. In 36ème* (pp. 11–12). Lyon, France: Colloque International de la Societas Linguistica Europaea.

Aouiche, K., Lemire, D., & Godin, R. (2009). *Web 2.0 OLAP: From data cubes to tag clouds.* In 4th International Conference on Web Information Systems and Technologies (WEBIST'09), Madeira, Portugal (pp. 51-64).

Arigon, A. M., Miquel, M., & Tchounikine, A. (2007). Multimedia data warehouses: A multiversion model and a medical application. [Springer.]. *Journal of Multimedia Tools and Applications, 35*(1), 91–108. doi:10.1007/s11042-007-0118-7

Baril, X., & Bellahsène, Z. (2003). Designing and managing an XML warehouse. In Chaudhri, A. B., Rashid, A., & Zicari, R. (Eds.), *XML data management: Native XML and XML-enabled database systems* (pp. 455–473). Addison Wesley.

Bebel, B., Eder, J., Koncilia, C., Morzy, T., & Wrembel, R. (2004). *Creation and management of versions in multiversion data warehouse.* In 19th ACM Symposium on Applied Computing (SAC'04), Nicosia, Cyprus (pp. 717-723). ACM Press.

Bellatrèche, L., Giacometti, A., Marcel, P., Mouloudi, H., & Laurent, D. (2005). *A personalization framework for OLAP queries.* In 12th ACM International Workshop on Data Warehousing and OLAP (DOLAP'05), Hong Kong, China (pp. 9-18).

Ben Messaoud, R., Boussaïd, O., & Loudcher Rabaséda, S. (2006). A data mining-based OLAP aggregation of complex data: Application on XML documents. [Idea Group Inc.]. *International Journal of Data Warehousing and Mining, 2*(4), 1–26. doi:10.4018/jdwm.2006100101

Ben Messaoud, R., Boussaïd, O., & Loudcher Rabaséda, S. (2007b). A multiple correspondence analysis to organize data cubes. *Databases and Information Systems IV: Frontiers in Artificial Intelligence and Applications, 155*(1), 133–146.

Ben Messaoud, R., Loudcher Rabaséda, S., Missaoui, R., & Boussaïd, O. (2007a). *OLEMAR: An online environment for mining association rules in multidimensional data. Advances in Data Warehousing and Mining Series* (*Vol. 2*). Hershey, PA: Idea Group Inc.

Bentayeb, F., Favre, C., & Boussaïd, O. (2008). A user-driven data warehouse evolution approach for concurrent personalized analysis needs. *Integrated Computer-Aided Engineering, 15*(1), 21–36.

Beyer, K., Chamberlin, D., Colby, L. S., Özcan, F., Pirahesh, H., & Xu, Y. (2005). *Extending XQuery for analytics*. In 24th ACM SIGMOD International Conference on Management of Data, Baltimore, Maryland, USA (pp. 503-514).

Bimonte, S., Tchounikine, A., & Miquel, M. (2007). *Spatial OLAP: Open issues and a Web based prototype*. In 10th International Conference on Geographic Information Science (AGILE'07). Aalborg, Denmark (pp. 1-11).

Blaschka, M., Sapia, C., & Höfling, G. (1999). *On schema evolution in multidimensional databases*. In 1st International Conference on Data Warehousing and Knowledge Discovery (DaWaK'99), Florence, Italy, (LNCS 1676, pp. 153-164). Springer.

Bliujute, R., Saltenis, S., Slivinskas, G., & Jensen, C. (1998). *Systematic change management in dimensional data warehousing*. In 3rd International Baltic Workshop on Databases and Information Systems.

Body, M., Miquel, M., Bédard, Y., & Tchounikine, A. (2002). *A multidimensional and multiversion structure for OLAP applications*. In 5th ACM International Workshop on Data Warehousing and OLAP (DOLAP'02), McLean, Virginia, USA (pp. 1-6).

Boukraa, D., Ben Messaoud, R., & Boussaïd, O. (2006). Proposition d'un Modèle physique pour les entrepôts XML. In *Atelier Systèmes Décisionnels (ASD'06), 9th Maghrebian Conference on Information Technologies (MCSEAI'06)*. Agadir, Morocco: MIPS-Maroc.

Boussaïd, O., Ben Messaoud, R., Choquet, R., & Anthoard, S. (2006). *X-warehousing: An XML-based approach for warehousing complex data*. In 10th East-European Conference on Advances in Databases and Information Systems (ADBIS'06), Thessaloniki, Greece (LNCS 4152, pp. 39-54). Springer.

Boussaïd, O., Tanasescu, A., Bentayeb, F., & Darmont, J. (2008). Integration and dimensional modeling approaches for complex data warehousing. *Journal of Global Optimization, 37*(4), 571–591. doi:10.1007/s10898-006-9064-6

Calvanese, D., Giacomo, G. D., Lenzerini, M., Nardi, D., & Rosati, R. (1998). *Description logics framework for information integration*. In 6th International Conference on Principles of Knowledge Representation and Reasoning (KR'98), Trento, Italy (pp. 2-13).

Chaudhuri, S., & Dayal, U. (1997). An overview of data warehousing and OLAP technology. *SIGMOD Record, 26*(1), 65–74. doi:10.1145/248603.248616

Chaudhuri, S., Fayyad, U., & Bernhardt, J. (1999). *Scalable classification over SQL databases*. In 15th International Conference on Data Engineering (ICDE'99), Sydney, Australia (pp. 470-479).

Chen, B. C., Chen, L., Lin, Y., & Ramakrishnan, R. (2005). Prediction cubes. In *Proceedings of the 31st International Conference on Very Large Data Bases (VLDB 2005)*, (pp. 982–993). Trondheim, Norway: ACM Press.

Chen, M., Zhu, Q., & Chen, Z. (2001). An integrated interactive environment for knowledge discovery from heterogeneous data resources. *Information and Software Technology, 43*, 487–496. doi:10.1016/S0950-5849(01)00159-8

Chen, Q., Dayal, U., & Hsu, M. (2000). *An OLAP-based scalable Web access analysis engine.* In 2nd International Conference on Data Warehousing and Knowledge Discovery (DAWAK'00), London, UK, (pp. 210-223).

Codd, E. (1993). *Providing OLAP (On-Line Analytical Processing) to user-analysts: An IT mandate. Tech. rep.* E.F. Codd and Associates.

Domshlak, C., & Joachims, T. (2007). Efficient and non-parametric reasoning over user preferences. *User Modeling and User-Adapted Interaction, 17*(1-2), 41–69. doi:10.1007/s11257-006-9022-5

Dong, G., Han, J., Lam, J. M. W., Pei, J., & Wang, K. (2001). *Mining multi-dimensional constrained gradients in data cubes.* In 27th Very Large Data Bases Conference (VLDB'01), Rome, Italy (pp. 321-330).

Espil, M. M., & Vaisman, A. A. (2001). Efficient intentional redefinition of aggregation hierarchies in multidimensional databases. In 4th ACM International Workshop on Data Warehousing and OLAP (DOLAP'01), Atlanta, Georgia, USA (pp. 1-8).

Favre, C., Bentayeb, F., & Boussaïd, O. (2007). *Dimension hierarchies updates in data warehouses: A user-driven approach.* In 9th International Conference on Enterprise Information Systems (ICEIS'07), Funchal, Madeira, Portugal (pp. 206-211).

Fu, L. (2005). Novel efficient classifiers based on data cube. [Idea Group Inc.]. *International Journal of Data Warehousing and Mining, 1*(3), 15–27. doi:10.4018/jdwm.2005070102

Garrigós, I., Pardillo, J., Mazón, J., & Trujillo, J. 2009. A conceptual modeling approach for OLAP personalization. In 28th international Conference on Conceptual Modeling (ER'08), Gramado, Brazil (LNCS 5829, pp. 410-414). Springer.

Goasdoué, F., Lattès, V., & Rousset, M. C. (2000). The use of CARIN language and algorithms for information integration: The PICSEL system. *International Journal of Cooperative Information Systems, 9*(4), 383–401. doi:10.1142/S0218843000000181

Goil, S., & Choudhary, A. (1998). *High performance multidimensional analysis and data mining.* In High Performance Networking and Computing Conference (SC'98), Orlando, USA (pp. 1-2).

Golfarelli, M., Maio, D., & Rizzi, S. (1998). The dimensional fact model: A conceptual model for data warehouse*s. International Journal of Cooperative Information Systems, 7*(2-3), 215–247. doi:10.1142/S0218843098000118

Golfarelli, M., Rizzi, S., & Vrdoljak, B. (2001). *Data warehouse design from XML sources.* In 4th International Workshop on Data Warehousing and OLAP (DOLAP'01), Atlanta, USA (pp. 40-47). ACM Press.

Hachicha, M., Mahboubi, H., & Darmont, J. (2008). *Expressing OLAP operators with the TAX XML algebra.* In 3rd International Workshop on Database Technologies for Handling XML Information on the Web (DataX-EDBT'08), Nantes, France.

Han, J. (1998). Toward online analytical mining in large databases. *SIGMOD Record, 27*, 97–107. doi:10.1145/273244.273273

Hümmer, W., Bauer, A., & Harde, G. (2003). *XCube: XML for data warehouses.* In 6th International Workshop on Data Warehousing and OLAP (DOLAP'03), New Orleans, Louisiana, USA (pp. 33-40). ACM Press.

Hurtado, C. A., Mendelzon, A. O., & Vaisman, A. A. (1999a). *Maintaining data cubes under dimension updates.* In 15th International Conference on Data Engineering (ICDE'99), Sydney, Australia (pp. 346-355). IEEE Computer Society.

Hurtado, C. A., Mendelzon, A. O., & Vaisman, A. A. (1999b). *Updating OLAP dimensions*. In 2nd ACM International Workshop on Data Warehousing and OLAP (DOLAP'99), Kansas City, Missouri, USA (pp. 60-66). ACM Press.

Imielinski, T., Khachiyan, L., & Abdulghani, A. (2002). Cubegrades: Generalizing association rules. *Data Mining and Knowledge Discovery*, *6*(3), 219–257. doi:10.1023/A:1015417610840

Inmon, W. H. (2005). *Building the data warehouse*. John Wiley & Sons.

Jagadish, H. V., Lakshmanan, L. V. S., & Srivastava, D. (1999). *What can hierarchies do for data warehouses?* In 25th International Conference on Very Large Data Bases (VLDB'99), Edinburgh, Scotland, UK, (pp. 530-541).

Jaimes, A., Tseng, B. L., & Smith, J. R. (2003). *Modal keywords, ontologies, and reasoning for video understanding*. In 2nd International Conference of Image and Video Retrieval (CIVR'03), Urbana-Champaign, Illinois, USA (pp. 248-259).

Jensen, M. R., Muller, T. H., & Pedersen, T. B. (2001). *Specifying OLAP cubes on XML data*. In 13th International Conference on Scientific and Statistical Database Management, Fairfax, Virginia, USA (pp. 101-112).

Kießling, W. (2002). *Foundations of preferences in database systems*. In 28th International Conference on Very Large Data Bases (VLDB'02), Hong Kong, China (pp. 311-322).

Kimball, R., & Ross, M. (2002). *The data warehouse toolkit: The complete guide to dimensional modeling* (2nd ed.). John Wiley & Sons.

Krill, P. (1998). XML builds momentum as repository standard. *InfoWorld*, *20*(25).

Lassila, O., & Swick, R. (1999). *RDF model and syntax specification*. Retrieved from http://www.w3.org/TR/REC-rdf-syntax/

Luján-Mora, S., Trujillo, J., & Song, I. (2006). A UML profile for multidimensional modeling in data warehouses. *Data & Knowledge Engineering*, *59*(3), 725–769. doi:10.1016/j.datak.2005.11.004

Maedche, A., Hotho, A., & Wiese, M. (2000). *Enhancing preprocessing in data-intensive domains using online-analytical processing*. In 2nd International Conference on Data Warehousing and Knowledge Discovery (DaWaK'00), London, UK. (LNCS 1874, pp. 258-264). Springer.

Mahboubi, H., Hachicha, M., & Darmont, J. (2009). XML warehousing and OLAP. In Wang, J. (Ed.), *Encyclopedia of data warehousing and mining* (2nd ed.). Hershey, PA: IGI Publishing.

Manjunath, B., Salembier, P., & Sikora, T. (2002). *Introduction to MPEG-7: Multimedia content description interface*. Wiley.

Mendelzon, A. O., & Vaisman, A. A. (2000). *Temporal queries in OLAP*. In 26th International Conference on Very Large Data Bases (VLDB'00), Cairo, Egypt (pp. 242-253). Morgan Kaufmann.

Morzy, T., & Wrembel, R. (2004). *On querying versions of multiversion data warehouse*. In 7th ACM International Workshop on Data Warehousing and OLAP (DOLAP'04), Washington, District of Columbia, USA (pp. 92-101). ACM Press.

Nassis, V., Rajugan, R., Dillon, T. S., & Rahayu, J. W. (2004). *Conceptual design of XML document warehouses*. In 6th International Conference Data Warehousing and Knowledge Discovery (DaWaK'04), Zaragoza, Spain (pp. 1-14). Springer.

Nassis, V., Rajugan, R., Dillon, T. S., & Rahayu, J. W. (2005). Conceptual and systematic design approach for XML document warehouses. *International Journal of Data Warehousing and Mining*, *1*(3), 63–86. doi:10.4018/jdwm.2005070104

Palpanas, T. (2000). Knowledge discovery in data warehouses. *SIGMOD Record*, *29*, 88–100. doi:10.1145/362084.362142

Park, B. K., Han, H., & Song, I. Y. (2005). *XML-OLAP: A multidimensional analysis framework for XML warehouses*. In 7th International Conference on Data Warehousing and Knowledge Discovery (DaWaK'05), Copenhagen, Denmark. (LNCS 3589, pp. 32-42). Springer.

Parsaye, K. (1997). OLAP and data mining: Bridging the gap. *Database Programming and Design*, *10*, 30–37.

Pedersen, B. T., Pedersen, D., & Pedersen, J. (2008). Integrating XML data in the TARGIT OLAP system. *International Journal of Web Engineering and Technology*, *4*(4), 495–533. doi:10.1504/IJWET.2008.019945

Perez, J. M., Berlanga, R., Aramburu, M. J., & Pedersen, T. B. (2008). Integrating data warehouses with Web data: A survey. *IEEE Transactions on Knowledge and Data Engineering*, *20*(7), 940–955. doi:10.1109/TKDE.2007.190746

Pinto, H., Han, J., Pei, J., Wang, K., Chen, Q., & Dayal, U. (2001). *Multi-dimensional sequential pattern mining*. In 10th ACM International Conference on Information and Knowledge Management (CIKM'01), Atlanta, USA (pp. 81-88).

Pokorny, J. (2001). *Modelling stars using XML*. In 4th ACM International Workshop on Data Warehousing and OLAP (DOLAP'01), Atlanta, Georgia, USA (pp. 24-31). ACM Press.

Rajugan, R., Chang, E., & Dillon, T. S. (2005). *Conceptual design of an XML FACT repository for dispersed XML document warehouses and XML marts*. In 5th International Conference on Computer and Information Technology (CIT'05), Shanghai, China (pp. 141-149). IEEE Computer Society.

Ramakrishnan, R., & Chen, B. C. (2007). Exploratory mining in cube space. *Data Mining and Knowledge Discovery*, *15*(1), 29–54. doi:10.1007/s10618-007-0063-0

Ravat, F., & Teste, O. (2008). Personalization and OLAP databases. *New Trends in Data Warehousing and Data Analysis*, *3*, 71–92.

Rousset, M. C. (2002). *Knowledge representation for information integration*. In 13th International Symposium on Methodologies for Intelligent Systems (ISMIS'02), Lyon, France. (LNCS 2366, pp. 509-513). Springer.

Rusu, L. I., Rahayu, J. W., & Taniar, D. (2005). A methodology for building XML data warehouses. *International Journal of Data Warehousing and Mining*, *1*(2), 67–92. doi:10.4018/jdwm.2005040102

Sarawagi, S., Agrawal, R., & Megiddo, N. (1998). *Discovery-driven exploration of OLAP data cubes*. In 6th International Conference on Extending Database *Technology* (EDBT'98), Valencia, Spain. Volume (LNCS 1377, pp. 168-182). Springer.

Sifer, M. (2005). *Exploring Web logs with coordinated OLAP dimension hierarchies*. In 4th International Workshop on Databases in Networked Information Systems (DNIS'05), Aizu-Wakamatsu, Japan (pp. 213-224).

Stoffel, K., Saltz, J., Hendler, J., Dick, J., Merz, W., & Miller, R. (1997). *Semantic indexing for complex patient grouping*. In Annual Conference of the American Medical Informatics Association.

Stohr, T., Muller, R., & Rahm, E. (2002). *An integrative and uniform model for metadata management in data warehousing environment*. In 5th ACM International Workshop on Data Warehousing and OLAP (DOLAP'02), McLean, USA (pp. 35-42).

Tjioe, H. C., & Taniar, D. (2005). Mining association rules in data warehouses. [Idea Group Inc.]. *International Journal of Data Warehousing and Mining, 1*(3), 28–62. doi:10.4018/jdwm.2005070103

Trujillo, J., Lujan-Mora, S., & Song, I. (2004). Applying UML and XML for designing and interchanging information for data warehouses and OLAP applications. *Journal of Database Management, 15*(1), 41–72. doi:10.4018/jdm.2004010102

Vrdoljak, B., Banek, M., & Rizzi, S. (2003). *Designing Web warehouses from XML schemas.* In 5th International Conference on Data Warehousing and Knowledge Discovery (DaWaK'03), Prague, Czech Republic, (LNCS 2737, pp. 89-98). Springer.

Wang, H., Li, J., He, Z., & Gao, H. (2005). *OLAP for XML data.* In 5th International Conference on Computer and Information Technology (CIT'05), Shanghai, China (pp. 233-237). IEEE Computer Society.

Wiwatwattana, N., Jagadish, H. V., Lakshmanan, L. V. S., & Srivastava, D. (2007). *X^3: A cube operator for XML OLAP.* In 23rd International Conference on Data Engineering (ICDE'07), Istanbul, Turkey (pp. 916-925). IEEE Computer Society.

Xyleme. (2001). *Xyleme: A dynamic warehouse for XML data of the Web.* In International Database Engineering & Applications Symposium (IDEAS'01), Grenoble, France (pp. 3-7). IEEE Computer Society.

Zhang, J., Wang, W., Liu, H., & Zhang, S. (2005). *X-warehouse: Building query pattern-driven data.* In 14th International Conference on World Wide Web (WWW'05), China, Japan (pp. 896-897). ACM Press.

KEY TERMS AND DEFINITIONS

Analysis Personalization: Technique that provides the user with the most relevant answer set. It consists of taking user preferences into account when answering a decision query.

Complex Data: Data represented in various formats (databases, texts, images, sounds, videos...), diversely structured (relational databases, XML documents repository...), originating from several different sources (distributed databases, the Web...), described through several channels or points of view (radiographies and audio diagnosis of a physician, data expressed in different scales or languages...), changing in terms of definition or value (temporal databases, periodical surveys...).

Complex Data Warehouse: Warehouse of complex data.

Coupling OLAP and Data Mining: Analysis approach that allows extending OLAP capabilities from exploration to explanation and prediction.

Data Warehouse: Subject-oriented, integrated, time-variant, and nonvolatile collection of data in support of management's decision-making process.

Online Analytical Processing (OLAP): Class of means that enable the user to gain insight into data through interactive access to a wide variety of possible views of information

Web Warehouse: Warehouse of Web data. The Web or World Wide Web is a distributed global information resource.

XML Data Warehouse: XML database (database in which XML data are natively stored and queried as XML documents) that is specifically modeled to support decision-support and XML analytic queries.

ENDNOTE

[1] http://clapi.univ-lyon2.fr

Chapter 3

An Extraction, Transformation, and Loading Tool Applied to a Fuzzy Data Mining System

Ramón A. Carrasco
University of Granada, Spain

Miguel J. Hornos
University of Granada, Spain

Pedro Villar
University of Granada, Spain

María A. Aguilar
University of Granada, Spain

ABSTRACT

In this chapter, we address the problem of integrating semantically heterogeneous data (including data expressed in natural language), which are collected from various questionnaires published in different websites, into a Data Warehouse. We present an extension of the sentences and architecture of data mining Fuzzy Structured Query Language as an extraction, transformation, and loading tool to integrate semantically heterogeneous data from these websites. Moreover, we show a case study using the questionnaires (carried out during several years) about the courses on Information and Communication Technologies which are taught in the Business Studies implanted at the University of Granada (Spain). With this integrated information, the Data Warehouse user can make several analyses with the benefit of an easy linguistic interpretability. The solution proposed here can be used to similar integration problems.

DOI: 10.4018/978-1-61350-038-5.ch003

INTRODUCTION

A *Data Warehouse* (DW) is defined as "a subject-oriented, integrated, time-variant, non-volatile collection of data in support of management's decision-making process" (Inmon, 2005). Data is extracted from the sources and then loaded into the DW using various data loaders and *Extraction, Transformation* and *Loading* (ETL) tools. We can define *Data Mining* (DM) as the process of extracting interesting information from the data stored in databases. According to (Frawley et al, 1991), a discovered knowledge is interesting when it is novel, potentially useful and non-trivial to compute. A series of new functionalities there exists in DM, which reaffirms that it is an independent area (Frawley et al, 1991): high-level language on the discovered knowledge and for showing the results of the user's information requests (e.g. queries); efficiency on large amounts of data; handling of different types of data; etc. There is a symbiotic relationship between the activity of DM and the DW. The DW sets the stage for effective DM. DM can be done where there is no DW, but the DW greatly improves the chances of success in DM (Wang, 2009; Inmon, 1996). The *World Wide Web* (WWW) has become an important resource of information for the DM process. Consequently, the integration of the WWW information into a DW is important in order to get a more effective DM.

One of the most complex issues about the integration and transformation interface is the case where there are multiple sources for a single element of data in the DW. Our proposal is to integrate semantically heterogeneous data from various websites with opinions about educational issues in order to obtain a more effective DM on this information. Similar integration problems have already been solved in various platforms of the so-called Web 2.0, where people are encouraged to post reviews or express their opinions on several subjects, such as: education (PlanetRate, 2010), tourism (Booking.com, 2010; eDreams.com, 2010; TripAdvisor.com, 2010), etc., using numerical values and/or natural language (forums, news groups, etc.). The general approach of these websites is to compute only the accurate numerical information given by users in order to provide a ranking value (e.g. see Figure 1). However, the opinions expressed by the users in natural language are an important source of information. Therefore, the overall problem is the integration of information collected in these questionnaires which are available on various websites and formats, including also linguistic information.

Many aspects of different activities in the real world cannot be assessed in a quantitative form, but rather in a qualitative one (i.e., with vague or imprecise knowledge). In these cases, a better approach may be to use linguistic assessments instead of numerical values. The fuzzy linguistic approach, which was introduced by (Zadeh, 1975), is a theory that facilitates the coding of human knowledge in the form of linguistic concepts, and proposes a tool for modelling qualitative information in a problem. Consequently, the fuzzy linguistic approach seems to be an appropriate framework for solving our problem.

Figure 1. Example of rating on education in http://www.planetrate.com/category/education

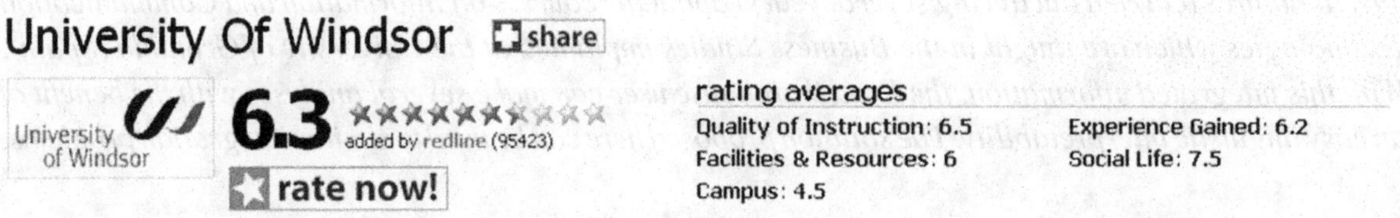

University Of Windsor 🔲share

University of Windsor	*UW* **6.3** ★★★★★★★☆☆☆ added by redline (95423)

⭐ **rate now!**

rating averages

Quality of Instruction: 6.5	Experience Gained: 6.2
Facilities & Resources: 6	Social Life: 7.5
Campus: 4.5	

There are some DM tools based on this concept (Galindo, 2008). One of these tools is dmFSQL (data mining Fuzzy Structured Query Language) (Carrasco et al, 2006), which integrates flexible queries, clustering, fuzzy classification techniques (Carrasco et al, 2002) and fuzzy global dependencies (GDs) (Carrasco et al, 2000). There is a dmFSQL server, programmed in PL/SQL, which allows us to use the language dmFSQL on DW implemented on Oracle© Databases. This enables us to evaluate the DM process at both theoretical and practical levels. This dmFSQL architecture has been satisfactorily used in many problems, such as: finances, marketing, tourism, information retrieval, decision-making, RFID systems, etc. The WWW has become an important resource of information in such applications. However, the ETL process to convert the original information stored in websites to the dmFSQL architecture has been developed ad-hoc, depending on the particular problem. In fact, the standardization of the fuzzy ETL process is not solved and we can find in the literature authors (e.g. Sapir et al, 2008), who leave this task as a future work.

Therefore, our objective is to define and implement a new architecture with these desirable functionalities:

- It must solve the integration and transformation in the case, where there are multiple sources for a single element of data in the DW.
- It must allow identifying any fuzzy information from the websites analyzed and convert it to the internal representation used by the fuzzy types.
- It must fulfil the above explained desirable functionalities of DM systems.

In this chapter, and in order to fulfil these objectives, we propose an architecture with two elements:

- A *conventional integration methodology* based in the model (Araque et al, 2006; Araque et al, 2007), which consists of a set of processes that define the rules for capturing a parameter from a single source as well as integrate a set of values semantically equivalent coming from different data sources. It has three phases: *Temporal metadata extraction*, *Generation of refresh metadata*, and *Refreshment process*. The last phase is responsible to carry out the incremental capture of data sources and to integrate them into a temporal DW table.

- A *fuzzy integration methodology*, which consists of an extension of the sentences and architecture of dmFSQL in order to include functionalities focused on integrating conventional information (obtained in the conventional integration methodology) into fuzzy information. We call this process *Fuzzy Extraction, Transformation and Loading* (FETL), and propose the use of the FETL functionalities of the dmFSQL language for the semantic integration needed in the refreshment process of the conventional integration methodology.

This new model is applied to integrate semantically heterogeneous data from various websites. In particular, several website questionnaires, with distinct answer formats (natural language included) and questions, have been used during the last years to survey the students enrolled on Information and Communication Technologies (ICT) courses taught at the Business School of the University of Granada. The objective is to integrate these questionnaires into a DW. Furthermore, we show examples of DM analysis that the user can make using the integrated information.

The chapter is structured as follows. In the next sections, we revise the background literature and the preliminaries concepts, including the dmFSQL language and architecture. Then, we present an extension of this model in order to include sentences focused on the FETL process. Afterwards, we use the proposed system to solve the complete ETL task based on a particular architecture (Araque et al, 2006; Araque et al, 2007) in order to integrate semantically heterogeneous data got from various questionnaires placed on different websites. Finally, we point out some concluding remarks and future works.

BACKGROUND

After designing the basic schema of the DW, data staging and ETL processes are used to extract the business oriented data from the organization's transaction-oriented operational databases and load it into the DW. There are already well established methodologies for the construction of a DW (Inmon, 2005). One of the most complex issues of the integration and transformation interface is the case where there are multiple sources for a single element of data in the DW. ETL architecture (Araque et al, 2006; Araque et al, 2007) has proved an effective tool for achieving such integration tasks in several applications.

The fuzzy linguistic approach (Zadeh, 1975) is a tool used for modelling qualitative information in a problem. It is based on the concept of linguistic variable and has been satisfactorily used in many problems, such as information retrieval (Bordogna & Passi, 1993), decision-making (Delgado et al, 1992), etc. It is based on the concept of linguistic variable. Briefly speaking, linguistic variables are variables whose values are not numbers but words or sentences in a natural or artificial language.

When important business data or business measures or entities are fuzzy, it may be useful to construct a fuzzy DW that can directly support the analysis of fuzzy data. To the best of our knowledge, no one has ever investigated the fuzzy DW. Fuzzy relational databases extend the relations of the classic relational database and allow the storing and mapping of fuzzy data. An extensive literature exists on fuzzy relational databases (Medina et al.

1995; Sapir et al, 2008). (Galindo, 2008) reviews most of the previous work. The processing of fuzzy data in the DW model has been studied by (Burdick et al, 2006). However, commercial tools did not fit the need for a customized software that supports the fuzzy ETL processes. We can find in the literature authors (e.g. Sapir et al, 2008), who leave this task as a future work.

PRELIMINARIES

In this section, we present the basic elements of the dmFSQL language and the architecture that supports it.

dmFSQL Language

Here we explain the basic elements of the dmFSQL language: fuzzy attributes, fuzzy comparators, the representation of the fuzzy attributes on a conventional Relational Database Management System (RDBMS) and the syntax of the language: Data Definition Language (DDL) and Data Manipulation Language (DML). A more detailed description can be found in (Carrasco et al, 2006):

Fuzzy Attributes

In day-to-day activities we have to solve different problems, and depending on the aspects presented by each problem, we can deal with different types of precise numerical values, but in other cases, the problems present qualitative aspects that are complex to assess by means of precise and exact values. dmFSQL has provided very good results managing both types of data. Therefore, in dmFSQL the attributes are classified as:

- **Fuzzy Type Over an Ordered Underlying Domain:** For simplicity, this kind of data is called *Type 2* (FTYPE2 or POSSIBILISTIC in dmFSQL syntax) and is classified as follows:

○ **Linguistic Label:** It is based on the concept of linguistic variable (Zadeh, 1975) with a parametric representation achieved by the 4-tuple $[\alpha,\beta,\gamma,\delta]$ for each label of the set $S=\{s_i\}$, $i \in \{0...g\}$, where β and γ indicate the interval in which the membership value is 1, with α and δ indicating the left and right limits of the definition domain of the trapezoidal membership function. We show several linguistic labels defined on a fuzzy attribute in Figure 6.

○ **Fuzzy Number:** Defined in the interval $[0,1]$, described by trapezoidal membership functions as well.

○ **Interval $[\alpha,\delta]$:** With a semantic significance "between α and δ," it can be defined as a trapezoidal function $[\alpha,\alpha,\delta,\delta]$,

○ **Approximate Value $\alpha\pm m$:** With a semantic significance "approximately α with margin $\pm m$," it can be defined with a triangular function that can be expressed as a trapezoidal function $[\alpha-m,\alpha,\alpha,\alpha+m]$.

○ **Crisp Value α:** It can be defined as a trapezoidal function $[\alpha,\alpha,\alpha,\alpha]$;
 Missing Values. *Unknown*, defined as $[1,1,1,1]$, and *Undefined*, defined as $[0,0,0,0]$.

• **Fuzzy Type Over a Non-Ordered Underlying Domain:** We denominate this kind of data *Type 3* (FTYPE3 or SCALAR in dmFSQL syntax). They are attributes over data of discrete non-ordered dominion with analogy defined on a non-ordered underlying domain. In these attributes, a set $E=\{e_i\}$, $i \in \{0...n\}$ is defined, with labels e_i that are scalars with a similarity (or proximity) relationship $\Theta'='$ defined over them, so that this relationship indicates to what extent each pair of labels is similar to each other (see Figure 2). This group

can represent data either as simple scalars or as possibility distributions in discrete domains:

○ **Simple:** it is represented as a pair of data with a possibility value $\{1/ e_i\}$, $i \in \{0...n\}$ (i.e. the unique possible value is e_i) since the possibility degree is 1 (i.e. the maximum).

○ **Possibility Distributions:** they are represented as $\{e_1/p_1, e_2/p_2,..., e_n/p_n\}$ $\forall i /i \in \{0...n\}$, where each value e_i has assigned a membership degree p_i to the fuzzy set.

• **Precise Data:** We call this kind of data *Type 1* (FTYPE1 or CRISP in dmFSQL syntax). It uses the data representation provided by the host RDBMS. These attributes are totally crisp (traditional, with no imprecision), but they have some linguistic trapezoidal labels defined on them.

Fuzzy Comparators

The conventional comparators $(=, <, >, ...)$ are not usable on fuzzy attributes. In order to manage these attributes, the fuzzy comparators specified in Table 1 are available in dmFSQL. This usage is useful for DM as well as for flexible queries:

• **DM:** Using the fuzzy equal comparator (FEQ, NFEQ), it is possible to model the distance or similarity measures of hierarchical clustering, k-means algorithms, fuzzy classification, etc. Besides, all the fuzzy comparators can be useful to model fuzzy global dependencies (GDs) of similarity (e.g. "similar age implies similar salary") and monotonicity (e.g. "greater age implies greater salary") between attributes.

• **Flexible Queries:** They are very similar to conventional SQL queries. Instead of the common comparator $(=, <, ...)$ we use the corresponding fuzzy comparators (FEQ,

Table 1. Fuzzy comparators

Fuzzy Comparators		Significance	Usage
Possibility	Necessity		
FEQ	NFEQ	Possibly/Necessarily Fuzzy EQual	Clustering Classification GDs Flexible Queries
FGT	NFGT	Possibly/Necessarily Fuzzy Greater Than	GDs Flexible Queries
FGEQ	NFGEQ	Possibly/Necessarily Fuzzy Greater or Equal	
FLT	NFLT	Possibly/Necessarily Fuzzy Less Than	
FLEQ	NFLEQ	Possibly/Necessarily Fuzzy Less Than or Equal	
MGT	NMGT	Possibly/Necessarily Much Greater Than	
MLT	NMLT	Possibly/Necessarily Much Less Than	

NFEQ, FGT, NFGT...) into the WHERE clause.

The definition of the fuzzy comparator is different depending on the fuzzy attribute. Thus, possibility and necessity theory are used to define fuzzy comparator on Type 2 (i.e. on two trapezoidal distributions). This definition is applicable on Type 1 as well (e.g. to compare with linguistic labels). The Type 3 only admits the fuzzy equal comparator (FEQ) which is implemented with the similarity relationship $\Theta'^=$' defined over them (e.g. see Figure 2).

Representation of Fuzzy Attributes

This representation is different depending on the fuzzy attribute:

- **Type 1:** They are represented as usual attributes using the data representation provided by the host RDBMS.
- **Type 2:** A fuzzy attribute of Type 2, called F, needs five classic attributes, as Table 2 shows.

- ○ F_T: It stores the kind of value which the attribute in question can take (0 for *Unknown*, 1 for *Undefined*, etc.). The letter T is concatenated with the name of the attribute.
- ○ F_1, F_2, F_3 and F_4: These store the description of the parameters which define the data and depend on the type of value (F_T); the name of these attributes is formed by the concatenation of numbers 1, 2, 3 and 4 respectively with the name of the attribute to which they belong.
- **Type 3:** They are represented by a variable number of traditional attributes according to the form described in Table 3.
  - ○ F_T: It is similar to the classic attribute F_T used in an attribute of Type 2.
  - ○ $(F_{P1},F_1),...,(F_{Pn},F_n)$: These attributes store data of the possibility distribution. For example, in a value of simple scalar type, only the first couple is used and the value of possibility will be 1 (standardized).

Figure 2. Definition example of an attribute of Type 3

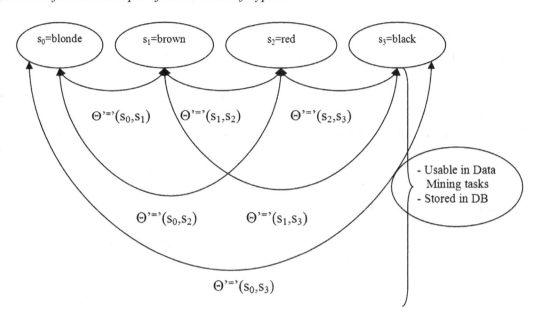

Table 2. Representation of an attribute of Type 2

Type of Value	Value of the attributes of the host RDBMS				
	F_T	F_1	F_2	F_3	F_4
Unknown	0	NULL	NULL	NULL	NULL
Undefined	1	NULL	NULL	NULL	NULL
Null	2	NULL	NULL	NULL	NULL
crisp: d	3	d	NULL	NULL	NULL
linguistic label: s_i	4	s_i	NULL	NULL	NULL
interval: $[\alpha,\delta]$	5	α	NULL	NULL	δ
approximate: $\alpha \pm m$	6	α	$\alpha - m$	$\alpha + m$	m
trapezoid: $[\alpha,\beta,\gamma,\delta]$	7	α	$\beta - \alpha$	γ	δ

Table 3. Representation of an attribute of Type 3

Type of Value	Value of attributes of the host RDBMS					
	F_T	F_{P1}	F_1	...	F_{Pn}	F_n
Unknown	0	NULL		...	NULL	NULL
Undefined	1	NULL		...	NULL	NULL
Null	2	NULL		...	NULL	NULL
simple scalar: e_i	3	p_i	e_i	...	NULL	NULL
dist. pos.: $\{e_1/p_1, e_2/p_2, ..., e_n/p_n\}$	4	p_1	e_1	...	p_n	e_n

DDL of dmFSQL

dmFSQL includes an extension of the DDL of SQL for defining the following objects: tables, labels and projects of DM. They are sentences to create, alter, drop, grant and revoke privileges on these objects. We will explain briefly the creation semantics for the objects of this language:

- **Table:** dmFSQL includes a series of options included into the CREATE TABLE statement in order to define the previously explained fuzzy attributes.
- **Label:** dmFSQL includes a series of formats to create the labels depending on the attribute type:
  - **Type 1 and 2:** It allows specifying its trapezoidal possibility distribution using the CREATE LABEL statement.
  - **Type 3:** It allows specifying their similarity relationships using the CREATE NEARNESS statement.
- **Project:** We define a new type of object, called *project*, which does not exist in SQL. This object has mainly the following task: It is the structure to keep the initial conditions, intermediate results (in order to improve the performance of the iterative DM process), and the final results of the DM process. A new project can be created with the sentence CREATE_MINING PROJECT. In a project, the process conditions are set to carry out DM depending on the DM technique used, since several techniques can be used in the same project (e.g. Clustering, Classification and GDs).

DML of dmFSQL

We have explained the form to define a table with fuzzy attributes, labels and DM projects by means of the DDL of dmFSQL. Now we can carry out the true DM process or the flexible query using the DML of dmFSQL:

- **Execution of a Project:** The DML of dmFSQL has a unique SELECT_MINING sentence by means of which we will carry out the different processes of DM previously described.
- **Extension of the Original DML of SQL for Fuzzy Data Management:** dmFSQL extends the DML SQL commands in order to manage the fuzzy attributes. Therefore, we can use the fuzzy constants described in Table 4 in these commands.

dmFSQL Architecture

We have developed an architecture that allows using the dmFSQL language for Oracle© Databases.

The architecture (Figure 3) is made up of Data, dmFSQL Server and dmFSQL Clients, elements that we will explain now:

Data: Traditional Database and dmFMB

The data can be classified into two categories:

- **Traditional Database:** It contains data from our relations with a special format to store the 4 types of fuzzy attributes.

Table 4. Fuzzy Constants in dmFSQL

F. Constant	Significance
Unknown	Unknown value but the attribute is applicable
Undefined	The attribute is not applicable or it is meaningless
Null	Total ignorance: we know nothing about it
$\$[\alpha_A, \beta_A, \gamma_A, \delta_A]$	Fuzzy trapezoid
$\$label$	Label
$[\alpha, \delta]$	Interval "Between α and δ"
$\#n$	Fuzzy value "Approximately n" with margin $\pm m$

Figure 3. Architecture of dmFSQL

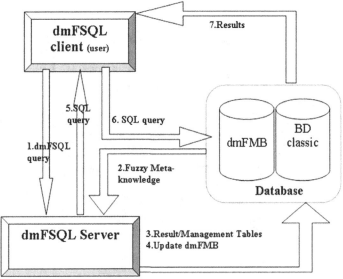

- **Data Mining Fuzzy Meta-Knowledge Base** (dmFMB): It is the support for the project object and contains information about the Fuzzy Relational Database in a relational format. It stores attributes which admit fuzzy treatment for DM, each of them save different information, depending on their type.

dmFQL Server

It has been mainly programmed in PL/SQL and carries out a lexical, syntactic and semantic analysis of dmFSQL statements. The dmFSQL Sever, which always generates a standard SQL sentence, works depending on the kind of dmFSQL sentence, by carrying out a different semantic treatment:

- **DDL Sentences:** Normally, the treatment consists of either inserting information in the dmFMB or executing grant sentences on the host RDBMS.
- **DML of Fuzzy Sentences** (fuzzy SELECT command): The dmFSQL query is translated into a standard SQL sentence.

- **DML of Data Mining Sentences** (SELECT_MINING command): The treatment consists of calling the DM process: clustering, classification, or obtaining GDs. These processes obtain a SELECT command or a table; in this case, the Server returns a conventional SELECT command on this table.

dmFQL Clients

They are independent programs which serve as an interface between the users and the dmFSQL Server. The user introduces the dmFSQL query and the client programs communicate with the Server and with the database in order to obtain the final results (see Figure 3). We have several client programs that work on dmFSQL architecture.

EXTENDING THE DMFSQL LANGUAGE FOR FUZZY ETL

Regarding the problem to be solved, the extension of DML of SQL to manage fuzzy attributes is considered, with constrains in the following aspects:

Figure 4. Schema of the FETL process

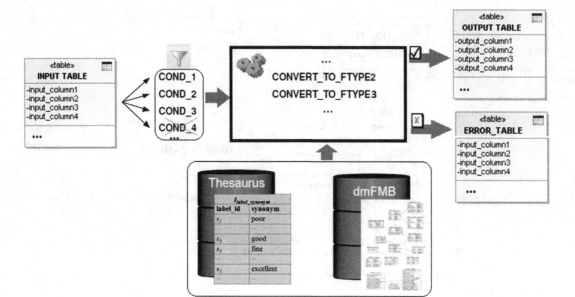

- The INSERT and UPDATE sentences allow including fuzzy constants with the format showed in Table 4. In a practical level, these formats are not common in the textual or numeric information found in the data sources (i.e. websites). Therefore, it is necessary an ad-hoc transformation from the original data to these formats depending on the website to be loaded. The final results are atomic DML sentences including the fuzzy constants.

- The unique common characteristic across all DW systems is that they are designed to handle large scale query processing. Thus, atomic INSERT and UPDATE sentences are considered very inefficient for processing a large data set.

The aim of this section is to develop an extension of the language and architecture for overcoming these limitations, in order to automate the process of:

- **Extraction** of the textual or numeric information from a conventional repository (table) with data loaded from websites.
- **Transformation** of such information into the fuzzy constants identified according to the internal format of the fuzzy attributes.
- **Loading** the fuzzy table with this transformed information.

We call this process Fuzzy Extraction, Transformation and Loading (FETL), which consists of the following elements:

Input Table: Repository (table or view) with the input data for the FETL process loaded from one or more websites.

Input Conditions: Conditions applied on the rows of the input table in order to select such rows for the FETL process.

Output Table: Fuzzy table with the correct output data for the FETL process.

Transformation Functions: These functions convert conventional information into fuzzy information. If the output attribute it is not a fuzzy attribute, we can use any transformation function defined on the RDBMS. There are special transformation functions to obtain the fuzzy attributes from conventional attributes. The functionality of these functions is primarily based on the identification of regular expressions and on the text mining process with a specific thesaurus, in order to identify the fuzzy constants and labels in several formats and languages. The four transformation functions to obtain fuzzy values are the following ones:

- **CONVERT_TO_FTYPE2:** It is applied to a numerical or text attribute to obtain a Type 2 attribute and convert it in its internal representation (showed in Table 2). Therefore, this function identifies in the attribute of the input table any possible value of a Type 2 attribute:

  ○ **Crisp:** We obtain a precise numerical value d expressed as text or numeric values, identifying regional settings (decimal point,…).

  ○ **Linguistic Label:** In order to obtain the linguistic labels s_i, we use some specific thesauruses of terms that contain synonyms (including formal and informal terms and abbreviations), higher-level terms, and words that have the same root as the specified term.

  ○ **Interval:** We obtain an interval value $[\alpha,\delta]$ identifying the crisp value α and δ (as we have previously explained) and some near keywords included in the thesaurus (e.g. "from … to …," "between … and …," etc.).

  ○ **Approximate:** we obtain an approximate value $\alpha \pm m$ identifying the crisp value α (as we have previously explained) and some near keywords included in the thesaurus (e.g. "about," "around," etc.). Normally, the value m is not identified; in this case, we will use the value *margin* specified

in the corresponding clause FTYPE2 added to the CREATE or ALTER TABLE sentence; please, see the syntax in (Carrasco et al, 2006).

  ○ **Trapezoid:** We obtain a trapezoid $[\alpha,\beta,\gamma,\delta]$ identifying the crisp values α, β, γ and δ. However, these values are not at all common in conventional data sources.

  ○ **Missing Values** (*Unknown, Undefined* and *Null*)**:** They can be explicitly identified using a specific thesaurus of terms. Besides, we obtain a missing value if no one of the previous values has been identified according to the DEFAULT clause specified in the CREATE or ALTER TABLE sentence for a Type 2 attribute, see the syntax in (Carrasco et al, 2006).

- **CONVERT_N_TO_FTYPE2:** It is applied to several numerical or text attributes to obtain a Type 2 attribute and convert it in its internal representation (showed in Table 2). For each attribute is first applied the previously explained CONVERT_TO_FTYPE2 function. This function uses fuzzy arithmetic based on the Extension Principle (Bonissone & Decker, 1986) to integrate the fuzzy values obtained from the input attributes.

- **CONVERT_TO_FTYPE3:** It is applied to a numerical or text attribute to obtain a Type 3 attribute and convert it in its internal representation (showed in Table 3). Therefore, this function identifies any possible value of a Type 3 attribute in the attribute of the input table:

  ○ **Label:** In order to obtain the scalar labels e_i, we use some specific thesauruses of terms that contain synonyms (including formal and informal terms and abbreviations), higher-level terms, and words that have the same root as the specified term.

○ **Missing Values** (*Unknown, Undefined* and *Null*)**:** They can be explicitly identified using specific thesauruses of terms. Besides, we obtain a missing value if no one of the previous values has been identified according to the DEFAULT clause specified in the CREATE or ALTER TABLE sentence of a Type 3 attribute, see the syntax in (Carrasco et al, 2006).

• **CONVERT_TO_FTYPE1:** It is applied to a numerical or text attribute to obtain a Type 1 attribute. Therefore, this function identifies then only possible value of a Type 1 attribute:

○ **Crisp:** We obtain a precise numerical value *d* expressed as textual or numeric values, identifying regional settings (decimal point,…).

Error Table: Exception table to insert in it the wrong transformed rows of the input table as the result of the FETL process. This allows an interactive FETL process, because we can make a new FETL process using as input table an error table of the previous FETL process. For example, let us consider an input table with a Type 2 attribute "age." If after a FETL process, in the error table has been inserted one row with the value of the attribute "teenager," we can define this new linguistic label with the corresponding dmFSQL sentence and make a new FETL process using as input table this error table.

Algorithm 1.

```
{fINSERT [WITH_TRUNCATE] | fINSERT_OR_UPDATE | fUPDATE}
INTO output_table_fetl
WITH_COLUMNS list_output_columns_fetl
SELECT trans_list_input_columns_fetl
FROM input_table_fetl
[WHERE input_condition_fetl]
[EXCEPTION INSERT INTO error_table_fetl]
```

Extending the dmFSQL Language for Fuzzy ETL

We propose a new set of DML sentences of dmFSQL in order to implement the previously mentioned FETL process. The syntax of these sentences is shown in Algorithm 1.
where:

• *input_table* is a table or view name that contains the input data for the FETL process.

• *input_condition* is a condition in SQL format, which is applied to the rows of *input_table* in order to select the rows satisfying it for the FETL process.

• *output_table* is a fuzzy table name where the right transformed rows of the *input_table* have to be inserted or updated as a result of the FETL process.

• *list_output_columns_fetl* is the list of prominent columns of the *output_table* for the FETL process:

output_column_fetl$_1$, ..., output_column_fetl$_n$.

• *trans_list_input_columns_fetl* is the list of prominent columns of the *input_table* for the FETL process with their corresponding transformation functions:

[*trans_func_input_column_fetl$_1$*] *list_input_column_fetl$_1$*, ..., [*trans_func_input_column$_n$*] *list_input_column_fetl$_n$*.

- ○ Each column *output_column_fetl$_i$* with *i*∈{1...*n*} will obtain the data from the corresponding list of columns *list_input_column_fetl$_i$* of the *input_table*, once applied the transformation function *trans_func_input_column_fetl$_i$*. As we have explained, we can use four special transformation functions to obtain the fuzzy attributes from conventional attributes: CONVERT_TO_FTYPE1, CONVERT_TO_FTYPE2, CONVERT_N_TO_FTYPE2 and CONVERT_TO_FTYPE3.

- ○ *error_table_fetl* is the exception table name where the wrong transformed rows of the *input_table* have to be inserted as the result of the FETL process.

There are four DML sentences regarding the loading strategy over the output table:

- fINSERT: The rows will be inserted into the *output_table*. If the record already exists, it will be inserted into the *error_table_fetl*.
- fINSERT WITH_TRUNCATE: The rows will be inserted into the *output_table*, which will be previously truncated (i.e. all its records will be deleted).
- fINSERT_OR_UPDATE: The rows will be inserted into the *output_table*. If the record already exists, it will be updated into the *output_table*.
- fUPDATE: The rows will be updated into the *output_table*. If the record does not exist, it will be inserted into the *error_table_fetl*.

Extending the dmFSQL Architecture for Fuzzy ETL

The new features of the dmFSQL language have been implemented into the architecture of dmFSQL.

Data

We have added to the dmFMB the specific thesaurus with the keywords to obtain the explained fuzzy values, including the labels in several formats and languages.

dmFQL Server

We have modified the dmFSQL Server in order to include the news dmFSQL sentences to manage the FETL process. Therefore, this new server carries out a lexical, syntactic and semantic analysis of the new dmFSQL statements: fINSERT, fINSERT WITH_TRUNCATE, fINSERT_OR_UPDATE, fUPDATE.

For each sentence, the semantic analysis generates large (non-atomic) DML sentences of standard SQL language, because they are more efficient for DW systems (which are designed to handle large scale query processing). Within these SQL statements, the transformation functions from conventional to fuzzy information are included. Oracle Text© (Shea, 2008) has been used as a tool for the text mining process in order to manage textual information in English and Spanish languages. In particular, we use the *contains* operator (Shea, 2008) in combination with the *near* operator (Shea, 2008) to return a score based on the proximity of the searched terms. In order to search such terms, we use some specific thesauruses of terms that contain: synonyms (including formal and informal terms and abbreviations), higher-level terms, and words that have the same root as the specified term (using the *stem* operator (Shea, 2008)). Moreover, we use helpful operators for finding more accurate results when there are frequent misspellings in the original data sources: words that sound like the specified terms (*soundex* operator (Shea, 2008)) and words that are spelled similarly to the specified terms (*fuzzy* operator (Shea, 2008)).

USING THE EXTENDED dmFSQL LANGUAGE IN AN ETL ARCHITECTURE APPLIED TO INTEGRATION OF QUESTIONNAIRES

In this section, we show the application of the FETL functionalities of the dmFSQL language, defined in the above section. This new functionalities will be part of a complete ETL process (Araque et al, 2006; Araque et al, 2007), with the aim of integrating semantically heterogeneous data from various websites. In particular, several questionnaires placed in different websites, with distinct formats and items (questions), have been used during the last years to survey the students of Information and Communication Technologies (ICT) courses taught at the Business School of the University of Granada. The objective is to integrate these questionnaires into a temporal DW. With this integrated information, the user can make several DM analyses. In particular, we show an application example using a clustering analysis, in order to extract interesting educational information and knowledge from the DW.

Fuzzy Integration of Web Data Sources for Data Warehousing

One of the most complex issues of ETL is the case where there are multiple sources for a single element of data in the DW. This is the proposed case, where the selected web pages for data extraction are included in (Google Docs, 2010; SurveyMonkey, 2010; Tutor, 2010). Now, we will explain the extraction and integration process chosen. In this explanation, we are going to simplify the process.

Thus, there will be only two sources of information. If it is possible to temporally integrate the data from both sources, semantic integration is undertaken and the result is stored in the DW. The integration methodology (Araque et al, 2006; Araque et al, 2007), which is shown in Figure 5, consists of a set of processes that define the rules for capturing a parameter from a single source as well as integrating a set of values semantically equivalent coming from different data sources. It has three phases:

- **Temporal Metadata Extraction (A):** In the information extraction process, it is necessary to maintain the temporal consistency. To solve this problem, this phase uses tools to define and generate wrappers for data sources accessible via web.
- **Generation of Refresh Metadata (B):** The most suitable instants are chosen to carry out the data refreshment process.
- **Refreshment Process (C):** It is responsible of making the incremental capture of data sources and integrating them into a temporal DW table. We propose the use of the FETL functionalities of the dmFSQL language for the semantic integration that we need in this phase. In the next subsection, we will explain this process in more detail.

Fuzzy Semantic Integration

The input questionnaires are very heterogeneous. Therefore, we need a standard format of questionnaire to be included into the DW system. We decide to use a widely used form called *Course Experience Questionnaire* (CEQ). The basic form of CEQ was developed for initial graduates in the United Kingdom (Ramsden & Entwistle, 1981). A later version was tested in Australian universities during 1989 (Ramsden et al, 1989). Since then, the GCCA's Survey Management Group has progressively refined the contents of this instrument. The

Figure 5. ETL architecture

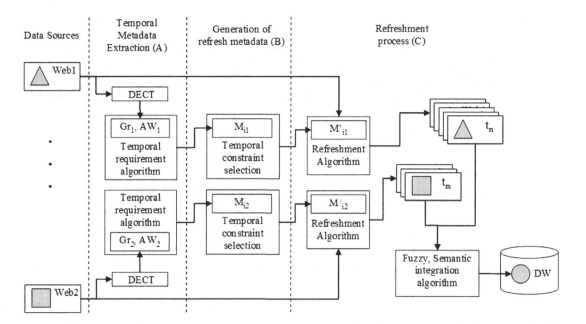

items included in the questionnaire have changed, and the wording of some items has been modified in response to data obtained from the application of the instrument in different contexts. In (Wilson et al, 1997) there is a report on the validity and usefulness of CEQ as a performance indicator of the perceived quality of university teaching. The final five scales recommended for CEQ are:

- The *Good Teaching Scale* (GTS) is characterised by practices such as providing students with feedback on their progress, explaining things, making the course interesting, motivating students, and understanding students' problems. High scores on GTS are associated with the perception that these practices are present. Lower scores reflect a perception that these practices are carried out less frequently. There is a body of research that links these practices to positive learning outcomes.
- The *Generic Skills Scale* (GSS) is an attempt to take into account the extent to which university courses add to the generic

skills that their graduates might be expected to possess. While discipline-specific skills and knowledge are often crucial to prospects of employment and further studies, the emphasis on generic skills stems from the belief that knowledge quickly becomes obsolete, and generic skills that may have been acquired in the learning process should endure and be applicable in a broader context. Skills typically identified in this context include communication skills, the capacity to learn new skills and procedures, the capacity to make decisions and solve problems, the ability to apply knowledge to the workplace, and the capacity to work with minimum supervision.
- The *Student Support Scale* (SSS) attempts to measure access to, and satisfaction with, key university facilities and services supporting student learning outcomes.
- The *Graduate Qualities Scale* (GQS) focuses on qualities typically associated with university outcomes, especially attitudes

Figure 6. Linguistic labels defined on the CEQ scales

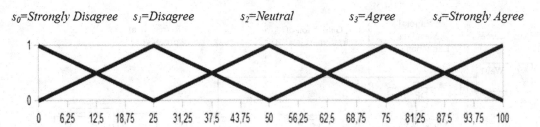

s_0=Strongly Disagree s_1=Disagree s_2=Neutral s_3=Agree s_4=Strongly Agree

and perspectives related to the relevance of the course for lifelong learning.

- *Overall Satisfaction Index* (OSI): students indicate their overall level of satisfaction with the course through one question: "Overall, I was satisfied with the quality of this course."

Given the requirement to integrate the existing questionnaires, we cannot use the more granular CEQ items, because generally they are not available in the original questionnaires. Therefore, we have to use the major conceptual CEQ scales previously explained. Thus, we have the following framework in the problem we are trying to solve:

- $Y=\{y_1,...,y_n\}$ is a set of n opinions included in the selected web pages for data extraction, which is obtained after the *temporal metadata extraction* (showed in Figure 5) for each questionnaire belongs to the set $H=\{Q_k\}$, with $k\in\{1...s\}$, in a specific interval of dates corresponding to a higher hierarchy of time (usually year) symbolized as *date*.

- $C=\{C_1,...,C_r\}$, with $r=5$, is a set of fact attributes characterizing such opinions using the five scales previously explained: C_1=GTS; C_2=GSS; C_3=SSS; C_4=GQS; and C_5=OSI.

The objective of this phase is the data semantic integration, which is represented in the table $t_{DW}(date\_id, questionnaire\_id, C_1,...,C_r)$, where

date_id is a temporal attribute with value *date* for the current extraction; *questionnaire_id* is the identification of the questionnaire in the set H (i.e. Q_k, and C_j, with $j\in\{1...r\}$) are the integrated characteristics of the data sources. Table 5 shows all the questions of the three questionnaires to be integrated, together with the website in which they are placed, the typology of the answers, and the CEQ assigned by experts to each question.

We consider that this information can be represented as a fuzzy type over an ordered underlying domain. Thus, we decide to define each C_j, with $j\in\{1...r\}$, of the t_{DW} as Type 2 attributes. Besides, in the CREATE TABLE sentence, we specify the DEFAULT UNKNOWN clause in order to manage the missing values. Usually, we cannot obtain some values for the attributes in this case study.

The CEQ scale asks students to agree or disagree each question on a 5-point Likert scale: "Strongly Disagree," "Disagree," "Neutral," "Agree" and "Strongly Agree." Therefore, each of the attributes C_j could be expressed linguistically. With this purpose, the set of primary terms $S=\{s_i\}$, $i\in\{0...g\}$, with $g=4$, is defined for each the attributes with the following values: s_0=*Strongly Disagree*, s_1=*Disagree*, s_2=*Neutral*, s_3=*Agree* and s_4=*Strongly Agree*. Figure 6 shows the semantics of each one, based on the expert users' criterion, using the domain [0,100] (as we will show below, this domain provides the most accurate answers to the question included in the questionnaires). The CREATE LABEL statements are used to define adequately these labels.

Table 5. Questionnaires used as data source and websites where they are placed

Questionairre_id and Website	Question_id and Wording		CEQ scale	Answer type
Q1 http://www.survey-monkey.com/	1	The teaching staff worked hard to make Information and Communication Technology (ICT) subjects interesting.	GTS	1-5
	2	The teaching staff of the course motivated me to do my best work.	GTS	1-5
	3	The teaching staff normally gave me helpful feedback on how I was doing.	GTS	1-5
	4	The course helped me develop my ability to work as a team member using ICT tools.	GSS	1-5
	5	The course improved my skills in communication using ICT tools.	GSS	1-5
	6	The course helped me develop my ability to plan my work using ICT tools.	GSS	1-5
	7	I was able to access ICT resources via Tutor (https://tutor2.ugr.es) when I needed them.	SSS	1-5
	8	Relevant learning resources were accessible when I needed them.	SSS	1-5
	9	I consider what I learned about ICT valuable for my future business job.	GQS	1-5
	10	The course developed my confidence to investigate new ICT applications on business.	GQS	1-5
	11	Overall, I was satisfied with this course.	OSI	1-5
Q2 https://spreadsheets.google.com/	1	How would you rate the teaching staff for the theoretical part of this course?	GTS	[0,100]
	2	How would you rate the teaching staff for the practical (laboratory) part of this course?	GTS	[0,100]
	3	As a result of this course, how would you rate your analytic skills to approach conventional business problems?	GSS	[0,100]
	4	How would you rate the access to electronic resources provided when you needed?	SSS	[0,100]
	5	As a result of this course, how would you rate your confidence to investigate new application of ICT in business?	GQS	[0,100]
	6	How would you rate the overall quality of this course?	OSI	[0,100]
Q3 https://tutor2.ugr.es/	1	Your assessment about the staff member's teaching activities?	GTS	free text
	2	As a result of this course, what is your assessment of the improved analytic skills to approach business problems?	GSS	free text
	3	What is your assessment of the advices provided for your future career?	SSS	free text
	4	What is your assessment about the value of what you learned on information and communication technology for your future business job?	GQS	free text
	5	What is your assessment of the overall value of this course?	OSI	free text

For each one of the fact attributes to obtain, we have decided to extract information of the following typology (see Table 5):

- **Crisp:** Q2 is the only questionnaire of the ones studied with precise numerical ratings by the students. The scores are numbers in the interval [0,100] as Figure 7 shows. The information extracted from this questionnaire is stored in the temporary table $t_{ETL\_Q2}(id\_date, question\_id\_1,...,question\_id\_6)$, where each attribute *question_id_i*, with $i \in \{1...6\}$, identifies the corresponding question of the questionnaire Q2 shown in Table 5. In order to integrate the table t_{ETL_Q2} into the table t_{DW}, we use the dmF-SQL sentence shown in Algorithm 2, where the attribute $C_1=GTS$ will correspond to the

Figure 7. Example of questionnaire with crisp answer type

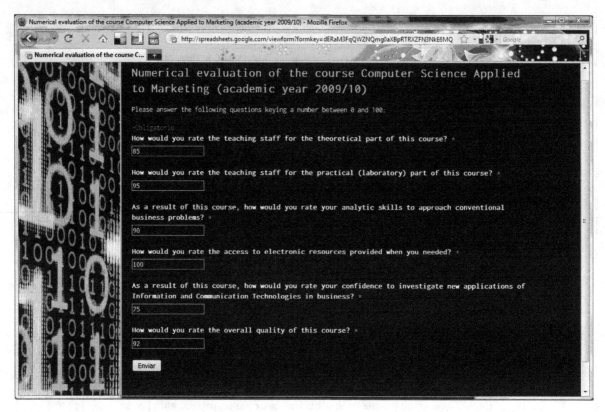

Algorithm 2.

```
        fINSERT INTO TDW
WITH_COLUMNS C1, C2, C3, C4, C5
SELECT          CONVERT_TO_FTYPE2 (QUESTION_ID_1+QUESTION_ID_2)/2,
        CONVERT_TO_FTYPE2 QUESTION_ID_3,
        CONVERT_TO_FTYPE2 QUESTION_ID_4,
        CONVERT_TO_FTYPE2 QUESTION_ID_5,
        CONVERT_TO_FTYPE2 QUESTION_ID_6
FROM TETL_Q2
        EXCEPTION INSERT INTO ERROR_TETL_Q2;
```

average between *question_id_1* and *question_id_2*; the rest is obvious.

- **Approximate:** Certain questionnaires, as the identified by Q1 in Table 5, ask the students to rate the questions in the range from 1 to 5 without decimals (i.e. 5-point Likert scale). Since the score that can give

the users in this case is far less accurate than the previously described, we will assume this information as approximate values according to Figure 8. An example of this type of rating is shown in Figure 9. The information extracted from the website is stored in a temporary table $t_{ETL\_Q1}(id\_$

Figure 8. Membership functions defined for approximate values in the range from 1 to 5

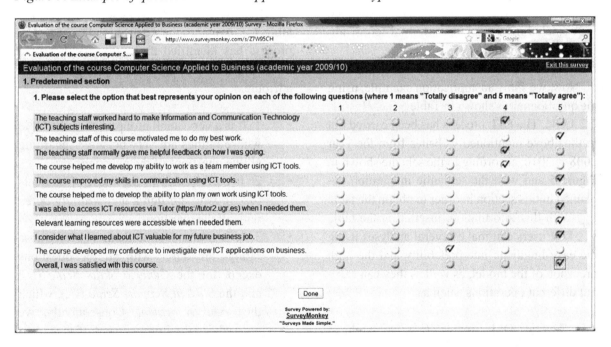

Figure 9. Example of questionnaire with approximate answer type

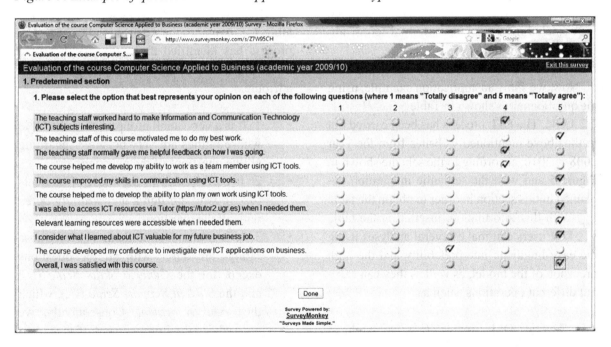

date,   question_id_1,…,question_id_11) with the same considerations previously described for t_{ETL_Q2}. In order to insert the table t_{ETL_Q1} into the table t_{DW}, we use the dmFSQL sentence shown in Algorithm 3.

- **Linguistic Label:** If the questionnaire does not have any numerical value, we decide to get the values of the answers from the students' textual commentaries and expressed them as linguistic labels. This is the case of questionnaire Q3. Given the heterogeneity of users that exists, we de-

cide to use a unique semantics for these labels, represented in Figure 10. These labels are defined with the corresponding dmFSQL sentence. Figure 11 shows an example of this type of answers. The information extracted from the website is stored in a temporary table t_{ETL_Q3}*(id_date, question_id_1,…,question_id_5)* with the same considerations previously described for t_{ETL_Q1} and t_{ETL_Q2}. In order to integrate the table t_{ETL_Q3} into the table t_{DW}, we used the dmFSQL sentence (see Algorithm 4) that

Algorithm 3.

```
        fINSERT INTO TDW
WITH_COLUMNS C1, C2, C3, C4, C5
SELECT       CONVERT_N_TO_FTYPE2 QUESTION_ID_1 QUESTION_ID_2 QUESTION_ID_3,
       CONVERT_N_TO_FTYPE2 QUESTION_ID_4 QUESTION_ID_5 QUESTION_ID_6,
       CONVERT_N_TO_FTYPE2 QUESTION_ID_7 QUESTION_ID_8,
       CONVERT_N_TO_FTYPE2 QUESTION_ID_9 QUESTION_ID_10,
       CONVERT_TO_FTYPE2 QUESTION_ID_11
FROM TETL_Q1
       EXCEPTION INSERT INTO ERROR_TETL_Q1;
```

identifies the linguistic labels explained (including synonyms, informal terms, abbreviations, etc.):

Now, we show an application example, using the questionnaires shown in Table 5 (i.e. $H=\{Q1, Q2, Q3\}$). The ETL process has been carried out in the above mentioned websites from the year 2008 to 2010, according to the scheme shown in Figure 5 and with the semantic integration explained in this section in order to obtain the table t_{DW}. With this information, inserted in the table t_{DW}, DW users can make several analyses using the easy linguistic interpretability and the high precision of the model, as well as they can carry out different operations, such as:

- Several DM studies (e.g. hierarchical clustering analysis of the questionnaires). Thus, with the two sentences in Algorithm 5 we obtain three clusters described by the linguistic labels previously defined (in Figure 6):

After the execution of these sentences, the table t_{CEN} contains the centroids obtained. The process has identified three groups (shown in Table 6), which are identified by the *cluster_id* attribute.

- 1: It is a very small group of students (1%) whose ratings are very negative regarding all the questions of the questionnaire.
- 2: It corresponds to the most of students (82%), who are *agree* and *strongly agree* with all the questions.
- 3: It is a group of students (17%) whose ratings are *agree* with all the questions except for the *Generic Skills Scale* (C_2) and the *Student Support Scale* (C_3), which they rate as *neutral*. Consequently, we may advise the improvement of these two characteristics.
  - Historical evolutions of the characteristics of the questionnaires.
  - Integration of very heterogeneous questionnaires (included in *H*) with other external CEQ studies, etc.

Figure 10. Linguistic labels defined for the questionnaire Q3

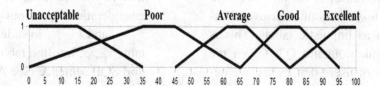

Figure 11. Example of questionnaire with free text answer type, with the following label extraction: 1=average; 2=good; 3, 4 and 5=excellent

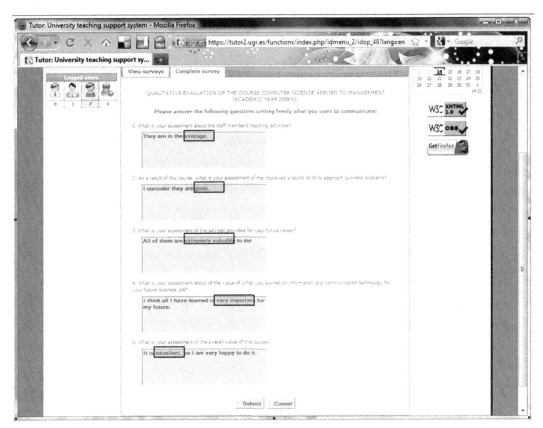

Algorithm 4.

```
        fINSERT INTO TDW
WITH_COLUMNS C1, C2, C3, C4, C5
SELECT         CONVERT_TO_FTYPE2 QUESTION_ID_1,
        CONVERT_TO_FTYPE2 QUESTION_ID_2,
        CONVERT_TO_FTYPE2 QUESTION_ID_3,
        CONVERT_TO_FTYPE2 QUESTION_ID_4,
        CONVERT_TO_FTYPE2 QUESTION_ID_5
FROM TETL_Q3
        EXCEPTION INSERT INTO ERROR_TETL_Q3;
```

CONCLUSION

In this paper, we have extended the dmFSQL language and architecture in order to include a Fuzzy Extraction, Transformation and Loading (FETL) process. We have used the new approach as a tool which is included in a complete ETL architecture (Araque et al, 2006; Araque et al, 2007), with the aim of integrating semantically heterogeneous data from various questionnaires placed in different websites. Therefore, the answers expressed in different formats (i.e. in natural language) and

Algorithm 5.

```
CREATE_MINING PROJECT WEQUEST
ON TABLE TDW
WITH COLUMNS FOR CLUSTERING
C1      WEIGHT_CLUSTERING 0.2 FCOMP_CLUSTERING FEQ
        WEIGHT_CENTROID 0.2 FCOMP_CENTROID FEQ
        ABSTRACTION_LEVEL_CENTROID LABEL,
C2      WEIGHT_CLUSTERING 0.2 FCOMP_CLUSTERING FEQ
        WEIGHT_CENTROID 0.2 FCOMP_CENTROID FEQ
        ABSTRACTION_LEVEL_CENTROID LABEL,
C3      WEIGHT_CLUSTERING 0.2 FCOMP_CLUSTERING FEQ
        WEIGHT_CENTROID 0.2 FCOMP_CENTROID FEQ
        ABSTRACTION_LEVEL_CENTROID LABEL,
C4      WEIGHT_CLUSTERING 0.2 FCOMP_CLUSTERING FEQ
        WEIGHT_CENTROID 0.2 FCOMP_CENTROID FEQ
        ABSTRACTION_LEVEL_CENTROID LABEL,
C5      WEIGHT_CLUSTERING 0.2 FCOMP_CLUSTERING FEQ
        WEIGHT_CENTROID 0.2 FCOMP_CENTROID FEQ
        ABSTRACTION_LEVEL_CENTROID LABEL;
SELECT_MINING KMEANS_CLUSTERING WEBQUEST
INTO TABLE_CLUSTERING TCLU, TABLE_CENTROIDS TCEN
OBTAINING 3 CLUSTERS;
```

Table 6. Extract of the table t_{CEN}

cluster_id	Number of rows	C1	C2	C3	C4	C5
1	9	Strongly Disagree	Strongly Disagree	Strongly Disagree	Strongly Disagree	Strongly Disagree
2	755	Agree	Strongly Agree	Agree	Strongly Agree	Strongly Agree
3	158	Agree	Neutral	Neutral	Agree	Agree

by means of approximate, numerical and missing values, have been integrated into a DW. With this information, the user can make several DM analyses with the benefit of an easy linguistic interpretability.

FUTURE RESEARCH DIRECTIONS

Since there are not commercial tools that support the fuzzy ETL processes, we consider that this chapter can help to achieve this type of tools.

Moreover, we are working on a friendlier client program for the FETL task of dmFSQL, as well as on extending the solution proposed here to similar integration problems.

REFERENCES

Araque, F., Salguero, A. G., Carrasco, R. A., & Delgado, C. (2007). Fuzzy integration of Web data sources for data warehousing. *Lecture Notes in Computer Science*, *4739*, 1208–1215. doi:10.1007/978-3-540-75867-9_151

Araque, F., Salguero, A. G., Delgado, C., Garví, E., & Samos, J. (2006). *Algorithms for integrating temporal properties of data in data warehousing.* In 8th Int. Conf. on Enterprise Information Systems (ICEIS) (pp. 193-199).

Bonissone, P. P., & Decker, K. S. (1986). Selecting uncertainty calculi and granularity: An experiment in trading-off precision and complexity. In Kanal, L. H., & Lemmer, J. F. (Eds.), *Uncertainty in artificial intelligence* (pp. 217–247). Amsterdam, The Netherlands: North-Holland Publishers.

Booking.com. (n.d.). *Europe's leading online hotel reservations agency by room nights sold.* Retrieved October 25, 2010, from http://www.booking.com/

Bordogna, G., & Passi, G. (1993). A fuzzy linguistic approach generalizing Boolean information retrieval: A model and its evaluation. *Journal of the American Society for Information Science American Society for Information Science, 44,* 70–82. doi:10.1002/(SICI)1097-4571(199303)44:2<70::AID-ASI2>3.0.CO;2-I

Burdick, D., Deshpande, P. M., Jayram, T. S., Ramakrishnan, R., & Vaithyanathan, S. (2006). OLAP over uncertain and imprecise data. [VLDB]. *The International Journal on Very Large Data Bases, 16*(1), 123–144. doi:10.1007/s00778-006-0033-y

Carrasco, R. A., Vila, M. A., & Araque, F. (2006). dmFSQL: A language for data mining. In R. S. Bilof (Ed.), *Proceeding of the 17th International Conference on Database and Expert Systems Applications (DEXA)* (pp. 440-444). IEEE Computer Society.

Carrasco, R. A., Vila, M. A., & Galindo, J. (2002). FSQL: A flexible query language for data mining. In Piattini, M., Filipe, J., & Braz, J. (Eds.), *Enterprise Information Systems* (pp. 68–74). Kluwer Academic Publishers.

Carrasco, R. A., Vila, M. A., Galindo, J., & Cubero, J. C. (2000). FSQL: A tool for obtaining fuzzy dependencies. In Universidad Politécnica de Madrid (Eds.), *Proceeding of the 8th International Conference on Information Processing and Management of Uncertainty in Knowledge-Based Systems (IPMU)*, vol. 3 (pp. 1916-1919).

Delgado, M., Verdegay, J. L., & Vila, M. A. (1992). Linguistic decision making models. *International Journal of Intelligent Systems, 7,* 479–492. doi:10.1002/int.4550070507

eDreams.com©. (n.d.). *eDreams.com© offers the widest selection and the best prices on the market for flights, hotels and vacation packages.* Retrieved October 25, 2010, from http://www.edreams.net

Frawley, W. J., Piatetsky-Shapiro, G., & Matheus, C. J. (1991). Knowledge discovery in databases: An overview. In Piatetsky-Shapiro, G., & Frawley, W. J. (Eds.), *Knowledge discovery in databases* (pp. 1–31). The AAAI Press.

Galindo, J. (Ed.). (2008). *Handbook of research on fuzzy information processing in databases.* Hershey, PA: Information Science Reference. doi:10.4018/978-1-59904-853-6

Google. (2010). *Google Docs – Online documents, spreadsheets, presentations, surveys, file storage and more.* Retrieved from https://spreadsheets.google.com

Inmon, W. H. (1996). The data warehouse and data mining. *Communications of the ACM, 39*(11), 49–50. doi:10.1145/240455.240470

Inmon, W. H. (2005). *Building the data warehouse* (4th ed.). New York, NY: Wiley.

Medina, J. M., Vila, M. A., Cubero, J. C., & Pons, O. (1995). Towards the implementation of a generalized fuzzy relational database model. *Fuzzy Sets and Systems, 75*(3), 273–28. doi:10.1016/0165-0114(94)00380-P

PlanetRate. (n.d.). *Education ratings, reviews and opinions*. Retrieved October 25, 2010, from http://www.planetrate.com/ Category/Education

Ramsden, P., & Entwistle, N. J. (1981). Effects of Academic Departments on Students' Approaches to Studying. *The British Journal of Educational Psychology*, *51*, 368–383. doi:10.1111/j.2044-8279.1981.tb02493.x

Ramsden, P., Martin, E., & Bowden, J. (1989). School environment and sixth form pupil's approaches to learning. *The British Journal of Educational Psychology*, *59*, 129–142. doi:10.1111/j.2044-8279.1989.tb03086.x

Sapir, L., Shmilovici, A., & Rokach, L. (2008). A methodology for the design of a fuzzy data warehouse. In *Proceeding of the IEEE Conference on Intelligent Systems, Volume 1*, 6-8 (pp. 2-14 - 2-21).

Shea, C. (2008). *Oracle text reference, 11g release 1*. (Part Number B28304-03).

SurveyMonkey. (2010). *Questionnaires online*. Retrieved from http://www.surveymonkey.com/

TripAdvisor.com. (n.d.). *Branded sites alone make up the most popular and largest travel community in the world*. Retrieved October 25, 2010, from http://www.tripadvisor.es/

Tutor. (2010). *University teaching support system*. Retrieved from https://tutor2.ugr.es

Wang, J. (Ed.). (2009). *Encyclopedia of data warehousing and mining*. Hershey, PA: Information Science Reference.

Wilson, K., Lizzio, A., & Ramsden, P. (1997). The development, validation and application of the course experience questionnaire. *Studies in Higher Education*, *22*(1), 33–53. doi:10.1080/0 3075079712331381121

Zadeh, L. A. (1975). The concept of a linguistic variable and its applications to approximate reasoning. *Information Sciences*, *8*(1-2), 199–249, 301–357. doi:10.1016/0020-0255(75)90036-5

KEY TERMS AND DEFINITIONS

Centroid: The centroid of a cluster is an average point in the multidimensional space defined by the dimensions. In a sense, it is the center of gravity for the respective cluster.

Classification: It is the systematic arrangement of elements based on everything we know about them.

Clustering: It consists on identifying elements with similar characteristics, and grouping cases with similar characteristics together.

Data Mining: Process extracting interesting information from the data in databases.

Data Warehouse: It is the storage of consolidated information dedicated to easily and quickly provide simple or preaggregated data for analysis.

ETL: Process in the data warehousing usage that involves three operations: extracting data from outside sources; transforming it to fit operational needs; and loading it into the end target (data warehouse).

Linguistic Labels: They are values of linguistic variables, which are variables whose values are not numbers, but words or sentences in a natural or artificial language.

Chapter 4
Incorporating Text OLAP in Business Intelligence

Byung-Kwon Park
Dong-A University, Korea

Il-Yeol Song
Drexel University, USA

ABSTRACT

As the amount of data grows very fast inside and outside of an enterprise, it is getting important to seamlessly analyze both data types for total business intelligence. The data can be classified into two categories: structured and unstructured. For getting total business intelligence, it is important to seamlessly analyze both of them. Especially, as most of business data are unstructured text documents, including the Web pages in Internet, we need a Text OLAP solution to perform multidimensional analysis of text documents in the same way as structured relational data. We first survey the representative works selected for demonstrating how the technologies of text mining and information retrieval can be applied for multidimensional analysis of text documents, because they are major technologies handling text data. And then, we survey the representative works selected for demonstrating how we can associate and consolidate both unstructured text documents and structured relation data for obtaining total business intelligence. Finally, we present a future business intelligence platform architecture as well as related research topics. We expect the proposed total heterogeneous business intelligence architecture, which integrates information retrieval, text mining, and information extraction technologies all together, including relational OLAP technologies, would make a better platform toward total business intelligence.

DOI: 10.4018/978-1-61350-038-5.ch004

INTRODUCTION

Using a business intelligence solution, people get business insight from the vast amount of data they manage. In general, there are three categories of data: structured, semi-structured, and unstructured. Mostly, structured data are represented in a relational form; semi-structured in XML; and unstructured in text. It is known that only 20% of the data available are structured and are stored in relational databases, while about 80% are unstructured text and are stored in various forms of documents such as reports, news articles, e-mails, and largely web pages. Thus, in order to obtain complete business intelligence, incorporating and analyzing text data are essential.

Sullivan (2001) proposed to associate relational data warehouses with a text document warehouse for that purpose. Through analyzing the former, such information as where, when, and who did how many of what can be extracted. Through analyzing the latter, such information as why it was done can be figured out. For example, if we found that the sales volume of wide television set was cut down especially in an urban area, we can understand the reason by analyzing such documents as sales report, marketing report, product catalogs, and news articles at that time. Google Finance is another example of associating numerical data with web pages. The Google Finance web page contains a graph showing the stock price changes over time, and also hyperlinks from the extreme points of the graph to the web pages describing what happened at that time.

For multidimensional analysis, in general, online analytical processing (OLAP) technology is used. OLAP helps to perform multidimensional analysis of a vast amount of data from many perspectives. In this chapter, we call the multidimensional analysis on text documents using OLAP technology as *Text OLAP*. The major technologies handling text data are Text Mining (TM), Information Retrieval (IR), and Information Extraction (IE). A TM system mines, from a document set, such information as top keywords, text summary, text classification, and text clustering. An IR system retrieves, from a document set, the documents containing the keywords given as a user query. An IE system extracts, from a document set, the structured information according to the schema given by a user. Integration of TM and IR technologies can contribute to the TEXT OLAP and IE technology to the linkage of unstructured text documents to the structured data in a relational database. We describe each approach with some examples, and discuss the future directions.

In this chapter, Section 2 focuses on analyzing text documents only (i.e. Text OLAP). Through Text OLAP over the reports on market trends, news articles, and web pages in Internet, business people can obtain important business information such as new competitors or competitive products coming out in market and consumer demand patterns changing. Section 3 focuses on linking structured relational data and unstructured text documents for the multidimensional analysis on the consolidated information. Section 4 focuses on the future research direction toward total business intelligence platform. Finally, we conclude in Section 5.

ANALYZING TEXT DOCUMENTS

Analyzing Based on Text Mining

Using TM technology, we can perform the operations of classifying, clustering, summarizing, or extracting top keywords from a set of text documents. Through those TM operations, we can perform multi-perspective analysis such as what documents belonging to each category, what clusters being formed, what being the summary in brief, and what being the top keywords from a set of text documents. In other words, we can perform a macro-level analysis and investigate the characteristics of a whole document set from various perspectives. For more information on

Figure 1. Multidimensional model of XML-OLAP

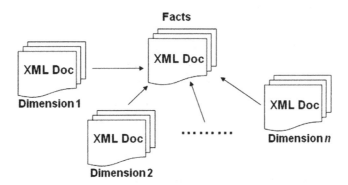

TM technology, Kroeze et al.(2003) and Simitsis et al.(2008) are good references. In this section, we first introduce the framework of Text OLAP based on TM technology, and then introduce the special dimension of *topic* which is important for analyzing text documents.

Framework

The XML-OLAP proposed by Park et. al.(2005) is a good example of Text OLAP Framework based on TM technology. Although XML-OLAP is a multidimensional analysis framework for a document-centric XML document warehouse, we use it to show how Text OLAP can be done based on TM. In XML-OLAP, it is assumed that both fact and dimension data are all represented in an XML document as shown in Figure 1. XML-OLAP uses the TM operations in aggregating text contents of XML documents for Text OLAP. The advantage of the framework is that it can be easily applied to a collection of any XML documents.

Figure 2 shows an example of XML-OLAP query on the US patent document warehouse. A text cube is returned as the query result, where each cell has a textual content such as top keywords, a summary, a set of classes, and a set of clusters. The FROM clause, using the XPath expression, specifies the text segments of XML

documents to analyze - the title segments of US patents, and also specifies a TM operation for aggregation – 'TOP_KEYWORD.' The WHERE clause is optional and specifies the slice condition that the patents related with the topic 'AI' or 'database' are selected for analysis. The SELECT clause specifies the axis dimensions of the resulting cube. In the example, a two-dimensional cube is returned with the two axes: one is the registration year having values 2003 and 2004, and the other the inventor's institution type having values 'university' and 'industry.' Each cell of the cube has some number of top keywords extracted from the title texts of the selected patents. Figure 3 is an example of the resulting cube.

There are several other works on the methods of efficiently performing TM operations and special TM operations used for the analysis of Bioinformatics papers.

DocCube

The DocCube system proposed by Mothe et al.(2003) also is an example of the Text OLAP system that can be used to explore and visualize the whole document collection using the classification (or categorization) technology. It treats a different facet of a document as a document dimension. Examples of facets are authors,

Figure 2. An example of an XML-OLAP query

```
SELECT  {/regTime//year[@num=2003],
         /regTime//year[@num=2004] } ON COLUMNS
        {/inventor//instType[@name='University'],
         /inventor//instType[@name='Industry'] } ON ROWS
FROM    /usPatent//title/text : TOP_KEYWORD
WHERE   (/topic//high[@area='AI'], /topic//high[@area='database']);
```

Figure 3. A resulting cube example as the result of an XML-OLAP query

	2003	2004
University	ML, genome	XML, sequence
Industry	Robot, vision	Grid, stream

affiliations, and creation or last modification dates. These dimension tables are not different from the ones used in traditional OLAP systems. However, the fact table content is different. A fact table contains a link that associates a fact row to a document. Hence, the document represented by the dimension values can be easily retrieved. In addition, the link can be weighted according to the confidence degree on the association of the document with the dimension values. This weight results from the document categorization method, 'vector voting method.' The link is represented as the 'Doc. Ref' field, which corresponds to the document identifier or the document URL. Figure 4 is an example of such a multidimensional model of DocCube.

DocCube provides two and three dimensional visualization as shown in Figure 5 so that a user can visually know how many documents are related to each other in the multidimensional space and directly access to the document content. For example, when scientific monitoring is involved, DocCube allows one to visualize global information such as the number of publications per author and per year, or who are the main authors in a given area. The knowledge on the relationships

between authors and topics of documents, the strength of these links, and their evolution in the time can also be discovered. Whatever the application, DocCube provides global views of the contents of a document collection. By browsing the dimensions, the user knows the dispersion of the documents according to the dimension values and can change the level of aggregation he wants to visualize. At any moment, he can have direct access to the documents associated with selected dimension values.

Topic Cube

When analyzing text data using TM technology, it is important to support an analyst to drill-down or roll-up text data on a topic dimension according to some meaningful hierarchy defined for the analysis task. Drill-down or roll-up along the topic dimension will allow users to view the text data from different granularities of topics. Figure 6 shows such an example of such a topic dimension especially used for analyzing various kinds of anomaly events that may happen in the domain of aviation. The root represents the aggregation of all the topics, the second level some general

Figure 4. A multidimensional model of DocCube [Mothe 2003]

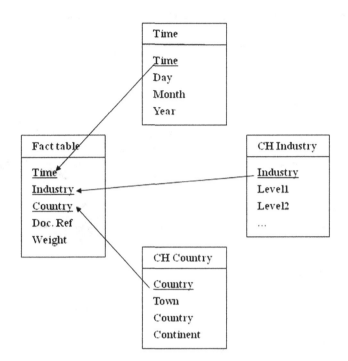

types, and the child level specialized types of their parent nodes. While drilling down and rolling up along such a topic hierarchy, the TM operations would be applied for aggregating text data.

The Topic Cube proposed by Zhang et al.(2009) is a good example of Text OLAP using a topic dimension as well as TM technology. It is a new cube model using a topic dimension and a text content measure which carries parameters of a probabilistic model that serves to indicate how well the text content matches with the topic. Figure 7 shows the star schema of a topic cube. The dimension table for the topic dimension is built based on the hierarchical topic tree. Two kinds of measures are stored in a topic cube cell: word distribution of a topic $p(w_i|topic)$ and topic coverage by documents $p(topic|d_j)$. The topic coverage means the probability that document d_j covers the topic. Thus we can easily predict which topic is dominant in the set of documents by aggregating the coverage over all the documents in

the set. For further explanation of the probabilistic topic model used for topic cubes, you can refer to the reference by Zhang et al.(2009).

Figure 8 shows an example of a topic cube. The topic dimension is added from the hierarchical tree shown in Figure 6 to the standard dimensions such as "Time" and "Location" dimensions. The left cuboid shows some finer topics like "overshoot" at "LAX" in "Jan. 99," while the right cuboid shows some coarse topics like "Deviation" at "LA" in "1999." Figure 9 shows two example cells of a topic cube (with only word distribution measure). The meaning of the first record is that the top words of aircraft equipment problem occurred in flights during January 1999 are (engine 0.104, pressure 0.029, oil 0.023, checklist 0.022, hydraulic 0.020, ...). So when an expert gets the result from the topic cube, she will soon know what the main problems of equipments are during January 1999, which shows the power of a topic cube.

Figure 5. The 3D visual representation of documents in DocCube [Mothe 2003]

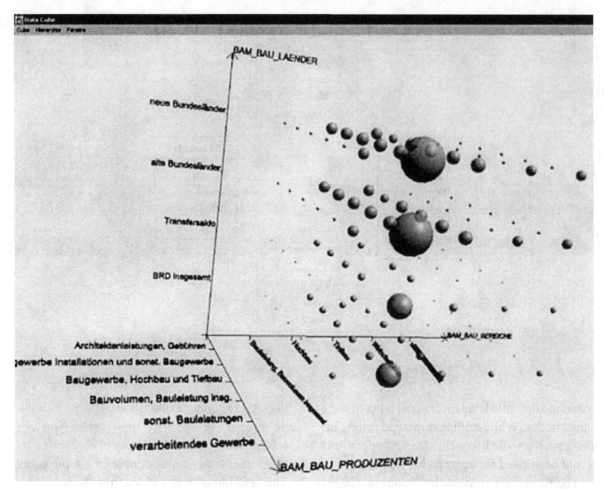

Figure 6. An example of topic dimension for anomaly events [Zhang 2009]

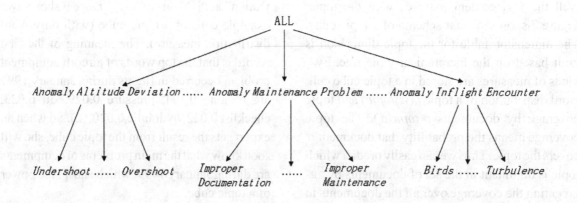

Figure 7. A star schema of Topic Cube [Zhang 2009]

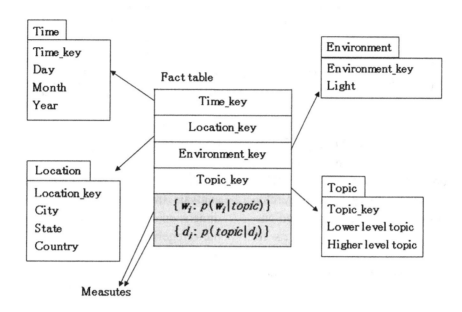

Figure 8. An example of Topic Cube [Zhang 2009]

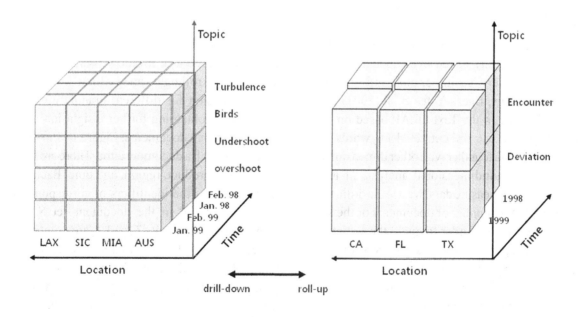

Figure 9. Two example cells of Topic Cube [Zhang 2009]

Time	Anomaly Event	Word Distribution
1999.01	**equipment**	engine 0.104, pressure 0.029, oil 0.023, checklist 0.022, hydraulic 0.020, . . .
1999.01	**ground encounters**	tug 0.059, park 0.031, pushback 0.031, ramp 0.029, brake 0.027, taxi 0.026, tow 0.023, . . .

Based on the Topic Cube, Yu et al.(2009) proposed iNextCube (Information Network-Enhanced Text Cube) which integrated the capability of automatic formation of topic hierarchy through information network analysis. It is tedious and error-prone to rely on human experts to specify topic hierarchy, so it is desirable to automatically construct topic hierarchy by information network analysis.

Analyzing Based on Information Retrieval

Using IR technology, we can extract keywords from and compute their weights for text documents. In an IR system, every document is assumed to consist of keywords, and a keyword-based query is used to retrieve the documents that are most related with the keywords given in the query. For a certain retrieval model (e.g. the vector space model) the retrieved documents are ranked in the query result. For more information on IR technology, Baeza-Yates et. al (2001) is a good reference. In the Text OLAP based on IR technology, we use the extracted keywords as dimensional data together with other dimensional ones for the multidimensional analysis of text documents. For measure data, we use the ordinary ones such as the number of documents or the set of document ID's in order to apply the ordinary aggregation operation such as addition. In this section, we first introduce a framework of Text OLAP based on IR technology, and then introduce the concept of multidimensional IR.

Framework

Tseng et al.(2006) proposed a multidimensional analysis framework for text documents. For dimensional data, they used the metadata and the categories of documents, and the keywords extracted from document contents. However, they did not mention how the metadata and the keywords could be organized in a hierarchical form. For measure data, they used the identifiers and the number of corresponding documents. Figure 10 shows a star schema example of a document warehouse according to the framework. The keywords and the metadata such as title, creator, date, and rights are shown as dimensions. We can perform a multidimensional analysis for the document warehouse, for example, how many documents were created regarding 'business intelligence' between 2009 and 2010?

We can derive a document cube from the document warehouse to allow users to browse documents by rolling up and drilling down along some dimension for different granularities and perspectives, obtaining further insight into relationships among documents. Figure 11 shows an example of such a document cube. There are three dimensions: product, region, and time. Each cell of the cube has the identifiers of corresponding documents stored in the document set S. For example, the documents T_1 and T_3 are pointed by the cell a, and the documents T_1 and T_2 are pointed by the cell d. In other words, T_1 and T_3 are the corresponding documents related with the product *printer* of the region *Taipei* at some time; T_1 and T_2 the corresponding documents related

Figure 10. A star schema example of a document warehouse[Tseng 2006]

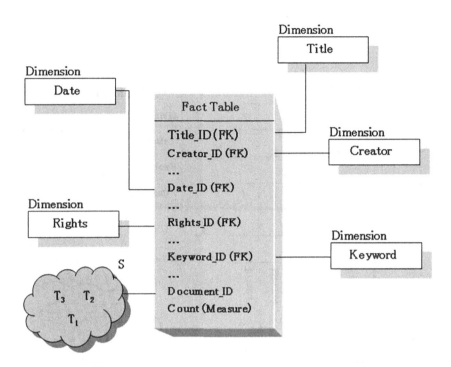

with the product *printer* of the region *Tainan* at some time.

For the document cube, we can submit a multidimensional query. Tseng et. al.(2006) proposed a new kind of query language called *MD²X (Multi-Dimensional Document eXpression)* specially designed for the document cube. Figure 12 illustrates a sample query in MD²X for the document cube *DC*, saying *"Find the documents related with the products of TV, Refrigerator, Cellular Phone, Radio, Monitor, and Printer that are sold at North and South region on Apr. 2003."* Figure 13 shows a sample result for the query in Figure 12. The result displays the identifiers of the related documents for each product and each region.

Text Cube

Lin et al.(2008) proposed a new data cube called *text cube*. It has a new dimension for semantic navigation of text data, *term hierarchy*, which involves two new OLAP operations of *pull-up* and *push-down*. It also has two special IR measures, *term frequency* and *inverted index* so that other IR techniques and applications can be efficiently built. A term hierarchy is newly introduced in text cube to specify the semantic levels of and relationships among text terms. Figure 14 shows an example. Each term extracted from the document set becomes a node at base level, the parent node at upper level consists of all the children at lower level, and the node at top level consists of all the terms. A user can pull-up or push down term level along the hierarchy. The measures, term frequency and inverted index, are

Figure 11. An example of a document cube[Tseng 2006]

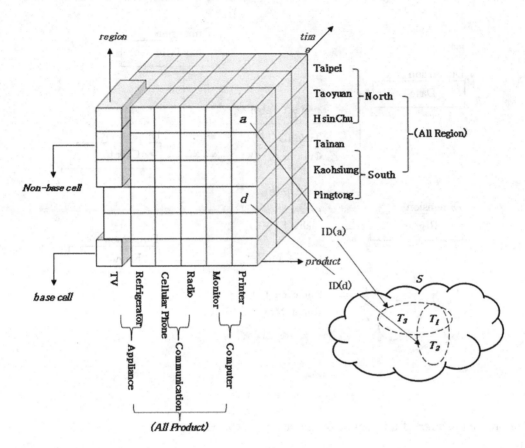

Figure 12. A sample query on a document cube[Tseng 2005]

```
SELECT {P.[Appliance].[TV],
        P.[Appliance].[Refrigerator],
        P.[Communication].[Cellular Phone],
        P.[Communication].[Radio],
        P.[Computer].[Monitor],
        P.[Computer].[Printer]} ON COLUMNS, {R.[North],
        R.[South]} ON ROWS,

FROM DC
WHERE Time.[2003].[Apr]
```

Figure 13. A sample query result on a document cube[Tseng 2005]

		Appliance		Communication		Computer	
		TV	Refrigerator	Cellular Phone	Radio	Monitor	Printer
North		Doc 024 Doc 001	Doc 021 Doc 008 Doc 017 Doc 012 Doc 016 Doc 010 Doc 020 Doc 002	Doc 007 Doc 006	Doc 018 Doc 023 Doc 022 Doc 019	Doc 001 Doc 010 Doc 023	Doc 002 Doc 006
South		Doc 011	Doc 003 Doc 015	Doc 004 Doc 005	Doc 013 Doc 009 Doc 014	Doc 013 Doc 014	Doc 009 Doc 015

Figure 14. A sample term hierarchy[Lin 2008]

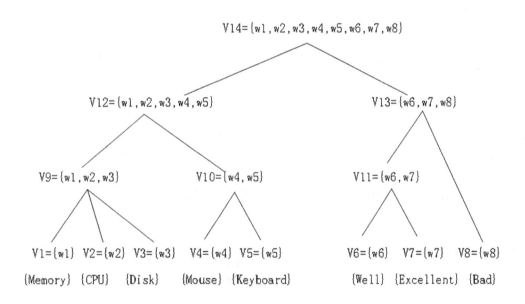

essential for IR tasks, and are redefined for aggregated text data. Suppose D is the aggregated text data for a cuboid cell. For term w and document d, $tf_{w,d}$ denotes the total times w appear in d, $TF(w,D) = \sum tf_{w,d}$ denotes the total times w appear in D, and $IV(w,D) = \{(d, tf_{w,d}) \mid tf_{w,d} > 0\}$ denotes the list of documents in D containing w.

Multidimensional IR

Lee and McCabe et al.(2000) proposed a multidimensional IR engine (MIRE) which is based on a multidimensional data model to utilize OLAP technology. The approach is simply to build a multi-dimensional data model for text, and allows users to search with the ease of OLAP techniques. The MIRE system can provide for a multidimensional IR query such as "Find all documents that has terms *Information Retrieval*, which are published in Illinois during year 2000." The MIRE system provides new functionalities such as browsing through a document collection and quickly identifying patterns surrounding where, when, and on what topic documents are written.

Figure 15 shows the model used in MIRE. The measure is 'Term Occurrence' and the dimensions are 'Category,' 'Time,' 'Location,' 'Document,' and 'Term.' The Time dimension has a hierarchy of (time, year, month, day), and the Location has a hierarchy of (Region, Country, State, City). The Document dimension contains structured, bibliographic information about the document. The Term dimension includes information on each term such as the term's name, its category (what kind of word it is) and the weight of the term. The Category dimension describes various subject categories used to find the document (e.g.; medical, legal, etc.). Each term is placed into a category of related words. This category can be obtained from a thesaurus or from the concept hierarchy such as WordNet or from a manually derived set of related words. The fact table contains: Category Id, Time Id, Location Id, Term Id, Doc Id, and Term Occurrence.

MIRE is an approach to build an IR system on top of OLAP facility where fact tables contain the measure, word-appears-in-document, and dimensional tables contain hierarchical structured data. MIRE is a new IR system integrating an inverted index for text and a multidimensional access method for dimensional data. The multidimensional access method is used for handling dimensional data, and it can provide OLAP functionalities such as drilling up and down on specific dimensions. In order to address scalability issues, MIRE builds an inverted index and uses a single multidimensional access structure (modified k-d-b tree) to access the data of Loca-

Figure 15. A data model for multidimensional IR[Lee 2000]

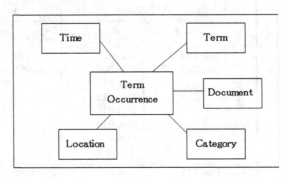

tion, Time, Category, and Document dimension together.

The query, "Find all documents that has terms *Information Retrieval*, which are published in Illinois during year 2000" is processed in two steps. Location and Time dimensions are retrieved from the multidimensional access structure. The set of documents retrieved from this structure is stored in an intermediate document collection. From the inverted index, the documents that contain the terms *Information Retrieval* can be obtained and stored in another intermediate set. Final set of ranked documents can be obtained by merging these two intermediate document sets. MIRE is designed to combine the functionality of a multidimensional access method and an inverted index into a single unified framework.

Analyzing Based on Information Extraction

Using IE technology, we can extract structured data from text documents. Based on the schema of structured data, we can process text documents using natural language processing technology to extract some entity instances or relationship instances between entities. For more information on basic IE technology, Grishman (1997) and Moens (2006) are good references. The extracted structured data can be stored in a relational database so that we can use conventional OLAP as we do in a relational data warehouse.

There are some other examples than using conventional OLAP. Castellanos et al.(2010) proposed a platform called SIE-OBI (Streaming Information Extraction Platform for Operational Business Intelligence) which can be used for a situational-awareness application by relating two text sources (e.g., internal contracts collection and external news feeds) for detecting potentially relevant situations through the common facts extracted from both sources. Lauw et al.(2007) proposed a framework called TUBE (Text-cUBE) which can be used for discovering documentary evidence of associations among entities. A document supports an association among a set of entities if all the entities co-occur within this document. The set of all such documents forms the documentary evidence of the association.

LINKING TEXT DOCUMENTS WITH STRUCTURED DATA

Linking Based on Information Extraction

The most important reason of using IE technology is that, through the extracted data from text documents, we can relate the text documents with relational databases. In other words, we can connect a lot of text documents with relational databases; they were separated from each other before. In an IE system, every document is assumed to contain information about entities or relationships between entities.

We consider two different approaches for that purpose. One is to search a relational database for finding the associated data with a given text document; the other to search for finding the associated text documents with the retrieved data from a relational database. An example of the former is the R-Cubes, proposed by Perez et al.(2007), which are OLAP cubes contextualized

with text documents. Another example is the EROCS system, proposed by Chakaravarthy et al.(2006), which takes as input a text document and finds the best matching entities stored in a relational database. With this system, we can further analyze the structured data associated with the given text documents. An example of the latter is the SCORE system, proposed by Roy et al.(2005), which takes as input an SQL query on a relational database and returns the relevant text documents associated with the query results executed on the relational database. With this system, we can easily understand the global context of an SQL query result by dynamically associating text documents with the query result without any facility to consolidate the schemas of the individual data sources. In this section, we introduce each approach, and then introduce an application to a banking environment.

R-Cube

Perez et al.(2007) proposed an architecture for integrating a warehouse of structured data with a warehouse of text documents. The resulting warehouse is called a contextualized warehouse that is a new kind of decision support system allowing users to obtain strategic information by combining all their sources of structured data and unstructured documents, and by analyzing the integrated data under different contexts. A context is defined as a set of text documents that can provide analysts with strategic information important for decision-making tasks. Since the document warehouse may contain documents about many different topics, a user first specifies an analysis context by supplying a sequence of keywords, and then an *R-cube* (*Relevance Cube*) is materialized by retrieving the documents and the facts related to the selected context. Each fact in the R-cube is linked to the set of documents that describe its context, and has a numerical value representing its relevance with respect to the specified context.

Figure 16. Contextualized warehouse architecture[Perez 2005]

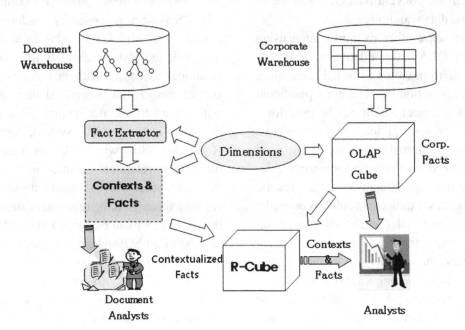

Figure 16 shows the architecture of the contextualized warehouse. Building a contextualized warehouse mainly means relating each fact of the corporate data warehouse with its context. The main components are a corporate data warehouse, a text document warehouse and the fact extractor module. In order to evaluate keyword-based searches over the document collection, the document warehouse keeps an inverted index. The fact extractor module relates each fact with the documents that describe its context by looking for the dimension values in the document contents. The fact extractor tool uses the dimensions defined in the corporate warehouse to detect and build the facts described in the documents. Finally, an R-cube is materialized, over which analysis capabilities are provided.

An R-cube is an OLAP cube contextualized with text documents. It has two new dimensions: the Context and the Relevance dimension, which have special meanings for associating the cube with the text documents that constitute the contexts of the cube. In other words, the two dimensions

provide for further information about the facts of the cube. The Context dimension has the links to the text documents that describe the context of the fact and can be used to gain insight into the circumstances of a fact by retrieving its related text documents; the Relevance dimension has a numerical value that represents its relevance with respect to the specified analysis context and can be used to explore the most relevant portions of an R-cube.

In order to create an R-cube, the analyst must supply a query of the form (Q, MDX) where Q is an IR condition consisting of a sequence of keywords that specifies the context under analysis; MDX (Multi-Dimensional eXpression) are conditions over the dimensions and measures of the analysis. The query process takes place as follows: First, the IR condition Q is evaluated in the document warehouse. The result is a set of documents satisfying Q along with their relevance with respect to Q. Second, the fact extractor parses the obtained documents and, using IE technology, returns the set of facts described by each document along with their frequency. Next, the MDX conditions are evaluated on the corporate data warehouse. Then, each document is assigned to those facts of the corporate data warehouse whose dimension values can be rolled-up or drilled-down to some (possibly imprecise or incomplete) fact described by the document. Finally, the relevance value of each fact is calculated, resulting in an R-cube.

EROCS

Chakaravarthy et al.(2006) addressed the problem of linking a text document with related structured data in a relational database, and proposed a novel system, called *EROCS* (*Entity RecOgnition in Context of Structured data*), for linking the given document with the relevant structured data in the database. EROCS views the structured data in a relational database as a predefined set of entities and identifies the entities from the set that best match the given document. EROCS further finds embeddings of the identified entities in the document; these embeddings are essentially the linkages that relate relevant structured data with segments within the given document. EROCS identifies such links even when the relevant entity is not explicitly mentioned in the document.

For what can we use EROCS? Suppose a company that has a steady inflow of complaints into a centralized complaint repository via a web-form, e-mail, fax, or voice mail transcription. Such complaint is a free-flow narrative text about sales transactions, and not guaranteed to contain the respective transaction identifiers; instead, it divulges the store name, a partial list of items bought, the purchase dates, etc. Using the limited information, EROCS discovers the potential matches with the transactions present in the sales transaction database, and links the given complaint with the matching transactions.

Such linkage provides actionable context to a typically fuzzy, free flow narrative, which can be profitably exploited in a variety of ways. We can build an automated complaint routing sys-

tem. Given the transaction automatically linked with the complaint, the system retrieves from the relational database additional information about the transaction, and routes the complaint to an appropriate department or customer service center. Furthermore, the association between complaints and transactions can be exploited in OLAP to derive useful information such as what regions or product categories have shown a recent upsurge in complaints.

EROCS takes as input a given document, suitably filtered to retain only the relevant terms, and a given database viewed as a set of predefined entities and associated context information. These entities are defined in terms of a collection of entity templates that specify the location of each entity and its context information in the relational database. In a retail company, for example, each sales transaction is an entity; the customer, the store, and the product information associated with the given transaction form its context. Given those input, as illustrated in Figure 17, EROCS matches the document with the context information of the candidate entities, and finds the best matching entities and their embeddings.

EROCS deals with the problem of semantic integration across structured relational data and unstructured text documents through matching entities across both of them. In the entity model of EROCS, an entity is a thing of significance about which the relational database holds information; an entity template specifies the entities to be matched in the document and, for each entity, the context information that can be exploited to perform the match. Formally, an entity template is a rooted tree with a designated root node. Each node in this tree is labeled with a table in the given relational database schema, and there exists an edge in the tree only if the tables labeling the nodes at the two ends of the edge have a foreign-key relationship in the database schema. The table that labels the root node is called the pivot table of the entity template, and the tables that label the other nodes are called the context tables. Each

Figure 17. EROCS overview[Chakaravarthy 2006]

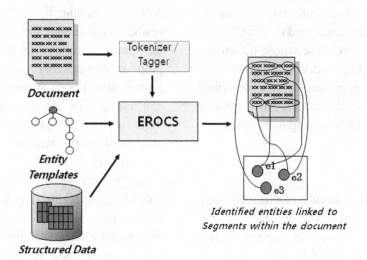

row e in the pivot table is identified as an entity belonging to the template, with the associated context information consisting of the rows in the context tables that have a path to row e in the pivot table through one or more foreign-keys covered by the edges in the entity template.

EROCS views a document as a set of terms that are noun-phrases; the rest filtered out, assuming only nouns appear as values in the relational database. Further, each noun identified is looked up in the database and annotated with the database columns it occurs in. This filtering and annotating reduces the amount of work to be performed in the matching step. For the detailed matching method, you can refer to the paper [Chakaravarthy 2006].

Linking Based on SQL Query Results

Roy et al.(2005) proposed the *SCORE (Symbiotic Context-Oriented Information REtrieval)* system for seamlessly integrating critical business information distributed across both structured and unstructured data sources. In existing information integration solutions, the application needs to formulate the SQL logic to retrieve the needed structured data on one hand, and identify a set of keywords to retrieve the related unstructured data on the other. In the SCORE system, the application specifies its information needs using only a SQL query on the structured data, and this query is automatically translated into a set of keywords that can be used to retrieve relevant unstructured data.

For automatically associating related unstructured content with the SQL query result, thereby eliminating the need for the application to specify a set of keywords in addition to the SQL query, some techniques are used in SCORE in order to obtain keywords from the query result and additional related information in the underlying database. First, the application specifies its information needs using only a SQL query on the structured data. SCORE executes the query on the RDBMS. Second, SCORE translates the given SQL query into a set of keywords that, in effect, reflect the same information needs as the input query. This set of keywords constitutes the context of the query. Finally, SCORE uses these keywords to retrieve relevant unstructured content using a search engine. This unstructured content is then associated with the result of the given SQL query computed earlier, and returned to the application.

Figure 18. An application scenario of the SCORE system[Roy 2005]

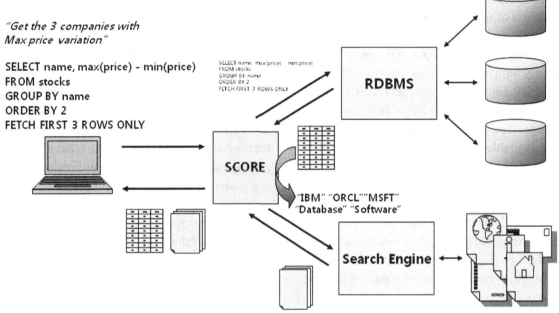

Figure 18 shows an application scenario of the SCORE system. Consider an investment information system that helps to analyze stock market data. There are maintained such structured data as stock ticker archived, company profile, information about institutional investors, mutual-fund portfolios, etc. There are maintained such unstructured data as a searchable repository of past week's news stories, advisories and recent analyst reports. Now, the application submits a query asking for the names of the three companies with maximum stock price variation in the past week. With this query as input, SCORE explores the query's result, and identifies the keywords that are most relevant to the profiles of these stocks. These keywords form the context of the input query. In this example, these keywords are "IBM," "ORCL," "MSFT" (obtained from the stocks table) and "Database," "Software" (obtained from the company profile tables). These keywords are then used to retrieve relevant news stories and related advisories and reports using the search engine,

which are then returned to the application along with the SQL query result.

The SCORE's approach to integrating structured and unstructured information has several advantages. First, SCORE dynamically associates documents with the SQL query result based on the context of the result. Second, SCORE does not maintain static association of documents and relational data. This implies that administrator does not have the onus of maintaining SCORE in face of data and/or schema updates on the data sources. Third, SCORE does not require any external semantic information (e.g. ontologies). In effect, it uses the semantics embedded in the structured data. Finally, SCORE does not require any non-standard interface to the data sources being integrated. It interfaces with the structured data source using standard SQL queries over JDBC/ODBC, and with the unstructured data source using keyword queries over HTTP. SCORE can thus work with any DBMS supporting SQL and any unstructured data source with a keyword-based search interface.

The hardest task in SCORE is identifying the context of the input query—that is, deriving the set of keywords that succinctly represent the information need of the input SQL query. Deriving every term available in the query result is not appropriate since the resulting set is very likely to be a potpourri of unrelated terms. In order to pick relevant and informative keywords from the entire set of available terms in the database, SCORE uses an algorithm to automatically compute the context of a SQL query from the result of the query as well as by exploring related data in the underlying database; the algorithm determines what relevant tables to explore without any help from the user. (Recall that the computed context is used to retrieve the relevant unstructured content to be associated with the SQL query result.)

Application to Banking Environment

Bhide et al.(2007) introduced a tool, called *LIPTUS* (*LInking and Processing Tool for Unstructured and Structured information*), which links unstructured customer interactions (e-mails and transcribed phone calls) with structured customer and account profiles in a banking environment. Unstructured information such as those customer interactions exists as silos with limited use in business intelligence which is based on structured information. LIPTUS bridges this gap, enabling consolidated analysis of both the structured and unstructured data. LIPTUS is now extensively used in a large bank in India [Bhide 2007].

Customers regularly interact with a bank by sending e-mails, calling up or meeting a banker. The interactions may involve complaints about a service or inquiry about a new product. The customer intelligence analytics should be able to exploit the valuable customer interactions. However, the interactions are free-flow unstructured text and are not tagged with customer or account ids. LIPTUS automatically associates the interac-

tions with customer and account profiles stored in a database. The associations discovered enable analytics spanning the customer and account profiles on one hand and the meta-data extracted from the interactions using IE technology on the other.

The components of LIPTUS and the process flow are shown in Figure 19. Each customer interaction has a ticker-id for identification. LIPTUS takes as input the customer interactions and extracts the customer and account identifiers mentioned in the text. These extracted identifiers are then matched with the identifiers present in the customer and account profiles, and the best matching profile is then linked with the interaction. This linkage consolidates the information available in the customer profile (customer product holding, profitability, etc.) and account profile (account type, usage, loyalty, age, etc.) with the information available with the interaction (date, purpose, etc.). In addition, as shown in the figure, LIPTUS also applies IE techniques (such as sentiment analysis, keyword extraction) to mine additional information from the interaction text. This combined information can be used for customer intelligence analysis.

The linking of customer profiles with customer interactions brings together the factual information about the customer (such as the customer's demographics, profitability, product holdings) with the factual information about the interaction (purpose of the interaction, the product or service it concerned, etc.). However, useful additional information can be gained by analyzing the content of the interaction. For example, interesting events (a customer traveling outside the country), relationship with a competitor (a customer holding a competitor product), introduction of new products or services, market trends, and customer's satisfaction levels can be inferred. Getting such information without the need of extensive customer surveys is indeed of significant value to the organization.

There can be many possible applications using LIPTUS. First, the aggregate customer analytics

Figure 19. LIPTUS Overview[Bhide 2007]

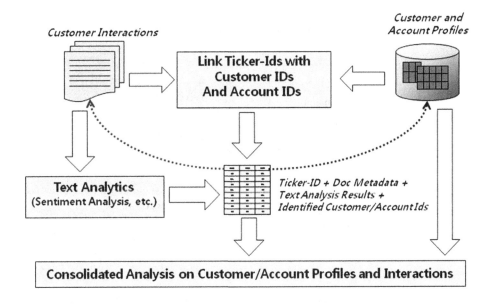

can be tapped through the following analytical queries without having to spend time, effort, and money in gathering the data through explicit customer surveys: *what are the ten categories that over the past month have received the greatest upsurge in "dissatisfied" complaints from the most profitable (top band) customers?*; *which product category has been receiving most inquiries from salaried customers between 25 and 35 years of age?*; *what are the most common phrases appearing in the interactions in each category?* Second, the individual customer analytics can be gathered through the following consolidated analysis queries on the entire history of the interactions for a customer: *has the customer been upset in the past?*; *what is the frequency of the customer's interaction with the bank?*; *On the average, what is the duration of the interaction with a given customer? How many messages on the average are exchanged per interaction?*; *Are the interactions (especially the "dissatisfied" ones) focused on a single category?*; *If the customer holds multiple products, what is the spread of her interactions across these products?* Finally,

stale customer profiles can be easily detected by extracting customer signatures from the interactions. For instance, if a customer uses a mail id different from that in her profile, the current profile is stale and needs to be updated. The bank can note the email addresses of such customers as their alternate contacts, and send an request asking them to update their contact information.

FUTURE RESEARCH DIRECTIONS

In this chapter, we have first reviewed the representative works on Text OLAP that handles multi-dimensional analysis of unstructured text documents, and then on linking text documents with structured data through the common facts extracted from the text documents. Most of the works are based on one of the three text handling technologies: TM, IR, and IE technologies. For fully exploiting the power of them, the three technologies should all be used appropriately. Furthermore, for getting total business intelligence, Text OLAP should be integrated with relational

Figure 20. TOBI Architecture

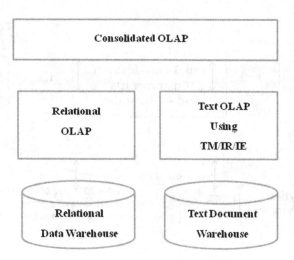

OLAP that handles multi-dimensional analysis of a corporate structured data warehouse.

We can consider two alternative methods of integrating Text OLAP with relational OLAP: tightly coupled or loosely coupled integration. As tightly coupled integration is expected much more difficult, we leave tightly coupled integration as a future research problem. In loosely coupled integration, as Text OLAP and relational OLAP may independently exist, we need a third module that consolidates Text OLAP and relational OLAP.

The loosely coupled architecture of total business intelligence platform (which we call *TOBI* in short) may be illustrated as shown in Figure 20. There exist two data sources: a relational data warehouse storing structured data and a text document warehouse storing various kinds of documents including web pages from Internet. The Relational OLAP module handles the former, and the Text OLAP module based on TM/IR/IE handles the latter. The Consolidated OLAP module handles consolidating relational OLAP and Text OLAP modules.

A user can get total business intelligence using the tool based on TOBI. A scenario is as follows. The user may first analyze the relational data using relational OLAP. When he needs some context

knowledge of the data, he can use the IR-based Text OLAP. At this moment, only the related documents may be selected using the keywords in the output of relational OLAP. He can also use the TM-based Text OLAP for further understanding of the overall characteristics of the selected document set. If the documents have information about some entities, he can use the IE-based Text OLAP which links the entities in the documents to the corresponding data in the relational data warehouse. We can consider another scenario where the user can start using Text OLAP first.

We need more research for implementing TOBI that contains two heterogeneous components: relational data warehouses (RDWs) and text data warehouses (TDWs). To fully take advantage of the TOBI architecture in federated environments, we suggest the following research topics:

OLAP Operations: Identification of complex heterogeneous OLAP operations that can be applied to the TOBI architecture for advanced OLAP applications

Query Language: Single OLAP query language that integrates both an RDW and a TDW and their efficient processing

Metadata Maintenance: Automatic maintenance of metadata between RDW and TDW for consistency maintenance and evolution of the RDW and TDW

ETL Processes: Development of systematic ETL processes for both RDWs and TDWs for a single application

Applications: Application of the TOBI architecture to spatial and temporal applications, and development of procedures to effectively apply it to CRM applications

CONCLUSION

Using a business intelligence solution, people get business insight from vast amounts of data they manage. Since it is known that only 20% of the data available are structured and are stored in relational databases, while about 80% are unstructured text and are stored in various forms of documents such as reports, news articles, e-mails, and largely web pages, incorporating and analyzing text data is essential for total business intelligence. In this chapter, we surveyed the representative works selected for demonstrating how the technologies of TM, IR, and IE can be applied for multidimensional analysis of text documents and eventually for business intelligence by associating unstructured text data with structured relational databases.

First, we surveyed the representative works selected for demonstrating how the technologies of TM can be applied for multidimensional analysis of text documents. XML-OLAP can be an example framework for Text OLAP based on TM technology. DocCube is an example system that can be used to explore and visualize the whole document set based on TM technology. Topic-Cube is another example system that supports an analyst to drill down or roll up text data along a topic dimension, which is a meaningful hierarchy defined for the analysis task.

Second, we surveyed the representative works selected for demonstrating how the technologies of IR can be applied for multidimensional analysis of text documents. The work by Tseng et al. (2006) is a good framework for Text OLAP based on IR technology. TextCube is an example system that has a special IR dimension, term hierarchy, for semantics navigation of text data and two special IR measures, term frequency and inverted index. MIRE is a multidimensional IR engine based on a multidimensional data model for text and utilizing OLAP technology.

Third, we surveyed the representative works selected for demonstrating how we can, using IE technology, associate and consolidate both unstructured text documents and structured relation data for obtaining total business intelligence. R-cube is an example of consolidated OLAP cube constructed from relational data warehouse and contextualized with a set of documents that are selected as an analysis context. Each cell of R-cube has a measure representing its relevance with respect to the context. EROCS is another example system of linking text documents to the related structured data in a relational database. In contrast, SCORE is a system that relates a SQL query result with the relevant text document constituting the context of the query. LIPTUS is an application system in a banking environment, which links unstructured customer interactions with structured customer and account profiles, enabling consolidated analysis of structured and unstructured customer data.

Finally, we discussed a total business intelligence platform architecture that integrates IR, TM, and IE technologies all together including relational OLAP technologies as well for giving a better service toward total business intelligence. We believe it can be achieved in the near future. We also suggested some research topics in the heterogeneous total business intelligence platform that integrates both relational data warehouses and text data warehouses.

REFERENCES

Adomavicius, G., Sankaranarayanan, R., Sen, S., & Tuzhilin, A. (2005). Incorporating contextual information in recommender systems using a multidimensional approach. *ACM Transactions on Information Systems, 23*(1), 103–145. doi:10.1145/1055709.1055714

Baeza-Yates, R., & Ribeiro Neto, B. (2001). *Modern information retrieval.* Addison-Wesley.

Baid, A., Balmin, A., Hwang, H., Nijkamp, E., Rao, J., & Reinwald, B. (2008). DBPubs: Multidimensional exploration of database publications. *Journal of Proceedings of VLDB Endowment, 1*(2), 1456–1459.

Bernstein, P. A., & Haas, L. M. (2008). Information integration in the enterprise. *Communications of the ACM, 51*(9), 72–79. doi:10.1145/1378727.1378745

Bhide, M., Chakravarthy, V., Gupta, A., Gupta, H., Mohania, M., Puniyani, K., et al. (2008). Enhanced business intelligence using EROCS. *ICDE '08: Proceedings of the 24th IEEE International Conference on Data Engineering,* (pp. 1616-1619).

Bhide, M. A., Gupta, A., Gupta, R., Roy, P., Mohania, M. K., & Ichhaporia, Z. (2007). LIPTUS: Associating structured and unstructured information in a banking environment. *SIGMOD '07: Proceedings of the 2007 ACM SIGMOD International Conference on Management of Data,* Beijing, China, (pp. 915-924).

Burdick, D., Deshpande, P. M., Jayram, T. S., Ramakrishnan, R., & Vaithyanathan, S. (2005). OLAP over uncertain and imprecise data. *VLDB '05: Proceedings of the 31st International Conference on very Large Data Bases,* (pp. 970-981). Trondheim, Norway.

Castellanos, M., Gupta, C., Wang, S., & Dayal, U. (2010). Leveraging Web streams for contractual situational awareness in operational BI. *EDBT '10: Proceedings of the 1st International BEWEB Workshop at EDBT,* (pp. 1-8). Lausanne, Switzerland.

Castellanos, M., Wang, S., Dayal, U., & Gupta, C. (2010). SIE-OBI: A streaming information extraction platform for operational business intelligence. *SIGMOD '10: Proceedings of the 2010 ACM SIGMOD International Conference on Management of Data,* (pp. 1-6). Indianapolis, USA.

Chakaravarthy, V. T., Gupta, H., Roy, P., & Mohania, M. (2006). Efficiently linking text documents with relevant structured information. *VLDB '06: Proceedings of the 32nd International Conference on very Large Data Bases,* (pp. 667-678). Seoul, Korea.

Chaudhuri, S., & Dayal, U. (1997). An overview of data warehousing and OLAP technology. *SIGMOD Record, 26*(1), 65–74. doi:10.1145/248603.248616

Chu, E., Baid, A., Chen, T., Doan, A., & Naughton, J. (2007). A relational approach to incrementally extracting and querying structure in unstructured data. *VLDB '07: Proceedings of the 33rd International Conference on very Large Data Bases,* (pp. 1045-1056). Vienna, Austria.

Connelly, R. (2004). Introducing data mining. *Journal of Computing Sciences in Colleges, 19*(5), 87–96.

Danger, R., & Berlanga, R. (2006). Inferring multidimensional cubes for representing conceptual document spaces. *Current Topics in Artificial Intelligence, 4177,* 280–290. doi:10.1007/11881216_30

Doan, A., Ramakrishnan, R., & Vaithyanathan, S. (2006). Managing information extraction: State of the art and research directions. *SIGMOD '06: Proceedings of the 2006 ACM SIGMOD International Conference on Management of Data,* (pp. 799-800). Chicago, IL, USA.

Goldstein, J., & Larson, P. (2001). Optimizing queries using materialized views: A practical, scalable solution. *SIGMOD '01: Proceedings of the 2001 ACM SIGMOD International Conference on Management of Data,* (pp. 331-342). Santa Barbara, California, United States.

Gray, J., Chaudhuri, S., Bosworth, A., Layman, A., Reichart, D., & Venkatrao, M. (1997). Data cube: A relational aggregation operator generalizing group-by, cross-tab, and sub-totals. *Data Mining and Knowledge Discovery, 1*(1), 29–53. doi:10.1023/A:1009726021843

Grishman, R. (1997). Information extraction: Techniques and challenges. *Lecture Notes in Computer Science, 1299,* 10–27.

Hsieh, M.-J., Chen, M.-S., & Yu, P. S. (2007). Approximate query processing in cube streams. *IEEE Transactions on Knowledge and Data Engineering, 19*(11), 1557–1570. doi:10.1109/TKDE.2007.190622

Inokuchi, A., & Takeda, K. (2007). A method for online analytical processing of text data. *CIKM '07: Proceedings of the Sixteenth ACM Conference on Conference on Information and Knowledge Management,* (pp. 455-464). Lisbon, Portugal.

Kroeze, J. H., Matthee, M. C., & Bothma, T. J. D. (2003). Differentiating data- and text-mining terminology. *SAICSIT '03: Proceedings of the 2003 Annual Research Conference of the South African Institute of Computer Scientists and Information Technologists on Enablement through Technology,* (pp. 93-101).

Lauw, H. W., Lim, E., & Pang, H. (2007). TUBE (text-cUBE) for discovering documentary evidence of associations among entities. *SAC '07: Proceedings of the 2007 ACM Symposium on Applied Computing,* (pp. 824-828). Seoul, Korea.

Lee, J., Grossman, D., Frieder, O., & McCabe, M. C. (2000). Integrating structured data and text: A multi-dimensional approach. *Proceedings of the International Conference on Information Technology: Coding and Computing,* (pp. 264-269).

Lee, J., Grossman, D., & Orlandic, R. (2002). MIRE: A multidimensional information retrieval engine for structured data and text. *Proceedings of the International Conference on Information Technology: Coding and Computing,* (pp. 224-229).

Lin, C. X., Ding, B., Han, J., Zhu, F., & Zhao, B. (2008). Text cube: Computing IR measures for multidimensional text database analysis. *Proceedings of the 2008 Eighth IEEE International Conference on Data Mining,* (pp. 905-910).

McCabe, M. C., Lee, J., Chowdhury, A., Grossman, D., & Frieder, O. (2000). On the design and evaluation of a multi-dimensional approach to information retrieval (poster session). *SIGIR '00: Proceedings of the 23rd Annual International ACM SIGIR Conference on Research and Development in Information Retrieval,* (pp. 363-365). Athens, Greece.

Moens, M. F. (2006). *Information extraction: Algorithms and prospects in a retrieval context.* Springer.

Mothe, J., Chrisment, C., Dousset, B., & Alaux, J. (2003). DocCube: Multi-dimensional visualisation and exploration of large document sets. *Journal of the American Society for Information Science and Technology, 54*(7), 650–659. doi:10.1002/asi.10257

Nonomura, K., Hattori, M., Sakurai, S., Isobe, S., & Sueda, N. (2002). Text-based OLAP using XML for knowledge management and the development environment. *Transactions of Information Processing Society of Japan, 43*, 75–86.

Park, B. K., Han, H., & Song, I. Y. (2005). XML-OLAP: A multidimensional analysis framework for XML warehouses. *Proceedings Data Warehousing and Knowledge Discovery, 3589,* 32–42. doi:10.1007/11546849_4

Perez, J. M., Berlanga, R., & Aramburu, M. J. (2004). A document model based on relevance modeling techniques for semi-structured information warehouses. *Proceedings Database and Expert Systems Applications, 3180,* 318–327. doi:10.1007/978-3-540-30075-5_31

Perez, J. M., Berlanga, R., Aramburu, M. J., & Pedersen, T. B. (2005). A relevance-extended multi-dimensional model for a data warehouse contextualized with documents. *DOLAP '05: Proceedings of the 8th ACM International Workshop on Data Warehousing and OLAP,* (pp. 19-28). Bremen, Germany.

Perez, J. M., Berlanga, R., Aramburu, M. J., & Pedersen, T. B. (2007). R-cubes: OLAP cubes contextualized with documents. *ICDE '07: Proceedings of the 23rd IEEE International Conference on Data Engineering,* (pp. 1477-1478).

Perez, J. M., Berlanga, R., Aramburu, M. J., & Pedersen, T. B. (2008). Integrating data warehouses with Web data: A survey. *IEEE Transactions on Knowledge and Data Engineering, 20*(7), 940–955. doi:10.1109/TKDE.2007.190746

Perez, J. M., Berlanga, R., Aramburu, M. J., & Pedersen, T. B. (2008). Towards a data warehouse contextualized with Web opinions. *ICEBE '08: Proceedings of the IEEE International Conference on e-Business Engineering,* (pp. 697-702).

Perez, J. M., Pedersen, T. B., Berlanga, R., & Aramburu, M. J. (2005). IR and OLAP in XML document warehouses. *Advances in Information Retrieval, 3408,* 536–539. doi:10.1007/978-3-540-31865-1_43

Perez-Martinez, J. M., Berlanga-Llavori, R., Aramburu-Cabo, M. J., & Pedersen, T. B. (2008). Contextualizing data warehouses with documents. *Decision Support Systems, 45*(1), 77–94. doi:10.1016/j.dss.2006.12.005

Priebe, T., & Pernul, G. (2003). Ontology-based integration of OLAP and information retrieval. *Proceedings of the 14th International Workshop on Database and Expert Systems Applications,* (pp. 610-614).

Qi, Y., Candan, K. S., Tatemura, J., Chen, S., & Liao, F. (2008). Supporting OLAP operations over imperfectly integrated taxonomies. *SIGMOD '08: Proceedings of the 2008 ACM SIGMOD International Conference on Management of Data,* (pp. 875-888). Vancouver, Canada.

Ravat, F., Teste, O., & Tournier, R. (2007). *OLAP aggregation function for textual data warehouse.* 9th International Conference on Enterprise Information Systems (ICEIS 2007), (pp. 151-156).

Ravat, F., Teste, O., Tournier, R., & Zurfluh, G. (2008). Top-keyword: An aggregation function for textual document OLAP. *Lecture Notes in Computer Science, 5182,* 55–64. doi:10.1007/978-3-540-85836-2_6

Roy, P., Mohania, M., Bamba, B., & Raman, S. (2005). Towards automatic association of relevant unstructured content with structured query results. *CIKM '05: Proceedings of the 14th ACM International Conference on Information and Knowledge Management,* (pp. 405-412). Bremen, Germany.

Simitsis, A., Baid, A., Sismanis, Y., & Reinwald, B. (2008). Multidimensional content eXploration. *Proceedings of the Journal of the Very Large Database Endowment, 1*(1), 660–671.

Sullivan, D. (2001). *Document warehousing and text mining*. John Wiley & Sons.

Theeramunkong, T., & Lertnattee, V. (2002). Multi-dimensional text classification. *Proceedings of the 19th International Conference on Computational Linguistics*, (pp. 1-7). Taipei, Taiwan.

Thomsen, C., & Pedersen, T. B. (2006). Building a Web warehouse for accessibility data. *DOLAP '06: Proceedings of the 9th ACM International Workshop on Data Warehousing and OLAP*, (pp. 43-50). Arlington, Virginia, USA.

Tseng, F. S. C. (2005). Design of a multi-dimensional query expression for document warehouses. *Information Sciences, 174*(1-2), 55–79. doi:10.1016/j.ins.2004.08.010

Tseng, F. S. C., & Chou, A. Y. H. (2006). The concept of document warehousing for multi-dimensional modeling of textual-based business intelligence. *Decision Support Systems, 42*(2), 727–744. doi:10.1016/j.dss.2005.02.011

Tseng, F. S. C., & Lin, W. P. (2006). D-tree: A multidimensional indexing structure for constructing document warehouses. *Journal of Information Science and Engineering, 22*(4), 819–841.

Vassiliadis, P., & Sellis, T. (1999). A survey of logical models for OLAP databases. *SIGMOD Record, 28*(4), 64–69. doi:10.1145/344816.344869

Wang, E. D., Luo, Q., Yang, D., & Tang, S. (2006). Binary search join between an IR system and an RDBMS. *WI '06: Proceedings of the 2006 IEEE/WIC/ACM International Conference on Web Intelligence*, (pp. 782-785).

Wu, P., Sismanis, Y., & Reinwald, B. (2007). Towards keyword-driven analytical processing. *SIGMOD '07: Proceedings of the 2007 ACM SIGMOD International Conference on Management of Data*, (pp. 617-628). Beijing, China.

Yang, Y., & Luk, W. (2002). A framework for Web table mining. *WIDM '02: Proceedings of the 4th International Workshop on Web Information and Data Management*, (pp. 36-42). McLean, Virginia, USA.

Yu, Y., Lin, C., Sun, Y., Chen, C., Han, J., & Liao, B. … Zhao, B. (2009). iNextCube: Information network-enhanced text cube. *VLDB '09: Proceedings of the 35th International Conference on very Large Data Bases*, Lyon, France.

Zhang, D., Zhai, C., & Han, J. (2009). Topic cube: Topic modeling for OLAP on multidimensional text databases. *SDM '09: Proceedings of the 2009 SIAM International Conference on Data Mining*, (pp. 1124-1135). Sparks, NV, USA.

Zhou, N., Cheng, H., Chen, H., & Xiao, S. (2007). The framework of text-driven business intelligence. *WiCom '07: Proceedings of the International Conference on Wireless Communications, Networking and Mobile Computing*, (pp. 5468-5471).

Chapter 5
A Semantic Approach for News Recommendation

Flavius Frasincar
Erasmus University Rotterdam, The Netherlands

Wouter IJntema
Erasmus University Rotterdam, The Netherlands

Frank Goossen
Erasmus University Rotterdam, The Netherlands

Frederik Hogenboom
Erasmus University Rotterdam, The Netherlands

ABSTRACT

News items play an increasingly important role in the current business decision processes. Due to the large amount of news published every day it is difficult to find the new items of one's interest. One solution to this problem is based on employing recommender systems. Traditionally, these recommenders use term extraction methods like TF-IDF combined with the cosine similarity measure. In this chapter, we explore semantic approaches for recommending news items by employing several semantic similarity measures. We have used existing semantic similarities as well as proposed new solutions for computing semantic similarities. Both traditional and semantic recommender approaches, some new, have been implemented in Athena, an extension of the Hermes news personalization framework. Based on the performed evaluation, we conclude that semantic recommender systems in general outperform traditional recommenders systems with respect to accuracy, precision, and recall, and that the new semantic recommenders have a better F-measure than existing semantic recommenders.

DOI: 10.4018/978-1-61350-038-5.ch005

INTRODUCTION

Finding the news items of interest is a critical task in many business processes. One such process is business intelligence which aims to gather, analyse, and use company-related data in order to support decision making (Luhn, 1958). While a lot of this information is represented by company internal data (e.g., product sales, costs, incomes, etc.), in the recent years, we observed a growing focus of attention for company external data whose processing is aimed to answer questions as how is the company perceived by the public? (business marketing), how are competitors reported in the media? (competitive intelligence), what are possible collaborators in other countries? (business internationalization), etc., (Saggion, Funk, Maynard, & Bontcheva, 2007) (Pang & Lee, 2008) (Castellanos, Gupta, Wang, & Dayal, 2010). News items, as rich sources of external company-related information, are increasingly exploited in business intelligence tasks.

The Web is one of the most popular platforms for distributing and consuming news items. There are several factors that contributed to this success story as for example the reduced cost for distributing and accessing news items, Web availability on a multitude of browsing platforms, world-wide information delivery and consumption, short amount of time required for news publication, etc. Unfortunately, the Web's success is also the cause of one of its most serious liabilities: the large number of daily published news items makes the process of finding the ones relevant to particular interests difficult. For business intelligence, companies are only interested in news items deemed relevant for their analytical processes, which for competitive reasons should be made available with minimal delay times.

One possible solution to deal with the news items overload problem is the use of recommender systems, which aim to propose previously unseen items, in our case news items, that are of interest to a certain user. Typically such recommenders employ a user profile and aim to recommend news items that best match this user profile. Currently, there are four types of recommender systems: content-based, collaborative filtering, semantics-based, and hybrid (Adomavicius & Tuzhilin, 2005). While the user profile is usually represented by the user's previously browsed items, the recommendation methods differ per employed recommendation method. The content-based recommenders propose items based on the lexical content of the previously viewed items, semantic recommenders use the semantic information of the earlier browsed items, collaborative filtering recommenders exploit profile similarities between different users, and hybrid recommenders are combinations of the previous recommenders.

In this chapter we focus on recommenders that use the information content in news items, be it lexical (as in content-based approaches) or semantic (as in semantics-based approaches). While content-based recommenders have previously been thoroughly investigated, it is only in the last years that researchers started to focus on semantics-based approaches for recommender systems. Also, a comprehensive study that compares the content-based recommenders with semantics-based recommenders is currently missing. Therefore one of the aims of this chapter is to produce such an investigation in the context of recommending news items. In addition, we would like to investigate multiple semantics-based approaches and compare their performances. The collaborative filtering and hybrid recommenders are considered outside the scope of this chapter.

In previous work (IJntema, Goossen, Frasincar, & Hogenboom, 2010) we have proposed a semantic recommender for news called Ranked-based Semantic Recommender (RSR). In this chapter we extend our previous work by considering not only the concepts directly related to the concepts from the user profile but also the concepts directly related to the concepts present in unread news items, which can help recommend more relevant news items than before. Our research is circumscribed to Hermes, a framework for news personalization that we have developed during the last five years (Borsje, Levering, & Frasincar, 2008; Frasincar, Borsje, & Levering, 2009; Schouten et al., 2010). For this purpose we have developed Athena, which extends Hermes with news recommendation functionality.

The chapter is organized as follows. In the first section we discuss the background on recommendation methods, including content-based recommenders and semantics-based recommender systems, with a special attention being given to news recommenders. In the next section we present a new semantic recommender for news items. We describe the evaluation we performed using the implementation of the proposed recommender as well as existing content-based and semantics-based recommenders in the following section. The last two sections discuss future work and present our conclusions.

BACKGROUND

Recommendation helps users to focus on what is interesting by selecting new content based on previously read news articles, Web pages, research papers or other kind of documents. In this chapter we focus on recommendation of news items. First we discuss the user profile that is used to collect information about the interests of the user. Secondly a detailed description of content based-recommendation and semantics-based recommendation is given. The third and fourth part of this section discuss Hermes, a framework for building personalized news services, and Athena, an extension to Hermes which provides a news recommendation system employing both content- and semantics-based recommendation methods.

User Profile

In order to recommend news items to the user, a user profile needs to be constructed. The user's interests can be determined based on the news items which have been read. How the user profile is represented depends on the recommendation approach employed. For the content-based recommendation method the user profile consists of terms with corresponding frequencies. Semantics-based recommendation methods rely on the concepts that appear in the news items. For concept equivalence, binary cosine, and Jaccard, the user profile consists of all concepts that appear in the news items that have been read. The semantic relatedness approach uses a vector with distinct concepts and assigns a weight to each concept. In a similar way the rank-based semantic recommender assigns a rank to each concept, which is also stored in a vector.

Content-Based Recommendation

Term Frequency-Inverse Document Frequency (TF-IDF) (Salton & Buckley, 1988) is a well-known term weighting method which is often used in information retrieval. It is employed to determine the importance of a word within a document relative to the frequency of the word within a collection of documents (or corpus). TF-IDF is often used in conjunction with the cosine similarity measure in order to compare the similarity between two documents.

Many content-based recommenders make use of TF-IDF and the cosine similarity measure for news personalization. Before the TF-IDF values are calculated, first the stop words are removed, followed by stemming the remaining words. The latter means, determining the root of each word, such as 'recommending,' 'recommender,' and 'recommended' all become 'recommend,' with the advantage that the TF-IDF values are not calculated for each individual morphological form.

The TF-IDF value of a word can be calculated as follows. First we determine the term frequency (TF) $f_{i,j}$ for a term t_i within a news article a_j:

$$tf_{i,j} = \frac{n_{i,j}}{\sum_k n_{k,j}} \tag{1}$$

where $n_{i,j}$ is the number of occurrences of term t_i in news article a_j and the denominator is the total number of terms in the document. The second step is the calculation of the inverse document frequency (IDF), which is the relative importance of a term in a set of news items. This is computed as follows:

$$idf_i = \log \frac{|A|}{|\{a : t_i \in a\}|} \tag{2}$$

where the numerator is the total number of news items and the denominator denotes the number of news items containing term t_i. The final value is computed by taking the product of the term frequency and inverse document frequency:

$$tfidf_{i,j} = tf_i \times idf_i \tag{3}$$

In order to obtain the user profile, one has to calculate the TF-IDF values for each term in the news items that user has read. The user profile consists of a relatively large number of words (e.g., 100 words, as we have used later in our experiments) with the highest TF-IDF value. Subsequently an unread news item, which can be represented by vector N can be compared to the user profile P by computing the cosine similarity between these vectors N and P:

$$similarity = \frac{P \cdot N}{\|P\| \times \|N\|} \tag{4}$$

where the numerator is the dot product of vectors and the denominator is the product of the magnitude of vectors. The news items with the highest similarity are considered to match best with the user profile.

Implementations

Many existing systems employ content-based methods in order to recommend content to the user. They differ in aspects like article representation, user profile representation, and similarity measure. We discuss several existing methods and the similarities and differences with our implementation.

YourNews (Ahn, Brusilovsky, Grady, He, & Syn, 2007) is a personalized news system. It employs TF-IDF for representing news items and the user profile, and cosine similarity measure to compute the degree of similarity between news items and the user profile. Differently than other traditional approaches it aims to increase the transparency of recommended news items by allowing the user to inspect and modify the user profile. Unfortunately this added functionality seems to harm the system, as users observe a lower system performance when making use of this functionality.

NewsDude (Billsus & Pazzani, 1999) is a personalized news recommender agent. It uses a two step approach for making recommendations, first it employs the user's short term interests to find relevant news items and if this returns an empty result it filters news items based on the user's long term interests. For short term model construction NewsDude uses TF-IDF in combination with Nearest Neighbour (NN), which is able to represent user's multiple interests and takes in consideration the changing user's short term interests (concept drift problem). Long term interests or user's general interests are modeled by means of the Naïve Bayes classifier.

Personalized Recommender System (PRES) (van Meteren & van Someren, 2000) is another example of a news personalization system that uses TF-IDF and the cosine similarity measure. A specific aspect of this system is that each time a news items is added to the profile, the weights of the terms previously stored in the profile are diminished by a certain factor. This diminishing factor aims to decrease the importance of terms originating from news items read before the current news item in order to allow for possible changes of user interests over time. The optimal diminishing factor is determined by experimentation.

TF-IDF favors long documents in the cosine similarity computations over short ones. While it is true that long documents have in general more information and possibly select many relevant documents, TF-IDF reduces the chance of relevant short documents to be selected (Singhal, Salton, Mitra, & Buckley, 1996). Also, the vector space model is prone to produce many false negatives, as it does not take into account the term semantics, failing for example to consider synonyms of the query terms for occurrence in documents.

SEMANTICS-BASED RECOMMENDATION

In traditional content-based recommendation the degree of interestingness of a news item is determined by considering all terms in a document. In semantics-based recommendation only the most important words, called concepts, are considered. Furthermore, semantics are added by providing an underlying knowledge base, which contains relations between these concepts. The availability of concepts and relations to the recommendation process makes it possible to introduce news items to the user, which are semantically related to the ones read. For instance a user interested in news about Apple might also be interested in news about Microsoft, because both are of type Company and the knowledge base contains a relation defining a competitor relation between those two companies.

To illustrate how concepts can be used in the recommendation process, we explain three simple methods. The first is based on concept equivalence, followed by binary cosine and then Jaccard. With the semantic relatedness approach and our own ranked semantic recommendation method we show how relations between concepts can be employed in the recommendation process.

Concept Equivalence

The first method we discuss is a simple technique we proposed in (IJntema et al., 2010), where only equivalent concepts are considered. The idea is to recommend only news items which contain concepts appearing in the user profile. Each concept is stored in the underlying ontology. We define the ontology by the following set of concepts (concepts have the ontology properties attached):

$$C = \{c_1, c_2, c_3, \cdots, c_n\} \qquad (5)$$

A concept is present in a news item if one of its lexical representations is found in the news item. The news article can be defined by a set of p concepts:

$$A = \{c_1^a, c_2^a, c_3^a, \cdots, c_p^a\} \qquad (6)$$

The user profile consists of q concepts found in the news items read by the user and is defined by:

$$U = \{c_1^u, c_2^u, c_3^u, \cdots, c_q^u\} \qquad (7)$$

Due to the use of sets it is easy to compute the similarity between the news item and the user profile. In this method it is only relevant whether or not a concept from the user profile exists in the unread news item and if it does, it is considered to be interesting. The similarity between a news article and the user profile can consequently be computed by:

$$Similarity(U, A) = \begin{cases} 1 & \text{if } |U \cap A| > 0 \\ 0 & \text{otherwise} \end{cases} \quad (8)$$

Binary Cosine

In the previous subsection we have shown how TF-IDF is often used in conjunction with the cosine similarity measure. In a similar fashion we can employ binary cosine to compute the similarity between two sets of concepts:

$$B(U, A) = \frac{|U \cap A|}{|U| \times |A|} \quad (9)$$

where $|U \cap A|$ is the number of concepts in the intersection of the user profile and the unread news article and $|U| \times |A|$ is the product of the number of concepts in respectively U and A. The returned value gives an indication of the interestingness of the article compared to the news items the user has read so far.

Jaccard

Analogous to the binary cosine measure, Jaccard (Jaccard, 1901) computes the similarity between two sets of concepts as follows:

$$J(U, A) = \frac{|U \cap A|}{|U \cup A|} \quad (10)$$

where $|U \cap A|$ is the number of concepts in the intersection of U and A and $|U \cup A|$ represents the number of concepts in the union of U and A. Unlike concept equivalence, binary cosine and Jaccard take into account the number of concepts found in a news item.

Semantic Relatedness

(Getahun, Tekli, Chbeir, Viviani, & Yetongnon, 2009) proposes a method to determine the similarity between two texts which takes into account the semantic neighborhood of a concept. In this approach only linguistic relations (i.e., synonymy, hyponymy, and meronymy) are considered, while in our approach many more types of relations are covered by the ontology. Calculating the similarity between the user profile and a news article based on the semantic neighborhood of concepts is applicable to our approach.

The semantic neighborhood of a concept c_i is defined as all concepts directly related to c_i including c_i and can be denoted as:

$$N(c_i) = \{c_1^i, c_2^i, c_3^i, \cdots, c_n^i\} \quad (11)$$

A news item a_k, which consists of m concepts can be described as the following set:

$$A_k = \{c_1^k, c_2^k, c_3^k, \cdots, c_m^k\} \quad (12)$$

In order to compare two new items n_i and n_j, a vector in n-dimensional space can be created according to the vector space model:

$$V_l = \left(\left\langle c_1^l, w_1^l \right\rangle, \cdots, \left\langle c_p^l, w_p^l \right\rangle\right) \quad (13)$$

where $l \in \{i,j\}$ and w_i represents the weight associated to the concept c_i and $p = |A_i \cup A_j|$, which is the number of distinct concepts in A_i and A_j (the set of concepts in n_i and the set of concepts in n_j, respectively). The weights are calculated as follows:

$$w_i = \begin{cases} 1 & \text{if } freq(c_i \text{ in } A_j) > 0 \\ \max_j(ES(c_i, c_j)) & \text{otherwise} \end{cases}$$

$$(14)$$

If the concept c_i occurs once or more in A_j the weight assigned is equal to 1, otherwise it is calculated according to the maximum enclosure similarity, which takes into account the semantic neighborhood of a concept:

$$ES(c_i, c_j) = \frac{|N(c_i) \cap N(c_j)|}{|N(c_i)|} \qquad (15)$$

Once the weights are computed, the similarity between the news items a_i and a_j is determined by using the following equation:

$$\text{SemRel}(a_i, a_j) = \cos(V_i, V_j) = \frac{V_i \cdot V_j}{\|V_i\| \times \|V_j\|} \in [0,1] \qquad (16)$$

where the numerator represents the dot product of the vectors V_i and V_j and the denominator is the product of the magnitude of each vector.

Compared to the previous discussed approaches, this method has the advantage of taking into account the semantics of a text by also considering the related concepts to the concepts appearing in the text. The user profile is defined by the set of concepts appearing in the read news items.

Implementations

Some existing systems use semantics-based methods in order to recommend content to the user. They differ in aspects like article representation, user profile representation and similarity measure. We briefly describe existing methods and the commonalities and differences with our implementation.

PersoNews (Banos, Katakis, Bassiliades, Tsoumakas, & Vlahavas, 2006) is a personalized news reader that is based on semantic filtering and machine learning. First the reader filters news items that contain lexical representations associated to the selected concepts of interest from a taxonomy. Then, it applies the Naïve Bayes classification algorithm in order to determine if an article is interesting. In this approach the user is expected to manually update the concept lexical representations, which is a laborious process especially when the taxonomy size is large.

Quickstep (Middleton, Shadbolt, & De Roure, 2004) is recommender system for academic research papers. Academic papers are classified by means of the boosted IBk classifier (Aha, Kibler, & Albert, 1991) which makes use of k-Nearest Neighbour (k-NN) algorithm applied on a vector space representation of papers. Paper topics are stored in an ontology and are also used for modeling user interests. This ontology is also exploited to solve the user or item cold-start problems, by offering an initial set of user interests based on the topics of authors' previous papers. The recommendation is based on correlations between user's topic of interest and the paper's topics. Quickstep considers only type relationships failing to exploit other ontology relationships (e.g., part-of, domain specific relationships, etc.) that are also rich in semantics.

PVA, a self-adaptive Personal View Agent (Chen & Chen, 2002) introduces a recommender system that tries to recommend Web pages based on personal views. The world view is a predefined category hierarchy. A personal view is a subset of the world view. After Web pages are collected by a proxy, they are classified using the Automatic Classifier for Internet Resource Discovery (ACIRD) (Lin et al., 1998) in order to determine the category they belong to. The constructed user profile is compared with unviewed pages by using the cosine similarity measure. Different from our approach, no Semantic Web techniques are employed. In addition, only hierarchical structures are used, while our recommendation system employs many more types of relationships, such as 'CompetitorOf,' 'ProductBy,' 'CEOOf,' etc.

Unlike previous semantic approaches that are based on machine learning, we use linguistic techniques for text classification. Differently than machine learning approaches linguistic techniques offer easy explanations of why a certain news item is classified to a certain topic or why a news item is recommended to a certain user. Also, linguistic techniques are easily extensible to incorporate information semantics capturing the meaning behind textual descriptions. In this way we aim to improve the classifications and recommendations with respect to both precision and recall compared to traditional recommenders based on TF-IDF. We exploit General Architecture for Text Engineering (GATE) (Cunningham, Maynard, Bontcheva, & Tablan, 2002) in order to classify news and extract concept lexical representations in an automated manner from WordNet (Fellbaum, 1998). Also, we use more ontology relationships than just type relationships better capturing the news semantics.

Hermes

Hermes (Borsje et al., 2008; Frasincar et al., 2009; Schouten et al., 2010) is a framework that can be used for building a personalized news service. Based on a set of concepts, selected by the user, Hermes is able to determine which news items are relevant. In order to do so Hermes uses state-of-the-art classification techniques for categorizing news items from various sources. At the heart of this process lies the knowledge base, the formal representation of our domain.

The knowledge base is a domain ontology consisting of classes, relationships and instances of classes. For instance in the financial ontology used as an example in this chapter 'Company' and 'Product' are classes and between them there exists a relation like 'hasProduct' and its inverse 'isProducedBy.' We define a concept as being a class or an instance of a class, such as 'Google' is an instance of 'Company' and 'iPhone' is an instance of 'Product.' The knowledge base has initially been extracted from Yahoo! Finance and is maintained by a domain expert. At the current

moment it contains more than 300 concepts and their descriptions.

The Hermes News Portal (HNP) is a Java implementation of the Hermes framework. It allows the user to formulate queries and execute them in order to retrieve relevant news items. When news items are gathered from various RSS feeds, they are classified using a GATE (Cunningham et al., 2002) text processing pipeline and the WordNet (Fellbaum, 1998) semantic lexicon. GATE has the advantage of having a modular structure. This allows developers, aside from using out-of-the-box components, to build their own components and adapt the system to their needs. The components that are part of the pipeline used by Hermes are in the usage order: Document Reset, ANNIE English Tokeniser, ANNIE Gazetteer, ANNIE Sentence Splitter, ANNIE Part-Of-Speech Tagger, ANNIE Named Entity (NE) Transducer, and the ANNIE Ortho Matcher. Furthermore, the implementation employs various Semantic Web techniques. The ontology is represented in OWL (Bechhofer et al., 2004), which is queried by using SPARQL (Prud'hommeaux & Seaborne, 2008) and tSPARQL (Borsje et al., 2008), an extension to SPARQL with time-based functionalities.

Athena

Athena is our extension to the Hermes framework for news item recommendation. In Athena we use two types of recommenders, content-based recommenders and semantics-based recommenders. The first type of recommenders determine the similarity between the user profile and a news item based on the frequency of words, while the second type of recommenders determine the similarity between the user profile and a news item based on the meaning of the text by employing concepts and relations.

Athena is written in Java as a plug-in for the existing Hermes News Portal (HNP), which is the implementation of the Hermes framework. The HNP provides Athena with classified news items,

Figure 1. Athena recommendations

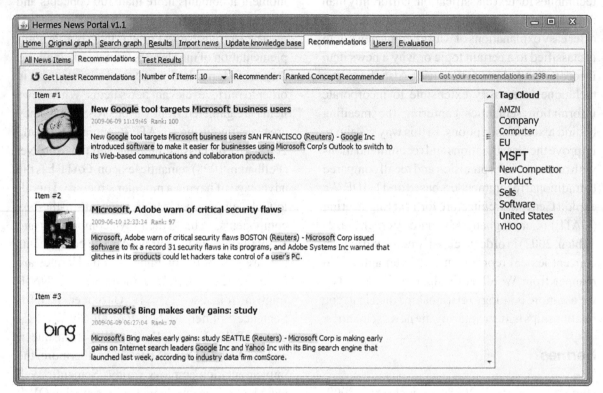

which are used in the semantics-based recommendation methods. The content-based method relies on news items from which the stop words are removed and the remaining words are stemmed. For the latter we have used an implementation of the Krovetz Stemmer (Guzman-Lara, 2007). Due to the object-oriented design of Athena it is easily extended with new recommendation methods.

The recommendations tab in Figure 1 corresponds to the Athena plug-in in HNP. The user is shown three subtabs. The first is a list with news items sorted by date in ascending or descending order. For each news item the user is provided with the title, the content, and the date. If the user double clicks a news item it is registered in the user profile and opened in the Web browser.

The second tab contains the recommendation functionality. The user is able to select which recommendation method he prefers and how many news items should be shown. Clicking the refresh

button starts the recommendation process by determining which news items are of most interest to the user. Generally this process does not take longer than a few seconds, depending on the number of articles and concepts. To give the user insight into his user profile we display a concept list on the right panel. It is similar to the well-known tag cloud. The font size of the concept is dependent on the number of articles read containing this concept.

Once the recommended news items are determined, they are shown in a list, displaying the title, date, and content. An additional feature is to highlight concepts from the user profile (yellow) and concepts related to them (green), which makes it easy to scan news items for concepts of interest. In the third tab we built a test environment used to evaluate the recommendation methods.

RANKED SEMANTIC RECOMMENDATION 2

In Ranked Semantic Recommendation (RSR), we rely on an intuitive approach described in (Bra, Aerts, Houben, & Wu, 2000) applied to adaptive hypermedia. Even though it is used in a different research field, the idea suits our purpose. When applied to our problem, the method assumes that the user reading news articles about a concept means that he might also be interested in directly related concepts. A user profile can be constructed by increasing the rank, which determines the importance of a concept in the user profile, with each article the user has read about a concept and concepts related to them. In addition to increasing the ranks of concepts which appear in the article and concepts related to them, we also assume that if a concept is neither referred to in the text nor is it related to a concept from the text, the rank should be decreased reflecting the user's current disinterest in the concept.

The method proposed in this chapter is an extension to Ranked Semantic Recommendation 1 (RSR1) (IJntema et al., 2010). The difference between RSR1 and RSR2 is that the latter also takes into account the concepts related to the concepts from the unread news items rather than only the concepts that appear in the article. For instance, if the concept 'Microsoft' appears in a news item, RSR2 will also take into account related concepts like 'Google,' 'Apple,' 'Windows' or 'Steve Ballmer.' We discuss this in more detail later in this section.

We first start with explaining how the extended user profile is constructed followed by how to determine the rank for each concept and end with computing the similarity between an article and the extended user profile. We define the set of related concepts to c_i as follows:

$$r(c_i) = \left\{ c_1^i, c_2^i, \cdots, c_k^i \right\} \qquad (17)$$

The user profile U is the set of concepts that appear in the news items read by the user. Subsequently we define R as the set with concepts related to the concepts from the user profile U:

$$R = \bigcup_{u_i \in U} r(u_i) \qquad (18)$$

Finally the extended user profile U_R is the union of both the user profile U and the related concepts of the concepts from the user profile R:

$$U_R = U \cup R \qquad (19)$$

The next step is computing the rank for each concept in the extended user profile. In order to do this we organize the concepts in a matrix, where the rows represent concepts appearing in read news items (user profile) and the columns represent concepts from the extended user profile (Table 1):

The ranks r_{11} through r_{mq} are determined as follows:

Table 1. Rank matrix

	c_1	c_2	$\cdots$	c_q
u_1	r_{11}	r_{12}	$\cdots$	r_{1q}
u_2	r_{21}	r_{22}	$\cdots$	r_{2q}
M	M	M	M	M
u_m	r_{m1}	r_{m2}	$\cdots$	r_{mq}

$$r_{ij} = w_i \times \begin{cases} +0.90 & \text{if } e_j = u_i \\ +0.75 & \text{if } e_j \neq u_i \text{ and } e_j \in r(u_i) \\ -0.05 & \text{otherwise} \end{cases}$$

(20)

where the weight w_i is equal to the number of read articles containing the concept u_i and is contained in the following vector:

$$W = (w_1, w_2, \cdots, w_m)$$

(21)

The values 0.9, 0.75, and -0.05 are determined empirically by evaluating the recommender performance (i.e., F-measure) on the training set (explained later in the chapter) by trying all combinations between -1 and +1 with a step of 0.05 and are different from RSR1 (as the methods are different). By taking the sum of each column in the matrix, we can compute the final rank for each concept in the extended user profile:

$$Rank(e_j) = \sum_{i=1}^{m} r_{ij}$$

(22)

Before comparing the extended user profile with an unread news article, we have to ensure that the ranks are between 0 and 1. Therefore we normalize the ranks as follows:

$$v_i^{new} = \frac{v_i^{old} - \min_{v_u^{old} \in V_U^{old}} (v_u^{old})}{\max_{v_u^{old} \in V_U^{old}} (v_u^{old}) - \min_{v_u^{old} \in V_U^{old}} (v_u^{old})}, v_i^{new} \in V_U$$

(23)

where V_U is a vector containing the ranks as determined by Eq. 22.

The last step of the approach is comparing an unread news item with the just created extended user profile in order to determine which articles are of interest to the user. We define the news article as:

$$A = \{a_1, a_2, \cdots a_t\}$$

(24)

The new semantics-based recommender proposed in this chapter, RSR2, extends RSR1 (IJntema et al., 2010) by also including the concepts related to the concepts appearing in the news item. This results in a set E:

$$E = \bigcup_{a_i \in A} r(a_i)$$

(25)

The extended article is then defined as:

$$A_E = A \cup E$$

(26)

Similar to the user profile a vector with ranks is defined for the extended news article:

$$V_{AE} = (s_1, s_2, \cdots, s_t)$$

(27)

where

$$s_i = \begin{cases} Rank(e_i) & \text{if } e_i \in A_E \\ 0 & \text{if } e_i \notin A_E \end{cases}$$

(28)

The rank corresponding to the concepts from the extended user profile in the vector V_{AE} is equal to the value in the matrix we constructed in the first step if it appears in the unread news item or is related to one of the concepts that appear in the news item, otherwise it is equal to zero. Subsequently we compare vector V_U and vector V_{AE} in order determine the similarity between the user profile and the unread article. We compute to what degree the article fits the user profile by dividing the sum of the ranks of the concepts in A_E by the sum of the ranks in U_R:

$$Similarity(V_{AE}, V_U) = \frac{\sum\limits_{v_a \in V_{AE}} v_a}{\sum\limits_{v_u \in V_U} v_u} \quad . \tag{29}$$

The article with the highest similarity is considered to be most interesting to the user.

We conclude this section with an example of RSR2. The example is simplified in order to illustrate the method at hand by limiting the number of concepts and it therefore does not reflect the contents of our knowledge base, which contains many more concepts and relationships. The user profile is defined as follows:

U = {Yahoo!, Obama, China}

The weights W for the corresponding concepts are:

$W = (4,3,2)$

which means that the user in this example has read four articles which contained the concept 'Yahoo!,' three articles with 'Obama' and two articles with 'China.' The sets of related concepts for each concept in the profile are as follows:

r(Yahoo!) = {Google, Apple}

r(Obama) = {USA}

r(China) = {USA}

The set R with related concepts to the concept in U is defined as:

$R = r$(Yahoo!) ∪ r(Obama) ∪ r(China) = {Google, Apple, USA}

By combining R with U the extended user profile is constructed:

$U_R = U \cup R$ = {Yahoo!, Obama, China, Google, Apple, USA}

Table 2 shows how the rank for each concept can be computed by applying Equations 20 and 22. The columns show the extended user profile and the rows show the user profile.

After normalizing these ranks within a range of [0,1], the following vector is constructed:

V_U = (0.950, 0.452, 0, 0.619, 0.619, 1.000)

The next step is to determine the interestingness of an unread article based on this user profile. The article that is being examined for this example contains three concepts and can be represented as:

A = {Google, Apple, Toyota}

Let us assume for this example that the concepts related to these concepts are:

r(Google) = {Yahoo!, Apple}

r(Apple) = {Yahoo!, Google}

r(Toyota) = {Prius}

Table 2. Example rank matrix

	Yahoo!	Obama	China	Google	Apple	USA
Yahoo!	3.6	-0.2	-0.2	3.0	3.0	-0.2
Obama	-0.15	2.7	-0.15	-0.15	-0.15	2.25
China	-0.1	-0.1	1.8	-0.10	-0.10	1.5
Rank	3.35	2.4	1.45	2.75	2.75	3.55

The union of *A* with these related concepts (extended article) becomes:

A_E = {Google, Apple, Toyota, Yahoo!, Prius}

The corresponding vector is determined by looking up the value for each concept in V_U:

V_A = (0.619, 0.619, 0, 0.905, 0)

The similarity between article *A* and the user profile is now computed by dividing the sums of both vectors V_U and V_A:

$$Similarity = \frac{0.619 + 0.619 + 0 + 0.905 + 0}{0.905 + 0.452 + 0 + 0.619 + 0.619 + 1.000} = 0.596$$

EVALUATION

The goal of this chapter is to evaluate and compare traditional recommenders and semantic recommenders for news items. For this purpose we have developed a test environment based on the implementation from the previous section. The test environment is based on a supervised learning method.

Setup

The performed tests are based on a corpus of 300 news items that have been assembled by the designer of the test. We have used 5 users with different but well-defined interests in our experiments. An example of a user interest is "Google and all its competitors." Each user has manually rated the news items as relevant or non-relevant for his interest.

For each user we split the news items corpus in two different sets: 60% of the news items are the training set and 40% of the news items are the test set. We have split the news items in such a way that two sets are filled with relatively equal number of interesting news items (which are user

dependent). The training set is used to learn the (extended) user profile, each news item marked by the user as relevant will contribute to the construction of the (extended) user profile. The test set is used to evaluate how well each recommender performs. The recommenders compute the similarity between the news items (from the test set) and the previously computed (extended) user profile (based on the training set). If the computed similarity value is higher than a predefined cut-off value the news item is recommended, otherwise the news item is ignored.

The evaluation of the different recommenders is performed by measuring accuracy, precision, recall (also known as sensitivity), specificity, and F-measure (the harmonic mean of precision and recall). In order to compute these measures we have used a confusion matrix for each user which stores the true positives, true negatives, false positives, and false negatives. Using these measurements we evaluate each recommender and compare them to each other.

Results

Table 3 shows the results of the evaluations of the considered recommenders. The reported results are user-based averages of the considered measures. RSR1 scores better than TF-IDF in terms of accuracy, precision, recall, and equally good for specificity. RSR2, which extends RSR1 so that the indirect concepts that appear in previously unseen news items are also considered in the recommendations, as expected, improves the recall of RSR1, although by decreasing the precision. Nevertheless, the F-measure of RSR2 is higher than RSR1, which means that the increase in recall in higher than the loss in precision. Also, by analyzing the F-measures it is clear that the Jaccard, RSR1, and RSR2 perform better than TF-IDF, showing that the (advanced) semantic recommenders outperform traditional recommenders.

When comparing the winners for each of the investigated performance measures we notice that

Table 3. Evaluation results

	Accuracy	Precision	Recall	Specificity	F-Measure
TF-IDF	90%	90%	45%	99%	60%
Concept Equivalence	44%	22%	98%	32%	36%
Binary Cosine	47%	23%	95%	36%	37%
Jaccard	93%	92%	58%	99%	71%
Semantic Relatedness	57%	26%	92%	47%	41%
RSR 1	94%	93%	62%	99%	74%
RSR 2	94%	80%	86%	97%	83%

the best recommenders for accuracy are RSR1 and RSR2, for precision is RSR1, for recall is concept equivalence, for specificity are TF-IDF, Jaccard, and RSR1, and for F-measure is RSR2. RSR algorithms score well on accuracy as they make relatively small amount of errors for both recommended news as well as discarded news items. For precision, RSR1 algorithm scores the best for precision as most recommended news items are relevant. The good results for recall obtained by the concept equivalence are due to the optimistic nature of the algorithm: any news item which involves previously viewed concepts (in news) is recommended. TF-IDF, Jaccard, and RSR1 score well on specificity as these algorithms do not recommend most of the non-relevant news items. The best performing recommender with respect to the F-Measure is RSR2, the newly introduced algorithm in this chapter. Based on these evaluations we suggest the use of RSR2 for news items recommendations in a business intelligence setup feeding on news items as it provides the best trade-off between precision and recall.

The conclusions are drawn for this particular experimental setup. Despite the experiment limitations (in the number of users and news items), it clearly shows the good performance of RSR1 and RSR2 with respect to the other considered recommenders.

FUTURE RESEARCH DIRECTIONS

In the future we plan to extend the evaluation with a larger user base and a statistical test. Furthermore, the results presented in this chapter are dependent on the quality of the used knowledge base. A manual maintenance of the knowledge base is a time-intensive and expensive process. Also, as the information in a business domain is continuously changing, it is imperative to provide an automatic solution for the knowledge base maintenance problem. In (Schouten et al., 2010) we have devised lexico-semantic rules that allow for extracting information from news items and used them for updating the knowledge base, closing thus the information processing loop. At the current moment we are extending this language, formally defining its grammar, and applying it for extracting financial events from news.

Another possible research direction relates to considering the importance of terms in news items. For example concepts appearing in the title of news items are possibly more important than the ones that appear in the body of new items. Also, we would like to experiment with advanced traditional weighting schemes that outperform TF-IDF as logarithmic TF functions (Buckley, Allan, & Salton, 1995), in the context of semantic recommendations. Another research direction closely related to the term weighting method is the considered similarity function. We would like to evaluate alternatives for cosine similarity as

Lnu.ltu which seem to remove some of the cosine similarity bias favoring long documents over short documents (Singhal, Buckley, & Mitra, 1996).

Regarding RSR, our semantics-based recommender, we would like to consider not only concepts directly related to concepts from the user profile or unread news items but also concepts that are indirectly related (via one or more concepts) to the concepts from the user profile or unread news items. Also, for building such concept neighborhoods the nature of semantic relationships needs to be taken in account (as for example a gloss relationship provides for less semantic similarity than a hyponym or hypernym relationship). By using machine learning techniques the semantic weights between the knowledge base concepts can be learned providing for a more accurate representation of the semantic neighborhood of a concept. These improved specifications can be exploited to recommend more relevant news items, further improving recall.

As additional further work we would like to consider other types of news recommendation services as collaborative filtering or hybrid approaches. In this way we will be able to compare semantic recommenders to these recommenders too. As hybrid approaches combining content-based recommendations and collaborative filtering have already been widely studied, we would like to investigate hybrid recommenders that combine semantic recommenders with collaborative filtering for addressing the user or item cold start problems. Also, we would like to investigate the performance of this type of recommenders with respect to existing hybrid recommenders.

CONCLUSION

In this chapter we have presented several semantic recommenders that can be employed for recommending news items in a business intelligence process. News items, due to their timeliness and rich information content can provide for a com-

petitive advantage in business decision activities. Currently there are hundreds of news items posted daily on the Web, which, combined with a historical analysis of news information, pose considerable challenges to decision makers facing time pressure while making important decisions that may impact companies for many years to come. News recommender systems are useful tools in such processes offering almost instantaneously access to the news items of interest.

A selection of traditional and semantic recommenders for news has been implemented in Athena, an extension of Hermes. Hermes is a framework for building news personalization services that makes use of advanced natural language processing techniques and Semantic Web technologies. Athena benefits from the Hermes classification of news items with respect to domain concepts as well as the available concept semantic relationships it exploits in similarity measures. As traditional methods we have implemented TF-IDF with cosine similarity, and as semantic recommenders we have implemented concept equivalence, binary cosine, Jaccard, semantic relatedness, and ranked semantic recommenders.

In a previous paper we have proposed the Ranked Semantic Recommender which have been proven to perform better not only than the traditional recommenders but also than many of the existing semantic recommenders (IJntema et al., 2010). In this chapter we go one step further, by improving our previous algorithm with respect to recall at the expense of a slight decline in precision. This has been achieved by taking into account not only the concepts directly found in unseen news items but also the concepts directly related to these ones when computing the similarity to the (extended) user profile. The new recommender has a better F-measure than any of the considered traditional and semantic recommenders.

Even though the evaluation was performed with a limited number of users, the results obtained with our semantic recommenders show a better performance of this class of recommenders with respect to traditional content-based recommenders. This is due to the fact that differently than terms, concepts have well-defined semantics and this provides for a more precise definition of user interests, which boosts the precision of the recommendations. Also, concepts have semantic relationships to other concepts that allow considering the "invisible" news information that have the potential to improve the recall rates. In our approach we have used concepts related to the ones of interest or the ones present in unread news items.

REFERENCES

Adomavicius, G., & Tuzhilin, A. (2005). Toward the next generation of recommender systems: A survey of the state-of-the-art and possible extensions. *IEEE Transactions on Knowledge and Data Engineering, 17*(6), 734–749. doi:10.1109/TKDE.2005.99

Aha, D. W., Kibler, D., & Albert, M. K. (1991). Instance-based learning algorithms. *Machine Learning, 6*(1), 37–66. doi:10.1007/BF00153759

Ahn, J., Brusilovsky, P., Grady, J., He, D., & Syn, S. Y. (2007). *Open user profiles for adaptive news systems: Help or harm?* In 16th International Conference on World Wide Web (WWW 2007) (pp. 11-20). ACM.

Banos, E., Katakis, I., Bassiliades, N., Tsoumakas, G., & Vlahavas, I. P. (2006). *PersoNews: A personalized news reader enhanced by machine learning and semantic filtering*. In 5th International Conference on Ontologies, DataBases and Applications of Semantics (ODBASE 2006) (vol. 4275, pp. 975-982). Springer.

Bechhofer, S., Harmelen, F. v., Hendler, J., Horrocks, I., McGuinness, D. L., Patel-Schneider, P. F., et al. (2004). *OWL Web ontology language reference*. W3C Recommendation 10 February 2004.

Billsus, D., & Pazzani, M. J. (1999). *A personal news agent that talks, learns and explains*. In Third International Conference on Autonomous Agents (Agents 1999) (pp. 268-275). ACM.

Borsje, J., Levering, L., & Frasincar, F. (2008). *Hermes: A Semantic Web-based news decision support system*. In 23rd Annual ACM Symposium on Applied Computing (SAC 2008) (pp. 2415-2420). ACM.

Bra, P. D., Aerts, A. T. M., Houben, G. J., & Wu, H. (2000). *Making general-purpose adaptive hypermedia work*. In World Conference on the WWW and Internet (WebNet 2000) (pp. 117-123). AACE.

Buckley, C., Allan, J., & Salton, G. (1995). Automatic routing and retrieval using smart: TREC-2. *Information Processing & Management, 31*(3), 315–326. doi:10.1016/0306-4573(94)00049-9

Castellanos, M., Gupta, C., Wang, S., & Dayal, U. (2010). *Leveraging Web streams for contractual situational awareness in operational BI*. In EDBT/ICDT International Workshop on Business Intelligence and the Web (BEWEB 2010). ACM.

Chen, C. C., & Chen, M. C. (2002). PVA: A self-adaptive personal view agent. *Journal of Intelligent Information Systems, 18*(2/3), 173–194. doi:10.1023/A:1013629527840

Cunningham, H., Maynard, D., Bontcheva, K., & Tablan, V. (2002). *GATE: A framework and graphical development environment for robust NLP tools and applications*. In 40th Anniversary Meeting of the Association for Computational Linguistics (ACL 2002) (pp. 168-175). ACL.

Fellbaum, C. (1998). *WordNet: An electronic lexical database*. MIT.

Frasincar, F., Borsje, J., & Levering, L. (2009). A Semantic Web-based approach for building personalized news services. *International Journal of E-Business Research, 5*(3), 35–53. doi:10.4018/jebr.2009082103

Getahun, F., Tekli, J., Chbeir, R., Viviani, M., & Yetongnon, K. (2009). *Relating RSS news/items*. In 9th International Conference on Web Engineering (ICWE 2009) (vol. 5648, pp. 442-452). Springer.

Guzman-Lara, S. (2007). *KStem Java implementation*. Retrieved from http://ciir.cs.umass.edu/cgi-bin/downloads/ downloads.cgi

IJntema. W., Goossen, F., Frasincar, F., & Hogenboom, F. (2010). *Ontology-based news recommendation*. In EDBT/ICDT International Workshop on Business Intelligence and the Web (BEWEB 2010). ACM.

Jaccard, P. (1901). Étude comparative de la distribution florale dans une portion des Alpes et des Jura. *Bulletin de la Société Vaudoise des Sciences Naturelles, 37*, 547–579.

Lin, S.-H., Shih, C.-S., Chen, M. C., Ho, J.-M., Ko, M.-T., & Huang, Y.-M. (1998). *Extracting classification knowledge of Internet documents with mining term associations: A semantic approach*. In 21st Annual International ACM SIGIR Conference on Research and Development in Information Retrieval (SIGIR 1998) (pp. 241-249). ACM.

Luhn, H. P. (1958). A business intelligence system. *IBM Journal of Research and Development, 2*(4), 314–319. doi:10.1147/rd.24.0314

Middleton, S. E., Shadbolt, N. R., & De Roure, D. C. (2004). Ontological user profiling in recommender systems. *ACM Transactions on Information Systems, 22*(1), 54–88. doi:10.1145/963770.963773

Pang, B., & Lee, L. (2008). Opinion mining and sentiment analysis. *Foundations and Trends in Information Retrieval, 2*(1-2), 1–135. doi:10.1561/1500000011

Prud'hommeaux, E., & Seaborne, A. (2008). *SPARQL query language for RDF*. W3C Recommendation 15 January 2008.

Saggion, H., Funk, A., Maynard, D., & Bontcheva, K. (2007). *Ontology-based information extraction for business intelligence*. In 6th International Semantic Web Conference (ISWC 2007) (pp. 843-856): Springer.

Salton, G., & Buckley, C. (1988). Term-weighting approaches in automatic text retrieval. *Information Processing & Management, 24*(5), 513–523. doi:10.1016/0306-4573(88)90021-0

Schouten, K., Ruijgrok, P., Borsje, J., Frasincar, F., Levering, L., & Hogenboom, F. (2010). A Semantic Web-based approach for personalizing news. In 25th Symposium on Applied Computing (SAC 2010) (pp. 854-861). ACM.

Singhal, A., Buckley, C., & Mitra, M. (1996). *Pivoted document length normalization*. In 19th Annual International ACM SIGIR Conference on Research and Development in Information Retrieval (SIGIR 1996) (pp. 21-29). ACM.

Singhal, A., Salton, G., Mitra, M., & Buckley, C. (1996). Document length normalization. *Information Processing & Management, 32*(5), 619–633. doi:10.1016/0306-4573(96)00008-8

van Meteren, R., & van Someren, M. (2000). *Using content-based filtering for recommendation*. In ECML/MLnet Workshop on Machine Learning in the New Information Age 2010 (MLNIA 2010) (pp. 47-56).

ADDITIONAL READING

Billsus, D., & Pazzani, M. J. (1999). A Hybrid User Model for News Story Classification. In *Seventh International Conference on User Modeling (UM 1999)* (pp. 99-108): Springer.

Bogers, T., & Bosch, A. d. (2007). Comparing and Evaluating Information Retrieval Algorithms for News Recommendation. In *2007 ACM Conference on Recommender Systems (RecSys 2007)* (pp. 141-144): ACM.

Cantador, I., Bellogín, A., & Castells, P. (2002). News@hand: A Semantic Web Approach to Recommending News. In *5th International Conference on Adaptive Hypermedia and Adaptive Web-Based Systems (AH 2002)* (Vol. 5149, pp. 279-283): Springer.

Cantador, I., Bellogín, A., & Castells, P. (2008). Ontology-based Personalised and Context-aware Recommendations of News Items. In *2008 IEEE/WIC/ACM International Conference on Web Intelligence and Intelligent Agent Technology (WI 2008)* (Vol. 1, pp. 562-565): IEEE Computer Society.

Chedrawy, Z., & Abidi, S. S. R. (2009). A Web Recommender System for Recommending, Predicting and Personalizing Music Playlists. In *10th International Conference on Web Information Systems Engineering (WISE 2009)* (Vol. 5802, pp. 335-342): Springer.

Chen, Y.-S., & Shahabi, C. (2001). Automatically Improving the Accuracy of User Profiles with Genetic Algorithm. In *IASTED International Conference on Artificial Intelligence and Soft Computing (ASC 2001)* (pp. 21-24): ACTA Press.

Claypool, M., Gokhale, A., Miranda, T., Murnikov, P., Netes, D., & Sartin, M. (1999). Combining Content-based and Collaborative Filters in an Online Newspaper In *ACM SIGIR Workshop on Recommender Systems (SIGIR-Rec 1999)*.

Conlan, O., O'Keeffe, I., & Tallon, S. (2006). Combining Adaptive Hypermedia Techniques and Ontology Reasoning to produce Dynamic Personalized News Services. In *4th International Conference on Adaptive Hypermedia and Adaptive Web-Based Systems (AH 2006)* (Vol. 4018, pp. 81-90): Springer.

Das, A. S., Datar, M., Garg, A., & Rajaram, S. (2007). Google News Personalization: Scalable Online Collaborative Filtering. In *16th International Conference on World Wide Web (WWW 2007)* (pp. 271-280): ACM.

Gauch, S., Chaffee, J., & Pretschner, A. (2003). Ontology-Based Personalized Search and Browsing. *Web Intelligence and Agent Systems*, *1*(3/4), 219–234.

Gauch, S., Speretta, M., Chandramouli, A., & Micarelli, A. (2007). User Profiles for Personalized Information Access. In *The Adaptive Web (Vol. 4321*, pp. 54–89). Springer. doi:10.1007/978-3-540-72079-9_2

Gruber, T. R. (1993). A Translation Approach to Portable Ontology Specifications. *Knowledge Acquisition*, *5*(2), 199–220. doi:10.1006/knac.1993.1008

Guarino, N. (1998). Formal Ontology and Information Systems. In *First International Conference Formal Ontology in Information Systems (FOIS 1998)* (pp. 3-15): IOS Press.

Hopfgartner, F., & Jose, J. M. (2010). Semantic User Profiling Techniques for Personalised Multimedia Recommendation. *Multimedia Systems*, *16*(4/5), 255–274. doi:10.1007/s00530-010-0189-6

Jannach, D., Zanker, M., Felfernig, A., & Friedrich, G. (2010). *Recommender Systems: An Introduction*. Cambridge University Press.

Lavrenko, V., Schmill, M., Lawrie, D., Ogilvie, P., Jensen, D., & Allan, J. (2000). Language Models for Financial News Recommendation. In *Conference on Information and Knowledge Management (CIKM 2000)* (pp. 389-396): ACM.

Liu, J., Dolan, P., & Pedersen, E. R. (2010). Personalized News Recommendation Based on Click Behavior. In *14th International Conference on Intelligent User Interfaces (IUI 2010)* (pp. 31-40) : ACM.

Middleton, S. E., Alani, H., & De Roure, D. C. (2002). Exploiting Synergy Between Ontologies and Recommender Systems. In *WWW Semantic Web Workshop 2002 (SWW 2002)* (Vol. 55): CEUR-WS.org.

Middleton, S. E., De Roure, D. C., & Shadbolt, N. R. (2001). Capturing Knowledge of User Preferences: Ontologies in Recommender Systems. In *First International Conference on Knowledge Capture (K-CAP 2001)* (pp. 100-107): ACM.

Middleton, S. E., Shadbolt, N. R., & De Roure, D. C. (2003). Capturing Interest Through Inference and Visualization: Ontological User Profiling in Recommender Systems. In *2nd International Conference on Knowledge Capture (K-CAP 2003)* (pp. 62-69): ACM.

Resnick, P., & Varian, H. R. (1997). Recommender Systems. *Communications of the ACM, 40*(3), 56–58. doi:10.1145/245108.245121

Sieg, A., Mobasher, B., & Burke, R. (2007). Web Search Personalization with Ontological User Profiles. In *Sixteenth ACM Conference on Conference on Information and Knowledge Management (CIKM 2007)* (pp. 525-534): ACM.

Tan, A.-H., & Teo, C. (1998). Learning User Profiles for Personalized Information Dissemination. In *International Joint Conference on Neural Networks (IJCNN 1998)* (pp. 183-188): IEEE Computer Society.

Trajkova, J., & Gauch, S. (2004). Improving Ontology-Based User Profiles. In *7th International Conference on Adaptivity, Personalization and Fusion of Heterogeneous Information (RIAO 2004)* (pp. 380-390): CID.

Wang, J., Li, Q., Chen, Y. P., & Lin, Z. (2010). Recommendation in Internet Forums and Blogs. In *48th Annual Meeting of the Association for Computational Linguistics* (pp. 257-265): ACL.

Wang, J., Li, Q., Chen, Y. P., Liu, J., Zhang, C., & Lin, Z. (2010). News Recommendation in Forum-Based Social Media. In *Twenty-Fourth AAAI Conference on Artificial Intelligence (AAAI 2010)* (pp. 1449-1454): AAAI.

Ziegler, C.-N. (2005). Semantic Web Recommender Systems. In *Joint EDBT/ICDT PhD Workshop 2004* (Vol. 3268, pp. 78-89).

Ziegler, C.-N., Lausen, G., & Konstan, J. A. (2008). On Exploiting Classification Taxonomies in Recommender Systems. *AI Communications, 21*(2/3), 97–125.

KEY TERMS AND DEFINITIONS

Concept: A concept is a class or an instance of a class from a domain ontology. For example, a class is 'Company' and an instance of this class is 'Google.'

Content-Based Recommendation: A content-based recommendation is based solely on the terms that appear in the text content of an item. Terms have often associated importance values based on weighting schemes (e.g., the frequencies of a term in an item). A popular content-based recommendation technique is TF-IDF combined with the cosine similarity measure.

Domain Ontology: A domain ontology is a formal explicit specification of a shared domain conceptualization. It is composed of concepts and concept relationships that characterize a certain domain.

Ranked Semantic Recommendation: A ranked semantic recommender is a news recommendation method where concepts and relations from an ontology are employed for determining the user's interests and recommending items previously unseen. It makes use of domain ontology concepts and their relationships that goes beyond the user profile/item content.

Related Concept: A related concept is a concept that is connected by any relationship to the current concept. For instance 'Apple' and 'iPhone' are connected through the 'hasProduct' relation. The related concepts are used to better specify the context of the user interests and item information.

Semantic Web: The Semantic Web is a collection of methods and technologies that enable machines to understand the 'meaning' of Web content. It aims to make available Web information for processing by intelligent Web agents.

Semantics-Based Recommendation: A semantics-based recommendation is a recommendation technique that uses concepts and relations between them to determine the meaning of the text, rather than by only analyzing terms occurrences as is the case for content-based recommendations.

User Profile: A user profile is a formal description of the user's current interests often based on previously read items. Based on the user profile, recommender systems suggest to the user items that match his domain of interest.

Chapter 6
Interaction Mining:
Making Business Sense of Customers Conversations through Semantic and Pragmatic Analysis

Vincenzo Pallotta
Webster University, Switzerland

Lammert Vrieling
Webster University, Switzerland

Rodolfo Delmonte
Università "Ca Foscari," Italy

ABSTRACT

In this chapter we present the major challenges of a new trend in business analytics, namely Interaction Mining. With the proliferation of unstructured data as the result of people interacting with each other using digital networked devices, classical methods in text business analytics are no longer effective. We identified the causes of their failure as being related to the inadequacy of dealing with conversational data. We propose then to move from Text Mining towards Interaction Mining, and we make several cases for this transition in areas such as marketing research, social media analytics, and customer relationship management. We also propose a roadmap for the future development of Interaction Mining by challenging the current practices in business intelligence and information visualization.

1 INTRODUCTION

Via the Web a wealth of information for business research is ready at our fingertips. Analyzing this—unstructured—information, however, can be very difficult. *Analytics* has become the business buzzword distinguishing traditional competitors from 'analytics competitors' who have dramatically boosted their revenues. The latter competitors distinguish themselves through "expert use of statistics and modeling to improve a wide variety of functions" (Davenport, 2006, p. 105). However, not all information lends itself to statistics and

DOI: 10.4018/978-1-61350-038-5.ch006

models. Actually, most information on the Web is made for, and by, people communicating through 'rich' language. This richness of our language is typically missed or not adequately accounted for in (statistical) analytics (e.g. Text-mining)—and so is its real meaning—because it is hidden in *semantics* rather than form (e.g. syntax). In our efforts of turning unstructured data into structured data, important information—and our ability to distinguish ourselves from competitors—gets lost.

Search engines (Büttcher, Clarke, & Cormack, 2010) have exploited statistical (frequency-based, TF-IDF[2]) methods to its extreme, but building indexes of Web content with keywords is not enough for understanding beyond keyword-based search. The use of semantics in search would be a great improvement and new generation search engines (Grimes, 2010) are starting to address this. Semantic search can be approached from several perspectives. The most common one is to go beyond word forms and consider concepts with their semantic relationships. Concepts can be extracted implicitly or explicitly. In the first case, the contexts of words in a document base determine the concept (Landauer, Foltz, & Laham, 1998). In the second case, concepts are assigned to word forms through a semantic lexicon or ontology such as WordNet[3].

However, semantics is not only necessary for search, it is necessary for any processing of information from the Web. After all, semantics simply means "making sense" and we would like to argue that sophisticated semantic analysis of content is a necessary tool for quality business research of Web data.

For instance, any business analyst in *fast moving consumer goods* (FMCG) is looking for so much more than just text when analyzing online focus group interview data. A FMCG analyst would analyze interaction, which would reveal shared language, beliefs and myths, argumentative reasoning, justifications, and changes of opinion or (re)interpretation of experiences (Catterall & Maclaran, 1997).

Focus group interview data is both qualitative and interactive. It is not just text; it is conversational data as people are responding to one another. As such traditional (manual) analysis of focus group data is labor intensive, complex, analyst dependent, inconsistent and subjective[4].

The key problem is that good analysis of unstructured data is costly, complex and time-consuming

However, the power of current state-of-the-art NLU[5] systems makes automated analysis of these—and other—types of unstructured data feasible and possible (Delmonte, Bristot, & Pallotta, 2010).

This chapter will put to rest the myth that computers cannot extract rich information from unstructured data[6] even from conversational data. We will put forward a new generation of "Interaction Mining" technology that is analyst independent, consistent regardless of the quantity of data, 'Machine-like' precision in its analysis in multiple languages and—compared to manual analysis—a quantum leap faster.

First, we will conduct first a survey of current technology for Interaction Mining by assessing the strengths, weaknesses and limits of current approaches such as Text Mining. Additionally, we will present a study in eliciting business requirements for Interaction Mining in different domains. We will present a new approach, which exploits information extracted from automatic analysis of conversational data, which solves some of the challenges highlighted in the requirements section. We will conclude the chapter by outlining a roadmap for research in Interaction Mining.

2 INTERACTION MINING

In this section we review some current approaches to Business Analytics such as Data Mining and Text Mining by assessing their benefit, strengths, weaknesses and limits to deal with conversational data. We then propose a novel paradigm that we advocate being more suitable for the analysis of interactions between customers. We call the new paradigm Interaction Mining and it stems from and extends standard approaches to Text Mining. We define Interaction Mining as analyzing *interaction* (or *conversational*) *business data* generating actionable insights.

2.1 Standard Approaches in Business Analytics

Gartner defines *[business] analytics* (BA) as "leveraging data in a particular functional process (or application) to enable context-specific insight that is actionable" (Kirk, 2006). In BA, data collected from data collected through structured customers' data (e.g. transactions, forms) are typically analyzed through *Data Mining* tools (Shmueli, Patel, & Bruce, 2010).

When dealing with unstructured data, data mining tools alone are insufficient. Text Business Analytics (TBA) aims at understanding business data using quantitative (statistical) methods resulting in actionable insights by means of *Text Mining* technologies. Text Mining looks at more unstructured data, which typically come in form of textual documents. Text Mining tools typically extract features from textual content in order to discover interesting patterns or classify these according to similarity. In a sense, Text Mining includes data mining as one of its component.

Text Mining is about extracting statistically relevant (possibly unknown) patterns (or themes) from textual documents (Feldman & Sanger, 2006). Text Mining can be decomposed into three distinct components:

1. a feature extraction component, which transforms unstructured input into structured data;
2. a data mining component, which discovers statistically significant patterns from data;
3. a visualization component, which allows the user to visualize the relationships between

the discovered patterns and map them into pre-defined categories.

For instance, a Text Mining system could help in building clusters of documents in a document base by looking at the similarity of their extracted features (e.g., words, concepts, named entities). The clusters are then visualized with their associated themes.

A Text Mining approach is more about coping with large-sized unstructured textual data repositories than about looking at finer-grained information contained in conversations. While we believe that Text Mining is extremely useful pattern discovery tool, it does not answer alone the questions of *why* these patterns are linked to the actual customer's behaviors and opinions.

2.2 From Text Mining to Interaction Mining

The presence of customers on the Web—through several communication channels—provides companies with a wealth of unstructured data, which is hardly transformed into actionable insights. Most of this unstructured information is user-generated and provided by customers in natural language, either in textual or in speech form.

With the establishment of Web 2.0 (Tapscot & Williams, 2006) we moved from user-generated content to user-generated conversations. Conversational data is clearly unstructured as the customers interact through free-text or speech and they are not constraint by any pre-defined structures when to use natural language.

By looking at conversations (i.e. interlinked contributions produced by several authors) as a process, we need to take a substantial different approach than Text Mining. It is the *process* itself that carries the semantics (true meaning) of the conversation and not just the aggregation of features extracted from individual contributions. In other words, we need to understand not only what is said, but also why and how it has been said.

Figure 1. Comparison of text business analytics (based on text mining) and interaction business analytics (based on interaction mining)

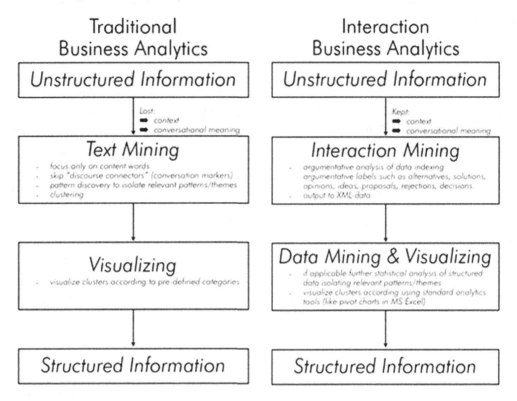

Interaction Mining extracts rich information (semantic and pragmatic) from unstructured customers' interactions, namely conversations held between people and organizations through various communication channels (e.g. phone calls, email, social media, recorded meetings). Moreover, Interaction Mining makes sense of extracted information by means of appropriate data mining and visualization tools thus enabling what we call Interaction Business Analytics.

The main similarities and differences between the two approaches are portrayed in Figure 1. The main difference lies in what type of information is extracted from conversation. We basically advocate that an Interaction Mining system should be able to make sense to the actions performed by language. In other words, the system should be able to analyze the *process* of conversation rather than just the *content* of conversation.

Conversations are indeed difficult to process with standard BA tools not only because it is unstructured language data but also because each individual contribution needs to be understood within its context (e.g. with respect to its position in the conversation).

The role of a contribution in conversations is no longer only informative as in a text documents. A contribution carries a *pragmatic force* that can steer the conversation along different directions and outcomes. Moreover, when dealing with unstructured data, Text Mining tools only look at content-bearing words and typically skip discourse connectors (e.g. conjunctions, prepositions) (Blakemore, 2002). These are extremely important in conversations since they carry a lot of the conversational meaning of each contribution. In other words, it is no longer possible to rely to the distributional semantics of documents based on the frequency of content-bearing words.

A simple but illustrative example is when negation is used in language. The sentence: "The judge declared that the CEO did not pay bribes" would always match the query "CEO pays bribes" in a standard content analysis system, but never will the query "CEO was innocent." There are two main reasons for this simple failure:

1. Negative markers such as "not" are normally removed from indexes;
2. Even if negation would be accounted for, there is no way to infer that "not paying" entails "innocence."

The above example is only one and maybe the simplest of the challenges posed by interaction mining. Other challenges are those related to various discourse-level phenomena such as anaphora and temporal resolution, detection of rhetorical relations, speech and dialogue acts, ellipsis, presupposition and conversational implicatures. Discussion of these issues is outside the scope of this chapter. The interested reader can refer to (Mitkov, 2003) for an overview.

Another case that clarifies the objectives of Interaction Mining and highlights the limitations of standard Text Mining techniques when applied to conversational data is Opinion Mining and Sentiment Analysis (Pang & Lee, 2008) and (Liu, 2010). Basically, nearly all approaches look at individual contribution and classify them into pre-defined categories (e.g. positive, negative, neutral attitudes). These approaches trivially fail in making sense of complex customer interactions where participant argue about a topic. Whatever algorithm is applied (e.g. based on machine learning or on a lexicon), the *context of the text* (i.e. where and when it appears) is never taken into account. In some cases it might be enough as long as the contribution directly refers to the topic under discussion (e.g. a review of a product). Very often, the text appears within a discussion or a conversation (e.g. comments, replies in blogs or micro-blogs) and negative contribution can refer to other contributions and not to the topic under discussion. A full example of this phenomenon is discussed in more details in section 3.3.

Of course, we also take into account other sources of context beyond the mere conversation, which are also neglected by Text Mining, such as knowledge of the user models and profiles, user's interaction history, cultural and language settings. Any account of these contexts would improve the quality of understanding of the conversation. Any system that relies on features extracted from the surface form of text (e.g. words) will fail in taking into account such contexts that are implicit and not manifested in the text. In contrast, systems that encode extensive knowledge bases and ontologies will have better chances to contextualize their analysis on multiple dimensions as long as the context of the conversation can be detected and classified by the system. For lack of space and because it would result into a too specific discussion, we do not address purposely these aspects in this chapter.

2.3 Making Sense of Customers' Interactions

Until now, using automation in making sense of unstructured customer information was particularly challenging as it must first be turned into structured information and then analyzed with the appropriate tools. Often, the richness of the information source makes it impossible to perform a trivial transformation into quantitative data.

For instance, just counting the occurrence of certain terms is not enough to make sense of opinions expressed in users' product reviews such as those in e-pinions[7]. Looking at ratings and doing standard Opinion Mining is not enough if the company wants to discover the *root cause* of customers' disappointment. In such a case, one has to look closer at the reviews and "understand" exactly why the customers say what they say.

Typically, this process is very time-consuming and complex especially in case where information must be harvested from multiple channels (e.g. blogs, social media, contact-centers, forums). The challenge here is to understand exactly what type of information needs to and can be extracted from unstructured conversational data and which methods can efficiently perform that task.

The term multichannel (or cross-channel) Interaction Mining has been introduced by several companies (Autonomy), (NICE) and (Verint) to describe the process of gathering the customers' voice from several communication channels and build actionable knowledge from it. All these products show an interesting trend: companies need to monitor customers' behavior from multiple sources in order to spot any arising issue in due time. Having this knowledge at hand, allow companies to react fast and fix the problem before it becomes unmanageable. An example of this is an organization that has a large amount of information spread across more than 100 different sources. Employees would spend about 50% of their time searching for the right type of information among these sources to answer customers' questions. What was needed was a system that would provide access to aggregate information over all different sources. Information needed to be automatically categorized, linked and delivered to the employees so that they can respond fast and accurate.

The minimum common denominator of these approaches is that unstructured data is extracted from several sources and turned into structured data for statistical quantitative analysis. Very few details are provided on what type of information is extracted but essentially most of the products are based on Search and Text Mining techniques and as such do not take real conversational data into account.

In summary, we believe that the benefit of applying Text Mining to conversational data is already major. However, we also believe that Text Mining provides only a slight contribution to what can be really extracted through a comprehensive account of natural language interaction between customers. Improvement of Text Mining techniques can be achieved by shifting the focus from content to process and have ways to extract features that allow us to understand the key points of interaction. One possible approach we present in this chapter is based on argumentative analysis and it will be detailed in section 4.1.

2.4 Related Work

As we already mentioned, Interaction Mining is a novel and emerging approach to business analytics and so far there are very few work that we can consider as strictly related. Loosely, we consider relevant Text Mining and Opinion Mining because these techniques can be used as a starting point for more elaborate analysis required for Interaction Mining's interaction mining. Data Mining and Information Visualization are clearly useful tools to further making sense to information extracted from conversational data.

One area of investigation we believe very relevant to Interaction Mining is that of Social Analytics[8]. This new trend includes the analysis of user-generated content published in social networks. Many big and small companies such as, for instance, SAS[9], ViralHeat[10], and Alterian[11] are trying to impose their signature on this area. However, we notice that the tools deployed for analyzing social media conversations are still based on standard Text Mining technology, with a social network analysis twist (Watt, 2003).

Relevant to Interaction Mining are also software architectures for deploying applications. Interaction Mining tools can be standalone or integrated with standard analytics architecture such as IBM's UIMA[12] or GATE[13]. While outside the scope of this chapter, we believe that industry standards for application development are fundamental and we advocate for an extensive use of them in the framework of Interaction Mining in order to ensure interoperability of applications.

Another area that is somehow related to Interaction Mining is Customer Relationship Management[14] (CRM). In CRM, the goal is to analyze the interactions with customers in order to predict future trends and improve the relationship over time. Of course, Interaction Mining would be beneficial in the analysis phase since it would enable better understanding of customers' behavior. So far, analysis of customers' behavior in CRM system is limited to Data Mining of transactional data (e.g. purchases, returns, churn rate in e-commerce websites). Very little work has been done in the area of analyzing unstructured interactions with customers (e.g. contact centers), let alone interaction between customers themselves. We see here a substantial impact of Interaction Mining for leveraging interaction information for boosting CRM performance.

In the following section we outline some specific requirements for Interaction Mining beyond those that are already met by standard Text Mining techniques, namely the context-unaware analysis of semantic content of text for classification and clustering purposes.

3 ELICITING USER REQUIREMENTS FOR INTERACTION MINING

The goal of this section is making a case for Interaction Mining by looking at limitations of current BA approaches, in particular of Text Mining and Opinion Mining. For that purpose, we look closer at the intrinsic nature of customers' interactions. Based on our observations, we distinguish between three broad classes of customer's interactions:

1. **Direct interaction between the company and the customer**. This type of interaction is either initiated by the customer by, for instance, calling the contact-center, or solicited by the company through feedback forms or surveys. These interactions are much more focused and issue-oriented and typically synchronous (with the exception of email exchanges).

2. **Indirect interaction between the company and customer**. This typically happens through the public broadcast of corporate messages or consumer-generated content in public forums. This interaction is often asynchronous and with a larger purpose than solving a particular issue. Both the customer and the company can initiate interactions of this kind. Channels used are typically social media, discussion forums, blogs and corporate websites.

3. **Customer-to-customer interaction**. This type of conversations are publicly recorded in discussion forums, chats, and other Web 2.0 collaborative tools, with the purpose of discussing about products or services provided by companies by sharing experiences and best practices.

Standard Text Mining tends to blur these distinctions that we want to make more explicit. We believe that the types of interaction are substantially different and different information extraction techniques need to be used.

For example, in direct interaction of customers with contact centers, one analysis goal can be to monitor agents' performance (e.g. the conversion rate, the problems solved rate). It is apparent that techniques for Opinion Mining are probably inappropriate here. Issue-oriented conversations show little sentiment towards the product but rather concerning the faced issue. A successful method should be able to provide information about whether or not the interaction leads to the customer's satisfaction (i.e. issue solved). This is usually signaled by a conventionalized exchange between the agent and the customer. While it might be possible to spot successful calls through Text Mining technique, the opposite is not, especially if one wants to figure out why the issue was not solved.

For instance, the occurrence of many questions and less assertions might signal a situation where the problem is not yet solved. Subsequently, a *conversational analysis system* must be able to at least detect the occurrence of questions and understand if the question is left unanswered or not.

In summary, applying inadequate analysis methods a great deal of information can be ost. The more interactive the conversation is, the higher is the need of focusing on micro-linguistic phenomena such as those that signal the real attitudes of participants and the roles of their contributions in the conversation.

We now examine three possible (among many others) domains of application for Interaction Mining: online focus groups research, quality monitoring of contact centers and mining public opinions in social networks. For each domain we first provide a summarized view on requirements for Interaction Mining. Then, we will provide some solutions in Section 4 and guidelines for future development in Section 5.

3.1 (Online) Focus-Group Research

We conducted a number of interviews with experts in the domain of qualitative analysis of focus group data and we summarize below our findings about the types of information that is typically considered relevant for the analysis:

- Group transcript into questions (or in our terminology "raised issues") made by the facilitator.
- For each question/issue/problem, report those that appear to be direct answers to the question (e.g. proposals, ideas, solutions, and opinions).
- Identify requests for clarification/explanations to the initial question and/or to participants' answers.
- Identify those conversations between participants that focus on a specific aspect of

the initial question (e.g. elaboration of a theme).
- Identify those conversations between participants that seem to be off topic or that start a new theme.
- Classify participant's contribution as factual and opinions/wishes.
- Highlight consensus patterns.
- Highlight agreement/disagreement patterns.

It is apparent that these elements are strongly related to the conversational process rather than to the textual content. One has to look at how themes are discussed and not just identify those themes.

Having a clear framework to understand what types of information is relevant for conducting qualitative analysis of focus group data is helpful also because it creates a minimum common denominator among analyses of comparable data.

Anybody who has analyzed even a few interviews knows how difficult this is. Skilled business analysts using qualitative analysis of conversations typically analyze unstructured data from customer interactions manually (e.g. online focus groups). This approach is expensive and complex but it has the advantage of providing rich explanations of the phenomenon. Proper analysis begins with a careful reading of all data. Next, one will need to assign open codes to all text by identifying the key word or words. Next, the codes will be grouped into broader categories or themes relevant to the research question, which will provide the basis for building the theory and interpretation of the findings. These themes are only verified when two or more groups include them in their discussion. Aforementioned process is often simplified in order to save time and cost through merely listening and/or reading and then summarizing the information.

Ideally, good analysis of focus group data would be consistent, systematic and objective[15]. Moreover, good analysis highlights shared language, what was taken for granted, what needs to be clarified, what was proposed, and what were the positives, negatives, and neutrals. Finally, good analysis distinguishes between facts, opinions, wishes, and statements, and it tracks opinions, agreements and disagreements. Unfortunately, this is typically not the case even if the researchers use advanced tools like Nvivo[16] or Atlas[17]. The latter tools facilitate consistent and systematic analysis but are only as smart as the user and consistently, let alone objectively, tracking the elements mentioned above requires more than a "mere human." According to our research most analysts do not use these tools but 'trust' on their memory and summarizing skills.

Above-mentioned requirements of focus group data indicate that Interaction Mining with fast, objective and 'Machine-like' precision would be a differentiator.

3.2 Contact Centers

Contact center analytics or "call analytics" is a very active field with many competitors. However, even "whole call analytics" is limited to the logistics of how a call is handled (call volume, call duration, time-to-answer, unnecessary transfers, managing partner transfers, and maximizing Interactive Voice Response (IVR)). Notable exceptions are companies specialized in Speech Analytics[18]. They use statistical analysis of (speech) calls and as such provide improvement to talk times and, for example, reduce the volume of audio for review. However, even if we consider the latter, there is still a lot that conversation analysis can improve for a contact center. For example, careful analysis of transcribed calls can discover correlation between call operators' utterances types and conversion rate or the number of unmatched requests. The use of 'association rules' is often used in Market Basket Analysis[19] (customers who bought this book, also bought these…) but with the use of conversation analysis this can also be used in contact centers. For example, agents who simply ask, "Shall I make the booking for you?" make more book-

ings (Subramaniam, 2008). In the case of contact centers, conversation analysis combined with data mining would make a "killer app."

3.3 Opinion Mining

As mentioned in Section 2.3, Opinion Mining approaches typically fail in making sense of complex customer interactions where participants argue about a topic. In Figure 2 we show an excerpt from a public conversation on Google Wave[20]. The topic of this conversation is Facebook's privacy policy changes. If we just look at the last contribution, there are several positive terms (e.g. agree, understand, care, good), but the comment is clearly negative as it supports the previous negative statement stating that Facebook's privacy changes are difficult to understand. For this specific case, most of Opinion Mining system would erroneously recognize the last contribution as positive, while it only confirms the previous negative comment on Facebook's privacy policy and it should actually count as a negative one. In other words, each contribution must be interpreted within its conversational context and not in absolute terms as it is mostly done in current Opinion Mining technology.

Similarly, casually searching for the company Nestlé on Twitrratr.com will provide a list of positive, neutral, and negative opinions on this company as shown in Figure 3. The percentages suggest a very exact result: 12.71% positive, 84.75 neutral, and 2.54% negative. However, 4 of the 12 opinions on the page are already wrong. A more careful analysis that we performed manually shows 34% positive, 40% neutral, 16% negative and 10% not clear. A clear example that existing tools cannot deal with these types of statements. In Figure 3, we circled in red those contributions that were misclassified

We recognize that sentiment analysis of Twitter can be extremely tricky due to the fact that tweets are difficult to put in context of a conversation. Moreover, Twitter users tend to engage

Figure 2. Excerpt of a public conversation on Google Wave

Figure 3. Twittratr's sentiment analysis of Néstlé search term

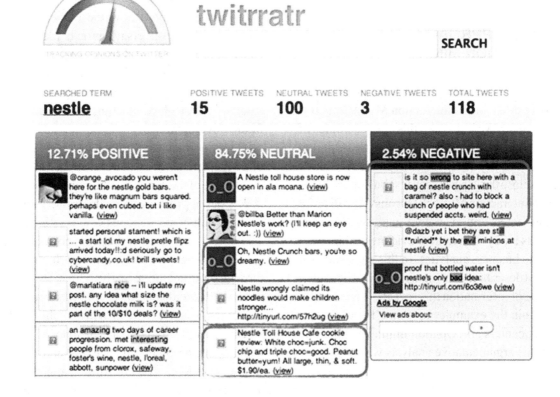

very little in conversations (i.e. reply to other user's Tweets) but they use the system to post their opinions as a form of public speech. Nevertheless, when conversational structure is present, accounting for this context would prove beneficial in ruling out false positive cases.

There is an interesting trend in Opinion Mining that tries to move the focus from sentence-level towards discourse-level sentiment analysis. In (Somasundaran, Wiebe, & Ruppenhofer, 2008) work has been carried out to automatically label contributions in discussions (i.e. meetings) with discourse-level opinion categories. These categories highlight the role of contributions in the conversation with a polarity twist. While this is not sufficient to fully characterize the discussion process it is nevertheless a serious attempt in framing discussion from argumentative perspective, which we believe is one of the right ways to go if we want to capture the full understanding of conversations.

4 A NEW APPROACH FOR INTERACTION MINING

So far we have demonstrated that in moving beyond Text Mining to Interaction Mining much is to be gained. We illustrated this with examples of online focus groups, contact centers and Opinion Mining. The key question in this paragraph is how can we close the gap between text business analytics and Interaction Mining? Our answer will point to automated argumentative analysis (Pallotta, 2006) as a way to include the richness of interaction into business analytics. In this paragraph we will first describe argumentative analysis including the type of information this reveals. Then we will take again the examples of online focus groups, contact centers and Opinion mining to illustrate what this argumentative analysis will add.

4.1 Argumentative Analysis

Our proposal for a new approach to Interaction Mining is to leverage the pragmatic information (automatically extracted through deep linguistic processing of conversations) into structured actionable knowledge. In order to achieve this goal we advocate that the most difficult task is to choose the right level of representation of pragmatic information. This choice substantially affects the linguistic processing required to extract the relevant information.

We believe that a good starting point to address the Interaction Mining requirements is to focus on *argumentative analysis of conversations* as it has already been demonstrated being adequate in (Pallotta, Seretan, & Ailomaa, 2007) for post-meetings information retrieval. Argumentation is pervasive in conversations because people tend to defend their opinions through arguments. At one extreme of the types of conversations we find multi-party dialogs such as face-to-face meetings. These conversations show the highest level of interactivity in conversations and they can be considered as the most difficult case for Interaction Mining. We will make a case for an effective approach in Interaction Mining by providing a study of face-to-face meetings as a baseline for future developments.

It is important to note that looking at dynamics of conversations does not presuppose extensive knowledge of the domain of the conversation. This makes our approach very scalable and robust for dealing with heterogeneous conversational data. The only assumption is that conversations have purpose, which we are aimed at highlighting through argumentative analysis.

To better understand the impact of argumentative analysis we will provide in this section a real example of how it can help in solving outstanding problems in indexing and retrieval of conversational content. In our approach, we adopt a representation of conversational structure based on argumentation theory (Pallotta, 2006).

Figure 4. Argumentative structure of a conversation (excerpt)

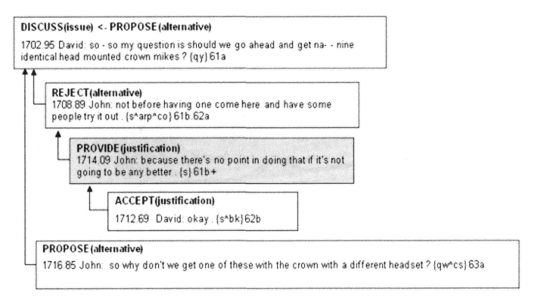

The argumentative structure defines the different patterns of argumentation used by participants in the dialog, as well as their organization and synchronization in the discussion.

The argumentative structure of a conversation is composed of a set of topic discussion episodes (a discussion about a specific topic). In each topic discussion, there exists a set of issue episodes. An issue is generally a local problem in a larger topic to be discussed and solved. Participants propose alternatives, solutions, opinions, ideas, etc. in order to achieve a satisfactory decision. Meanwhile, participants either express their positions and standpoints through acts of accepting or rejecting proposals, or by asking questions related to the current proposals. Hence, for each issue, there is a corresponding set of proposal episodes (solutions, alternatives, ideas, etc.) that are linked to a certain number of related position episodes (for example a rejection to a proposed alternative in a discussed issue) or questions and answers.

In Figure 4, we show a diagram representing the argumentative analysis of an episode of a conversation on the topic "microphone." Each box contains the argumentative role of the turn and its textual transcription as well as some additional metadata already contained in the corpus from which the excerpt has been taken (Janin, et al., 2003). This analysis would allow an analyst to answer a question such as: "*Why was the proposal on microphones rejected?*" by looking for a turn with an argumentative label, "justification." Of course, finding a justification is not enough because the justification must have been provided for a rejection to a "proposal" (or "alternative") made to an issue on the topic of "microphones." This can be done by navigating back through the argumentative links up to the "issue" episode whose content thematically matches the "microphone" topic.

A system capable of identifying and linking argumentative elements of a conversation has been presented and evaluated in (Pallotta, Delmonte, & Bistrot, 2009). This system is also able to provide for each turn sentiment (e.g. positive, negative and neutral) and subjectivity (e.g. factual or subjective) analysis (Delmonte & Pallotta, 2010).

The core of our solution for argument extraction is based on adapting and extending GETARUNS

Figure 5. Cooperativeness levels of each participant

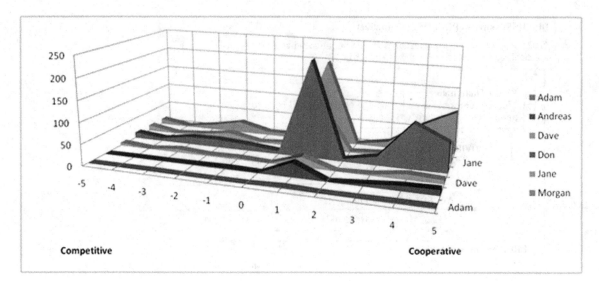

(Delmonte. 2007; 2009), a natural language understanding system developed at the University of Venice. Automatic argumentative annotation is carried out by a special module of GETARUNS activated at the very end of the analysis of each conversation, taking as input its complete semantic representation.

To produce argumentative annotation, the system uses the following 21 discourse relations: Statement, Narration, Adverse, Result, Cause, Motivation, Explanation, Question, Hypothesis, Elaboration, Permission, Inception, Circumstance, Obligation, Evaluation, Agreement, Contrast, Evidence, Hypoth, Setting, Prohibition.

These are then mapped onto five general argumentative labels: ACCEPT, REJECT/DISAGREE, PROPOSE/SUGGEST, EXPLAIN/JUSTIFY, REQUEST.

The subjectivity module is able to assign to each turn a combination of labels along several dimensions discussed in (Delmonte, 2007). For the purposes of the examples provided in this chapter, the labels are collapsed into three generic broad categories: FACTIVE, OPINION, and QUESTION.

4.2 The Interaction Mining Dashboard

We provide in this section a number of visualizations that we see as good candidates for building Interaction Mining dashboards. The examples are only illustrative of what type of insights can be captured from information extracted from conversations using argumentative, opinion, and subjectivity analysis.

The visualizations are obtained by means of pivot tables and charts in Microsoft Excel. We have found that readers often assume the data for these charts "must have been manually generated." Hence, we emphasize that the data for the diagrams below were automatically generated without any analyst intervention.

The first diagram in Figure 5 highlights the cooperativeness of participants in a conversation. The X axis displays the level of cooperativeness of turns according to the mapping in Table 1, while the Y axis displays the number of turns of each participants falling in those categories. The chart also highlights the level of participation of each participant.

Table 1. Mapping table for argumentative categories to levels of cooperativeness

Argumentative Categories	Level of Cooperativeness
Accept explanation	5
Suggest	4
Propose	3
Provide opinion	2
Provide explanation or justification	1
Question	-1
Raise issue	-2
Request explanation or justification	-3
Provide negative opinion	-4
Disagree	-5
Reject explanation or justification	-5

Note that from a strict business perspective "competitive" has a positive connotation. In this context, we consider "competitive behavior" as uncooperative. As shown in Table 1, uncooperativeness (i.e. negative scores) is linked to high level of criticism, which is not balanced by constructive contributions (e.g. suggestions and explanations). We acknowledge that this is a rough classification and a better mapping is needed. One possibility for improving the quality of group behavior assessment would be mapping the argumentative categories into Bales's Interaction Process Analysis framework (Bales, 1950).

Besides the level of participation the system also automatically highlights the number of participants, participants who talked the most, participants who has undergone the majority of overlaps (interruption) and who has done the majority of overlaps (dominance). This is highlighted in diagram of Figure 6 focusing on group social behavior in terms of both dominance and pairwise interaction among participants. The size of nodes is proportional to the replies provided and the thickness of edges represents the proportion of turns exchanged between two participants.

The diagram in Figure 7, not only confirms that most interaction was between Don, Jane and Morgan, but also that Morgan and Don dominated the conversation. Notably, Andreas and Adam never talked to each other. This type of analysis is only possible if the information extraction component can detect which participant is replying to a previous turn.

If we restrict ourselves to the "disagreement" category, we can understand from Figure 8 that Jane shows proportionally more dissent than other participants and that only Don dares to argue with Morgan while others disagree substantially less with Morgan or between each other. This might also highlight the power relationships between members of a group.

The diagram in Figure 8 shows the attitudes of participants towards the top 10 themes of the discussion. The system automatically generates the discussion topics, who introduced these topics, and whether their attitudes where positive, negative or neutral.

The diagram in Figure 9 shows a subjectivity analysis displaying the proportion of factual and subjective (opinion) statements (see Section 4.1) made by participants for the top 10 discussed topics. This type of analysis is interesting because it reveals how much of a perception is based on facts or 'mere opinion' and whether or not they have many doubts.

The spider diagrams in Figure 10 and Figure 11 show the consensus and dissent levels around the discussed topics.

Figure 10 highlights only the top 10 topics. This information can be helpful in retrospectively analyzing the decision process by looking at how much a decision was supported. If, hypothetically, a decision was made on "data," although a consensus was present, it is clear that it was not a major one. If this revealed to be a wrong decision, one can track who was effectively responsible.

We also provide in Table 2 a breakdown analysis of consensus that highlights who agreed

Figure 6. Group Social behavior

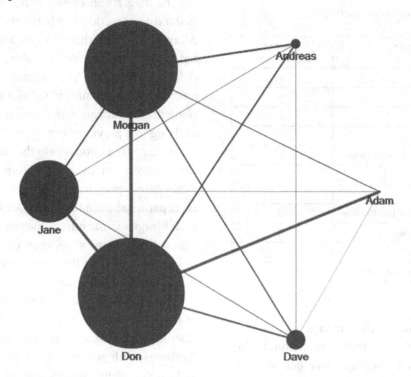

Figure 7. Social behavior for disagreement

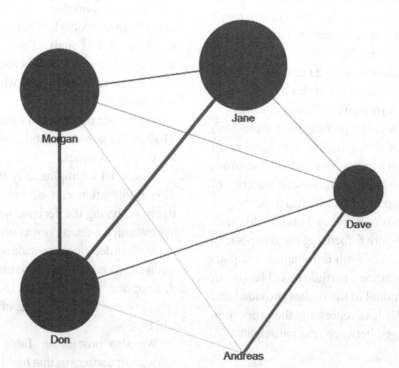

Figure 8. Participants' attitude towards top 10 topics

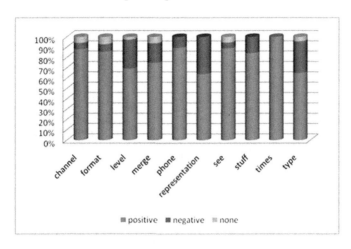

Figure 9. Subjectivity analysis for top 10 discussed topics

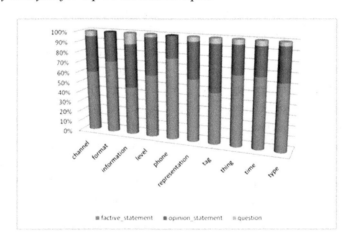

Figure 10. Consensus on top 10 topics

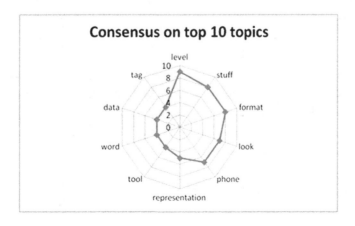

Figure 11. Dissent on all detected topics

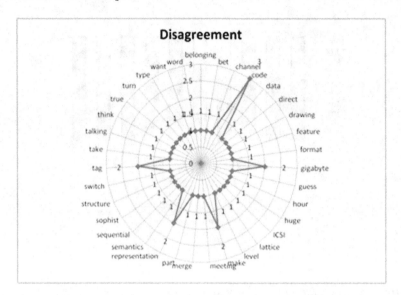

for each of the selected topic topics in terms of number of turns labeled with the Agree label. As one can check, Adam, Jane and Morgan did not explicitly agree on "data." If they have also expressed dissent on that, they could be relieved from any responsibility on that decision.

In Figure 11, we have an overview of dissent for all the topics discussed in the meeting. In a dashboard containing this diagram, the user can drill down on the topic and visualize the turns where the dissent happens[21].

In the following and last example, we show how Data Mining techniques can be used on top of data extracted from argumentative analysis. For this purpose we used a standard Data Mining tool for Excel, XLMiner[22] that we used to induce association rules. Table 3 shows the results.

We can see that there are a few interesting facts emerging from data:

Table 2. Breakdown analysis of consensus

Topics \ Speaker	Adam	Andreas	Dave	Don	Jane	Morgan
data		2	1	1		
format			1	4	1	2
level				1	1	7
look				1	3	3
phone					1	6
representation				3	1	1
stuff		1		3		4
tag				2		2
tool				2	1	1
word				1	2	1
Grand Total	1	3	2	22	14	34

Table 3. Associative Mining on argumentative data

Conf. %	Antecedent (a)	Consequent (c)
89.36	factive_statement, say=>	positive
80.30	positive, provide_expl_just=>	factive_statement
78.57	provide_expl_just=>	factive_statement
77.99	factive_statement, provide_expl_just=>	positive
76.32	provide_expl_just=>	positive
75.68	positive, say=>	factive_statement
71.18	factive_statement, positive=>	provide_expl_just
71.12	factive_statement=>	positive
68.81	Morgan=>	positive
64.91	factive_statement=>	provide_expl_just
63.09	positive=>	factive_statement
61.28	provide_expl_just=>	factive_statement, positive
56.06	Don=>	positive
55.92	positive=>	provide_expl_just
53.79	Don=>	factive_statement
52.17	factive_statement=>	positive
50.62	factive_statement=>	positive, provide_expl_just

- We can confirm that Don and Morgan were consistently positive.
- We can observe that Explanations are provided as factual statements and in positive way.
- We can observe that Statements (i.e. those marked with the "say" predicate) are consistently positive.

These results may appear quite obvious. In fact the conversation we have analyzed does not present any particular issue. We might, however, expect radically different results in cases where the conversation is highly controversial.

These are merely some examples of what automated argumentative analysis can do with the conversations. As mentioned, these face-to-face conversations are the most difficult cases for Interaction Mining.

We conclude this section with applications of the Interaction Mining analyses in our three cases: Focus Groups, Contact Centers and Opinion Mining.

4.3 (Online) Focus-Group

If we apply the above analysis to focus group interviews it would reveal the nature of the focus group, the level of interactivity, the different levels of contribution of the participants, the topics discussed, facts, opinions (positives, negatives, and neutrals), wishes, doubts, statements, consensus and dissent.

In the above example, the system would indicate that Adam, Andreas and Dave are not very helpful as focus group participants, and that, for example, Jane was quite competitive and not really open. Moreover, the system would list the main topics discussed (format, phone, representation) and the respective attitudes on these topics.

In short the system would analyze the focus group conversations in a consistent, systematic and objective manner.

4.4 Contact Centers

If we apply the analysis to contact centers and in particular to contact center operators the level of cooperativeness of some operators (Adam, Andreas, and Dave) would be 'flagged' for an evaluation conversation. We could compare the level of cooperation to the level of success of an operator. Furthermore, we could mine association rules between argumentative labels (e.g. reject, disagree, propose, suggest) and the conversion rate of operators. These rules would provide a list of specific statements beneficial to these conversion rates. If this would then be linked to an operator assistance system it could within milliseconds suggest 'helpful phrases' to better serve the customer. Indeed, the combination of argumentative analysis and data mining provides many very interesting opportunities for contact centers.

4.5 Opinion Mining

Even though the majority of current Opinion Mining systems are not technically conversational, argumentative and subjectivity analysis tools are much better equipped to handle these types of responses. The level of precision of qualifying opinions as positive, neutral of negative would be very high (about 90%). The real power of argumentative analysis, however, is only released when dealing with truly conversational data such as in the example of Google Wave in Section 3.3. These and other types of review conversations would provide very helpful and correct information on topics discussed.

In this section we introduced an effective approach to Interaction Mining. We demonstrated how argumentative analysis is essential for this approach and illustrated what kind of difference this can make in the area of focus group interviews, contact centers and opinion mining of user-generated content.

5 A ROADMAP FOR INTERACTION MINING

Interaction Mining is clearly in its infancy. The traditional works on Business Analytics, Business Intelligence and Text Mining have shown their intrinsic limitations to cope with conversational data. However, the power of recent NLP/NLU technology make a new generation of analytics tools possible that will eventually meet the requirements we detailed in Section 3.

We suggest a roadmap for research and development in this new area by highlighting the domains where work is still needed in order to solve outstanding problems.

First, we need to improve the quality of conversation analysis. For instance, the evaluation of accuracy of the state-of-the-art argumentative labeling system is still around 80%. To fully unleash the power of argumentative analysis, any system should also be able to compute the back-link between turns (e.g. the "replies to" and "elaborates" relations). This is fundamental if one wants to fully understand the conversation dynamics and detect relevant patterns of consensus/disagreement between participants.

Substantial work needs to be done in understanding, which Data Mining technique would help in discovering relevant patterns from conversation analysis data. We outlined a simple, but powerful technique, association mining, which might help the analyst in spotting issues in contact centers conversations. It might also help in generating a handy knowledge base from which contact center agents can look up during their interaction with clients. We believe that argumentative features can be leveraged to classification tasks as well, for instance in order to aggregate conversations as documents by their similarity (e.g. two conversations can be considered as similar regardless of the word uttered but on the basis of the type of interaction).

Another important aspect is related to visualization of results. We made our case by providing

Figure 12. Dashboard for Interaction Mining applications

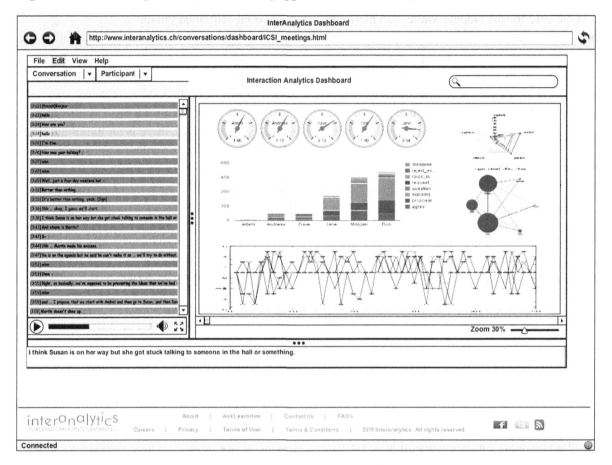

visualizations of analyzed data through off-the-shelf tools such as Microsoft Excel. Already with a low-end visualization tool we are able to provide relevant insights for Interaction Mining. We also did an exercise to imagine how an Interaction Mining dashboard would look like. In Figure 12, we provide a mock-up of a web-based Interaction Mining dashboard, which displays the conversation transcription on the left, as well as the video (if any) of the recorded conversation. This might look very similar to meeting browser such as those described in (AMI Consortium, 2007). However, we also present some other information that is missing in such tools. In the central part of the dashboard, we show a spider diagram, which displays the participants' attitudes. Below, we display a timeline where each participant contribution is

plotted on a scale of cooperativeness. The diagram is similar to the conversation graph proposed in (Pallotta, Delmonte, & Ailomaa, 2010).

All the diagrams we have shown in Section 4 could be integrated in the dashboard at the analyst's convenience. Moreover, we also believe that effort should be done to ensure interoperability between Interaction Mining tools sources of conversations such as Social Media, VoIP systems, and qualitative research tools.

Finally, we believe that it is of fundamental importance to build a repository of sample data for experimenting new techniques and tools. At the current state, it is very difficult to put hands on significant data. On the one hand, corporate conversational data is typically confidential. On the other, conversations from the Web are sometimes difficult to extract due to lack of APIs[23]. As it is the case for the Google Wave, this platform provides an excellent conversational space on the web. We suggest that extracting[24] and analyzing conversations from Wave would be an excellent example of integration of a collaborative conversational platform with Interaction Mining tools.

CONCLUSION

Today there is a wealth of unstructured information available to businesses; a wealth that remains mostly untapped. So far, tapping into this information richness was costly, complex and time-consuming because it needed to be done manually. Automated analysis (Text Mining) would typically miss this richness altogether. Nowadays, much of our competitiveness is based on the robustness of our business analytics. Since traditional business analytics is quickly becoming a hygiene factor, Interaction Mining—we believe—will become the new differentiator.

Business Analytics typically aims at understanding business data using quantitative (statistical) methods resulting in actionable insights. Interaction Mining extends these standard approaches as it extracts rich information from unstructured customers' interactions. The difficulty is that conversations are difficult to process with standard Text Mining tools because it is unstructured data, which need to be understood within its pragmatic context.

We indicated that the user requirements for Interaction Mining are distinctly different and more demanding and illustrated this in three business domains (focus groups, contact centers, and opinion mining). We then took the hardest conversational data (face-to-face conversations) and build a case what argumentative analysis can contribute. The examples (again in focus groups, contact centers, and opinion mining) showed that automated argumentative analysis, when necessary combined with association mining, could

unlock the wealth of unstructured information that so far remained untapped.

However, much research still remains to be done. We need to improve the quality of analysis, understand which Data mining technique aids the discovery of relevant patterns from conversation analysis data, and improve the visualization of results. Furthermore, there is an important need for sample data to facilitate the above.

REFERENCES

Autonomy. (n.d.). Multichannel customer interaction strategy: Identify customer patterns to drive world class customer experience.

Bales, R. (1950). *Interaction process analysis: A method for the study of small groups.* Cambridge, MA: Addison-Wesley.

Blakemore, D. (2002). *Meaning and relevance: The semantics and pragmatics of discourse markers.* Cambridge University Press. doi:10.1017/CBO9780511486456

Büttcher, S., Clarke, C., & Cormack, G. (2010). *Information retrieval: Implementing and evaluating search engines.* MIT Press.

Catterall, M., & Maclaran, P. (1997). Focus group data and qualitative analysis programs: Coding the moving picture as well as the snapshots. *Sociological Research Online, 2*(1), par. 4.6.

Cohen, J. (1960). A coefficient of agreement for nominal scales. *Educational and Psychological Measurement, 20,* 37–46. doi:10.1177/001316446002000104

Consortium, A. M. I. (2007). *State of the art report: Meeting browsing.* Retrieved July 15, 2010, from http://www.amiproject.org/ami-scientific-portal/documentation/annual-reports/pdf/D9_3_5.pdf

Davenport, T. (2006). Competing on analytics. *Harward Business Review* (Special issue on Decision Making), 99-107.

Delmonte, R. (2007). *Computational linguistic text processing – Logical form, semantic interpretation, discourse relations and question answering.* New York, NY: Nova Science Publishers.

Delmonte, R., Bristot, A., & Pallotta, V. (2010). Deep linguistic processing with GETARUNS for spoken dialogue understanding. *Proceedings of LREC 2010 Conference.* Malta: LREC Press.

Delmonte, R., & Pallotta, V. (2010). Opinion mining and sentiment analysis need text understanding. *Proceedings of 4th International Workshop on Distributed Agent-based Information Retrieval,* Geneva.

Feldman, R., & Sanger, J. (2006). *The Text Mining handbook. Advanced approaches in analyzing unstructured data.* Cambridge University Press. doi:10.1017/CBO9780511546914

Grimes, S. (2010, January 21). *Breakthrough analysis: Two + nine types of semantic search.* Retrieved July 1st, 2010, from http://www.informationweek.com/ news/showArticle.jhtml ?articleID=222400100

Intertek. (2002). *Management report on leveraging unstructured data in investment management.* Paris, France: The Intertek Group.

Janin, A., Baron, D., Edwards, J., Ellis, D., Gelbart, D., Morgan, N., et al. (2003). The ICSI meeting corpus. *Proceedings of IEEE/ICASSP* (pp. 364-367). Hong Kong: IEEE Press.

Kirk, J. (2006, February 7). *Analytics buzzword needs careful definition.* Retrieved October 29, 2010, from http://www.computerworld.com /s/ article/108460/ _Analytics_buzzword_ needs_ careful_definition

Landauer, T. K., Foltz, P. W., & Laham, D. (1998). Introduction to latent semantic analysis. *Discourse Processes, 25,* 259–284. doi:10.1080/01638539809545028

Liu, B. (2010). Sentiment analysis and subjectivity. In Indurkhya, N., & Damerau, F. J. (Eds.), *Handbook of natural language processing* (2nd ed.).

Mitkov, R. (2003). *Oxford handbook of computational linguistics.* Oxford University Press.

NICE. (n.d.). *Cross-channel interaction analytics.* Retrieved July 1st, 2010, from http://www.nice.com/ solutions/enterprise /interaction_analytics.php

Pallotta, V. (2006). Framing arguments. *Proceedings of the International Conference on Argumentation ISSA.* Amsterdam, NL.

Pallotta, V. (2010). Content-based retrieval of distributed multimedia conversational data. In Vargiu, E., Soro, A., Armano, G., & Paddeu, G. (Eds.), *Information retrieval and mining in distributed environments. Springer Verlag series: Studies in Computational Intelligence.*

Pallotta, V., Delmonte, R., & Ailomaa, M. (2010). Summarization and visualization of digital conversations. *Proceedings of the 1st Workshop on Semantic Personalized Information Management, part of LREC 2010 Conference.* Malta.

Pallotta, V., Delmonte, R., & Bistrot, A. (2009). Abstractive summarization of voice communications. *Proceedings of the LTC'09 Conference on Language Technology and Computers.* Poznan, PL.

Pallotta, V., Seretan, V., & Ailomaa, M. (2007). User requirements analysis for meeting information retrieval based on query elicitation. *Proceedings of the 45th Annual Meeting of the Association for Computational Linguistics.* Prague, Czech Republic: ACL Press.

Pang, B., & Lee, L. (2008). *Opinion mining and sentiment analysis*, vol. 2 (pp. 1-2). Now Publisher: Foundations and Trends in Information Retrieval.

Shmueli, G., Patel, N., & Bruce, P. (2010). *Data mining for business intelligence*. Wiley.

Somasundaran, S., Wiebe, J., & Ruppenhofer, J. (2008). *Discourse level opinion interpretation*. The 22nd International Conference on Computational Linguistics (COLING-2008).

Tapscot, D., & Williams, A. (2006). *Wikinomics*. Penguin Group.

Verint. (n.d.). *Customer interaction analytics*. Retrieved July 1st, 2010, from http://www.bps.nl/brochures /intelli/IntelliFind.pdf

Watt, D. (2003). *Six degrees: The science of a connected age*. New York, NY: W. W. Norton.

KEY TERMS AND DEFINITIONS

Argumentation: The study of how language is used to support claims. It is a type of pragmatic analysis. In it simplest form, it studies how people use language for agreeing and disagreeing. In our specific context, it also aims at modeling the process of decision-making and conflict resolution during multi-party discussion.

Business Intelligence: Intelligence as in "Intelligence Services" aimed at discovering relevant patterns from data so that they can be used for strategic or tactical purposes in the enterprise. Business Intelligence suites might include tools for data analysis, reporting and visualization as well as tools for supporting decision such as trend analysis and forecasting.

Data Mining (Knowledge Discovery): It is part of Business Intelligence and it aims at discovering statistically relevant patterns from data. The most common types of analysis are: Classification, Clustering, Association Mining and Regression Analysis. Data Mining typically applies to structured data (e.g. data bases). In order to apply Data Mining to unstructured data (e.g. text or conversations) one has to transform it into structured data. Text Mining is one possible approach to turn textual data into structured data.

Focus Group: An intentionally orchestrated series of group discussions aimed to get perceptions on a certain subject (product, interest, etc.) in a relaxed, open environment.

Natural Language Processing/Understanding: NLP/NLU technology is made of algorithms for processing and understanding natural language input and linguistic resources such as lexica, grammars, corpora and ontologies. Processing can be done at different linguistic levels such as syntax, semantics or pragmatics. Understanding of language happens when a system is capable to recognize user's intentions expressed through languages.

Pragmatics: The study of pragmatics pertains to the use of language to perform actions. It is based on the notion of "speech act," namely the action that is performed through the production of a linguistic expression. The language unit of pragmatic analysis is the "utterance." An utterance can be just a word (e.g. "yes" as an agreement) or even a discourse made of several sentences (e.g. a monologue made as an appraisal). In the specific case of this chapter, one form of pragmatic analysis is "argumentative" analysis.

Semantics: The study of language meaning. Semantics is relative to the language unit chosen. It can be word's semantics, sentence's semantics or discourse semantics. It usually refers to the link between expressions and objects (being real of fictive). In other words, semantics is about WHAT is referred by language.

Social Media: media supporting the production of content through social interaction. The content results as the byproduct of conversations between socially connected people that interact by using social communication channel. Social Media are possible because of i) a social connection infrastructure and ii) user-generated content.

Social Media subvert the conventional publishing model, which is mediated by "editors." In Social Media, authors and readers are the same entity. Content can be (and is indeed) created by users. Social Media have larger reach for users as the content is often indexed by search engines. This means that topic of interest and their attached communities can be easily discovered by new users, who will eventually become members and (hopefully) contributors. Social Media foster dialogue over monologues.

Syntax: A basic level of language structure that considers grammatical functions of the words and their aggregation into larger structures within the boundaries of the sentence. Syntax is usually used to check the "well-formedness" of a sentence (e.g. in orthographic checkers) and for determining what are the semantic relations between the sentence constituents (e.g. the subject, objects, predicate in a phrase).

Text Business Analytics: All kind of computer tools that analyze unstructured data and turn qualitative information in textual form into measurable data. Also referred as Text Mining, it focus in extracting content from textual data and aggregate the content extracted from large number of similar documents (e.g. news, emails, web pages). Usually, standard Text Business Analytics tools do not take the context (e.g. location, author, time, relationships with other information) of the information pieces into account.

ENDNOTES

[1] The authors are co-founders of InterAnalytics, Geneva, Switzerland, www.interanalytics.ch.

[2] TF-IDF stands for Term Frequency-Inverse Document Frequency. It is a common weighting schema in information retrieval and a statistical measure used to evaluate how important a word is to a document in a collection or corpus.

[3] http://wordnet.princeton.edu/

[4] Methods can be used to assess the level of subjectivity in analysis by comparing analyses of the same data performed by different analysts. This can be achieved by computing the Kappa agreement between the analysts (Cohen, 1960). Usually, subjectivity focus group analysis lies on the choice of the coding scheme and not just on the assignments of codes to text. This makes Kappa agreement test unusable.

[5] Natural Language Understanding

[6] See for example (Intertek, 2002): "The technology for searching and analyzing textual data is based on the ability of computers to handle the meaning (i.e., semantics) of content. While humans can read and understand texts, computers can not."

[7] www.epinions.com

[8] Gartner group mentioned Social Analytics as one of the top 10 strategic technologies that will have "significant impact" on the enterprise over the next three years (2011-2013).

[9] http://www.sas.com/software/customer-intelligence/social-media-analytics/

[10] http://www.viralheat.com/

[11] http://www.alterian.com/

[12] www.research.ibm.com/UIMA/

[13] http://gate.ac.uk/

[14] http://en.wikipedia.org/wiki/Customer_relationship_management

[15] Objectivity is often not even included because it is typically considered to be impossible to be objective in analyzing interviews. There are, however, ways to increase objectivity such as using more analysts for the analysis and having a threshold of cross-analyst agreement. In reality this is most of the time too expensive and time consuming.

[16] http://www.qsrinternational.com

[17] http://www.atlasti.com

[18] http://en.wikipedia.org/wiki/Speech_analytics

[19] Also referred to as Affinity Analysis: http://en.wikipedia.org/wiki/Affinity_analysis

[20] http://wave.google.com

[21] This is already possible in Excel. When clicking on an element of a pivot table or chart, a new sheet is created that contains the relevant rows.

[22] http://www.resample.com/xlminer/index.shtml

[23] See (Pallotta, 2010) for more details on digital and online conversations.

[24] FerryBot (http://ferrybot.appspot.com/) is a simple Wave robot that exports a conversation into Google docs. At the current state it does not preserve the names of the speakers for each turn.

Chapter 7
OpAL:
A System for Mining Opinion from Text for Business Applications

Alexandra Balahur
University of Alicante, Spain

Ester Boldrini
University of Alicante, Spain

Andrés Montoyo
University of Alicante, Spain

Patricio Martínez-Barco
University of Alicante, Spain

ABSTRACT

The past years have marked the birth and development of the Social Web, where people freely express and search for opinions on all possible topics. This phenomenon has been proven to have a great impact on many business sectors globally. Given the proven importance of the subjective data on the Web, but bearing in mind the difficulties inherent to their textual peculiarities and large volume, efficient techniques must be employed to process this data, so that it can be fully exploited to the benefit of potential users and companies. We present the OpAL system, which implements an efficient approach to mine, classify and statistically summarize opinions, grounded on the feature-based Opinion Mining paradigm. In this approach, all components are studied, implemented and optimized using different NLP techniques. Results of different in-house and competition evaluations show that the system components have a good performance and that the techniques considered are efficient. We finally complete the proposed approach by presenting a method for opinion retrieval, which is robust and multilingual. Thus, we offer an integrated solution to build a system that is able to fully respond to user needs, from the querying to the summarized output stage. Implemented at a large scale, such systems can benefit the business environment and its customers everywhere.

DOI: 10.4018/978-1-61350-038-5.ch007

INTRODUCTION

Humans are social beings. They cannot reach the level of what we call "human" unless they develop in organized societies, where they are taught norms, rules and laws governing the existence and co-existence of people. Although most of the times unconsciously, we continuously shape our behavior and attitudes on the basis of these social conventions, of public and private opinions and events of the world surrounding us. We give and accept advice as part of our every-day lives, as part of a ritual to knowing, better understanding and integrating into our surrounding reality.

In a globalized world, however, the whole idea of context changes. Supported by the fast development of the Internet and the Web 2.0 technologies, with the predominant presence of social networks, forums, "blogging" and reviewing as world-wide phenomena, giving and receiving advice has become a global phenomenon. One that we give into more and more every day, as decisions to buy products or contract services, for example, are nowadays preceded by an internet search for opinions in many of the cases [Pang and Lee, 2008]. People express and search for such opinions on blogs, forums, in reviews and comments - a phenomenon which led to the creation of extensive quantities of subjective data that cannot be manually processed, although the knowledge they enclose is crucial to the business and social environments.

At the economic level, the globalization of markets combined with the fact that people can freely express their opinion on any product or company on forums, blogs or e-commerce sites led to a change in the companies' marketing strategies, in the rise of awareness for client needs and complaints, and a special attention for brand trust and reputation. Specialists in market analysis, but also IT fields such as Natural Language Processing, demonstrated that in the context of the newly created opinion phenomena, decisions for economic action are not only given by factual information, but are highly affected by rumors

and negative opinions. Studies showed that financial information presented in news articles have a high correlation to social phenomena, on which opinions are expressed in blogs, forums or reviews. Investigations carried out in market analysis, as for example the Technorati survey series[1], assesses that opinions found in blogs and news correlate with the subsequent changes in sales. This is also exemplified by Mishne and Glance(2005), where the authors demonstrate that references to movies in blogs correlate well with the previous and subsequent success rate of a movie. Koppel and Shtrimberg(2004) investigate the influence of news of positive and negative polarity on rises and falls in stock market. Lexical-based opinion analysis models have shown up to 70% accuracy in predicting the corresponding actual price change and other research [Devitt and Ahmad, 2007] suggests that markets react to the same extent to affect-related parts of text as to the informative sections.

On the other hand, many tasks that involved extensive efforts from the companies' marketing departments are easier to perform. An example is related to market research for business intelligence and competitive vigilance. New forms of expression on the web made it easier to collect information of interest, which can help to detect changes in the market attitude, discover new technologies, machines, markets where products are needed and detect threats. Moreover, using the opinion information, companies can spot the market segments their products are best associated with and can enhance their knowledge on the clients they are addressing and on competitors. The analysis of the data flow on the web can lead to the spotting of differences between the companies' products and the necessities expressed by clients and between the companies' capacities and those of the competitors. Last, but not least, the interpretation of the large amounts of data and their associated opinions can give companies the capacity to support decision through the detection of new ideas and new solutions to their technological or economic problems. The advantage and, at the same time, issue related to these new capabilities is the large amount of information available and its fast growing rate. As lack of information on markets and their corresponding social and economical data leads to wrong or late decisions and finally to important financial losses, the opinion data needs to be processed automatically, by high-accuracy systems capable to work in real-time.

Motivated by this proven necessity to research on automatic methods to mine the opinions, the past years have registered the birth and rapid development of a new task within the field of Natural Language Processing: opinion mining (OM), also known as sentiment analysis (SA).

In this chapter, we first present an overview of the task, as it was defined and approached within different scenarios of use. We then concentrate on describing the opinion mining task in the context of product reviews, which in the literature bears the name of "feature-based opinion mining and summarization" [Hu and Liu, 2004]. Subsequently, we show the manner in which we build, within this context, the OpAL system that detects, classifies and summarizes opinions on products and their features, in English and Spanish. In order to demonstrate the challenges of this task, we present an external evaluation performed on one of the components of the system, within the SemEval 2010 forum and show that our approach can be easily ported to other languages. As the feature-based opinion mining and summarization task is performed on already-extracted reviews, we further on investigate methods to appropriately retrieve the opinionated texts on which the built system is applied. We present the results of the evaluation of these approaches in the NTCIR-8 MOAT (Multilingual Opinion Analysis Task) forum, demonstrating their performance and scalability in a multilingual environment. We conclude by summarizing our findings on the opinion mining task in the product review domain and by reflecting on the need, usefulness and maturity of such technologies in the business landscape.

BACKGROUND

Subjectivity is defined by Wiebe (1994) as the "linguistic expression of somebody's opinions, sentiments, emotions, evaluations, beliefs and speculations." In her definition, the author was inspired by the work of the linguist Ann Banfield [Banfield, 1982], who defines as subjective the "sentences that take a character's point of view" [Uspensky, 1973] and that present *private states* [Quirk, 1985] (that are not open to objective observation or verification) of an experiencer, holding an attitude, optionally towards an object. Subjectivity is opposed to objectivity, which is the expression of facts. The NLP task of subjectivity analysis aims at detecting subjectivity in text.

SA was formally defined as "a recent discipline at the crossroads of information retrieval and computational linguistics which is concerned not with the topic a document is about, but with the opinion it expresses." [Esuli and Sebastiani, 2006]

For practical applications, SA can be briefly defined as the task of extracting, from a given set of documents, the opinion expressed on a certain "target," by an a priori given "source" and classifying it depending on the *polarity* (orientation of the opinion) it has, into positive or negative. Sometimes the neutral category is defined, which, in fact, is considered in many research approaches as being the correspondent of "objectivity" in subjectivity analysis. Sentiment analysis can be dependently or independently done from subjectivity analysis. Nevertheless, authors such as Pang and Lee (2003) state that subjectivity analysis performed prior to the sentiment analysis leads to better results in the latter.

Sentiment analysis can be done at different levels, depending on the degree of detail that one wishes or requires in order to take an informed decision. While detecting the general sentiment expressed in a review on a movie suffices to take the decision to see it or not, when buying an electronics product, booking a room in a hotel or travelling to a certain destination, users weigh different arguments in favor or against, depending on the "features" they are most interested in (e.g. "weight" versus "screen size," "good location" versus "price").

There are three main research areas within sentiment analysis:

1. *Creation of resources* (corpora annotated with opinion and lexica of polar words) for sentiment analysis/ opinion mining;
2. *Classification of text*, whose main aim is finding expressions of emotion and classifying the texts into positive and negative. This task has been approached at a document, sentence, phrase and word level;
3. *Opinion extraction*, which is concerned with finding parts of text with opinion, identifying the polarity of the sentiment expressed and determining the source and target of the sentiment expressed. This category also includes the retrieval of opinionated snippets that comply with the conditions specified in the query (i.e. to find opinions of the required polarity, given by the source that is stated in the query, towards the target specified).

Further on, we will detail the background of these three research directions, specifying their relatedness to our approach.

1. In the first research area, a series of techniques were used to obtain lexicons of subjective words (e.g. the Opinion Finder lexicon [Wilson et al., 2005] and opinion words with associated polarity). Hu and Liu (2004) start with a set of seed adjectives ("good" and "bad") and apply synonymy and antonymy relations in WordNet. A similar approach was used in building WordNet Affect [Strapparava and Valitutti, 2004], starting from a larger set of seed affective words, classified according to the six basic categories of emotion (joy, sadness, fear, surprise, anger and disgust) and expanding the lexicon using paths in WordNet. Another

related method was used in the creation of SentiWordNet [Esuli and Sebastiani, 2005], employing a set of seed words whose polarity was known and expanded using gloss similarity. The collection of appraisal terms in [Whitelaw et al., 2005], the terms also have polarity assigned. MicroWNOp [Cerini et al., 2007], another lexicon containing opinion words with their associated polarity, was built on the basis of a set of terms extracted from the General Inquirer lexicon and by subsequently adding all the synsets in WordNet where these words appear. Other methods built sentiment lexicons using the local context of words. Pang et al. (2002) built a lexicon of sentiment words with associated polarity value, starting with a set of classified seed adjectives and using conjunctions ("and") disjunctions ("or," "but") to deduce the orientation of new words in a corpus. Turney (2002) classifies words according to their polarity on the basis of the idea that terms with similar orientation tend to co-occur in documents. Thus, the author computes the Pointwise Mutual Information score between seed words and new words on the basis of the number of AltaVista hits returned when querying the seed word and the word to be classified with the "NEAR" operator. In our work [Balahur and Montoyo, 2008a], we compute the polarity of new words using "polarity anchors" (words whose polarity is known beforehand) and Normalized Google Distance [Cilibrasi and Vitanyi, 2006] scores. In a subsequent approach, we compare the performance obtained using this metric to the one resulted using Latent Semantic Analysis [Deerwester et al., 1990]. Another approach that uses the polarity of the local context for computing word polarity is the one proposed by Popescu and Etzioni (2005), who use a weighting function of the words around the context to be classified.

Given the proven importance of the context to the correct classification of adjectives according to their polarity, the SemEval-2010 evaluation forum set up Task 18 [Wu and Jia, 2010], whose aim was to disambiguate 14 sentiment ambiguous adjectives in context. The language of the competition was Traditional Chinese. 7 systems participated in this task, with a total of 16 runs. The top scoring systems, YSC-DSAA [Yang and Liu, 2010] and HITSZ_CITYU [Xu et al., 2010], which ranked first to 4th use extensive manually crafted rules, dictionaries and heuristics. They determine the polarity of the adjectives in the context as a relation between opinion words and the target of the text or as a relation between surrounding local context (at a clause level) and the clause containing the sentiment ambiguous adjective. Our OpAL system [Balahur and Montoyo, 2010], for which we submitted one run, ranked fifth in terms of micro-accuracy. This system used three strategies, combining supervised methods with web validation and a set of heuristics for computing local polarity based on the presence of modifiers. The CityUHK [Lu and Tsou, 2010] system employed machine learning on the NTCIR[2] (NII Test Collection for IR Systems Project) data at clause and sentence levels. Another interesting approach is that is used in the Twitter sentiment system [Pak and Paroubek, 2010], which employs as training corpus tweets, automatically classified into positive and negative based on the emoticons they contain.

2. Regarding the second class of approaches, previous work includes document level sentiment classification using unsupervised methods [Turney, 2002], lexicon-based techniques [Pang et al., 2002], scoring of features [Dave et al., 2003], using PMI, syntactic relations and other attributes with SVM [Mullen and Collier, 2004], sentiment classification considering rating scales [Pang et al., 2002], supervised and unsupervised methods [Chaovalit and Zhou, 2005] and

semi-supervised learning [Goldberg and Zhu, 2006]. Research in classification at a document level included sentiment classification of reviews [Ng et al., 2006], sentiment classification on customer feedback data [Gamon et al., 2005], comparative experiments [Cui et al., 2006]. Other research has been conducted in analyzing sentiment at a sentence level using bootstrapping techniques [Riloff and Wiebe, 2003], considering gradable adjectives [Hatzivassiloglou and Wiebe, 2000], semi-supervised learning with the initial training set identified by some strong patterns and then applying NB or self-training [Wiebe and Riloff, 2006], finding strength of opinions [Wilson et al., 2004] sum up orientations of opinion words in a sentence (or within some word window) [Kim and Hovy, 2004], [Lin et al., 2006], determining the semantic orientation of words and phrases [Turney, 2002], [Turney and Littman, 2003], identifying opinion holders [Stoyanov and Cardie, 2006], comparative sentence and relation extraction and feature-based opinion mining and summarization [Hu and Liu, 2004].

The latter performs sentiment analysis at the feature level. This task is also known as "feature-based opinion mining and summarization" [Hu and Liu, 2004, Liu, 2007, Ding, 2008] (previously defined by Dave et al.in 2003) and is defined as the task of extracting, given an "object" (product, event, person etc.), the features of the object and the opinion words used in texts in relation to the features, classify the opinion words and produce a final summary containing the percentages of positive versus negative opinions expressed on each of the features. Feature-based opinion mining involves a series of tasks:

• Task 1: Identify and extract object features that have been commented on by an opinion holder (e.g., a reviewer).

- Task 2: Determine whether the opinions on the features are positive, negative or neutral.
- Task 3: Group feature synonyms.

Subsequently, once all the groups of words referring the same feature are gathered and the polarity of the opinion is computed, the result is presented as a percentage of positive versus negative opinion on each feature (feature-based opinion summary of multiple reviews). This is accomplished by computing the percentage of positive and negative opinions per feature; it is not a summarization in the sense of the traditional NLP task. For the identification of features, authors used "pros and cons" reviews and label sequential rules based on training sequences, employed to define extraction rules [Popescu and Etzioni, 2005]. Frequent features were mined using sequential pattern mining (frequent phrases) and patterns for "part of" relations were defined [Ding et al., 2008]. Infrequent features were discovered with similarity in WordNet. Polarity classification was done using as start point the "good" and "bad" adjectives and exploring the synonyms and antonyms of these words in WordNet [Hu and Liu, 2004], using weighting functions depending on surrounding words [Popescu and Etzioni, 2005] or using local conjunction or disjunction relations with words with priory known polarity [Ding et al., 2008]. Grouping of feature synonyms was done using relations in WordNet.

Present research has not included the discovery of implicit features and furthermore, it has left the problem of explicit features dependent on the mentioning of these features in the individual user reviews or not. The authors describe approaches that are lexicon-based and consist in discovering frequent features using association mining and determining the semantic orientation of opinions as polarity of adjectives (as opinion holders) that features are described by. The classification of adjectives is done starting with a list of seeds and completing it using the WordNet synonymy

and antonym relations. Infrequent features are deduced using the opinion holders. However, the fact that there is no well-organized structure of features and sub-features of products leads to the fact that, for example, the summarization of opinions is done for 720 features for an mp3 player [Ding et al., 2008].

The question that arises is: would a user in a real-life situation be interested on whether the edges of a camera are round or flat and what the previous buyers think about that, or would a potential buyer like to see if the design of the product is fine or not, according to the many criteria developed by buyers to assess this feature?

Another issue with the current research in the field is that the work does not approach implicit features and does not classify the orientation of adjectives depending on the context. A solution to the latter problem is presented by Ding et al. (2008) where the authors take a holistic approach to classifying adjectives, that is, consider not only the local context in which they appear next to the feature they determine, but also other adjectives appearing with the feature and their polarity in different contexts. In the research by Popescu and Etzioni (2005), a more complex approach is used for feature-based summarization of opinions, employing web Pointwise Mutual Information (PMI) statistics for the explicit feature extraction and a technique called relaxation labeling for the assignment of polarity to opinions. In this approach, dependency parsing is used together with ten extraction rules that were developed intuitively. The method we propose is language and customer-review independent. It extracts a set of general product features, finds product specific features and feature attributes and is thus applicable to all possible reviews in a product class.

3. The third direction for research in opinion mining concentrates on the challenges raised by more complex systems that aim not only at classifying the already-found opinionated texts, but also at retrieving them and extract-

ing answers to opinionated questions. As we have seen, classifying products according to the opinions expressed on their features is in itself a challenging task. Nonetheless, it is alone insufficient, as real systems must first be able to interpret queries or questions given by users to accurately extract what he/ she is looking for. Therefore, an important related task, which has to be solved in order to create real-life application systems, is opinion retrieval, or, in a more complex setting, Opinion Question Answering (OQA). This field has only recently been approached and there are only few studies that focus on the development of OQA systems. An example of such an approach is the one proposed by Cardie et al. (2003), who took advantage of opinion summarization to support Multi-Perspective QA system, aiming at extracting opinion-oriented information answering a non-factual question. Yu and Hatzivassiloglou (2003) discriminated opinions from facts and summarized them as answers to opinion questions. Kim and Hovy (2005) identified opinion holders, which are an important component to be determined when analyzing and answering opinion questions. In the past years, efforts have also concentrated in organizing international conferences encouraging the creation of effective QA systems, both for fact as well as subjective texts. The TAC 2008[3] Opinion QA track proposed a collection of factoid and opinion queries called "rigid list" (factoid) and "squishy list" (opinion) respectively, to which the traditional systems had to be adapted. Some participating systems treated opinionated questions as "other" and thus did not employ opinion- specific methods. However, systems that performed better in the "squishy list" questions than in the "rigid list" implemented additional components to classify the polarity of the question and of the extracted answer snippet. The

Alyssa system [Wiegand et al., 2008] uses a Support Vector Machines (SVM) classifier trained on the MPQA corpus [Wiebe et al., 2005], English NTCIR[4] data and rules based on the subjectivity lexicon [Wilson et al., 2005]. Varma et al. (2008) performed query analysis to detect the polarity of the question using defined rules. Furthermore, they filter opinion from fact retrieved snippets using a classifier based on Naïve Bayes with unigram features, assigning for each sentence a score that is a linear combination between the opinion and the polarity scores. The PolyU system [Wenjie et al., 2008] determines the sentiment orientation of the sentence using the Kullback-Leibler divergence measure with the two estimated language models for the positive versus negative categories. The QUANTA system [Li et al., 2008] performs opinion question sentiment analysis by detecting the opinion holder, the object and the polarity of the opinion. It uses a semantic labeler based on PropBank[5] and manually defined patterns. Regarding the sentiment classification, they extract and classify the opinion words. Finally, for the answer retrieval, they score the retrieved snippets depending on the presence of topic and opinion words and only choose as answer the top ranking results.

Another competition that has been organized in the past years is the NTCIR MOAT (Multilingual Opinion Analysis Task) evaluation forum. This challenge aims at creating a benchmark for building not only monolingual systems that are able to retrieve opinionated snippets and answer opinionated questions, but porting the technologies used in these systems to the cross-lingual level. In the most recent edition of this competition, NTCIR-8 MOAT [Seki et al., 2010], 5 subtasks were proposed, either for the monolingual setting (in English, Japanese, Simplified and Traditional Chinese) or the cross-lingual one (in any combination of these three languages). The participants were given a set of 20 opinion questions and, for each of these, a set of documents split at the sentence level and the same set split at the opinion unit level. In the first two subtasks, the aim was to annotate each of the sentences pertaining to the first test set as to whether they are opinionated, and if yes, relevant to the given question. In the last three subtasks, the participating systems had to employ the test set annotated at the opinion level to detect their polarity, source (opinion holders) and target. Best scoring systems used lexicon-based approaches, different machine learning algorithms (Maximum Entropy, Support Vector Machines) and combinations of the two using voting schemes.

MAIN FOCUS OF THE CHAPTER

OpAL: A System for Feature-Based Opinion Mining and Summarization

The main focus of this chapter is to present the OpAL system, an application developed on the feature-based opinion mining paradigm. The methodology employed to build OpAL was first put forward in [Balahur and Montoyo, 2008c, Balahur and Montoyo, 2008d, Balahur and Montoyo, 2008e]. This system automatically analyzes and extracts the values of the features for a given product, independently of the language the customer review is written in. It can then show the potential buyer the percentages of positive and negative opinions expressed about each of the product features (opinion summarization) and make suggestions based on buyer preferences. The system works for Spanish and English. However, the algorithm is language independent and can be extended to work in any language where similar NLP resources and tools as the ones used herein exist. In order to detect the product category, we use a modified system for person names classification. The raw review text is split

into sentences and depending on the product class detected, only the phrases containing the specific product features are selected for further processing. The phrases extracted pass through a process of anaphora resolution, Named Entity Recognition and syntactic parsing. Furthermore, applying syntactic dependency and part of speech patterns, we extract pairs containing the feature and the polarity of the feature attribute the customer associates to the feature in the review. On top of this system, we add a set of manually built patterns that were built to spot the opinions expressed in an indirect manner. Eventually, we statistically summarize the polarity of the opinions different customers expressed about the product on the web as percentages of positive and negative opinions about each of the product features. We show the results and improvements over baseline, together with a discussion on the strong and weak points of the method and the directions for future work. In the proposed approach, we concentrated on two main problems. The first one was that of discovering the features that will be quantified. As previously noticed in [Liu, 2007], features can be implicit or explicit. To this respect, apart from a general class of features and their corresponding attributes, that are applicable to all products, we propose a method to discover product specific features and feature attributes using knowledge from WordNet [Miller et al., 1990] and Concept-Net[6]. The second problem we address is that of quantifying the features in a product-dependent manner, since, for example, small for the size of a digital camera is a positive fact, whereas for an LCD display it is a rather negative one. We accomplish this by classifying the feature attributes using positive and negative examples from a customer opinions corpus annotated with the polarity depending on the product category and SMO SVM Machine Learning [Platt, 1998] with the Normalized Google Distance and Latent Semantic Analysis.

In order to demonstrate the validity our classification method for adjectives whose polarity

Figure 1. Preprocessing stage

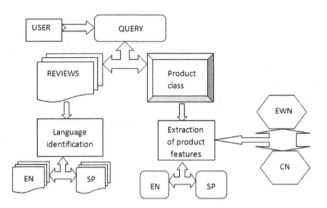

depends on the local context, we present the approach we used in the OpAL system's participation in the SemEval-2 Task 18[7] (Disambiguation of Sentiment-Ambiguous Adjectives). In this challenge, we extend the initial system, employing three different modules to assign the appropriate polarity to such adjectives, in close dependency to the local context; we thus intent to offer a solution to local context dependency of adjective polarity, in a multilingual setting. We illustrate the manner in which we solved the abovementioned problems with examples and discuss on the issues raised at each step by using different methods, tools and resources. Finally, we complete OpAL system for opinion mining and classification, by proposing adequate solutions to the retrieval and filtering of relevant, opinionated data, in a multilingual setting. We present and discuss on the evaluation of these approaches in the NTCIR 8 MOAT[8] competition.

Preprocessing

We start from the following scenario: a user enters a query about a product that the user is interested to buy. The search engine retrieves a series of documents containing the product name, in different languages, from a specific source of information (usually an e-commerce review site

such as "ciao.es," "amazon.com," "epinions.com"). This operation is done on-line, whereas the subsequent processing is performed offline. Further on, two parallel operations are performed: the first one uses the Lextek[9] language identifier software to filter and obtain two categories one containing the reviews in English and the other the reviews in Spanish. The second operation implies a modified version of the system described in [Kozareva et al., 2007] for the classification of person names to determine the class of products the query refers to (e.g. digital camera, laptop, printer), using similar and discriminatory terms for it. This is important at the time of determining the product features. Once the product category is determined, we extract the product specific features and feature attributes using WordNet and ConceptNet and the corresponding mapping to Spanish using EuroWordNet[10]. We also consider a core of features and feature attributes that are product-independent and whose importance determines their frequent occurrence in customer reviews. Figure 1 summarizes the steps performed at this preprocessing stage. Each component of this figure is explained in the following sections.

Product-Independent Features and Feature Attributes

There are a series of features that are product independent and that are important to any prospective buyer. We consider these the core of product features. For each of these concepts, we retrieve from WordNet the synonyms, which have the same Relevant Domain [Vázquez et al., 2004], the hyponyms of the concepts and their synonyms and attributes, respectively.

Using WordNet to Extract Product Specific Features and Feature Attributes

Once the product category has been identified, we use WordNet to extract the product specific features and feature attributes. We should notice that, contrary to the observation made in [Dave et al., 2003], once we establish the product, its corresponding term in WordNet is sense disambiguated and thus the obtained meronyms, synonyms and corresponding attributes are no longer ambiguous. Moreover, the terms obtained in this manner, should they appear in customer reviews, have the intended meaning. We accomplish this in the following steps:

1. For the term defining the product category, we search its synonyms in WordNet [Fellbaum (ed.), 1998].
2. We eliminate the synonyms that do not have the same top relevant domain [Vázquez et al., 2004] as the term defining the product category
3. For the term defining the product, as well as each for each of the remaining synonyms, we obtain their meronyms from in WordNet, which constitute the parts forming the product.
4. Since WordNet does not contain much detail on the components of most of new technological products, we use ConceptNet

to complete the process of determining the specific product features. We explain the manner in which we use ConceptNet in the following section.

After performing the steps described above, we conclude the process of obtaining the possible terms that a customer buying a product will comment on. The final step consists in finding the attributes of the features discovered by applying the attributes relation in WordNet to each of the nouns representing product features. In the case of nouns which have no term associated by the *"has attribute"* relation, we add as attribute features the concepts found in ConceptNet under the OUT relations PropertyOf and CapableOf. In case the concepts added are adjectives, we add their synonyms and antonyms from WordNet. As result we have for example, in the case of "photo," the parts "raster" and "pixel" with the attributes "blurry," "clarity," "sharp."

Using ConceptNet to Extract Product Specific Features and Feature Attributes

ConceptNet [Liu and Singh, 2004] is a freely available commonsense knowledgebase and natural-language-processing toolkit, which supports many practical textual reasoning tasks over real-world documents. Commonsense knowledge in ConceptNet encompasses the spatial, physical, social, temporal, and psychological aspects of everyday life. It contains relations such as CapableOf, ConceptuallyRelatedTo, IsA, LocationOf etc. In order to obtain additional features for the product in question, we add the concepts that are related to the term representing the concept with terms related in ConceptNet by the OUT relations UsedFor and CapableOf and the IN relations PartOf and UsedFor. For example, for the product "camera," the OUT UsedFor and CapableOf relations that will added are "take picture," "take photograph," "photography," "create image," "record image" and for the IN PartOf and UsedFor relations "shutter," "viewfinder," "flash," "tripod."

Mapping Concepts Using EuroWordNet

EuroWordNet (EWN) is a multilingual database with WordNets for different European languages (Dutch, Italian, Spanish, German, French, Czeck and Estonian). Each language has its own designed WordNet, structured as the Princeton WordNet. Having these connections, it is possible that parting from one word, one can consult similar words in any other language of the EWN. The main advantage of this lexical resource is that all the terms discovered in one language can be easily mapped to another one. We employ EuroWordNet and map the features and feature attributes, both from the main core of words, as well as the product specific ones that were previously discovered for English, independent of the sense number, taking into account only the preservation of the relevant domain. We are aware of the noise introduced by this mapping. However in the preliminary research we found that the concepts introduced that had no relation to the product queried did not appear in the user product reviews.

Discovering Overlooked Product Features

The majority of product features we have identified so far are parts constituting products. However, there remains a class of undiscovered features that are indirectly related to the product. These are the features of the product constituting parts, such as battery life, picture resolution, auto mode. Further, we propose to extract these overlooked product features by determining bigrams made up of target words constituting features and other words in a corpus of customer reviews. In the case of digital cameras, for example, we considered a corpus of 200 customer reviews on which we ran Pedersen's Ngram Statistics Package to determine

target co-occurrences of the features identified so far. As measure for term association, we use the Pointwise Mutual Information score, which is calculated according to the following Equation 1.

$$PMI(x, y) = \frac{P(x, y)}{P(x) P(y)} \qquad (1)$$

where x and y are two words and P(x) stands for the probability of the word x occurring in the corpus considered. In this manner, we discover bigram features such as "battery life," "mode settings" and "screen resolution."

After all the product features are identified, the reviews together with the set of features for the corresponding products are passed on to the main processing modules.

Main Processing

The main processing in our system is done in parallel for English and Spanish. In the next section, we will briefly describe the steps followed in processing the initial input containing the customer reviews in the two considered language and offer as output the summarized opinions on the features considered. Figure 2 presents the steps included in the processing. We start from the reviews filtered according to the language they are written in. For each of the two language considered, we used a specialized tool for anaphora resolution- JavaRAP for English[11] and SUPAR [Ferrández et al., 1999] for Spanish. Further on, we separate the text into sentences and use a Named Entity Recognizer to spot names of products, brands or shops. Using the lists of general features and feature attributes, product-specific features and feature attributes, we extract from the set of sentences contained in the text only those containing at least one of the terms found in the lists.

Figure 2. System architecture

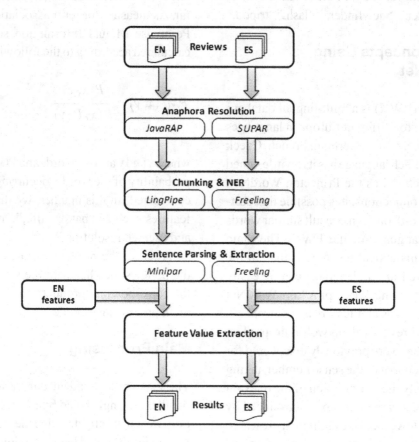

Anaphora Resolution

In order to solve the anaphoric references on the product features and feature attributes, we employ two anaphora resolution tools - JavaRAP for English and SUPAR for Spanish. Using these tools, we replace the anaphoric references with their corresponding referents and obtain a text in which the terms constituting product features could be found. JavaRAP is an implementation of the classic Resolution of Anaphora Procedure (RAP) given by [Lappin and Leass, 1994]. It resolves third person pronouns, lexical anaphors, and identifies pleonastic pronouns. Using JavaRAP, we obtain a version of the text in which pronouns and lexical references are resolved. For example, the text: "I bought this camera about a week ago,

and so far have found it very simple to use, takes good quality pics for what I use it for (outings with friends/family, special events). It is great that it already comes w/ a rechargeable battery that seems to last quite a while...," by resolving the anaphoric pronominal reference, becomes "I bought this camera about a week ago, and so far have found) <this camera > very very simple to use, takes good quality pics for what I use <this camera >for (outings with friends/family, special events). It is great that <this camera> already comes w/ a rechargeable battery that seems to last quite a while...."

We use SUPAR in the same manner as JavaRAP, to solve the anaphora for Spanish.

Sentence Chunking and NER

Further on, we split the text of the customer review into sentences and identify the named entities in the text. Splitting the text into sentences prevents us from processing sentences that have no importance as far as product features that a possible customer could be interested in are concerned. LingPipe[12] is a suite of Java libraries for the linguistic analysis of human language. It includes features such as tracking mentions of entities (e.g. people or proteins), part-of-speech tagging and phrase chunking. We use Lingpipe to split the customer reviews in English into sentences and identify the named entities referring to products of the same category as the product queried. In this manner, we can be sure that we identify sentences referring to the product queried, even the reference is done by making use of the name of another product. For example, in the text "For a little less, I could have bought the Nikon Coolpix, but it is worth the extra money." Anaphora resolution replaces <it> with <Nikon Coolpix>, but this step will replace <Nikon Coolpix> with <camera>. The FreeLing[13] package consists of a library providing language analysis services. The package offers many services, among, which are text tokenization, sentence splitting, POS-tagging, WordNet-based sense annotation and rule-based dependency parsing. We employ FreeLing in order to split the customer reviews in Spanish into sentences and identify the named entities referring to products of the same category as the product queried.

Sentence Extraction

Having completed the feature and feature attributes identification phase, we proceed to extracting for further processing only the sentences that contain the terms referring to the product, product features or feature attributes. In this manner, we avoid further processing of text that is of no importance to the task we wish to accomplish.

For example, sentences of the type "I work in the home appliances sector." will not be taken into account in further processing. Certainly, at the overall level of review impact, such a sentence might be of great importance to a reader, since it proves the expertise of the opinion given in the review. However, for the problems we wish to solve by using this method, such a sentence is of no importance.

Sentence Parsing

Each of the sentences that are filtered by the previous step are parsed in order to obtain the sentence structure and component dependencies. In order to accomplish this, we use Minipar [Lin, 1998] for English and FreeLing for Spanish. This step is necessary in order to be able to extract the values of the features mentioned based on the dependency between the attributes identified and the feature they determine.

Feature Value Extraction

Further on, we extract features and feature attributes from each of the identified sentences, using the following rules:

We introduce the following categories of context polarity shifters [Polanyi and Zaenen, 2004], in which we split the modifiers and modal operators in two categories: positive and negative:

- **Negation:** No, not, never etc.
- **Modifiers:** Positive (extremely, very, totally etc.) and negative (hardly, less, possibly etc.)
- **Modal Operators:** Positive (must, has) and negative (if, would, could, etc.)

For each identified feature that is found in a sentence, we search for a corresponding feature attribute that determines it. Further on, we search to see if the feature attribute is determined by any of the defined modifiers.

We consider a variable we denote "valueOf-Modifier," with a default value of -1, which will account for the existence of a positive or negative modifier of the feature attribute. In the affirmative case, we assign a value of 1 if the modifier is positive and a value of 0 if the modifier is negative. If no modifier exists, we consider the default value of the variable. We extract triplets of the form (feature, attribute of feature, "valueOfModifier"). In order to accomplish this, we use the syntactic dependency structure of the phrase, we determine all attribute features that determine the given feature (in the case of Minipar, they are the ones connected by the "det" or "mod" relation).

If a feature attribute is found without determining a feature, we consider it to implicitly evoke the feature that it is associated with in the feature collection previously built for the product. "The camera is small and sleek." becomes (camera, small, -1) and (camera, sleek, -1), which is then transformed by assigning the value "small" to the "size" feature and the value "sleek" to the "design" feature. This implicit assignment is based on the relations with coordinate terms in WordNet.

Assignment of Polarity to Feature Attributes

In order to assign polarity to each of the identified feature attributes of a product, we employ SMO SVM machine learning and the Normalized Google Distance (NGD). The intuition behind using this method is the fact that words that are similar in meaning tend to be used in the same manner [Cilibrasi and Vitanyi, 2006]. The main advantage in using this type of polarity assignment is that NGD is language independent and offers a measure of semantic similarity taking into account the meaning given to words in all texts indexed by Google from the World Wide Web. The set of anchors contains the terms {name of the feature, "happy," "unsatisfied," "nice," "small," "buy"} that have possible connection to all possible classes of products. Further on, we build the classes of

positive and negative examples for each of the feature attributes considered. From the corpus of annotated customer reviews, we consider all positive and negative terms associated to the considered attribute features. We then complete the lists of positive and negative terms with their WordNet synonyms. Since research in this field has shown that machine learning algorithms function better with an equal number of positive and negative and given that the training examples are given manually, we will consider from each of the categories a number of elements equal to the size of the smallest set among the two, with a size of at least 10 and less or equal with 20. We give as example the classification of the feature attribute "tiny," for the "size" feature. The set of positive feature attributes considered contains 15 terms such as (big, broad, bulky, massive, voluminous, large-scale etc.) and the set of negative feature attributes considered is composed as opposed examples, such as (small, petite, pocket-sized, little etc). We use the anchor words to convert each of the 30 training words to 6-dimensional training vectors defined as $v(j,i) = NGD(w_i, a_j)$, where a_j with j ranging from 1 to 6 are the anchors and w_i, with i from 1 to 30 are the words from the positive and negative categories. After obtaining the total 180 values for the vectors, we use the (polynomial kernel) SMO SVM implementation in Weka[14] to learn to distinguish the product specific nuances. For each of the new feature attributes we wish to classify, we calculate a new value of the vector $vNew(j,word) = NGD(word, a_j)$, with j ranging from 1 to 6 and classify it using the same anchors and trained SVM model. This step must be repeated for each of the product features and each of the attributes that have been found in the text as referring to them. In the example considered, we had the following results (we specify between brackets the word to which the scores refer to):

(small)1.52,1.87,0.82,1.75,1.92,1.93,positive
(little)1.44,1.84,0.80,1.64,2.11,1.85,positive
(big)2.27,1.19,0.86,1.55,1.16,1.77,negative

(bulky)1.33,1.17,0.92,1.13,1.12,1.16,negative

The vector corresponding to the "tiny" attribute feature is:

(tiny)1.51,1.41,0.82,1.32,1.60,1.36.

This vector was classified by SVM as positive, using the training set specified above. The precision value in the classifications we made was between 0.72 and 0.80, with a kappa value above 0.45.

Summarization of Feature Polarity

For each of the features identified, we compute its polarity depending on the polarity of the feature attribute that it is determined by and the polarity of the context modifier the feature attribute is determined by, in case such a modifier exists. Finally, we statistically summarize the polarity of the feature attributes, as ratio between the number of positive quantifications and the total number of quantifications made in the considered reviews to that specific feature and as ratio between the number of negative quantifications and the total number of quantifications made in all processed reviews. The formulas can be summarized in Equation 2.

$$F_{pos}(i) = \frac{\# \, pos\_feature\_attributes(i)}{\# \, feature\_attributes(i)}$$
$$F_{neg}(i) = \frac{\# \, neg\_feature\_attributes(i)}{\# \, feature\_attributes(i)}$$

$$(2)$$

The results shown are triplets of the form (feature, percentage of positive opinions, percentage of negative opinions).

Evaluation

For the evaluation of the system, we annotated a corpus of 50 customer reviews for each language, collected from sites as amazon.com, newegg.com, dealsdirect.com, ciao.es, shopmania.es, testfreaks.es and quesabesde.com. The corpus was annotated at the level of feature attributes, by the scheme shown in Box 1.

It is difficult to evaluate the performance of such a system, since we must take into consideration both the accuracy in extracting the features that reviews comment on, as well as the correct assignation of identified feature attributes to the positive or negative category. Therefore, we introduced three formulas for computing the system performance. The accuracy of the feature extraction method (denoted as Accuracy in Table 1) is computed as the normalized sum of the ratios between the number of identified positive feature attributes and the number of existing positive attributes and the ratio of identified negative feature and the total number of negative feature attributes for each of the considered features existing in the text. Secondly, we compute the Feature Identification Precision (Precision) as ratio between the number of features correctly identified from the features identified and the number of identified features. Thirdly, we compute the Feature Identification Recall (Recall) as the number of correctly identified features from the features identified and the number of features that were manually labeled in the review corpus.

Box 1.

```
<attribute>[attribute name]<feature>[feature determined]
</feature><value>[positive/negative]</value> </attribute>
```

Table 1. System results on the annotated review corpus

Feature extraction performance	English	Spanish	Combined	Baseline Eng	Baseline Sp
Accuracy	0.82	0.80	0.81	0.21	0.19
Precision	0.80	0.78	0.79	0.20	0.20
Recall	0.79	0.79	0.79	0.40	0.40

The results obtained are summarized in Table 1. We show the scores for each of the two languages considered separately and the combined score when using both systems for assigning polarity to feature attributes of a product. In the last column, we present a baseline, calculated as average of using the same formulas, but taking into consideration, for each feature, only the feature attributes we considered as training examples for our method.

We can notice how the use of NGD helped the system acquire significant new knowledge about the polarity of feature attributes. There are many aspects to be taken into consideration when evaluating a system identifying features, opinion on features and summarizing the polarity of features. First of all, customers reviewing products on the web frequently use informal language, disregard spelling rules and punctuation marks. At times, phrases are pure enumerations of terms, containing no subject or predicate. In this case, when there is no detectable dependency structure between components, an alternative method should be employed, such as verifying if the terms appearing near the feature within a window of specified size are frequently used in other contexts with relation to the feature.

Secondly, there are many issues regarding the accuracy of each of the tools and language resources employed and a certain probability of error in each of the methods used. In this initial research, we presented a method to extract, for a given product, the features that could be commented upon in a customer review. Further, we have shown a method to acquire the feature attributes on which a customer can comment in a review. Moreover, we presented a method to extract and assign polarity to these product features and statistically summarize the polarity they are given in the review texts in English and Spanish. The method for polarity assignment is largely language independent (it only requires the use of a small number of training examples) and the entire system can be implemented in any language for which similar resources and tools as the ones used for the presented system exist. The main advantage obtained by using this method is that one is able to extract and correctly classify the polarity of feature attributes, in a product dependent manner. Furthermore, the features in texts are that are identified are correct and the percentage of identification is high. Not lastly, we employ a measure of word similarity that is in itself based on the "word-of-mouth" on the web. The main disadvantage consists in the fact that SVM learning and classification is dependent on the NGD scores obtained with a set of anchors that must previously be established. This remains a rather subjective matter. Also, the polarity given in the training set determines the polarity given to new terms, such that "large" in the context of "display" will be trained as positive and in the case of "size" as negative. However, there are many issues that must be addressed in systems identifying customer opinions on different products on the web. The most important one is that concerning the informal language style, which makes the identification of words and dependencies in phrases sometimes impossible.

Subsequently to this first approach, we improved the system by adding extra features, taking into consideration the product technical specifications and defining patterns for indirectly expressed opinions using WordNet Affect categories [Balahur and Montoyo, 2008c], as well as enriching our feature-dependent method of opinion classification using Latent Semantic Analysis (LSA) relatedness scores; in the case of LSA scores, the context is given by the corpus from which the model is learnt, as opposed to the Normalized Google distance score (NGD), which is computed at the web level. We show the manner in which all these factors influence the system performance and at what cost. Last, but not least, many of the opinions on products are expressed in an indirect manner, that is, not relating the product or its features with polarity words, but expressing an emotion about them. We propose a set of patterns to extract such indirectly expressed opinions using the emotion lists from WordNet Affect. Our solution to the problem of feature attributes classification is using machine learning with two measures of similarity. On the one hand, we employ the Normalized Google Distance, which gives a measure of the strength of relationship between two considered words at the level of the entire WWW and on the other hand, we use the LSA, which gives the same measure of strength, but at a local corpus level. Classifying the feature attributes according to these scores and taking into consideration 6 anchor words that relate each word with the feature and known polarities, we show how the classification of feature attributes can be done in the feature context. Last, but not least, in the reviews to be mined and summarized, however, other opinion words can be found and other manners of expressing opinion can be encountered, such as those describing emotional states related to the product (for example, "I love this camera") or to using it. We discuss different methods to solve these problems and we show the list of patterns we used to extract from the reviews such phrases containing emotions to

express opinions of the different product features using the words associated to different emotions from WordNet Affect. In the evaluation section, we show how the use of such patterns raised with 12% the recall of the system, while the precision of classification rose to the same degree. In our previous approach, in order to assign polarity to each of the identified feature attributes of a product, we employed SMO SVM machine learning and the Normalized Google Distance (NGD). In this approach, we complete the solution with a classification employing LSA with Support Vector Machines classification. The LSA models are built and employed using the Infomap NLP[15] software. On the one hand, a model is build from a corpus of texts retrieved from the web using as queries the product classes our review corpus contained. On the other hand, another model is built from a corpus of reviews extracted on the product classes included in our test corpus. The Infomap software builds models from these corpora and reduces the dimensionality to 100. We calculate the relatedness of the words according to our LSA models, by using the "associate" command.

Subsequently, we build the classes of positive and negative examples for each of the feature attributes considered. From the list of classified feature attributes in the pros and cons reviews, we consider all positive and negative terms associated to the considered attribute features. We then complete the lists of positive and negative terms with their WordNet synonyms. We will again consider an equal number of positive and negative examples; this number of elements is equal to the size of the smallest set among the two, with a size of at least 10 and less or equal with 20. We give as example the classification of the feature attribute "tiny," for the "size" feature. The set of positive feature attributes considered contains 15 terms such as "big," "broad," "bulky," "massive," "voluminous," "large-scale" etc. And the set of negative feature attributes considered is composed as opposed examples, such as "small," "petite," "pocket-sized," "little" etc. We use the anchor

Table 2. LSA scores on non-specialized corpus (containing not only product reviews)

Feature attribute	V1	V2	V3	V4	V5	V6	Polarity
small	0.76	0.74	---	0.71	1	0.71	pos
big	0.80	0.75	---	0.74	0.73	0.68	neg
bulky	---	---	---	---	---	---	pos
little	---	---	---	---	---	---	neg
tiny	0.81	0.71	---	0.80	0.73	0.72	---

words to convert each of the 30 training words to 6-dimensional training vectors defined as $v(j,i) = LSA(w_i, a_j)$, where a_j with j ranging from 1 to 6 are the anchors and w_i, with i from 1 to 30 are the words from the positive and negative categories. After obtaining the total 180 values for the vectors, we use SMO SVM to learn to distinguish the product specific nuances. For each of the new feature attributes we wish to classify, we calculate a new value of the vector $vNew(j, word) = LSA(word, a_j)$, with j ranging from 1 to 6 and classify it using the same anchors and trained SVM model. We employed the classification on the corpus present for training in the Infomap software pack. The blank lines represent the words which were not found in the corpus; therefore a LSA score could not be computed. The results are presented in Table 2. On the other hand, we employed the classification on a corpus made up of reviews on different electronic products, gathered using the Google API and a LSA on the features attributes classified for the feature "size."

In Table 3, we show an example of the scores obtained with the similarity given by the LSA scores on a specialized corpus of reviews on products. The vector for the feature attribute "tiny" was classified by SVM as positive, using the training set specified above.

Precision values in classifications we made with NGD and LSA for different product features for the examples of digital camera reviews and the mobile phones reviews vary from 0.75 to 0.8 and kappa statistics shows high confidence of classification [Balahur and Montoyo, 2008c]. The conclusion that can be drawn from the results presented is that the main advantage in using the first method of polarity assignment is that NGD is language independent and offers a measure of semantic similarity taking into account the meaning given to words in all texts indexed by Google from the World Wide Web. On the other hand, using the whole Web corpus can also add significant noise. Therefore, we employ Latent Semantic Analysis at a local level, both on a non-specialized corpus, as well as on a corpus

Table 3. LSA scores on a specialized corpus of product reviews

Feature attribute	V1	V2	V3	V4	V5	V6	Polarity
small	0.83	0.77	0.48	0.72	1	0.64	pos
big	0.79	0.68	0.74	0.73	0.77	0.71	neg
bulky	0.76	0.67	0.71	0.75	0.63	0.78	pos
little	0.82	0.76	0.52	0.71	0.83	0.63	neg
tiny	0.70	0.70	0.65	0.67	0.71	0.71	pos

containing customer reviews. As we will show, the classification using LSA on a specialized corpus brings an average of 8% of improvement in the classification of polarity and a rise of 0.20 in the kappa measure, leading to an 8% overall improvement in the precision of the summarization system. However, these results were obtained using a specialized corpus of opinions, which was previously gathered from the WWW. To this respect, it is important to determine sources (web sites, blogs or forums) specific to each of the working languages, from which to gather the corpus on which the LSA model can be built. Using LSA on a non-specialized corpus improved the classification to the same degree as the classification on a specialized corpus in the cases where the specific pairs of words to be classified were found in the corpus. However, in 41% of the cases, the classification failed due to the fact that the words we tried to classify were not found in the corpus. Further on, we developed a method for feature polarity extraction using subjective phrases. As observed before, some opinions on the product or its features are expressed indirectly, with subjective phrases containing positive or negative emotions which are related to the product name, product brand or its features. In order to identify those phrases, we have constructed a set of rules for extraction, using the emotion lists from WordNet Affect.

For the words present in the "joy" emotion list, we consider the phrases extracted as having a positive opinion on the product or the feature contained. For the words in the "anger," "sadness" and "disgust" emotion lists, we consider the phrases extracted as having a negative opinion on the product or the feature contained. Apart from the emotion words, we have considered a list of "positive words" (pos list), containing adverbs such as "definitely," "totally," "very," "absolutely" and so on - as words positively stressing upon an idea - [Iftene and Balahur-Dobrescu, 2007], that influence on the polarity of the emotion expressed and that are often found in user reviews. We pres-

ent the extraction rules in table 6 (verb emotion, noun emotion and adj emotion correspond to the verbs, nouns and adjectives, respectively, found in the emotion lists from WordNet Affect under the emotions "joy," "sadness," "anger" and "disgust"). In case of "surprise," as emotion expressed about a product and its features, it can have both a positive, as well as negative connotation. Therefore, we have chosen not to include the terms expressing this emotion in the extraction patterns.

1. I [pos list*][verb emotion][this||the||my] [product name||product feature]
2. I ([am||'m||was||feel||felt])([pos list**]) [adj emotion][with||about||by] [product name||product feature]
3. I [feel||felt][noun emotion][about||with] [product name ||product brand]
4. I [pos list*][recommend][this||the][product name||product brand]
5. I ([don't])[think ||believe][sentence***]
6. It ['s||is] [adj emotion] [how||what][product name||product feature][product action]
7. You ||Everybody||Everyone||All||He||She||They][will||would][verb emotion][this||the] [product name brand||feature]

We have performed a comparative analysis of the system employing the SMO SVM polarity classification using NGD and LSA on a specialized corpus, the subjective phrases and combined, with the corpus used in [Balahur and Montoyo, 2008c] and also the corpus of 5 reviews from [Hu and Liu, 2004]. Results obtained in Table 4 are obtained when evaluating on our own annotated corpus. In the case of the [Hu and Liu, 2004] 5-reviews corpus, the observation that is important to make is that, as opposed to the annotation made in the corpus, we have first mapped the features identified to the general feature of the product (for example "fit" refers to "size" and "edges" refers to "design"), as we relieve that in real life situations, a user benefits more from a summary on coarserclasses of product features.

Table 4. System results on the review test set in [Balahur and Montoyo, 2008c]

NGD	NGD	LSA	LSA	Rules	Rules	NGD+RULES	NGD+RULES	LSA+RULES	NGD+RULES
P	R	P	R	P	R	P	R	P	R
0.80	0.79	0.88	0.87	0.32	0.6	0.89	0.85	0.93	0.93

Also, a set of sentences that were not annotated in the corpus, such as "You'll love this camera," which expresses a positive opinion on the product. The results shown in Table 5 are compared against the baseline of 0.20 precision and 0.41 recall, which was obtained using only the features determined as in the proposal by Balahur and Montoyo [Balahur and Montoyo, 2008f] and the feature attributes whose polarity was computed from the "pros and cons" -style reviews. As it can be seen, the best results are obtained when using the combination of LSA with the rules for subjective phrases extraction. However, gathering the corpus for the LSA model can be a costly process, whereas NGD scores are straightforward to be obtained and classifying is less costly as time and resources used. What is interesting to study is the impact of employing LSA for gradual learning and correction of a system that uses NGD for classifying the polarity of feature attributes. In such a self-learning scheme, the "online" classification would be that of NGD. However, the classification of the new feature attributes can be later improved "offline" using the classification given by LSA, which can then be used as better training for learning the polarity of new feature attributes by the "online" NGD classification. From this subsequent research, we could draw some conclusions on the advantages and disadvantages of using different scenarios for computing opinion polarity. The main advantage in using polarity assignment depending on NGD scores is that this is language independent and offers a measure of semantic similarity taking into account the meaning given to words in all texts indexed by Google from the World Wide Web. The main advantage in using

LSA on a specialized corpus, on the other hand, is that it eliminates the noise given by the multiple senses of words. We completed the opinion extraction on different product features with rules using the words present in WordNet Affect, as indicative of indirectly expressed opinions on products. We showed how all the employed methods led to significant growth in the precision and recall of our opinion mining and summarization system. Future work in this task includes a more thorough and systematic organization of product categories and features with their corresponding attributes and the fuzzy analysis of text for the detection of misspellings and grammar errors.

EXTENDING OPAL FOR THE DISAMBIGUATION OF ADJECTIVE POLARITY USING LOCAL CONTEXT

As we have seen in the previous section, one of the challenges faced in opinion mining is the fact that some adjectives have a different polarity depending on the context in which they appear. Our initial approach consisted in classifying adjective polarity using a set of anchors and the NGD and LSA scores, respectively. However, this component was not evaluated separately. With the participation in the SemEval-2 Task Number 18 (Disambiguation of Sentiment Ambiguous Adjectives [Wu and Jin, 2010]) we aimed at extending the OpAL system to resolve this task in a more general opinion mining scenario. Thus, we aimed at proposing a suitable method to tackle this issue, in a manner that is independent from the feature-based opinion mining framework.

Table 5. System results on [Hu and Liu, 2004] corpus

NGD	NGD	LSA	LSA	RULES	RULES	NGD+RULES	NGD+RULES	LSA+RULES	LSA+RULES
P	R	P	R	P	R	P	R	P	R
0.81	0.80	0.85	0.88	0.28	0.5	0.89	0.85	0.93	0.93

Our approach is based on three different strategies: a) the evaluation of the polarity of the whole context using an opinion mining system; b) the assessment of the polarity of the local context, given by the combinations between the closest nouns and the adjective to be classified; c) rules aiming at refining the local semantics through the spotting of modifiers. The final decision for classification is taken according to the output of the majority of these three approaches. The method used yielded good results, the OpAL system run achieving approximately 76% micro accuracy on a Chinese corpus. In the following subsections, we explain more in detail the individual components employed.

The OpAL Opinion Mining Component

First, we process each context using Minipar[16]. We compute, for each word in a sentence, a series of features, computed from the NTCIR 7 data and the EmotiBlog annotations. These words are used to compute vectors of features for each of the individual contexts:

- the part of speech (POS)
- opinionatedness/intensity: if the word is annotated as opinion word, its polarity (i.e. 1 and -1 if the word is positive or negative, respectively and 0 if it is not an opinion word) its intensity (1, 2 or 3) and 0 if it is not a subjective word
- syntactic relatedness with other opinion word: if it is directly dependent of an opinion word or modifier (0 or 1), plus the polarity/

intensity and emotion of this word (0 for all the components otherwise)
- role in 2-word, 3-word, 4-word and sentence annotations: opinionatedness, intensity and emotion of the other words contained in the annotation, direct dependency relations with them if they exist and 0 otherwise.

We add to the opinion words annotated in EmotiBlog the list of opinion words found in the Opinion Finder, Opinion Finder, MicroWordNet Opinion, General Inquirer, WordNet Affect, emotion triggers lexical resources. We train the model using the SVM SMO implementation in Weka17.

Assessing Local Polarity Using Google Queries

This approach aimed at determining the polarity of the context immediately surrounding the adjective to be classified. To that aim, we constructed queries using the noun found before the adjective in the context given, and issued six different queries on Google, together with six pre-defined adjectives whose polarity is known (3 positive: "positive," "beautiful," "good" and 3 negative: "negative," "ugly," "bad"). The form of the queries was "noun+adjective+AND+pre-defined adjective." The local polarity was considered as the one for which the query issued the highest number of total results (total number of results for the 3 queries corresponding to the positive adjectives or to the negative adjectives, respectively).

Modifier Rules for Contextual Polarity

This rule accounts for the original, most frequently used polarity of the given adjectives (e.g. *high* is *positive*, *low* is *negative*). For each of them, we define its default polarity. Subsequently, we determine whether in the window of 4 words around the adjective there are any modifiers (valence shifters). If this is the case, and they have an opposite value of polarity, the adjective is assigned a polarity value opposite from its default one (e.g. *too high* is *negative*). We employ a list of 82 positive and 87 negative valence shifters.

Evaluation Results for OpAL in the SemEval-2010 Task 18

Table 6 presents the results obtained by the 16 participating systems—including OpAL—in the SemEval 2010 Task 18 competition. As it can be seen in this table, the system ranked fifth, with a Micro accuracy of 0.76037 and sixth, with a Macro accuracy of 0.7037. The data is reproduced from [Wu and Jin, 2010].

Since the gold standard was not provided, we were not able to perform an exhaustive analysis of the errors. However, from a random inspection of the system results, we could see that a large number of errors was due to the translation—through which modifiers are placed far from the word they determine or the words are not translated with their best equivalent.

EXTENDING THE OpAL SYSTEM FOR OPINION RETRIEVAL AND QUESTION ANSWERING IN A MULTILINGUAL SETTING

The OpAL feature-based opinion mining and summarization system, in its initial phase, was designed to work with texts that were retrieved from specific e-commerce sites that we knew con-

Table 6. Results for the 16 system runs submitted (micro and macro accuracy)

System	Micro Acc.(%)	Macro Acc.(%)
YSC-DSAA	94.20	92.93
HITSZ_CITYU_1	93.62	95.32
HITSZ_CITYU_2	93.32	95.79
Dsaa	88.07	86.20
OpAL	76.04	70.38
CityUHK4	72.47	69.80
CityUHK3	71.55	75.54
HITSZ_CITYU_3	66.58	62.94
QLK_DSAA_R	64.18	69.54
CityUHK2	62.63	60.85
CityUHK1	61.98	67.89
QLK_DSAA_NR	59.72	65.68
Twitter Sentiment	59.00	62.27
Twitter Sentiment_ext	56.77	61.09
Twitter Sentiment_zh	56.46	59.63
Biparty	51.08	51.26

tained relevant reviews. In order to complete the approach and make it directly implementable at a large scale, we added the OpAL system an opinion retrieval and question answering component. The methods we implemented therein were evaluated within the first 3 NTCIR-8 MOAT subtasks—sentence opinionated judgment, sentence relevance judgment and polarity classification. Further on, we detail on the implementation of this additional component, according to the subtask in which it was evaluated, in an English monolingual and English-Traditional Chinese cross-lingual setting.

Judging Sentence Opinionatedness

The "opinionated" subtask required systems to assign the values YES or NO (Y/N) to each of the sentences in the document collection provided. This value is given depending on whether the sentence contains an opinion (Y) or it does not (N).

In order to judge the opinionatedness of the sentence, we employed two different approaches (the first one corresponding to system run number 1 and the second to system runs 2 and 3). Both approaches are rule-based, but they differ in the resources employed. We considered as opinionated sentences the ones that contain at least two opinion words or one opinion word preceded by a modifier. For the first approach, the opinion words were taken from the General Inquirer, Micro WordNet Opinion and Opinion Finder lexicon and in the second approach we only used the first two resources.

Determining Sentence Relevance

In the sentence relevance judgment task, the systems had to output, for each sentence in the given collection documents per topic, an assessment on whether or not the sentence is relevant for the given question. For the sentence relevance judgment task stage, we employ three strategies (corresponding to the system runs 1,2 and 3, respectively):

1. Using the JIRS (JAVA Information Retrieval System) IR engine [Gómez et al., 2007] to find relevant snippets. JIRS retrieves passages (of the desired length), based on searching the question structures (n-grams) instead of the keywords, and comparing them.

2. Using faceted search in Wikipedia and performing Latent Semantic Analysis (LSA) to find the words that are most related to the topic. The idea behind this approach is to find the concepts that are contained in the query descriptions of the topics. In order to perform this task, we match the query words, starting from the first, to a category in Wikipedia. Subsequently we match each group of two consecutive words to the same categories, then groups of 3, 4, etc. until the highest match is found. The concepts determined through this process are considered

as the topic components. For each of these topic components, we determine the most related words, applying LSA is to the first 20 documents that are retrieved using the Yahoo search engine, given the query. For LSA, we employ the Infomap NLP[18] software. Finally, we expand query, using words that are very similar to the topic (retrieved through the LSA process) and retrieve snippets that contain at least two such words.

3. The third approach consists in judging, apart from the topic relevance characteristic, the temporal appropriateness of the given sentences. In order to perform this check, we employ TERSEO [Saquete et al., 2006]. We then filter the sentences obtained in the second approach depending on whether or not the document in which they appear have a date matching the required time interval or the sentence with the resolved temporal expressions contains a reference to the required time interval.

Polarity and Topic-Polarity Classification for Judging Sentence Answerness

The polarity judgment task required the system to assign a value of POS, NEG or NEU (positive, negative or neutral) to each of the sentences in the documents provided. In order to determine the polarity of the sentences, we passed each sentence through an opinion mining system employing SVM machine learning over the NTCIR 7 MOAT corpus, the MPQA corpus and EmotiBlog. Each sentence is preprocessed using Minipar19. For the system training, the following features were considered, for each sentence word:

*   the part of speech (POS)
*   opinionatedness/intensity: if the word is annotated as opinion word, its polarity (i.e. 1 and -1 if the word is positive or negative, respectively and 0 if it is not an opinion

word) its intensity (1.2 or 3) and 0 if it is not a subjective word, its emotion (if it has, none otherwise)

- syntactic relatedness with other opinion word: if it is directly dependent of an opinion word or modifier (0 or 1), plus the polarity/intensity and emotion of this word (0 for all the components otherwise).

The difference between the submitted runs consisted in the lexicons used to determine whether a word was opinionated or not. For the first run, we employed the General Inquirer, MicroWordNet and the Opinion Finder opinion resources. For the second one, we employed, apart from these three sources, the "emotion trigger" resource [Balahur and Montoyo, 2008].

Cross-Lingual Opinion Retrieval and QA

In the Cross-lingual setting, the task of the participating systems was to output, for each of the twenty topics and their corresponding questions (in a language), the list of sentences containing answers (in another language). For this task, we submitted three runs of the OpAL system, all of them for the English- Traditional Chinese cross-lingual setting (i.e. the topics and questions are given in English; the output of the system contains the sentences in set of documents in Traditional Chinese which contain an answer to the given topics). In the following part, we explain the approaches we followed for each of the system runs.

Given that we had no previous experience with processing Chinese text, the approaches taken were quite simple. The first step we performed was to tokenize the Chinese texts using LingPipe[20]. Further on, we applied a technique known as "triangulation" to obtain opinion and subjectivity resources for Chinese. This technique requires the existence of two correct parallel resources in two different languages to obtain correct resources for

a third language. We have previously translated and cleaned the General Inquirer, MicroWordNet and Opinion Finder lexicons for Spanish. The "emotion triggers" resource is available both for English, as well as for Spanish. In order to obtain these resources for Traditional Chinese, we translated simultaneously, using the Google translator, these resources, from English and from Spanish. Subsequently, we performed the intersection of the obtained translations. These were considered as "clean" resources. We mapped each of these resources to four classes, depending on the score they are assigned: of "high positive," "positive," "high negative" and "negative" and we give each word a corresponding value (4, 1, -4 and 1), respectively.

On the other hand, we translated the topic words determined in English. For each of the sentence, we compute a score, given by the sum of the values of the opinion words that are matched in it. In order for a sentence to be considered as answer to the given question, we set the additional conditions that it contains at least one topic word and that the polarity determined corresponds to the required polarity, as given in the topic description. The three runs differ in the resources that were employed to calculate the sentiment score: in the first run, we employed the General Inquirer and MicroWordNet resources; in the second run we added the "emotion trigger resource" and the third run used only the Opinion Finder lexicon.

Evaluation Results and Discussion

Table 7 presents the results of the system runs for the three subtasks in which we took part in English and the cross-lingual English - Traditional Chinese task.

From the results obtained, we can see that although the extensive filtering according to the topic and the temporal restrictions increases the system precision, we obtain a dramatic drop in the recall. On the other hand, the use of simpler

Table 7. Results of system runs for the different tasks in NTCIR-8 MOAT

Task	System RunID	P	R	F
Opinonatedness	OPAL 1	17.99	45.16	25.73
	OPAL 2	19.44	44	26.97
	OPAL 3	19.44	44	26.97
Relevance	OPAL 1	82.05	47.83	60.43
	OPAL 2	82.61	5.16	9.71
	OPAL 3	76.32	3.94	7.49
Polarity	OPAL 1	38.13	12.82	19.19
	OPAL 2	50.93	12.26	19.76
Cross-lingual English-Traditional Chinese (agreed measures)	OPAL 1	3.54	56.23	6.34
	OPAL 2	3.35	42.75	5.78
	OPAL 3	3.42	72.13	6.32
Cross-lingual English-Traditional Chinese (non-agreed measures)	OPAL 1	14.62	60.47	21.36
	OPAL 2	14.64	49.73	19.57
	OPAL 3	15.02	77.68	23.55

methods in the cross-lingual task yielded better results, the OpAL cross-lingual run 3 obtaining the highest F score for the non-agreed measures and ranking second according to the agreed measures.

From the error analysis performed, we realized that, on the one hand, the LSA-based method to determine topic-related words is not enough to perform this task. The terms obtained by employing this method are correct and useful, but they should be expanded using language models, to better account for the language variability.

Finally, we have seen that systems performing finer tasks, such as temporal expression resolution, are not mature enough to be employed in such tasks. This was confirmed by in-house experiments using anaphora resolution tools such as JavaRAP[21], whose use also led to lower performances of the system and dramatic loss in recall.

FUTURE RESEARCH DIRECTIONS

Future research directions contemplate improvements in all the system components: at the retrieval, classification and summarization steps. At the retrieval stage, joint topic-sentiment models must be further investigated, in order to adjust the search process to the opinion component (which is, at the moment, only contemplated once the retrieval has been done). We have shown a method to perform retrieval in such a manner, by using LSA; but, nonetheless, LSA methods can only account for some of the topic-related words. In this sense, our future work will include the development of language models that are specific to the opinion retrieval task. As far as the opinion classification stage is concerned, our future work contemplates the integration of other models we have developed in the feature-based opinion mining system (e.g. the ones built for the SemEval and MOAT 2010 tasks). Finally, we plan to enhance the opinion summarization component to include textual summaries. Although we have undergone efforts in this direction [Kabadjov et al., 2009; Balahur et al., 2010], opinion summarization still remains a challenge, for which appropriate tackling methods have to be found.

CONCLUSION

Nowadays, the decision to buy a product or another, to book a hotel or visit a specific location is highly dependent on the opinions expressed on these objects in e-commerce sites, forums or blogs. However, given the growing amount of such data on the Internet, sifting through it is a time-consuming task for human users. Thus, specialized systems must be built to *automatically retrieve* the information needed by these users, *extract the relevant content, classify the opinions expressed* according to their polarity and finally *create statistical summaries*. In this chapter, we presented methods to tackle each of these tasks, and measured the performance of the different approaches taken. We have described the feature-based opinion mining paradigm and presented a method to build a system performing this task, in two different languages. Furthermore, have shown how product features can be obtained and presented three different methods to classify the polarity of adjectives within opinions in a feature-dependent manner. Last, but not least, we presented a method to perform opinion retrieval in a mono- and cross language setting, in close connection to describing a simple approach to generating opinion lexicons for other languages. Following the good accuracy results obtained in in-house and open competitions, we can conclude that these methods are appropriate for the tasks at hand, as many errors occur due to the performance of the different NLP tools used (although this is not valid for all the settings – as we could see, anaphora resolution with one and the same tool can improve one task and decreased performance in another). Nevertheless, apart from determining ways to cope with this drop in accuracy, a large number of other improvements can be made at the different steps. Such add-ons can help to better capture the semantics of the text, for example through the use of joint topic-sentiment retrieval (using language models to account for data sparseness) and classification, the enhancement of the extraction phase by employing machine learning to a greater extend and linguistic knowledge to a lesser extent. As we have mentioned, subjectivity is closely related to individual interpretations of meaning and personal preferences. Therefore, the OpAL system can greatly benefit from the adaptation to user-specific profiles and classification according to them.

As we have seen, the performance of our opinion mining system varies depending on the task and on the type of texts considered. However, the high performance of the system implementing the feature-based opinion mining task, at a multilingual level, leads us to believe that this technology is mature enough to be used in real world, multi- or cross-lingual business applications. Existing large-scale services, such as swotty.com, textmap. com or the Thomson Reuters analytics programs prove that there is a high business interest in mining opinions from the web. This is constantly growing, as companies realize the importance of gathering subjective data and transforming it into competitive advantage and, finally, revenue.

ACKNOWLEDGMENT

This chapter has been supported partially by Ministerio de Ciencia e Innovación - Spanish Government (grant no. TIN2009-13391-C04-01), and Conselleria d'Educación - Generalitat Valenciana (grant no. PROMETEO/2009/119 and ACOMP/2010/286).

REFERENCES

Balahur, A., & Montoyo, A. (2008a). Applying a culture dependent emotion triggers database for text valence and emotion classification. *Procesamiento del Lenguaje Natural, 40*.

Balahur, A., & Montoyo, A. (2008b). *Building a recommender system using community level social filtering.* Paper presented at the 5th International Workshop on Natural Language and Cognitive Science (NLPCS).

Balahur, A., & Montoyo, A. (2008c). Determining the semantic orientation of opinions on products - A comparative analysis. *Procesamiento del Lenguaje Natural, 41.*

Balahur, A., & Montoyo, A. (2008d). Multilingual feature-driven opinion extraction and summarization from customer reviews. *Lecture Notes in Computer Science, 5039.*

Balahur, A., & Montoyo, A. (2008e). *A feature-driven approach to opinion mining and classification.* Paper presented at the International Conference on Application of Natural Language to Information Systems (NLDB 2009).

Balahur, A., & Montoyo, A. (2008f). *Semantic approaches to fine and coarse-grained feature-based opinion mining.* Paper presented at the NLPKE 2008.

Balahur, A., & Montoyo, A. (2008g). *Applying a culture dependent emotion triggers database for text valence and emotion classification. Artificial Intelligence and Simulation of Behaviour.* Aberdeen: AISB.

Balahur, A., & Montoyo, A. (2008g). *A feature-driven approach to opinion mining and classification.* Paper presented at the NLPKE 2008.

Balahur, A., & Montoyo, A. (2010). OpAL: Applying opinion mining techniques for the disambiguation of sentiment ambiguous adjectives in SemEval-2 task 18. In *Proceedings of SemEval 2010, Satellite Workshop to ACL 2010.*

Balahur, A., & Steinberger, R. (2009, November 13). *Rethinking sentiment analysis in the news: From theory to practice and back.* Paper presented at the 1st Workshop on Opinion Mining and Sentiment Analysis (WOMSA), CAEPIA-TTIA Conference, (pp. 1–12). Seville, Spain.

Banfield, A. (1982). *Unspeakable sentences: Narration and representation in the language of fiction.* Routledge and Kegan Paul.

Boldrini, E., Balahur, A., Martínez-Barco, P., & Montoyo, A. (2009). *EmotiBlog: An annotation scheme for emotion detection and analysis in non-traditional textual genre.* Paper presented at the 2009 World Congress in Computer Science, Computer Engineering, and Applied Computing.

Boldrini, E., Balahur, A., Martínez-Barco, P., & Montoyo, A. (2009). *EmotiBlog: A finer-grained and more precise learning of subjectivity expression models.* Paper presented at LAW IV, ACL 2010.

Cardie, C., Wiebe, J., Wilson, T., & Litman, D. (2003). *Combining low-level and summary representations of opinions for multi-perspective question answering.* Paper presented at the AAAI Spring Symposium on New Directions in Question Answering.

Cerini, S., Compagnoni, V., Demontis, A., Formentelli, M., & Gandini, G. (2007). *Micro-WNOp: A gold standard for the evaluation of automatically compiled lexical resources for opinion mining.* Paper presented at The Sixteenth Text Retrieval Conference (TREC 2007), Gaithersburg, MD, USA.

Chaovalit, P., & Zhou, L. (2005). *Movie review mining: A comparison between supervised and unsupervised classification approaches.* Paper presented at the HICSS-05, the 38th Hawaii International Conference on System Sciences.

Cilibrasi, D., & Vitanyi, P. (2006). Automatic meaning discovery using Google. *IEEE Journal of Transactions on Knowledge and Data Engineering, 19*(3), 370–383.

Cui, H., Mittal, V., & Datar, M. (2006). *Comparative experiments on sentiment classification for online product reviews.* Paper presented at the 21st National Conference on Artificial Intelligence AAAI 2006.

Dave, K., Lawrence, S., & Pennock, D. (2003). *Mining the peanut gallery: Opinion extraction and semantic classification of product reviews.* Paper presented at the WWW-03.

Deerwester, S., Dumais, S., Furnas, G. W., Landauer, T. K., & Harshman, R. (1990). Indexing by latent semantic analysis. *Journal of the American Society for Information Science American Society for Information Science, 3*(41).

Devitt, A., & Ahmad, K. (2007). *Sentiment polarity identification in financial news: A cohesion-based approach.* Paper presented at the 45th Annual Meeting of the ACL, (pp. 984–991).

Ding, X., Liu, B., & Yu, P. (2008). *A holistic lexicon-based approach to opinion mining.* Paper presented at the WSDM 2008.

Esuli, A., & Sebastiani, F. (2005). *Determining the semantic orientation of terms through gloss analysis.* Paper presented at CIKM 2005.

Esuli, A., & Sebastiani, F. (2006). *SentiWordNet: A publicly available resource for opinion mining.* In Paper presented at the 6th International Conference on Language Resources and Evaluation.

Fellbaum, C. (1998). *WordNet: An electronic lexical database (Language, Speech, and Communication).* The MIT Press.

Ferrández, A., Palomar, M., & Moreno, L. (1999). *An empirical approach to Spanish anaphora resolution* (pp. 191–216). Machine Translation, Special Issue on Anaphora Resolution.

Gamon, M., Aue, S., Corston-Oliver, S., & Ringger, E. (2005). Mining customer opinions from free text. *Lecture Notes in Computer Science*, 3646.

Gómez, J. M., Rosso, P., & Sanchis, E. (2007). *JIRS language-independent passage retrieval system: A comparative study.* Paper presented at the 5th International Conference on Natural Language Proceeding (ICON 2007).

Hatzivassiloglou, V., & Wiebe, J. (2000). Effects of adjective orientation and gradability on sentence subjectivity. In *Proceedings of COLING 2000.*

Hu, M., & Liu, B. (2004). *Mining opinion features in customer reviews.* Paper presented at the Nineteenth National Conference on Artificial Intellgience AAAI-2004.

Kim, S.-M., & Hovy, E. (2004). *Determining the sentiment of opinions.* Paper presented at COLING 2004.

Kim, S. M., & Hovy, E. H. (2005). *Identifying opinion holders for question answering in opinion texts.* Paper presented at the Workshop on Question Answering in Restricted Domain at the Conference of the American Association of Artificial Intelligence (AAAI-05). Pittsburgh, PA.

Koppel, M., & Shtrimberg, I. (2004). *Good news or bad news? Let the market decide.* Paper presented at AAI Spring Symposium on Exploring Attitude and Affect in Text, (pp. 86–88).

Kozareva, Z., Vázquez, S., & Montoyo, A. (2007). *Discovering the underlying meanings and categories of a name through domain and semantic information.* Paper presented at the Conference on Recent Advances in Natural Language Processing RANLP 2007.

Lappin, S., & Leass, H. (1994). *Recognizing referential links: An information extraction perspective.* Paper presented at ACL/EACL Workshop on Operational Factors in Practical, Robust Anaphora Resolution, (pp. 46-53). Madrid, Spain.

Li, F., Zheng, Z., Yang, T., Bu, F., Ge, R., & Zhu, X. ... Huang, M. (2008). *QUANTA at TAC 2008. QA and RTE track.* Paper presented at the Human Language Technologies Conference/Conference on Empirical methods in Natural Language Processing (HLT/EMNLP), Vancouver, BC, Canada.

Lin, D. (1998). *Dependency-based evaluation of MINIPAR.* Paper presented at Workshop on the Evaluation of Parsing Systems.

Lin, W., Wilson, T., Wiebe, J., & Hauptman, A. (2006). *Which side are you on? Identifying perspectives at the document and sentence levels.* Paper presented at the Tenth Conference on Natural Language Learning CONLL'06.

Liu, B. (2007). *Web data mining: Exploring hyperlinks, contents and usage data* (1st ed.). Springer.

Liu, H., & Singh, P. (2004). ConceptNet: A practical commonsense reasoning toolkit. *BT Technology Journal*, 22.

Lu, B., & Tsou, B. K. (2010). CityU-DAC: Disambiguating sentiment-ambiguous adjectives within context. In *Proceedings of SemEval 2010, Satellite Workshop to ACL 2010.*

Miller, G. A., Beckwith, R., Fellbaum, C. D., Gross, D., & Miller, K. (1990). WordNet: An online lexical database. *International Journal of Lexicography*, *3*(4), 235–244.

Mishne, G., & Glance, N. (2005). *Predicting movie sales from blogger sentiment.* Paper presented at AAAI Symposium on Computational Approaches to Analysing Weblogs (AAAI-CAAW), (pp. 155–158).

Mullen, T., & Collier, M. (2004). *Sentiment analysis using support vector machines with diverse information sources.* Paper presented at the EMNLP 2004.

Ng, V., Dasgupta, S., & Arifin, S. M. N. (2006). *Examining the role of linguistic knowledge sources in the automatic identification and classification of reviews.* Paper presented at the 40th Annual Meeting of the Association for Computational Linguistics.

Pak, A., & Paroubek, P. (2010). Twitter based system: Using Twitter for disambiguating sentiment ambiguous adjectives. In *Proceedings of SemEval 2010, Satellite Workshop to ACL 2010.*

Pang, B., & Lee, L. (2003). Seeing stars: Exploiting class relationships for sentiment categorization with respect to rating scales. In *Proceedings of the 43rd Annual Meeting of the ACL*, (pp. 115–124).

Pang, B., & Lee, L. (2008). Opinion mining and sentiment analysis. *Foundations and Trends in Information Retrieval*, *2*(1-2), 1–135.

Pang, B., Lee, L., & Vaithyanathan, S. (2002). *Thumbs up? Sentiment classification using machine learning techniques.* Paper presented at the EMNLP-02, the Conference on Empirical Methods in Natural Language Processing.

Panicheva, P., Cardiff, J., & Rosso, P. (2009). *A co-occurrence based personal sense approach to opinion mining.* Paper presented at the 1st Workshop on Opinion Mining and Sentiment Analysis (WOMSA), CAEPIA- TTIA Conference, (pp. 205–212). Seville, Spain.

Platt, J. (1998). *Sequential minimal optimization: A fast algorithm for training support vector machines.* (Microsoft Research Technical Report MSR-TR-98-14).

Polanyi, L., & Zaenen, A. (2004). *Exploring attitude and affect in text: Theories and applications.* (Technical Report SS-04-07).

Popescu, A. M., & Etzioni, O. (2005). *Extracting product features and opinions from reviews.* Paper presented at the HLTEMNLP 2005.

Quirk, R. (1985). *A comprehensive grammar of the English language*. Longman.

Riloff, E., & Wiebe, J. (2003). Learning extraction patterns for subjective expressions. In *Proceedings of the 2003 Conference on Empirical Methods in Natural Language Processing*.

Saquete, E., Muñoz, R., Martínez-Barco, P. (2006). Event ordering using TERSEO system. *DKE Journal, 58*(1).

Seki, Y., Ku, L.-W., Sun, L., Chen, H.-H., & Kando, N. (2010). Overview of multilingual opinion analysis task at NTCIR-8 – A step towards cross lingual opinion analysis. In *Proceedings of NTCIR-8 Workshop Meeting*, Tokyo, Japan, 2010.

Shen, D., Wiegand, M., Merkel, A., Kazalski, S., Hunsicker, S., Leidner, J. L., & Klakow, D. (2007). *The Alyssa system at trec qa 2007: Do we need blog06?* Paper Text Analysis Conference, at the joint annual meeting of TAC and TREC. Gaithersburg, Maryland, USA.

Stoyanov, V., & Cardie, C. (2006). *Toward opinion summarization: Linking the sources*. Paper presented at the COLING ACL 2006 Workshop on Sentiment and Subjectivity in Text. Transactions on Information Systems, 21.

Strapparava, C., & Valitutti, A. (2004, May). *WordNet-Affect: An affective extension of Word-Net*. Paper presented at the 4th International Conference on Language Resources and Evaluation (LREC 2004), Lisbon, May 2004, (pp. 1083-1086).

Turney, P. (2002). *Thumbs up or thumbs down? Semantic orientation applied to unsupervised classification of reviews*. Paper presented at the 40th Annual Meeting of the Association for Computational Linguistics.

Turney, P., & Littman, M. (2003). *Measuring praise and criticism: Inference of semantic orientation from association*. ACM.

Uspensky, B. (1973). *A poetics of composition*. Berkeley, CA: University of California Press.

Varma, V., Pingali, P., Katragadda, S., Krishna, R., Ganesh, S., & Sarvabhotla, K. … Bharadwaj, R. (2008). *Text Analysis Conference, Joint Annual Meeting of TAC and TREC*. Gaithersburg, Maryland, USA.

Vázquez, S., Montoyo, A., & Rigau, G. (2004). *Using relevant domains resource for word sense disambiguation*. Paper presented at the International Conference on Artificial Intelligence.

Wenjie, L., Ouyang, Y., Hu, Y., & Wei, F. (2008). *PolyU at TAC 2008*. Paper presented at the Human Language Technologies Conference/Conference on Empirical methods in Natural Language Processing (HLT/EMNLP), Vancouver, BC, Canada.

Whitelaw, C., Garg, N., & Argamon, S. (2005). *Using appraisal groups for sentiment analysis*. Paper presented at the CIKM 2005.

Wiebe, J. (1994). Tracking point of view in narrative. *Computational Linguistics*, 20.

Wiebe, J., & Riloff, E. (2006). *Creating subjective and objective sentence classifiers from unannotated texts*. Paper presented at the 6th International Conference on Computational Linguistics and Intelligent.

Wiebe, J., Wilson, T., & Cardie, C. (2005). Annotating expressions of opinions and emotions in language. *Language Resources and Evaluation, 39*(2-3), 165–210.

Wiegand, M., Momtazi, S., Kazalski, S., Xu, F., Chrupala, G., & Klakow, D. (2008). The Alyssa system at TAC 2008. In Proceedings of the Text Analysis Conference, 2008.

Wilson, T., Wiebe, J., & Hoffmann, P. (2005). *Recognizing contextual polarity in phrase-level sentiment analysis.* Paper presented at the Human language Technologies Conference/Conference on Empirical methods in Natural Language Processing (HLT/EMNLP), Vancouver, BC, Canada.

Wilson, T., Wiebe, J., & Hwa, R. (2004). *Just how mad are you? Finding strong and weak opinion clauses.* Paper presented at the AAAI 2004.

Wu, Y., & Jin, P. (2010). SemEval-2010 Task 18: Disambiguating sentiment ambiguous adjectives. In *Proceedings of SemEval 2010, Satellite Workshop to ACL 2010.*

Xu, R., Xu, J., & Kit, C. (2010). HITSZ_CITYU: Combine collocation, context words and neighboring sentence sentiment in sentiment adjectives disambiguation. In *Proceedings of SemEval 2010, Satellite Workshop to ACL 2010.*

Yang, S.-C., & Liu, M.-J. (2010). YSC-DSAA: An approach to disambiguate sentiment ambiguous adjectives based on SAAOL. In *Proceedings of SemEval 2010, Satellite Workshop to ACL 2010.*

Yu, H., & Hatzivassiloglou, V. (2003). *Towards answering opinion questions: Separating facts from opinions.* Paper presented at the EMNLP-03.

KEY TERMS AND DEFINITIONS

Automatic Summarization: The process of creating a shortened version of a text by a computer program.

New Textual Genres: The text types born with the Social Web (blogs, forums, reviews)

Opinionated Data: Subjective information which presents the users' opinions and points of view

Sentiment Analysis: Area of natural language processing, which aims to determine the attitude of a speaker or a writer with respect to some topic.

ENDNOTES

[1]   http://technorati.com/
[2]   http://research.nii.ac.jp/ntcir/index-en.html
[3]   http://www.nist.gov/tac/
[4]   http://research.nii.ac.jp/ntcir/
[5]   http://verbs.colorado.edu/~mpalmer/projects/ace.html
[6]   http://web.media.mit.edu/~hugo/conceptnet/
[7]   http://semeval2.fbk.eu/semeval2.php
[8]   http://research.nii.ac.jp/ntcir/
[9]   http://www.lextek.com/langid/
[10] http://www.illc.uva.nl/EuroWordNet/
[11] http://www.comp.nus.edu.sg/qiul/NLP-Tools/JavaRAP.html
[12] http://www.alias-i.com/lingpipe/
[13] http://garraf.epsevg.upc.es/freeling/
[14] http://www.cs.waikato.ac.nz/ml/weka/
[15] http://infomap-nlp.sourceforge.net/
[16] http://webdocs.cs.ualberta.ca/~lindek/minipar.htm
[17] http://www.cs.waikato.ac.nz/ml/weka/
[18] http://infomap-nlp.sourceforge.net/
[19] http://webdocs.cs.ualberta.ca/~lindek/minipar.htm
[20] http://alias-i.com/lingpipe/
[21] http://aye.comp.nus.edu.sg/~qiu/NLPTools/JavaRAP.html

Chapter 8
A Unified Approach for Taxonomy–Based Technology Forecasting

Andreas Henschel
Masdar Institute of Science and Technology, UAE

Erik Casagrande
Masdar Institute of Science and Technology, UAE

Wei Lee Woon
Masdar Institute of Science and Technology, UAE

Isam Janajreh
Masdar Institute of Science and Technology, UAE

Stuart Madnick
Massachusetts Institute of Technology, USA

ABSTRACT

For decision makers and researchers working in a technical domain, understanding the state of their area of interest is of the highest importance. For this reason, we consider in this chapter, a novel framework for Web-based technology forecasting using bibliometrics (i.e. the analysis of information from trends and patterns of scientific publications). The proposed framework consists of a few conceptual stages based on a data acquisition process from bibliographic online repositories: extraction of domain-relevant keywords, the generation of taxonomy of the research field of interests and the development of early growth indicators which helps to find interesting technologies in their first phase of development. To provide a concrete application domain for developing and testing our tools, we conducted a case study in the field of renewable energy and in particular one of its subfields: Waste-to-Energy (W2E). The results on this particular research domain confirm the benefit of our approach.

DOI: 10.4018/978-1-61350-038-5.ch008

INTRODUCTION

Any given research field is composed of many subfields and underlying technologies which are related in intricate ways. A solid understanding of how these subfields are linked together as well as how important the different regions of this research landscape are will confer a significant competitive advantage. Currently, information regarding past and current research is available from a variety of channels, providing a rich source of data with which effective research strategies may be formed. These two important trends strongly motivate the development of computational tools for exploiting this data: firstly, the proliferation in technical and academic publications has greatly increased the rate at which relevant knowledge and data are produced and disseminated; secondly, access to this information is constantly improving thanks to the advances in the technologies underlying the web.

Motivation

In order to clarify the intended use of our system, it must be stressed that we are not using "forecasting" in the sense of weather forecasting, where future outcomes are predicted with a reasonably high degree of certainty. It is also important to note that certain tasks remain better suited to human experts. For example, where a particular technology of interest has already been chosen, we believe that a traditional literature review would prove superior to an automated approach. Instead, the proposed framework targets the preliminary stages of technology management, where breadth rather than depth is emphasized. The main focus of our system is on analyzing broad trends occurring in a very large number of documents or other textual sources. By scanning and digesting large amounts of information, promising but less obvious developments can be detected and subsequently brought to the attention of a human expert. This way we capitalize on the strength of computational approaches before making more efficient use of valuable expert time in the critical latter stages of the decision making process.

Knowledge that facilitates forecasting the likely growth and consequences of emergent technologies is essential for well-informed technology management, which is currently relying largely on expert opinion. However, expert decisions can be influenced by personal perspectives or biases. Moreover, acquiring and analyzing such knowledge is hampered by the vast amount of data available in publications. Consequently, sifting through the—often electronically—available R&D literature is time consuming, yet non-exhaustive and subjective. In order to cope with this problem, automated forecasting techniques have been developed in recent years (see Background section). A remaining challenge is related to the knowledge organization of the acquired data. For example, in order to elucidate the advances of technologies, we want to answer questions like: "How many scientific articles have been published in peer-reviewed journals on the topic of solar energy recently?" Intelligent search techniques capable of grouping semantically similar concepts are therefore needed, such that the term "parabolic trough" is subsumed under solar energy related technologies and hence articles about it should be included in the analysis. This underlying challenge of managing and structuring the vast amount of available knowledge from web resources is similar in web-based Technology Forecasting and general Semantic Web applications. However the former has yet to fully benefit from the advances of the latter. In particular, the state-of-the-art Technology Forecasting tools hardly make use of ontologies or taxonomies, the standard form of knowledge representation for the Semantic Web (Shadbolt, 2006).

The major novel aspect in the presented work is a modular and automated approach, which streamlines data acquisition, keyword extraction and taxonomy creation as the basis for trend detection. The framework provides evidence for growing technologies to decision makers in a logically structured manner. We therefore believe that it carries an enormous business potential within the realm of technology management.

BACKGROUND

Technology Forecasting. In order to assist purely expert-based technology management, automated bibliometrics techniques (i.e. the analysis of scientific publications) have been developed (Kostoff, 2001; Daim et al., 2006; Martino, 2003; Porter, 2005; Porter, 2007). These works perform bibliometric analyses in various ways: most commonly used are publication per year statistics for single keywords; other approaches deal with the inter-relationships between research topics, the identification of key authors and their collaboration patterns, the study of research performance and the core competences per country, institute or company.

The open problems with the existing approaches are related to the lack of structuring of the available input data: for example, when analyzing the trend of "Solar cells", the conventional methods will ignore documents on "Amorphous silicon", if they do not explicitly mention the main category. Also, within a research field, such as Photovoltaics, conventional approaches cannot detect the strongest contributing subfields (Organic Photovoltaics) because of the lacking concept hierarchy. Finally, they do not deal with vocabulary mismatch (synonyms, alternative wording).

Data acquisition and corpus generation. The main challenge of general data acquisition and data integration is that data has to be represented using the same abstraction principles. This challenge is frequently tackled with ontology-based approaches (Noy 2004, Kalfoglou 2003). They allow for the semantic integration of heterogeneous databases (i.e. the detection of correspondences in database schemata). In the case of web-based

Technology Forecasting, we can draw from a number of diverse sources such as scientific publication databases, patent collections and blogs, however, the actual challenge of data integration boils down to the identification of entities that include a textual representation (abstracts or full text documents, blog entries, patent abstracts, claims), timestamps, and possibly keyword/tag annotations and authors including their affiliation/country. Ideally, the relevant, distributed databases would be accessible as a seamless, unified virtual data warehouse, interlinked through query interfaces such as SPARQL. Unfortunately, many database web front-ends are not configured for automated querying and data acquisition and access to large scale document and patent collections in machine-readable formats is rarely permitted to the public. Notable exceptions include the Open Archive Initiative (OAI) repositories machine. The OAI provides standards for web content interoperability such as a unified protocol for harvesting meta-data of publications. In the context of bibliometric analysis it is promising to see that as of 2009, 20% of all publications are now freely available, though not all in OAI archives (Björk, 2009). Blogs are commonly provided as RSS feeds but as a data source, it is important to keep in mind that they often contain only poorly structured information with the least amount of peer review.

Term Extraction. With the advent of the semantic web era, many communities and distributed companies simultaneously access and update textual online resources. For several web applications it is important to model the knowledge domain of such virtual communities. One of the fundamental steps of this modeling process is the modeling of the used vocabulary (i.e. the identification of domain-relevant terms). This step is often referred to as "keyword extraction" or "term extraction", in this context we also include keyphrase extraction, as English research terminology often includes compound word phrases.

The goal is to identify significant terms from a given corpus. The algorithms therein describe term extraction methods using statistical and linguistic features. In general, terms are detected after removal of stop words (words of little or no information gain such as "and", "the", "like"). The state of the art of automated techniques includes four different approaches:

- Techniques from Statistical Natural language processing. In order to detect potential candidates, N-gram (often unigram, bigram and trigram) models have been suggested (Manning, 1999). They provide a mean to estimate the probability of observing a phrase in a text using conditional probabilities of the n-1 preceding words. Further estimates for the significance of a term in a document are term frequency (TF), inverse document frequency (IDF), their product (TFIDF) and the position of a term in a document.

- Linguistic features for keyword extraction have been proposed, such as part of speech tags and part of speech tag patterns (for phrases), have been proposed (Hulth, 2003)

- Supervised Machine Learning techniques. They take as training data a set of documents for which keywords have been assigned manually. Documents are represented with features using the abovementioned techniques (Turney, 2000; Hulth, 2003).

It is important to emphasize that simple features as employed in KEA (Witten, 1999) using TFIDF and Naive Bayesian Classifiers perform reasonably well in comparison to sophisticated Machine Learning approaches. Moreover, statistical methods do not require any training data, are straightforward to implement and run fast. For a thorough review of keyword extraction methods, the reader is referred to (Pazienza et al., 2005).

A number of online web tools for term extraction from text corpora exist, such as TerMine[1] (Frantzi, 2000) and in Yahoo!'s Query Language YQL[2]. In the case of the Yahoo! term extraction, a programmable interface (API) is provided. These web-based tools are useful as long as the demand of the user does not exceed the limitations, these web servers are commonly afflicted with. The limitations include volume restricted corpus size, the number of queries or restricted amount network traffic.

Taxonomy Creation. Taxonomies for scientific research bodies facilitate the organization of knowledge. They are applied in Information Retrieval tasks such as Semantic Web search engines (Shadbolt et al., 2006) and semantic database integration (Noy, 2004), where it is beneficial to abstract from plain words to hierarchical concepts. Many approaches for Ontology learning (Maedche, 2001) include the creation of taxonomies as a preliminary step. The commonly used techniques can be summarized as follows:

- Lexico-syntactic patterns (Hearst, 1992)
- Hyponymy information from WordNet (Miller, 1990)
- Noun phrase head matching (Navigli, 2003)
- Information theoretic approaches (Sanderson, 1999);
- Graph-theoretic approaches (Heymann, 2006)

The first approach is afflicted with a low recall in most corpora, whereas the latter approaches rely on the distributional hypothesis introduced by (Harris, 1968). It states that two words that appear in many similar linguistic contexts are semantically similar. However, this view is afflicted with the challenge that general terms such as "energy" and "fossil", or terms that somehow interact (e.g., "hammer" and "nail"), frequently co-occur and hence exhibit a misleadingly high co-occurrence similarity. Yet neither are subsumable in the strict sense ("is-a" or "part-of" relations) of standard taxonomies. Therefore, machine learning approaches have been used as meta-classifiers

Figure 1. The generic technology forecasting framework described in this chapter

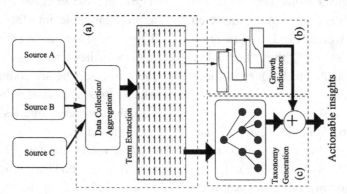

(Cimiano, 2004). They combine several of the above mentioned techniques. Yet, the authors report that the best of these classifiers, a Support Vector Machine, only reached 33% percent F-measure. Likewise, a comparison of seven fully automated state-of-the-art taxonomy creation tools exhibited mediocre results with F-measures not exceeding 50% (Waechter, 2009). These results explain, why semi-automated methods are still frequently used.

The remainder of this chapter is organized as follows: The next section introduces a generic framework for a complete Technology Forecasting workflow. We discuss each module individually and how it is integrated in the framework. The usefulness of this methodology is demonstrated in the subsequent section, where we describe proof of concept implementations and their applications to case studies. Finally, we outline potential future research directions and draw conclusions in the last section.

FRAMEWORK

Over the past two years we have been working on a variety of taxonomy-based techniques for performing Web-based Technology Forecasting, (Woon and Madnick, 2009; Woon et al., 2009). While there are existing studies which address various aspects of this problem, it appears that an integrated and automated framework which can produce concrete, actionable results has not yet been satisfactorily presented. This chapter presents a detailed explanation of our approach, which goes some way towards addressing this need.

The high-level organization of our system is shown in Figure 1. To facilitate discussion, the system has been divided into the following conceptual blocks:

1. Data collection from web sources,
2. Term extraction,
3. Design of growth indicators,
4. Taxonomy generation,
5. Visualization of accumulated growth indicators.

These blocks and their inter-relations are shown respectively in Figure 1. In the following subsections these will be discussed in more detail. However, we would like to stress that the modular nature of this framework means that individual parts can be exchanged or modified without affecting the overall functionality of the system.

Data Acquisition and Corpus Generation

The initial process of data acquisition, shown in Figure 1(a), can draw from a broad variety of available sources. They differ in the breadth of their respective focus areas, accuracy, recency and machine readability. The corpus generation process unifies these heterogeneous data sources and ensures the integrity of important meta-data such as time stamps, document identifiers, authors and possibly keyword annotations and document titles/headers. In principle we consider blogs, conference papers, journal papers and patents (listed in order of increasing accuracy and decreasing recency). Data from the latter three is preferably acquired through professionally curate citation repositories such as Scopus, Google Scholar, Scirus, Compendex, PubMed, ISI Web of Science, the European Patent Office (EPO), the United States Patent and Trademark Office (USPTO), and the Derwent World Patents Index.

Further improvements could include author network analyses (see refs in the Future work section), which would impose additional requirements such as authors, their affiliations and possibly further information in order to disambiguate author names.

Term Extraction

Once a corpus of sufficient relevant documents is generated, we proceed with the task of Term Extraction (see Figure 1 (b)). Where applicable, i.e when documents are annotated already in scientific databases, keyword annotations can be used to guide the term extraction process: a simple approach would be rank these keywords according to their respective frequencies, where the most frequent keywords are collected and used as the domain vocabulary.

Multiple-word noun phrases are essential for Technology Forecasting, since many technology descriptions in the English language are composed of more than one word. Noun phrases can be detected with reasonable accuracy using a chain of state-of-the-art tools from Natural Language Processing, typically sentence and word tokenization, part-of-speech tagging and noun phrase chunking (Bird et al., 2009). Noun phrases can be compounds of nouns ("waste combustion"), adjective noun phrases ("thermal treatment"), prepositional and noun phrases ("board of directors"). Statistical significance of words or word phrases can then be estimated using information retrieval measures, in order to avoid irrelevant terms which are not specific for a certain technology (e.g. "review" or "approach"). These terms cause confusion in the downstream data processing such as the taxonomy creation. Ideally the extracted terms should be of low ambiguity and high specificity. These properties are preconditions for the conceptualization of a knowledge domain and the creation of a domain taxonomy/ontology.

One advantage of using an automated term extraction tool in addition to a manual one is that emerging technology terms and research field names can be potentially detected before they are recognized and consistently attached as keywords to articles. It also allows for working with data sources having poor or no keyword annotations, such as a variety of blogs.

Because of the aforementioned limitations in state-of-the-art web-tools we describe a small, powerful tool for offline usage in the next section. It provides full control over the selection of linguistic and statistical features in the term extraction process. Moreover, full control of the term extraction process is useful, if more customization towards a certain purpose is desirable (e.g. in the context of technology forecasting, it is easily possible in combination with the local literature database to extract only terms from a certain subset of the corpus, such as only recent documents).

Finally, it should be mentioned that corpus generation and term extraction can be viewed as an iterative, co-evolving process: newly extracted keywords can be used to extend the corpus, which in turn effects the next iteration of term extraction.

Growth Indicators

Given a set of keywords, we strive to find a suitable measure of their prevalence (Figure 1(c)). We hereby focus on keywords with relatively low but recently increasing occurrence frequency, which we refer to as "Early Growth" phase. As an easily derivable indicator in the context of bibliometric trend analysis it is helpful to look at the absolute amount of the growth rate of recent publications. A second step is to normalize the annual publication rates either by total volume of that particular technology or by total publication rate for all technologies. One particular growth indicator we focus on is the average publication year for a certain technology, defined in the following Equation 1.

$$\theta_i = \frac{\sum_y \in y \cdot TF_y[t_i]}{\sum_y \in y TF_y[t_i]} \tag{1}$$

where θ_i is the growth potential for keyword t_i and $TF_y[t_i]$ is the term frequency for term t_i for a given year time span Y under consideration. This measure reflects the majority of publications, irrespective of its volume. Consequently, it facilitates the detection of recent topics, even small ones. Conclusions about trends with low publication volume must be drawn cautiously though, as they are prone to artifacts.

While curve fitting approaches are also commonly utilized, we refrain from using this approach for two main reasons: firstly, data might often follow an unexpected distribution that cannot be fitted using a preconceived shape. Renewable Energy technologies are influenced by political issues such as oil price regulations. As a consequence, it can be seen that "Solar thermal power" experienced a revival in recent years after being a hot topic in the early 80's (coinciding with the oil crisis of 1979) followed by a decrease of activity during the mid-80's until the mid-90's. For instance see (Dawelbait et al, 2010). The concept of technol-

ogy revival or other turbulences is generally not reflected by trend discovery techniques such as the Fisher-Pry model and Gompertz (S-shaped) curves. Secondly, the statistical stability of a trend discovery relies on the exclusion of artifacts such as noisy term frequencies combined with low document coverage. As will be seen, our use of accumulated term statistics mitigates this problem to some extent. Yet, fluctuations are still present, especially when working with small corpora. For those cases, curve fitting methods would be equally inappropriate.

Taxonomy Generation

Taxonomies and ontologies (which additionally include non-taxonomic semantic relations for concepts) have been used for similar problems in the field of information retrieval (Wang, 2009). A feature of this approach is that a technology can be further analyzed in terms of its subcategories. If a general technology such as "Solar power" is on the rise, it is possible to retrieve a more differentiated view of the individual contributors thanks to the hierarchical nature of the used taxonomy. Unfortunately, in many cases a suitable taxonomy is not available. Moreover, manual taxonomy construction is costly and subjective.

In order to make our framework broadly applicable, we developed automatic and semi-automatic taxonomy creation algorithms (Figure 1(d)). In particular, in this study we consider a taxonomy creation process based on the Heymann-Algorithm (Heymann and Garcia-Molina, 2006). We previously considered as well two other approaches as described in (Woon and Madnick, 2009). The original aim of the Heymann-algorithm was the analysis of social tagging systems, where users collaboratively annotate a body of documents via the use of topical labels, also known as "tags". Inversion of this information results in a look-up table where each tag is associated with a vector that contains the frequencies of annotations for all documents. The Heymann-algorithm consists of the following two stages:

1. Firstly, a similarity scores are used to create a weighted graph of tags; this is then used to calculate the centrality of each of the tags. In graph theory, centrality is a measure of the connectedness of a node in a graph (a few approaches to calculating graph centrality exist (see our description in [Henschel et al., 2009] for example).

2. The tags are then ranked according to their respective centralities, and are inserted into a growing taxonomy in accordance to this ranking; the attachment of the tags is also determined by the similarity measure described above, where each tag is attached to either the most similar tag or to the taxonomy root.

Both parts involve similarity measures between terms. Originally the authors in (Heymann and Garcia-Molina, 2006) used vectors $\mathbf{x}_t=[x_1,\ldots,x_N]$ of length equal to the number of documents N, where x_1 describes, how many times a numbered document *i* in a user community has been annotated with term t. In Equation 2, we adapt this to binary term-vectors (or set representations) indicating whether a term occurs in a document (1) or not (0). Standard cosine vector similarity is therefore applicable.

$$S_{\cos}(x, y) = \frac{x \cdot y}{\| x \| \| y \|} \quad (2)$$

where **x** and **y** are binary term vectors. Hence, the similarity between two terms is simply the dot product of its normalized term vectors. We discuss several aspects that can be modified in order to boost the algorithm: generality ordering, similarity measures and weight functions insertion of new nodes. Other measures of distance are possible. For example, in (Woon and Madnick, 2009) we

proposed an asymmetric distance function which is used to reflect the distances of terms that are in a taxonomic "is-a" relationship.

Complementary to fully automated taxonomy generation methods, we explore in this study the utilization of ontological background knowledge. This knowledge can be assumed to be previously indicated by an expert of the particular field of interest. Alternatively, such information may be extracted from online resources such as Wikipedia, a large-scale and accurate resource well-suited for Semantic Web and Information Extraction applications. (Giles, 2005, Auer et al., 2007). In both cases, the previous Heymann-algorithm is modified by starting its computation by a preexisted prior taxonomy. While the initial structure of such taxonomy maybe suboptimal by overconstraining the previous exploratory analysis and may hide interesting patterns in the data, it is possible that a semi automatic algorithm may be of a better interpretation by an expert in the field. This may help to refine his knowledge and modify in case his prior taxonomy. In the following case study section, we discuss both automatic and semiautomatic generation modality.

Growth Indicator Accumulation and Visualization

Finally, with the keyword taxonomies we can recalculate the early growth indicators based on aggregate scores of each of the individual scores of subordinate keywords contained in the according subtree of the taxonomy (Figure 1(e)). Several ways of aggregation are possible (i.e. the growth indication scores of subordinate terms can be either weighted equally or, for example, in terms their associated publication volume). We describe and implement both in the following case of study.

Single and accumulated growth indicators can be visualized in order to provide intuitive and actionable insights about the hot topics of a certain domain. Most commonly, trends are visualized by plotting over time as in (Woon et al., 2010). We further seek to integrate the visualization of growth indicators with the underlying knowledge structure (i.e. the taxonomy as provided by the taxonomy creation algorithm of Section "Taxonomy Generation"). To this end we developed two visualization techniques: color coded hierarchies and hierarchical tag clouds. The font size or color of a node reflects the average publication year of the branch under that node. This visualization technique is adapted from tag clouds that are useful as visual information retrieval interfaces (Lohmann et al., 2009). The hierarchical arrangement of tag clouds places semantically related terms nearby which are reported to be advantageous (Hassan-Montero and Herrero-Solana, 2006) for the viewer's perception of the research field. By using font sizes or node colorings to represent growth potential, we are able to overlay this important information on top of the structural information conveyed by the keyword taxonomies. A further important advantage is that encoding the growth indicators in this way allows provides the growth of entire regions in the landscape to be detected – this would be very difficult to do, for example, if the indicators were merely presented as a ranked list of terms.

RESULTS: PROOF OF CONCEPT INSTANTIATIONS APPLIED TO SELECTED CASE STUDIES IN RENEWABLE ENERGY

It is important to note that the system described in Figure 1 is merely a high-level framework, and that each of the five components can be implemented in a variety of different ways. In the following sections we discuss proof-of-concept instantiations in an instructive manner.

To provide a concrete application domain for developing and testing our tools, it was decided that a case study in a specific domain of technology was required. As our research has been supported by the Masdar Initiative, the natural choice was to conduct a study of the field of renewable energy

(RE). It is an active area of research, the ultimate goal of which is to find and exploit new forms of energy; prominent examples include a variety of "green" energy technologies such as wind power, solar heating or biomass. The advancement of RE technologies is of critical importance as traditional resources such as coal, oil and natural gas are finite in nature and are also damaging to the environment. In addition, the research landscape of RE is rapidly evolving and is extremely rich in that research in RE is intricately linked with research in a variety of seemingly unrelated scientific disciplines. The framework outline above provides a decision maker with an eagle eye perspective over a research landscape. Previously, we studied trends in Renewable Energy Desalination and Power Generation (Dawelbait et al, 2010). To further focus our efforts, the examples presented in this chapter will be centered on the research landscape of a particular RE subfields, amongst them biofuel and Waste-to-energy (W2E).

W2E is described as the process in which waste is used to generate electricity or heat. There is a growing interest in this technology since it helps to avoid waste disposal related environmental problems, while serving as a valuable source of renewable fuel. Supported by our web mining methodology, we are interested to undertake an exploratory analysis of the W2E research. Firstly, we will produce a comprehensive hierarchical map which represents the state-of-art of W2E topics, processes, products and infrastructures. Secondly, we are keen to use this map to identify recently growing W2E areas in order to inform the decision making process of science and technology management for possible investments and/or to propose solutions for a sustainable and clean world.

Waste to Energy Publication Corpus

After an initial survey of possible web sources we chose SCOPUS as the central source of data acquisition. SCOPUS is a subscription based,

Figure 2. Algorithm

Algorithm 1 Most Frequent TFIDF Keywords

Require: corpus $\mathbb{C}$, extended corpus $\mathbb{C}'$
  for all documents $d \in \mathbb{C}$ **do**
    Tokenize d
    Add Part-of-speech tags to d
    Identify Noun-phrases $t_1^d, \ldots, t_{d_k}^d$
  end for
  Initialize Frequency distribution F
  for all documents $d \in \mathbb{C}$ **do**
    for all tokens t_i^d **do**
      Calculate TFIDF(t_i^d) wrt. $\mathbb{C}'$
    end for
    Update F with $\arg\max\{t_i^d | \text{TFIDF}(t_i^d) > \text{threshold}\}$
  end for
---

professionally curate publication database provided by Elsevier. It provides document records generally of high quality in terms of Meta-data annotation, publication coverage and search term relevance. Assuming that a large selection of relevant documents can be retrieved in a machine readable format, the entire corpus is then preferably stored in a relational database, as in our case study. This solution provides fast and easy access to subsets such as documents from a certain year range. The database also features search enhancing tools such as search indices, full text search and the storage of secondary data such as word-stemmed abstracts and identified noun phrases of abstracts.

Extraction of Waste to Energy Terms

For term extraction we used the most frequent keywords associated to documents by SCOPUS. Additionally we apply the NLP based term extraction algorithm described in Figure 2. The algorithm generates keywords for each abstract by identifying noun phrases and we use a set of tools that are part of the NLTK toolbox (Bird et al., 2009) such as its built-in sentence word Tokenizer.

The identified keywords are scored by the TFIDF scheme [Salton and McGill, 1984], which we refer as TFIDF-keywords. The TFIDF of a keyword t_i is given in Equation 3.

$$TFIDF[t_i^d] = TF[t_i^d] \cdot IDF[t_i] \qquad (3)$$

which is the product of the term frequency $TF[t_i^d]$ (i.e. the number of times a term t_i occurs in a document d divided by the number of words in that document) and the inverse document frequency $IDF[t_i]$ (i.e. the logarithm of the number of all documents divided by the number of documents where the term occurs). While the former accounts for the emphasis of a word in terms of repetitions in a document, the latter makes sure that words occurring almost everywhere are downgraded. We then select the most frequent of these TFIDF-keywords.

As a result, the most frequently occurring words of the Waste to energy corpus (shown in Table 1) such as "results", "effect", "study", "paper" are not present in the list of most frequent TFIDF-keywords. Unfortunately, general or more abstract terms that are still useful for taxonomy creation such as "process", "temperature" or "biomass" are also eliminated because they are abundant in the selected corpus. This effect can be mitigated by extending the corpus with unrelated scientific documents (denoted $\mathbb{C}'$ in the algorithm), such that it will be distinguishable whether terms are specific for a certain research field only or whether they are generally used.

In effect, general research terms such as "experiment" still receive a low inverse document

Table 1. The first column contains the ranked list of the most frequent keywords as annotated by SCOPUS together with its frequencies. The second column list the most frequent, self extracted TFIDF-keywords and their respective frequencies.

Ranking	Keyword	Term Frequency	Keyword	Term Frequency
1.	results	4124	soil	106
2.	study	3562	ethanol	103
3.	biomass	2933	mg/l	98
4.	effect	1876	model	98
5.	paper	1761	hydrogen	90
6.	production	1671	coal	87
7	process	1606	reactors	87
8.	addition	1565	pyrolysis	84
9.	treatment	1520	phenol	83
10.	order	1465	sludge	80
11.	removal	1447	gasification	79
12.	days	1380	sewage sludge	78
13.	waste	1352	biosorption	77
14.	effects	1332	methanol	71
15.	temperature	1325	heavy metals	69
16.	reactor	1298	food waste	67
17.	sludge	1216	reactor	66
18.	presence	1144	biofilm	65
19.	system	1117	biosolids	60
20.	wastewater	1107	membrane	57

frequency, whereas frequent yet domain specific terms such as "biomass" score a higher inverse document frequency and are hence ranked higher. In our case study we therefore offset significant W2E-terms with respect to their occurrences in biomedical literature, extracted from PubMed Central, a freely available database of scientific abstracts. The extracted terms are shown in the rightmost column of Table 1. The final selection is subject to a careful choice of the extended corpus and the involved thresholds (i.e. how many TFIDF-keywords per document and which minimal TFIDF value should be chosen).

Afterwards we applied manual post-processing and stop lists (e.g., geographic terms from SCOPUS' controlled keyword vocabulary can be useful for classifying publications by geographic location). However, for technology taxonomies these terms are generally irrelevant.

Taxonomy Creation: Fully Automated Taxonomies

Firstly, the fully automated taxonomy creation process was used to analyze the data. As mentioned previously, our approach is based on the Heymann-Algorithm as described in Section "Taxonomy Creation". To demonstrate the applicability of this approach to technology forecasting, we apply it to a number of different domains. In general, the taxonomies resulting from these analyses are quite large, so what we show in the following pages is

Figure 3. Taxonomy subtree for semiconducting cadmium compounds

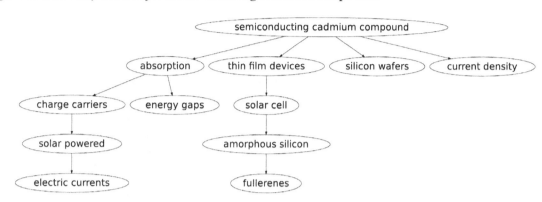

Figure 4. Taxonomy subtree for silicon

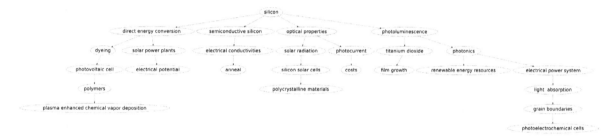

a sampling of interesting sub-trees which have been extracted from the corresponding publication corpora.

It is also important to note that the algorithms demonstrated here have a number of variations or "settings" which control the execution of the algorithm. Examples of these include the number and selection of keywords used, the type of centrality measure and the type of similarity metric used to compare the tags. We concede that varying these settings can significantly alter the resulting taxonomy. However it is not within the scope of this chapter to systematically investigate the effect each of these settings has on the taxonomy generation process; instead, readers are referred to (Henschel et al., 2009, Camina, 2010), which provide a much more detailed treatment of this issue. The subtrees presented here are chosen to be typical of the kinds of results that were obtained, and are aimed at providing the reader with an idea of the capabilities of our approach.

Example subtrees from the following three RE-related research domains have been selected and are presented here:

- **Solar PV:** Example subtrees were gen\ erated for the "semiconducting cadmium compounds" (Figure 3) and "silicon" subtrees (Figure 4).
- **Geothermal Energy:** Example subtree for "rocks" was generated (Figure 5).
- **Waste to Energy (W2E):** Example subtrees for this domain were generated for "biomass" (Figure 6) and "wastewater" (Figure 7)

All taxonomies were generated using the Heymann algorithm, and the Sine distance was used to create the distance matrices (this is the distance-based analog of the Cosine distance). The number of keywords used for each taxonomy ranged from 100 to 400.

Figure 5. Taxonomy subtree for rocks

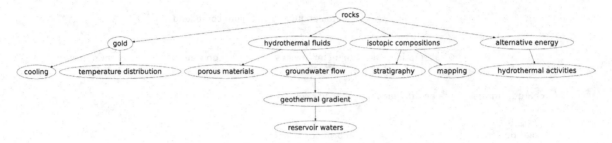

Figure 6. Taxonomy subtree for biomass

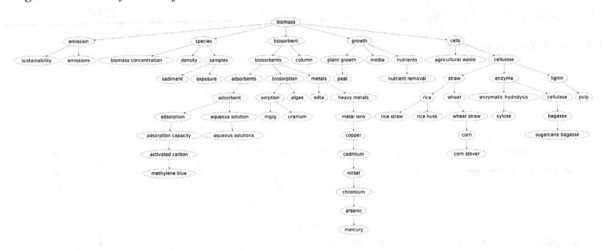

Figure 7. Taxonomy subtree for wastewater

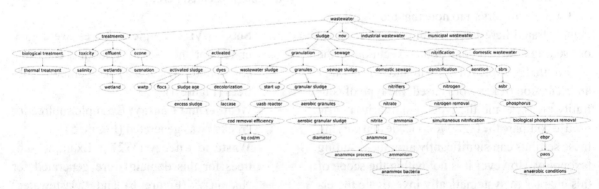

Our main observations are as follows:

1. The quality of the results varied significantly between domains and between subtrees within the same domain.

2. For the "semiconducting cadmium compounds" subtree (Figure 3), it can be seen that a number of related topics were correctly attached, for example *absorption* and the related sub-topics (related to the physics of light absorption), and *thin film devices*, which are an important application of these cadmium compounds.

3. One interesting example where the results are not as good as in "semiconducting cadmium compounds" is in the case of the "rocks" subtree (extracted from the geothermal taxonomy). In this case, we see that the four sub-topics are *gold*, *hydrothermal fluids*, *isotopic combinations* and *alternative energy*. While it is possible to conceive of each of these topics as being related to "rocks", it is quite clear that in this case the algorithm has not produced an informative taxonomic structure. What appears to have happened is that an extremely general term ("rocks"), has, by virtue of its generality, artificially grouped a collection of terms which are otherwise unrelated (or only weakly related).

4. The two W2E subtrees ("biomass" and "wastewater") are significantly larger and more complex than the other subtrees shown here, and helped to highlight the performance of the algorithm with respect to very complex taxonomies. Broadly speaking, the two taxonomies seemed to provide a good illustration of their respective subject areas. However, upon closer inspection, we see that there are a number of irregularities, which would merit further study.

5. In Figure 7, the series of nodes from "heavy metal" to "mercury" represent compounds which are related but which are clearly not subclasses of each other. A similar situation is encountered with the "granulation" to "diameter" path in Figure 8, where we see that each of the three intervening nodes contain some variant of the term "granule". In this example, the similarity function would appear to be picking up semantic relationships rather than actual technological dependencies.

6. As a further example, consider the *thin film devices* → *solar cells* → *amorphous silicon fullerenes* branch in Figure 3. On the one hand, these are all topics which are closely related while on the other hand, it is still difficult to explain how *solar cells* came to be a sub-topic of *thin film devices*. We can surmise that the taxonomic structure induced on the keywords might work in a similar fashion to the related technique of hierarchical clustering.

7. These questions raise one of the main problems with the approach, which is that it is difficult to find a clear interpretation of the taxonomic links. While a traditional taxonomy is commonly defined by "is-a" relationships, it is clear that the automatically generated taxonomies do not necessarily follow this rule.

Taxonomy Creation: Incorporation of Expert Knowledge

In conclusion, we note that fully automated taxonomy generation techniques are able to produce results that are interesting. However, it is also faced with a variety of problems. Firstly, automated taxonomy generation is a somewhat inconsistent process which can, under unfavorable conditions, result in inaccurate or noisy results. Secondly, the choice of algorithm settings is also a difficult problem for which there is no straightforward solution.

A viable alternative might be to opt for a semi-automatic process which would allow some prior knowledge to be incorporated into the taxonomy generation process. This allows for the best of both worlds to be enjoyed. On the one hand, we benefit from the advantages of the automatic approach, namely the ability to quickly incorporate the latest developments as well as to efficiently utilize very large quantities of data; on the other hand, taking a semi-automatic approach allows for valuable input from experts and other manually curate sources to be taken into account. By providing a scaffold or framework with which the taxonomies may be initialized, this approach helps to significantly reduce the uncertainty and inconsistency experienced when purely automatic approaches are used.

Depending on the desired accuracy and the final purpose of taxonomies, their fully automated creation remains a very ambitious endeavor. Many researchers have therefore suggested semi-automated protocols, in which experts have manual influence during various stages of the taxonomy/ontology creation process. The field of Ontology Engineering deals with these aspects. Cimiano points out that automatic extension of existing ontologies have been shown to work successfully (Cimiano, 2006). As a consequence, tools have been created which help to extend ontologies by suggesting terms and their location in the ontology (e.g. within the context of the Gene Ontology project). We therefore investigate the possibility to capitalize on available expert knowledge as an initial guidance to the taxonomy creation process. Note that this approach is an appropriate alternative to the fully automated procedure where expert knowledge is available. We emphasize that we can easily extend the formalism of the Heymann-Algorithm to accommodate initial expert knowledge. The precondition is that terms -at least the expandable nodes- of the expert guidelines must occur frequently in the corpus in order to provide compatibility in terms of the similarity measure. In that case, expert knowledge can be formalized as an initial taxonomy, which is then extensible in the same way, the automatic Heymann algorithm extends a growing taxonomy.

Visualization

Figure 8 shows a taxonomy which has been constructed in collaboration with an expert of W2E technologies. The taxonomy largely consists of predefined taxonomic relations, which are subsequently extended with 100 TFIDF keywords (larger taxonomies can be found in the Supplementary material). In addition, as mentioned in section "Growth indicator accumulation and visualization", the growth indicators were also incorporated into the figure by modulating the font sizes. As mentioned previously, we have used both font sizes and color-codings to convey growth indicators; however using font sizes has an important advantage in that these are preserved when the document is printed in black and white, which is the reason for its use here.

If such a semi-automatically created taxonomy is embedded in the general framework (Figure 1), it is interesting to inspect the growth indicators (i.e. the recency and the volume of the research bodies associated to each node [shown respectively in all nodes]). In particular we note that the font-size modulation allows the growth potential of the nodes to be very clearly visualized. It can for example be seen that the top level categories at taxonomy level 1 and 2 are all balanced out in terms of recency (all are within 1999-2001) due to the average of their associated subtopics. "Plasma Gasification" is the most recent topic (2006). Moreover, it becomes apparent that recently "Biodiesel production" is frequently discussed in the context of "Transesterification". This is evidenced by a body of 105 publications with average publication year 2007. The findings for Biodiesel are consistent with earlier results reported in (Dawelbait et al, 2010) even though a different corpus and a different keyword set was used. The taxonomy created with frequent keywords (Supplementary material S1) unravels that "Removal experiments" have been mentioned in 272 documents with an average date of 2007. A further inspection into the corpus reveals that indeed a large number of recent papers mention different kinds of removal experiments, such as nitrogen removal. Another term that grew to recent popularity is "Wastewater reclamation". We found its mention in 433 papers.

In general, it must be said that the recency of subordinate terms are generally independent from each other (i.e. the W2E research landscape developed rather heterogeneous). This is in contrast to the related study on Renewable Energy (Supplementary material, Figure 2). There, com-

Figure 8. Semi-automatic taxonomy for W2E, incorporating expert knowledge and 100 TFIDF keywords. Average publication year and associated research body is provided for each term. Large fonts indicate strong recent growth.

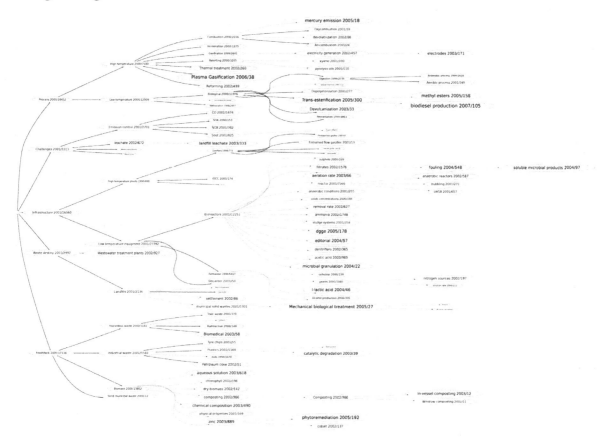

plete branches including subordinate terms could be identified as hot topics, for example most subordinate terms of "Biofuels".

CONCLUSION

Summary of Findings and Analysis

In this chapter, a novel framework for analyzing and forecasting the growth of technology has been presented. This framework has been developed to efficiently mine online databases in order to enhance R&D operations and inform technological decision-making in a given field of science and technology. The high-level organization of our system comprises a series of computational steps:

1. Data collection from web sources
2. The extraction of domain-relevant keywords
3. The design of growth indicators
4. Automatic and semi-automatic taxonomy generation

In order to validate the technical implementation of our framework we consider possible examples of analysis in the domain of the renewable energy and particularly in the subfield of Waste-to-Energy (W2E). The results of our analysis, as validated by an expert in the field, confirm the benefits of using our approach.

Table 2. A listing of possible future research organized by respective system block

Block	Current approach	Possible future techniques/research directions
Data/ Sources **(A)**	Currently, the Scopus publication database is used.	Future research in this area can be divided into two main topics: • Determination of broader/more diverse sources of publication statistics. Examples include internet-based sources like Google scholar, scirus and Microsoft Academic search, patent databases like Lexis-Nexis, "social" resources like blogs and twitter feeds, technical reports and even the popular press. • Incorporation of more intelligence into the process – a particularly interesting idea would be to place a weighting over the sources depending on the quality or degree of confidence in the database. A simple example would be to use the journal impact factors to determine the weighting of publications appearing in the different databases.
Term extraction **(B)**	Selection of terms is based on term frequencies	A variety of term extraction algorithms have been presented in the literature; these have already been detailed above but briefly, many use more sophisticated methods based on natural language processing (NLP). One notable avenue that we hope to pursue is the extraction of significant or frequently occurring tuples of words (n-grams) or noun-phrases. A further direction that could prove important is to involve subject matter experts in the term collection process. This could either be via direct methods (i.e. asking the experts to list interesting terms), or through relevance feedback methods, where the experts is asked to evaluate an automatically generated subset, allowing it to be further fine-tuned.
Growth indicators **(C)**	Average publication year	In other publications, we have already attempted other growth indicators, generally based on estimating the first or second derivative of the publication growth. Avenues for future investigation include: • Identification of more advanced growth indicators, possibly based on technical indicators from the field of finance • Another promising direction is the creation of hybrid indicators that involve the combination of a number of basic growth indicators via committee-based or averaging schemes.
Taxonomy genera-tion **(D)**	In this publication both fully automatic and semi automatic techniques have been explored. However, both approaches are based on variants of the Heyman algorithm.	This is an area that is under intense development and research. The following areas, in particular, have looked promising: • One problem with the Heymann-algorithm is that it is used primarily in batch mode, where a large set of keywords are structured into a taxonomy based on their usage patterns. An alternative strategy would be to use document classification techniques in an iterative manner to partition the research landscape into a hierarchy of categories. The advantage of this approach is that new and previously unseen materials can be quickly added to the existing taxonomy. • Probabilistic topic models are a special class of machine learning methods which represent the content of a document as a mixture of latent variables (i.e. topics) (Steyvers and Griffiths, 2007). A topic is a semantic entity that describes an idea, a concept or an argument the author of a document is expressing through a mixture of words and sentences. In particular, we are keen on using these hidden concepts instead of single keywords as in this chapter to analyze a collection of scientific documents related to the technologies of interest, link their relationships and track their evolution over time. Moreover, since these models are based on a Bayesian framework they can be designed to incorporate prior knowledge to extend and improve the process of taxonomy creation and keyword extraction in the previous stages. • Finally, alternative visualization schemes such as topographic maps are also being considered. These still allow the relationships between domains of research to be easily visualized but, unlike taxonomies, do not impose restrictive and *a priori* structural constraints on these relationships. Such maps can be generated using a variety of techniques such as multidimensional scaling and spring force models.
Growth indicator accumulation **(E)**	Growth indicators for nodes attached to a common ancestor are simply averaged to obtain the overall score.	• Different weighted averaging approaches could be attempted, for example one could devise a scheme that prioritizes more immediate descendants over "distant relatives". • We are also interested in trying more sophisticated approaches that analyze the growth indicators for attached nodes and detects patterns beyond simply aggregate growth. For example, one cluster could contain nodes that are uniformly "high growth", while another might have a mix of extremely high and low growth nodes. While these two example could theoretically have the same average growth rates, there are important qualitative differences between the two which might be important.

However, the results also point to some limitations of a completely automatic process of taxonomy generation, where several inconsistencies in the relationships between keywords have been found. These observations highlight the inherent difficulty of inferring a taxonomic structure from incomplete and noisy observations (such as those obtained from locally cached publication databases). To address this problem, our framework permits the incorporation of prior knowledge (by an expert or by a previously built taxonomy) into the taxonomy generation process, and this was shown to result in more stable results. Such an approach was demonstrated and was able to extract and highlight trends and patterns that were consistent with actual developments in the field of W2E.

Future Directions

As indicated in previous sections, it is important to note that the system described here does not represent the primary value of our work; rather the main innovation is in the overall framework, which describes how a number of separate activities can be combined in a novel way to facilitate the process of technology forecasting. However, the specific selection of algorithms used is by no means optimal (in fact they are intended only as an early demonstration of the potential capabilities of our methodology).

In the context of this formulation, the future development of this work could naturally be organized as the identification of optimal methods for conducting each of the activities depicted in blocks (a)→(d) (Fig. 1). These have been tabulated in the Table 2, as follows.

REFERENCES

Auer, S., Bizer, C., Kobilarov, G., Lehmann, J., Cyganiak, R., & Ives, Z. G. (2007). DBpedia: A nucleus for a Web of open data. In *ISWC* [Berlin, Germany: Springer.]. *Lecture Notes in Computer Science, 4825*, 722–735.

Bird, S., Klein, E., & Loper, E. (2009). *Natural language processing with Python: Analyzing text with the natural language toolkit.* Beijing, China: O'Reilly.

Björk, B.-C., Welling, P., Laakso, M., Majlender, P., & Hedlund, T. (2010). Open access to the scientific journal literature: Situation 2009. *PLoS ONE, 5*(6), e11273.

Camina, S. (2010). *A comparison of taxonomy generation techniques using bibliometric methods: Applied to research strategy formulation.* Meng., Massachusetts Institute of Technology.

Cimiano, P., Pivk, A., Schmidt-Thieme, L., & Staab, S. (2004). Learning taxonomic relations from heterogeneous sources. *Proceedings of the ECAI 2004 Ontology Learning and Population Workshop.*

Cimiano, P., Völker, J., & Studer, R. (2006). *Ontologies on demand: A description of the state-of-the-art, applications, challenges and trends for ontology learning from text.*

Daim, T. U., Rueda, G., Martin, H., & Gerdsri, P. (2006). Forecasting emerging technologies: Use of bibliometrics and patent analysis. *Technological Forecasting and Social Change, 73*(8), 981–1012.

Dawelbait, G., Mezher, T., Woon, W. L., & Henschel, A. (2010). Taxonomy based trend discovery of renewable energy technologies in desalination and power generation. In *Management of Engineering. Technology. PICMET.*

Frantzi, K., Ananiadou, S., & Mima, H. (2000). Automatic recognition of multi-word terms: the c-value/nc-value method. *International Journal on Digital Libraries*, *3*(2), 115–130.

Giles, J. (2005). Internet encyclopaedias go head to head. *Nature*, *438*(7070), 900–901.

Griffiths, T. L., Steyvers, M., & Tenenbaum, J. B. (2007). Topics in semantic representation. *Psychological Review*, *114*(2), 211–244.

Harris, Z. (1968). *Mathematical structures of language*. Wiley.

Hassan-Montero, Y., & Herrero-Solana, V. (2006). *Improving tag-clouds as visual information retrieval interfaces*. In InScit2006: International Conference on Multidisciplinary Information Sciences and Technologies.

Hearst, M. A. (1992). Automatic acquisition of hyponyms from large text corpora. *Proceedings of the Conference on Computational Linguistics*

Henschel, A., Wächter, T., Woon, W. L., & Madnick, S. (2009). Comparison of generality based algorithm variants for automatic taxonomy generation. *Proceedings of the International Conference on Innovations in Information Technology*, Al Ain, UAE.

Heymann, P., & Garcia-Molina, H. (2006). *Collaborative creation of communal hierarchical taxonomies in social tagging systems*. Technical Report 2006-10, Stanford University.

Hulth, A. (2003). Improved automatic keyword extraction given more linguistic knowledge. In *Proceedings of the Conference on Empirical Methods in Natural Language Processing (EMNLP'03)*, (pp. 216-223).

Kalfoglou, Y., & Schorlemmer, M. (2003). Ontology mapping: The state of the art. *The Knowledge Engineering Review*, *18*(1), 1–31.

Kostoff, R. N. (2001). Text mining using database tomography and bibliometrics: A review. *Technological Forecasting and Social Change*, *68*, 223–253.

Lohmann, S., Ziegler, J., & Tetzlaff, L. (2009). Comparison of tag cloud layouts: Task-related performance and visual exploration. In T. Gross, J. Gulliksen, P. Kotz, L. Oestreicher, P. A. Palanque, R. O. Prates, & M. Winckler (Eds.), *Proceedings of INTERACT, Lecture Notes in Computer Science*, *5726*, (pp. 392–404). Springer.

Maedche, A., & Staab, S. (2001). Ontology learning for the Semantic Web. *IEEE Intelligent Systems*, 16.

Manning, C. D., & Schütze, H. (1999). *Foundations of statistical natural language processing*. MIT Press.

Martino, J. P. (2003). A review of selected recent advances in technological forecasting. *Technological Forecasting and Social Change*, *70*(8), 719–733.

Miller, G. A., Beckwith, R., Fellbaum, C. D., Gross, D., & Miller, K. (1990). WordNet: An online lexical database. *International Journal of Lexicography*, *3*(4), 235–244.

Navigli, R., Velardi, P., & Gangemi, A. (2003). Ontology learning and its application to automated terminology translation. *IEEE Intelligent Systems*, *18*(1), 22–31.

Noy, N. F. (2004). Semantic integration: A survey of ontology-based approaches. *SIGMOD Record*, *33*(4), 65–70.

Pazienza, M., Pennacchiotti, M., & Zanzotto, F. (2005). *Terminology extraction: An analysis of linguistic and statistical approaches* (pp. 255–279). Berlin/ Heidelberg, Germany: Springer.

Porter, A. (2005). Tech mining. *Competitive Intelligence Magazine*, *8*(1), 30–36.

Porter, A. (2007). How tech mining can enhance R&D management. *Research Technology Management, 50*(2), 15–20.

Salton, G., & McGill, M. (1984). *Introduction to modern information retrieval.* McGraw-Hill Book Company.

Sanderson, M., & Croft, B. W. (1999). *Deriving concept hierarchies from text.* In ACM SIGMIR Conference on Research and Development in Information Retrieval, (pp. 206–213).

Shadbolt, N., Hall, W., & Berners-Lee, T. (2006). The Semantic Web revisited. *Intelligent Systems, 21*(3), 96–101.

Steyvers, M., & Griffiths, T. (2007). Probabilistic topic models. In Landauer, T., McNamara, D. S., Dennis, S., & Kintsch, W. (Eds.), *Handbook of latent semantic analysis.* Hillsdale, NJ: Erlbaum.

Wächter, T., & Schroeder, M. (2010). Semi-automated ontology generation within OBO-Edit*Bioinformatics, 26(10).* Oxford University Press.

Wang, P., Hu, J., Zeng, H. J., & Chen, Z. (2009). Using Wikipedia knowledge to improve text classification. *Knowledge and Information Systems, 19*(3), 265–281.

Witten, I., Paynte, G., Frank, E., Gutwin, C., & Nevill-Manning, C. (1999). KEA: Practical automatic keyphrase extraction. *In Proceedings of the 4th ACM Conference on Digital Library.*

Woon, W. L., Henschel, A., & Madnick, S. (2009). A framework for technology forecasting and visualization. In *Proceedings of the International Conference on Innovations in Information Technology*, Al Ain, UAE.

Woon, W. L., & Madnick, S. (2009). Asymmetric information distances for automated taxonomy construction. *Knowledge and Information Systems, 21*(1), 91–111.

Woon, W. L., Zeineldin, H., & Madnick, S. (2010). (in press). Bibliometric analysis of distributed generation. *Technological Forecasting and Social Change.*

ENDNOTES

[1]   http://www.nactem.ac.uk/software/termine
[2]   http://developer.yahoo.com/yql/

Section 2
Engineering Web–Enabled BI

Chapter 9
Business Intelligence-as-a-Service:
Studying the Functional and the Technical Architectures

Moez Essaidi
Université Paris-Nord, France

Aomar Osmani
Université Paris-Nord, France

ABSTRACT

In recent years, the data warehousing infrastructures have undergone many changes in various aspects. This is usually due to many factors: the emergence of Software-as-a-Service (SaaS) architecture model; the success of agile and iterative Data Warehouse (DW) development approaches; the introduction of new approaches based on the Model Driven Architecture (MDA); the changing needs of organizations and the extension of the DW into new application areas; and the evolving of standards and open-source technologies. This chapter explores several aspects that may influence the next-generation of data warehousing platforms: the architectural aspects for business intelligence-as-a-service deployment, the promising open industry standards and technologies recommended for use, and the emerging methodological aspects for DW components engineering.

DOI: 10.4018/978-1-61350-038-5.ch009

1. INTRODUCTION

Software-as-a-Service (SaaS) is a model for software delivery that allows lower total cost of ownership and better return on investment for subscribers (Software & Information Industry Association, 2006). Recently, several Business Intelligence (BI) platforms including some well known names have embraced this new model of architecture. These solutions present many advantages derived in general from the advantages of the SaaS concept. However, few solutions offer integrated platforms that cover all functional and technical aspects of the data warehousing architecture. Indeed, these tools focus only on the problem of the business intelligence services deployment. They provide a partial on-demand solution to the problem of data warehousing design. Furthermore, none of these solutions offers an integrated model-driven Data Warehouse (DW) development approach and a web-based environment that supports this approach. Finally, there are few studies on open standards and open-source business intelligence tools integration in this context.

This chapter deals with two important aspects of BI-as-a-service architectures: (i) the functional aspects to deliver business intelligence services covering the Model-Driven Data Warehousing (MDDW) services; and (ii) the technical aspects covering the recommended open industry standards and open-source tools. The chapter provides several recommendations for data warehousing standards and development technologies. It, mainly, helps project managers and organizations involved in developing web-based business intelligence solutions.

We study the advantages of SaaS deployment model. Some industry experiences (BusinessObjects, MicroStrategy, etc.) are, also, presented. Then, a proposal for a common functional business intelligence as-a-service architecture is described. We focus on the data warehousing projects management and components design services. We discuss the model-driven DW approaches integra-tion. Indeed, such approaches of DW engineering provide several advantages and their integration in a SaaS environment seem more promising. So, we introduce the model-driven DW development in the cloud using our approach (Essaidi & Osmani, 2009) based on the Model Driven Architecture (MDA) and the 2 Track Unified Process (2TUP). The MDA/2TUP based process for DW engineering and its advantages are thus presented.

Moreover, we study the data warehousing standards and open-source business intelligence and web-applications development tools integration. Indeed, only a few solutions propose a standard and integrated DW design framework like the Common Warehouse Metamodel (CWM). Other MDA-compliant metamodels are useful, but they are not yet integrated as the Ontology Definition Metamodel (ODM). In addition, little information is available on the technical architecture of data warehousing platforms. Consequently, we give several recommendations concerning the standard industry tools, languages, and business intelligence APIs which can be integrated. Then, a technical architecture for the business intelligence-as- a-service based on the most popular open-source frameworks is described. The proposed technical architecture is based on Java Enterprise Edition (JEE) technologies using spring framework.

The chapter is organized as follows: the next section gives a review of the literature and an overview of main concepts related to our proposal. Section 3 describes the proposed architectures (functional and technical) for Business Intelligence-as-a-Service including our approach for the MDDW-as-a-Service. In section 4, we discuss the main future research directions related to the BI-as-a-Service. Finally, section 5 depicts our conclusions and future work.

Figure 1. The Data warehousing architecture

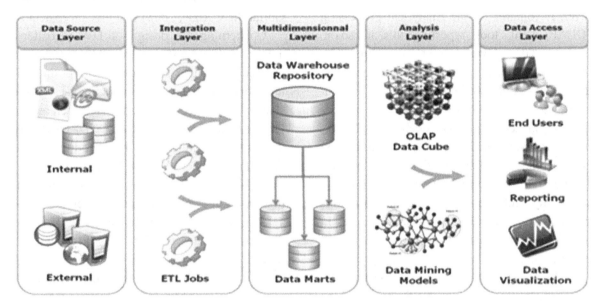

2. BACKGROUND

The section is divided into four parts: in section 2.1 we present the main issues around the data warehousing architecture development; section 2.2 present the Model Driven Architecture and its transformation process; in section 2.3 we explain the 2 Track Unified Process and its goals; finally, the Software-as-a-Service model and examples of applications are presented in section 2.4.

2.1. Data Warehousing Architecture (DWA)

The data warehousing architecture is defined through several heterogeneous and interrelated layers. Moreover, each layer contains different components, using different modeling profiles, and depends on several technologies. We distinguish five main layers (figure 1) that compose the data warehousing architecture: the data source layer, the integration layer, the multidimensional layer, the analysis layer, and the data access layer. In this architecture, we consider that the staging area is a part of the integration layer, and the meta-data

layer is an implicit layer shared between all other layers.

Data Source layer defines the sources of information used to feed the Data Warehouse. It can be internal sources (transactional information systems, content management systems or files) or external sources (remote systems, web data). Integration layer is responsible for data extraction, data transformation and data loading (ETL) into DW. It defines the ETL jobs and the mapping between data sources and data warehouse. Multidimensional layer defines the structure of the DW repository. The dimensional modeling techniques (Kimball & Ross, 2002; Inmon, 2002) are used to design the multidimensional structures (i.e. facts and dimensions) of this layer. The multidimensional layer can be organized as one companywide warehouse or/and multiple independent data marts. Analysis layer defines the mapping between the multidimensional layer and end-user applications. It contains special data structures (data cube and data mining models) that are used by the end-user applications for goals of analysis. Data Access layer defines the end-user applications used to access and to analyze data from DW repository through the analysis layer. It contains Online Analytical Processing (OLAP) client's tools, reporting tools, and so on.

Each of these layers presents its own specificities, such as semantic schemas integration (Noy, 2004; Polo et al., 2007), semantic data integration (Skoutas & Simitsis, 2006), ETL process design and generation (Dessloch et al., 2008), multidimensional and analysis models derivation (Pardillo et al., 2008a; Pardillo et al., 2008b). Interoperability between layers, components portability and adaptability are the commons problems encountered in such architecture. In addition, business intelligence projects are still exposed to several technical risks and require more knowledge about the underlying business domain. These aspects increase the costs and the time of DW development and make it a very difficult and challenging task.

Current DW development approaches can fall within three categories: (i) approaches for the DW design framework, (ii) approaches for DW engineering process, and (iii) methods that address the two problems. Some framework-oriented approaches are discussed in this section. Related works on MDA-based design approaches are presented in next section. The process-oriented approaches and general methods are discussed in section 1.3.

The framework-oriented approaches focus on DW system design. In this category, we distinguish the approaches that focus on the design of one layer of the data warehousing architecture (Luján-Mora et al., 2006; Vassiliadis et al., 2002; Dessloch et al., 2008), and those dealing with more than one layer or all DW layers (Mazón & Trujillo, 2008). In this chapter, we focus more on research efforts on DW repository design and ETL process development. For data sources reverse and integration efforts you can refer to (Noy, 2004; Polo et al., 2007; Hakimpour & Geppert, 2005), and to (Pardillo et al., 2008a) for analysis layer modeling, and concerning data access layer

the works presented in (Chowdhary et al., 2006; Golfarelli & Rizzi, 2008) will give more details.

Concerning the design of DW repository, authors in (Luján-Mora et al., 2006) propose a Unified Modeling Language profile for multidimensional modeling in data warehouses. Some standards are used in this approach such as, the Object Constraint Language (OCL) to specify the constraints attached to the multidimensional model and the Query/View/Transformation (QVT) for an automatic generation of the implementation in a target platform. In (Prat et al., 2006) a UML-based data warehouse design method that spans the three design phases (conceptual, logical and physical phases) are presented. A set of metamodels is used to design each phase, as well as a set of OCL transformations to map schemas. However, these approaches focus only on the design of the DW repository and other DW components like ETL or analysis are not considered. Thus, these UML profiles do not provide a general standard framework like the Common Warehouse Metamodel for integrated modeling covering other layers of the DW. Different other approaches (Kimball & Ross, 2002; Giorgini et al., 2005; Tryfona et al., 1999; Lechtenbörger & Vossen, 2003) for the DW conceptual design are also proposed. These approaches share the same disadvantages with those previously presented and have other limitations such as: no standard notation and framework are adopted, no formal transformations are defined, and so on.

Concerning the development of extraction, transformation, and loading (ETL) processes, several approaches are proposed since decade. First approach like (Vassiliadis et al., 2002) proposes a conceptual model for ETL scenarios without taking account a standard notation such as UML. A second work is proposed in (Trujillo & Luján-Mora, 2003). Authors present a standard UML-based approach for modeling ETL processes in data warehouses (DWs). However, this conceptual metamodel is not a CWM-compliant profile, therefore metadata interchange becomes difficult.

The logical design of ETL scenarios was presented in (Vassiliadis et al., 2005) using a generic and customizable framework. In (Simitsis, 2005) a formal transformation between these conceptual and logical ETL models has proposed, the physical design and optimization of the ETL processes were studied in (Simitsis, 2003). However, these transformations (conceptual to logical and logical to physical) are not based on the QVT standard. An approach for designing ETL processes using semantic web technologies is presented in (Skoutas & Simitsis, 2006; Simitsis et al., 2008) when an ontology is used to model the domain and formally specify the semantic of the data-store schemata. However, the definition of the ontology does not use a standard metamodel such the Ontology Definition Metamodel that can be easily integrated in a Model Driven Architecture approach. In (Dessloch et al., 2008), authors present Orchid, a system that converts declarative mapping specifications into data flow specifications (ETL jobs) and vice versa. Orchid provides the Operator Hub Model (OHM); a model for representing data transformation operations independently of specific ETL platforms. However, the definition of this model is not UML or CWM compliant, and no standard approach using MDA and QVT is defined to generate mapping and ETL jobs.

2.2. Model Driven Architecture (MDA)

MDA is an Object Management Group (OMG) standard (Miller & Mukerji, 2003). MDA starts with the well-known and long established idea of separating the specification of the operation of a system from the details of the way that system uses the capabilities of its platform. The three primary goals of MDA are portability, interoperability and reusability. The MDA standard base includes also many specifications. These include UML, MOF, specific platforms models (i.e. CORBA, JEE), CWM and CWM extension (CWMX) to design DW components, ODM to design ontologies and to enable semantic model-driven development,

Query/View/Transformation as a standard language for model transformation, and the XML Metadata Interchange (XMI) as a standard format for models exchange and serialization.

An MDA approach specifies several viewpoints on a system: the computation-independent model (CIM) viewpoint, the platform-independent model (PIM) viewpoint, the platform-dependent model (PDM), the platform-specific model viewpoint (PSM) and the system code. The MDA transformation process (see figure 2) starts by the definition of a CIM model. The CIM model contains the requirements for a system. Using the CIM, MDA encourages specifying a PIM model that contains no specific information to the platform or the technology which is used to realize it. Then, this PIM can be mapped into a platform-specific model (PSM) in order to include information about a specific technology or platform already defined in a PDM. The PDM represents the design viewpoint of technical requirements. The technical requirements model is known as TCIM (technical CIM). Afterwards, each PSM is transformed into code to obtain the final implementation.

The MDA is based on architecture with four meta-levels described as follows: (i) The meta-metamodeling level forms the foundation of the metamodeling hierarchy. The primary responsibility of this level is to define the language for specifying a metamodel. The level is often referred to as M3; Meta-Object Facility (MOF) and Eclipse Modeling Framework (EMF) are examples of meta-metamodels. (ii) A metamodel is an instance of a meta-metamodel, meaning that every element of the metamodel is an instance of an element in the meta-metamodel. The primary responsibility of the metamodel layer is to define a language for specifying models. The metamodel layer is often referred to as M2. The Unified Modeling Language, the Common Warehouse Metamodel, and the Ontology Definition Metamodel are examples of metamodels. (iii) A model is an instance of a metamodel. The primary responsibility of the model layer is to define languages that describe

Figure 2. The MDA transformation process

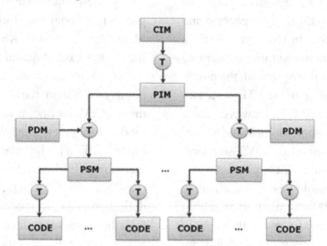

semantic domains (i.e., to allow users to model a wide variety of different problem domains, such as software, business processes, and requirements). This layer is often referred to as M1. (iv) The metamodel hierarchy bottoms out at M0, which contains the runtime instances of model elements defined in a model. In general, this level is not detailed in the MDA based approaches, because it depends on the parameters of each execution.

In (Mazón & Trujillo, 2008; Zepeda et al., 2008), MDA oriented approaches for the development of DWs are presented. These approaches provide several advantages (simplified development, reusability, interoperability, etc.) resulting from the use of the MDA and QVT. The approach presented in (Zepeda et al., 2008) describes derivation of OLAP schemas from ER schemas. The source and target PIMs are conform to ER and OLAP metamodels of CWM. Authors describe how an ER schema is mapped to an OLAP schema and provide, also, a set of QVT rules (e.g., EntityToCube, AttributeToMeasure, RelationShipToDimension, etc.) to ensure this. The approach presented in (Mazón & Trujillo, 2008) describes an integrated framework for DW layers development with MDA and QVT. Authors focus on MDA for multidimensional modeling and

provide an extension of UML and CWM to build the different MDA models. They, provide, using QVT language, transformations (e.g., Fact2Table, Dimension2Table, etc.) between the multidimensional PIM and the multidimensional PSM.

2.3. Two Track Unified Process (2TUP)

The process-oriented approaches focus on DW development process. These approaches can fall within three major groups: data-driven, goal-driven and user-driven. A detailed comparison and discussion about the three approaches are presented in (List et al., 2002). For example, Inmon (Inmon, 2002) argues that DW environments are data driven, while the Kimball et al. (Kimball and Ross, 2002) approach focuses on business processes in order to deliver consistent information throughout the organization. The DW development process can also be a mix of these three approaches. In (Golfarelli et al., 1998) a data-driven approach has been presented. Authors propose a semi-automated methodology to build a dimensional DW model from the pre-existing E/R schemas that represent operational databases. In (Böhnlein & Ulbrich-vom Ende, 2000) authors present an approach based on the SOM (Semantic

Object Model) process modeling technique in order to derive the initial DW structure. Finally, user-driven approaches are presented in (Westerman, 2001; List et al., 2000), and a mix-driven approach is proposed in (Kaldeich & e Sá, 2004).

The main shortcomings of these approaches are as follows: (i) there is no proposal for an iterative and an incremental development using a standard process such as the Unified Process (UP) or 2TUP; (ii) they do not propose a clear set of steps or phases including development best practices; (iii) the definition of the technical requirements is not taken into account; (iv) they do not address the whole DW process; in most case only the DW repository is considered.

2 Track Unified Process is a software development process that implements the Unified Process and uses UML as a modeling language (Roques & Vallée, 2004). The 2TUP process (also called Y shaped process or Y lifecycle) answers to the constraints of change of the information systems that are subjected to two types of constraints: (1) the functional constraints and (2) the technical constraints. Thus, 2TUP is modeled by two branches (or tracks): The left branch makes an inventory of the functional needs and analyzes it, which produces a model focused on the needs of business users. The right branch contains a study of the technical needs and defines the technical architecture of the solution. The two branches are then merged into a medium branch which supports preliminary design, detailed design, coding, tests and validation steps.

The choice of 2TUP comes owing to the fact that the evolution of the 2TUP process is similar to the transformation process of MDA. It will simplify the mapping between the MDA concepts and 2TUP disciplines, and the integration of the MDA transformation process in our final process. Figure 3 shows the mapping between 2TUP activities and MDA transformation process.

In (Belangour et al., 2006), authors present a software development process for MDA called M2T. The M2T process provides an implementa-

tion of the MDA approach while relying on a Y shaped development cycle. The left branch of the Y cycle corresponds to the PIM model, while the right one corresponds to what we call an explicit PDM representing the target platform. Authors propose the Design Decision Metamodel (DDM) to merge the PIM and the PDM models, in order to produce the PSM model. However, the DDM is not a standard and MOF-compliant language for models transformation such as the Query/View/Transformation. In our process, the 2TUP activities are adapted to enable the transformation process of MDA using QVT and to take into account the DW development constraints.

Other general methods for the DW development (Luján-Mora & Trujillo, 2004) and the Decision Support Systems (DSS) development (Brandas, 2007) using UP and UML are proposed. These methods offer the advantage of integrating the engineering process part and the design framework part. But, they present several disadvantages such as: (i) they do not use any model driven approach to generate DW diagrams and no transformation process using QVT is defined; (ii) no standards metamodels for DW development such as the Common Warehouse Metamodel or the CWM extension (CWMX) are explicitly defined to design DW layers; (iii) the development process does not take into account the definition of the technical architecture of DW.

2.4. Software-as-a-Service (SaaS)

Software-as-a-Service is a model for software delivery where a software company publishes one copy of their software on the Internet. It allows individuals and companies (multi-tenant architecture) to "rent" it through a subscription model (pay as you go model). The software company centrally operates, maintains and supports all its customers using this centralized service. The on-demand and "pay-as-you-go" models mean that in SaaS architecture, costs are directly aligned with usage. The cost may increase as the usage

Figure 3. MDA / 2TUP integration

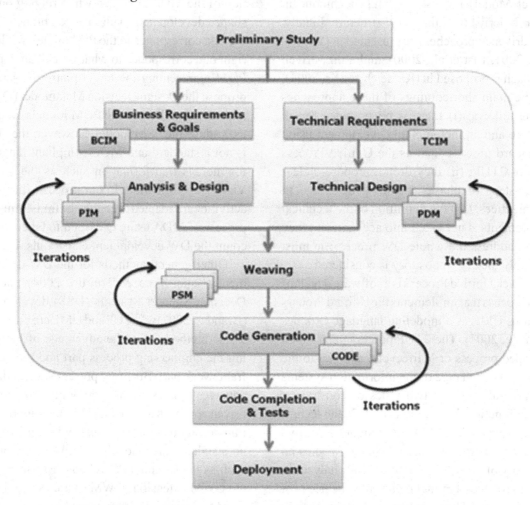

of the application increases. Multi-tenant architecture model means that the physical backend hardware infrastructure is shared among many different customers but logically is unique for each customer (Software & Information Industry Association, 2006).

Lower total cost of ownership (TCO) and better return on investment (ROI) constitute the major benefits of SaaS. Indeed, several factors contribute to making it considerably less expensive to implement a SaaS application than a traditional on-premises application. These factors include: (i) lower IT costs; since when you subscribe to a SaaS application, you avoid the overhead associated with implementing conventional software (installing and maintaining servers, etc.). (ii) Economies of scale; subscription costs for SaaS applications reflect the economies of scale achieved by multi-tenancy; as example on database is used to store all customers data, so, this makes the overall system scalable at a far lower cost. (iii) Pay as you go; companies who subscribe to a SaaS application pay a monthly or annual subscription fee, sometimes depending also on the number of users or transactions. Others key variables such as simplicity, flexibility and accessibility constitute the advantages of SaaS deployment model.

In recent years, SaaS is gaining momentum with more and more successful adoptions. Several companies including some well known names have embraced this new model for software distribution. As SaaS providers, we cite Salesforce.com for on-demand Customer Relationship Management (CRM) services; PeopleSoft On-Demand from Oracle provides SaaS infrastructure for enterprise applications; ShareMinds that offers an on-demand Enterprise Content Management (ECM). Google maps and apps (mail, docs, sites, etc.); and recently Microsoft, that announces office web apps.

Several business intelligence software solutions are exposed in a SaaS model. SAP BusinessObjects, the world's leading business intelligence software company launched a hosted on-demand platform (available at http://www.ondemand.com) to deliver analytic and reporting functionality. PivotLink is one of the major actors of the on-demand business intelligence (http://www.pivotlink.com). PivotLink offers a SaaS business intelligence solution covering data analysis, reporting and dashboards. MicroStrategy (http://www.microstrategy.com) is a leading business intelligence applications provider. MicroStrategy introduces in (MicroStrategy, 2009) the MicroStrategy platform architecture for hosted reporting, analysis and monitoring applications. LogiXML provides a web-based ad-hoc reporting, analysis, dashboard and data integration applications. LogiXML solution (http://www.logixml.com) is one of the few solutions that offer a fully web-based data integration environment. Talend (http://www.talend.com) one of the most known open-source data integration solutions, starts recently the Talend on-demand project. Talend on-demand is a centralized and shared repository hosted by Talend in order to consolidate Talend Open Studio metadata and project information in online and to facilitate collaboration, object and code reuse. However, it consists of a partial SaaS solution since the design of ETL package is made with Talend Open Studio, the on-demand service covers only uploading, sharing and collaboration functions. Finally, Pentaho Ad-Hoc Reporting (http://www.pentaho.com) and OpenI (http://openi.org) are examples of open-source solutions for web-based business intelligence deployment that allow build and publish reports, analyses, and dashboards.

These solutions present many advantages derived in general from the advantages of the SaaS concept. But, not much information on the architecture of these on-demand solutions is provided. In addition, few solutions offer integrated platforms that cover all functional and technical aspects of the data warehousing architecture. Indeed, these tools focus only on the problem of the business intelligence services deployment and they provide a partial on-demand solution to the problem of data warehousing design. Furthermore, none of these solutions offer an integrated model-driven DW development approach and a web-based environment that supports this approach.

Thus, the goal of our work is to provide an integrated business intelligence-as-service architecture covering the main data warehousing aspects (integration, analysis, reporting, design, etc.). In addition, we give a description of the role of each module in the architecture and recommendation for enterprise-class technologies to implement it. The study of a web-based DW design and derivation architecture using a model-driven approach represents the key contribution of this work.

3. BI-AS-A-SERVICE ARCHITECTURES

This section is divided into three parts: in section 3.1 we propose a unified and complete functional architecture for Business Intelligence-as-a-Service; in section 3.2 we focus on the model-driven DW design component and we introduce the MDDW-as-a-Service; and in section 3.3 the technical architecture is explained.

Figure 4. Business intelligence-as-a-service functional aspects

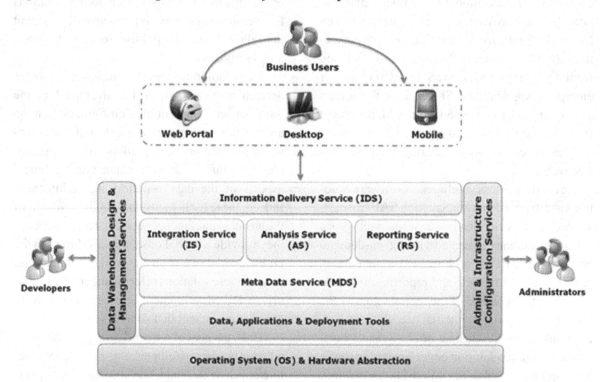

3.1. Functional Architecture

The proposed BI-as-a-service architecture is defined through five main layers (see figure 4): (i) the technical-resources layer (data, applications & deployment tools); (ii) the DW design and management layer; (iii) the infrastructure administration and configuration layer; (iv) the core business intelligence services layer (meta-data, integration, analysis, reporting, and delivery services); (v) and the end-users access tools layer (web portal, desktop, mobile). The operating system and hardware layer is not discussed in this chapter. In fact, it corresponds to the Platform-as-a-Service (PaaS) and the Infrastructure-as- a-Service (IaaS) concepts of the cloud computing which are out of scope of the chapter.

The technical-resources layer (data, applications & deployment tools) contains the data warehousing components (database servers, ETL engine, analysis server, reporting engines, etc.)

used to deploy and to execute the designed DW models. This layer corresponds also to data stored in the cloud, web data, and accessible web services useful for the platform. The integration of these data and the interoperability between all of these tools and APIs can be ensured using an Enterprise Service Bus (ESB) like apache ServiceMix (http://servicemix.apache.org/) or JBossESB (http://www.jboss.org/jbossesb). A detailed technical analysis is given in the next section (technical architecture).

The design and management layer contains services to design DW models (ETL jobs, multidimensional models, reports, etc.) and services to manage DW development projects. It represents model-driven data warehouse services part of a web-based environment to design and manage DW projects using our model-driven approach for DW development presented in (Essaidi & Osmani, 2009). This layer offers an on-demand DW design in order to ensure platform integrity (same technologies for all layers). It also simplifies the deployment and the access to the development environment for developers whom want to subscribe to this service. This reduces the installation time of development infrastructure and its costs.

The core BI services layer represents the basic applications provided to users. We identify five essential business intelligence services: (i) the meta-data service (MDS), which allows meta-data and business information definition to facilitate information sharing and exchange between all services. (ii) the integration service (IS), which offers an ad-hoc way to define data integration jobs, jobs scheduling, etc. (iii) the analysis service (AS), which allows definition of analysis data models (OLAP data cube), data cube visualization and navigation. (iv) the reporting service (RS) can be defined using existing reporting APIs like BIRT (web viewer, http://www.eclipse.org/birt/), or it can present same ad-hoc reporting functionalities; the current version of the RS implementation supports BIRT reporting and ad-hoc reporting. (v) the information delivery service (IDS) is an abstraction level to support many client interfaces and technologies (web browser, mobile, office tools). It can be also presented as a web service for more flexibility to access the platform.

The infrastructure administration and configuration layer offers a web-based tool for administrators to manage user's accounts, to customize services configuration and to report same information on platform usage and performance. Finally, the end-users access tools layer contains client applications used to access the platform and use its services. The web browser, web services, desktop/office tools, and mobile applications are examples of client-side technologies to support.

3.2. Towards MDDW-as-a-Service

Model-Driven Data Warehouse (MDDW) represents an approach that aligns the development of data warehousing systems with a general model-driven development paradigm. Model-driven DW development approaches are presented in (Mazón & Trujillo, 2008; Zepeda et al., 2008; Pardillo et al., 2008a). Such approaches have several advantages (adaptability, integrity, extensibility and standard development) and seem more promising. Recently, we have contributed to improve current MDDW approaches by providing a complete and integrated method (Essaidi & Osmani, 2009) based on the Model Driven Architecture and the 2 Track Unified Process standards. MDDW-as-a-Service applications aims to provide web-based data warehousing services based on the model-driven approach.

This section describes the dimensions of our unified method, the DW design framework dimension and the DW engineering process dimension. It introduces also the architecture of a DW development environment that implements this method, in order to provide a complete support for DW engineering approaches and to contribute to improve current DW development tools. Then, the section presents the MDDW-as-a-Service concept objectives and its advantages. Finally, the section lists main technical challenges around the MDDW-as-a-Service and provides recommendations for tools that can be used to implement it.

The DW design framework is structured on three main layers (figure 5) showing the use of MDA meta-levels for data warehousing components and services development. The DW design framework is part of the proposed technical architecture (defined in next section). The Meta-Object Facility (MOF), the M3 meta-level of MDA metamodeling architecture, represents the first layer. Standards metamodels (CWM, UML, etc.) which corresponds to M2 meta-level, are used to define the second layer of the design framework. The domain objects (or business objects) and the data warehousing services, the M1 meta-level, form the third layer. The third layer contains also the MDA viewpoints (CIM, PIM, PDM, PSM, and CODE) which are derived by transformation services using the Query/View/Transformation.

Each DW component has all viewpoints of MDA, and each component model in a specific

Figure 5. The DW design framework

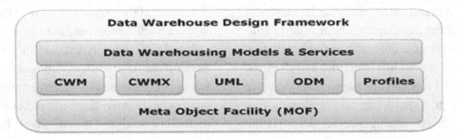

viewpoint is defined by the MDA four-level architecture (meta-levels). For example, to design the multidimensional layer we define the multidimensional computation-independent model (multidimensional CIM), the multidimensional platform independent model (multidimensional PIM), the multidimensional platform dependent model (multidimensional PDM), and the multidimensional platform specific model (multidimensional PSM) viewpoints. These viewpoints correspond also to the M1 meta-level (multidimensional models), and are instantiated using a set of DW design metamodels (M2 meta-level) conform to Meta-Object Facility meta-metamodel (M3 meta-level) as discussed before. Note that the CODE viewpoint and the instance (M0) meta-level are not detailed because CODE represents another form of the PSM and M0 is specific to every execution. In the following paragraphs, we describe in details which metamodels (or packages) are used to design the DW layers (data source, integration, multidimensional, analysis, and data access).

The data source layer is obtained by reverse engineering and by the integration of data sources models. The data source platform specific model (data source PSM) diagrams represent the logical views of data sources. So, suppliers platforms metamodels, and CWM Relational packages are used to design relational databases. The CWM XML package can be used to represent semi-structured and unstructured data. The data source PDM describes the platforms where the sources

are deployed; therefore platforms metamodels (provided by platforms suppliers) are used to define data source PDM in order to facilitate the reverse engineering process. The data source PIM represents the conceptual view of the data sources; it is instantiated using CWM ObjectModel (i.e. UML). In data source layer, we need a unified schema that gives a standard representation of the data, thus offering a way to deal with the heterogeneity in the sources. Thus, the data source computation independent model (data source CIM) defines information for the semantic integration of schemas. This data source CIM represents the domain ontology containing matching concepts to solve heterogeneity during the generation of the integrated schemas (intentional level of integration). We propose the Ontology Definition Metamodel an MDA-compliant metamodel to define this ontology.

Concerning the integration layer, we propose also ODM to design the integration computation independent model (integration CIM) model. The integration CIM defines a semantic mapping between data sources and DW repository to solve heterogeneity during data integration (extensional level of integration). Thus, the role of integration CIM is to improve the transformation process and solve data quality issues. The integration PIM represents the conceptual view of integration process. We propose the CWM Transformation package to design data transformation activities, the CWM WarehouseProcess package to design maintenance tasks and events. However, these metamodels are too generic to represent explicit extraction, transformation, and loading operations. Therefore, we recommend the use of CWM-profiles to simplify the ETL design and to ensure meta-data interchange at the same time. The metamodels of ETL platforms such as SQL Server Integration Services and DB2 Warehouse Manager (with CWMX DB2 WarehouseManager package) are used to design integration PDM and to generate the integration PSM model.

In our approach, the multidimensional CIM level represents the enterprise goals and business needs. In (Mazón et al., 2008), UML profiles for i* modeling in the DW domain have been presented. This i* extension is used to define a CIM and it can be easily integrated in a MDA approach through a set of QVT transformation in order to derive the conceptual multidimensional models. In our framework, this conceptual multidimensional model is defined through the multidimensional PIM viewpoint, and we use CWM OLAP metamodel to instantiate it. The multidimensional PDM is used to personalize the multidimensional PSM and to adapt it to the context of the target platform. Platforms metamodels such as Oracle and Microsoft SQL Server are used to design the multidimensional PDM model. The multidimensional logical view is given by multidimensional PSM model, which is developed using the CWM Relational package.

For the analysis layer, we recommend also i* framework to design analysis CIM (goals and requirements for analysis). This layer contains customs data structures such as Online Analytical Processing (OLAP) data cubes and data mining models used for analysis by end-users tools. Regarding the analysis PIM, we recommend CWM OLAP and CWM DataMining metamodels to design, respectively, data cubes and data mining components. Concerning analysis PDM, some platforms are described in CWMX metamodel; as examples CWMX Express for the Oracle Express server, CWMX Hyperion for Hyperion OLAP platform, etc. Other platforms metamodels such

as Mondrian for OLAP, SAS Data Mining for data mining can also be used to define specific platforms representations. For the analysis PSM of the OLAP data cube, we have the choice between a relational implementation (ROLAP) and a multidimensional implementation (MOLAP). So, we propose the CWM Relational package to implement ROLAP case; and for MOLAP case we propose the CWM Multidimensional package.

The goal of data access layer is to generate specific user interfaces in order to develop reports and for information visualization. At the computation independent model level (data access CIM), UML metamodel (use cases package part) or other adapted profiles are used to define users requirements. Several CWM metamodels can be used to design the data access PIM. In our approach, we propose the CWMX InformationReporting package for reports construction and CWM InformationVisualization package to support information visualization. UML class diagram metamodel is also used with these metamodels to design applicative and Graphical User Interface layers at data access PIM level. Java Enterprise Edition and Microsoft .NET frameworks are, in general, used to generate these tools, so we adopt them to define the data access PDM and the data access PSM levels.

The main advantages of the proposed data warehouse design framework are: (i) Completeness: since, our framework covers the design of all DW components, and integrates all MDA viewpoints and meta-levels. (ii) Extensibility: in our approach the metamodeling architecture using MOF simplifies the extension of the framework through metamodeling techniques. (iii) Standard development: indeed, all DW layers design diagrams are identified using a standard metamodels for DW development such as CWM, CWMX, ODM, etc.

The MDA transformation process does not include all engineering disciplines such as preliminary study and tests. Moreover, result of a MDA process is a semi-complete system code.

Figure 6. Model-driven data warehouse engineering process

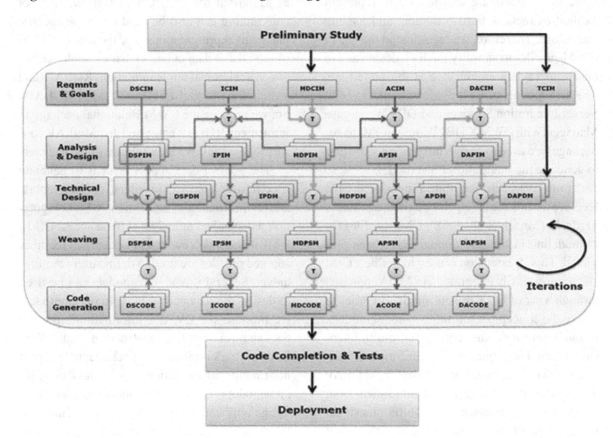

Thus, it is necessary to define a code completion activity in the global development process. Finally, transformation process of MDA is not an iterative and incremental process. To overcome these limits, we propose to use the 2TUP process in order to develop DW components while keeping the MDA approach in order to ensure coherence between the DW design framework and the DW engineering process. Therefore, in our DW engineering process, the MDA transformation process is a sub-process. Figure 3 shows the disciplines and the iterations applied to develop the components of a one layer of the data warehousing architecture. It represents, also, the mapping between the 2TUP activities and the MDA transformation process steps. Below we adapt the process of figure 3 for the development of all DW layers in order to define the DW engineering process.

The DW engineering process starts by the preliminary study activity. The preliminary study contains a study of the enterprise business process to collect business information's, identifying preliminary requirements, and a study of market platforms to prepare the technical requirements modeling. Each DW layer is developed using a MDA transformation process starting by the definition of the layer BCIM (Business CIM), using the common TCIM (Technical CIM) and ends with components code generation. So, the MDA process is repeated for the construction of each DW layer. If several components are defined in a layer, then several 2TUP iterations may be applied (for example, runs iteration per component). The final DW engineering process showing the development of all DW layers is given by Figure 6. In the following paragraphs, we describe in more details the execution of the DW engineering process.

The MDA process starts by the development of the data source layer. A reverse engineering process is applied since data source code to obtain the data source logical model (data source PSM). Then the reverse engineering process is applied on data source PSM using information's given by data source PDM and data source CIM, to obtain the data source conceptual model (data source PIM). The data source PDM is used to solve the technical errors related to reverse process and the data source CIM is used to solve the problems related to the semantic heterogeneity of sources.

The next step of the DW engineering process is the derivation of the multidimensional components (DW repository and/or data marts). The data source PIM and the multidimensional CIM are merged using a QVT transformation to generate the multidimensional conceptual model (multidimensional PIM). The multidimensional PIM is an instance of CWM OLAP metamodel already defined in our DW design framework. Then, the multidimensional logical model (multidimensional PSM) and code (multidimensional CODE) are generated for a specific platform using the description given by the multidimensional platform dependent model (multidimensional PDM).

The development of the conceptual ETL jobs (integration PIM) requires three models: the integration CIM (semantic transformation rules), the data source PIM (source model), and the multidimensional PIM (target model). The data source PIM and the multidimensional PIM are used to define mapping between sources and the DW repository (or data marts). The integration CIM is used to solve problems related on heterogeneous data and to make semantic data cleansing, correction, and integration. The integration PSM and integration CODE (XML files in general) describing the mapping and transformations are finally generated for a specific ETL tool.

The fourth step of the DW engineering process is the customization of analysis models. So, a set of OLAP cubes and mining models (analysis PIM) can then derived from the multidimensional layer according to business requirements and goals defined in the analysis CIM model.

The DW engineering process ends with the derivation of the data access layer (fifth step). The data access tools and reporting interfaces are developed using the analysis layer models (analysis PIM) and user requirements provided by the data access CIM. The MDA transformation process using QVT is also applied to generate the data access PIM and data access PSM models. Finally, end-users applications are generated for a specific framework (JEE or .NET) to obtain the data access CODE.

The main advantages of the proposed DW engineering process are: (i) the whole DW development is tackled in an iterative and incremental way; (ii) it is component oriented, offering flexibility to the model and supporting the re-use; (iii) it allows a better technical risk management and thus constitutes the deadlines and the costs control; (iv) the MDA transformation process is fully integrated in the global engineering process, which includes additional disciplines to improve quality.

The model-driven data warehouse services (MDDWS) module is part of the DW management and design layer of figure 4. It represents an implementation of the proposed metamodeling architecture (mainly the DW design framework). The services set contains: (i) the services for the DW engineering process management based on the integration of 2TUP and the transformation process of MDA; (ii) the services for the data warehousing models design based on metamodeling architecture of MDA; and (iii) the services for models deployment, exportation, and importation through meta-data (merged with the metadata service).

Thus, we introduce the architecture of a DW development environment that implements our unified method, in order to provide a complete support for DW engineering approaches and to contribute to improve current DW development tools. This DW design environment is called MDDWS for model driven data warehouse services. MDDWS is a web-based model-driven data warehouse development environment and it's developed under the ODBIS platform (Essaidi, 2010). The MDDWS application offers an innovative architecture to deliver on-demand model-driven data warehouse design services that reduce time and costs of DW components implementation. Current ODBIS version provides complete administration, meta-data and reporting services. The MDDWS, integration and analysis services are under incubation and beta-versions will be available soon.

The MDDWS services stack includes the DW project management service (or methodology), the DW design service, and the DW refinement and deployment services. The project management service covers project steps definition and control, and project team roles definition. We study the integration of existing web-based and open-source project management tool like dotProject (http://www.dotproject.net/).

The DW design service allows web-based diagramming features. Indeed, interactive and rich web solutions (Adobe AIR, Microsoft Silverlight, AJAX, etc.) are the key technologies to provide these features. Currently, we study existing web-based diagramming tools: several products with different technologies options (Ajax, Flex, and Silverlight) are provided by yWorks (http://www.yworks.com/). Gliffy (http://www.gliffy.com/) offers online modeling solution for different diagrams types (Flowchart, Network, UML, Business Process, etc.). Gliffy is based on OpenLaszlo (http://www.openlaszlo.org/) an open source platform for the development and delivery of rich Internet applications. Mx- Graph (http://www.mxgraph.com/) is a JavaScript library that uses built-in browser capabilities to provide an interactive drawing and diagramming solution. MxGraph allows several modeling options: Graph, Database, Org Chart, and Workflow. Finally, js-

graph-it (http://js-graph-it.sourceforge.net) and Jalava (http://jalava.buildyourownapps.com/) are open-source JavaScript libraries to develop web-based diagram editors.

3.3. Technical Architecture

The proposed technical architecture (figure 7) is based on Java Enterprise Edition technologies using spring framework (http://www.springsource.org). Spring framework is a very popular framework for enterprise Java applications development and integration. It allows easy platform configuration and extension using several reusable modules (JavaConfig, Security, Web, Integration, etc.). Spring framework and Spring tools are provided by the SpringSource company. Since 2009, SpringSource is a division of VMware, a leader in virtualization and cloud solutions.

At the data layer, we use PostgreSQL to store metadata. PostgreSQL is one of the most mature and advanced open-source database management systems. For the customer data (used for reporting, analysis, etc.) the platform supports many databases such as Oracle, MSSQL, MySQL using configuration capabilities of Spring. To facilitate access to customer data (in general is stored in a cloud-based database), the integration of web data and the interoperability between remote database management systems and local data warehousing tools we need an ESB. For this purpose, we plan to use Spring Integration which provides a simple model for building enterprise integration solutions via many supported ESB-features.

The data access layer allows a simplified way to access metadata and offers an abstraction level for the services layers to manipulate much heterogeneous persistent storage. The object-relational mapping tools, called also persistence APIs such as Hibernate or iBatis, are in general used to support the implementation of this layer. So, for persistence layer, we use the Java Persistence API (JPA) to define the object-relational mapping using

Figure 7. The proposed technical architecture

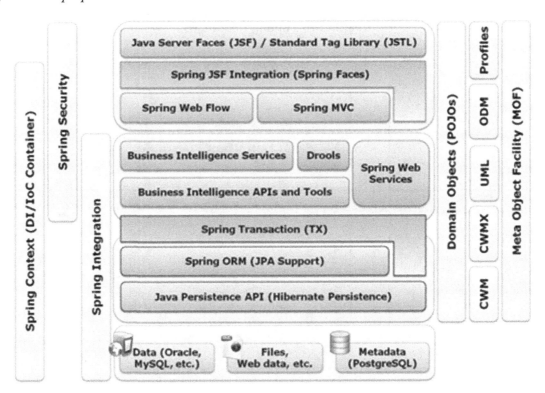

Java metadata annotations and Hibernate is used as persistence provider for JPA.

The domain model layer contains domain objects that represent the business concepts of the information system. The domain objects are used by all layers can represent a large proportion of meta-data that are serialized into the data repository. Current domain model implements the Common Warehouse Metamodel and CWMX metamodels. For the future, we plan to integrate other metamodels and profiles as the Ontology Definition Metamodel. The implementation of these meta-models is based on the Meta-Object Facility (MOF) meta-metamodel. More details about this layer (also called the framework layer) and the packages used are discussed in section 3.2.

Spring integration, Spring security, Spring web services and Spring context represent the main configuration layers of the platform. Spring Integration supports the well-known Enterprise Integration Patterns and offers many ESB-features.

So, it simplifies integration of existing business intelligence tools, the access to remote customer databases and interoperability through java messaging services. Spring security is a highly customizable, extensible authentication and authorization framework for securing Spring-based applications. Spring Web Services is used to expose business intelligence services on the web. Finally, Spring context offers automatic mechanisms to create objects and configuration (defines the ApplicationContext) via dependency injection.

The business rules brick (with Drools component) plays an important role in a service oriented infrastructure and any business intelligence system (essentially performance management). Indeed, a SaaS platform is shared by several customers that have different business processes, the definition of a business rules engine is essential for the orchestration of services. The Business Process Management defines the process logic while the Business Rules Management implements the deci-

Figure 8. Dashboard example for healthcare

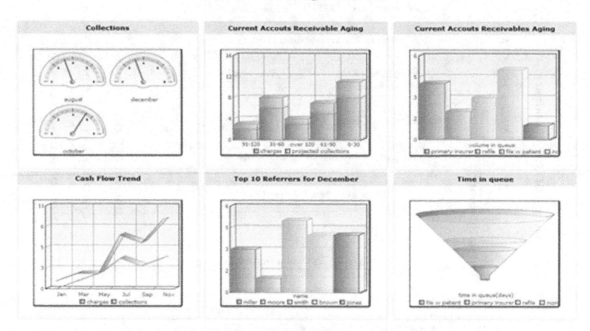

sion logic. Thus, we recommend Drools (http://www.jboss.org/drools) an open-source business rules management tools that can be easily integrated with spring context.

For the presentation layer, we use Java Server Faces (JSF) technology. Sun Mojarra, and Spring Faces are the JSF libraries used to defines user interfaces. Finally, all services are configured with spring context and run under Apache Tomcat (http://tomcat.apache.org/) web server, a standard container for Java server technologies.

Currently, we are working on a prototype of a platform integrating the concepts discussed in this paper. The project is named ODBIS, for On-Demand Business Intelligence Services presented in (Essaidi, 2010). A first release covering the administration, metadata and reporting services is available at http://odbis-project.sourceforge. net/. The administration service provides a secure web-based application to manage authorities (privileges), roles, users, and groups. It offers also some search futures. The reporting services

provides: (i) features to manage report-groups and reports; (ii) a BIRT reporting module that allows upload and execute BIRT reports under the integrated BIRT Viewer; (iii) an ad-hoc reporting module which offers an easy way to defines chart reports, data-table reports and to build dashboards. The meta-data service provides features to define data-sources and datasets. DataSource objects provide a set of information (database url, user, password, etc.) used to connect to database servers. DataSet objects are a SQL query abstraction used by charts, data-tables and dashboards. Figure 8 shows a dashboard example using the ad-hoc reporting module for Healthcare case.

The main contributions presented in this section are: (i) a unified functional architecture to support on-demand business intelligence services; (ii) a DW development approach based on MDA and 2TUP to support MDDWS-as-a-Service. This approach allows DW models design and derivation in order to reduce DWs development complexity (multilayer and multi-component architecture, goals definition, etc.); (iv) a flexible multi-layered technical architecture based on spring, standard Java enterprise and the most popular open-source tools.

4. FUTURE RESEARCH DIRECTIONS

The book entitled "DW 2.0: The Architecture for the Next Generation of Data Warehousing" (Inmon et al., 2008) describes an architecture of the second-generation data warehouses. It presents the differences between DW2.0 (introduced as the new generation) and the first generation data warehouses. Authors start by an overall architecture of DW 2.0 and give its key characteristics. Then, they present the DW 2.0 components and the role of each component in the architecture.

The proposed architecture focuses on three key features: (i) the DW repository structure (organization on four sectors: interactive, integrated, near line, and archival); (ii) unstructured-data integration and organization; and (iii) unified meta-data management. We confirm that unstructured data and web-data integration constitutes a future challenge. Thus, we support semantic-based approaches (Nebot & Llavori, 2010) for web-data integration and DWs contextualization with documents (Pérez et al., 2009). This kind of approaches will probably represent the essential part of what we call "the DW 3.0 architecture." The DW 3.0 concept (or content data warehouse) is a unified architecture that includes the data warehouse, the document warehouse and the web warehouse.

According to authors (Inmon et al., 2008), DW 2.0 represents the way corporate data needs to be structured in support of web access and Service Oriented Architecture (SOA). For this purpose, an effort is provided by (Wu et al., 2007). So, we believe that BI-as-a-Service platforms need a more efficient, personalized and intelligent web-services discovery and orchestration engines. The perfect marriage of SOA/SaaS infrastructures is a key issue to design future on-demand business intelligence services.

In (Philip Russom, 2009), the author studies the evolving state of DW platforms and gives some options available for next generation data warehousing. Those options include the concepts presented in this chapter: SaaS and open-source business intelligence tools. He presents, also, many important features such as: real-time data warehousing, data management practices and advanced analytics. In (Pedersen, 2007), the author discusses other remaining challenges to extend traditional DW architecture. The focus is mainly given for the DW full-scale problem (world warehouse) and the privacy in DW.

Metadata management for BI-as-a-Service infrastructures and cloud-based databases will be an interesting research direction. Indeed, current standards and models should be extended in this new architectural context. Finally, we believe that our proposal for MDDWS-as-a-Service is a key characteristic to provide future DW design in the cloud.

5. CONCLUSION

This chapter provides a study on the benefits of the SaaS model for the design of business intelligence architectures. First, we define current data warehousing and business intelligence applications deployment issues. We discuss some of the most important related work and we present the Model Driven Architecture and the 2 Track Unified Process standards to support model-driven DW services. Then, we describe the proposed architecture to support common on-demand business intelligence services (functional architecture). We introduce MDDWS-as-a-Service based on our approach to support model-driven DW services. We define, also, a flexible multi-layered technical architecture based on standard Java enterprise with spring and the most popular open-source tools. Finally, we discuss the research orientations, the development perspectives and the opportunities related this topic.

Concerning the core business intelligence services, we're working to improve current realized services: administration, reporting and metadata. We will start soon the development of the integration and analysis services, the development of model-driven data warehouse services and security improvements. For the future, we plan to study other dimensions of the cloud-computing in order to improve scalability and configurability of data warehousing platforms. So, we will explore the Platform-as-a-Service (PaaS) and the Infrastructure-as-a-Service (IaaS) concepts. For example, we will study the VMware vFabric Cloud Application Platform, a solution for building, running, and managing spring applications in the cloud. We will explore others open-source tools in order to complete current architecture. For example, an interesting survey of open-source tools for business intelligence (including databases, ETL, analysis, etc.) is presented in (Thomsen & Pedersen, 2005). We will explore, also, an advanced distributed data management platform like GemFire (http://www.gemstone.com/).

REFERENCES

Belangour, A., Bézivin, J., & Fredj, M. (2006, July). *Towards a new software development process for MDA*. Paper presented at the European Workshop on Milestones, Models and Mappings for Model-Driven Architecture, Bilbao, Spain.

Böhnlein, M., & Ulbrich-vom Ende, A. (2000, November). Business process oriented development of data warehouse structures. In *Proceedings of Data Warehousing 2000*, Friedrichshafen, Germany.

Brandas, C. (2007). Unified approach in the DSS development process. *Economy Informatics Review, 11*(1), 98–102.

Chowdhary, P., Palpanas, T., Pinel, F., Chen, S.-K., & Wu, F. Y. (2006, October). Model-driven dashboards for business performance reporting. In *Proceedings of the International Enterprise Distributed Object Computing Conference*, Hong Kong, China.

Dessloch, S., Hernández, M., Wisnesky, R., Radwan, A., & Zhou, J. (2008, April). Orchid: Integrating schema mapping and ETL. In *Proceedings of the International Conference on Data Engineering*, Cancún, México.

Essaidi, M. (2010, March). ODBIS: Towards a platform for on-demand business intelligence services. In *Proceedings of EDBT/ICDT Workshops*, Lausanne, Switzerland.

Essaidi, M., & Osmani, A. (2009, June). *Data warehouse development using MDA and 2TUP*. In International Conference on Software Engineering and Data Engineering, Las Vegas, Nevada, USA.

Giorgini, P., Rizzi, S., & Garzetti, M. (2005, November). Goal-oriented requirement analysis for data warehouse design. In *Proceedings of the International Workshop on Data Warehousing and OLAP*, Bremen, Germany.

Golfarelli, M., Maio, D., & Rizzi, S. (1998, January). Conceptual design of data warehouses from E/R schema. In *Proceedings of the Annual Hawaii International Conference on System Sciences*, Kohala Coast, Hawaii, USA.

Golfarelli, M., & Rizzi, S. (2008, September). UML-based modeling for what-if analysis. In *Proceedings of the International Conference on Data Warehousing and Knowledge Discovery*, Turin, Italy.

Hakimpour, F., & Geppert, A. (2005). Resolution of semantic heterogeneity in database schema integration using formal ontologies. *Journal of Information Technology Management, 6*(1), 97–122.

Inmon, W. (2002). *Building the data warehouse* (3rd ed.). New York, NY: John Wiley & Sons, Inc.

Inmon, W., Strauss, D., & Neushloss, G. (2008). *DW 2.0: The architecture for the next generation of data warehousing*. San Francisco, CA: Morgan Kaufmann Publishers Inc.

Kaldeich, C., & Sá, J. O. (2004, June). Data warehouse methodology: A process driven approach. In *Proceedings of Advanced Information Systems Engineering*, Riga, Latvia.

Kimball, R., & Ross, M. (2002). *The data warehouse toolkit: The complete guide to dimensional modeling*. New York, NY: John Wiley & Sons, Inc.

Lechtenbörger, J., & Vossen, G. (2003). Multidimensional normal forms for data warehouse design. *Journal of Information Systems*, *28*(5), 415–434.

List, B., Bruckner, R. M., Machaczek, K., & Schiefer, J. (2002, September). A comparison of data warehouse development methodologies: Case study of the process warehouse. In *Proceedings of the International Conference on Database and Expert Systems Applications*, Aix-en-Provence, France.

List, B., Schiefer, J., & Tjoa, A. M. (2000, September). Process-oriented requirement analysis supporting the data warehouse design process - A use case driven approach. In *Proceedings of the International Conference on Database and Expert Systems Applications*, London, UK.

Luján-Mora, S., & Trujillo, J. (2004, October). A data warehouse engineering process. In *Proceedings of the International Conference on Advances in Information Systems*, Izmir, Turkey.

Luján-Mora, S., Trujillo, J., & Song, I.-Y. (2006). A UML profile for multidimensional modeling in data warehouses. *Journal of Data & Knowledge Engineering*, *59*(3), 725–769.

Mazón, J.-N., Pardillo, J., Soler, E., Glorio, O., & Trujillo, J. (2008, February). Applying the i* framework to the development of data warehouses. In *Proceedings of the International i* Workshop*, Recife, Brazil.

Mazón, J.-N., & Trujillo, J. (2008). An MDA approach for the development of data warehouses. *Journal of Decision Support Systems*, *45*(1), 41–58.

MicroStrategy. (2009). *An architecture for software-as-a-service (SaaS) business intelligence*. Retrieved December 16, 2009, from http://www.b-eye-network.com /files/SaaS_WP.pdf

Miller, J., & Mukerji, J. (2003). *MDA guide version 1.0.1*. Technical report, Object Management Group (OMG). Retrieved April 23, 2008, from http://www.omg.org/mda/

Nebot, V., & Llavori, R. B. (2010, March). Building data warehouses with semantic data. In *Proceedings of the EDBT/ICDT Workshops*, Lausanne, Switzerland.

Noy, N. F. (2004). Semantic integration: A survey of ontology-based approaches. *Journal of ACM SIGMOD Record*, *33*(4), 65–70.

Pardillo, J., Mazón, J.-N., & Trujillo, J. (2008a, September). Model-driven metadata for OLAP cubes from the conceptual modelling of data warehouses. In *Proceedings of the International Conference on Data Warehousing and Knowledge Discovery*, Turin, Italy.

Pardillo, J., Zubcoff, J., Mazón, J.-N., & Trujillo, J. (2008b, July). Towards a model-driven engineering approach of data mining. In *Proceedings of the International Association for Development of the Information Society*, Amsterdam, The Netherlands.

Pedersen, T. B. (2007, November). Warehousing the world: A few remaining challenges. In *Proceedings of the International workshop on Data warehousing and OLAP*, Lisboa, Portugal.

Pérez, J. M., Berlanga, R., & Aramburu, M. J. (2009). A relevance model for a data warehouse contextualized with documents. *International Journal of Information Processing and Management, 45*(3), 356–367.

Polo, M., García-Rodríguez, I., & Piattini, M. (2007). An MDA-based approach for database re-engineering. *Journal of Software Maintenance and Evolution, 19*(6), 383–417.

Prat, N., Akoka, J., & Comyn-Wattiau, I. (2006). A UML-based data warehouse design method. *Journal of Decision Support Systems, 42*(3), 1449–1473.

Roques, P., & Vallée, F. (2004). *UML 2 en action: De l'analyse des besoins à la conception J2EE.* Eyrolles Editions.

Russom, P. (2009). *Next generation data warehouse platforms.* Retrieved September 29, 2010, from http://www.oracle.com/us/solutions /data-warehousing/040119.pdf

Simitsis, A. (2003, September). Modeling and managing ETL processes. In *Proceedings of the VLDB 2003 PhD Workshop*, Berlin, Germany.

Simitsis, A. (2005, November). Mapping conceptual to logical models for ETL processes. In *Proceedings of the International Workshop on Data Warehousing and OLAP*, Bremen, Germany.

Simitsis, A., Skoutas, D., & Castellanos, M. (2008, October). Natural language reporting for ETL processes. In *Proceedings of the International Workshop on Data warehousing and OLAP*, Napa Valley, California.

Skoutas, D., & Simitsis, A. (2006, November). Designing ETL processes using Semantic Web technologies. In *Proceeding of the International Workshop on Data warehousing and OLAP*, Arlington, Virginia, USA.

Software & Information Industry Association. (2006). *Software-as-a-service: A comprehensive look at the total cost of ownership of software applications.* Retrieved March 12, 2009, from http://www.winnou.com /saas.pdf

Thomsen, C., & Pedersen, T. (2005, August). A survey of open source tools for business intelligence. In *Proceedings of Data Warehousing and Knowledge Discovery*, Copenhagen, Denmark.

Trujillo, J., & Luján-Mora, S. (2003, October). A UML based approach for modeling ETL processes in data warehouses. In *Proceedings of the International Conference on Conceptual Modeling*, Chicago, Illinois, USA.

Tryfona, N., Busborg, F., & Borch Christiansen, J. (1999, November). starER: A conceptual model for data warehouse design. In *Proceedings of the International Workshop on Data warehousing and OLAP*, Kansas City, Missouri.

Vassiliadis, P., Simitsis, A., Georgantas, P., Terrovitis, M., & Skiadopoulos, S. (2005). A generic and customizable framework for the design of ETL scenarios. *Journal of Information Systems, 30*(7), 492–525.

Vassiliadis, P., Simitsis, A., & Skiadopoulos, S. (2002, November). Conceptual modeling for ETL processes. In *Proceedings of the International Workshop on Data Warehousing and OLAP*, McLean, Virginia, USA.

Westerman, P. (2001). *Data warehousing: Using the Wal-Mart model.* San Francisco, CA: Morgan Kaufmann Publishers Inc.

Wu, L., Barash, G., & Bartolini, C. (2007, June). A service-oriented architecture for business intelligence. In *Proceedings of the International Conference on Service-Oriented Computing and Applications*, Newport Beach, California, USA.

Zepeda, L., Celma, M., & Zatarain, R. (2008, June). A mixed approach for data warehouse conceptual design with MDA. In *Proceedings of the International Conference on Computational Science and Its Applications*, Perugia, Italy.

Chapter 10
A Data Mining Service to Assist Instructors Involved in Virtual Education

Marta E. Zorrilla
University of Cantabria, Spain

Diego García
University of Cantabria, Spain

ABSTRACT

In this chapter we present a BI application delivered as a service on-demand. In particular, it is a data mining service that aims to help instructors involved in distance education to discover their students' behavior profiles and models about how they navigate and work in their virtual courses offered in Learning Content Management Systems such as Blackboard or Moodle. The main characteristic is that the users do not require data mining knowledge to use the service; they only have to send a data file according to one of the templates provided by the system and request the results. The service carries out the KDD process itself. Furthermore, the service provides an interface based on Web services, which can be called by external software. In short, the chapter talks about the necessity of a service with these characteristics and includes the description of its architecture and its method of operation as well as a discussion about some of the patterns it offers and how these provide instructors valuable knowledge to make decisions.

DOI: 10.4018/978-1-61350-038-5.ch010

INTRODUCTION

Business Intelligence (BI) refers to the use of company data and data from other external sources like the Web to help managers and executives to make decisions in their businesses. This means understanding what is currently happening in their business, and if possible in their competitors' business by means of the analysis of key performance indicators, behavior patterns or the analysis of trends, among others. In this way, decision makers, having a more comprehensive knowledge of the factors affecting their business, can take actions for better-informed management of their enterprise.

Business Intelligence tools encompass a wide range of techniques and technologies: the data warehouse as integrated repository of strategic information, the OLAP (On-Line Analytical Processing) technology for the exploration of information under different perspectives, dashboards, scorecards and reporting tools for the analysis and visualization of information and trends, and data mining techniques to discover meaningful patterns and rules in large volumes of data by automatic or semi-automatic means.

In this chapter we focus on this last aspect, and in particular, in the use of data mining techniques applied to educational data. Our goal is to describe a data mining service implemented in the University of Cantabria which assists the instructors involved in virtual education in their teaching activity in the sense that the system helps instructors to discover on one hand, the distance students' behaviors based on their navigation and demographic data and on the other hand, how they surf and work in a distance course offered in an e-Learning platform such us Moodle (Moodle, 2007) or Blackboard (Blackboard, 2006). These patterns will help instructors to better understand the learning process, and to analyze the course organization effectiveness (design, tasks, resources used, and so on).

Our application has been developed as a BI-Service which can be consumed from the cloud, since no e-learning platform, as far as we know, provides a similar tool and a clear necessity for a tool which addresses this issue exists according to the extensive research activity which is being carried out in this field (Baker & Yacef, 2009).

The two main characteristics of this Data Mining Web Service are that: it offers a set of templates which resolves some of the common questions of instructors involved in virtual courses and it is configured to be used by non-data mining experts (although it also offers an interface for advanced users with data mining knowledge).

The chapter is organized as follow. First, we describe the problems instructors involved in virtual courses encounter in their day-to-day activity, discuss the limitations of reporting tools that LCMSs offer and explain the necessity of developing specific tools based on data mining techniques to provide instructors with additional information which help them to understand the underlying relationships behind the actions of the learners and make the student's learning behavior more interpretable. Next, we relate works published in the educational data mining field and talk about the different data mining tools which exist and compare these with our proposal. In section 3, we describe the architecture of our service based on the most popular open-source framework, Java Enterprise Edition (JEE) and other standard web technologies. In section 4, we present the functionality of our service with real data from two virtual courses registered in Blackboard Learning CMS and offered by the University of Cantabria at the largest virtual campus in Spain, called G9, in the present academic year. Next, we comment open research issues related to data mining and its delivery as a service and, finally we close by summarizing the contents of this chapter and discuss our future work.

MOTIVATION

The well-established field of study of Computer-Supported Learning has seen, after the advent of Learning Content Management Systems (LCMS) and the Web 2.0, a great impulse; powerful systems supporting virtual learning activities have been very widely deployed and are now used daily in many institutions, and in particular, in universities and other educational centers.

According to (Kahiigi, Ekenberg, Hansson, Tusubira & Danielson, 2008) Learning Management Systems (LCMS) are Web-based software applications used to plan, implement, and assess a specific learning process. Typically, an LCMS provides an instructor with a way to create and deliver content, monitor student participation, and assess student performance. It may also provide students with the ability to use interactive features such as threaded discussions, video conferencing, and discussion forums. Some systems also include cooperative working tools such as blogs and wikis. Examples of most commonly used LCMSs are Blackboard (Blackboard, 2006), Moodle (Moodle, 2007) and Claroline (Claroline, 2005)

The advantages which LCMSs provide are many and well-known: they support many of the activities that occur in the classroom and allow the use of different multimedia resources, facilitate communication and feedback, support different styles of learning, allow time and location flexibility, to name some (Britain & Liber, 1999). But, unfortunately, they also present some disadvantages for both students and instructors mainly as a consequence of the lack of face-to-face contact.

There is a list of problems encountered by students studying on-line courses, including the students' feeling of isolation due to lack of contact with the instructor, disorientation in the course hyperspace, loss of student motivation and lack of institutional support (Conrad, 2002; Mazza & Dimitrova, 2007). On the other hand, instructors face three major problems: a) assuring that students will reach a satisfactory level of involvement

in the learning processes (Juan, Daradoumis, Xhafa, Caballé & Faulin, 2009), b) avoiding high abandonment rates (Jusung, 2005; Lykourentzou, Giannoukos, Nikolopoulos, Mpardis & Loumos, 2009) and c) reducing the high workload which this kind of teaching supposes (Castro, Nebot & Mugica, 2008). As is said in (Juan, Daradoumis, Xhafa, Caballé & Faulin, 2009) monitoring and tracking tools are a solution since they can help in identifying non-attending students or groups and consequently, permit intervention to ensure student involvement in the collaborative learning process.

In fact, LCMSs provide instructors with certain information but this is limited and not very significant when assessing the teaching-learning process. In general, they offer a report with summarised access information such as the dates of the first and the last connection, the number of visited pages, the number of read/sent mails and so on by each student; and another report, about the use of resources (announcements, discussions, etc.) with parameters such as number of accesses and spent time on each one. Furthermore, this is shown in a tabular format and not in an intuitive and graphical way so that the instructor, with just a glimpse, can ascertain the students' situation in the course. As a consequence of this, getting a clear vision of each student or group academic progression during the course is difficult and time consuming for instructors (Douglas, 2008). A detailed comparison of the monitoring and tracking tools offered by the most-used LCMSs and a proposal of more interesting reports to help instructors in their work is found in (Zorrilla & Álvarez, 2009). With these reports, instructors can easily find out how their students progress in the virtual course, compare their activity with respect to the average student activity, get an idea of the learning style according to the resources students use and assess the course design seeing the click stream carried out by the students.

The architecture which gives support to this reporting tool follows the general guidelines of design of Business Intelligence (BI) applications: a dimensional database feed with the activity registered in LCMS databases, OLAP cubes to provide quick answers and a graphical user interface with dynamic reports and dashboards.

But, regretfully, there are still questions that these BI-Reports can not yet answer such as: what are students' profiles according to demographic and navigation information?, what kind of sessions do the students carry out when connected?, how to group students according to the their style of learning?, what is the drop-out students' profile?, what are the resources which are frequently used together? or what are the questions in a test which students fail more frequently? In order to answer these questions, the use of data mining techniques is required. In the Service Functionality section of this chapter we explain how the system answers three of these questions.

Thanks to the fact that LCMSs log all the activity carried out by instructors and students in the system from when they connect to it until they close the session, they provide a data set suitable for data mining purposes.

Then, why do LCMSs not provide a tool to answer these questions? In our opinion, one of the main reasons is the difficulty in carrying out the Knowledge Discovery in Databases (KDD) process (Kaplan, 2007) and showing the results in an understandable way to end-users who are non-expert in data mining techniques.

The overall process of knowledge discovery from data involves the repeated application of the following steps (Fayyad, Piatesky-Shapiro & Smyth, 1996):

1. Developing an understanding of the application domain and the goals of the end-user.
2. Creating a target data set: selecting a dataset or focusing on a subset of variables, to which the discovery process is to be applied. This step in general requires one or more of the following tasks: data cleaning and preprocessing, removal of noise or outliers, data

transformation, adding context information, etc.

3. Choosing the data mining task, this means, deciding whether the goal of the KDD process is descriptive or predictive, and based on this decision, choosing the data mining algorithm(s) and the most appropriate parameters for its execution.
4. Executing the algorithm on the dataset.
5. Interpreting mined patterns.
6. Consolidating discovered knowledge.

Regretfully, in each step of the process, there is such a number of decisions to be taken with little or no formal guidance, that, often, the outcome of the process just results in the necessity to start over: either with more (or less, but cleaner) data, or using different data mining tools, or setting different values for some parameters. Often, the outcome of each round, instead of profound knowledge distilled from large amounts of data, is very large amounts of modeled information; for instance, it is common that the output of an association rule miner on a moderately large dataset consists of tens of thousands of rules which are not manageable for a human-being.

Although the difficulty is real, we consider it necessary to make the effort to resolve it. Thus, we have designed and developed a web service called ElWM (E-learning Web Miner) which aims to provide a solution applied to educational field. This has been designed following a service-oriented architecture (SOA) in such a way it can be easily hosted in a server in the cloud and can be used directly by any instructor or any LCMS platform as on-demand software (also called software-as-a-service) (Srinivasa, Nageswara & Ekusuma, 2009).

RELATED WORK

In this section we review the context of data mining applied to educational data and we relate works published in this field. Likewise we discuss different educational data mining tools and compare these with our proposal.

Educational Data Mining

According to the International Working Group on Educational Data Mining, Educational data mining is an emergent discipline concerned with developing methods for exploring the unique types of data that come from educational settings, and using those methods to better understand students and the settings which they learn in (http://www. educationaldatamining.org/).

A characteristic of data mining from e-learning environments is the fact that, in general, the a posteriori comparison of various methods or measures is impossible, or, at the very least, extremely difficult (Merceron & Yacef, 2008), quoting an excellent example from that reference: "Take the example of building a system to transform hand-written documents into printed documents". This system has to discover the printed letters behind the hand-written ones. It is possible to try several sets of measures or parameters and experiment what works best. Such an experimentation phase is difficult in the educational field because the data is very dynamic and can vary a lot among samples; indeed, we encounter different course design, students with different skills, different methods of assessment, different resources used and so on. To avoid the risk of such variability heavily distorting the data mining results, there is no option but to reduce the amount of data available to mine to only the students enrolled in one single course edition. This means that the dataset size with which our ElWM works is small or medium. Furthermore, as the data comes from an LCMS database, it is usually very clean (i.e., its values are correct and thus, few pre-processing tasks are

required). Another additional advantage is that there are many proven data mining algorithms which work suitably with this kind of transactional data (Han, 2006; Witten & Frank, 2005). These reasons make our system adequate and efficient for solving the problem. Of course, if LCMSs register contextual data about each course in a standardized way, more accurate and profitable patterns could be discovered.

There are a great number of works in which data mining techniques are used on educational data. Some of them address understanding learner behavior (Hung & Zhang, 2008; Talavera & Gaudioso, 2004), others recommend activities, topics, etc. (Zaïane, 2002), offer learning experiences (Au, 2009) or provide instructional messages to learners (Ueno & Okamoto, 2007) with the aim of improving the effectiveness of the course and producing better outcomes. In other works the goal is to promote group-based collaborative learning (Perera, Kay, Koprinska, Yacef & Zaïane, 2009) or to predict students' performance (Hung & Zhang, 2008), among others. In the particular case of Educational Adaptive Hypermedia Systems (EAHS), such as ALFANET (Van der KlinkBoon, Rusman, Rodrigo, Fuentes, Arana & Barrera, 2002), LON-CAPA (Minaei-Bidgoli, 2004) or AHA! (Romero, Porras, Ventura, Hervás & Zafra, 2006), data mining techniques have been incorporated in the system in order to adapt the course to the students' navigational behavior.

Two interesting papers which summarize the application of data mining to educational systems are (Romero & Ventura, 2007; Castro, Vellido, Nebot, & Mugica, 2007).

Data Mining as a Service

Currently, most data mining tools such as Weka (Witten & Frank, 2005), Keel (Alcalá-Fdez, Sánchez, García, Jesus, Ventura, Garrell, Otero, Romero, Bacardit, Rivas, Fernández, & Herrera, 2009), R (R, 2010), and so on, aim to provide different utilities with which to construct simple as well as complex KDD processes. But these software applications are designed more for power and flexibility than for simplicity which prevents non-expert data miners from being able to use them. As Romero et al. (2008) say, most of the current data mining tools are too complex for educators to use and their features go well beyond the scope of what an educator may want to do.

As far as we know there are two tools which try to solve this issue. TADA-Ed (Merceron, & Yacef, 2005), a data mining platform dedicated to instructors, which allows them to preprocess, visualize and discover pedagogically relevant patterns and Moodle Data Mining Tool (Romero, Ventura, Espejo, & Hervas, 2008) which is a similar tool to this but connected to the Moodle platform. But in both of them instructors still have to have certain knowledge of data mining to use them, since they are responsible for doing the phases of selection and preprocessing of attributes and selection of algorithms and their parameters.

There are also other educational data mining tools but these are for solving a specific issue, such as EPRules (Romero, Ventura, Bra & Castro, 2003) for discovering predictive rules in EAHS, O3R (Becker & Vanzin, 2010) for carrying out the analysis of navigation patterns, MINEL (Bellaachia, Vommina, & Berrada, 2006) for mining learning paths or Simulog (Bravo and Ortigosa, 2006) a tool able to simulate student behaviour by generating log files according to specified profiles.

Until now, the related applications were developed as stand-alone versions, and none of them is offered as a service in the cloud. In this context there are some initiatives such as ADAPA (Adapa, 2009) which is the first standards-based, real-time scoring engine available on the market and the first scoring engine accessible as a service on the Amazon Cloud and other non-commercial data mining tools such as Anteater (Guedes, Meira & Ferreira, 2005), GridMiner (Brezany, Janciak, Wöhrer & Tjoa, 2004) or ADaM (Rushing, Ramachandran, Nair, Graves, Welch & Lin, 2005) which provide data mining services to construct

KDD processes. Given that these non-commercial tools were built according to a service-oriented architecture, in the near future, they could offer services on-demand. Finally, Ohri Framework (Ohri, 2009) tries to create an economical alternative to proprietary data mining software by giving more value to the customer and utilizing open source statistical package R, with the GUI Rattle, hosted on a cloud computing environment.

But, once again, the services they offer are addressed to expert data miners. In contrast, our proposal hides the KDD process to the user. It only shows a set of templates that specify the data which must be sent to the service in order to obtain certain patterns which have been previously defined from a rigorous experimentation. Thus, the templates contain the definition of the attributes (data) as well as the mining algorithms which are adequate for obtaining the patterns. Since one of the difficulties which data miners face is the selection of parameters and how these affect the result, in our service, the parameters of the algorithms are established by the system itself, through a previous analysis of the data and/or using other mining algorithms as explained in the Service Functionality section.

Furthermore as it has been designed following a serviced-oriented architecture and implemented based on web services, the ElWM can be hosted in an internet server and run in the cloud, being able to be used by multiple end users through its user interface as well as by LCMSs which would consume the offered services through SOAP messages.

ARCHITECTURE

ElWM is a service-oriented application (SOA) built on the most popular open-source framework, Java Enterprise Edition (JEE) and standard web technologies and languages such as SOAP (Simple Object Access Protocol), WSDL (Web Services Description Language), XML, etc.

Figure 1. Architecture

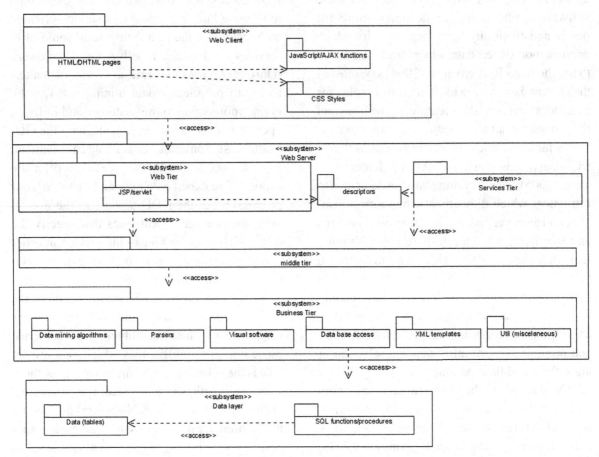

SOA implementations rely on a mesh of software services. Services comprise unassociated, loosely coupled units of functionality that have no embedded calls to each other. Each service implements one action and the calls to each service are done by means of defined protocols that describe how services pass and parse messages, using description metadata. Developers commonly build SOAs using web services standards as SOAP that have gained broad industry acceptance (Erickson & Siau, 2008).

The advantages which the service-oriented architecture provides are summed up as follows: it allows re-use of software and the building of scalable software; it makes interoperability easier, this means, the integration of third-party services is quick and easy; and it has lower maintenance costs. Furthermore, software built with this architecture can be offered effortlessly as a service in the cloud. Therefore our proposal follows a service-oriented architecture with the aim of being easily configured and hosted in the web and can be deployed as a Business intelligent software-as-a-service (BiaaS). Software-as-a-service (SaaS) is a current term used to refer to business software rather than consumer software since its delivery model avoids the need to install and run the applications on the computer of the user and to carry out the maintenance and support tasks (Essaidi & Osmani, 2011). At the moment, our system can be classified as a SaaS level-1 maturity according to (Traudt & Konary, 2005).

Figure 1 shows a high-level abstraction view of the components in our architecture and how

Figure 2. User interface

they are connected, as has been implemented in the current ElWM prototype. It follows a 3-layer design: web-client layer, web server layer and data layer.

Web client layer is the user interface built for instructors using the service (see Figure 2). It is programmed with AJAX technology (shorthand for Asynchronous JavaScript and XML) which is a group of interrelated web development techniques used on the client-side to create rich internet applications (RIA). The interface offers two possible forms of use: one for instructors without data mining knowledge in which users only have to send the data file according to the template and request its execution (amateur user) and another in which instructors, before running the process, can establish the parameters of the algorithms (advanced user).

The second layer, called server layer, is in turn divided in 3 tiers. The first tier is made up of two components: a server application which is responsible for linking user interface with business logic, programmed by means of servlets, and a module which gathers three web services deployed to be used by external software, one which offers the whole functionality of the ElWM, another for using a concrete data mining method, and the last using a concrete data mining method, and the last

which provides the visualization services. As is usual, these services are described in WSDL and they use SOAP for the exchange of messages. Furthermore, this tier includes the service descriptors, also called service repository.

The middle-tier acts as an interface through which the web tier and the service tier accede to the functionality of the business logic. Its role is, therefore, to isolate these tiers, so that changes carried out in one of them do not affect the working of the others. This guarantees a simpler maintenance and extension of the tool in the future.

The business tier consists of several modules. A data mining module which wraps data mining algorithms and the pre-processing tasks, a module which implements the visualization tools and other modules necessary for the parsing of files, connection to a database and other utilities. All elements have been programmed in java except the visualization module which uses the graphical capabilities provided by Matlab. All of them are deployed as web services.

Finally, the data layer stores the necessary information (metadata) for the configuration of the system.

As can be observed, our service has been designed to offer a complete and autonomous functionality, although in the future, it could be orchestrated with other services in order to offer a more powerful functionality. That is the main reason for which this has been designed following the SOA principles and implemented by means of Web Services.

Lastly we recommend reading the chapter entitled Business Intelligence-as-a-service: Studying the Functional and the Technical Architectures (Essaidi & Osmani, 2011) where an architecture for implementing on-demand software is proposed and discussed.

SERVICE FUNCTIONALITY

In this section we describe the service built specifically to be used with information from LCMSs logs. First we relate the data commonly registered in LCMS and describe some of templates defined to answer instructors' questions. Next, we demonstrate the functionality of our service using two virtual courses taught in the University of Cantabria as case studies and finally, discuss the usefulness of the service for instructors, showing the models and patterns obtained and how they can be applied to the teaching process.

Data from a LCMS Database

As we said previously, our service aims to offer information which complements that provided by LCMSs in their reporting tools. Thus, the templates have to be constituted by variables which can be obtained from their databases. After the study carried out in (Zorrilla & Álvarez, 2009) about the monitoring and tracking tools provided by LCMSs and our work developing MATEP (Zorrilla & Álvarez, 2008), we can determine that the attributes listed in Table 1 can be read from LCMS repositories with different level of detail. For example it is possible to read the number of sessions carried out by a student in a term or in a week, or calculate its average value. It is also

Table 1. Some of available variables

Demographic	Learner gender
	Learner age
Navigation	Nº sessions
	Delay among sessions
	Time spent in any resource
	Nº hits in any resource
Content activity	Nº content pages viewed
Forum activity	Nº messages post to forum
	Nº messages read on forum
	Nº messages replied to forum
	Mark in forum
Assignment activity	Nº assignments read
	Nº assignments submitted
	Mark in assignment
Activity Mail	Nº messages sent by mail
	Nº messages read on mail
Chat activity	Nº chat room entered
Wiki activity	Nº wiki page edited
Quizzes	Nº quizzes done
	Nº quizzes passed
	Nº quizzes failed
	Nº items in test
	Nº attempts in item
	Grade in item
Course evaluation	Final mark

possible to know which day of the week a certain session corresponds to. All the power of SQL language can be used to generate the variables that make up the templates.

We define session as a series of requests by the same identified student (user) from the moment he or she connects to the course until he or she disconnects or leaves it. We consider hit as each click in a web page. Resource is any tool available in the LCMS such as mail, forum, wiki, and so on. Lastly, we define action as any activity inside a resource, for example sending a mail, browsing content pages, etc.

It is important to point out that the data used by the service is read directly from the e-learning database without carrying out any kind of supposition or using any heuristic as is usual in web usage mining where the information is read from log files and the session definition must be defined (Srivastava, Cooley, Deshpande & Tan, 2000).

Proposal of Patterns

Initially, the set of models which we propose use only descriptive techniques such as clustering and association because these easily allow instructors to gain an insight into students' characteristics and depict students' learning patterns.

Later, we will deal with prediction and classification tasks, once we have studied what kind of questions can be answered and how to manage the fact of having a low number of transactions. In general, there are no more than 80 or 100 learners per virtual course which does not allow us to build very accurate classifiers. A possible solution would be using data from several editions of the same course but it must be guaranteed that the design and organization of the course have not changed, if for example instructors want to know what the average activity necessary in each resource to pass the course is.

For the case studies, we have used the data from two courses offered in the 2009/2010 academic year at the largest virtual campus in Spain, called G9 Group, which is composed of 9 Spanish universities, one of which is the University of Cantabria. Both courses are eminently practical. The first one, entitled "Introduction to multimedia methods", has the objective of teaching the students how to use a particular multimedia tool (in what follows, we refer to it as the Multimedia dataset) and the second one, "Basic administration of a UNIX-LINUX system" (the Linux dataset) teaches the students the basic utilities and tools to install and configure correctly a LINUX operating system.

The multimedia course is designed by means of web pages and includes some video tutorials,

flash animations and interactive elements. The students must perform 4 exercises, 2 projects and one final exam online. The course is open to all degrees. The number of students enrolled in the multimedia course was 80, of which only 37 did the first assignment, the deadline being 15 days after the beginning of the course. Finally, 24 students followed the course up to the end and 17 passed.

In the case of the Linux course, 20 students enrolled, all of them from a telecommunication degree (it is limited to these students) and all of them passed at the first or second opportunity. This course is organized as follows: the instructor indicates the topics and self-tests that they must perform every week on the calendar. Additionally, during the course, they must deliver 6 practical exercises and pass two online exams. The course includes 38 self-tests, one for each topic of the course.

Next, we show three of the templates designed, one for building the student profile, another for the session profile and another for discovering the resources which are used together as example of application.

Student Profile

This template utilizes the following input parameters: gender, age, number of sessions in the course, time spent in the course, average sessions per week, average time spent per week. These variables were chosen with the aim of grouping students according to their activity in the e-learning platform and their demographic data. The number of attributes is reduced with objective of obtaining a model which is easy to understand and interpret, since the model is explained depending on these variables.

The algorithms chosen for obtaining the patterns are EM (Expectation-Maximization) and SimpleKMeans (Witten & Frank, 2005). Thanks to the fact that EM algorithm provides a probability distribution that can be used as a similarity criterion to characterize the data, we utilize it first in

Figure 3. Student profile for the Linux dataset

Attribute	Full Data (20)	Cluster# 0 (1)	1 (5)	2 (12)	3 (2)
gender	m	f	m	m	f
TotalTime	794.7	4048	1124.4	385	802
NumberOfSessions	100.1	385	143	54.9167	121.5
averageTimePerWeek	28.95	149	41.2	13.75	29.5
avergareSessionPerWeek	3.25	14	4.8	1.5833	4

Clustered Instances

0   1 (5%)
1   5 (25%)
2   12 (60%)
3   2 (10%)

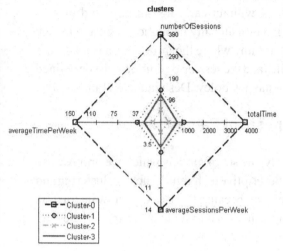

order to know the number of clusters with which the SimpleKMeans algorithm will be executed (required parameter). We generate the patterns with SimpleKMeans (MacQueen, 1967) because it is one of the most-used in practical problems, its execution is quick and furthermore the results which it offers are easy to understand statistically and graphically. Each cluster is represented by its centroid, which means, the "average" of all its points (average for numerical data and most-frequent value for categorical data).

The left-hand side of Figure 3 shows the textual result obtained from the Linux dataset (without user intervention). It must be pointed out that this dataset has the gender and age attributes with null value, consequently they were eliminated in the pre-processed task.

The instructor can find out that students are grouped in four clusters. Cluster-0 gathers a woman with high activity in the system (one hour and twenty minutes on average per week), Cluster-1 which is characterized by a lower activity to the previous one but higher than the average and mainly carried out by men. Cluster-3 collects women with an activity at near-average levels and Cluster-2 gathers men with a very low dedication.

The same information is drawn graphically on the right-hand side of Figure 3. This spider graph helps to compare, at a glance, the clusters obtained. It can only represent numerical variables, so that the service offers other graphic results in which the distribution of each attribute in each cluster is shown.

Now we analyze the results obtained in the Multimedia dataset (Figure 4). As can be observed the service generates three clusters, one of them (Cluster-1) with a very low activity which corresponds to students who dropped out in the first days of the course, Cluster-0 which gathers learners with an average activity in time and number of sessions which is half of the activity carried out by the students collected in Cluster-2. It must be pointed out that there are 13 students who never accessed to the course (there are only 67 transactions of 80) and most of the students who enrolled in the course are men.

The first conclusion which we reach is that the system is able to show the different behavior of learners in each course which was contrasted and validated by the instructors involved. Furthermore, it allows the instructors to assess whether the average activity carried out by students matches

Figure 4. Student profile for the multimedia dataset

Attribute	Cluster# Full Data (67)	0 (21)	1 (31)	2 (15)
age	22.3226	21.9662	22.2799	22.9097
gender	Man	Man	Man	Man
totalTime	1138.1791	1394.7143	103.6129	2917.1333
numberOfSessions	73.6418	93.9524	8.2903	180.2667
averageTimePerWeek	56.4776	69.1905	4.8065	145.4667
averageSessionsPerWeek	3.2836	4.1905	0.0645	8.6667

Clustered Instances

0   21 (31%)
1   31 (46%)
2   15 (22%)

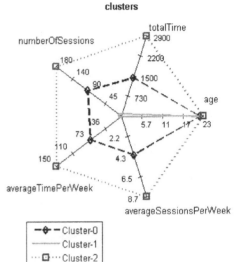

with the predicted effort for the course. Additionally, instructors can run the algorithm again with a higher or lower number of clusters in order to compare the results.

Pattern of Resources which are Frequently Used Together

This template is directed towards the discovery of the resources which are more commonly used together in each session, thus allowing instructors to find out which tools are used more frequently (wiki, chat, forum, etc.) by their students and which ones are basically ignored, and gain an insight into the learning process followed by the students. This information is very valuable in order to propose tasks according to the learners' learning styles.

This template contains the following parameters: session identification and a list of all resources used in the session, for example content-pages, mail, forum, chat, etc.

The algorithm chosen for this template is the implementation of Apriori developed by Borgelt

(Borgelt, 2003). It is an efficient implementation which generates an irredundant rule set. This requires two parameters to run, support and confidence. For a given dataset D, consisting of n transactions, the support of a rule $s(X \rightarrow Y)$ is defined as the number of transactions which have the items X and Y and the confidence is the support of the rule divided by the support of its antecedent, $c(X \rightarrow Y) = s(X \rightarrow Y) / S(X)$.

ElWM uses some heuristics with the aim of establishing these two parameters, and in this way, automating the process (towards parameter-free data mining algorithms). The closed frequent itemset is calculated and the confidence is taken as the median of the frequencies and the support as the minimum frequent itemset. Once again it must be remembered that the user can run the algorithm several times in order to increase or decrease the number of rules, which implies changing the support and confidence parameters, augmenting or reducing these respectively.

In Figure 5, the textual and graphic results obtained in the Linux dataset are shown. In this case, the system established the confidence as 0.7

Figure 5. Resources more frequently used together for the Linux dataset. The antecedent of the rule is drawn in grey and the consequent in black. The last two columns represent the support and the confidence respectively (Wong, Whitney, & Thomas, 1999).

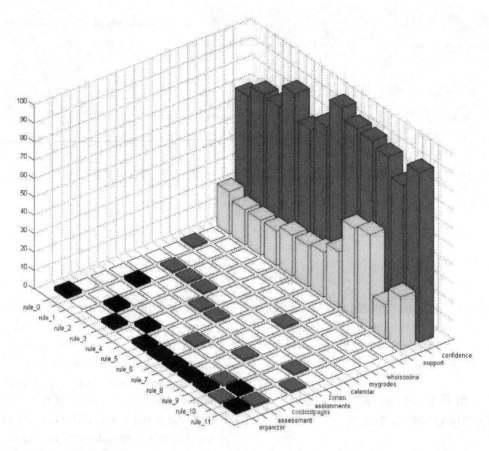

Rule_0: organizer <- who_is_online (23.0, 71.1)
Rule_1: assignments <- calendar (19.0, 77.7)
Rule_2: assessment <- calendar (19.0, 76.9)
Rule_3: organizer <- calendar (19.0, 89.5)
Rule_4: assessment <- forum (22.5, 75.8)
Rule_5: organizer <- forum (22.5, 83.3)
Rule_6: organizer <- content-page (24.5, 99.2)
Rule_7: organizer <- my_grades (30.5, 93.5)
Rule_8: organizer <- assignments (49.1, 92.5)
Rule_9: organizer <- assessment (51.2, 89.7)
Rule_10: assessment <- forum organizer (18.7, 79.5)

and the support as 0.18. The instructor can see that the organizer is the most used tool (more frequent itemset with support 100% and confidence 86,1%), but this does not come as a surprise, given the fact that the organizer is the initial page of the course. The remaining sessions, close to 15%, correspond to accesses to the system through the forum. Assessment is the following tool utilized (rule_9) with 51.2% of the sessions, followed by assignments with 49.1% (rule_8), mygrades with 30.5% (rule_7) and by content pages with 24.5% (rule_6). The instructor was surprised to discover this behavior because this suggested to him that students learn the topics answering the self tests instead of reading the html pages. The remaining rules inform the instructor about some small groups of two or three resources that are often used jointly such as assignments and calendar (rule_1), assessment and calendar (rule_2) or forum with assessment (rule_4) or assignment with assessment and organizer (rule_11). This is a consequence of the organization of the course. The date of exams and the tasks to be submitted are announced in the calendar tool weekly and this is the reason for visiting assessment and assignment tools. Forum is used to discuss the date of the exams since the exams are done online on a fixed date. So, the instructor observes that the course was used as he intended. Another interesting rule is that learners are interested in knowing who is connected (rule_0). This allows the instructor to think about proposing some collaborative tasks.

Next, we discuss the rules obtained in the Multimedia dataset (see Figure 6). In this case, the system established the confidence as 0.7 and the support as 0.10. As in the previous dataset, the organizer is the tool most often used followed by the forum (rule_3), assignments (rule_4) and content-pages (rule_2). The rules in this case are not very informative since the organizer is always in the consequent of the rule. In this course, the instructor could observe that the students visited the forum in the study sessions (rule_10) as well as in sessions of doing tasks (rule_12). So, she could conclude that this resource is suitable for solving problems or doubts since chat and mail were scarcely used. Unlike the Linux dataset, in this course the content-pages were visited and used to do the assignments (rule_11). The instructor was surprised to discover the use of the assessment tool since this was used for an exam and two surveys. After analysing the session profile (next section) and seeing the low time spent in the tool, the instructor could conclude that learners acceded to the assessment tool in order to see if there was something new. Perhaps using the calendar tool would avoid this abnormal behaviour.

Session Profile

Next, we describe the session profile which helps instructors to better understand the usage pattern of the resources and complements the knowledge provided by the pattern of the resources which are frequently used together in the sense that it allows the measuring of the level of use of each tool measured in time and hits. The input variables of this template are the number of hits and time spent in each session (minutes) in each resource. As before, we use some heuristics with the aim of selecting only the course resources which are relevant to the process. In this case, we calculate the average time of usage as well as the average number of clicks in each resource, and eliminate those resources whose usage is lower than 1% of the value of the resource with the highest activity. As the activity by hits and by time can be quite different depending on the resource, we intersect the lists of resources with both criteria and the result is the final list of resources.

The algorithm chosen for this template is x-means (Pelleg & Moore, 2000), an extension of k-means which estimates the number of clusters. Its limitation is it only works with numerical data.

Observing Figure 7, we can discover that cluster_0 gathers sessions where the learners use mainly forum assessment and content-pages tools. These seem to be sessions near an exam. Cluster_1 collects sessions mainly focused on reading the content-pages and doing assignments. Finally, cluster_2 gathers very brief sessions which can be considered as consulting visits to forum and submission tasks. This cluster concentrates most of the activity of the course. In the instructor's opinion the pattern depicts the behavior that he expected, one or two sessions for carrying out each task (cluster 1), one or two sessions for preparing the exam and the rest for following the course.

Analysing the Multimedia dataset (see Figure 8), it can be observed that forum and assessment are the more used tools since cluster_2 and cluster_3 sum up 89% of the sessions in which prac-

Figure 6. Resources more frequently used together for the multimedia dataset

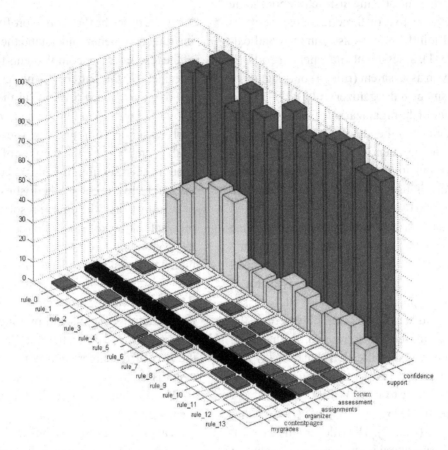

Rule_0: organizer <- my_grades (22.9, 84.4)
Rule_1: organizer <- assessment (31.3, 87.5)
Rule_2: organizer <- content-pages (38.4, 99.0)
Rule_3: organizer <- forum (42.4, 78.7)
Rule_4: organizer <- assignments (41.4, 93.4)
Rule_5: organizer <- my_grades assessment (11.5, 86.2)
Rule_6: organizer <- my_grades forum (11.9, 78.8)

Rule_7: organizer <- assessment content-pages (11.3, 98.7)
Rule_8: organizer <- assessment forum (18.7, 88.4)
Rule_9: organizer <- assessment assignments (17.0, 92.2)
Rule_10: organizer <- content-pages forum (14.0, 97.7)
Rule_11: organizer <- content-pages assignments (16.0, 99.1)
Rule_12: organizer <- forum assignments (17.7, 90.8)
Rule_13: organizer <- assessment forum assignments (10.3, 92.7)

tically only these resources and organizer are used. In both clusters, the students seem to consult the forum and/or submit an assignment since the time spent and hits done are low.

Cluster_1 collects mainly study sessions with an hour of dedication and an average of 27 viewed-pages. Clusters_0 gathers sessions in which learners are developing the tasks and looking up content-pages at the same time. It must be said

that in this course the assignments are described in several html pages and that is the reason for having several clicks. This last cluster also gathers the activity in the assessment tool.

In the opinion of the instructors involved in these two virtual courses, these patterns allow them to gain an insight into the characteristics of their students with relation to the time spent and the use of resources available in the course.

Figure 7. Session profile for the Linux dataset

Attributes	Cluster 0 (28)	Cluster 1 (126)	Cluster 2 (1805)
time_mail	0.3513	0.5213	0.1634
time_forum	5.4324	0.3504	0.1939
time_content-page	17.9189	26.8632	0.6958
time_organizer	1.7297	4.5042	0.1412
time_assignments	0.9189	8.3589	0.4216
time_who_is_online	4.3243	2.2905	0.3961
time_calendar	0.6756	0.2136	0.0548
time_syllabus	0.1891	0.2222	0.0554
time_media_library	1.5675	0.2735	0.0182
time_assessment	24.3513	1.9401	1.2332
time_my_grades	0.0810	0.3589	0.1412
hit_correo	3.0810	0.5299	0.2144
hit_forum	46.9189	1.0598	1.3412
hit_content-page	13.8918	9.7521	0.6853
hit_organizer	10.1081	4.7777	1.4703
hit_assignments	8.1081	2.7435	1.0326
hit_who_is_online	11.6486	1.4102	0.3623
hit_calendar	6.2702	0.4957	0.3440
hit_syllabus	2.0810	0.2051	0.1063
hit_media_library	2.5675	0.2905	0.0581
hit_assessment	46.3783	2.2051	1.5689
hit_my_grades	1.5945	0.4700	0.4033

Filtered clusters

0	28 (1%)	
1	126 (6%)	
2	1805 (92%)	

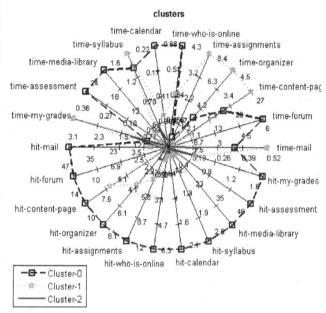

Figure 8. Session profile for the multimedia dataset

Attributes	Cluster 0 (271)	Cluster 1 (256)	Cluster 2 (1051)	Cluster 3 (3356)
time_mail	1.3476	0.4169	0.8051	0.4140
time_forum	4.1622	3.8892	2.0904	0.7084
time_content-page	11.0927	68.6051	1.4502	3.3794
time_organizer	2.6655	6.7933	0.5586	0.7770
time_assignments	20.9470	4.4243	5.2296	0.5603
time_filemanager	0.9801	0.1697	0.1729	0.0128
time_who_is_online	0.1655	0.3321	0.0715	0.0619
time_assessment	4.4437	1.2952	0.6003	0.0566
time_my_grades	0.7185	0.3726	0.4135	0.1552
time_compiler	0.1721	1.9926	0.0347	0.1087
hit_mail	1.0264	0.4760	0.6610	0.3868
hit_forum	10.2682	6.4538	6.5029	1.9123
hit_content-page	3.5033	27.3763	0.6083	1.2411
hit_organizer	5.9304	11.5682	2.0039	1.8634
hit_assignments	5.6490	1.5202	2.4642	0.3511
hit_filemanager	0.5562	0.1217	0.1978	0.0220
hit_who_is_online	0.3973	0.2140	0.1153	0.0837
hit_assessment	2.7152	0.9409	1.1292	0.1642
hit_my_grades	0.6225	0.2546	0.5367	0.2131
hit_compiler	0.0695	0.4280	0.0049	0.0268

Filtered clusters

0	271 (5%)	
1	256 (5%)	
2	1051 (21%)	
3	3356 (68%)	

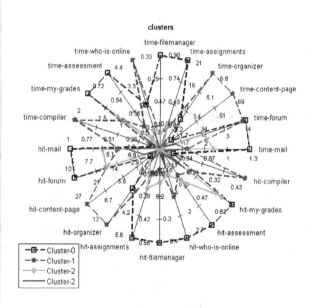

Although it is true that the learning process can be carried out without being connected, the interaction of the students with the different resources contains information to improve their use. This allows instructors to validate or refute hypothesis used in the design of the learning process. For example, knowing that there are few sessions in which students accede to content-pages makes instructors suppose that most of the students do not connect to study or, what would be worse, they do not read the content-pages. This data can alert instructors and they can detect, for example, a bad design of content-pages. Likewise, knowing that students use the assessment tool half the times they connect to the e-learning platform confirms his effort in preparing this kind of material although, at the same time, it can be dangerous if this is the only source of learning the students use.

Given that the reports offered by Blackboard do not show this kind of information, the instructors feel satisfied with the results which ElWM provides although they point out that adding a descriptive output of the results in natural language would make the reading of the results easier.

Finally we must say that as a consequence of the fact that the organization and design of the courses is very varied, the interpretations of the patterns can only be carried out by the courses' instructors, as is reflected in these cases studies.

FUTURE RESEARCH DIRECTIONS

Data mining techniques are more and more used in many different fields such as business, marketing, bioinformatics or science. The main goal of data mining is to discover valid, novel, non-trivial and potentially useful information from data which helps decision-makers to take better actions in their "business". As said previously, the KDD process involves multiple stages and, currently, the process is carried out more as an "art" than as a "science" due to the lack of a theoretical framework that unifies different data

mining tasks (Yang & Xindong, 2005). Thus, developing this framework and implementing tools which automate (to the degree possible) the KDD process are two great challenges of this era. A possible approach may be to use theories and principles proven to be successful in other established fields and branches of computer science, such as conceptual modeling, model-driven engineering and software engineering with which to raise a formal framework that provides a solid foundation for a systematic study in the KDD area and allows developing methodologies and tools for developing KDD projects.

On the path to this goal, designing mining algorithms with as few parameters as possible, ideally none, is another challenging work. This would avoid finding patterns that are not correct, or greatly overestimating the significance of a pattern because of a failure to understand the role of parameter searching in the data mining process (Keogh, Lonardi & Ratanamahatana, 2004). Some advances in this field are arising such as Yacaree, a parameter-free closure-based association rule miner (Balcazar, 2010) or the parameter-free classification method proposed by Boullé (2009) which not only automates the modelling task but also the data preparation task by selecting the more suitable variables.

Another additional difficulty of the KDD process is to compare the results across methods and decide which one is the right. Thus mathematical tools which address this issue are necessary. A good reference which deals with this subject is (Guillet & Hamilton, 2007) which summarizes quality and interestingness measures for data mining and proposes new measures.

From a high performance computational point of view, designing data mining services which take advantage of the resources that cloud computing offers is another important task to be carried out (Grossman, Gu & Sabala, 2008). But, cloud computing is still in its infancy (Joshi, 2010) and there are still some other challenges that need to be overcome in order to make the BI on cloud model work: a) moving data to the cloud is an expensive proposition due to the network costs, b) storing data in the cloud and assuring its recovery and protection is also expensive and c) there are regulatory and compliance restrictions in some countries which do not allow personal information and other sensitive information to be physically located outside the state.

Lastly, another challenging area of work, not directly related with data mining but useful in the e-learning context, is opinion mining and sentiment analysis. As a consequence of the fact that the use of blogs and wikis to carry out activities in virtual courses is very extended, these techniques, enclosed in the Information Retrieval field, can greatly help instructors and students to search and summarize the different opinions about a certain subject. Likewise academics can also discover students' appreciation of virtual courses based on sentiment analysis of opinions expressed by students on web surveys (Binali, H., Potdar, V., & Wu, C., 2009.). In this book, the chapter entitled Feature-based opinion mining and summarization is a good starting point for reading about this topic (Balahur, Boldrini, Montoyo, & Martínez-Barco, 2011).

CONCLUSION

In this chapter we relate some problems which instructors involved in virtual teaching face every day as a consequence of the lack of face-to-face contact and the lack of tools to help them to analyze and assess how their students work and progress in the course. We discuss some tools developed in order to solve some of these issues and compare these with our proposal.

Next we present our educational data mining service, called ElWM (E-learning Web Miner), which can also be offered as a service in the cloud. Its main characteristic is that its use is oriented to instructors without data mining knowledge since it hides the KDD process from the user. Its

mode of working is very simple; instructors only have to send a data file according to one of the templates offered by the system and request the results. ElWM carries out the tasks of preprocessing, selection of algorithms and parameters automatically using mining algorithms and some heuristics. The designed templates gather the data and the algorithms which answer some of the common questions of the instructors, such as what is my student profile? Or which resources of the course do they frequently use?

An additional advantage of this system is that it can be easily connected to any LCMSs by simply calling the web services offered through SOAP messages. In fact, we have linked the University of Cantabria Blackboard instance with our service.

Likewise, its modular architecture facilitates its extension with other data mining algorithms and visualization tools developed ad-hoc or consumed from a provider in the cloud (data mining as a service).

Finally, we point out that the instructors in charge of the analyzed courses have a good opinion of the service. It allows them to gain an insight into the characteristics of their students with relation to their behavior in the course and with this information they can validate or refute the hypothesis used in the design of the learning process.

Currently our research is focused on the specification of new templates to be incorporated in the service and as consequence of this fact to add other data mining algorithms and visualization techniques. Next, we will develop a service to connect our system with Moodle. The security is other important aspect we are going to consider. Our idea is to incorporate WS-Security (Web Services Security), a flexible and feature-rich extension to SOAP to apply security to Web services. Lastly, we will study and choose the suitable cloud environment in which to deploy our solution.

ACKNOWLEDGMENT

The authors are deeply grateful to CEFONT, the department of the University of Cantabria which is responsible for LCMS maintenance, for their help and collaboration. This work has been partially financed by Spanish Ministry of Science and Technology under project 'TIN2007-67466-C02-02' and 'TIN2008 – 05924'.

REFERENCES

Adapa. (2009). *Adapa on the cloud.* Retrieved from http://www.zementis.com/on-the-cloud.htm

Alcalá-Fdez, J., Sánchez, L., García, S., Jesus, M., Ventura, S., & Garrell, J. (2009). KEEL: A software tool to assess evolutionary algorithms to data mining problems. *Soft Computing, 13*(3), 307–318.

Au, T., Sadiq, S., & Li, X. (2009). *Learning from experience: Can e-learning technology be used as a vehicle?* 4th International Conference on e-Learing (pp. 32-39). Toronto, Canada: Academic Publishing Limited.

Baker, R. S., & Yacef, K. (2009). The state of educational data mining in 2009: A review and future visions. *Journal of Educational Data Mining, 1*(1), 3–17.

Balahur, A., Boldrini, E., Montoyo, A., & Martínez-Barco, P. (2011). Feature-based opinion mining and summarization. In Zorrilla, M., Mazon, J., Ferrández, O., Garrigós, I., Daniel, F., & Trujillo, J. (Eds.), *Business intelligence applications and the Web: Models, systems and technologies.* Hershey, PA: IGI Global.

Balcázar, J. L. (2010). *Parameter-free association rule mining with yacaree.* Submitted to International Conference on Data Engineering, 2011. Retrieved from http://personales.unican.es/ balcazarjl/yacaree-v04.pdf

Becker, K., & Vanzin, M. (2010). O3R: Ontology-based mechanism for a human-centered environment targeted at the analysis of navigation patterns. In Fujita, H., & Lu, J. (Eds.), *Knowledge-based systems* (pp. 455–470). Elsevier B.V.

Bellaachia, A., Vommina, E., & Berrada, B. (2006). Minel: A framework for mining e-learning logs. *Proceedings of the 5th IASTED International Conference on Web-Based Education* (pp. 259-263). Puerto Vallarta: Mexico: International Association Of Science And Technology For Development.

Binali, H., Potdar, V., & Wu, C. (2009). A state of the art opinion mining and its application domains. In *Proceedings of the 2009 IEEE International Conference on Industrial Technology*, IEEE Computer Society, Washington, DC, (pp. 1-6).

Blackboard Inc. (2006). *Blackboard.* Retrieved from http://www.blackboard.com

Borgelt, C. (2003). *Efficient implementations of Apriori and Eclat.* 1st Workshop of Frequent Item Set Mining Implementations, Melbourne, Australia.

Boullé, M. (2009). A parameter-free classification method for large scale learning. *Journal of Machine Learning Research, 10*, 1367–1385.

Bravo, J., & Ortigosa, A. (2006). Validating the evaluation of adaptive systems by user profile simulation. In *Proceedings of the Workshop on User-Centred Design and Evaluation of Adaptive Systems* (pp. 52-56). Dublin, Ireland: Springer.

Brezany, P., Janciak, I., Wöhrer, A., & Tjoa, A. M. (2004). Grid miner: A framework for knowledge discovery on the Grid - From a vision to design and implementation. *Proceedings of the Cracow Grid Workshop.* Cracow.

Britain, S., & Liber, O. (1999). *A framework for the pedagogical evaluation of virtual learning environments.* Retrieved from http://www.jisc.ac.uk/ uploaded_documents/jtap-041.doc

Castro, F., Nebot, À., & Mugica, F. (2008). A soft computing decision support framework to improve the e-learning experience. *Proceedings of the 2008 Spring Simulation Multiconference* (pp. 781-788). Ottawa, Canada: Society for Computer Simulation International.

Castro, F., Vellido, A., Nebot, A., & Mugica, F. (2007). Applying data mining techniques to e-learning problems. In Kacprzyk, J. (Ed.), *Studies in computational intelligence* (pp. 183–221). Springer-Verlag.

Claroline Society. (2005). *Claroline*. Retrieved from http://www.claroline.net/

Conrad, D. L. (2002). Engagement, excitement, anxiety and fear: Learners' experiences of starting an online course. *American Journal of Distance Education, 16*(4), 205–226.

Douglas, I. (2008). Measuring participation in Internet supported courses. *Proceedings of the 2008 International Conference on Computer Science and Software Engineering* (pp. 714-717). Washington, DC: IEEE Computer Society.

Erickson, J., & Siau, K. (2008). Web services, service-oriented computing, and service-oriented architecture: Separating hype from reality. *Journal of Database Management, 19*, 42–54.

Essadi, M., & Osmani, A. (2011). Business intelligence-as-a-service: Studying the functional and the technical architectures. In Zorrilla, M., Mazon, J., Ferrández, O., Garrigós, I., Daniel, F., & Trujillo, J. (Eds.), *Business intelligence applications and the Web: Models, systems and technologies*. Hershey, PA: IGI Global.

Fayyad, U., Piatetsky-Shapiro, G., & Smyth, P. (1996). The KDD process for extracting useful knowledge from volumes of data. *Communications of the ACM, 39*, 27–34.

Grossman, R. L., Gu, Y. S., & Zhang, W. (2008). Compute and storage clouds using wide area high performance networks. In Sloot, P. (Ed.), *Future generation computer systems* (pp. 179–183). Elsevier B.V.

Guedes, D. Jr, W. M., & Ferreira, R. (2006). Anteater: A service-oriented architecture for high-performance data mining. *IEEE Internet Computing, 10*(4), 36–43.

Guillet, F., & Hamilton, H. J. (2007). *Quality measures in data mining* (43rd ed.). Springer Series: Studies in Computational Intelligence.

Han, J. (2006). *Data mining: Concepts and techniques*. Morgan Kaufmann.

Hung, J., & Zhang, K. (2008). Revealing online learning behaviors and activity patterns and making predictions with data mining techniques in online teaching. *Journal of Online Learning and Teaching, 8*(4), 426–436.

Joshi, S. (2010, June 7). *Use the potential of BI on cloud*. Retrieved from http://www.channelworld.in/ opinions/use-potential-bi-cloud

Juan, A., Daradoumis, T., Xhafa, F., Caballé, S., & Faulin, J. (2009). *Monitoring and assessment in online collaborative environments: Emergent computational technologies for e-learning support*. Hershey, PA: IGI Global.

Jusung, J. (2005). Understanding e-dropout? *International Journal on E-Learning, 4*(2), 229–240.

Kahiigi, E., Ekenberg, L., Hansson, H., Tusubira, F., & Danielson, M. (2008). Exploring the e-learning state of art. *Electronic Journal of e-Learning, 6*(2), 77- 88.

Kaplan, J. (2007, July). *Data mining as a service: The prediction is not in the box*. Retrieved from http://www.information-management.com/ issues/20070701/1087703-1.html?pg=1

Keogh, E., Lonardi, S., & Ratanamahatana, C. A. (2004). Towards parameter-free data mining. *Proceedings of the Tenth ACM SIGKDD international Conference on Knowledge Discovery and Data Mining* (pp. 206-215). Seattle, WA: ACM.

Lykourentzou, I., Giannoukos, I., Nikolopoulos, V., Mpardis, G., & Loumos, V. (2009). Dropout prediction in e-learning courses through the combination of machine learning techniques. *Computers & Education, 53*(3), 950–965.

MacQueen, J. B. (1967). *Some methods for classification and analysis of multivariate observations*. 5th Berkeley Symposium on Mathematical Statistics and Probability (pp. 281-297). Berkeley, CA: University of California Press.

Mazza, R., & Dimitrova, V. (2007). CourseVis: A graphical student monitoring tool for supporting instructors in Web-based distance courses. *International Journal of Human-Computer Studies, 65*(2), 125–139.

Merceron, A., & Yacef, K. (2005). TADA-Ed for educational data mining. *Interactive Multimedia Electronic Journal of Computer-Enhanced Learning, 7*, 267–287.

Merceron, A., & Yacef, K. (2008). *Interestingness measures for associations rules in educational data*. 1st International Conference on Educational Data Mining (pp. 57-66). Montreal, Canada: EDM.

Minaei-Bidgoli, B. (2004). *Data mining for a Web-based educational system*. Doctoral Thesis. Michigan.

Moodle Trust. (2007). *Moodle*. Retrieved from http://moodle.org/

Ohri, A. (2009). *Data mining through cloud computing: Ohri framework-data mining through cloud computing*. Retrieved from http://knol.google.com/k/ajay-ohri/ data-mining-through-cloud-computing/ d8o4tiw9xa68/3

Pelleg, D., & Moore, A. (2000). X-means: Extending K-means with efficient estimation of the number of clusters. *Proceedings of the Seventeenth International Conference on Machine Learning* (pp.727-734). San Francisco, CA: Morgan Kaufmann.

Perera, D., Kay, J., Koprinska, I. Y., & Zaïane, O. R. (2009). Clustering and sequential pattern mining of online collaborative learning data. *IEEE Transactions on Knowledge and Data Engineering, 21*(6), 759–772.

R Development Core Team. (2010). *R: A language and environment for statistical computing*. R Foundation for Statistical Computing.

Romero, C., Porras, A., Ventura, S., Hervás, C., & Zafra, A. (2006). *Using sequential pattern mining for links recommendation in adaptive hipermedia educational systems*. International Conference Current Developments in Technology-Assisted Education, (pp. 1016-1020). Sevilla.

Romero, C., & Ventura, S. Bra., P. & Castro C. (2003). *Discovering prediction rules in AHA! courses*. 9th International Conference on User Modeling (pp. 25-34). Johnstown, PA: Springer-Verlag.

Romero, C., & Ventura, S. (2007). Educational data mining: A survey from 1995 to 2005. *Expert Systems with Applications, 33*(1), 135–146.

Romero, C., Ventura, S., Espejo, P., & Hervas, C. (2008). *Data mining algorithms to classify students*. International Conference on Educational Data Mining (pp. 8-17). Montreal, Canada: EDM.

Rushing, J., Ramachandran, R., Nair, U., Graves, S., Welch, R., & Lin, H. (2005). ADaM: A data mining toolkit for scientists and engineers. *Computers & Geosciences, 31*(5), 607–618.

Srinivasa R.V., Nageswara, R. N. K., & Ekusuma, K. (2009). Cloud computing: An overview. *Journal of Theoretical and Applied Information Technology, 1.*

Srivastava, J., Cooley, R., Deshpande, M., & Tan, P. (2000). Web usage mining: Discovery and applications of usage patterns from Web data. *SIGKDD Explorations, 1*(2), 12–23.

Talavera, L., & Gaudioso, E. (2004). *Mining student data to characterize similar behaviour groups in unstructured collaboration spaces.* Workshop on Artificial Intelligence in Computer Supported Collaborative Learning. 16th European Conference on Artificial Intelligence (pp. 17–23). Valencia.

Traudt, E., & Konary, A. (2005). *Software as a service taxonomy and research guide.* Retrieved from http://www.idc.com/getdoc.jsp?containerId= 33453&pageType= PRINTFRIENDLY#33453-S-0001

Ueno, M., & Okamoto, T. (2007). Bayesian agent in e-learning. *Proceedings of the Seventh IEEE International Conference on Advanced Learning Technologies* (pp. 282-284). Niigata, Japan: INTECH.

Van der Klink, M., Boon, J., Rusman, E., Rodrigo, M., Fuentes, C., Arana, C., et al. (2002). *Market study. (*ALFanet/IST-2001-33288 Deliverable D72). Retrieved from http://learningnetworks.org/downloads/alfanet-d72- initialmarket-studies.pdf

Witten, I. H., & Frank, E. (2005). *Data mining: Practical machine learning tools and techniques* (2nd ed.). Morgan Kaufmann.

Wong, P. C., Whitney, P., & Thomas, J. (2009). *Visualizating association rules for text mining.* IEEE Symposium on Information Visualization (pp. 120-128). San Francisco, CA: IEEE Computer Society.

Yang, Q., & Wu, X. (2006). 10 challenging problems in data mining research. *International Journal of Information Technology & Decision Making, 5*(4), 597–604.

Zaïane, O. (2002). Building a recommender agent for e-learning systems. *Proceedings of the International Conference on Computers in Education* (pp. 55–59). Auckland, New Zealand: Springer.

Zorrilla, M., & Álvarez, E. (2008). MATEP: Monitoring and analysis tool for e-learning platforms. *Proceedings of the 8th IEEE International Conference on Advanced Learning Technologies* (pp. 611 - 613). Santander, Spain: IEEE.

Zorrilla, M. E., & Álvarez, E. E. (2009). Proposal of a set of reports for students' tracking and assessing in e-learning platforms. In Juan, A. A., Faulin, J., Caballé, S., Xhafa, F., & Daradoumis, T. (Eds.), *Monitoring and assessment in online collaborative environments: Emergent computational technologies for e-learning support* (pp. 235–261). Hershey, PA: IGI Global.

Chapter 11
BIN:
Business Intelligence Networks

Matteo Golfarelli
University of Bologna, Italy

Federica Mandreoli
University of Modena & Reggio Emilia, Italy

Wilma Penzo
University of Bologna, Italy

Stefano Rizzi
University of Bologna, Italy

Elisa Turricchia
University of Bologna, Italy

ABSTRACT

Cooperation is seen by companies as one of the major means for increasing flexibility and innovating. Business intelligence (BI) platforms are aimed at serving individual companies, and they cannot operate over networks of companies characterized by an organizational, lexical, and semantic heterogeneity. In this chapter we propose a framework, called Business Intelligence Network (BIN), for sharing BI functionalities over complex networks of companies that are chasing mutual advantages through the sharing of strategic information. A BIN is based on a network of peers, one for each company participating in the consortium. Peers are equipped with independent BI platforms that expose some querying functionalities aimed at sharing business information for the decision-making process. After proposing an architecture for a BIN, we outline the main research issues involved in its building and operating, and we focus on the definition of an ad hoc language for expressing semantic mappings between the multidimensional schemata owned by the different peers, aimed at enabling query reformulation over the network.

DOI: 10.4018/978-1-61350-038-5.ch011

INTRODUCTION

Cooperation is seen today by companies as one of the major means for increasing flexibility and innovating so as to survive in today uncertain and changing market. Companies need strategic information about the outer world, for instance about trading partners and related business areas (Hoang & Nguyen, 2009). Indeed, it is estimated that above 80% of waste in inter-company and supply-chain processes is due to a lack of communication between the companies involved. Traditional information systems, that were devised for individual companies and for operating on internal information, give limited support to inter-company cooperation. Even business intelligence (BI) platforms, that support decision making and strategic management activities, are aimed at serving individual companies, and they cannot operate over networks of companies characterized by an organizational, lexical, and semantic heterogeneity (Abiteboul, 2003). The existing approaches in this direction are basically aimed at data mart integration (Banek et al., 2008; Torlone, 2008), so they cannot support dynamic scenarios like those of mergers and acquisitions, nor can they preserve autonomy of individual actors.

In this chapter we propose a framework, called *Business Intelligence Network* (BIN), for sharing BI functionalities over complex networks of companies that, though they may operate in different geographical and business contexts, are chasing mutual advantages by acting in a conscious and agreed upon way, through the sharing of strategic information. A BIN is based on a network of peers, one for each company participating in the consortium; peers are equipped with independent BI platforms that expose some functionalities aimed at sharing business information for the decision-making process, in order to create new knowledge.

In order to get maximum benefit and effectiveness from the BIN framework, some key issues must be taken into account:

- BIN participants are *collaborative*, even if with different grades: local bodies and health-care agencies, as well as enterprises belonging to the same holding, show higher inclination to sharing management information than companies belonging to an individual product supply-chain or companies that belong to the same business area but operate in different geographical markets.

- Inclination to collaboration should not reduce *autonomy* of each participant, that must be allowed to define and change the set of shared information as well as its own terminology and schema without being subject to a shared schema.

- A BIN must be completely *decentralized* and *scalable* because the number of participants, the complexity of business models, and the user workload are unknown a priori and may change during the BIN lifetime.

The main benefits the BIN approach aims at delivering to the corporate world are the possibility of building new inter-organizational relationships and coordination approaches, and the ability to efficiently manage inter-company processes and safely sharing management information besides operational information. Other practical benefits arising from activating a BIN depend on the specific corporate context. In companies that belong to the same supply-chain or operate in the same market, (partial) business information sharing is required by users to allow inter-company processes to be monitored and markets to be accurately controlled. Remarkably, the BIN approach can be applied both to large enterprises and small-medium size companies. As to companies belonging to the same holding, a BIN can lead to a faster activation of shared BI services; this topic is particularly relevant in case of mergers and acquisitions, that are very frequent in the banking area. Finally, as to networks of municipalities, local health-care departments, or chambers of commerce, a BIN enables users to thoroughly compare analytical data about events to discover meaningful trends that could hardly be detected through local analyses.

The working example adopted in this chapter falls in the latter case: a set of local health-care departments participate a BIN to integrate their data about admissions so as to increase the effectiveness of governmental analysis of epidemics and health-care costs. Each local department autonomously developed its BI system, thus resulting into a set of different multidimensional schemata. The heterogeneity between the shared information is increased by different codings adopted for data, as well as be the adoption of different privacy policies. A medical-director at the Florence local department could be interested in comparing the efficiency of its wards with that of another department, thus he could submit a query asking for the average admission costs and durations of stay for each ward and diagnosis. The query is run locally, and it is also forwarded it to the other peers participating the BIN. Each contacted peer locally answers the query and returns its results, according to the security and trust policies set for the requesting peer. The (possibly partial or approximate) results are then integrated and returned to the user based on his local vocabulary and using a friendly interface; this interface should support the user in understanding the returned information by emphasizing inter-data relationships (e.g., data obtained from the Rome peer may be aggregated by disease instead of single diagnosis) as well as the approximations introduced (e.g., the admission costs transmitted from the Rome peer may not include medicine costs).

BUILDING A BIN: RESEARCH ISSUES AND CHALLENGES

A BIN is a complex system, whose construction and management requires sophisticated techniques, mostly devised to cope with the peculiarities of decision-making oriented information. In the following we outline the main issues to be solved to ensure that a BIN operates in a reliable, effective, and efficient way:

- Query reformulation is one of the basic building blocks of a BIN. In the PDMS architecture, reformulation of OLAP queries first of all requires a *language* for properly expressing the semantic mappings between each couple of neighboring peers; this language must accommodate the peculiar characteristics of the multidimensional model, on which the representation of business information at each peer is founded. Then, a *reformulation algorithm* must be devised that takes as input an OLAP query on a local schema *ls* and the mappings between *ls* and the schema of one of its neighbors, the remote schema *rs*, and outputs an OLAP query expressed on *rs*. This is made particularly challenging due to the need of correctly handling the different aggregation operators while preserving summarizability.

- Answering queries in a BIN may be a very resource-consuming task both for the computational effort which is required to each queried peer and for the amount of exchanged messages. In order to avoid this, techniques for *optimizing the reformulation process* in the network must be adopted. We propose to make use of query routing strategies which prune redundant paths and forward queries to the most promising peers only, and of distributed caching models and online aggregation techniques which minimize query execution costs.

- A BIN must provide a unified, integrated vision of the heterogeneous information collected from the different peers to answer a user query. To this end, *object fusion* functionalities must be adopted to properly reconcile the multidimensional results returned; this task is made more complex by the fact that, due to heterogeneity of multidimensional schemata, the information returned may be not completely compliant with the original user query (e.g., it may have a different granularity).

- As stated above, when a user performs a query, the other peers will often return results that are not exactly conformed to the schema of that query. For this reason, a BIN requires smart interfaces capable of emphasizing the differences and relationships between the returned data, as well as techniques to *rank* the returned data depending on how compliant they are with the original local query.

- A BIN should include mechanisms for controlling *data provenance and quality* in order to provide users with information they can rely on. A mechanism for *data lineage* is also necessary to help users understand the semantics of the retrieved data and how these data have been transformed to handle heterogeneity.

- Last but not least, the nature of the exchanged information, as well as the presence of participants that belong to different organizations, require advanced approaches for *security*, ranging from proper access policies to data sharing policies that depend on the degree of trust between participants, as well as techniques for protecting against undesired information inference.

The focus of this chapter is on the first issue, namely query reformulation.

BACKGROUND

Federation-Based Approaches

Although the integration of heterogeneous databases has been widely discussed in the literature, only a few works are specifically focused on strategies for data warehouse integration and federation. Indeed, in this context, problems related to data heterogeneity are usually solved by ETL (Extraction, Transformation, and Loading) processes that read data from several data sources and load them in a single multidimensional repository to be accessed by users. While this centralized architecture may fit the needs of old-style, stand-alone companies, it is hardly feasible in the context of a BIN, where the dynamic nature of the business network, together with the independence and autonomy of peers, call for more sophisticated solutions.

In the context of a federated data warehouse architecture, Torlone (2008) describes two methods for integrating dimensions belonging to different data marts and provides a set of rules to check for their compatibility. The problem of how to define mappings between concepts and how to evaluate their quality with reference to user queries is not considered. In this direction, the work proposed by Banek et al. (2008) presents a complete algorithm for matching multidimensional structures, with a strong emphasis on the process of calculating similarity between complex concepts. However, the data-related aspects—that could enrich the matching definitions—are not considered, and the issues related to the reconciliation of query results are not faced; besides, no model is provided to formalize mapping predicates and relate them with multidimensional data. Another work centered on interoperability issues among heterogeneous data warehouses is the one by Kehlenbeck & Breitner (2009), that emphasizes the importance of a semantic layer to enable communication among different entities. This approach supports the exchange of business calculation definitions and enables their automatic linking to specific data warehouses through semantic reasoning. Three models are suggested: a business ontology, a data warehouse ontology, and a mapping ontology between them. The approach is flexible because it could be implemented by adopting different formalisms for each layer (e.g., the

Common Warehouse Metamodel [CWM] or the Unified Modeling Language [UML] for the data warehouse ontology). However, the work proposes specific techniques to deal with measures only, so it cannot be used to completely solve a typical aggregate query.

Mediation-Based Approaches

On the other hand, decentralized sharing of data among autonomous sources has been deeply studied in the context of OLTP databases as an evolution of mediator systems in the data integration field. In this context, *Peer Data Management Systems* (PDMSs) have been proposed as powerful decentralized and easily extensible architectures that blend database world semantic expressiveness and P2P network flexibility (Mandreoli et al., 2008). A PDMS consists of a set of peers, where each peer has an associated schema representing its domain of interest; peer mediation is implemented by means of semantic mappings between portions of schemata that are local to a pair or a small set of peers (Halevy et al., 2004). Anytime, every peer can act freely on its data, and in the meantime access data stored by other participants. The main advantages of PDMSs are: (1) peers can share data in diverse and overlapping domains without a mediated schema; (2) joining a PDMS can be done opportunistically (i.e., a peer can provide a mapping to the most convenient [e.g., similar] peer[s] already in the PDMS); and (3) a peer can pose a query using its *own* schema without having to learn a different one (Tatarinov & Halevy, 2004). Although PDMSs well meet the characteristics of a BIN, specific extensions are needed to support BI aspects.

As to the languages for knowledge representation, in the BI context the OMG (Object Management Group) proposed the Common Warehouse Metamodel (CWM) (OMG, 2003) in order to support the interoperability among BI platforms. However, there is no mechanism that can capture the complex semantic relations on which applica-

tions of a BIN are based. OWL (OWL, 2004) is a W3C standard designed for applications that need to process the content of information by themselves, instead of just presenting information. Thus, OWL proves to be suitable for knowledge representation and for the context of heterogeneous networks for data-sharing. Moreover, in PDMS networks, the need for inter-peer sharing of data modeled on heterogeneous schemata lead to the development of languages that can also represent semantic mappings, for instance using XQuery queries (Halevy et al., 2004). As to query languages, SPARQL is the W3C standard proposed in order to query data modeled on graph schemata (SPARQL, 2008). All these languages, even if general and flexible, need extensions to express BI specifications and to define privacy and trust requirements.

As to the semantic mediation between peers schemata, a wide range of tools for generating schema mapping have been proposed in the literature (Fagin et al., 2005; Fuxman et al., 2006; Mecca et al., 2009). In distributed environments, the schema mapping generation phase and the preceding schema matching phase pose new issues with reference to simpler centralized contexts: consistency problems are studied by Cudré-Mauroux et al. (2006) and innovative learning techniques are presented by Madhavan et al. (2005). Nevertheless, no proposals exist on how the overall process could be influenced by the collaborative aspects characterizing a BIN.

As to query answering in a PDMS, a query is formulated on a peer local schema and, in order to be answered by other peers in the network, it needs to be reformulated over their schemata, according to the established semantic mappings. Reformulation algorithms have been proposed for the PDMS scenario (Halevy et al., 2004; Tatarinov & Halevy, 2004); however, these proposals do not deal with the reformulation of aggregate queries, that are typical of the BI context. The problem of rewriting aggregate queries with arbitrary aggregation functions has been investigated by Cohen et al. (2006) with the purpose of query optimization in OLTP databases.

A further issue of uppermost importance regarding query reformulation in heterogeneous and distributed scenarios is how to effectively and efficiently translate queries by taking into account differences in operators and data formats (Chang & Garcia-Molina, 1999). This is even more evident for the reformulation of OLAP queries in a BIN, where potentially different understandings of information, due to the possibility of having data represented at different granularities and under different perspectives, necessarily have to be considered.

Efficiency

The work by Tatarinov & Halevy (2004) focuses on techniques for optimizing the reformulation process in a PDMS. As we already mentioned, whenever the reformulation reaches a peer that stores data, the appropriate query is posed on that peer and additional answers may be found. Since peers typically do not contain complete information about a domain, any relevant peer may add new answers. Furthermore, different semantic paths to the *same* peer may yield different answers. Following all such paths in a naïve way leads to several inefficiencies. Many paths can be pruned early on because they result in redundant reformulations that significantly degrade performance. Besides, in many cases reformulations may be inefficient, in that queries must be heavily optimized before they can be efficiently executed on peers. Thus, pruning and minimizing reformulations are crucial issues to be investigated. An additional efficiency benefit for query reformulation would be obtained by pre-computing some semantic paths in the network. This leads to the problem of composing inter-peer mappings in a PDMS. This issue has been considered in the works by Bernstein et al. (2008), Fagin et al. (2005)a, Madhavan & Halevy (2003), where a semantics for the composition operator has been proposed. Also in this direc-

tion, challenges arise when dealing with BI data management.

Efficiency issues in the distributed data warehouse context have been examined by Kalnis et al. (2002), who propose a peer-to-peer architecture for supporting OLAP queries focusing on the definition of a caching model to speed up query rewriting. They also define adaptive techniques that dynamically reconfigure the network structure in order to minimize the query cost. This solution, however, presents a structured-P2P-network-based approach, which is inherently inadequate for the BIN scenario since it does not support peer's autonomy as to both data representation and neighbor selection. Similar architectural limits apply to the works by Wu et al. (2009) and Jiang et al. (2007). The former aims at efficiently supporting the evaluation of computationally expensive aggregate queries in a distributed context by extending the online aggregation technique to a scenario where sources are maintained in Distributed Hash Table (DHT) network (i.e., a typical structured P2P network). The latter describes a hybrid approach between the centralized and the full-federation configuration, suggesting the use of a federation server to store aggregated data from different remote sources. The goal is to improve the performance of complex OLAP queries exploiting the correlation among different queries. In both approaches data heterogeneity is not supported.

Quality

Since peers' autonomy in local data representation may induce *information loss* in the instance transformation process specified in the mappings, repeated reformulations inevitably have an impact on the quality of results due to repeated approximations. Preliminary studies on the concept of information loss and its estimation in distributed contexts are presented by Mena et al. (2000) who, however, assume that sources share a common vocabulary.

How to quantify information loss in a BIN is a challenging task because of both the heterogeneity of the data sources and of the possible security policies which affect the availability of information. In the literature, it is known that information loss in a PDMS is also deeply influenced by the adopted network organization (Halevy et al., 2004). This is because most P2P systems create a random overlay network and queries are blindly forwarded from node to node (Crespo & Garcia-Molina, 2004). To this end, particularly useful are the Semantic Overlay Networks - SONs (Lodi et al., 2008), where semantically similar nodes are logically placed close (i.e., they are clustered together). An optimal SON organization able to minimize the information loss in a BIN is indeed essential.

In this context, it is also of the utmost importance to adopt query routing techniques to identify the paths which minimize information loss in the reformulation processes. Particularly relevant to a BIN are the proposals which exploit semantic information, such as those by Mandreoli et al. (2006, 2009); nevertheless, in a BIN context, the aspects related to the specificity of the adopted BI model must also be considered.

The quality problem is strictly connected to the application of data lineage techniques. The data lineage problem arises in many contexts of computer science and it can be generally described as a set of techniques and algorithms to provide rich and descriptive information about data in order to make sense of it and reuse it (Simmhan et al., 2005). The presence of auxiliary metadata for deriving data provenance becomes particularly strategic in the context of a BIN. As a matter of fact, because of data heterogeneity as well as due to security restrictions imposed by the sensitive nature of business information, query results are possibly approximate and/or incomplete. Additional information about their provenance would remarkably improve their interpretation by the user as well as their reconciliation, which is a critical step because of possible duplicate and conflicting results. In the literature, Cui &

Widom (2003) formally define how to trace warehouse data back to the original source items from which they were derived, and they also present algorithms for lineage tracing. However, their work is mainly aimed at supporting the ETL process. Finally, data lineage can be also exploited to improve data quality, with strong attention to trustworthiness, accuracy and consistency of data (Simmhan et al., 2005). In particular, lineage can be used to estimate data reliability based on the source data and transformations, and can also provide proof statements on data derivation (da Silva et al., 2003).

Reconciliation

In the context of mediator systems this issue is referred to as *object fusion* (Papakonstantinou et al., 1996). This involves grouping together information (from the same or different sources) about the same real-world entity. In doing this fusion, the mediator may also "refine" the information by removing redundancies, resolving inconsistencies between sources in favor of the most reliable source, and so on. As to this issue, in the data warehousing context, Miller et al. (1998) present an object-oriented approach to design, implement and populate a data warehouse from distributed data sources. However, also in this work, the approach is oriented to ETL processes.

A typical requirement in the BIN context is the merging of results at different levels of aggregation. In this direction, the work proposed by Dubois & Prade (2004) discusses a general approach on the use of aggregation operations in information fusion processes and suggests practical rules to be applied in common scenarios. However, these aspects need to be specifically addressed according to the peculiarities of the BIN mapping language.

Security

In OLAP systems, the lack of sufficient countermeasures against security attacks may lead to disclose sensible information and privacy breaches. The Access Control (AC) techniques proposed for relational databases can be only partially applied in the multidimensional context and many aspects must be revisited. Pernul & Priebe (2000) define the requirements for an AC model and stress the need for specific solutions to the security policy definition and the inference control. The first issue concerns the definition of policies capable of handling the access to specific portion of a cube; such portion should be specified according to the involved dimensions and measures, instances, and users (Wang et al., 2004). The second issue concerns the definition of techniques specifically devised to avoid the inference of detailed (i.e., disaggregated) values of data through the access to summary (i.e., aggregated) ones. Specific techniques for single OLAP applications have been developed for inference control through data perturbation and restrictions by Sung et al. (2006) and by Cuzzocrea et al. (2008).

These issues become even more relevant within a P2P architecture, where inter-company collaboration raises further problems related to accessing remote peers for which no AC rules have been directly defined. This gives a primary role the *trust* among participants. The trust management problem is considered a distinct and important component of security in network services (Blaze et al., 1996); it includes formulating security policies and security credentials, determining whether particular sets of credentials satisfy the relevant policies, and deferring trust to third parties. In general, trust is a subjective notion and depends on specific situations (Marsh, 1994). Trust may vary according to the risk degree and the sensitivity of exchanged data; it is not necessarily transitive or monotone; it is context-dependent. The essence of trust handling is not trust itself, but the ability to decide to what extent we are willing to trust and how to establish and develop relationships based on trust (Josang et al., 2007).

AN ARCHITECTURE FOR A BIN

The architectural solution we propose for a BIN is that of a PDMS (Halevy et al., 2004), that ensures large-scale data sharing while preserving full peer autonomy, network scalability and dynamism. The companies involved in a BIN are enabled to expose selected business information and use the information made available over the network through cooperation techniques aimed at achieving their own business goals while ensuring full autonomy in managing local BI systems. Each company participates in the BIN through a peer that relies on a local multidimensional schema to represent the business information to be shared. Peers are organized into a PDMS as sketched in Figure 1, and semantic mappings between pairs of network nodes relate different local representations of information (Kehlenbeck & Breitner, 2009).

In this architecture, a user formulates OLAP queries by accessing the local multidimensional schema of his peer (Figure 1, peer *i*, flow #1); answers can come from any peer that is connected to the peer *i* through a chain of semantic mappings. Peers interact with each other through a message-passing protocol. Each query is first processed locally by accessing the peer BI platform (flows #2, 3, and 4) and it is then forwarded to the network (flows #5 and 7). The query is sent to the immediate neighbors of the querying peer (flows #7 and 8), then to their immediate neighbors (flow #13), and so on. In order to be answered, the query has to be first reformulated according to the vocabularies of the peers it is forwarded to (flows #6 and #12). Query reformulation uses the semantic mappings established between the peers; hence, a query undergoes a chain of reformulations along the semantic paths it passes through. Each involved peer (e.g., peer *j*) locally processes the query (flow #9) and returns its results to the querying peer (flows #10 and 14). The results, even if partial or approximate, are integrated (flow #15) and returned to the user based

Figure 1. General architecture of a BIN

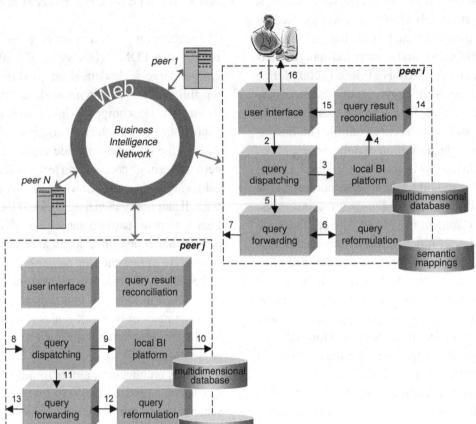

on the vocabulary used to formulate the initial query (flow #16).

The architecture of each peer is shown in more detail in the dashed box of Figure 1. As commonly happens with BI platforms, the *user interface* is web-based, which leads to a number of advantages in terms of ubiquity, customizability, installation and upgrade simplicity, and familiarity. The *query dispatching module* receives queries coming either from local users or from other peers and transmits them to both the local BI platform and the query forwarding module. The *query forwarding module* delivers queries to the network; to perform this task, it implements smart routing policies to

select the most relevant peers to forward a query to, thus impacting on both the effectiveness and the efficiency of query answering. The *query reformulation module* takes advantage of the semantic mappings established towards the peer neighbors to reformulate queries accordingly. Finally, the *query result reconciliation module* collects and integrates the results coming from the local database and from the peers in the BIN, and provides the user with sophisticated tools to cope with different granularities of results that could not be automatically reconciled (e.g., results having a higher level of aggregation than the requested one).

Figure 2. Multidimensional schemata of related facts at two peers

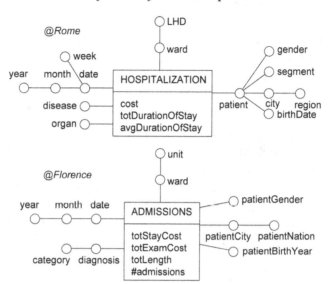

QUERY REFORMULATION FOR A BIN

In this section, after discussing the requirements for a language to establish inter-peer semantic mappings in a BIN, we propose a mapping language specifically devised to cope with a basic multidimensional model, and we informally show how it can be used to enable the query reformulation process.

Mapping Language

Devising a language for declaring inter-peer semantic mappings in a BIN requires, first of all, to decide on a reference model for representing the information to be mapped. Though different BI platforms adopt slightly different models for information representation with different expressiveness, they all share a common denominator: the core multidimensional model. In this model, a *fact* (e.g., patient admissions) is associated to a set of alphanumerical coordinates called *dimensions* (e.g., ward and admission date) and is quantified by a set of numerical *measures* (e.g., the admission cost). Noticeably, we assume that each

measure is associated with a specific distributive operator that must be used to aggregate it (e.g., the totDurationOfStay measure is aggregated by summing up values, whereas the avgDurationOfStay measure is aggregated by averaging values). A dimension can be further described by a set of hierarchically-structured *attributes* connected by many-to-one associations (e.g., a ward belongs to one area, that in turn is part of one Local Health-Care Department (LHD)). With reference to our health-care example, Figure 2 shows the multidimensional schemata of related facts at the peers in Rome and Florence, using the Dimensional Fact Model notation (Golfarelli & Rizzi, 2009); small circles represent attributes, while measures are listed inside the fact boxes. Note that, while an event in the Rome schema corresponds to a single hospitalization, in the Florence schema an event may aggregate several admissions (because there is no patient dimension).

Even in this basic form, the multidimensional model suggests some requirements for the mapping language:

1. One of the basic features of the multidimensional model is the asymmetry between

dimensions and measures: dimensions are used as a key to selection and aggregation, measures are used for computing. This asymmetry should be reflected in the mapping language by providing different predicates for mapping dimensions/attributes and measures.

2. Aggregation at different granularities is inherently part of the multidimensional model, and is supported by hierarchies. To accommodate this key feature, the mapping language should be capable of specifying the relationship between two attributes of different multidimensional schemata in terms of their granularity.

3. A measure is inherently associated with an aggregation operator. Then, when mapping a measure onto another, their aggregation operators must be taken into account to avoid the risk of inconsistent query reformulations.

4. While in the literature on PDMSs the problems of data formats and differences in operators have been only marginally considered, declaring useful mappings in the BI context necessarily requires also the instance level to be taken into account. This can be done if there is a known way to transcode values of an attribute/measure belonging to a multidimensional schema into values of an attribute/measure belonging to another multidimensional schema and the related aggregation operations.

Clearly, the mapping language is also related to the expressiveness of the query language. In this work, we consider OLAP queries that can be expressed in GPSJ (Generalized Projection - Selection - Join) form (Gupta et al., 1995): $\pi_{G,AGG(m)}$ σ_P χ, where π denotes a generalized projection (i.e., an aggregation of measure m using aggregate function AGG over the attributes in G); σ_P is a selection based on Boolean predicate P; and χ denotes the star join between the fact table and the dimension tables. For instance, the following

query expressed at the Rome peer computes the total hospitalization cost of female patients for each region and year:

$$\pi_{region,year,SUM(cost)} \, \sigma_{gender='F'} \, \chi_{Rome}$$

Now, let p and q be two peers in a BIN. The language we propose to express how the local multidimensional schemata of p maps onto the one of q includes five mapping predicates, namely same, equi-level, roll-up, drill-down, and related. Each mapping establishes a semantic relationship from an ordered list c of concepts (either measures or attributes) of p ($p.c=<p.a_1, ..., p.a_n>$, on the left side of the mapping predicate) to an ordered list d of concepts of q ($q.d=<q.b_1, ..., q.b_k>$, on the right side of the mapping predicate), and enables a query formulated on p to be (exactly or approximately) reformulated on q. Optionally, a mapping can be associated with an encoding predicate, which relates c and d by means of a *data conversion function* that specifies how values of c can be obtained from values of d (or vice versa). If this predicate is available, it is used during query reformulation and data integration to return more query-compliant results to users. Note that mappings on measures (same predicate) take a simpler form (exactly one measure on the left side) to avoid incorrect reformulations due to a wrong use of aggregation operators.

In the following we provide a detailed description of the five mapping predicates, leaning on some examples summarized in Figure 3. We remark that the choice of these very predicates strictly depends on both the reference multidimensional model adopted and the class of OLAP queries selected. Adopting an extended multidimensional model (e.g., one where dimensions and measures have interchangeable roles) and/or referring to a broader class of queries (e.g., one where a given measure can be aggregated using different operators) would obviously lead to determining a larger set of predicates.

Figure 3. Examples of inter-schema mappings

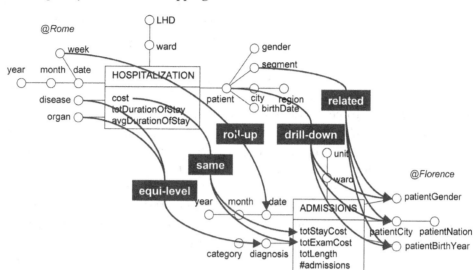

Same Predicate

$p.m$ same$_f$ $q.d$

where m is a measure and d only includes measures. This mapping predicate is used to state that measure m in measures in p has the same semantics than a set of measures in q. If knowledge is available about how values of m can be derived from values of d, it can be expressed by a data conversion function f: dom(d)→dom(m) (where dom(d)=dom(b$_1$)×…×dom(b$_k$)). The semantics of this function is that, whenever m is asked in a query on p, it can safely be rewritten as $f(d)$ on q. For instance,

```
<Rome.cost> same_f
<Florence.totStayCost,
Florence.totExamCost>
```

with

```
f(<totStayCost,totExamCost>) =
totStayCost+totExamCost
```

states that measure cost at the Rome peer can be derived by summing totStayCost and totExamCost at the Florence peer.

Equi-Level Predicate

$p.c$ equi-level$_f$ $q.d$

where c and d only include attributes. This predicate is used to state that a set of attributes in p has the same semantics and granularity than a set of attributes in q. If knowledge is available about a transcoding between c and d, it can be expressed by an injective data conversion function f: dom(d)→dom(c) that establishes a one-to-one total relation between values of c and values of d, and is used in the query result integration phase to integrate data returned by p and q. For instance,

```
<Rome.disease, Rome.organ>
equi-level_f <Florence.diagnosis>
```

with

```
f(<diagnosis>) =
<substring(diagnosis, 1, 20),
substring(diagnosis, 21, 40)>
```

states that the diagnosis codes used in Florence are obtained by concatenating the fixed-length disease and organ codes used in Rome.

Roll-Up Predicate

$p.c$ roll-up$_f$ $q.d$

where c and d only include attributes. This predicate is used to state that c in p is a roll-up of (i.e., it aggregates) d in q. If knowledge is available about how to roll-up values of d to values of c, it can be expressed by the data conversion function f: $dom(d) \rightarrow dom(c)$ that establishes a one-to-many relation between values of c and values of d, and is used to aggregate data returned by q and integrate them with data returned by p. For instance,

```
<Rome.week> roll-up_f <Florence.date>
```

with

```
f(<date>) = <weekOf(date)>
```

states that weeks are an aggregation of dates.

Drill-Down Predicate

$p.c$ drill-down$_f$ $q.d$

where c and d only include attributes. This predicate is used to state that c in p is a drill-down of (i.e., it disaggregates) d in q. If knowledge is available about how to drill-down values of d to values of c, it can be expressed by the data conversion function f: $dom(c) \rightarrow dom(d)$, which establishes a many-to-one relation between values of c and values of d. Function f cannot be used to integrate data returned by p and q because this would require disaggregating data returned by q, which obviously cannot be done univocally; however, it can be used to empower the presentation of results given to users. For instance,

```
<Rome.patient> drill-down
    <Florence.patientGender, Florence.
    patientCity,
    Florence.patientBirthYear>
```

with no data conversion function, states that several patients can have the same gender, city, and birth year.

Related Predicate

$p.c$ related$_F$ $q.d$

where c and d only include attributes. This predicate is used to state that c in p has a many-to-many relationship with d in q. Function F: $dom(c) \rightarrow 2^{dom(d)}$ establishes a many-to-many relation between values of c and values of d. Like in the previous case, though F cannot be used neither for query rewriting nor for result integration, it could be used to improve result presentation. For instance,

```
<Rome.segment> related
    <Florence.patientGender,
    Florence.patientCity,
    Florence.patientBirthYear>
```

states that several combinations of gender, city, and birth year can correspond to a single patient segment, and vice versa.

With reference to our health-care example in Figure 2, Function 1 shows all the mappings from the Rome peer to the Florence peer. Function 2 shows the related encoding predicates. Assuming that all the units at the Florence peer belong to the same Local Health-Care Department identified at Rome with code 'LHD39 - Florence', the #4 encoding predicate uses a constant function. weekOf(), yearOf(), and substring() are common SQL functions and completeGender() transcodes values 'M' and 'F' (Florence vocabulary) into 'Male' and 'Female' (Rome vocabulary). regionOf() can be implemented as a user-defined function that returns the region a city belongs to by accessing a CITIES relational table stored at the Florence peer. When a data conversion function is not explicitly specified, we assume the use of the identity function.

Function 1. Complete mapping from Rome to Florence

```
#1   <Rome.cost> same <Florence.totalStayCost, Florence.totExamCost>
#2   <Rome.totDurationOfStay> same <Florence.totLength>
#3   <Rome.avgDurationOfStay> same <Florence.totLength, Florence.#admissions>
#4   <Rome.LHD> roll-up <Florence.unit>
#5   <Rome.ward> equi-level <Florence.ward>
#6   <Rome.year> equi-level <Florence.year>
#7   <Rome.month> equi-level <Florence.month>
#8   <Rome.date> equi-level <Florence.date>
#9   <Rome.week> roll-up <Florence.date>
#10  <Rome.disease, Rome.organ> equi-level <Florence.diagnosis>
#11  <Rome.patient> drill-down <Florence.patientGender, Florence.patientCity,
     Florence.patientBirthYear>
#12  <Rome.gender> equi-level <Florence.patientGender>
#13  <Rome.segment> related <Florence.patientGender, Florence.patientCity,
     Florence.patientBirthYear>
#14  <Rome.birthDate> drill-down <Florence.patientBirthYear>
#15  <Rome.city> equi-level <Florence.patientCity>
#16  <Rome.region> roll-up <Florence.patientCity>
```

Function 2. Encoding predicates for the mapping in Function 1

```
#1   Rome.cost = Florence.totStayCost+Florence.totExamCost
#2   Rome.totDurationOfStay = Florence.totLength
#3   Rome.avgDurationOfStay = Florence.totLength / Florence.#admissions
#4   Rome.LHD = 'LHD39 - Florence'
#5   Rome.ward = Florence.ward
#6   Rome.year = Florence.year
#7   Rome.month = Florence.month
#8   Rome.date = Florence.date
#9   Rome.week = weekOf(Florence.date)
#10  Rome.disease = substring(Florence.diagnosis, 1, 20), Rome.organ =
     substring(Florence.diagnosis, 21, 40)
#11  —
#12  Rome.gender = completeGender(Florence.patientGender)
#13
#14  yearOf(Rome.birthDate) = Florence.patientBirthYear
#15  Rome.city = Florence.patientCity
#16  Rome.region = regionOf(Florence.patientCity)
```

Query Reformulation by Examples

As already mentioned, the mappings specified by means of the mapping language allow each OLAP query formulated on the multidimensional schema of peer p to be reformulated on the multidimensional schema of peer q. For space reasons we do not report here the complete set of reformulation rules we adopt; however, we illustrate the underlying principles with a few examples.

To start simple, consider the OLAP query (formulated at Rome) asking for the monthly average duration of staying for each patient gender during the last year:

$$\pi_{\text{month,gender,AVG(avgDurationOfStay)}} \; \sigma_{\text{year='2009'}} \; \chi_{\text{Rome}}$$

This query group-by and selection clauses are easily reformulated on the Florence peer by using three equi-level mappings (see Function 1), while measure avgDurationOfStay is derived using the same mapping #3, where $f(<\text{totLength,\#admissions}>) = \text{totLength/\#admissions}$:

$$\pi_{\text{month,completeGender(patientGender),SUM(totLength)/SUM(\#admissions)}} \; \sigma_{\text{year='2009'}} \; \chi_{\text{Florence}}$$

where SUM is the aggregation operator for both totLength and #admissions. The resulting tuples from the Florence peer are transcoded using completeGender() and then returned to the Rome peer to be properly integrated with the tuples retrieved locally at Rome.

As a second, more complex example, consider the query asking in Rome for the total hospitalization cost by LHD and disease for male patients only:

$$\pi_{\text{LHD,disease,SUM(cost)}} \; \sigma_{\text{gender='Male'}} \; \chi_{\text{Rome}}$$

The LHD granularity is not available at the Florence peer, so grouping is done by unit instead, as suggested by the #4 roll-up mapping, that employs the corresponding encoding predicate based on a constant data conversion function. Unfortunately, no mapping exists for the single disease concept towards the Florence peer; however, mapping #10 states that the disease-organ combination in Rome has the same granularity than diagnosis in Florence, which implies that disease is a roll-up of diagnosis. This means that the total hospitalization costs at the Florence peer can be aggregated by unit and disease; disease values are computed from diagnosis using the first component of the data conversion function f (i.e., disease = substring(diagnosis, 1, 20)). The query is then reformulated as:

$$\pi_{\text{'LHD39 − Florence',substring(Florence.diagnosis,1,20),SUM(totStayCost)+SUM(totExamCost)}} \; \sigma_{\text{completeGender(patientGender)='Male'}} \; \chi_{\text{Florence}}$$

In absence of a data conversion function available for units, the results returned by the Florence peer could not be directly integrated with those from the Rome peer, thus they would be shown to the user together with the local ones, but in a separate report, since they represent data at a different granularity level.

Finally, the following query

$$\pi_{\text{week,birthDate,SUM(totDurationOfStay)}} \; \sigma_{\text{ward='Cardiology'}} \; \chi_{\text{Rome}}$$

can be reformulated as

$$\pi_{\text{weekOf(date),patientBirthYear,SUM(totLength)}} \; \sigma_{\text{ward='Cardiology'}} \; \chi_{\text{Florence}}$$

considering that week rolls-up date and birthDate drills-down patientBirthYear. The resulting tuples are transcoded through the encoding function weekOf(date); however, the granularity obtained is

Figure 4. Results with different granularities from different peers

@Rome

	totDurationOfStay	week			
birthYear	birthDate	1st week 2010	2nd week 2010	3rd week 2010	....
1945	13/01/1945	4			....
	24/07/1945	2		3	....
1957	14/03/1957	1			....
1960	24/07/1960	3		8	....
1964	12/09/1964		5		....
....	....	....	....	....	....

@Florence

	totLength	week		
patientBirthYear	1st week 2010	2nd week 2010	3rd week 2010	....
1933	22	12	7	....
1936	19		33	....
1955	22	11		....
1964	36			....
1969		14	14	....
....	....	....	....	....

not the same asked by the original query, because there is no way to disaggregate values of totLength according to patient birth dates. Figure 4 shows possible results obtained from the two peers. The birthYear column in Rome has been added since it can be easily obtained from birthDate via the yearOf() function. The results coming from Rome are sparser than those from Florence, since data have finer granularity.

FUTURE RESEARCH DIRECTIONS

Several interesting research directions can be explored to enrich and improve the BIN approach. Most of them are inspired by research issues already tackled for OLTP data in P2P systems. Indeed, a lot of work has been done as to both effectiveness and efficiency of transactional data management in distributed environments. However, as already mentioned, the works presented in those contexts do not adequately apply to the specific scenario of a BIN, in that they do not effectively deal with the peculiarities of BI data and OLAP query processing.

In this section we specifically focus on how our mapping language could be effectively coupled with a language for expressing user preferences, aimed at better tailoring the reformulation process to the user's wishes. As a first step in this direction, the specification of mappings can be enriched with a *similarity score* to express the semantic correlation of the source and target sets of concepts. Similarity may depend on the differences

in the peers' vocabularies as well as on different perspectives of data representation (e.g., different granularities), and should clearly be influenced by the absence or presence of encoding functions that make source and target values compatible. Such a score, representative of the semantic strength of a mapping, can be profitably employed in query reformulation where, in presence of alternative mappings for a given set of concepts onto a remote peer, it can be used to identify the mapping that best approximates this set of concepts, so as to translate the query as accurately as possible.

Then, the similarity scores of the mappings involved in the reformulation process can be combined to determine how compliant the results obtained from a remote peer are, overall, with respect to the original query (Banek et al., 2008). This *compliance score* can be profitably used by users to rank (and, possibly, filter) the results obtained from different remote peers. Finally, the scoring of mappings is also a fundamental means for improving the organization of the network. In fact, it is well-known from the literature (Crespo & Garcia-Molina, 2004; Halevy et al., 2004) that heterogeneous P2P systems benefit from the organization of peers in Semantic Overlay Networks, where peers with similar contents are close to each other. Mapping scores could guide the optimal placement of a node in the BIN, as done for instance by Lodi et al. (2008), where the best neighbors are selected according to their similarity to the new peer entering the network.

The scores described above can be seen as a way to express *quantitative preferences* on mappings and data. A further issue to be explored is the alternative use of *qualitative preferences*. Under this perspective, the nature of the mapping predicates as well as the user's preferences on the mappings, which could be either expressed independently for each query or collected into a user profile, would be taken into account for query reformulation. For instance, the user may prefer using a roll-up mapping associated with an encoding function than an equi-level mapping for which no encoding function is available. Indeed, the former enables the remote results to be integrated with local data after aggregation, whereas the latter, while returning data at the required aggregation, prevents the integration of results because of different encodings adopted by the local and the remote peers.

Golfarelli et al. (2010) proposed the MYOLAP algebra for expressing qualitative preferences to annotate OLAP queries. In MYOLAP, the user can express preferences not only on values of attributes and measures, but also on the aggregation level of results. In the context of a BIN, a user could annotate an OLAP query with a preference stating for instance that data grouped by month and patient region are preferred to the others, that are ranked according to the distance of their aggregation level from the preferred one. In this case, if the month-region granularity is not available at a remote peer, data grouped at a "near" level—such as quarter and nation—can be returned instead.

Overall, thanks to the specification of preferences, the quality and reliability of query reformulation can be substantially improved, by making it most likely up to the users' expectations. But preferences also affect the efficiency of query execution since they enable the selection of the most promising directions to forward a query to, thus supporting smart query routing (Crespo & Garcia-Molina, 2002; Mandreoli et al., 2006). Indeed, techniques such as those introduced by Mandreoli et al. (2009) for data-sharing P2P networks leverage on the presence of semantic approximations for query routing purposes and use mapping scores to inform users of the returned answers through a ranking mechanism that promotes the most semantically-related results. Most of these techniques could be adapted/extended to deal with aggregate queries as needed in a BIN context.

CONCLUSION

BI transformed the role of computer science in companies from a technology for passively storing data into a discipline for timely detecting key business factors and effectively solving strategic decisional problems. However, to meet the new user needs in the current changeable and unpredictable market scenarios, a new generation of BI systems—the so-called BI 2.0—has been emerging during the last few years. One of the key features of BI 2.0 is the ability to become pervasive and extend the decision-making process beyond the boundaries of a single company. In this direction, we presented the BIN framework for sharing querying functionalities between collaborating and autonomous BI peers. We outlined the main research challenges related to this framework, and we proposed a language for establishing a mapping between the multidimensional schemata exposed by two peers, showing how it enables a query formulated on one peer to be reformulated on the other.

Although many problems must be solved to allow BIN to become fully operative, we believe that this chapter takes an important step forward in this direction since the query reformulation module is at the core of the proposed architecture.

REFERENCES

Abiteboul, S. (2003). Managing an XML warehouse in a P2P context. In *Proceedings of International Conference on Advanced Information Systems Engineering* (pp. 4-13). Klagenfurt, Austria.

Banek, M., Vrdoljak, V., Min Tjoa, A., & Skocir, Z. (2008). Automated integration of heterogeneous data warehouse schemata. *International Journal of Data Warehousing and Mining, 4*(4), 1–21.

Bernstein, P. A., Green, T. J., Melnik, S., & Nash, A. (2008). Implementing mapping composition. *The VLDB Journal, 17*(2), 333–353.

Blaze, M., Feigenbaum, J., & Lacy, J. (1996). Decentralized trust management. In *Proceedings of IEEE Symposium on Security and Privacy* (pp. 164-173). Oakland, CA, USA.

Chang, C. C. K., & Garcia-Molina, H. (1999). Mind your vocabulary: Query mapping across heterogeneous information sources. In *Proceedings of ACM SIGMOD International Conference on Management of Data* (pp. 335-346). Philadelphia, USA.

Cohen, S., Nutt, W., & Sagiv, Y. (2006). Rewriting queries with arbitrary aggregation functions using views. *ACM Transactions on Database Systems, 31*(2), 672–715.

Crespo, A., & Garcia-Molina, H. (2002). Routing indices for peer-to-peer systems. In *Proceedings of International Conference on Distributed Computing Systems* (pp. 23-30). Vienna, Austria.

Crespo, A., & Garcia-Molina, H. (2004). Semantic overlay networks for P2P systems. In *Proceedings of International Workshop on Agents and Peer-to-Peer Computing* (pp. 1-13). New York, USA.

Cudré-Mauroux, P., Aberer, K., & Feher, A. (2006). Probabilistic message passing in peer data management systems. In *Proceedings of International Conference on Data Engineering* (pp. 41-53). Atlanta, USA.

Cui, Y., & Widom, J. (2003). Lineage tracing for general data warehouse transformations. *International Journal on Very Large Data Bases, 12*(1), 41–58.

Cuzzocrea, A., Russo, V., & Saccà, D. (2008). A robust sampling-based framework for privacy preserving OLAP. In *Proceedings of International Conference on Data Warehousing and Knowledge Discovery* (pp. 97-114).

da Silva, P. P., McGuinness, D. L., & McCool, R. (2003). Knowledge provenance infrastructure. *A Quarterly Bulletin of the Computer Society of the IEEE Technical Committee on Data Engineering, 26*(4), 26–32.

Dubois, D., & Prade, H. (2004). On the use of aggregation operations in information fusion processes. *International Journal on Fuzzy Sets and Systems, 142*(1), 143–161.

Fagin, R., Kolaitis, P. G., & Popa, L. (2005). Data exchange: Getting to the core. *ACM Transactions on Database Systems, 30*(1), 174–210.

Fagin, R., Kolaitis, P. G., Popa, L., & Tan, W. C. (2005). a. Composing schema mappings: Second-order dependencies to the rescue. *ACM Transactions on Database Systems, 30*(4), 994–1055.

Fuxman, A., Hernández, M. A., Howard Ho, C. T., Miller, R. J., Papotti, P., & Popa, L. (2006). Nested mappings: Schema mapping reloaded. In *Proceedings of International Conference on Very Large Data Bases* (pp. 67-78). Seoul, Korea.

Golfarelli, M., & Rizzi, S. (2009). *Data warehouse design: Modern principles and methodologies.* New York, NY: McGraw-Hill.

Golfarelli, M., Rizzi, S., & Biondi, P. (2010). MYOLAP: An approach to express and evaluate OLAP preferences. To appear on *IEEE Transactions on Knowledge and Data Engineering*.

Gupta, A., Harinarayan, V., & Quass, D. (1995). Aggregate-query processing in data warehousing environments. In *Proceedings of International Conference on Very Large Data Bases* (pp. 358-369). Zurich, Switzerland.

Halevy, A. Y., Ives, Z. G., Madhavan, J., Mork, P., Suciu, D., & Tatarinov, I. (2004). The Piazza peer data management system. *IEEE Transactions on Knowledge and Data Engineering, 16*(7), 787–798.

Hoang, T. A. D., & Binh Nguyen, T. (2009). State of the art and emerging rule-driven perspectives towards service-based business process interoperability. In *Proceedings of International Conference on Computing and Communication Technologies* (pp. 1-4). Danang City, Vietnam.

Jiang, H., Gao, D., & Li, W. (2007). Exploiting correlation and parallelism of materialized-view recommendation for distributed data warehouses. In *Proceedings of International Conference on Data Engineering* (pp. 276-285). Istanbul, Turkey.

Josang, A., Ismail, R., & Boyd, C. (2007). A survey of trust and reputation systems for online service provision. *Decision Support Systems, 43*(2), 618–644.

Kalnis, P., Siong Ng, W., Chin Ooi, B., Papadias, D., & Tan, K. L. (2002). An adaptive peer-to-peer network for distributed caching of OLAP results. In *Proceedings of ACM SIGMOD International Conference on Management of Data* (pp. 25-36). Madison, Wisconsin.

Kehlenbeck, M., & Breitner, M. H. (2009). Ontology-based exchange and immediate application of business calculation definitions for online analytical processing. In *Proceedings of International Conference on Data Warehousing and Knowledge Discovery* (pp. 298-311). Linz, Austria.

Lodi, S., Mandreoli, F., Martoglia, R., Penzo, W., & Sassatelli, S. (2008). Semantic peer, here are the neighbors you want! In *Proceedings of International Conference on Extending Database Technology* (pp. 26-37). Nantes, France.

Madhavan, J., Bernstein, P. A., Doan, A., & Halevy, A. Y. (2005). Corpus-based schema matching. In *Proceedings of International Conference on Data Engineering* (pp. 57-68). Tokyo, Japan.

Madhavan, J., & Halevy, A. Y. (2003). Composing mappings among data sources. In *Proceedings of International Conference on Very Large Data Bases* (pp. 572-583). Berlin, Germany.

Mandreoli, F., Martoglia, R., Penzo, W., & Sassatelli, S. (2006). SRI: Exploiting semantic information for effective query routing in a PDMS. In *Proceedings of ACM International Workshop on Web Information and Data Management* (in conj. with CIKM) (pp. 19-26). Arlington, USA.

Mandreoli, F., Martoglia, R., Penzo, W., & Sassatelli, S. (2009). Data-sharing P2P networks with semantic approximation capabilities. *IEEE Internet Computing, 13*(5), 60–70.

Mandreoli, F., Martoglia, R., Penzo, W., Sassatelli, S., & Villani, G. (2008). Paving the way to an effective and efficient retrieval of data over semantic overlay networks. In Ma, Z., & Wang, H. (Eds.), *The Semantic Web for knowledge and data management: Technologies and practices* (pp. 151–175). Hershey, PA: Information Science Publishing.

Marsh, S. (1994). *Formalizing trust as a computational concept*. PhD thesis, University of Stirling, 1994.

Mecca, G., Papotti, P., & Raunich, S. (2009). Core schema mappings. In *Proceedings of ACM SIGMOD International Conference on Management of Data* (pp. 655-668). Providence, Rhode Island.

Mena, E., Kashyap, V., Illarramendi, A., & Sheth, A. P. (2000). Imprecise answers in distributed environments: Estimation of informationl for multi-ontology based query processing. *International Journal of Cooperative Information Systems*, 9(4), 403–425.

Miller, L. L., Honavar, V., Wong, J., & Nilakanta, S. (1998). Object-oriented data warehouses for information fusion from heterogeneous distributed data and knowledge sources. In *Proceedings of the IEEE Information Technology Conference* (pp. 27-30). Syracuse, New York.

OMG. (2003). Common warehouse metamodel specification. Retrieved from http://www.omg.org/ spec/CWM/1.1/

OWL. (2004). OWL Web ontology language overview. Retrieved from http://www.w3.org/ TR /owl-features/

Papakonstantinou, Y., Abiteboul, S., & Garcia-Molina, H. (1996). Object fusion in mediator systems. In *Proceedings of International Conference on Very Large Data Bases* (pp. 413-424). Bombay, India.

Pernul, G., & Priebe, T. (2000). Towards OLAP security design - Survey and research issues. In *Proceedings of 3rd ACM International Workshop on Data Warehousing and OLAP* (pp. 33-40). Washington, DC.

Simmhan, Y., Plale, B., & Gannon, D. (2005). A survey of data provenance in e-science. *SIGMOD Record*, 34(3), 1–14.

SPARQL. (2008). *SPARQL query language for RDF*. Retrieved from http://www.w3.org/TR / rdf-sparql-query/

Sung, S., Liu, Y., Xiong, H., & Ng, P. (2006). Privacy preservation for data cubes. *Knowledge and Information Systems*, 9(1), 38–61.

Tatarinov, I., & Halevy, A. Y. (2004). Efficient query reformulation in peer-data management systems. In *Proceedings of ACM SIGMOD International Conference on Management of Data* (pp. 539-550). Paris, France.

Torlone, R. (2008). Two approaches to the integration of heterogeneous data warehouses. *International Journal on Distributed and Parallel Databases*, 23(1), 69–97.

Wang, L., Jajodia, S., & Wijesekera, D. (2004). Securing OLAP data cubes against privacy breaches. In *Proceedings of IEEE Symposium on Security and Privacy* (pp. 1-15). Berkeley, California.

Wu, S., Jiang, S., Ooi, B. C., & Tan, K. (2009). Distributed online aggregation. In *Proceedings of International Conference on Very Large Data Bases* (pp. 443-454). Lyon, France.

ADDITIONAL READING

Agarwal, S., Agrawal, R., Deshpande, P., Gupta, A., Naughton, J. F., Ramakrishnan, R., & Sarawagi, S. (1996). On the computation of multidimensional aggregates. In *Proceedings of International Conference on Very Large Data Bases* (pp. 506-521). Mumbai (Bombay), India.

Akinde, M. O., Böhlen, M. H., Johnson, T., Lakshmanan, L. V. S., & Srivastava, D. (2003). Efficient OLAP query processing in distributed data warehouses. *International Journal of Information Systems*, 28(1-2), 111–135.

Androutsellis-Theotokis, S., & Spinellis, D. (2004). A survey of peer-to-peer content distribution technologies. *ACM Computing Surveys, 36*(4), 335–371.

Berger, S., & Schrefl, M. (2008). From federated databases to a federated data warehouse system. In *Proceedings of International Conference on Systems Sciences* (pp. 394). Waikoloa, Big Island, Hawaii.

Burdick, D., Deshpande, P. M., Jayram, T. S., Ramakrishnan, R., & Vaithyanathan, S. (2007). OLAP over uncertain and imprecise data. *International Journal on Very Large Data Bases, 16*(1), 123–144.

Calvanese, D., De Giacomo, G., Lenzerini, M., Nardi, D., & Rosati, R. (1999). A principled approach to data integration and reconciliation in data warehousing. In *Proceedings of International Workshop on Design and Management of Data Warehouses* (pp. 16). Heidelberg, Germany.

Cudré-Mauroux, P., Agarwal, S., & Aberer, K. (2007). GridVine: An Infrastructure for Peer Information Management. *IEEE Internet Computing, 11*(5), 36–44.

Cuzzocrea, A., Russo, V., Saccà, D., & Serafino, P. (2007). Advanced OLAP visualization of multidimensional data cubes: a semantics-driven compression approach. In *Proceedings of Italian Symposium on Advanced Database Systems* (pp. 365-372). Torre Canne, Italy.

Daniel, F., Casati, F., Palpanas, T., & Chayka, O. (2008). Managing Data Quality in Business Intelligence Applications. In *Proceedings of International Workshop on Quality in Databases and Mangement of Uncertain Data* (pp. 133-143). Auckland, New Zealand.

Daswani, N., Garcia-Molina, H., & Yang, B. (2003). Open Problems in Data-Sharing Peer-to-Peer Systems. In *Proceedings of International Conference on Database Theory* (pp. 1-15). Siena, Italy.

Fuxman, A., Kolaitis, P. G., Miller, R. J., & Tan, W. C. (2006). Peer data exchange. *ACM Transactions on Database Systems, 31*(4), 1454–1498.

Gribble, S. D., Halevy, A. Y., Ives, Z. G., Rodrig, M., & Suciu, D. (2001). What Can Database Do for Peer-to-Peer? In *Proceedings of International Workshop on the Web and Databases (in conj. with ACM PODS/SIGMOD)* (pp.31-36). Santa Barbara, USA.

Immon, W. H. (1996). *Building the data warehouse*. New York, NY: John Wiley & Sons.

Jarke, M., Lenzerini, M., Vassiliou, Y., & Vassiliadis, P. (2000). *Fundamentals of data warehouse*. Heidelberg, Germany: Springer.

Jarke, M., & Vassiliou, Y. (1997). Data warehouse quality: a review of the DWQ project. In *Proceedings of International Conference on Information Quality* (pp. 299-313). Cambridge, MA.

Kimball, R., Reeves, L., Ross, M., & Thornthwaite, W. (1998). *The data warehouse lifecycle toolkit expert methods for designing, developing & deploying data warehouse*. New York, NY: John Wiley & Sons.

Kossmann, D. (2000). The state of the art in distributed query processing. *ACM Computing Surveys, 32*(4), 422–469.

Melnik, S., Bernstein, P. A., Halevy, A. Y., & Rahm, E. (2005). Supporting Executable Mappings in Model Management. In *Proceedings of ACM SIGMOD International Conference on Management of Data* (pp. 167-178). Baltimore, USA.

Miller, R. J., Haas, L. M., & Hernández, M. A. (2000). Schema Mapping as Query Discovery. In *Proceedings of International Conference on Very Large Data Bases* (pp. 77-88). Cairo, Egypt.

Nejdl, W., Siberski, W., & Sintek, M. (2003). Design issues and challenges for RDF- and schema-based peer-to-peer systems. *SIGMOD Record, 32*(3), 41–46.

Rosenthal, A., & Sciore, E. (2000). View security as the basic for data warehouse security. In *Proceedings of International Workshop on Design and Management of Data Warehouses* (pp. 1-8). Stockholm, Sweden.

Rundensteiner, E. A., Koeller, A., & Zhang, X. (2000). Maintaining data warehouses over changing information sources. *Communications of the ACM, 43*(6), 57–62.

Skoutas, D., & Simitsis, A. (2006). Designing ETL processes using semantic web technologies. In *Proceedings of International Workshop on Data Warehousing and OLAP* (pp. 67-74). Arlington, USA.

Torra, V., & Narukawa, Y. (2007). *Modeling decisions. Information fusion and aggregation operators*. Berlin, Germany: Springer.

Triantafillou, P., Xiruhaki, C., Koubarakis, M., & Ntarmos, N. (2003). Towards High Performance Peer-to-Peer Content and Resource Sharing Systems. In *Proceedings of Biennal Conference on Innovative Data Systems Research*. Asilomar, USA.

KEY TERMS AND DEFINITIONS

Business Intelligence: A set of tools and techniques that enable a company to transform its business data into timely and accurate information for the decisional process, to be made available to the right persons in the most suitable form.

Data Warehouse: A repository for integrated, consistent, historical, and summarized information to be used for decision making.

Multidimensional Model: The model commonly used for storing information in a data warehouse; it is based on the cube metaphor featuring the concepts of fact, dimension, measure, and hierarchy.

OLAP Query: An analytical query aimed at computing summarized information to be used for decision making.

Peer Data Management System: A P2P architecture for decentralized data sharing, where each peer is associated with a schema that represents the peer's domain of interest, and semantic relationships (mappings) between peers are provided locally between pairs or small sets of peers.

Peer-to-Peer (P2P) Architecture: Any distributed network architecture composed of participants that make a portion of their resources (such as processing power, disk storage or network bandwidth) directly available to other network participants, without the need for central coordination instances (such as servers or stable hosts).

Query Reformulation: Given a query Q posed over a target schema and the mappings between a source schema and a target schema, query reformulation is the task of finding a query which is equivalent to Q and that refers only to the source schema.

Schema Mapping: Declarative specifications that describe the relationship between two schemas.

Chapter 12
Towards Ad-Hoc and Collaborative Business Intelligence

Henrike Berthold
SAP AG, Germany

Philipp Rösch
SAP AG, Germany

Stefan Zöller
BARC, Germany

Felix Wortmann
University of St. Gallen, Switzerland

Alessio Carenini
CEFRIEL, Italy

Stuart Campbell
TIE, Netherlands

ABSTRACT

The success of organizations and business networks depends on fast and well-founded decisions taken by the relevant people in their specific area of responsibility. To enable timely and well-founded decisions, it is often necessary to perform ad-hoc analyses in a collaborative manner involving domain experts, line-of-business managers, key suppliers, or customers. Current Business Intelligence (BI) solutions fail to meet the challenges of ad-hoc and collaborative decision support, thus slowing down and hurting organizations. To move towards ad-hoc and collaborative BI, we envision a highly scalable and flexible BI platform. The main building blocks of this platform are a flexible and efficient concept for the management of business context information, an intuitive and powerful methodology for the configuration of a BI system, a concept of an information self-service for business users over data sources within and across organizations, a collaborative decision making environment, and an architecture for the whole system that complements current BI systems.

DOI: 10.4018/978-1-61350-038-5.ch012

Figure 1. Envisioned platform

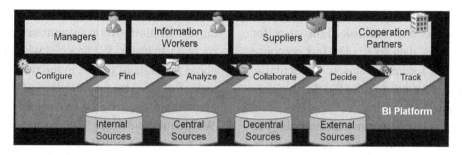

INTRODUCTION

Current Business Intelligence (BI) environments suffer from several shortcomings regarding the following characteristics:

- **Focus on individual needs**: Today, business users cannot fulfill their individual information needs but have to rely on standard reporting and predefined analytical content; they depend on either IT administration or enhanced technical skills to generate business reports.
- **Availability of business context information**: Highly relevant business context information, such as definitions, business goals and strategies that help to understand the results of an analysis are missing in current BI systems as well.
- **Support for collaboration**: Despite the fact that decisions making is a collaborative task, today's BI solutions only provide no or rather fundamental collaboration capabilities.
- **Open Business Intelligence world**: Today's BI solutions have a strong focus on structured, internal information but lack of integrating external and/or unstructured information.

Failing to meet the BI challenges described above inevitably leads to poor usage of BI systems. According to the world's largest BI study of the Business Application Research Center (BARC,

2009), in only 23% of all enterprises more than 20% of the employees use BI technologies; the overall mean ratio of employees using BI regularly is just 13.2%.

We envision a BI platform that allows business users to derive their own business information in an ad-hoc fashion, discuss the gained knowledge and shape their business strategies in a collaborative manner. This platform will reduce IT dependencies and put information acquisition directly into the business user's hands, be it managers or operative information workers, see Figure 1.

We propose techniques to significantly enhance the individual steps along the BI process. These techniques ease the business configuration and improve the capabilities to find the relevant information and to analyze the data; we make collaboration an essential part of the decision making process and enable the tracking of taken decisions. Further, the platform may utilize a variety of different data sources, which clearly positively impacts the analysis step. To accomplish these goals we need:

- **A flexible data model** to describe and adapt business relevant entities and their relationships within and across organizations. Such a data model allows to react on rapidly changing conditions by adding, removing or modifying new entities and relationships. Further, it allows to model various context information (i.e. information relevant for the decision making process that complements the data to be analyzed).

- **An efficient and scalable data store** for the business data to realize fast response times even for large datasets. Particularly, this data store has to take the flexible data model into account.

- **A business configuration methodology** to populate the data store in a pay-as-you-go fashion and to empower users to adapt the business data on their own.

- **An information self-service** allowing users to easily retrieve the business information of interest. The information self-service should enable business users to satisfy their information needs in an intuitive, fast, and efficient manner and to define a personalized environment for retrieving information of central data sources, integrating external data sources, and analyzing both kinds of information in an integrated manner.

- **An integrated collaboration environment** to discuss the results, derive conclusions and take decisions in a collaborative fashion. Important properties of this environment are synchrony, intuitiveness and traceability.

Our platform aims to empower business users to be able to configure business data and create analyses based on their specific requirements without technical skills or synchronization efforts using the language and terminology they are familiar with. Further, the information self-service enables business users to easily find and consume the relevant information; collaboration rooms additionally strongly support decision making by allowing information sharing, discussions, and joint problem solving. As data volumes are growing, we also take efficiency into account; business users want to interactively work the system and decisions have to be taken preferably fast.

To make the scenario more concrete and tangible we next describe the shortcomings of current BI platforms in a summarized form based on two use cases. We proceed with an overview about the state of the art in the relevant research areas followed by a description of our ideas and approaches towards the envisioned BI platform. We identify and describe components of a system for ad-hoc and collaborative BI. We point out future research directions and finally summarize the chapter. We oppose our proposed approaches to the shortcomings of current BI solutions and show how our platform complements them.

BACKGROUND

In the introduction, we briefly pointed out the shortcomings of current BI environments. We now address these problems in more detail and demonstrate their validity by means of two use cases.

Our first problem is related to the missing focus on the individual needs of the analysts and decision makers (i.e., the business users). These users have to rely on standard reporting and predefined analytical content that often rather insufficiently fulfills the individual information needs. They strongly depend on either IT administration or enhanced technical skills to generate the required business reports.

A second problem follows from the lack of business context information, such as definitions, business goals and strategies as well as business rules or best practices for the provided analytical data. Hence, business users have to understand the semantics of the data by themselves and they have to take decisions and derive strategies using additional information sources, which often leads to an escalation of efforts and costs.

Another shortcoming concerns the collaboration aspect: Well-founded decisions are often based upon opinions and expertise of several analysts. This implies that decision making is inherently a collaborative task and the combination of social software with Business Intelligence (collaborative BI) can dramatically improve the quality of decision making. However, current BI solutions only provide (in the best case) rudimentary collaboration capabilities. Collaborative decision making is done outside of the system using other tools or classical communication channels such as emails or phone conversations. Such cumbersome, lengthy, and expensive processes slow down organizations and have negative impact on the adoption and usage of analytical tools.

Furthermore, the setup and configuration of current BI systems requires deep insight in both the data to be analyzed and the intended analytical tasks. Here, content and data models have to be provided in advance by the IT department and tailored to the needs of a specific group of people within the company. This procedure usually ends up with several configuration (implementation or adaption) cycles; according to BARC (2009), the modal time for new BI implementations is between 3 and 6 months causing implementation and support costs that often deter companies of a wider BI deployment.

Finally, today's BI solutions have a strong focus on structured, enterprise-internal data but lack the capability of integrating external and/or unstructured information in an easy, (near) real-time and effective way. As a consequence, a lot of useful information is never included in the analyses. Not considering this information could provide a distorted or incomplete view of the actual world and consequently, it could lead to wrong business decisions.

To underpin the above listed problems we will describe the needs of two companies: a large globally acting chemical company and a large international electronics and systems company.

In the large globally acting chemical company, BI systems are in place to provide valuable business information to employees, e.g. the sales department is using predefined BI reports in order to analyze the latest sales data, compares them with plan or target values, conducts forecasts

and derives decisions to improve the company's performance. Basically, the business users are aware of the benefit of such systems but they also have some major concerns based upon their own experiences. The major challenges are:

a. *Need for fast retrieval of information and flexible adaption to business requirements.* In the chemical company, there are several thousand reports in tens of different applications. While globally defined reports are categorized, business users have lost the overview on the reports useful for them and spend a significant amount of time finding the reports they need. In spite of the vast amount of reports, users often have analysis requirements not covered by standard reports. Users have the possibility to create their own reports; however, two major issues prevent a major uptake: First, business users have only limited technical background. Current wizards and report designer tools are rather complicated and based upon technical vocabulary. Systems often require changes and additions to the underlying data models that are impossible to realize without expert IT know-how. Second, the BI systems do not provide all the business rules to be met in report definitions. Thus, users risk the generation of faulty reports providing wrong data outside the company's governance. As a consequence, today, business users conduct a development or change request at the respective IT service department. Each development or change request has to be evaluated, coordinated and prioritized and finally implemented causing high business and IT coordination costs and long lasting configuration cycles.

b. *Need for business context information.* The major constraint for the application of BI in this chemical company is the rich business knowledge: Specific rules, definitions of key performance indicators (KPIs), and respective business goals and strategies are inevitably required for a correct interpretation of the analyzed data. An evaluation and interpretation of such business context is needed to arrive at a harmonized and common understanding of analyzed data. However, currently most business context data is outside the BI application.

The large international electronics and systems company provides solutions in various areas to customers all over the world. There are a number of emerging challenges of BI within the solutions of this company.

a. *Need for a user-centric and role-specific analyses.* Many of the solutions provided by this company are large scale, cross organizational boundaries, and involve different actors or departments. Here, the traditional, system-centric provisioning of pre-defined reports is of limited use as different roles have different information needs that are not adequately reflected by current systems.

b. *Need for business context to explain BI results.* The BI systems suffer from limited facilities regarding the explanation of results. They lack enhanced business context on how to interpret analyzed data and derive better decisions, e.g. they do not provide common cross-company definitions for reports and KPIs. Due to missing relations to different company specific business goals the stakeholders are not able to align them to common cross-company business goals.

c. *Need for an integrated collaboration environment.* Some solutions comprise data that belong to different and distributed companies acting in the same area. The different physical locations and the incomplete data integration limit a collaborative analysis to identify business relevant aspects for the participating companies.

Those use cases clearly show that BI is perceived very important for well-running businesses and that there is a great demand to apply BI in several situations and applications fields. The current solutions, however, severely restrict the usage and thus, also limits the actual power of BI.

COMPONENTS OF A PLATFORM FOR AD-HOC AND COLLABORATIVE BUSINESS INTELLIGENCE

In this section, we present our envisioned platform for ad-hoc and collaborative BI. We argue that such a platform requires the following main building blocks: A flexible data model for the management of business context information, an efficient and scalable data store, an intuitive and powerful methodology for the configuration of a BI system, a concept of an information self-service for business users over data sources within and across organizations, and an integrated collaborative decision making environment. Finally, we need an architecture for the whole system that combines the individual building blocks and thus complements current BI systems.

The State of the Art of the Individual Components

Before we introduce our platform for ad-hoc and collaborative BI, we first give an overview about the current state of the art of the identified building blocks. For each building block, we name existing solutions and discuss their applicability and their limitations.

Flexible Data Models for Business Context Information

Data Warehousing and OLAP are the means of choice for the integration and consolidation of multi-dimensional data; their architectures and data models are well known (Kimball, Ross, Thornthwaite & Mundy, 2008). In addition, OLAP functions allow complex analyses of the data.

However, today's analysis tools provide a rather technical view on the analysis content and thus require technical skills of the analysts. Some BI solutions have already incorporated business metadata in a limited manner via a dedicated abstraction level based upon business terminology. Also some applications like dedicated performance management solutions cover enhanced business knowledge, comprising general and domain specific rules and interdependencies.

Current research efforts concentrate on introducing ontology-based approaches to improve decision making, tracking, progress monitoring and usage-information mining. For instance, Spahn, Kleb, Grimm, & Scheidl (2008) contribute a first attempt to enable end-user self-service BI with the help of ontology-based infrastructure and reasoning. By providing a target ontology capturing the business view the authors achieve a declarative and flexible decoupling between data sources and business-oriented models. Furthermore, Pedrinaci, Markovic, Hasibether, & Domingue (2009) propose an approach for strategy-driven business process analyses by providing an ontology formalizing performance management related aspects like strategies, goals, KPIs, processes, measures, etc. as well as their interrelationships. Cao, Zhang, & Liu (2006) present an alternative approach to achieve ontology-based integration of BI considering data warehouses, data mining and reporting systems as well as OLAP tools. The authors state that current BI solutions focus on structural integration, and, thus, enable semantic integration mechanisms to facilitate user-friendly and adaptive analyses. Clearly, ontologies are very powerful for the formalization of concepts and terms and for the representation of their interrelationships. However, the setup and the maintenance of ontologies is rather expensive which limits its application. This becomes particularly apparent in our envisioned flexible and dynamic environment.

In the Web community, the RDF (Resource Description Framework; W3C, 2004) data model is well established; it has been designed as a flexible representation of schema-relaxable or even schema-free information for the Semantic Web. To achieve our goals, we leverage the flexibility and expressiveness of RDF to add business metadata (i.e. a business view) to the technical terms. The resulting relationships between technical and business terms allow abstracting from the technical view.

Efficient and Scalable Data Stores

Representing business terms and their relations to technical terms and other business terms in a large organization or company may lead to a high data volume. In such a scenario, an efficient and scalable data store such as a distributed or a column-oriented main-memory data management system has to be used.

A distributed data management system consists of a collection of subsystems whose distribution is transparent to the user. The subsystems process the data in parallel. Therefore, high data volumes can be handled efficiently. The distributed system appears as one local system. The user may be unaware of the fact that there are several machines (i.e., their location, storage replication, load balancing, and functionality is transparent) (Özsu & Valduriez, 1997).

Main-memory databases like MonetDB (Boncz, Kersten, & Manegold, 2008) store and thus efficiently process the data in main memory. Column-store databases like MonetDB, Sybase IQ (Sybase Inc., 2010) or SAP NetWeaver BI Accelerator / TREX (Legler, Lehner, & Ross, 2006) store the data in a column-oriented way which allows high compression rates and a more effective exploitation of main memory and modern CPU features, like SIMD or pipelining (Willhalm et al., 2009). However, as the tuples are fragmented some query types require expensive joins.

In our system, we propose the application of main-memory processing to improve the overall performance of our RDF-based business data store explained below. To effectively utilize the main memory column-store techniques have to be applied; to be efficient special care on joins have to be taken (e.g. with enhanced index structures). Here, the solutions of Neumann and Weikum are promising starting points (Neuman & Weikum, 2009, 2010).

Business Configuration Methodologies

In the past, the usage of customized standard software (packaged applications) has been established in particular in the area of transaction-oriented information systems. Configuration and customizing approaches allow an enterprise-specific adaptation of the respective packaged application thereby addressing the individual needs of the enterprise (Arinze & Anandarajan, 2003; Barstow & Arango, 1991). Recently, basic customization and configuration functionalities have also been incorporated into analytical information systems in order to reduce development and implementation efforts of these systems and to meet user requirements in a better way (Gómez, Rautenstrauch, Cissek, & Grahlher, 2006). The reference content that is provided within packaged applications is called business content and forms the foundation for any customization and configuration task. For instance, SAP defines analytical business content as role- and task-specific information models. These information models may comprise amongst others queries, OLAP cubes, measures, dimensions etc. for a specific purpose like sales planning. In an implementation project business content has to be adapted to the needs of the enterprise. Accoring to Arinze & Anandarajan (2003), this is often a time-consuming and costly process.

To facilitate an effective and efficient configuration process a couple of concepts for configuring business content for transaction-oriented systems evolved over the years such as checklists, requirements navigation, reference models, and business configuration sets (Dittrich, Mertens, Hau, & Hufgard, 2006). All these approaches build upon one key idea: Enterprise applications have to be adapted to business needs and business processes of respective enterprises. Therefore the configuration of business software is first of all driven by business questions. Technical software settings are just a result of answering business questions and can thus be mostly derived automatically if all relevant business questions are answered properly. Requirements navigation for example is a checklist mechanism based on a configuration wizard and a knowledge-based system. While using the wizard, an end user with business expertise will be asked about business-related topics in a comprehensive way. During this configuration process potential dependencies of functional configurations will be checked in the background and automatically resolved if necessary. This dependency check and resolving mechanism is based on a dedicated rule system.

Until today, these *business-driven* configuration approaches have not been applied to the domain of analytical information systems. Comparable to the aforementioned approaches for configuring transaction-oriented systems, we propose to first provide business content for analytical information systems and second, to develop a configuration approach which is adequate for business users. One solution could be a wizard-based business-user tool instead of a complex, technical configuration environment built for IT experts.

Information Self-Service

In today's BI environments, there is often a clear separation of roles between (technical) BI experts—who configure the BI system and specify the underlying queries such that the reports and analyses are created according to the information needs of the (non-technical) business users—and the business users themselves who consume the standard reports and predefined analytical content. While the entrance barrier for defining information queries has been lowered in recent years by query generation tools such as the MySQL

Query Browser (Sun Microsystems, 2010) or the Microsoft Access 2007 Query Wizard or Query Designer (Microsoft, 2010), these tools nevertheless require the user to have a detailed knowledge of technical data schemas as well as query syntax and semantics, which is still too technical and complex for the business users we target with our approach. At the same time, there is a clear need and demand in companies to enable information self-service for business users. A good example for easy querying and report generation is the Tableau software (Tableau Software, 2010). Besides the need for some improvements in the handling of hierarchies within dimensions this tool provides a first step towards information self-service.

A key element of such an information self-service environment is the ability to seamlessly integrate (or mash-up) different information sources (that may come from different information providers). Easy but rather limited tools like the Intel Mash Maker (Intel, 2010) or iGoogle (Google, 2010) allow to mash up Web content. On the other side, with Damia (Simmen, Altinel, Markl, Padmanabhan, & Singh, 2008) small situational applications can be build mashing up distributed data. However, we do not only want to combine data but also query results. By combining several independent queries, business users will be able to develop their own analytical applications and dashboards. The solution of Ikeda, Nagamine, & Kamada (2008) enables the combination of different types of information in order to provide a new integrated information or view. For instance, geographic information can be combined with real estate services and yellow page services for a person looking for an apartment to rent. Yahoo! Pipes provides a graphical user interface for building applications that aggregate Web feeds, Web pages, and other services, creating Web-based applications from various sources, and publishing those applications. Yahoo! Pipes can be seen as communication channels between data sources and gadgets. Users can create mash-ups by dragging pipes from a toolbox and dropping

them in work area, specifying data input, interconnecting resources through pipes, and specifying data output formats. However, current mash-up technologies and in particular mash-up applications created using technologies like Yahoo! Pipes usually do not have an enterprise focus and do not support more complex data queries.

Integrated Collaboration Environments

It is widely agreed that the decision making process of a company has major impact on the success of a company in the market. Companies will only survive if they take the right decisions and if they can rely on a sound decision making process. Within the next decade the meaning of having a good and sophisticated decision making process in an enterprise will become even more important as companies have to face the increasing globalization and the impact of strongest market competitions. As stated by Golfarelli, Rizzi, & Cella (2004), Business Intelligence, data warehousing, and related technologies and approaches provide the technical mechanisms for decision makers to examine historical trends, to measure results, and to look for patterns in the data that might be missed otherwise. The kinds of decisions which need to be made in organizations and which are supported by these mechanisms are manifold. Decisions are made on different hierarchy levels of a company such as on the strategic level, the management level, and the operative level. Furthermore, the data, which form the base of decisions, differ regarding the degree of structuring (i.e., unstructured, semi-structured, and structured) (Gorry & Morton, 1971; Laudon & Laudon, 2006). A typical collaborative decision making process including different decision makers and business analysts is rather unstructured and dominated by efforts for coordination and inquiries. Today, email is the preferred communication means in such a process, so that the overall decision process is distributed in the form of multiple email threads over several mailboxes.

Intransparent decision processes and the loss of information are the ultimate result of these practices. Collaborative decision environments thrive to overcome these challenges by bringing together all relevant information and people in one place for effective and efficient decision making. On top of that, flexible process management support (Ceri, Daniel, Matera, & Raffio, 2009) could be applied to structure decision processes with collaboration tasks in a user-friendly manner. It allows users to create and modify processes including collaboration tasks easily to their needs. It has been applied successfully to eLearning processes.

In the portfolios of analytical software vendors a couple of collaboration techniques can be found that are partly integrated into their products. In addition to that, in the field of social software, "much of the technological foundation is [already] in place," which could be used for further enhancements of collaborative functionalities of analytic software. However, "no commercial offerings [exist] that comprehensively incorporate the vision of collaborative decision making" (Bitterer et al., 2009).

Regarding collaborative decision making processes, it can be said that today it mainly consists of adding simple collaboration aspects to existing software such as messaging functionalities.

A Platform for Ad-Hoc and Collaborative Business Intelligence

After reviewing the state of the art of the individual components, we now discuss ideas for their utilization, extension, and composition for our envisioned BI platform. Recall, we require the following building blocks to be part of our solution: A flexible data model for the management of business context information, an efficient and scalable data store, an intuitive and powerful methodology for the configuration of a BI system, a concept of an information self-service for business users over data sources within and across organizations, and an integrated collaborative decision making environment. We start with a detailed description of the components followed by a presentation of the overall architecture of our BI platform.

Flexible Data Models for Business Context Information

The flexible data model of our proposed platform consists of two concepts: *DataSpaces* that manage the base data (i.e., the actual data to analyze) and *InfoSpaces* that model the relations and provide context information for DataSpaces. This is motivated by our goal to have a clear separation of the IT point of view (DataSpaces) from the business point of view (InfoSpaces).

DataSpaces

Our platform builds upon data feeds from central and decentral data sources. Central data sources are managed by IT and cover internal transactional data sources (e.g. ERP, CRM) as well as data warehouses and data marts. Decentral data sources may be added by business users and may cover locally managed data (e.g. data managed by business departments or business users) as well as external data (e.g. external RSS feeds). Both the central and the decentral data sources are encapsulated as DataSpaces. Beside the data itself, DataSpaces comprise meta data like ETL definitions or basic post-processing rules like anonymization and data cleaning.

InfoSpaces

InfoSpaces are business representations of data abstracting from technical concepts such as data formats or schemas. They integrate data from different sources for the needs of a specific user group. In general, InfoSpaces may contain business objects (e.g. orders, customers), measures (e.g. quantities, amounts, KPIs), BI information provider definitions (e.g. tables, Cubes), query definitions, and strategic goals. The aim of InfoSpaces is to provide access to data on an appropriate end-user-oriented data-abstraction level. This requires

- to lift data to a standardized and domain independent data model,
- to provide business-related concepts and definitions, and
- to consider business knowledge and rules that allow user-driven configuration and adaption of InfoSpaces to changed requirements.

Efficient and Scalable Data Stores

With our flexible data model, we face the challenge to easily and efficiently manage a large amount and high diversity of InfoSpaces. The latter aspect makes RDF—due to its flexibility—a promising solution. Hence, for the management of business context information we propose a technological shift from heavy-weight ontologies and reasoning to a light-weight approach based upon a combination of RDF data and database technology in order to support performing BI analyses also over large scale data sets.

To realize efficiency, we propose a heavy use of main memory and distributed query processing. As main memory is rare we suggest the use of column-store databases and compression techniques for an effective utilization of the available memory. For further speed-up, optimized index structures for RDF-based (self-) joins have to be applied.

Business Configuration Methodology

While in traditional BI environments data integration is performed by IT departments, our proposed business configuration methodology enables power users to perform such configuration tasks by themselves. Power users create InfoSpaces in a pay-as-you-go-manner starting with few InfoSpaces and adapt and extend the set continu-

ously. As data integration can be a complex task, a specific power-user-oriented methodology will be necessary. Our business configuration process is based on interaction paradigms that allow business users to express their information needs in a simple and intuitive way. In order to facilitate a quick and easy configuration process, the business configuration uses a three-step approach. In the first step the scope of an InfoSpace is defined (scoping) while in the second step the detailed configuration is specified (fine-tuning). With the help of a wizard, the configuration process can be guided by questions like "Do you want analytical support for the sales planning?" (scoping) and "Do you perform a monthly or quarterly sales planning?" (fine-tuning). The third and final step is to select the DataSpaces to be used in the analysis. The user is provided with a set of candidate DataSpaces that have been suggested by the system as appropriate to deliver the needed data. IT engineers will be responsible for the required mapping between internal or external data sources and DataSpaces of the envisioned platform. Beside the integration of new data sources, the business configuration also manages the creation and adaption of business context information such as business strategies, KPIs and InfoSpaces.

BI Life Cycle

Our envisioned platform supports the life cycle of a BI analytical task as shown in Figure 2. The life cycle visualizes the recurrent adaptation of the BI environment to business needs. The lifting of the BI life cycle on a business level results in an environment that can be primarily used by business users. This entails that also configuration activities, which so far have been assigned to the software engineers with a direct effect on the increase of the business/IT coordination costs, is manageable by business users.

We aim to address the risk of poor data quality in analytics by using a two-step approach; we distinguish IT-dependent measures and business-dependent measures. The former ones are related to data cleaning and can be enforced at the data layer provided by the DataSpaces. The latter ones, which are related to centrally provided enterprise and legal rules as well as domain-specific interaction rules, can be enforced at a business level in the InfoSpaces.

By monitoring the creation and usage of the InfoSpaces as well as of the lightweight applications and reports, corporate IT will furthermore be able to help mitigating quality risks and discover information needs that have not been originally covered by the system. Based on this, they can enrich the built-in solutions offered by the BI environment, thereby "standardizing" content from the platform and bringing it back into the corporate BI environment

Information Self-Service

Traditional BI environments provide only limited capabilities to modify existing reports or to compose new ones. The envisioned information self-service (ISS) environment is the business user environment for self-service query design, query execution and information mash-ups; it enables business users to find required information using enhanced navigation and search techniques and to build lightweight analytical applications according to their individual needs based upon InfoSpaces. Intuitive portals and wizards are going to help the users to formulate their information needs on the basis of InfoSpaces and to browse the data along different dimensions. An intuitive query consumption environment may allow the user to consume information in a table format or as graphical chart. Additionally to the requested data, the ISS environment automatically provides context information, such as related reports, business goals or general/company specific business knowledge (KPI definitions, interdependencies), in order to improve and accelerate the business decision processes. The built-in evaluation of report usage information allows the system to

Figure 2. BI life cycle

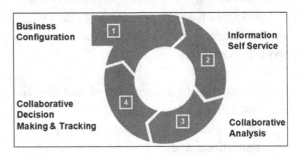

pro-actively make recommendations to business users (e.g. on related reports). Furthermore, different information elements like tables or charts could be composed into dashboards based on simple patterns. By linking content of different queries in a visual and intuitive way, the business users are empowered to create their own solutions that fit best their business requirements. No skills in technical or even programming concepts are required at this stage.

Regarding ad-hoc analyses, the combination of several data sources and linkages between single queries resembles an advanced development process by itself that may discourage business users. A viable alternative that we propose to investigate is a pattern-based approach, which provides templates of pre-defined and pre-linked queries that fulfill the needs of an explicit scenario or use case. In a Web 2.0-based approach, these templates could be collected from other users via a shared repository. Moreover, semi-automatic linkage of information queries can be a vital approach to business user mash-ups. Usage analyses ("How have other users linked information?") could serve as a basis to automatically generate information mash-ups and propose them to a user. Furthermore, the analysis of data models could also serve as a basis for automatic query linking and mash-up generation. One of the key objectives of our approach is therefore a business-oriented composition approach of analytical mash-ups comprising information queries while technical aspects are handled "behind the scenes" as much as possible.

Due to the multitude of queries that could be generated by business users, a management regarding their semantic content is essential (e.g., for realizing synergies by reusing predefined queries). For this purpose, metadata can be used for describing the data in the integration layer as well as the queries. Foshay, Mukherjee, & Taylor (2007) differentiate between the following categories of metadata, that is relevant for our purposes: definitional (What does this data mean from a business perspective?), data quality (Does this data possess sufficient quality for me to use it for a specific purpose?), navigational (Where can I find the data I need?), and lineage (Where did this data originate and what's been done to it?).

The ISS essentially deals with three types of content: internal data (from central data sources), external data (from decentral data sources) and business context information. Business context information enriches the business data with further information (e.g. definitions or best practices like "how to improve a KPI"). Metadata could be extended by domain specific information within the ISS or the collaboration rooms. To achieve this, business users must be enabled with corresponding tools (e.g., the Semantic MediaWiki) (MediaWiki, 2010).

Integrated Collaboration Environment

Our proposed BI platform provides collaboration rooms where business users are able to share, comment, and take joint decisions. For an effective collaboration, we require to allow users to work on business reports simultaneously and to allow them to collaborate in all phases of the decision making process including the formulation of queries and the interpretation of results. Live interaction facilities allow users of our platform to exchange ideas on the fly. Users may bring in information from various public and private sources and may use them as an information source when taking

decisions in a team. As such, we want to add a new level to the collaborative decision making process, thus, lifting it to the same level as if people would work together in the same room. Furthermore, collaboration rooms are the means to capture user feedback, community knowledge and best practices to improve decision making. Exploiting information usage data to proactively distribute information is a key feature of collaboration rooms.

Overall Architecture

For our envisioned platform for ad-hoc and collaborative BI, we propose an overall architecture consisting of two major layers and one key repository. As layers, we suggest an *Ad-hoc and Collaborative Analysis* layer and an *Integration and Enrichment* layer; the key repository provides the *Global Business Data Store*. The layers, the repository, and their interfaces to data sources and end users are depicted in Figure 3. This figure also shows how the individual components discussed above are placed within the overall architecture.

Ad-Hoc and Collaborative Analysis

The Ad-hoc and Collaborative Analysis layer facilitates information self-service and collaboration of business users. It consists of two main components: the *Information Self-Service Environment* for intuitive ad-hoc analyses and the *Collaboration Rooms* as seamlessly integrated means for collaborative decision making.

Integration and Enrichment

The Integration and Enrichment layer integrates and semantically enriches heterogeneous data sources within and across organizations. The two main components of this layer are the *Business Configuration*—the environment for business users with moderate data management skills to setup and configure InfoSpaces and DataSpaces—and

Figure 3. Proposed architectural components

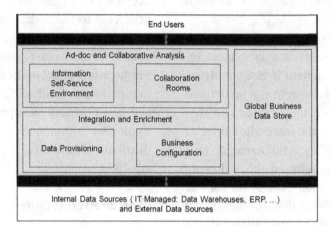

the *Data Provisioning* that ensures high flexibility and efficiency.

Global Business Data Store

The Global Business Data Store manages instance data specified in a flexible data model in an efficient and scalable way. It is the central repository of the platform. On the one hand, it serves to "translate" the IT terminology (e.g. data models, fields, etc.) into business terminology and thus, to support business users in configuring new information models (InfoSpaces) and creating new reports. On the other hand, it provides extended general, company- and user-specific context information for faster and more accurate business decisions. It contains InfoSpace definitions, navigational and lineage metadata (descriptions of ETL processes), definitional metadata (business object, KPIs, dimensions), integrated organizational data (contact persons, business functions, access rights), advanced business data (decisions, legal data strategies, objectives, tasks), and usage and evaluation data (logs on reports and KPI usages).

FUTURE RESEARCH DIRECTIONS

In short, as our platform for ad-hoc and collaborative BI is a recommendation or a vision for future

BI solutions, future research is required to verify the applicability, the feasibility, and the limitations of our ideas. Examples for those future research activities comprise a closer inspection of the InfoSpaces to see what can be expressed and where are the restrictions; also the final representation might require some research. The last point is closely connected with the application of RDF, column stores and in-memory techniques. Here, future research will reveal if there is a paradigm shift for certain application fields from traditional relational databases to those new techniques. Another topic of future research will be related to the realization of the business configuration to identify the details of the scoping, fine-tuning, and selection steps and to evaluate methodologies regarding their appropriateness for business users to perform ad-hoc BI. This also involves the question of how much automation or at least semi-automation is possible and meaningful in this process. For the information self-service and the collaboration environment the user interface is of major importance. Information has to be found and consumed in an intuitive way; the collaboration capabilities have to be seamlessly integrated. For all the developments, improvements and extensions of techniques towards an ad-hoc and collaborative BI environment, we will use the real-world uses cases described in the background section to evaluate their benefit.

CONCLUSION

In this chapter, we outlined the importance of providing business users with the means for ad-hoc and collaborative decision making. We presented the coarse-grained architecture for the envisioned system and identified the main building blocks that need to be developed. We further described ideas of how to realize the envisioned goals.

Regarding the shortcomings of current BI solutions identified above, our envisioned BI platform addresses the individual needs as follows:

- **Focus on individual needs**: Business users use the information self-service to identity appropriate reports, specify their analysis tasks and add business context information. The flexible data model enables the addition of new types of business context information. The interactive use of context information for BI tasks is realized by the efficient and scalable data store.
- **Availability of business context information**: Business context information is added by IT experts and can be extended by business users. The flexible data model allows an incremental design and creation of context information. The efficient and scalable data store supports the use of the growing amount of context information in an interactive BI system.
- **Support for collaboration**: An integrated collaboration environment supports collaborative decision making.
- **Open Business Intelligence world**: The information self-service allows to integrate and to use external data sources easily in the BI system.

Finally, we slightly change the view and show how our solution complements traditional BI systems. State-of-the-art BI environments are currently end-to-end developed and maintained by corporate IT. While their rigid processes guarantee high quality data and BI analysis, they tend to decrease flexibility, end-user centricity, and finally innovation. Our envisioned platform aims to complement such BI environments in order to overcome these challenges and empower the business users (see Figure 4).

Our proposed solution complements traditional BI in four major areas:

- **Data Sources**: The envisioned platform builds upon data feeds from central and decentral data sources. Central data sources are managed by IT and cover internal transactional data sources (e.g. ERP, CRM, SRM, SCM) as well as data warehouses and data marts. In contrast to traditional BI environments, our platform also enables business users to add own decentral data sources which cover locally managed data (e.g. data managed by business departments or business users) as well as external data (e.g. external RSS feeds).
- **Global Business Data Model:** The core elements of our data model are represented by the concept of InfoSpaces, which are business representations of data abstracting from technical concepts such as data formats or schemas. InfoSpaces integrate data from different sources for the needs of a specific user group. To enable the "average" business user to build his/her own queries on top of InfoSpaces, they provide access to data on an appropriate end-user-oriented data-abstraction level.
- **Business configuration methodology and tools**: While in traditional BI data integration is performed by IT departments, our platform enables business users to perform such configuration tasks by themselves. As data integration can be a complex task, a specific business-user-oriented design time is necessary. Our envisioned business configuration component will be the environment for business users with moderate data

Figure 4. Complementing traditional BI

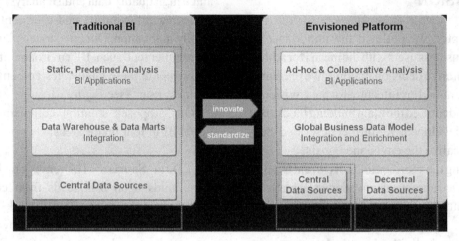

management skills to perform these activities (i.e., power users).

- **Ad-hoc and collaborative analysis:** Traditional BI environments only provide limited possibilities to change or compose new reports. The platform's information self-service environment enables business users to find required information using enhanced navigation and search techniques and to build lightweight analytical applications according to their individual needs based upon InfoSpaces. By linking content of different queries in a visual and intuitive way, the business users are empowered to create their own solutions that fit best their business requirements. No skills in technical or even programming concepts are required at this stage. Furthermore, our platform provides collaboration rooms where business users are able to share, comment, and take joint decisions.

State-of-the-art BI environments are the basis for standardized, high quality data analyses and reporting. Our BI platform builds on top of existing BI environments and lays the basis to foster innovation and to fulfill the individual user's reporting needs (see "innovate" in Figure 4).

In our envisioned BI platform, the risk of poor data quality in analytics will be addressed by centrally providing and enforcing enterprise and legal rules. By monitoring the creation and usage of the InfoSpaces as well as of the lightweight applications and reports, corporate IT will furthermore be able to help mitigating quality risks and discover information needs that have not been originally covered by the system. Based on this, they can enrich the built-in solutions offered by the BI environment, thereby "standardizing" content from our BI platform and bringing it back into the corporate BI environment (see "standardize" in Figure 4).

ACKNOWLEDGMENT

We thank Frank Strohmaier and Pascal Bisson for their input for the two real-world use cases given in the background section. These use cases are very helpful in revealing the shortcomings of current Business Intelligence solutions.

REFERENCES

W3C. (2004). *Resource description framework (RDF)*. Retrieved July 14, 2010, from http://www.w3c.org/RDF/

Arinze, B., & Anandarajan, M. (2003). A framework for using OO mapping methods to rapidly configure ERP systems. *Communications of the ACM, 46*(2), 61–65. doi:10.1145/606272.606274

BARC. (2009). *The BI survey 8*. Würzburg, Germany: Business Application Research Center.

Barstow, G., & Arango, D. (1991). Designing software for customization and evolution. *Proceedings of the 6th International Workshop on Software Specification and Design* (pp. 250-255). Los Alamitos, CA: IEEE Computer Society Press.

Bitterer, A., Sallam, R. L., Schlegel, K., Gassman, B., Richardson, J., Hostmann, B., … Friedman, T., (2009). *Hype cycle for business intelligence and performance management*. (Gartner, ID G00169443).

Boncz, P. A., Kersten, M. L., & Manegold, S. (2008). Breaking the memory wall in MonetDB. *Communications of the ACM, 51*(12), 77–85. doi:10.1145/1409360.1409380

Cao, L., Zhang, C., & Liu, J. (2006). Ontology-based integration of business intelligence. *Web Intelligence and Agent Systems, 4*(3), 313–325.

Ceri, S., Daniel, F., Matera, M., & Raffio, A. (2009). Providing flexible process support to project-centered learning. *IEEE Transactions on Knowledge and Data Engineering, 21*(6), 894–909. doi:10.1109/TKDE.2008.134

Dittrich, J., Mertens, P., Hau, M., & Hufgard, A. (2006). *Dispositionsparameter in der Produktionsplanung mit SAP* (pp. 21–32). Vieweg Verlag.

Foshay, N., Mukherjee, A., & Taylor, A. (2007). Does data warehouse end-user metadata add value? *Communications of the ACM, 50*(11), 70–77. doi:10.1145/1297797.1297800

Golfarelli, M., Rizzi, S., & Cella, I. (2004). Beyond data warehousing: What's next in business intelligence? *Proceedings of the 7th ACM International Workshop on Data Warehousing and OLAP* (pp.1-6).

Gómez, J. M., Rautenstrauch, C., Cissek, P., & Grahlher, B. (2006). *Einführung in SAP business information warehouse*. Heidelberg, Germany: Springer-Verlag.

Google Inc. (2010). *iGoogle*. Retrieved October 28, 2010 from http://www.google.com/ig

Gorry, G. A., & Morton, M. S. S. (1971). A framework for management Information Systems. *Sloan Management Review, 13*(1), 55–70.

Ikeda, S., Nagamine, T., & Kamada, T. (2008). Application framework with demand-driven mashup for selective browsing. *Proceedings of the 10th International Conference on Information Integration and Web-Based Applications & Services* (pp. 33-40). New York, NY: ACM.

Intel Inc. (2010) *Intel® mash maker*. Retrieved October 28, 2010 from http://mashmaker.intel.com/

Kimball, R., Ross, M., Thornthwaite, W., & Mundy, J. (2008). *The data warehouse lifecycle toolkit*. Wiley & Sons.

Laudon, J., & Laudon, K. (2006). *Management Information Systems: Managing the digital firm*. Upper Saddle River, NJ: Prentice Hall Press.

Legler, T., Lehner, W., & Ross, A. (2006). Data mining with the SAP Netweaver BI accelerator. *Proceedings of the 32nd International Conference on Very Large Data Bases* (pp. 1059-1068). VLDB Endowment.

MediaWiki. (2010). *Introduction to semantic MediaWiki*. Retrieved July 14, 2010 from http://semantic-mediawiki.org/wiki/Help:Introduction_to_Semantic_MediaWiki

Microsoft Inc. (2010). *Introduction to queries*. Retrieved July 14, 2010 from http://office.microsoft.com/en-us/ access/HA102098921033.aspx

Neumann, T., & Weikum, G. (2009). Scalable join processing on very large RDF graphs. *Proceedings of the 35th SIGMOD International Conference on Management of Data* (pp. 627-640). New York, NY: ACM.

Neumann, T., & Weikum, G. (2010). The RDF-3X engine for scalable management of RDF data. *The VLDB Journal, 19*(1), 91–113. doi:10.1007/s00778-009-0165-y

Özsu, M. T., & Valduriez, P. (1997). *Principles of distributed database systems*. Upper Saddle River, NJ: Prentice Hall Press.

Pedrinaci, C., Markovic, I., Hasibether, F., & Domingue, J. (2009). Strategy-driven business process analysis. *Proceedings of the 12th International Conference of Business Information Systems* (pp. 169-180). Springer.

Simmen, D., Altinel, M., Markl, V., Padmanabhan, S., & Singh, A. (2008). Damia: Data mashups for Intranet applications. *Proceedings of the ACM SIGMOD International Conference on Management of Data* (pp. 1171-1182). New York, NY: ACM.

Spahn, M., Kleb, J., Grimm, S., & Scheidl, S. (2008). Supporting business intelligence by providing ontology-based end-user information self-service. *Proceedings of the First International Workshop on Ontology-Supported Business Intelligence* (pp. 1-12). New York, NY: ACM

Sun Microsystems Inc. (2010). *MySQL query browser*. Retrieved July 14, 2010, from http://dev.mysql.com/doc/query-browser/en/index.html

Sybase Inc. (2010). *Sybase IQ*. Retrieved July 14, 2010, from http://www.sybase.com/products/datawarehousing/sybaseiq

Tableau Software. (2010). *Tableau desktop*. Retrieved October 28, 2010, from http://www.tableausoftware.com/ products/desktop

Willhalm, T., Popovici, N., Boshmaf, Y., Plattner, H., Zeier, A., & Schaffner, J. (2009). SIMD-Scan: Ultra fast in-memory table scan using on-chip vector processing units. *PVLDB, 2*(1), 385–394.

ADDITIONAL READING

Berger, R. (2003). *Sales Performance in Difficult Times*. Retrieved at July 14, 2010 from http://www.rolandberger.com/ company/press/releases/513-press_archive2003_sc_content/pr63.html

Berger, R. (2009). *Global Restructuring Study 2009*. Retrieved at July 14, 2010 from http://www.rolandberger.ch/media/pdf/ Roland_Berger_Global-restructuring-study-2009_20090824.pdf

Berger, R. (2009). *Working Capital – "Cash for Recovery"*. Retrieved at July 14, 2010 from http://www.rolandberger.com/media/pdf/Roland_Berger_Working_Capital_Eshort_20090723.pdf

Gilbert, S., & Lynch, N. (2002). Brewer's Conjecture and the Feasibility of Consistent, Available, Partition-tolerant Web Services. *SIGACT News, 33*(2), 51–59. doi:10.1145/564585.564601

Hufgard, A., Hecht, H., Walz, W., Hennermann, F., Brosch, G., Mehlich, S., & Bätz, C. (2004). *Business Integration mit SAP-Lösungen*. Heidelberg, Germany: Springer-Verlag.

IBIS Thome AG. (2009). *White Paper - SAP Business ByDesign - A new, highly adaptable Category of Software*. Retrieved at July 14, 2010 from http://www.ibis-america.com/fileadmin/ website/PDF/eng/White_Papers/ WhitePaper_SAPBusinessByDesign.pdf

Idreos, S., Kersten, M. L., & Manegold, S. (2009). Self-organizing Tuple Reconstruction in Column-Stores. *Proceedings of the ACM SIGMOD International Conference on Management of Data* (pp. 297-308). New York, USA: ACM.

Inmon, W. H. (2005). *Building the Data Warehouse*. Wiley & Sons.

Ivanova, M., Kersten, M. L., Nes, N. j., & Goncalves, R. (2009). An Architecture for Recycling Intermediates in a Column-Store. *Proceedings of the ACM SIGMOD International Conference on Management of Data* (pp. 309-320). New York, USA: ACM.

Neumann, T., & Weikum, G. (2008). RDF-3X: A RISC-style Engine for RDF. *PVLDB*, *1*(1), 647–659.

Plattner, H. (2009). A Common Database Approach for OLTP and OLAP Using an In-Memory Column Database. *Proceedings of the ACM SIGMOD International Conference on Management of Data* (pp. 1-2). New York, USA: ACM.

Sallam, R. L., Schlegel, K., Austin, T., & Rozwell, C. (2009). *The Rise of Collaborative Decision Making*. Gartner RAS Core Research Note G00164718.

SAP AG. (2009). *SAP Knowledge Warehouse: BI Content*. Retrieved at July 14, 2010 from http://help.sap.com/saphelp_nw04/ helpdata/en/37/5fb13cd0500255e10000000a114084/content.htm

Schlegel, K., & Rayner, N. (2009). *Key Issues for Business Intelligence and Performance Management Initiatives*. Gartner Research Note G00156014.

Schmidt, A. (2006). Sustainable Availability of Brewing Materials and Managing Volatility. *Proceedings of the Global Procurement Conference*. Retrieved at July 14, 2010 from http://www.rolandberger.com/media/ pdf/rb_press/RB_Brewing_20061112.pdf

Sidirourgos, L., Goncalves, R., Kersten, M. L., Nes, N. J., & Manegold, S. (2008). Column-Store Support for RDF Data Management: Not all Swans are White. *PVLDB*, *1*(2), 1553–1563.

TDWI. (2009). *TDWI BI Benchmark Report*. Retrieved at July 14, 2010 from http://tdwi.org/pages/research/ tdwi-bi-benchmark-reports.aspx

UPS. (2005) *Strategic Sourcing: Building a Foundation for Success*. Retrieved at July 14, 2010 from http://www.ups-scs.com/ solutions/whitepapers.html

KEY TERMS AND DEFINITIONS

Ad-Hoc: With ad-hoc (lat. "for this"), an approach or a solution is characterized to be designed for a specific problem or task. An ad-hoc solution cannot be generalized or adapted to other purposes.

Business Intelligence: The goal of Business Intelligence (BI) is to support better business decision making; therefore, BI systems are also referred to as decision support systems. BI provides complex means for the analysis of business data but also comprises techniques for spotting and digging out the relevant information. BI allows to analyze the history and the present but also provides predictive views on the business data. Typical functions of BI technologies are reporting, online analytical processing, data mining, and predictive analytics.

Business Metadata: As business metadata we consider all the information closely related to the actual business data or business objects. Those metadata include lineage metadata (descriptions of ETL processes), definitional metadata (measures, KPIs, dimensions), integrated organizational data (contact persons, business functions, access rights), advanced business data (decisions, legal data strategies, objectives, tasks), and usage and evaluation data (logs on reports and KPI usages).

Business User: As business users we consider business people that are unaware of IT. They know and understand business objects, their interrelationship, KPIs and the business logic but are not able to conduct database queries or even to integrate new data sources in the way as it is done by IT experts.

Collaboration: Collaboration is an iterative process with multiple people or organizations that work together on a common topic or with a common goal. It is highly relevant in areas of problem solving, consensus finding, knowledge sharing or even learning. Collaboration has the advantage of utilizing more resources or knowledge to reach the common goal.

Information Self-Service: Self-service in general is the practice of serving oneself. This, of course, also includes the *ability* of doing the respective action by yourself and not to rely on other (more experienced) people. With information self-service we refer to the case where a person is able to find and to consume information by itself, preferably in an easy and intuitive way.

Chapter 13
Real–Time BI and Situational Analysis

Maik Thiele
Technische Universität Dresden, Germany

Wolfgang Lehner
Technische Universität Dresden, Germany

ABSTRACT

In the past, data-warehouse systems served as information providers for key management members and knowledge workers; today, they are the central platform for the enterprise-wide integrated information provision. Aside from strategic analyses on historical data, this encompasses, above all, the submission of real-time data to operational processes. The clear separation of the operational and the analytical world, as it has been promoted until now, will thus become obsolete in the future. This development (i.e., the merging of the operational and the analytical world in context of Web technologies) is topic of this chapter. For this purpose, we take a closer look at current business intelligence (BI) and data warehouse trends from the perspective of both the applications and the database systems. We discuss scenarios which show the emerging trend to real-time business intelligence and present techniques that address the problems upcoming when building a real-time DWH. Additionally, we extend the concept of real-time business intelligence by the aspect of situational data analyses.

INTRODUCTION

Business intelligence and data warehousing have enjoyed immense popularity and success over the last years and now play a key role in strategic corporate decision-making. Through the evolution

DOI: 10.4018/978-1-61350-038-5.ch013

of web technologies, the ubiquitous presence of data and the increasing demand for current data in the recent years the requirements posed to business intelligence systems have changed: 1) On the back-end and system level this evolution raised the need for more up-to-date, so-called real-time, analyses. The real-time aspect in the context of business intelligence describes a new processing model where every change is automatically captured and pushed into the underlying data warehouse (DWH). Thus, the data in a real-time DWH is subject to continuous changes, denoted as a trickle-feed of updates. 2) On the end-user and application level the shift from static to dynamic web applications through modern web technologies leads to a raising demand for interactive and customizable reports as well as ad-hoc integrations of arbitrary data sources. Especially the latter aspect is not compatible with today's business intelligence and data warehouse architectures.

Some applications scenarios should strengthen the two challenges sketched above: One application scenario from the business sector is the avoidance of so-called out-of-stock items; these are situations in which goods are requested but not available for purchase any longer. In order to minimize the number of occurrences of such situations, we require historical sales transaction data as input for prediction models on the one hand but also information on the current inventory and transaction data for consistency checks and refinements of the prediction data on the other hand. Additionally, an analyst could build a situational application to see how weather is affecting sales at specific retail stores and the occurrences of out-of-stock situations. In order to do so the analyst has to integrate public information from weather Web sites together with the sales information.

In e-commerce scenarios the current behavior of customers must be analyzed with the help of click-streams and basket analyses and then compared to similar behavioral patterns of past customers. From such comparison, we can derive so-called cross-selling and/or up-selling opportunities (i.e., the chance to recommend complementary or better products and thereby increase the company's revenue).

Another real-time scenario focuses on supporting customer calls in call centers: Employees of a call center must always have access to current customer data in order to ensure the smooth and consistent communication with clients. Such in-formation must be gathered via all communication channels (web, e-mail, phone etc.) of a company and then made available in real-time.

Airport operators, whose business model is based on the optimal aviation management and ground handling, are highly dependent on operation information, too. A plane that is taking off or touching down can be assigned up to 1,000 attributes, including, for example, the airport weather, the plane's load, or the passengers' nationalities. These data are compared to past data, statistics, and predictions in order to control the mentioned processes. One example is the scheduling of ground personnel for visa processing in dependence on the passengers' nationalities. In order to compare the performance of the own aviation management with other airports, business analysts may build a situational application which integrate third-party flight delay statistics[1] with their own information. Furthermore, they may rely on external web services to improve and visualize their results.

These example scenarios show that the currently strict separation of operational and analytical systems on a system level, as it has been propagated until now, will thus become obsolete in the near future. As the central information provision platform within enterprises, data warehouses will thus simultaneously have to provide up-to-date information and qualitative, verified data that has been refined over the course of many processing steps. Data-warehouse systems are thus faced with a heterogeneous group of users who have different requirements in terms of freshness, query latency and the consistency and stability of data. Looking at our application scenarios, we see that a data warehouse does not only have to provide real-time data to detect out-of-stock items, but it also needs to provide data to classic applications such as controlling or marketing.

On an application level there is evident lack of support for ad-hoc integration in today's business intelligence and data warehouse architectures. The reason for this lies in the large amount of data sources and possible views to the data makes which makes it impossible to provide users with each potentially relevant report. Therefore, the IT has to provide appropriate services which enable the user to create new views on the data in order to generate added value for themselves and their enterprise. The thereby acquired new views on the data can subsequently be picked by the IT architects and—depending on its relevance—the user-made processes may be integrated into the classic data integration and production processes (i.e., the classic mass data integration with ETL remains as relevant as ever).

In the following we address both facets of real-time BI. First, we formulate the requirements of real-time BI-architectures, and analyze current trends, techniques and solutions. The concept of real-time BI with the aspect of information acquisition, the so-called situational BI, is stated in the subsequent section. In the conclusion section we give a brief summary of the chapter and discuss future research challenges.

REAL-TIME DATA WAREHOUSING

The terms "real-time" and "data warehouse" in the context of data analysis initially seem contradictory. The former calls for up-to-date data, and the latter relies on historical data. However, there are a multitude of applications that may generate decisive added value with this very combination of up-to-date and historical data as shown it the introduction section. In this section we will confirm the growing trend to real-time analytics, give an outline of problems which arise with real-time requirements and present current solutions and techniques.

Evolution of Data-Warehouse Systems

The concept of data-warehouse systems is applicable to a variety of use-case scenarios. Initially, however, data-warehouse projects are usually planned and implemented for very concrete application fields. Only when they are employed and accepted by an increasing user base does the number of applications grow, which increases the requirements posed to the system and to the data-warehouse architects. The following brief sketch of the evolution of data-warehouse applications can be observed both in the small (within specific data-warehouse projects) and in the large, as a general historic trend of the last years.

Types of Applications

At first, the four-step development process for data-warehouse applications is described (see Figure 1). In the first step of a data-warehouse installation, the applications are mostly used for reporting purposes. They are defined once and then recalculated during certain reporting cycles. A main feature of this type of applications is the availability of prior knowledge about the queries and the determined points in time when reports will have to be created. Due to the inflexible processing pattern, this approach is also called batch processing. For this type of applications, databases can be specifically optimized (e.g., by materializing sum data).

In the next application step, additional questions arise. Aside from the basic representation of facts, the analysis of causes is considered as well. Starting from raw-grained facts, the user can further refine the information (e.g., via drill-down navigation). Thus, the query patterns are no longer static, as they are in step 1, but the required interactivity leads to quite dynamic and unpredictable patterns. These interactive user queries are called ad-hoc queries. The point in

Figure 1. The four steps of evolution when using a data-warehouse system (according to Brobst, 2003)

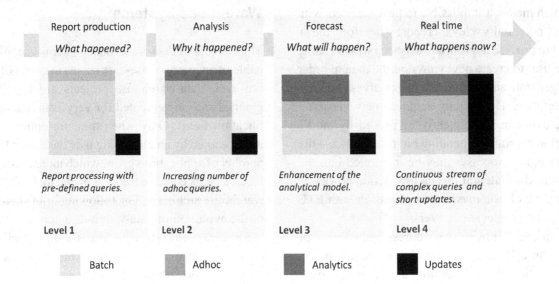

time when these queries are submitted to the system cannot be predicted, which can result in performance bottlenecks in scenarios with high concurrency.

Now that enterprises can answer the questions of "what" and "why" for past processes, the next application step consists of predicting future developments. In order to realize prediction models, the use of data-mining software, based on the data-warehouse system, is necessary. The complexity of such data-mining software, however, means that its user base is rather limited. Nevertheless, the resource consumption of such applications is very high due to the data intensity of the prediction algorithms. However, the parameterization of the prediction models is increasingly simplified, all the way to parameter-free algorithms, which will certainly increase the user base in the near future.

Previous applications normally served the purpose of supporting long-term or strategic decision-making processes. On a regular basis, the data-warehouse system was therefore loaded in weekly or monthly intervals. The achieved data freshness is insufficient to support daily business processes, the so-called operational decision-making. In the ideal case, modifications are propa-

gated immediately, so that a continuous stream of updates—in addition to the heterogeneous query workload—stresses the system. Another improvement of operational decision-making is given by *Active Data Warehouses*. These automate the decision-making process, so that the latency time incurred by human activity is avoided.

The presented application fields do not replace one another, but they are operated in coexistence to one another. For example, the workload in application step 4 will still consist of a significant part of batch queries for reporting purposes and of analytical queries. Due to the diversity of applications and the heterogeneity of user groups, a data-warehouse system is thus faced with a range of service-level requirements.

Classifying the Decision Levels

The sketched applications support business processes on different decision levels. These can be distinguished into a strategic, a tactical and an operational level, whose characteristics will be described in the following (see Figure 2).

Primarily, the three levels differ in the time horizon during which a decision has certain ef-

Figure 2. Comparison of strategic, tactical and operational decision-making

	Time horizont	Type of decision	Decision level	Data latency	Data sources
strategic	• Long-term	• Corporate policy	• Broad • Enterprise	• High, historical data • Time period	• Many data sources • Structured and unstructured data • Aggregated data
tactical	• Medium-term	• Control and implemenatation of business objectives	• Relatively broad • Enterprise and Departments	• Medium-High	• Few to many data sources • Structured and semi-structured data • Detailed and aggregated data
operational	• Short-term	• Pricing • Contract term • Partially automatable	• Focused • Processes	• Low, operational data • Point of time	• Few data sources • Structured • Very detailed data

fects. They also differ in the type and/or the reference object of the decision. Strategic decisions refer to the definition and the achievement of goals and are, therefore, long-term-oriented. In contrast to this, operational decisions refer to single processes and are only relevant within a short period of time. Let us look at the following example: The decision on the approval of a credit with a runtime of 20 years is rather long-term-oriented, but for the concerned bank, this only represents one operational decision.

The consideration of the time horizon is thus insufficient to differentiate between the decision levels. By adding the type of decision and/or its range of effect, this differentiation becomes much clearer. The approval of a credit does not affect a company's policy or its goals, but it only affects the individual case in the operational business sphere. In contrast to this, making a decision on a company's product or distribution policy is a strategic decision both in terms of the time horizon and the range of effects. Between these two levels, there is the tactical decision level, which is mostly concerned with controlling and implementing company goals and thus acts on a mid-term basis. This also includes, for example, the control of price developments and price adjustments (e.g., to successfully realize certain product policies).

The different decision levels require different data, which is also schematically sketched in Figure 2. The data serving as foundation for the decisions is differentiated in terms of its temporal point of reference and/or its data latency and the type of data sources. For example, strategic decisions require historic or time-period-related data, whereas operational decisions necessitate highly up-to-date and point-in-time-related data. The data latency (i.e., the delay between the occurrence of the event and the information extraction) must thus be quite low for operational decision-making. Opposed to this, the requirements posed to the data currency of strategic decisions are much lower. Due to the organization-wide range of effect of strategic decisions, the number of data sources to be considered is much higher than for operational decisions. The data sources on the strategic level also include unstructured data, such as text documents. In contrast, the data on the operational level is available in structured form, which makes it easy to automate decision-making processes. The high amount of information necessary for strategic decision-making usually means that the data is processed in aggregated form. On the operational decision level, in contrast, detailed data are absolutely required.

The three presented decision levels pose different requirements to the underlying data-warehouse system. In the context of a real-time system, the time horizon of decision levels and the resulting different needs in terms of data latency are particularly interesting here.

Changes in the ETL Processes

The extended application range of data warehouses as well as their inclusion on different decision levels incurs changes in the data provision processes, too. In a TDWI study from 2005 (White, 2005), 672 IT experts were surveyed on their usage of ETL (Extract, Transformation, Load), EAI (Enterprise Application Integration) and EII tools (Enterprise Information Integration). Part of this survey was, among other things, a question on the use of ETL in enterprises. For this purpose, the ETL process was differentiated into three categories: classic batch ETL processing, change-data-capture ETL (CDC-ETL) and online ETL (also known as real-time ETL or trickle-feed ETL). The latter describes a push-based propagation of changes into the data-warehouse system, whereas CDC-ETL only refers to the use of techniques that can detect changes (timestamp-, trigger-based approaches etc.). Amongst the interviewees, 57% mentioned a high degree of usage of batch ETL in their enterprises. When asked about the "high" usage in the next two years, the number only rose to 58%. On the one hand, this shows the high relevance of batch ETL, but on the other hand, this also indicates an already existing saturation for these processing semantics in enterprises.

Another picture emerges for the categories change-data-capture ETL and online ETL: in 2005, the degree of high usage was only 16% and 6%, respectively. In terms of estimated trends for the next two years, these values rose to 36% and 23%, respectively. The combination of the two categories "medium" and "high" for online ETL in the next two years leads to a value of 55%. This shows the clear trend towards online ETL and the inherent growing need for real-time analyses in enterprises.

Data-Warehouse Workload

The previous three sections showed that—in terms of both the update workloads and the query workloads of data-warehouse systems—quite some changes have happened over the last years. Continuously increasing data freshness requirements necessitate the continuous updating of the data warehouse via so-called online ETL or real-time ETL. The classic batch-oriented load processes are not replaced by this though, but they still have their reason of existence, since not all data in a data warehouse necessitate low latency times. With regard to queries, there are different applications that can be classified into different decision levels and thus pose various requirements to the data freshness. A Gartner study from 2008 (Gartner, 2008) confirms these trends again. In this study, the heterogeneity of today's data-warehouse workloads is described as the biggest challenge for database providers over the next three years.

The Concept of Real Time in the Data-Warehouse Context

For data-warehouse systems, which address the demand for highly up-to-date data, the term *real-time data warehouse* has been established in available literature, but it does not have much in common with the classic real-time concept. In general, a computer system is described as real-time-capable if it is guaranteed that results can be computed within fixed time intervals. In this context, the predictability (i.e., the question of when a result can be delivered) is particularly interesting. The system's performance remains a secondary aspect. This represents a clear contrast to the interpretation of the term *real-time* in the context of data warehouses. Here, the term *real-time* means that changes in the real world or in the modeled world are mapped to the data warehouse in a timely fashion. To achieve this, the data acquisition process and the insertion of updates as well as the query processing have to be implemented with the necessary performance. This also applies to the information back-flow in case of closed-loop architectures, such as those given in *Active Data Warehouses*.

Adding real-time functionality to a data-warehouse system—in the classic sense—creates miscellaneous difficulties: On the one hand, changes must be applied both to the source systems and to the data warehouse within one transaction. In loosely coupled data-warehouse systems, this is only possible via distributed transaction protocols, but those lead to long write locks on the source systems. The data acquisition process in data warehouses is, therefore, decoupled from the source systems or happens asynchronously. Another problem is posed by the response times of queries. The query optimizers used in relational database systems only return estimated costs and/or query times that cannot be guaranteed. To provide guarantees, real-time databases are required, which have their own research field due to the variety of open challenges that still have to be tackled (Ramamritham, 2004).

These aspects shall not be considered any further here. Instead, the main focus lies on the integration of highly up-to-date data in the data-warehouse system while preserving the classic data-warehouse functionality. Due to the ambiguity of the term *real-time*, available literature also uses the terms *near-real-time, right-time, on-time* or *living data warehouses*.

The Architecture of a Real-Time Data Warehouse

The fundamental differences in comparison to the classic architecture are found in the shorter update cycles on the one hand and in the query accesses on the other hand. The latter are not restricted to data marts here but may occur during any given process step in the data refinement process. Instead of following the previously used batch-oriented processing approach for updates, which keeps

queries and updates clearly separated from one another, the context of real-time data warehouses necessitates the simultaneous processing of read and write transactions. The functionality of the data integration process itself remains unchanged though. In (Inmon, 2005), Bill Inmon described the importance of the integration as follows:

"There is no point in bringing data ... into the data warehouse environment without integrating it. If the data arrives at the data warehouse in an unintegrated state, it cannot be used to support a corporate view of data. And a corporate view of data is one of the essences of the architected environment."

This means that both the demand for highly up-to-date data must be addressed and the classic added value of a data warehouse (as an integrated, stable data base) must be preserved. The users of a real-time data warehouse are aware of the data's volatility and may access specific data that has not yet been fully integrated and refined in order to meet the demand for highly up-to-date data. Data warehouse queries are annotated with the respective requirements and will be transparently forwarded to the individual process steps by a query layer (see Figure 3). This assumes the existence of the respective rewrite mechanisms for queries.

In order to guarantee the data stability demanded by data warehouses, a new data layer that is decoupled from the continuously updated real-time data warehouse is required as well. In Figure 3, this is shown as the reporting layer. The reporting layer, as the last step in the data production process, is also served by the query layer, which means that queries with the respective requirements for data stability (e.g., for reporting purposes) will automatically be forwarded to this step.

Figure 3. Architecture of a real-time data warehouse

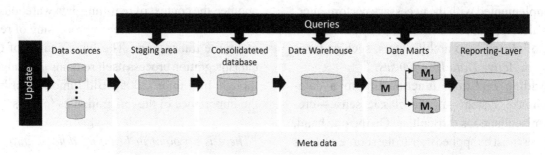

Requirements for Real-Time Data Warehouses

Based on the extended data-warehouse concept, as introduced in the previous section, the detailed requirements for real-time data warehouses as well as existing research work and techniques will be analyzed in the following.

Maximizing the Data Freshness

Real-time functionality of a data-warehouse system refers to the capability to quickly integrate data into the data warehouse and to transform the data into formats suitable for analyses. The process from the occurrence of an event to the resulting decision and its implementation is divided into five steps, where each step slightly delays the process. The first step is the data modification (in the context of data-warehouse systems, this refers to the ETL and the data production process, respectively). The temporal delay introduced by the ETL process is called *data delay*. A reduction in the data delay can be achieved, among other things, through the logical and physical optimization of the ETL processes and by the provision of sufficient hardware resources. If such measures are in place, significant reductions of the data delay, particularly through shorter load cycles, become possible. In this context, the batch-oriented load processes are replaced by a continuous stream of updates so that changes in the real world will be immediately propagated to the data warehouse.

Such update semantics allow for high data freshness but stand in contrast to the query latency and the data stability, as shown in Figure 4. However, the application analysis in the previous sections demonstrated that data-warehouse workloads are rather heterogeneously structured in terms of the data freshness requirements. This means that, regarding the relevance of an update, we find a certain gradation that may be used to determine the prioritization and the workflows. In order to express the degree of required data freshness on the part of the application, we need a user or workload model (Thiele, 2009).

Changed Data Capture

With regard to a real-time-capable architecture, source systems must meet several requirements: On the one hand, they must account for the need for faster visibility of data changes in the data-warehouse system by providing data net changes. Since each individual change is propagated to the data warehouse, this must be supported by the source system. From the perspective of supporting the extraction process, so-called *replication sources* or *active sources* should be preferred, since they propagate changes to the data-warehouse system on their own. This corresponds to the paradigm of the push-based propagation of data changes, which is a fundamental assumption in the context

Figure 4. Requirements for real-time data warehouses

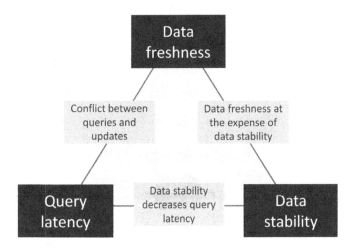

of real-time-capable data-warehouse systems. For less supportive source systems, this feature could be emulated by implementing an intermediate layer. In the case of snapshot-based data sources, we would have to compare two successive snapshots and then derive the data changes from this comparison. The required efforts, however, may significantly delay the extraction process, which would stand in clear contrast to the real-time requirements.

Optimizing ETL Processes

Up to now, a data warehouse's data has been committed in batch-based processes by relying on periodical snapshots of the operational sources. To support data integration in real-time, we need a paradigm change away from classic, pull-based batch processes towards continuous, push-based loading processes. Together with the update periodicity, we also need to change the ETL processes specialized in processing mass data in favor of stream-based processing.

Here, work on the logical optimization should be mentioned, which mostly focuses on restructuring ETL processes in order to minimize the cardinalities (Simitsis, 2005). On the other

hand, physical optimization is important, such as the insertion of artificial sorting operators (Tziovara, 2007) and the development of special non-blocking operators such as the mesh-join (Polyzotis, 2008) that support push-based processing semantics.

Another research area in the context of ETL processes focuses on the incremental loading of the data warehouse. For this purpose, we need to derive so-called incremental load jobs from the already existing ETL processes (Jörg, 2008; Jörg, 2009).

In order to resolve the conflict between many writing and long-running reading transactions in real-time data warehouses, the approach of isolated external caches or real-time partitions is used rather often (Thomsen, 2008). Updates write their modifications into the external cache to avoid the update-query contention problem in the data warehouse. Queries that require the real-time information are partially or completely redirected to the external cache.

In the classic data-warehouse reference architecture, there is a separation between the data warehouse and the operational data store in order to handle the different data freshness requirements. Thus, the historic data is separated from defined

Figure 5. Information provision process according to (Finger, 2006)

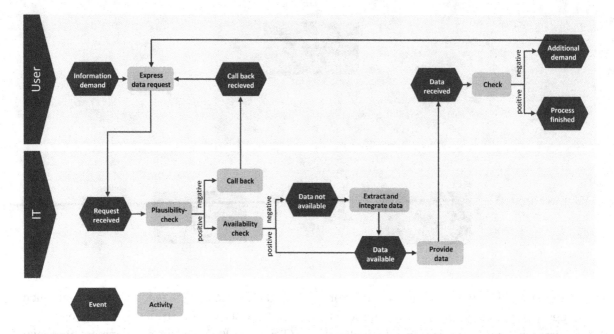

data ranges of high freshness. A prerequisite for this is that the data ranges needing to comply with special freshness requirements must be known during the development stage. However, we cannot guarantee the data freshness for arbitrary ad-hoc queries. Thus, we speak of a generalized approach of a real-time data-warehouse system in which the same data production process is applied to all data, and the prioritization is only decided at runtime or at the data production time, respectively.

Minimizing the Query Latency

In the second step in Figure 4, we formulate queries in order to derive information from the data. The latency incurred by the database system's query processing step is called *information delay* which is caused by the execution of queries and updates. In order to solve the conflict between data freshness and query latency (shown in Figure 4), we must extend the user model introduced in the previous section. Aside from the required data freshness, the

user must also be enabled to express the desired query latency. This means that updates must be prioritized in such a way that, on the one hand, the data freshness will be maximized and on the other hand, the query latency will be minimized. Since the two criteria cannot be optimized independent of one another, we get a multi-criteria optimization problem (Thiele, 2009).

Steps 3 to 5 in Figure 5 are fundamentally defined or delayed by human interaction and will thus not be considered any further.

The increasing requirements for data analysis systems have resulted in various architectural approaches over the last years. The most important techniques—parallelization, use of special hardware, and massive employment of the main memory—and some representatives of such approaches will be presented in the next paragraphs.

Parallelization

Another important approach towards achieving good response times in spite of rising numbers of queries and increasing data volumes is given by the parallelization of DBMS architectures. Here, we differentiate the following three approaches: Shared-Memory, Shared-Disk and Shared-Nothing. The simplest but also the least effective approach is the shared-memory architecture (e.g., Microsoft SQL Server[2]): All processors share a common main- and disk-memory, which simplifies the implementation of these systems, since there is no need for distributed lock protocols; at the same time though, this represents the biggest limitation. Since all processors must share the same bus for I/O operations and memory accesses, these systems are hardly scalable. Similar restrictions are imposed on the shared-disk architecture. Independent processing nodes, each with its own main memory, access a common disk-memory. Since there are no common main-memory ranges, we need distributed lock mechanisms, but with increasing numbers of processing nodes, these become a bottleneck for the whole system. Oracle RAC[3] is one example for such architectures. The most scalable of these approaches is the shared-nothing architecture, also known as massively-parallel-processing architecture (short MPP architecture). In this architecture, all processing nodes that are connected via LAN have their own hard-disk memory. The data tables are horizontally partitioned and distributed amongst the processing nodes. Buffers and lock tables are kept locally for each processing node and will thus never become a bottleneck. Known representatives of this architecture are, for example, Teradata[4], Netazza[5] and Greenplum[6]. MPP systems gain in additional interest when using simple commodity hardware, which allows the more cost-efficient development of high-performance systems.

Hardware Acceleration

Another path is chosen by systems that accelerate database operations via using special and often proprietary hardware. For example, Xtreme Data Appliance[7] uses main boards with two sockets and one standard processor extended by an FPGA chip (Field Programmable Gate Array). The FPGA chip serves to accelerate core routines during query processing. Netezza also uses FPGAs to complement the hard-disk controller for data preprocessing. Furthermore, there are research projects on the employment of special multi-core architectures, such as graphics card processors or IBM's Cell processor[8]. However, from the perspective of data-intensive data-warehouse applications, which are particularly limited by slow hard-disk access, main-memory-oriented approaches are especially interesting and will thus be described in the next section.

Main-Memory Databases

The optimization of data-warehouse queries achieved, above all, by reducing the I/O efforts. On the part of the algorithms and software, this is made possible particularly through the materialization of aggregations, the reduction of intermediate results through the optimizer, column-oriented storage, compression, etc. On the part of the hardware, the I/O efforts can be reduced through the extensive use of the main memory, by fully storing the data in the cache, thus making hard-disk accesses obsolete. By employing compression algorithms that allow a reduction of the data volume by a factor of 5-10, it is possible to store even very large databases completely in the main memory. For even higher requirements, the use of a shared-nothing architecture for main-memory databases allows for almost endless scalability (e.g., SAP BI Accelerator[9]). Another advantage of main-memory DBMS is given by the fact that access structures have been left out, which results in relatively constant and predictable response times. Aside from the stand-alone main-memory databases, there are also main-memory caches such as IBM solidDB Universal Cache[10] and Oracle In-Memory Database Cache[11]; these complement relational databases.

While classic database systems are particularly dominated by I/O operations, main-memory databases find their resource limits in the CPU. The special hardware architectures introduced in the previous section are thus a central component of many main-memory databases as well.

Scheduling in Mixed Workloads

In OLAP or BI application the processing time for individual queries can differ by several orders of magnitude. For example, in (Mehta, 2009), a number of practical workloads were evaluated and differences in the query runtime by a factor of 10,000 were detected. The distribution of the processing times for such workloads is thus described as *heavy-tailed*. Since the computation of the response time also considers the query's own processing time, the average response time is too blurry for heavy-tailed workloads and not fair from the user's perspective. That is to say, if a user is aware of the complexity—and hence of the runtime—for the query in question, this user will also expect a proportionally higher response time. Query scheduling in the context of BI systems, in which we often find heavy-tailed workloads, were discussed in detail in (Krompass 2007; Krompass, 2009; Mehta, 2009). Required mechanisms for interrupting the query execution and resuming it at a later point in time were introduced in (Chaudhuri, 2007).

In (Thiele, 2009), the workflow scheduling aspect was extended such that, in addition to queries, updates will also be integrated into workflow schedules. Thereby, the query response time could be minimized and the freshness could be maximized at the same time.

Preserving the Data Stability

The application analysis in the previous sections showed that data-warehouse systems are employed in applications both for operational and for classic, strategic decision-making pro-

cesses. The push-based update semantics of a real-time data-warehouse system might increase the data freshness (as it is required in operational processes) but this poses a problem for strategic analyses. The continuous data changes that stand in contrast to the classic data-warehouse concept lead to many inconsistencies in analysis and/or reporting processes. Furthermore, we find many data-warehouse scenarios in which the data base is continuously modified since the data production cannot be homogenized due to operational workflows. The data evaluation, however, still follows the classic approach—on the level of tactical and strategic decision-making processes—and mostly generates standard reports. The demand for data stability stands in contrast to the need for data freshness, as shown in Figure 4. In terms of the query latency, however, the data stability is an advantage, since it provides the chance to pre-compute aggregations.

The necessary stability can be achieved by introducing an additional data layer that is decoupled from the real-time operation of the data-warehouse system; in the following, we will call this the reporting layer. Stability means, above all, that reporting-relevant data cannot change in uncontrolled fashion, but there are defined publication points. The integration of the reporting layer into the architecture of a real-time data warehouse is illustrated in Figure 3. The design, organization, and operation of this data layer are explained in more detail in (Thiele, 2006).

SITUATIONAL BI

In connection to real-time data warehouses, we often hear the term "Situational BI." The nature of situational data analyses in comparison to real-time data-warehouse systems is marked by the fact that the data sources to be used are not known to the data-warehouse operator in advance and has to be provided to the user in ad-hoc fashion. The call for the timely integration of new data sources, however, confronts today's data-warehouse architectures with a serious problem. Given the demand for high data quality and consistency, they are rather inflexible and may only be modified within well-defined development cycles.

At this point, two trends of recent years have driven the development towards situational BI solutions: the first of these is the increasing release of government or enterprise data stocks. For example, the US Web site data.gov already provides free access to the data of more than 100 institutions. This includes demographic information, weather and climate statistics, geological data, etc. The trend towards making data stocks publicly accessible is intentionally pushed forward by government initiatives (Open Government) such as E-Government 2.0[12] in Germany or the initiative i2010[13] on a European scale. Enterprises also follow this trend and make their data publicly available in order to gain added value through the combination with other services. As an example, we find Google's OpenSocial API[14], which provides programming interfaces for functions and contents of social networks.

The second trend that drives situational BI developments is found in the various Web services that have emerged in the context of Web 2.0 developments, which offer valuable opportunities for computer-assisted decision-support processes. The implementation of complex calculations, visualizations or semantic analyses of documents does not have to be performed by the analyst any longer but can be integrated into the data analysis with the help of simple service calls. For example, WolframAlpha[15], which is based on the software Mathematica, offers services to calculate mathematical expressions and to represent information. The service OpenCalais[16], developed by Thomsen Reuters, receives unstructured documents and extracts entities (people, organizations, products, etc.), facts, and events and then adds them as metadata to documents. In addition, a knowledge base is used to create associations to other documents. By doing so, documents can be transferred into a structured form and used for further data analyses. For the visualization of analysis results, a variety of services are available, such as IBM Manyeyes[17], Swivel[18] or iCharts[19].

To support situational data analyses, there are diverse methods and solutions both on an organizational and on a technical level. In the former case, this includes the improvement of the communication between the IT unit (service provider) and the individual departments (users) as well as the project management. On the technical level, so-called spreadmart solutions are used which is presented in the following. Later on we present a second approach, based on service-oriented architectures and mashups. Finally, we summarize the advantages and disadvantages of these different approaches and compare their impact on the project costs for both the IT unit and the individual departments.

Interaction Between the IT Unit and Other Departments

The successful operation of a data-warehouse system absolutely necessitates the integration of expert knowledge. Only the respective individual departments are able to formulate their contextual and operational requirements, which then have to be implemented by the IT unit. Such cooperation between the IT unit and other departments, however, often causes problems in practical scenarios, which is worsened by the current trend towards situational data analyses. In the following, the points of interaction between the IT unit and other departments are considered, and solution approaches for optimizing workflows during the data-warehouse project management are presented.

Information Provision Process

Enterprises usually have organizationally distinguished departments that are catered by a central IT unit with the role of a service provider. Ideally, the individual departments state their requirements to the IT unit in the form of projects to be implemented within a certain timeframe. If the IT unit's data acquisition processes or development cycles, respectively, are too slow, this often leads to development activities by the individual departments themselves – without any participation of the IT unit. Such solo-developments foster the emergence of so-called data silos, which introduce unnecessary redundancy regarding the data storage and the loading or extraction processes.

The complete information provision process is illustrated in Figure 5. The first step consists of a data request with the goal to specify the individual department's information needs. The IT unit receives all requests and verifies their structural plausibility. In case of any ambiguities, further clarification by the respective department is required. Once the plausibility check has finished, the availability of the requested information is checked. The potential non-existence of information may have several causes: On the one hand, derived information may be missing and would have to be re-calculated. On the other hand, missing base information can be a root cause, which means that additional extractors and loading processes would have to be defined. In both cases, the integration of the data acquisition into existing data production processes is required. As soon as the needed data is available, the departments can verify its completeness and its match with the requirements. If additional information needs arise, a new data query must be formulated.

From the process description, it becomes apparent that the information provision process may occasionally be subject to significant complications and resulting delays. In the next section, these will be described in more detail, and recommendations on appropriate assignments of competencies to departments will be derived.

Resource Requirements and Distribution of Competencies

We can look at the interests and resources involved in the development of new data-warehouse applications from two perspectives. From the perspective of the individual departments, most resource requirements are driven by the necessity for an extensive specification of the departmental logics to be implemented, which is a prerequisite for a functional solution to be delivered by the IT unit. If the specification is incomplete or inconsistent, this will result in additional iteration steps, which then again causes additional overhead. Further costs are incurred by having to verify the data delivered by the IT unit in order to guarantee their technical accuracy. If the departments' requirements are subject to frequent changes—which is the case for situational analysis scenarios—the specification and verification costs will be multiplied.

As the operator of a data warehouse, the IT unit has the role of a service provider for the individual departments and is obliged to provide them with data and services according to certain defined service-level agreements. Thus, any change requests have to be implemented following systematic and standardized procedural models. In particular, already existing data must not be changed, and data production processes already in place must not be delayed beyond the period specified in the service-level agreements. Furthermore, the IT unit aims to operate the data warehouse in a cost-efficient way and thus, automated processes tend to be employed. The development efforts needed to automate data production processes is also in conflict with situational data analyses.

When implementing short-term data requirements, the IT unit—or the communication structure between the IT unit and the individual departments—is often organized too strictly. Alternatively, one should decide on a case-by-case basis which competencies to assign to which units. This decision can be made with the help of the following four criteria:

- Frequency of changes to the departments' requirements
- Possibility to automate processes and/or degree of interaction with the departments
- General validity of the data and processes (for a group of different departments)
- Legal warranties regarding the operation and the data quality.

Depending on the emphasis given to these different criteria, the competencies for data extraction, integration and management as well as for information retrieval and access to information have to be assigned appropriately to the IT unit and the departments.

Competence Centers

Aside from the optimal distribution of responsibilities to the IT unit and the departments, an improvement of the communication between these two organizational units is needed as well. For this purpose (Strange, 2003) was the first to suggest the creation of so-called *BI Competence Centers* (short BICC) as a link between the IT unit and all the departments. These centers are occupied by staff members both from the IT unit and from the individual departments, and they formulate the organization's BI strategy. In particular, this includes the proactive provision of data and/or the establishment of necessary infrastructures. A competence center is the first point of contact for the departments when retrieving information and it monitors the compliance with process standards.

The information retrieval process is significantly sped up through the creation of a competence center, since communication structures are improved and the information requirements can be planned in a strategic and predictive fashion. For situational data analyses, the competence center is thus a very important factor for success.

Spreadmart Solutions

If a department considers the information provision process too tedious or too expensive in terms of its suitability to support situational data analyses, this often results in individual solutions of the respective departments, which are referred to as *spreadmarts* in the available literature. In a TDWI study (Eckerson, 2008) these were defined as follows:

"A spreadmart is a reporting or analysis system running on a desktop database (e.g., spreadsheet, Access database, or dashboard) that is created and maintained by an individual or group that performs all the tasks normally done by a data mart or data warehouse, such as extracting, transforming, and formatting data as well as defining metrics, submitting queries, and formatting and publishing reports to others. Also known as data shadow systems, human data warehouses, or IT shadow systems."

However, such spreadmart solutions come with high risks. In particular, the quality and consistency of analyses generated with the help of spreadmarts cannot be guaranteed. Different departments use different calendar definitions, naming conventions, and calculations for their data analyses, which leads to inconsistent views on the data. The spreadmarts' lack of compliance with IT standards means that the data generated with them is less reliable. These errors are increased when deriving new spreadmarts from existing spreadmarts. Furthermore, the data integration and refinement are not part of the business analysis unit's tasks, which incurs further costs and time expenses for the departments. In (Eckerson, 2008), a survey illustrated that business analysts spend as much as 40% of their time on the creation of spreadmarts.

Despite the mentioned risks, spreadmarts are used in more than 90% of all organizations (Eckerson, 2008). One of the reasons – the delay in the information retrieval process – was mentioned above. Further causes that the TDWI study (Eckerson, 2008) identifies as particularly relevant include the high degree of autonomy, the lower costs, the desire to protect interests, and the lack of suitable analysis tools within the IT unit. Thus, spreadmart solutions do have their raison d'être, but they should not be employed for storing and managing central enterprise data. Instead, their usage should be restricted to data analyses and decision-support processes. Within the context of competence centers, the existing spreadmarts should be reviewed and used as the foundation to analyze the departments' requirements. The transformation and business rules determined through such procedure will then have to be integrated into data production processes.

Spreadmart Tools

One of the main reasons for the low costs of spreadmart solutions is found in the tools used for their creation. The three tools used most often, according to (Eckerson, 2008), are Microsoft Excel (with 41%), Microsoft Access (with 11%) and Microsoft Powerpoint (with 9%), which can be found on most office computers and, hence, do not incur any additional costs. The mightiness of these three tools, however, is rather limited. Therefore, for larger data volumes, one finds main-memory-based analysis tools, such as IBM Cognos TM1[20], QlikTech Qlikview[21], Tableau Desktop[22], Panoratio PANOSight[23], Comma Soft Infonea Cube[24], HumanIT InfoZoom[25], and PivotLink[26], which are all capable of analyzing several gigabytes of datasets on ordinary desktop computers. Particular focus should be given to Microsoft's PowerPivot for Excel 2010[27] (project name "Gemini"). PowerPivot integrates main-memory-based analysis methods in Excel and allows users to integrate, cleanse and analyze data as well as to create reports in their usual spreadsheet environment. Considering the general availability of Excel in enterprises and the already existing Excel know-how, an alarming increase in the number of spreadmart solutions in the near future may have to be expected.

Analytical Mashups and Service-Oriented Architectures

The goal of mashups is to combine existing data and services from a variety of sources in order to create new contents from them. Hence, the success of the mashup approach is closely tied to the availability of data and services. In this context, enterprise-internal information are not the only relevant source for mashup data analyses – on the contrary, external contents tend to be even more important.

The isolated operation of spreadmart solutions is counterproductive in terms of an enterprise-wide BI strategy. Important analysis results and insights reside within the spheres of the spreadmart operators' units, which means that valuable knowledge remains unused and often redundant analysis tasks have to be performed. Competence centers may provide some relief, but the range of different spreadmart tools as well as the lacking interface compatibility severely restrict the reusability of information.

The aspect of distributing data and staff competencies leads to the approach to combine the data-warehouse concept with service-oriented architectures (short SOA). The fundamental idea here is to provide the data-warehouse data as services that may be combined freely by the individual departments. Subsequently, the derived analysis results will also be provided as services again. As a means for the composition of services, the mashup concept has emerged over the last years. The use of mashups and service-oriented architectures to develop situational BI solutions is topic of the following sections. In particular, a discussion of current trends and developments will emphasize the added value of this approach in comparison to spreadmart-based solutions.

Analytical Mashups

Mashups represent a type of interactive Web applications that combine existing contents and services in order to offer new and innovative services. A typical example is the linking of news items with Google Maps to support the recipient with additional information on the location of the news event. This approach can be developed further and employed for data integration and analysis tasks in the form of so-called *analytical mashups*.

During a meeting of analysts of market research specialist Gartner in January 2009 (Gartner 2009), the following assumptions and predictions were made:

- By 2010, 20% of all organizations will have industry-specific analysis applications integrated into their BI portfolios via "Software as a Service" (SAAS) by default.
- In 2009, the collaborative decision-making will be established as new product category and combine social software with BI platform functionality.
- By 2012, one third of all analysis applications applied to business processes will be published in the form of mashups.

This stresses the importance of mashup technologies in the context of data-warehouse and BI environments and indicates another aspect of BI applications: While data analysis applications have been developed and operated by individual analysts so far, this will become a collaborative

process in the future. Web technologies, service-oriented architectures and mashups offer perfect conditions for this.

Distinction from Classic ETL

The ETL processes (extraction, transformation, loading) used for classic data integration are not replaced by analytical mashups though. While ETL addresses the scalable integration of mass data for persistent applications, the approach of analytical mashups focuses on situational data analyses. Due to the restricted amount of data—and also considering the temporal volatility of situational analyses—non-functional aspects such as performance and scalability only play a minor role for analytical mashups. Also, the requirements posed to the quality of mashup data are usually lower.

In general, the three-step ETL process model—consisting of extracting, transforming and loading the data—can be transferred to the mashup approach. In the context of mashups, these three steps are referred to as *fetch*, *shape* and *pick*. The fetch step describes the fetching of data by using internal or external services, which does not require any complex extraction logics as it is the case for ETL processes. The shape step refers to a weaker form of the transformation process, since it does not require any extensive cleansing steps or a transformation into a data-warehouse schema. No complex loading procedures are required, but the user can work with (i.e., pick) the data right away instead of having to store them in target databases. To summarize, ETL can be considered the IT-driven approach for data integration, while analytical mashups are driven by the individual departments.

The Role of SOA in the Mashup Development

The term SOA describes a concept for aligning an enterprise's IT environment with its business processes. This is achieved by providing loosely coupled atomic services that can be flexibly combined with one another. From a technical perspective, a SOA can be implemented with the help of any arbitrary service-based architecture. In practice, however, the three standards SOAP, WSDL and UDDI have come to dominate the scene. There, SOAP is used as the communication protocol between services, WSDL is the language to describe the services' interfaces, and UDDI is the index service for registering and localizing services.

Transferred to the vision of a mashup development platform, the data of a data warehouse have to be provided as data services and can then be employed by users of this platform for their data analyses. This type of usage is significantly different from the classic usage of data-warehouse data. The majority of data-warehouse users are only provided with pre-computed reports in different file formats. Only a minority of the users are allowed to directly access the data warehouse and/or the data marts. The usage of data in the form of services by a large and mostly anonymous user group thus leads to the following problems:

- Optimization: Given the arbitrary and unpredictable query behavior, the targeted optimization of the data warehouse is barely possible at all.
- Erroneous data usage: In contrast to classic database users, who are familiar with the data schema and the data itself, external users may misinterpret the data model and use the data in incorrect or inappropriate ways.
- Maintainability: Modifications on the database schema may have unexpected effects on applications on top of it.
- Security: When using data services, authorization is required.

A pragmatic solution that addresses these problems is to encapsulate and to provide only pre-defined queries as services. However, this stands in clear conflict with the idea behind situational data analyses. The aspect of maintainability does not pose any problems for short-lived analyses. Only when violating the philosophy behind situational data analyses by using mashups for long-term analysis projects will their maintenance have to be considered.

Organizational Classification of a Mashup Platform

A data-warehouse architecture that integrates a mashup platform while ensuring the organizational separation of IT unit, departments and competence centers at the same time is illustrated in Figure 6. The IT unit's responsibility is centered on the technical provision of the full infrastructure of the data warehouse and the mashup platform. In terms of the data provision, the IT unit is responsible for the data warehouse and the mostly application-neutral IT data marts. The application-specific departmental data marts are defined by a competence center consisting of IT unit and departmental staff members. The individual departments are still provided with pre-defined reports or cubes for strategic analyses (not shown in Figure 6). If a department requires situational data analyses, this is implemented with the help of the mashup development platform. The internal data services used for this purpose are provided by the IT unit and the competence center. As the operator of the mashup platform, the IT unit may transfer particularly frequently requested mashups or parts of mashups into the regular data production process, as long as this is agreed upon with the competence center.

The users of the mashup platform must be aware of the fact that the guarantees on the data consistency (structural guarantees) and on the operation (operational guarantees in Figure 6) will become weaker with increasing influence of the departments and decreasing influence of the IT unit.

Figure 6. Integration of the mashup platform into a DWH architecture

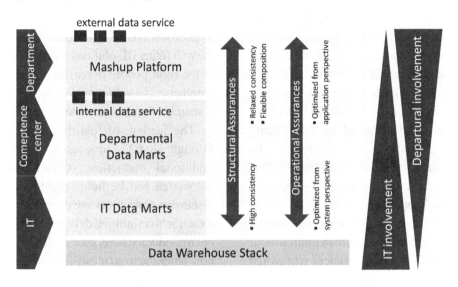

Figure 7. Implementation costs in dependence on the dynamics of the requirements

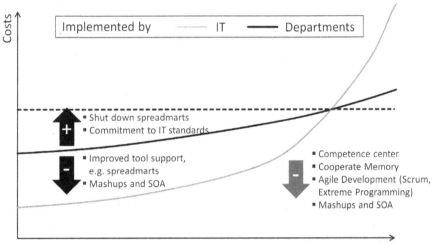

Cost Comparison of Tools and Methods

In a last step, the concepts and solutions for implementing situational data analyses, as described in this section, will be evaluated in a cost comparison. For this purpose, Figure 7 lists the costs for implementing a data analysis application in dependence on the dynamics of the requirements.

In a static environment, the development costs for the IT unit are always lower than for the individual departments without the respective competencies. This advantage, however, slowly vanishes with increasing dynamics of the requirements until the point is reached when the individual department can develop the required application in a cheaper way than the IT unit could. It should be noted,

303

though, that this point can be reached even sooner from the subjective perspective of the department.

Aside from the cost-efficient operation, the main goal of any IT unit is to offer its services at much lower costs compared to the individual departments (i.e., IT units attempt to lower the intersection point in Figure 7). On the part of the IT unit, this can be achieved by introducing stricter process standards that will have to be considered for each individual development. One example would be the requirement to shut down all spreadmarts. However, from an overall enterprise's perspective, higher IT standards do not represent the ideal way. Instead, the IT unit should also be able to act in a cost-efficient way when implementing analysis applications under quickly changing requirements. The organizational form of competence centers to improve the communication between departments and the IT unit contributes to this goal. Also, shortening and optimizing development processes by applying methods from the agile software development field, such as the *scrum* process model, may lower the IT costs. Now, the expenses on the part of the individual departments are more and more often lowered, too, through increasing improvements in the support for various tools, and thus, they stand in clear competition with the IT unit developments. The implementation of data analysis projects by applying mashup technology must be regarded neutrally in terms of costs, since it contributes to the optimization of process flows both for the IT unit and for the individual departments.

CONCLUSION

Over the last years business intelligence has been gradually growing in importance. In the past, BI was restricted to mathematicians and analysts only, for which expensive statistical tools had to be acquired. With the steadily improvement of web technologies and the advent of rich internet applications, BI is now spreading to nearly every part of organizations and enables nearly everybody to gain new business insights. So with the help of the web future BI solutions will deliver information to the right people in real-time across the whole enterprise. To achieve this objective many open research questions need to be solved.

The feeding of real-time data into a DWH through an ETL process is very similar to a traditional production process. Both should be automated and be lightweight as possible (i.e., disburden from blocking operators or human interaction to minimize delays). Some research has been conducted here, such as the development of a non-blocking join (mesh-join) to derive surrogate keys (Polyzotis 2008).

Whereas in traditional production processes for consumer goods it does not make sense to deliver a premature good, in ETL processes which handle the production of data it should be made possible to access data during the process itself. Today this is very challenging since the data model in the source OLTP system and in the data warehouse and OLAP system differs strongly from each other. Hence, a homogeneous enterprise wide data model would enable the usage of data during data integration and aggregation and thereby allow data access in a real-time manner.

The co-existence of strategic and operational support in a real-time data warehouse requires new solutions regarding the data production management and scheduling. On the part of the users of a real-time DWH this requires the formalization of requirements to the system (e.g. an analyst who conducts complex data mining analyses has lower currency requirements compared to an user who is part of an operational process). These requirements need to be determined query or session wise and have to be aligned with the data production process. In order to do so, there must be a common scheduling for updates and queries according to the user-specified needs. Additionally, the query processing has to be preemptive to stop and restart long-running queries.

Whereas first steps in these direction have been made in (Chauduri, 2007) and (Thiele, 2009), the query processing and scheduling of transactions in real-time data warehouse landscapes are still open research question.

Analytical mashups as proposed here in the chapter should enable nontechnical users to solve typical BI tasks, just using their browser and an analytical mashup platform provided by the IT. By lowering the responsibilities of IT in this way the paradigm of analytical mashups reduces the time to deliver new BI functionality to end-users and allows the IT and the departments to concentrate on their very own skills. In order to fulfill this vision the IT needs to provide a collaborative mashup development platform including a rich set of mashup patterns, a collaborative environment, version control, monitoring capabilities, a billing model etc. Complex data models should be hidden from the user by applying a service-oriented middleware, semantic data integration techniques and a priori domain-specific modeling on the part of the IT. To provide an interactive user experiences there should be no distinction between design and runtime mode within a mashup platform which is a high burden especially if large data set are processed. A very important feature in terms of data quality and trustability of data will be the support of data lineage techniques within an analytical mashup platform. For this purpose already existing research on lineage in data warehouses (Cui, 2001) need to reviewed and adapted to the new context of lightweight data integration.

In practical scenarios, we currently find only a limited number of data-warehouse architectures that integrate data in real-time. However, various applications are available that can generate added value by integrating the data warehouse in operational processes. According to a Gartner study (Gassman, 2006), until 2010, about 30% of all BI functionalities will need data with a freshness of 15 minutes and less. The reasons for the hesitation in the development process are manifold. On the one hand, data-warehouse systems are extremely complex, which means that modifications of many components, such as the source systems, ETL systems, analysis tools, data representation etc., would be required in order to benefit from the integration of highly up-to-date data. Considering the high development costs in the data-warehouse sector, this represents too big of an obstacle. On the other hand, there are fears that the necessary modifications and further developments might negatively affect the data quality and integrity. In this regard, enterprises will have to take the next steps and improve their data-warehouse systems in accordance to the latest research developments.

REFERENCES

Anderson, C. (2007, August). The long tail: The future of entertainment is in the millions of niche markets at the shallow end of the bitstream. Wired Magazine, 12(10), 170-177. New York, NY: The Conde Nast Publications. ISSN 1059-1028

Brobst, S., & Rarey, J. (June 2003). *Five stages of data warehouse decision support evolution.* Retrieved from DSSResources.com

Chaudhuri, S., Kaushik, R., Pol, A., & Ramamurthy, R. (2007). Stop-and-restart style execution for long running decision support queries. In *VLDB '07: Proceedings of the 33rd international conference on Very Large Databases,* (pp. 735-745).

Cui, Y., & Widom, J. (2001). Lineage tracing for general data warehouse transformations. In *Proceedings of the 27th International Conference on Very Large Data Bases* (VLDB'01).

Eckerson, W. W., & Sherman, R. P. (2008). *Strategies for managing spreadmarts.* TDWI Research Report, 13.

Feinberg, D., & Beyer, M. A. (December 2008). *Magic quadrant for data warehouse database management systems.* (Gartner RAS Core Research Note G00163473).

Finger, R. (2006). BI-Betriebsmodelle auf dem Pruefstand. *BI-Spektrum*, 21-25.

Gassman, B., & Schlegel, K., & Beyer, M. A. (2006). *Survey shows BI users want fresher data.* Gartner Research, September 2006.

Inmon, W. H. (1999). *Building the operational data store.* New York, NY: John Wiley & Sons.

Jörg, T., & Dessloch, S. (2008, September). Towards generating ETL processes for incremental loading. *IDEAS, 2008,* 101–110. doi:10.1145/1451940.1451956

Jörg, T., & Dessloch, S. (March, 2009). *Formalizing ETL jobs for incremental loading of data warehouses.* In Datenbanksysteme in Business, Technologie und Web (BTW 2009), 13. Fachtagung des GI-Fachbereichs Datenbanken und Informationssysteme, (pp. 327-346).

Krompass, S., Kuno, H., Dayal, U., & Kemper, A. (2007). Dynamic workload management for very large data warehouses: Juggling feathers and bowling balls. In *VLDB '07: Proceedings of the 33rd International Conference on Very Large Databases,* (pp. 1105-1115).

Krompass, S., Kuno, H., Wiener, J. L., Wilkinson, K., Dayal, U., & Kemper, A. (2009). Managing long-running queries. In *EDBT '09: Proceedings of the 12th International Conference on Extending Database Technology,* (pp. 132-143). New York, NY, USA.

Mehta, A., Gupta, C., Wang, S., & Dayal, U. (March, 2009). rFEED: A mixed workload scheduler for enterprise data warehouses. In *ICDE '09: Proceedings of the 2009 IEEE International Conference on Data Engineering,* (pp. 1455-1458). Washington, DC, USA.

Pettey, C., & Stevens, H. (January 2009). *Gartner reveals five business intelligence predictions for 2009 and beyond.*

Polyzotis, N., Skiadopoulos, S., Vassiliadis, P., Simitsis, A., & Frantzell, N.-E. (2008). Meshing streaming updates with persistent data in an active data warehouse. *IEEE Transactions on Knowledge and Data Engineering, 20*(7), 976–991. doi:10.1109/TKDE.2008.27

Ramamritham, K., Son, S. H., & Dipippo, L. C. (2004). Real-time databases and data services. *Real-Time Systems, 28*(2-3), 179–215. doi:10.1023/B:TIME.0000045317.37980.a5

Simitsis, A., Vassiliadis, P., & Sellis, T. K. (2005). *Optimizing ETL processes in data warehouses.* International Conference on Data Engineering, (pp. 564-575).

Strange, K., & Hostmann, B. (2003). *BI competency center is core to BI success.* Gartner Research.

Thiele, M., Bader, A., & Lehner, W. (March 2009). Multi-objective scheduling for real-time data warehouses. In *Proceedings der 12. GI-Fachtagung für Datenbanksysteme in Business, Technology und Web* (BTW'09, Münster), (pp. 307-326).

Thiele, M., Bader, A., & Lehner, W. (2009, October). Multi-objective scheduling for real-time data warehouses. *Computer Science - . Research for Development, 23*(3).

Thiele, M., Fischer, U., & Lehner, W. (November 2007). Partition-based workload scheduling in living data warehouse environments. *Proceedings of the 10th ACM international workshop on Data warehousing and OLAP,* Lisbon, Portugal.

Thiele, M., Fischer, U., & Lehner, W. (2009, July). Partition-based workload scheduling in living data warehouse environments. *Information Systems, 34*(4-5), 382–399. doi:10.1016/j.is.2008.06.001

Thomsen, C., Pedersen, T. B., & Lehner, W. (2008). Rite: Providing on-demand data for right-time data warehousing. In *ICDE '08: Proceedings of the 2008 IEEE 24th International Conference on Data Engineering*, (pp. 456-465). Washington, DC: IEEE Computer Society.

Tziovara, V., Vassiliadis, P., & Simitsis, A. (2007). Deciding the physical implementation of ETL workflows. In *DOLAP '07: Proceedings of the ACM tenth international workshop on Data warehousing and OLAP*, (pp. 49-56). New York, NY: ACM.

Tziovara, V., Vassiliadis, P., & Simitsis, A. (November 2007). *Deciding the physical implementation of ETL workflows*. ACM Sixth International Workshop on Data Warehousing and OLAP, (pp. 49-56).

White, C. (2005). *Data integration: Using ETL, EAI, and EII tools to create an integrated enterprise*. A 101communications Publication.

ADDITIONAL READING

Berthold, H., Rösch, P., Zöller, S., Wortmann, F., Carenini, A., & Campbell, S. (2010). *An architecture for ad-hoc and collaborative business intelligence*. EDBT/ICDT Workshops.

Braumandl, R., Kemper, A., & Kossmann, D. (2003). Quality of service in an information economy. *ACM Transactions on Internet Technology*, *3*(4), 291–333. doi:10.1145/945846.945847

Cohen, J., Dolan, B., Dunlap, M., Hellerstein, J. M., & Welton, C. (August 2009). *MAD skills: new analysis practices for big data*. Proceedings of the VLDB Endowment, v.2 n.2.

Dieu, N., Dragusanu, A., Fabret, F., Llirbat, F., & Simon, E. (2009). *1,000 tables under the form*. Proceedings of the VLDB Endowment, Volume 2, Issue 2.

Golab, L., Johnson, T., & Shkapenyuk, V. (March, 2009). *Scheduling Updates in a Real-Time Stream Warehouse*. Proceedings of the 2009 IEEE International Conference on Data Engineering, p.1207-1210.

Inmon, W. H. (2005). *Building the Data Warehouse*. John Wiley & Sons, Inc., New York, NY, USA, 4 edition.

Santos, R. J., & Bernardino, J. (2009, September). Optimizing data warehouse loading procedures for enabling useful-time data warehousing. *IDEAS, 2009*, 292–29. doi:10.1145/1620432.1620464

Simitsis, A., Wilkinson, K., Castellanos, M., & Dayal, U. (2009). *QoX-driven ETL design: reducing the cost of ETL consulting engagements*. In SIGMOD '09: Proceedings of the 35th SIGMOD international conference on Management of data, pages 953-960, New York, NY, USA.

Thiele, M., Kiefer, T., & Lehner, W. (November 2009). *Cardinality Estimation in ETL Processes*. Proceedings of the 12th ACM international workshop on Data warehousing and OLAP (DOLAP'09, Hongkong, China).

Thiele, M., & Lehner, W. (August 2009). *Evaluation of Load Scheduling Strategies for Real-Time Data Warehouse Environments*. Proceedings of the 3rd International Workshop on Business Intelligence for the Real-Time Enterprise, BIRTE 2009, Lyon, France.

Umeshwar, D., Castellanos, M., Simitsis, A., & Wilkinson, K. (2009). Data integration flows for business intelligence. *EDBT, 2009*, 1–11.

KEY TERMS AND DEFINITIONS

Analytical Mashup: Mashups represent a genre of interactive Web applications that draw upon content retrieved from external and often unrelated data sources to create new and innovative services. From the traditional point of view, a mashup is a composition of content provided for human consumption rather than for further computerized processing. In this aspect, the classic mashups differ from so-called analytical mashups, where the focus lies on the ad-hoc data consolidation and integration.

BI Competence Center: A BI Competence Center, short BICC, is an enterprise-internal organizational structure that schedules, coordinates, and strategically refines all BI activities. BICCs are founded in order to address problems such as end-user dissatisfaction, blurred responsibilities, the uncoordinated coexistence of different partial BI systems, missing requirements management, etc.

Data Silo: A Data Silo is a separate database within an enterprise that is not part of the enterprise-wide administration. Due to the lack of visibility, the data stored in data silos is not available for inter-departmental or global data analyses.

Mixed BI Workloads: The processing time for queries in BI workloads is mixed. That means that the distribution of the processing times is heavy-tailed and typical differs by several orders of magnitude.

Real-Time Business Intelligence: Real-Time Business Intelligence refers to data analyses on both historic and highly up-to-date data. The goal is to minimize the existing latency times of real-time BI systems when integrating and analyzing data in order to meet the requirements of typical business applications.

Situational Business Intelligence: Situational Business Intelligence denotes a Data-Warehousing discipline in which the data sources to integrate are not known in advance but still have to be available without delay for analyses. In order to achieve this, the various business departments must be provided with suitable tools to handle the ad-hoc data integration themselves. Since the term "Real-Time" is misleading, the alternative term "Right-Time Business Intelligence" has been coined.

Spreadmart: A Spreadmart is an analysis system that is normally implemented and operated with standard office software (spreadsheets, Access databases). The creators and those who benefit from these systems are usually individual users or small user groups. Spreadmarts emerge when the business departments' needs (in terms of data freshness or scope) cannot be met completely by the data warehouse. Due to the isolated character of Spreadmarts, we also speak of Shadow Data Warehouses or Data Silos.

ENDNOTES

1 http://www.flightstats.com
2 http://www.microsoft.com/germany/sql/2008/default.mspx
3 http://www.oracle.com/lang/de/database/rac_home.html
4 http://www.teradata.com
5 http://www.netezza.com
6 http://www.greenplum.com
7 http://www.xtremedata.com
8 http://www.research.ibm.com/cell/
9 http://www.sap.com/germany/plattform/netweaver/fsc.epx
10 http://www-01.ibm.com/software/data/soliddb/universal-cache/
11 http://www.oracle.com/database/in-memory-database-cache.html
12 http://www.cio.bund.de/DE/E-Government/e-government_node.html
13 http://europa.eu/legislation_summaries/employment_and_social_policy
14 http://code.google.com/intl/de-DE/apis/opensocial
15 http://www.wolframalpha.com
16 http://www.opencalais.com
17 http://manyeyes.alphaworks.ibm.com/manyeyes
18 http://www.swivel.com
19 http://www.icharts.net

[20]   http://www-142.ibm.com/software/products/de/de/cognostm1

[21]   http://www.qlikview.com

[22]   http://www.tableausoftware.com/products/desktop

[23]   http://www.panoratio.com

[24]   http://www.comma-soft.com

[25]   http://www.infozoom.com

[26]   http://www.pivotlink.com

[27]   http://www.powerpivot.com

Chapter 14
Semantic Web Technologies for Business Intelligence

Rafael Berlanga
Universitat Jaume I, Spain

Oscar Romero
Universitat Politècnica de Catalunya, Spain

Alkis Simitsis
Hewlett-Packard Co, USA

Victoria Nebot
Universitat Jaume I, Spain

Torben Bach Pedersen
Aalborg University, Denmark

Alberto Abelló
Universitat Politècnica de Catalunya, Spain

María José Aramburu
Universitat Jaume I, Spain

ABSTRACT

This chapter describes the convergence of two of the most influential technologies in the last decade, namely business intelligence (BI) and the Semantic Web (SW). Business intelligence is used by almost any enterprise to derive important business-critical knowledge from both internal and (increasingly) external data. When using external data, most often found on the Web, the most important issue is knowing the precise semantics of the data. Without this, the results cannot be trusted. Here, Semantic Web technologies come to the rescue, as they allow semantics ranging from very simple to very complex to be specified for any web-available resource. SW technologies do not only support capturing the "passive" semantics, but also support active inference and reasoning on the data. The chapter first presents a motivating running example, followed by an introduction to the relevant SW foundation concepts. The chapter then goes on to survey the use of SW technologies for data integration, including semantic

DOI: 10.4018/978-1-61350-038-5.ch014

data annotation and semantics-aware extract, transform, and load processes (ETL). Next, the chapter describes the relationship of multidimensional (MD) models and SW technologies, including the relationship between MD models and SW formalisms, and the use of advanced SW reasoning functionality on MD models. Finally, the chapter describes in detail a number of directions for future research, including SW support for intelligent BI querying, using SW technologies for providing context to data warehouses, and scalability issues. The overall conclusion is that SW technologies are very relevant for the future of BI, but that several new developments are needed to reach the full potential.

INTRODUCTION

The semantic web (SW) has been conceived as a means to build semantic spaces over web-published contents so that web information can be effectively retrieved and processed by both humans and machines in a great variety of tasks. The definition of these semantic spaces can have many different facets: to provide common terminology (e.g., thesauri), to semantically link published information (e.g., linked data) and to provide further knowledge to allow reasoning (e.g,. logical axioms). The SW is still an open research area although many interesting outcomes have been attained during the last years. Thus, we will use the term "SW technologies" rather than Semantic Web in order to refer to these results, since they can be applied to numerous tasks not necessarily associated to the web.

Despite the successful results of SW area, they have been timidly used in the data warehouse community. Multidimensional models (MD) and online analytical processing technologies (OLAP) have been successfully applied within the database community for analysis purposes, but always under a well-controlled and structured scenario. However, the eruption of XML and other richer semi-structured formats like RDF has shifted the attention of the data warehouse community to a much more heterogeneous and open scenario than that of traditional BI applications. Currently no one questions the need of adding all this external information to the traditional corporate analysis processes. On the other hand, there is a strong

agreement in the community about bringing more semantics to the analytical processes. As data warehousing mainly involves the integration of disparate information sources, semantic issues are highly required for effectively discovering and merging data. These semantic issues are similar to those faced in the SW.

This chapter is aimed at giving a new perspective to the BI and the web, which is the main topic of the book. SW technologies have been recently applied to some BI tasks such as extract, transform, and load processes (ETL), MD design and validation, and so on. However, they are usually limited to traditional BI scenarios. In this chapter we also describe the SW technologies that can be useful in highly heterogeneous and open scenarios, and what are their strong and weak points.

As far as we know, this is the first review of the combination of SW and BI technologies. Given that there is a great interest within the BI area about analyzing web-published data, SW technologies seem to be a promising way to approach the involved semantic integration issues as well as new operational capabilities such as automatic classification and deductive reasoning over (integrated) data.

The chapter is organized as follows. First, we present a motivating scenario for combining BI and SW, including a running example. Second, the chapter introduces the relevant foundations of SW technologies, including the resource description format (RDF) and the ontology web language (OWL), standard reasoning services, and technologies for storing and querying semantic annotations. Third, the chapter describes how to use SW technologies for data integration, including how to perform semantic data annotation and the operation of semantics-aware ETL processes. Fourth, the chapter goes into the heartland of BI, namely multidimensional data models and their relation to SW technologies, including how SW formalisms can be used to capture MD models, and how reasoning services can be applied to perform advanced reasoning about the models and their properties. Fifth, the chapter describes directions for future research in the area, including intelligent querying, contextualizing of data warehouses, and scalability issues. The chapter is rounded off with an overall conclusion.

MOTIVATING SCENARIO AND RUNNING EXAMPLE

BI technology is aimed at gathering, transforming and summarizing available data from existing sources to generate analytical information suitable for decision making tasks. A typical BI scenario can be roughly structured into three layers:

- the data sources layer, which regards all the potential data of any nature (e.g., relational, object-oriented, semi-structured, and textual) that can help to fulfill the analysis goals,
- the integration layer, which is in charge of normalizing and cleansing the data gathered from the sources, as well as of storing it in an appropriate format for the subsequent analysis, and
- the analysis layer, which contains a series of tools for generating the information from the normalized data so that it will be presented to analysts.

The most successful approach to BI has been the combination of data warehousing (DW) and online analytical processing technologies (OLAP).

These approaches propose for the integration layer a special model, called multidimensional model, where factual data gathered from the data sources layer must be expressed in terms of numerical measures and categorical dimensions. The semantics of this model consists of representing any interesting observation of the domain (measures) at its context (dimensions). The typical processes in charge of translating data from the data sources layer to the integration layer are called ETL processes (extract, load, and transform). In this chapter we will focus on this kind of architecture, although most topics treated in it can be also applied to other integration architectures such as service-oriented ones.

For illustrating the concepts introduced in this chapter, we will use the BI scenario of a consortium of EU car rental companies. This consortium is interested in generating and sharing strategic information about the sector so that they can improve their respective market strategies. In this scenario, each partner is fully autonomous in the design of their IT infrastructures, while at the same time requiring minimal overhead when sharing data and documentation of interest. As a result, data sources are prone to diverge in almost all the aspects: syntactic, linguistic and semantic ones. Notice that in this scenario, the main issue is about the integration of data formats, schemas, vocabularies, and so on. However, there are also many aspects in common for all the partners, mainly the domain (rent-a-car) and the business strategic goals they are interested in. These agreements are gathered in a conceptual model, which is the base of the intended data warehouse (see Figure 1). This conceptual model captures the main elements of the scenario required by analysts, and it will guide the data warehouse design and implementation process.

Before introducing the technical aspects of the SW technology, we discuss the role of knowledge-based representations in this scenario. In fact, for integration issues we need to define the agreed representations of the components involved in the scenario, namely:

Figure 1. A conceptual model for the proposed BI scenario

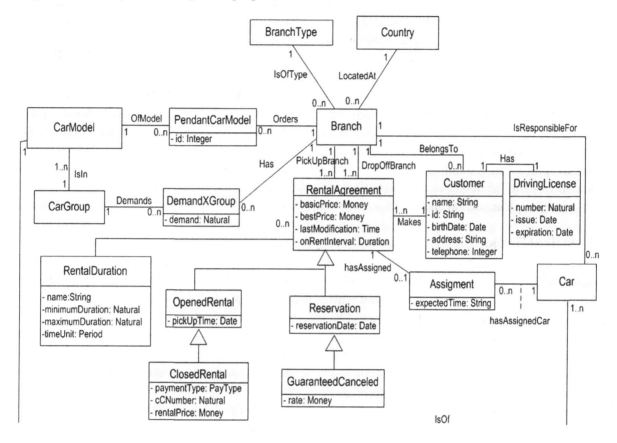

- Domain Ontology (DO), which describes the elements that characterize the business topics and subjects. In the example: cars, companies, locations, etc. Large taxonomies of products, taxonomies and generic business rules fall into this category.
- Technical Ontologies (TO), which describe the elements that characterize the information technology objects, mainly the schemas of the three BI layers. Logic representations of conceptual schemas fall into this category.
- Business Ontologies (BO), which describe the elements that characterize the business models, such as the semantics of the measures (Diamantini & Potena, 2008), their relation to strategic goals, etc. Also ontologies derived from the eXtensible Business Reporting Language (XBRL) fall within this category.

Following our running example, in Figure 1 yellow-colored classes correspond to knowledge pertaining to the DO elements, whereas blue-colored classes belong to TO elements, which are associated to the intended data warehouse. The business ontology will describe both the consortium's business activities and the BI measures used in their strategic goals (e.g., Return on Investment, Fraudulent Ratio, and so on). The other classes of the conceptual model can be represented either as properties between ontology classes (e.g. PendantCarModel) or ontology classes (e.g. RentalDuration).

SEMANTIC WEB FOUNDATIONS

This section covers the foundations of the Semantic Web, introducing the main concepts through the running example. First, we give a brief introduction of the semantic web technology origins and motivations. Second, we introduce the two main representation formalisms that are being used nowadays for semantic annotations, and their inference capabilities and limitations. Finally, we introduce the most widely used language for querying Semantic Web data, SPARQL, where we explain the structure, give examples, and discuss BI-related extensions. We then introduce the various approaches to building specialized RDF data stores, called triple-stores, including schema design and implementation choices.

Historical Background

Semantic Web technology is aimed at providing the necessary representation languages and tools to express semantic-based metadata. Prior to SW, there were several efforts to provide metadata formats to the web contents, resulting in well-known metadata formats such as Dublin-Core, whose main purpose was to improve information discovery and retrieval. However, these formats were shown very limited mainly due to their very poor expressivity and little web-awareness. As a result, the W3C proposed new representation formats, all relying on XML (Bray et al. eds., 2000), to overcome the limitations of existing metadata formats. The main idea behind these formats is that any concept or instance used for describing a web object must be referred through a unique resource identifier (URI). Thus, the most basic way to describe an object consists of creating a link to the URI that represents the intended semantics. With the resource description framework (RDF) (Keyne et al. eds., 2004), we can create more complex metadata elements allowing the representation of relationships between descriptors (e.g. triples). Additionally, the RDFS (Brikley & Guha eds., 2004) extension allows users to define a conformant schema for RDF descriptions. It is worth mentioning that the semantics of RDFS are quite similar to frame-based and object-oriented formalisms. More expressive semantic descrip-

tions have been also proposed by adopting logic-based frameworks: DAML+OIL (Horrocks et al. eds., 2001) and the ontology web language (OWL) (Dean et al., 2004). Contrary to RDFS, all these languages rely on description logics, which are tractable subsets of the first order logic (FOL). In this context, metadata is governed by logic axioms over both classes and instances (assertions). Like in RDFS, logic axioms in these formats must be defined over web-based references (i.e. URIs).

In the data warehouse field, the definition and use of metadata also have strong requirements (Chaudri & Dayal, 1997). Indeed, the traditional division of DW metadata into three categories (i.e. administrative, business, and operational) resembles the division we have proposed in the previous section. In the same way that web developers required more powerful mechanisms to express and manage web metadata, DW developers are requiring more powerful tools to face the increasingly heterogeneous, dynamic and open BI domains.

SW Formats: RDF(S) and OWL

In RDF there are three kinds of elements (Keyne et al. eds., 2004): resources, literals, and properties. Resources are web objects (entities) that are indentified through a URI, literals are atomic values such as strings, dates, numbers, etc., and properties are binary relationships between resources and literals. Properties are also identified through URIs. The basic building block of RDF is the triple: a binary relationship between two resources or between a resource and a literal. The resulting metadata can be seen as a graph where nodes are resources and literals, and edges are properties connecting them. RDFS extends RDF by allowing triples to be defined over classes and properties. In this way, we can describe the schema that rules our metadata within the same description framework.

The ontology web language (OWL) mainly differs from RDFS in the underlying semantic formalism, which is founded in description logics (DL) (Baader et al., 2003). Indeed, OWL languages provide RDF/XML serializations of different DL languages.

DL basic elements are concepts and individuals, being concepts the intentional representation of *individuals* sets. Concepts can be defined in terms of other concepts by using a series of constructors, which can be either set-oriented, like concept union ($\sqcup$), concept intersection ($\sqcap$), and concept complement ($\neg$), or relation-oriented, like the existential ($\exists R.C$) and universal ($\forall R.C$) restrictions. Relations can be also defined in terms of other simpler relations by using role constructors, like the inverse of a role (R^-). Different DL families can be defined depending on the constructors provided by their languages. The basic family is ALC, which contains the previous operators except the inverse of roles.

Ontologies in DL consist of two parts: the terminological box (TBox), which contains a set of axioms describing concepts, and the assertional box (ABox), which contains concept and role assertions involving individuals (i.e. the data). In our running example, the following axiom of the TBox describes the concept RentalAgreement:

```
RentalAgreement≡
CommercialTransaction ⊓
∃assignment.Car ⊓
    1hasPrice.(1hasCurrency.Currency
    ⊓ 1amount.Float)
```

The qualifier "1" of the properties hasPrice, hasCurrency and amount indicates that they are functional properties for this concept definition, that is, they are to-one relationships.

The following assertions describe an instance for the previous definition:

```
{  RentalAgreement:Contract112,
assignment(Contract112, MMT34),
price(Contract112,_p001),
hasCurrency(_p001,Euros), hasAmount(_
p001,"100"^^"float")   }
```

Notice that this axiom does not necessarily follow the model given in Figure 1, as ontologies are intended to describe semantics not database schemas. Indeed, unlike RDF schemas, not all the axioms of the ontology are designed to describe the "structure" of classes, properties, and instances. Some axioms can express the application business logic. For example, the following axiom may be used to identify taxed transactions according to their currency:

```
∃hasPrice.(∃hasCurrency.(Currency ⊓
∃usedIn⁻.(¬EuroZone)) ⊑
TaxedTransaction
```

In this way, we can encode implicit knowledge in our descriptions, resulting in much more concise metadata. For example, by just asserting that an instance *a* is of type "∃hasPrice.(∃hasCurrency. Dollars)", we can infer that "*a* is an amount of money expressed in the currency used in USA, and therefore it is associated to a taxed transaction". In the following section, we will introduce the inference tasks that can be performed by means of *reasoning* mechanisms.

DL axioms can be seen as a kind of logic rule of the form "body → head", because in DL the expression $C \sqcap D \sqsubseteq A$ is equivalent to the FOL expression $\forall x\, C(x) \wedge D(x) \rightarrow A(x)$. However, in DL we cannot express rules of the form: $\forall x.\, \forall y\, C(x) \wedge R(x, y) \rightarrow P(x, y)$, which can be useful to describe BI concepts as well as transformation rules necessary for integration tasks. For example, consider the following rule for the running example:

$\forall x. \forall y \; RentalAgreement(x) \; \wedge$
$hasCustomer(x, y) \; \wedge \; NonUECustomer(y)$
$\rightarrow \; TaxedTransaction(x, y)$

Several extensions of OWL have been proposed to support rules, mainly the semantic web rule language (SWRL) (Horrocks et al., 2004) and the recent integration between DL and rules (Motik & Rosati, 2010). However, these languages restrict the rule syntax in order to ensure they are safe: a safe rule has all individual variables bound to individuals named explicitly in the ontology. As a consequence, data variables are not allowed, and therefore they are not suitable for data-oriented transformations as those required in BI ETL flows.

Currently, there are several software platforms that give support to the development of ontologies by providing tools for edition, debugging, and querying. Among them, we emphasize Protégé and NeOn toolkits. Both platforms are based on java plug-ins, which can be easily added and removed according to the user requirements. These plug-ins allow a great variety of task associated to ontology development: editors, keyword searchers, module builders, ontology matching tools, reasoners, and so on.

Standard Reasoning Services

Logic-based systems can provide users with inference capabilities to manage the implicit knowledge derivable from the ontology axioms. Any inference can be expressed as $O \vDash \alpha$, where α is any axiom expressed with the same language as the ontology O. The typical inferences DL reasoning services usually provide are the following ones:

- Subsumption and equivalence inferences: $O \vDash C \sqsubseteq D$ and $O \vDash C \equiv D$
- Concept unsatisfiability: $O \vDash C \sqsubseteq \bot$
- Instance classification: $O \vDash C(a)$

A relevant task derived from the previous inference problems is that of query answering.

Basically, it consists of retrieving all the subsumed/subsuming concepts along with the individuals of a given DL concept description.

Reasoners

The main approaches to carry out DL inferences have mainly relied on the tableaux-based algorithms (Baader, 2009). A tableaux-algorithm is intended to incrementally build an ontology model (i.e. a finite interpretation of the ontology) by applying a series of transformation rules which express the semantics of each DL constructor in terms of models. Models in decidable DLs are always tree-shaped, where the branches represent relations between concepts (roles) and nodes represents interpretations of the involved concepts. Most of the popular reasoners for OWL-DL, like Pellet (Clark & Parsia, 2010), Racer (Haarslev & Möller, 2001) and FaCT++ (Horrocks, 1998), are implementations of these algorithms.

Computational Complexity Issues

Unfortunatelly, most of the significant OWL 1 languages proposed by the W3C (namely, OWL-DL and OWL-Lite) are actually coNP-hard in data complexity, i.e., when complexity is measured with respect to the size of the data layer only, which is indeed the dominant parameter in this context. This means that, in practice, computations over large amounts of data are prohibitively costly. A way to reduce the complexity of DLs is to impose restrictions on the ontology language, so as to guarantee that reasoning remains computationally tractable w.r.t. the TBox size. Possible restrictions that guarantee polynomial reasoning have been studied and proposed in the context of description logics, such as Horn SHIQ (Hustadt et al., 2005), EL++ (Baader et al., 2005) y DLP (Grosof et al., 2003). Among these fragments, we find a family of DLs, called DL-Lite (Artale, 2009), which is specifically tailored to capture basic ontology and conceptual data modeling

Figure 2. SPARQL query example and its graph pattern representation

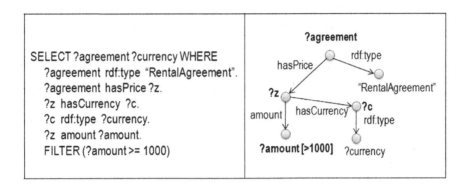

languages, while keeping low complexity w.r.t. the size of the data. These logics allow for answering complex queries (namely, conjunctive queries, i.e., SQL select-project-join queries, and unions of conjunctive queries) in LogSpace with respect to data complexity. More importantly, after a pre-processing phase which is independent of the data, they allow for delegating query processing to the relational DBMS managing the data layer.

Recently, OWL2 (W3C, 2009) introduces three profiles aimed to perform specific reasoning tasks (e.g. classification, query/answering, etc.) with tractable computational cost, namely:

- OWL2-EL profile, which is intended to produce complete inferences in polynomial time for large terminological requiring a limited expressivity resources (e.g. life sciences ontologies),
- OWL2-QL profile, which is intended to efficiently perform queries over large data bases with a expressivity equivalent to DL-Lite$_R$, and
- OWL2-RL, which is intended to make inferences over RDF (graph) data through rule-based query languages. More details about these profiles can be found at the official W3C site (Calvanese et al., 2008).

Currently, these profiles are supported by several reasoners: Mastro (Savo et al., 2010) is fully

conformant to OWL2-QL, CEL (Baader et al., 2006) is a reasoner for the OWL2-EL profile, and OWLRL (Herman, 2008) implements a reasoner for the OWL2-RL profile.

Apart from these efforts, other recent approaches aim to implement efficient reasoners for the complete DL expressivity as well as new reasoning problems. For example, (Motik et al, 2010) propose an extension of the tableaux-algorithms, called hypertableux-algorithms, which allows reasoning with rules. The HermiT reasoner (Hermit, 2010) implements this approach.

Storing and Querying Semantic Annotations

An RDF store, also called triplestore, is a database management system in charge of storing huge amounts of RDF triples as well as of providing a query language for sub-graph retrieval. As RDF data is basically graph data expressed with triples of the form "subject-predicate-object" (SPO), the query language consists of sub-graph patterns also expressed as a set of triples containing variables over any of the triple arguments. Additionally, pattern variables can be restricted by filtering expressions. SPARQL (Prud'hommeaux & Seaborne, 2008) is the query language proposed by the W3C for RDF stores. Basically, a SPARQL statement is a SELECT-FROM-WHERE expression (see Figure 2).

In a SPARQL query, variables start with "?", the WHERE clause contains triple patterns and filtering expressions over variables which are separated by ".", and the SELECT clause contains the variables that will be used in the result set. Result sets are just tuples with all the bindings of the variables that satisfy the WHERE clause. Although not yet part of the W3C Recommendation, several extensions have been proposed for SPARQL, e.g., by the ARQ query engine, that make it more applicable for BI-like queries, including ORDERBY, DISTINCT and GROUPBY clauses to manage resulting tuples. While SPARQL is the most prominent, other families of query languages capable of querying semantic web data exist, including XML query languages such as XQuery (Boag et al., 2007), topic map query languages, other RDF query languages such as RQL (Karvounarakis et al., 2002), and OWL query languages. A detailed survey of these is found in (Bailey et al., 2009), which also notes that a drawback of SPARQL is the weak support for schema or ontology information. From our BI perspective, this is a problem, since BI data, including MD models, require very strong schema/ontology support.

RDF stores have the main drawback of lacking a conformant schema that facilitates its physical database design and query optimization techniques. The simplest way to implement a RDF store is to create a single relational table with three columns (S-P-O) and perform queries through self-join operations. This approach is clearly inefficient for both large triple stores and large graph queries. Several optimization approaches have been proposed in the literature, which have derived to different RDF store systems. A common optimization that still maintains a generic database schema is to put long text values such as URIs and string literals into separate tables. This is done, e.g., by the well-known triplestore 3store (Harris et al., 2003). A further optimization consists of grouping triples by predicate and then creating a table for each group. Jena (Wilkinson et al., 2003)

and Sesame (Broekstra et al., 2003) use this strategy in their implementations. More sophisticated ways of clustering triples have been proposed in order to facilitate the generation of materialized joint views, like in the Oracle-RDF and C-Store (Abadi et al., 2007) implementations. The 3XL triple store (Liu et al. 2011) builds a specialized and optimized object-relational schema based on a supplied OWL-Lite ontology for the data in order to provide intelligent data partitioning, a strategy that proves very successful. Finally, the RDF-3X (Neumann & Weikum, 2008) and YARS2 (Harth et al., 2007) systems propose indexing the different SPO combinations under a B+-Tree, so that triple patterns can be solved through range queries.

The main issues addressed in query processing are the design of proper indexes for graph-pattern queries and gathering the most appropriate statistical information for join-order optimization. For the former, materialized join indexes, B+-trees and hash indexes have been proposed. For the latter, frequency statistics must go beyond S-P-O individual histograms and must take into account element co-occurrences for different graph shapes (Neumann & Weikum, 2010).

SW TECHNOLOGY FOR INTEGRATION ISSUES IN DATA WAREHOUSING

Current BI solutions face two main challenges. The first one is related to how to represent domain and business semantics, that is, how to model domain and business concepts and logic, so that decision makers can explore information repositories without using technical descriptions. The second challenge is concerned with the integration of heterogeneous information sources. The widespread adoption of new technologies in the Web, such as XML and other richer semi-structured formats like RDF, has widened the traditional BI scenario to a much more heterogeneous and open one. Dealing with the problem of accessing structured and non-structured data in an integrated and transparent way is still a challenge. *Semantic annotation* has been proposed to overcome these issues by providing a semantic abstraction to support both homogeneous access to disparate data sources and resource discovery. In this context, semantic-aware ETL processes are those that take into account these semantic annotations to improve the integration processes required in BI solutions. This section reviews these topics.

Semantic Annotation

An annotation is usually conceived as a comment attached to a section of a document, or more generally, an object. Annotations may be provided in different forms and formats, ranging from links to the information resources to embed in the annotated object and also as unstructured text or with formal structures. In general terms, semantic annotation is conceived as the process of discovering and assigning to the entities in the text links to their semantic descriptions, which are usually defined in a knowledge base (Kiryakov et al., 2004; Reeve & Han, 2005). In principle, semantic annotation is applicable to any kind of text – web pages, text documents, text fields in databases, and so on. It can be seen as a metadata generation/acquisition process so that data can be leveraged into a more expressive semantic level. We put special emphasis in the language used to describe the schema of the annotation since the more formal the semantics of this language the more machine-processable are the annotations.

In the BI scenario where applications are domain-dependent (e.g. retail sales, R&D), semantic annotation should be focused on assigning both domain and business concepts from specific known resources (e.g. thesauri, ontologies) to the data structures of the information system. It can be seen as a mapping of the sources to a homogeneous conceptual space where we capture the meaning of the integrated elements. This process will be usually performed in a semi-automatic way.

State-of-the-art research in the BI area proposes the use of semantic annotation by means of ontologies as a semantic middleware for integrating data from heterogeneous information systems. In (Spahn et al., 2008) a layered architecture is proposed where each data source schema is independently mapped to a technical ontology (TO) and the various TOs are connected to a business ontology (BO) to relate technical concepts to business-level concepts. At the application layer, the user can specify queries based on graph representation of the BO, which contains business-relevant vocabulary that is familiar to business users and therefore intuitive and easy to understand. In (Sell et al., 2008) they differentiate between the domain ontology, which provides the terminology of the business domain, and the BI ontology, which models the concepts used to describe how the data is organized in data sources (i.e. OLAP concepts) and to map such data to the concepts described in the domain ontology. In (Simitsis et al., 2010) ontology-based semantic annotation of data stores is used for deriving the conceptual design of ETL processes through reasoning. In a pre-processing phase the elements of each individual data store are analyzed and mapped to concepts using a domain specific thesaurus using both string and structure-based schema matching techniques in a semi-automatic way. Then, an ontology is constructed with the previous concepts and is used to annotate the data stores using OWL-DL constructs. These annotations embed both domain and technical concepts. Figure 3 shows an excerpt of the semantic annotations over one data source and the data warehouse.

In a similar way, a semi-automatic method exploiting ontology-based semantic annotation for the design of multidimensional data warehouses is presented in (Romero & Abelló, 2010b). The method assumes several heterogeneous data sources are represented by an ontology and identifies potential facts, dimensions and measures based on functional dependencies. In (Romero et al., 2009), the inference capabilities of the domain

Figure 3. Double underlined concepts refer to the technical ontology (i.e. application specific concepts) whereas single underlined ones refer to the domain ontology (i.e. BI domain specific concepts)

Source_Contract ≡ RentalAgreement ⊓ ∀hasPrice.(∀hasCurrency.Dollar) ⊓
    ∀DropOffBranch.{BranchType1,BracnhType2}
DW_Contract ≡ RentalAgreement ⊓ ∀hasDuration.LessThan20days ⊓ ∀hasPrice.(∀hasCurrency.Euros) ⊓
    ∀DropOffBranch.{BranchType2}

ontology encoded in DL-Lite are exploited to derive a multidimensional model that fully takes into account the semantics of the domain.

In recent years a lot of research and development has been carried out in the area of automatic information extraction (IE) from Web pages, text resources, semi-structured data such as HTML tables or Wikipedia *infoboxes*. The main goal of these approaches is to provide a comprehensive knowledge base of facts about named entities, their semantic classes and their mutual relations. Most pattern-based approaches follow the basic method outlined in (Brin, 98). In (Kiryakov et al., 2003; Maedche et al., 2003) extraction rules arise from an initial set of tagged entities. Other relevant approaches include (Cimiano et al., 2004) which present a tool for automatic pattern-based annotation based on the available knowledge on the Web, Text2Onto (Cimiano & Völker, 2005) a tool for ontology learning with improved statistical assessment of fact candidates and patterns and Omnivore (Cafarella et al., 2009) which aim to extract arbitrary relations from natural language texts. Moreover, most research along these lines has considered Wikipedia as key asset for the extraction of knowledge. Examples of such efforts include (Atserias et al., 2008) which provide semantic annotations for the English Wikipedia, DBpedia (Auer et al., 2008) which harvests RDF subject-predicate-object triples from Wikipedia and similar sources, Kylin/KOG (Weld et al., 2008; Wu & Weld, 2007; Wu & Weld, 2008) an ambitious work whose goal is to extract arbitrary relations from natural language texts and Wikipedia *infobox* templates and YAGO (Suchanek et al., 2007; Suchanek et al., 2008) which integrates relational knowledge from Wikipedia with the WordNet taxonomy. The prevalent methods under these IE tools are a combination of rule-based pattern matching, natural language processing, and statistical machine learning.

Although one of the goals of the previous approaches is to leverage data with semantics (similar to the goal of semantic annotation) they conceive the harvesting of knowledge in a broad, universal way. They are domain-independent in the sense that they try to capture in an automatic way as many entities as possible and link them to knowledge resources mainly to advance the functionality of search engines to a more expressive semantic level. These differences w.r.t. the specific and domain-oriented nature of BI scenarios along with the lack of standards and integration with formal knowledge hinders its usage for semantic annotation in the aforementioned BI scenarios. However, some approaches have tackled this issue by customizing and adapting existing IE tools so that they can be effectively applied to a specific BI scenario. In (Saggion et al., 2007; Declerk, 2008) the use of ontology-based IE in the context of BI is proposed for the internationalization domain. This approach requires the construction of a domain ontology by knowledge engineers and domain experts that gathers all the required domain concepts and relations. Furthermore, IE tools like NER have been customized to target the specific domain entities and map them to the ontology concepts.

Most of the classical IE annotation tools require a complete syntactic analysis, and in some cases, a semantic analysis too, which is usually an expensive operation not affordable for even medium-sized document collections. Methods based on manual pattern definition do not suffer from these issues, but require human effort and intervention for updating and customizing patterns to each application scenario. Finally, machine learning methods usually rely on training corpora, which is not always available. As an alternative to the previous approaches in (Danger & Berlanga, 2009) a tool for the extraction of complex instances from free text on the Web is presented. The approach is based on non-monotonic processing and uses a logic-based reference ontology, entity recognizers and disambiguators, in order to adequately create and combine instances and their relations. The complementary work in (Nebot & Berlanga, 2009) enables the customized use of available knowledge resources such as thesauri or ontologies to assist in the annotation process. The method allows the user to select and build tailored and logics-enabled ontologies from large knowledge repositories. Later, the extracted ontology can be used as an alternative to the use of training corpora in machine learning methods (Danger & Berlanga, 2009).

New research possibilities may arise if we consider the semantic descriptions delivered by the previous tools as a new type of data sources susceptible of being analyzed by BI applications. Along this line of research we can find a few approaches aimed at analyzing semantic annotations encoded in logic languages such as RDF(S) and OWL. (Nebot et al, 2009) propose a multidimensional framework for analyzing semantic annotations from a logical viewpoint using ontologies. In this approach semantic annotations are based on application and domain ontologies. The user can build a multidimensional integrated ontology (MIO) containing the required analysis measures and dimensions taken from the available ontologies. This approach is similar to the previous semantic BI approaches in the sense that it uses ontologies as an integrating tool among different sources. In such scenario where multiple ontologies co-exist together, ontology alignment and merging strategies play a key role.

Semantic-Aware ETL Processes

During the initial steps of an ETL project, the main goal is to construct a conceptual ETL design that identifies the useful to the project data sources and describes the corresponding data transformations needed to map these sources to the target data warehouse concepts. For achieving that, it is imperative to identify and understand the semantics of both the data sources and the target data stores. Several approaches have already been proposed for using Semantic Web technology to the design and construction of the ETL part. Naturally, most of them deal with the conceptual part of the ETL design, since the Semantic Web paradigm seems as a promising means to overcome the lack of handy ways for capturing the semantics of an ETL process.

The prevailing –so far– idea in using Semantic Web technology for ETL suggests using a global ontology for mapping all the involved data stores to it. This idea resembles the "local-as-view" paradigm (Lenzerini, 2002), where the application ontology, constructed as a conceptual model of the domain, corresponds to the global schema and the semantic descriptions of the data stores, in terms of classes and properties defined in the ontology, correspond to the views describing the local schemata. However, the use of an OWL ontology, instead of a global schema provides a formal model on which automated reasoning mechanisms may be applied. Furthermore, in ETL it is not sufficient to consider the integration problem as a query rewriting problem, since the transformations taking place in a real-case ETL scenarios usually include operations, such as the application of functions, that cannot be captured by a query rewriting process (see Skoutas & Simitsis, 2007).

(Niemi et al., 2007) discusses methods for OLAP cube construction using Semantic Web technology. They use a generic OLAP ontology as an upper ontology for all OLAP cubes. This ontology defines only general OLAP concepts and it is independent of the application area. Per application need, they consider domain-specific ontologies (e.g., CarModel, Branch, Country) based on the upper one. Such ontologies are defined based on common concepts that have global definitions shared among all domain-specific ontologies. The OLAP cubes are described based on the domain-specific ontologies and the data sources are defined using the global concepts. However, since in practice it is possible that some data sources are not defined using the domain-specific ontology and they are described in another way –for example, using the upper ontology– we may need to define ontology mapping transformations describing how the source data should be converted to conform to the global domain ontology. In order to integrate data from different sources, the authors consider an RDF data format and an RDF query language. The approach proposed by (Niemi et al., 2007) is as follows. They suggest starting with mapping the sources to an OWL/RDF ontology. Then, the user needs to design the structure of the OLAP cube. Next, the OLAP cube (presented using the XML serialisation of RDF) is constructed based on RDF queries issued on the data sources. At the instance level, the combined result of such queries represents an instance of the OLAP cube. As a constraint, the method requires that there is a common ontology base for the data sources and that each data source can be described in sufficient level of detail for enabling a mapping to RDF format.

An extension to this work discusses in more detail the method for automating the construction of OLAP schemas (Niinimäki & Niemi, 2009). Again, the source and target schemas are considered as known. The mapping among the source data and the OLAP schema is done by converting the data in RDF using ontology maps. Then,

the relevant source data are extracted using RDF queries generated using the ontology describing the OLAP schema. At the end, the extracted data are stored in a database and analyzed using typical OLAP techniques. Both works aim at an end-to-end design approach, but they have two main limitations. First, they both require prior knowledge of the source and target schemas and second, they consider simple data transformations.

Another research approach to ETL design using Semantic Web technology elaborates more on the complexity of the data transformations required for integrating source data from heterogeneous sources into a data warehouse (Skoutas & Simitsis, 2006; Skoutas & Simitsis, 2007). This research work deals with one of the major challenges of the ETL design: the structural and semantic heterogeneity. For example, two sources $S1$ and $S2$ may contain the same kind of information under two different schemata: S1.Rents(rentID, cartype, carplate, carmileage, customerID, …) and S2.Rents(rentID, carID, customerID, …); or they may use different representation formats, like: carmileage in kilometers (km) in $S1$ and in miles (mi) in $S2$. The core idea of this work is the use of ontologies to formally and explicitly specify the semantics of the data source and the data warehouse schemas and thus, to automate in a large extent the ETL generation. This work also assumes that the source and target schemas are previously known.

In more detail, the first step of this approach is to construct an ontology to model the domain of discourse as described by the data store schemas and the application specifications. For that and in order to deal with different naming schemes, first, an application vocabulary is constructed. The vocabulary involves information like terms denoting the primitive concepts of the domain of discourse (e.g., car, branch), the features that characterize such concepts (e.g., carID, carmileage), the different representation formats that may be used for a feature (e.g., for carmileage {km, mi}), the allowed values that an enumerated feature may take (e.g., for branch location {Athens, Barcelona, New York}), and functions associating features to concepts, representation format to features, values to representation formats or features, and so on. Then, the data sources and the data warehouse are annotated w.r.t. the application vocabulary. Each data store contains a set of relations that comprise one or more attributes. The process of annotating a data store refers to providing two types of information: establishing the appropriate mappings between the data store relations and attributes and the concepts and features of the vocabulary; and describing each relation in terms of the cardinality, representation format and (range of) values of its associated features. Based on these, this works elaborates on how the application ontology is generated.

The second step of the process is the generation of conceptual ETL design. This step involves an automatic means for deriving the mappings from the source attributes to the attributes belonging to the data warehouse, along with the appropriate ETL transformations. First, the method determines from which sources –i.e., from which attributes/relations of these sources– information needs to be extracted in order to populate each attribute/relation in the data warehouse. Next, the method determines the transformations required to integrate data from the source to the target relations using the specified mappings and the relative position of the source and target classes in the class hierarchy. This is realized in three phases. In the first, transformations like project, concatenate, and join are identified. In the second, other transformations like select, convert (functions), not null, aggregate, and so on are also discovered. Finally, the design is complemented with transformations like add attribute, union, distribute, detect duplicates, and so on. Although more complex transformations (e.g., pivot and slowly changing dimensions) are not captured by this process, the most frequently used ones can be automatically discovered. For example, assuming that location information was stored in the two sources $S1$ and $S2$ under different formats: S1.Branch(..., location,...) and S2.Branch(..., street, number, ...) and that the target data store has a different schema T(..., city, street,...), then a convert operation, namely concatenation $c(attr_1\_val, ..., attr_2\_val, property\_val)$, will be identified as: c(street, number, street).

Several extensions to the above two research works have been proposed. (Skoutas et al., 2009) proposes using a graph-based representation as a conceptual model for the source and target data stores and based on that, the ETL transformations can be identified by means of graph transformations. In other words, this work describes how the operations comprising the ETL process can be derived through graph transformation rules, the choice and applicability of which are determined by the semantics of the data with respect to an attached domain ontology. Thus, starting from an initial graph comprising the source and target data stores subgraphs, the ontology subgraph, and the semantic annotations, this works shows how to produce a final graph that contains the ETL process subgraph. In this context, the specification of the ETL process can be seen as a set of paths directed from source data store nodes towards target data store nodes. The nodes along these paths denote ETL operations and the edges connecting the nodes indicate the data flow. Figure 4 presents a simple rule for inserting a LOAD operation in the presence of a direct relationship, where the source and target elements correspond to the same concept; in Figure 4(a) a match is found and a rule is triggered causing the insertion of a LOAD operation Figure 4(b). Several transformations can be discovered by this process as Load, Filter, Convert, Extract, Split, Construct, and Merge.

The techniques discussed so far consider as given the source and target schemas and search for the mapping of one to the other. A more recent approach starts with the business requirements and the source data stores, and works toward the identification of both the target schema and the transformations needed for the realization of the

Figure 4. Rule for inserting LOAD operation (Skoutas et al., 2009)

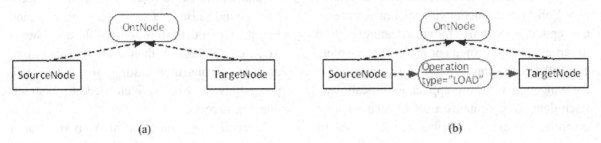

(a)   (b)

ETL process (Romero et al., 2010a). The method starts with a single business requirement, and after its validation, and possibly completion, it relates it to the source data stores in order to annotate a generic ontology. Then, the concepts are characterized either as factual or dimensional and correctness w.r.t. multidimensional design principles is checked. In the meantime, the annotations are used for extracting schema modification operators; e.g., selection, projection, union, set operations, aggregation, functions. At a next step, additional transformations can be added either based on functional requirements of the data –e.g., "make sure that each customer is considered once"– or based on standard business and design needs; e.g., "replace the production keys with surrogate keys" or "take care of the slowly changing dimensions". As a final step, all the results produced for each single business requirement are consolidated in order to produce the final multidimensional design and ETL process.

The abovementioned efforts work toward the facilitation and automation of ETL design, and thus, aim at making the life of the designer easier. Another crucial matter is to allow business people to comprehend and evaluate the design outcome. Several design notations, like UML or BPEL, require some knowledge and experience for their understanding. Providing a textual description of ETL designs is the most natural way for their representation. The ontology-driven techniques for conceptual ETL design can be exploited for producing such textual descriptions (Simitsis et al., 2008; Simitsis et al., 2010). In particular, after

the generation of the ETL design, the constructed ontology can be parsed and a template based method can be used for representing information about the data stores –using the data store annotations– and about the generated ETL process. Then, several reports can be customized using a template language for showing a list of annotations, ETL transformations, ETL statistics, and so on.

All the previous approaches are conceived for dealing with relational data sources. Recently, (Nebot & Berlanga, 2010) have presented a method to generate fact tables directly from semantic data expressed in RDF(S) and OWL. The proposed method starts with the target MD, which must be expressed in terms of concepts and properties of the source ontologies, and then it performs a series of transformations that guarantee that the generated factual data conforms to both the MD and the source semantics. This method could be incorporated to existing semantic-aware ETL processes in order to integrate SW annotations of unstructured and semi-structured data into data warehouses.

MULTIDIMENSIONAL MODELS AND THE SW

This section presents a brief introduction to the multidimensional model, and we highlight the strong dependence of multidimensional modeling of data warehouses on data found within the organizations. However, nowadays it is compulsory to consider external data to produce the data warehouse multidimensional schema. At this point, SW technologies arise as a valuable asset to help in the integration process of external data to complement the organizations own data. This section is divided in 3 subsections:

- In the "Relationships between MD models and SW formalisms" subsection we present the current straightforward solutions relating multidimensional modeling and the SW technologies.
- The "Advanced reasoning services for MD models" subsection discusses which advanced features from the SW become essential when modeling the data warehouse. We highlight two main reasoning tasks tightly related to data warehousing: reasoning on data aggregation and transitive functional dependencies.
- Finally, we wrap up the discussion in the "Advanced Reasoning and MD Modeling" subsection by presenting how these advanced features have been exploited by current modeling methods.

Multidimensional modeling is a well-known paradigm in the area of data warehouses and databases in general. It was firstly introduced by Ralph Kimball at the logical level (Kimball, 1996) and later by Matteo Golfarelli at the conceptual level (Golfarelli et al., 1998). Since then, many approaches have introduced, or improved, multidimensional models either at the logical or the conceptual level (Pedersen et al., 1999; Vassiliadis, 1998; Abelló et al., 2006). Multidimensionality is based on the dichotomy Fact-Dimension. This paradigm aims at analyzing the instances of a kind of fact (or subject of analysis), from different points of view (i.e., the analysis dimensions). For example, we may want to analyze "rental agreements" (our kind of fact) depending on the customer profile, the duration of the agreement, the branch where it was picked up, the branch where it was dropped off, and so on. Factual instances

can be placed in a multidimensional space (whose axis are the analysis dimensions), known as data cube. Thus, each factual instance is identified by a point on each analysis dimension.

Several measures (i.e., variables or metrics) use to be available for each fact instance. For example, we may be interested in analyzing the basic price (with no benefit considered) or the best price (the lowest price offered yet providing benefit) of the rental agreements. Furthermore, the multidimensional model also provides foundations to study / analyze the available measures at various aggregation levels hierarchically structured in the dimensions. For example, we would like to study the basic price we may offer regarding the kind of customer (instead of a specific customer), country (instead of the city from where the deal was done) and kind of branch (instead of the specific branch where the car was picked up). Indeed, aggregation is one of the main characteristics of the multidimensional model, setting foundations for the well-known roll-up and drill-down operators.

Usually, the multidimensional analysis of data has been restricted to the well structured information sources within the company. Nevertheless, (Inmon et al., 2008) outlines the opportunity and importance of using unstructured and semi-structured data (either textual or not) in the decision making process. These data could still come from the sources in the company, but also from the Web. It is clear the benefit of enriching our multidimensional model with information coming from the Web, since it can provide new points of view, new aggregation levels, or even new measures to analyze. Anyway, either coming from inside or outside the company, data must be annotated somehow in order to be used for decision making (it is the addition of data and metadata that generates information). Among the first attempts to include web data in analysis schemas were (Jensen et al., 2001) and (Vrdoljak et al., 2003). These works generate multidimensional schemas from XML. However, this can be clearly improved by using current semantic web

Figure 5. UML multidimensional schema

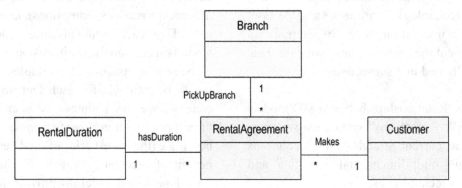

formalisms. A review and deep discussion of data warehouse approaches for XML and Web data can be found in (Pérez-Martínez et al, 2008a).

Relationships Between MD Models and SW Formalisms

To the best of our knowledge, there is only one work, (Hacid et al., 1997), that shows the relationship of multidimensionality and the SW by proposing a model based on DL. This work emphasizes on multidimensional operations and defines a data cube as follows:

```
Cube  ≡ ∀hasCell.(∀hasDuration.
RentalDuration ⊓ ∀makes.Customer ⊓
∀pickupBranch.Branch)
```

The problem with such definition is that strict role-typing is assumed (meaning that the range as well as the domain of a role is a subset of a concept and it cannot freely relate any instance in the database), which is a rather common assumption in the conceptual modeling area, but not for DL ontologies. For example, the has role in Figure 1 has two different ranges DemandXGroup and DrivingLicense. Thus, it cannot be represented by assuming strict role-typing.

In the last years, some multidimensional models based on UML have been presented. For example, (Abelló et al., 2006) proposed a UML

meta-model extension to capture and describe the multidimensional concepts in a UML class diagram (like that in Figure 5).

Relevantly, nowadays it is well known how to capture and represent UML and ER class diagrams by means of DL (Berardi et al., 2005). Indeed, most of the UML features are known to be captured by well-behaved DLs such as the DL-Lite family (Artale et al., 2009). This fact opens a new bridge between the semantic web and multidimensional formalisms, as the work presented in (Abelló et al. 2006) can be easily translated into DL. Thus, the multidimensional schema in Figure 5 would be translated into:

```
Cube ≡ RentalAgreement ⊓
∃hasDuration.RentalDuration ⊓
∃makes.Customer ⊓ ∃pickupBranch.
Branch
```

However, two issues still remain open: how to reason with aggregation relationships (which, in any case, can be represented by roles) and fact IDs (to be captured as keys).

Advanced Reasoning Services for MD Models

Logic frameworks are the foundations of the **SW** that provide standard reasoning services that, in turn, provide a theoretical and algorithmic basis that can be used for the design and evolution of the data warehouse.

Reasoning Services to Support Data Aggregation

In the field of ontology population we can find some approaches dealing with aggregated ontology instances. For example, (Danger & Berlanga, 2008) presents a system to extract complex ontological instances and relations from unstructured environments such as the web. This work, based on the DL language SHOIQ(D), presents a set of operations for merging and aggregating instances. Thus, aggregation of instances (by means of paths between concepts) can be asserted on a reference ontology. However, this work is thought to capture aggregation relationships between instances when parsing unstructured text related to an ontology, but no further reasoning aggregation services can be exploited. Many inference problems can be reduced to satisfiability and containment but this is not the case of aggregation, a new kind of inference problem crucial in the data warehouse scenario. (Jarke et al, 2000) outlines four different open problems associated to aggregation:

1. To decide whether queries (or views) are satisfiable,
2. whether one is contained in another,
3. whether one is refined by another (i.e., one can be calculated from the other despite not being a subset), and
4. to answer a query.

(Baader et al., 2003) introduced aggregates over concrete domains. The resulting language is called $ALC(\Sigma)$, and extends the basic language ALC with concrete domains, functional roles (i.e., relations between instances and values from these domains) with predicates expressing value comparisons, and a limited set of aggregation functions, namely: sum, min, max and count. Aggregates are introduced through complex functional roles

of the form $\Gamma(R \circ u)$, which relate each instance with the aggregate Γ over all the values reachable from R followed by the functional role u (note that $\circ$ doesn't stand for role composition, but for an ad-hoc constructor). For example, we can define the following complex functional role sum(monthPickUpTime $\circ$ basicPrice) to find out which was the income based on the rental agreements done per month, where the complex functional role sum(monthPickUpTime $\circ$ basicPrice) relates an individual to the sum over all values reachable from monthPickUpTime (extracted from the pickUpTime date from the Opened-Rental class) followed by basicPrice (inherited from RentalAgreement). Thus, a new, complex functional role is built using the aggregation function sum, the role name PickUpTime, and the functional role basicPrice.

However, DLs formalisms present important limitations for representing complex measures and aggregations. (Baader et al., 2003) also demonstrate that handling aggregates in DLs usually leads to undecidability for problems (1) and (2), even for very simple aggregates such as sum and count. Moreover, decidable cases present a level of computational complexity too high for practical real-world applications and thus, there are no reasoners able to deal with the advanced features required by these new constructors.

Problem (3) is also known as query rewriting from materialized views (i.e., if a query can be refined from materialized views, given that answering queries from views is cheaper than answering them from the sources). For example, consider that the user asks for a query Q asking for the average best price offered by every rental agreement done, per year and kind of customer (ranged by age). Let us consider now two complementary materialized views V and V', which are defined as rental agreements in EU countries and rental agreements in non-EU countries, per day and customer, respectively. Then, Q can be answered by computing the average best price (grouping the instances by year and date of birth and then, summing up the best prices of each group and dividing the result obtained by the number of deals on the group) from both views. In general, according to (Mannino, 2007), a view could be used to answer a certain aggregation query if:

1. the selection predicate of the query is subsumed by that of the view,
2. the aggregation level (i.e., the data granularity demanded) is coarser or equal than that in the query and
3. if the aggregation function used is the same (or compatible) with that of the view.

For example, the first condition states that a view storing data related to EU cannot be used to answer a query regarding the USA, as the query selection predicate is not contained into that of the view (thus, data needed is missing). The second condition states that data at month granularity level cannot be used to answer queries at day level. However, it can be used to answer queries at year level. Finally, a query using the average function to aggregate data can be answered from a view capturing both the sum and the number of instances involved, but it would not be possible if, for example, the number of instances is not captured in the view. In general, query rewriting is too complex to be exhaustively checked. Thus, DBMSs use heuristics to rewrite queries in terms of materialized views.

Recently, the problem of answering queries over ontologies (4) has also been addressed. Firstly, very expressive DLs (such as fragments of OWL 1 DL) have been considered and the data complexity (i.e., measured in the size of the intensional level) of the problem was characterized. It has been shown that for expressive ontology languages like SHIQ, answering unions of conjunctive queries (the typical scenario considered in this area) is coNP-complete in data complexity (Glimm et al., 2008) and (Ortiz et al., 2008). For this reason, most recent works have focused on less expressive languages providing a nice trade-off with data

complexity on query answering. One relevant result is that of the DL-Lite family (Artale et al., 2009), which is known to be LogSpace in data complexity (i.e., it can be reduced to standard query evaluation over DBs) when considering union of conjunctive queries. In this scenario, (Calvanese et al., 2008) studied the complexity of extending query answering of union of conjunctive queries with aggregates. However, the authors shown that there are some assumptions related to aggregate queries that are difficult to overcome in formalisms such as DL. DL ontologies deal with incomplete information (i.e., the intensional level –i.e., IL- is a partial description of the domain of interest that the ontology completes by characterizing the space of all the possible, compatible intensional levels – i.e. IL'-). This fact is known as the open-world assumption in contrast to the closed-world assumption assumed for relational databases. For this reason, the authors argue that assuming certain answers (**i.e.,** asking for an aggregate query Q over each IL') may produce meaningless answers, as it may return a different answer for each IL' and eventually obtain an empty intersection. The authors explore the conditions to be fulfilled so aggregate queries make sense; i.e., that the answer exists and can be computed (Calvanese et al., 2008) and (Thorne et al., 2009). However, although, in these cases, the computational complexity is yet LogSpace regarding data complexity, the result happens to be too restrictive and not feasible for most real cases.

Transitive Functional Dependencies

It is well-known that patterns used to look for multi-dimensional concepts in multidimensional design are based on functional dependencies (Kimball et al., 1996; Romero et al., 2010b) because of two reasons. On the one hand, the multidimensional space is arranged by the analysis dimensions of a given fact. Each instance of data is identified (i.e., placed in the multidimensional space) by a point in each of its analysis dimensions (i.e., the multidimensional space axis). Conceptually, it entails that the fact must be related to each analysis dimension by a to-one conceptual relationship. That is, a functional dependency. Furthermore, since two different instances of data cannot be placed in the same point of the multidimensional space, it is compulsory that a set of dimensions (known as the multidimensional base) functionally determine the fact. On the other hand, measures can be thought as class attributes (i.e., OWL properties with data types as range) and thus, they are functionally dependent on the fact. For this reason, computing functional dependencies is essential for data warehouse modelling.

Functional dependencies discovery has been tightly related to the databases field and it has been typically addressed either at the logical or physical level. Addressing this task at the logical level entails that results obtained are tied to the design decisions made when devising the system. Most approaches try to overcome the lack of semantics in a logical schema by addressing this task at the physical level (e.g., (Jensen et al., 2004) already addressed this approach for data warehousing), but these result in computationally expensive solutions that register drops in performance when a large number of attributes or instances are processed.

Given that DL ontologies provide a semantically rich formalism, (Romero et al., 2010b) discusses the benefits of computing the functional dependencies closure (i.e., by considering role chains, also known as role compositions) at the conceptual level, if the ontology provides multiplicities for the roles. Composition allows expressing joined relationships making the intermediate involved concepts implicit, but it was not supported by OWL 1 and it is not yet fully supported by current reasoners. For this reason, (Romero et al., 2010b) presented an ad hoc algorithm to compute transitive functional dependencies based, partially, on standard reasoning services. A refined approach to fully exploit DL reasoning services and compute functional dependencies is discussed in (Romero et al, 2009). This work shows that role composition

can be simulated by means of a well-behaved DL such as DL-Lite$_A$ (Artale et al., 2009), by exploiting its query answering services for conjunctive queries. Similarly, (Danger & Berlanga, 2008) presents the adaptation of an algorithm to select functional dependencies. This approach focuses on building dimension hierarchies, which are shaped to maximize the information gain.

Recently, OWL 2 provides a construct to assert a property that is the composition of several properties. Such axioms are known as complex role inclusions in SROIQ (in which OWL 2 is based on). However, SROIQ defines regularity conditions for decidability (mainly, prevent cyclic definitions involving hierarchies with property chains).

A specific case of functional dependency is the key concept, which is relevant for modeling tasks to identify instances. Thus, it is worth remarking that some recent works have addressed the issue of asserting keys on ontologies: OWL 2 allows asserting them under certain safe rules (Motik et al., 2005). With the same spirit, (Calvanese et al., 2008) shows how path-based identification constraints can be considered in both, very expressible DLs such as ALCQIbreg and the DL-Lite family. In general, path-based constraints are a powerful class of identification constraints (which allow using roles, inverses, and paths) that capture sophisticated forms of identifications (although it does not suit to the traditional key definition). This kind of constrains though, happen to be problematic in the general case and the authors propose a restricted form of these constraints, called local, that does not increase the complexity of reasoning both in very expressive DL and in the tractable DL-Lite family. Local path-based constraints still remain interesting for most real scenarios.

Advanced Reasoning and MD Modeling

Nowadays we can find several approaches exploiting the advanced reasoning services presented in previous section. We can classify its use in three areas: discovering dimension hierarchies from ontology fragments, fact extraction and integrating concepts from several ontologies to produce the multidimensional schema (i.e., carry out the fact extraction and dimension discovery from several sources).

Mainly, automatically discovering dimension hierarchies has attracted researchers' attention. Regardless of the data source formalisms, it can be thought as a way to summarize schemas (in the sense of allowing the user to grasp, at a glance, the information contained by the schema), as considered in (Yang et al., 2009). This approach summarizes relational databases by exploiting a metric distance over the schema to cluster the most relevant tables (i.e., facts) and present a summarization of the ontology topology around it (i.e., the analysis dimensions). In the data warehousing area, (Romero et al., 2010b) present a similar way of proceeding. There, distance metrics and multidimensional patterns are introduced to identify facts, measures and dimensional concepts (which, eventually, will form the analysis dimensions). (Danger & Berlanga, 2008) also present its own approach to identify dimension hierarchies based on functional dependencies. Both approaches foundations are based on discovering functional dependencies as discussed in previous section.

Note, however, that these two approaches assume a single domain ontology. However, in certain scenarios, like biomedicine, this is not a fair assumption, as several domain ontologies are available and should be considered. To overcome this limitation, (Nebot et al., 2009) introduces the Semantic Data Warehouse (SDW), which can contain semantic annotations defined in several large inter-linked ontologies. Thus, it presents an approach to tackle the semantic integration of ontologies. Specifically, the authors focus on only integrating the right amount of knowledge needed for specific multidimensional analysis (for example, data related to opened rental agreements, or data related to customers, etc.) and a

method for designing, validating and building these schemas is detailed.

Oppositely, (Romero et al., 2010a) presents a different approach for the same scenario. There, the authors propose to extract a multidimensional schema from each domain ontology (for example, as suggested in (Romero et al., 2010b)) and later conciliate those results in a single, detailed multidimensional schema. Thus, the semantic integration of the resulting schemas is performed a posteriori.

FUTURE RESEARCH DIRECTIONS

In this section, we discuss future and emerging trends in the collaboration of both OLAP and SW areas. First, we discuss the use of Semantic Web techniques for OLAP query recommendation. Second, the use of Semantic Web data to provide context information for multidimensional data warehouses is discussed. Finally, issues related to the scalable and efficient storage of Semantic Web data are treated.

Query Recommendation

The use of semantic web technologies has increased the amount of steps that can be (semi-) automatically performed in the data warehousing system design process. This scenario opens a new and interesting researching topic: query recommendation. Query recommendation has gained relevance in the database community in the last years. In the data warehousing community, (Giacometti et al., 2009a; 2009b) introduced their approach for multidimensional query recommendation. These works take advantage of the OLAP tool query log to exploit the knowledge it contains and assess the user in his / her future queries. However, it remains open if the knowledge extracted from performing some tasks automatically (mainly, when involving the user requirements in the design phase) can help the user when querying the DW.

A promising approach would be considering SW technologies to help in this process.

Contextualization of Data Warehouses with SW Data

Next generation of BI systems require further research on data warehouse contextualization. This is an alternative way of doing global search on separate structured and unstructured data sources and integrating both types of information in order to semantically enrich the process of analyzing business data. The process of analyzing contextualized data was initially defined by (Priebe & Pernul, 2003) with the purpose of communicating the user context among different *portlets* representing different data sources and, therefore, to support such integration in a generic way. With this approach, the system can provide the user with the documents that are related to the information that is being currently displayed in an OLAP report. In order to solve the problem of the heterogeneity of both systems, they propose to use ontological concept mapping.

The formal definition of contextualized warehouse was later proposed in (Pérez-Martínez et al., 2008a). This work consists in the integration of a corporate warehouse of structured data with a warehouse of text-rich XML documents. With this purpose they define a new information retrieval model to select the context of analysis from the document warehouse and to associate to each fact of the analysis cube the set of documents that are more related (Pérez-Martínez et al., 2009). In a contextualized warehouse, the user specifies an analysis context by supplying a sequence of keywords (i.e., an IR condition like "financial crisis"). The analysis is performed on a new type of OLAP cube, called R-cube, which is materialized by retrieving the documents and facts related to the selected context. A new set of OLAP operators allows users to find out the relationship that can occur between the data in the cubes and the information in the documents.

Another contribution someway related to data warehouse contextualization has been recently made by (Castellanos et al., 2010). With the purpose of identifying external events that may affect the enterprise operations, in this work, novel techniques of information extraction and correlation measurement are applied to extract relevant information from two disparate sources of unstructured data, and determine which documents are correlated. They have also developed several functions for information extraction and analytics.

All these systems have in common that the integration of data needs to be made on the fly, in a dynamic and efficient way. This is the only way of ensuring that the answer can satisfy the requirements of each specific analysis operation involved in a decision making process. The application of the technology developed in the context of Semantic Web research to this problem is a work that remains to be done and that surely would bring further benefits. As an example, semantic annotation technologies can help to identifies generic and domain specific entities, relationships as well as semantic time expressions. This would allow us to improve the integration and joint analysis of structured and unstructured data coming from heterogeneous data sources.

SW Storage Issues

A RDF store somewhat resembles a data warehouse in the sense that they are intended to store huge amounts of read-only data under very simple schemas (just three columns). Here, a very interesting direction is the application of data warehousing techniques like bulk-loading in order to manage huge amounts of triples more efficiently. For example, the 3XL system (Liu et al., 2011) have shown that using bulk-loading techniques in combination with main memory storage and intelligent data partitioning can result in huge speedups for bulk operations such as loading and querying large amounts of triples.

Unlike traditional multidimensional data warehouses, data in triple stores is not subject-oriented, and there is not a predefined set of dimensions and measures to which all data must refer. Identifying which concepts and properties are of interest for representing dimensions and measures is indeed one of the key points for integrating OLAP techniques and SW data. For example, the approach recently presented in (Niinimaki, M. & Niemi, 2009), proposes to build DWs from RDF data through SPARQL queries that identifies the target dimensions and measures. Similarly, (Nebot & Berlanga, 2010) proposes to define multidimensional schemas from the concepts of the ontology to which the triple store refers, and then semi-automatically generate an OLAP cube according to that schema.

A further promising direction is the application of bitmap indexing techniques to semantic web data management, including efficient reasoning. Bitmap indices have traditionally been applied for the dimensional data found in data warehouses. Recent advances in compressed bitmap indices (Deliege et al., 2010) have shown that significant speedups can be achieved for both storage and query speed when performing complex operations, and it is believed that these advantages can be exploited for more efficient SW data management.

Finally, a huge challenge related to both scalability and semantics lies in the transition of business intelligence into so-called "cloud intelligence", where the full potential of cloud computing is realized (Pedersen, 2010). Challenges related to the SW includes using SW technologies to achieve location and device independence, providing intelligence as a service, scaling intelligence services to a global level through techniques such as map-reduce and beyond, and providing agility, the ability to assemble the necessary resources on demand, not only in terms of computing power, but also in terms of data sources.

CONCLUSION

Business intelligence requires the integration of massive data coming from disparate data sources. Traditionally, these data sources were limited to corporate transactional databases, relying on the relational data model mostly. As a consequence, BI research has been mainly focused on this data model so far. However, the increasing availability of valuable knowledge resources, public databases, and a great variety of information sources in the Web are requiring new BI models and techniques for dealing with structured and unstructured data at the same time.

The Semantic Web is clearly targeted to facilitate the integration of all these web resources by providing semantic annotations that follow some agreed ontologies. In this chapter, we have firstly reviewed the major efforts to bring semantics to both web resources and BI application data, which is a previous step to a true integration of both worlds. Then, we have presented the main approaches that have utilized SW technology to face classical issues of data warehouse design and implementation. These approaches have brought BI methods closer to SW data and vice versa. However, several issues must be addressed before achieving the actual integration of BI and SW, to mention a few: new user recommendation methods, data warehouse contextualization, massive SW data storage for analytical tasks, and performing BI in the cloud regarding fully distributed data and services. These issues and many others to come constitute an open intelligent information systems research area of great interest.

REFERENCES

W3C OWL Working Group (Eds.). (2009). *OWL 2 Web ontology language document overview.* Retrieved from http://www.w3.org/TR/ owl2-overview/

Abadi, D. J., Marcus, A., Madden, S., & Hollenbach, K. J. (2007). Scalable Semantic Web data management using vertical partitioning. In *Proceedings of VLDB Conference,* (pp. 411–422).

Abelló, A., Samos, J., & Saltor, F. (2006). YAM²: A multidimensional conceptual model extending UML. *Information Systems, 31*(6), 541–567.

ARQ. (n.d.). A SPARQL processor for Jena. Retrieved from http://jena.sourceforge.net/ ARQ/

Artale, A., Calvanese, D., Kontchakov, R., & Zakharyaschev, M. (2009). The DL-Lite family and relations. *Journal of Artificial Intelligence Research, 36,* 1–69.

Atserias, J., Zaragoza, H., Ciaramita, M., & Attardi, G. (2008). Semantically annotated snapshot of the English Wikipedia. *Proceedings of the Sixth International Language Resources and Evaluation (LREC'08).*

Auer, S., Bizer, C., Kobilarov, G., Lehmann, J., Cyganiak, R., & Ives, Z. (2008). Dbpedia: A nucleus for a Web of open data. *Proceedings of the Conference on The Semantic Web,* (pp. 722–735).

Baader, F., Brandt, S., & Lutz, C. (2005). Pushing the EL envelope. *In Proceedings of the 19th International Joint Conference on Artificial Intelligence* (IJCAI) (pp. 364-369), Edinburgh, Scotland.

Baader, F., Calvanese, C., McGuinness, D. L., Nardi, D., & Patel-Schneider, P. F. (Eds.). (2003). *The description logic handbook: Theory, implementation, and applications.* Cambridge University Press.

Baader, F., Lutz, C., & Suntisrivaraporn, B. (2006) CEL-A polynomial-time reasoner for life science ontologies. In *Proceedings of the Third International Joint Conference of Automated Reasoning, IJCAR 2006,* (pp. 287-291).

Baader, F., & Sattler, U. (2003). Description logics with aggregates and concrete domains. *Information Systems, 28*(8), 979–1004.

Berardi, D., Calvanese, D., & De Giacomo, G. (2005). Reasoning on UML class diagrams. *Artificial Intelligence, 168*(1-2), 70–118.

Boag, S., Chamberlin, D., Fernándex, M. F., Florescu, D., Robie, J., & Siméon, J. (2007). *XQuery 1.0: An XML query language.* Retrieved from http://www.w3.org/ TR/xquery/

Bray, T., Paoli, J., Sperberg-McQueen, C. M., & Maler, E. (Eds.). (2000). *Extensible markup language* (XML) 1.0 (2nd ed.). W3C Recommendation, 6 October 2000. Retrieved from http://www. w3.org/ TR/REC-xml/

Brickley, D., & Guha, R. V. (Eds.). (2004). *RDF vocabulary description language 1.0: RDF schema.* Retrieved from http://www.w3.org/ TR/ rdf-schema/

Brin, S. (1998). *Extracting patterns and relations from the World Wide Web.* International Workshop on The World Wide Web and Databases, (pp. 172-183).

Broekstra, J., Kampman, A., & van Harmelen, F. (2003). An architecture for storing and querying RDF data and schema information. In *Spinning the Semantic Web* (pp. 197–222). Sesame.

Cafarella, M. (2009). Extracting and querying a comprehensive Web database. In *Proceedings of the Conference on Innovative Data Systems Research (CIDR).* Asilomar, CA. Retrieved from http://www.cs.washington.edu/ homes/mjc/papers/ cafarella-cidr09.pdf

Calvanese, D., Carroll, J., De Giacomo, G., Herman, I., Parsia, B., Patel-Schneider, P., & Ruttengerb, A. (2008). *OWL 2 Web ontology language: Profiles*. Retrieved from http://www.w3.org/TR/2008/WD-owl2- profiles-20081008/

Calvanese, D., De Giacomo, G., Lembo, D., Lenzerini, M., & Rosati, R. (2008). Path-based identification constraints in description logics. In *Proceedings of the 11th International Conference on Principles of Knowledge Representation and Reasoning* (KR) (pp. 231-241). Sydney, Australia.

Calvanese, D., Kharlamov, E., Nutt, W., & Thorne, C. (2008). *Proceedings of the 2nd International Workshop on Ontologies and Information Systems for the Semantic Web (ONISW)* (pp. 97-104). Napa Valley, California, USA.

Castellanos, M., Wang, S., Dayal, U., & Gupta, C. (2010) SIE-OBI: A streaming information extraction platform for operational business intelligence. In *Proceeding of SIGMOD Conference 2010*, (pp. 1105-1110).

Cimiano, P., Handschuh, S., & Staab, S. (2004). Towards the self-annotating Web. In *Proceedings of the 13th International Conference on World Wide Web* (pp. 462-471). New York, NY: ACM. doi:10.1145/988672.988735

Cimiano, P., & Völker, J. (2005). Text2Onto. In *Proceedings of the Conference on Natural Language Processing and Information Systems* (pp. 227-238). Retrieved from http://dx.doi.org/10.1007/ 11428817_21

Clark & Parsia. (2010). *Pellet: The OWL 2 reasoner*. Retrieved from http://clarkparsia.com/pellet/

Danger, R., & Berlanga, R. (2008). A Semantic Web approach for ontological instances analysis. *Software and Data Technologies. Communications in Computer and Information Science, 22*, 269–282.

Danger, R., & Berlanga, R. (2009). Generating complex ontology instances from documents. *Journal of Algorithms, 64*(1), 16–30.

Dean, M., Schreiber, G., Bechhofer, S., van Harmelen, F., Hendler, J., Horrocks, I., et al. Stein, L.A. (2004). *OWL Web ontology language reference*. W3C Recommendation 10 February 2004. Retrieved from http://www.w3.org/TR/owl-ref/

Declerck, T., Krieger, H., Saggion, H., & Spies, M. (2008). Ontology-driven human language technology for semantic-based business intelligence. In *Proceeding of the 2008 Conference on ECAI 2008: 18th European Conference on Artificial Intelligence* (pp. 841-842). IOS Press. Retrieved from http://portal.acm.org/ citation.cfm?id=1567281.1567497

Deliège, F., & Pedersen, T. B. (2010). Position list word aligned hybrid: Optimizing space and performance for compressed bitmaps. In *Proceedings of EDBT*, (pp. 228-239).

Dublin Core Metadata Initiative. (n.d.). *Website*. Retrieved from http://dublincore.org/

Giacometti, A., Marcel, P., & Negre, E. (2009a). Recommending multidimensional queries. In *Proceedings of the 11th International Conference on Data Warehousing and Knowledge Discovery* (DaWaK 2009), (pp. 453-466).

Giacometti, A., Marcel, P., Negre, E., & Soulet, A. (2009b). Query recommendations for OLAP discovery driven analysis. In *Proceedings of the ACM 12th International Workshop on Data Warehousing and OLAP* (DOLAP 2009), (pp. 81-88).

Glimm, B., Horrocks, I., Lutz, C., & Sattler, U. (2008). Conjunctive query answering for the description logic SHIQ. *Journal of Artificial Intelligence Research, 31*, 151–198.

Golfarelli, M., Maio, D., & Rizzi, S. (1998). The dimensional fact model: A conceptual model for data warehouses. *International Journal of Co-operative Information Systems, 7*(2-3), 215–247.

Grosof, B. N., Horrocks, I., Volz, R., & Decker, S. (2003). Description logic programs: Combining logic programs with description logic. *In Proceedings of the 12th International World Wide Web Conference* (WWW) (pp. 48-57). Budapest, Hungary.

Haarslev, V., & Möller, R. (2001). Description of the RACER system and its applications. In *Working Notes of the 2001 International Description Logics Workshop*. Retrieved from CEUR-WS.org

Hacid, M.-S., & Sattler, U. (1997). An object-centered multi-dimensional data model with hierarchically structured dimensions. In *Proceedings of the IEEE Knowledge and Data Engineering Exchange Workshop (KDEX)* (pp. 65-72).

Harris, S., & Gibbins, N. (2003). 3store: Efficient bulk RDF storage. In *Proceedings of PSSS*, 2003.

Harth, A., Umbrich, J., Hogan, A., & Decker, D. (2007). YARS2: A federated repository for querying graph structured data from the Web. In *Proc. of 6th International Semantic Web Conference/ 2nd Asian Semantic Web Conference*, (pp. 211-224).

Herman, I. (2008). *RDFS and OWL 2 RL generator service*. Retrieved from http://www.ivan-herman.net/Misc/2008/owlrl/

Hermit. (2010). *Hermit OWL reasoner*. Retrieved from http://hermit-reasoner.com/

Horrocks, I. (1998). Using an expressive description logic: Fact or fiction? *In Proceedings of 6th Conference on Principles of Knowledge Representation and Reasoning*, (pp. 636-649). Morgan Kaufmann. Retrieved from http://owl.man.ac.uk/factplusplus/

Horrocks, I., Patel-Schneider, P. F., Boley, H., Tabet, S., Grosof, B., & Dean, M. (2004). *SWRL: A Semantic Web rule language combining OWL and RuleML*. W3C Consortium, Member submission. Retrieved from http://www.w3.org/ Submission/ SWRL/

Horrocks, I., van Harmelen, F., & Patel-Schneider, P. (2001). *Reference description of the DAML+OIL ontology markup language*. Retrieved from http:// www.daml.org/ 2000/12/reference.html

Hustadt, U., Motik, B., & Sattler, U. (2005). Data complexity of reasoning in very expressive description logics. In *Proceedings of the 19th International Joint Conference on Artificial Intelligence* (IJCAI) (pp. 466-471), Edinburgh, Scotland.

Inmon, W. H., Strauss, D., & Neushloss, G. (2008). *DW 2.0: The architecture for the next generation of data warehousing*. Morgan Kauffman.

Jarke, M., Lenzerini, M., Vassiliou, Y., & Vassiliadis, P. (Eds.). (2000). *Fundamentals of data warehouses*. Springer.

Jensen, M. R., Holmgren, T., & Pedersen, T. B. (2004). Discovering multidimensional structure in relational data. In *Proceedings of the 6th International Conference on Data Warehousing and Knowledge Discovery (DaWaK)* (pp. 138-148).

Jensen, M. R., Møller, T. H., & Pedersen, T. B. (2001). Converting XML data to UML diagrams for conceptual data integration. In *Proceedings of the 1st International Workshop on Data Integration over the Web (DIWeb)* (pp. 17-31), Interlaken, Switzerland.

Karvounarakis, G., Alexaki, S., Christophides, V., Plexousakis, D., & Scholl, M. (2002). RQL: A declarative query language for RDF. In *Proceedings Eleventh International World Wide Web Conference*, (pp. 592-603).

Kimball, R. (1996). *The data warehouse toolkit: Practical techniques for building dimensional data warehouses*. John Wiley.

Kiryakov, A., Popov, B., Terziev, I., Manov, D., & Ognyanoff, D. (2004). Semantic annotation, indexing, and retrieval. *Web Semantic, 2*(1), 49–79.

Klyne, G., Carroll, J., & McBride, B. (Eds.). (2004). *Resource description framework (RDF) concepts and abstract syntax*. W3C Recommendation 10 February 2004. Retrieved from http://www.w3.org/ TR/rdf-concepts/

Lenzerini, M. (2002). Data integration: A theoretical perspective. In *Proceedings of the Twenty-first ACM SIGACT-SIGMOD-SIGART Symposium on Principles of Database Systems* (PODS), (pp. 233-246).

Liu, X., Thomsen, C., & Pedersen, T. B. (2010). *3XL: Supporting efficient operations on very large OWL lite triple-stores. Information Systems 36(4):765-781 (2011)*. Preprint available as DBTR no. 28. Retrieved from http://dbtr.cs.aau.dk

Maedche, A., Neumann, G., Staab, S., & Saarbruecken, G. (2003). *Bootstrapping an ontology-based information extraction system* (pp. 345–359). Intelligent Exploration of the Web.

Mannino, M. V. (2007). *Database design, application development, & administration*. McGraw Hill.

Motik, B., & Rosatti, R. (2010). Reconciling description logics and rules. *Journal of the ACM, 57*(5), 1–63.

Motik, B., Sattler, U., & Studer, R. (2005). Query answering for OWL-DL with rules. *Journal of Web Semantics: Science, Services and Agents on the World Wide Web, 3*(1), 41–60.

Nebot, V., & Berlanga, R. (2009). Efficient retrieval of ontology fragments using an interval labeling scheme. *Information Sciences, 179*(24), 4151–4173.

Nebot, V., & Berlanga, R. (2010). Building data warehouses with semantic data. *In Proceedings of the 1st International Workshop on Business Intelligence and the Web (BEWEB)*. Lausanne, Switzerland.

Nebot, V., Berlanga, R., Pérez, J., Aramburu, M., & Pedersen, T. (2009). Multidimensional integrated ontologies: A framework for designing semantic data warehouses. *Journal of Data Semantics. Special Issue on Semantic Data Warehouses, 13*, 1–36.

NeOn Project team. (2010). *Neon tool-kit*. Retrieved from http://neon-toolkit.org/wiki/Main_Page

Neumann, T., & Weikum, G. (2008). RDF-3X: A RISC-style engine for RDF. In *Proc. Of the VLDB Endowment, 1*(1), 647-659.

Neumann, T., & Weikum, G. (2010). The RDF-3X engine for scalable management of RDF data. *The VLDB Journal, 19*(1), 91–113.

Niemi, T., Toivonen, S., Niinimäki, M., & Nummenmaa, J. (2007). Ontologies with Semantic Web/Grid in data integration for OLAP. *International Journal on Semantic Web and Information Systems, 3*(4), 25–49.

Niinimäki, M., & Niemi, T. (2009). An ETL process for OLAP using RDF/OWL ontologies. *Journal of Data Semantics. Special Issue on Semantic Data Warehouses, 13*, 97–119.

ORACLE-RDF. (n.d.). *Oracle technical network, semantic technologies center*. Retrieved from http://www.oracle.com/technology /tech/semantic_technologies /index.html

Ortiz, M., Calvanese, D., & Either, T. (2008). Data complexity of query answering in expressive description logics via tableaux. *Journal of Automated Reasoning, 41*(1), 61–98.

Pedersen, T., & Jensen, C. (1999). *Multidimensional data modeling for complex data*. IEEE International Conference on Data Engineering (ICDE) (pp. 336-345).

Pedersen, T. B. (2010). Research challenges for cloud intelligence (invited talk). In *Proceedings of the Workshop on Business IntelligencE and the WEB (BEWEB), 2010*.

Pérez-Martínez, J. M., Berlanga, R., & Aramburu, M. J. (2009). A relevance model for a data warehouse contextualized with documents. *Information Processing & Management, 45*(3), 356–367.

Pérez-Martínez, J. M., Berlanga, R., Aramburu, M. J., & Pedersen, T. B. (2008a). Contextualizing data warehouses with documents. *Decision Support Systems, 45*(1), 77–94.

Pérez-Martínez, J. M., Berlanga, R., Aramburu, M. J., & Pedersen, T. B. (2008b). Integrating data warehouses with Web data: A survey. *IEEE Transactions on Knowledge and Data Engineering, 20*(7), 940–955.

Priebe, T., & Pernul, G. (2003). Towards integrative enterprise knowledge portals. In *Proceedings of the Twelfth International Conference on Information and Knowledge Management (CIKM)* (pp. 216-223)

Protégé. (2010). *Protégé Project*. Stanford Center for Biomedical Informatics Research. Retrieved from http://protege.stanford.edu/

Prud'hommeaux, E., & Seaborne, A. (2008). SPARQL query language for RDF. Retrieved from http://www.w3.org/TR/rdf-sparql-query/

Reeve, L., & Han, H. (2005). Survey of semantic annotation platforms. In *Proceedings of the 2005 ACM Symposium on Applied Computing* (p. 1638).

Romero, O., & Abelló, A. (2007). Automating multidimensional design from ontologies. In *Proceedings of the ACM Tenth International Workshop on Data Warehousing and OLAP* (pp. 1-8). Lisbon, Portugal: ACM. doi:10.1145/1317331.1317333

Romero, O., & Abelló, A. (2010a). Automatic validation of requirements to support multidimensional design. *Data & Knowledge Engineering, 69*(9), 917–942.

Romero, O., & Abelló, A. (2010b). A framework for multidimensional design of data warehouses from ontologies. *Data & Knowledge Engineering, 69*(11), 1138–1157.

Romero, O., Calvanese, D., Abelló, A., & Rodríguez-Muro, M. (2009). Discovering functional dependencies for multidimensional design. In *Proceeding of the ACM Twelfth International Workshop on Data Warehousing and OLAP* (pp. 1-8). Hong Kong, China: ACM. doi:10.1145/1651291.1651293

Romero, O., Simitsis, A., & Abello, A. (2010). (to appear). GEM: Requirement-driven generation of ETL and multidimensional conceptual designs. *DaWaK, 2011*.

Saggion, H., Funk, A., Maynard, D., & Bontcheva, K. (2007). Ontology-based information extraction for business intelligence. In *Proceedings of ISWC/ASWC* (pp. 843-856)

Savo, D. F., Lembo, D., Lenzerini, M., Poggi, A., Rodriguez-Muro, M., & Romagnoli, V. … Stella, G. (2010). Mastro at work: Experiences on ontology-based data access. In *Proc. of the 23rd International Workshop on Description Logics, CEUR Electronic Workshop* (pp. 20-31). Waterloo, Canada: CEUR. Retrieved from http://www.dis.uniroma1.it/quonto/

Sell, D., Silva, D. C. D., Beppler, F. D., Napoli, M., Ghisi, F. B., Pacheco, R. C. S., & Todesco, J. L. (2008). SBI: A semantic framework to support business intelligence. In *Proceedings of the First International Workshop on Ontology-Supported Business Intelligence* (pp. 1-11). Karlsruhe, Germany: ACM. doi:10.1145/1452567.1452578

Simitsis, A., Skoutas, D., & Castellanos, M. (2008). Natural language reporting for ETL processes. In *Proceedings of the 11th ACM International Workshop on Data Warehousing and OLAP* (DOLAP), (pp. 65-72).

Simitsis, A., Skoutas, D., & Castellanos, M. (2010). Representation of conceptual ETL designs in natural language using Semantic Web technology. *Data & Knowledge Engineering, 69*(1), 96–115.

Skoutas, D., & Simitsis, A. (2006). Designing ETL processes using Semantic Web technologies. In *Proceedings of the 9th ACM International Workshop on Data Warehousing and OLAP* (DOLAP), (pp. 67-74).

Skoutas, D., & Simitsis, A. (2007). Ontology-based conceptual design of ETL processes for both structured and semi-structured data. *International Journal on Semantic Web and Information Systems, 3*(4), 1–24.

Skoutas, D., Simitsis, A., & Sellis, T. (2009). Ontology-driven conceptual design of ETL processes using graph transformations. *Journal of Data Semantics. Special Issue on Semantic Data Warehouses, 13,* 120–146.

Spahn, M., Kleb, J., Grimm, S., & Scheidl, S. (2008). Supporting business intelligence by providing ontology-based end-user information self-service. In *Proceedings of the first international workshop on Ontology-Supported Business Intelligence* (pp. 1-12). Karlsruhe, Germany: ACM. doi:10.1145/1452567.1452577

Suchanek, F. M., Kasneci, G., & Weikum, G. (2007). YAGO: A core of semantic knowledge. In *Proceedings of the 16th International Conference on World Wide Web* (pp. 697-706). Banff, Alberta, Canada: ACM. doi:10.1145/1242572.1242667

Suchanek, F. M., Kasneci, G., & Weikum, G. (2008). YAGO: A large ontology from Wikipedia and WordNet. *Web Semantics, 6*(3), 203–217.

Thorne, C., & Calvanese, D. (2009). Controlled aggregate tree shaped questions over ontologies. In *Proceedings of 8th International Conference on Flexible Query Answering Systems (FQAS)* (pp.394-405).

Vassiliadis, P. (1998). Modeling multidimensional databases-Cubes and cube operations. In *Proceedings of the IEEE International Conference on Scientific and Statistical Database Management (SSDBM)* (pp. 53-62).

Vrdoljak, B., Banek, M., & Rizzi, S. (2003). Designing Web warehouses from XML schemas. In *Proceedings of the 5th International Conference on Data Warehousing and Knowledge Discovery* (DaWaK) (pp.89-98), Prague, Czech Republic.

Weld, D. S., Hoffmann, R., & Wu, F. (2008). Using Wikipedia to bootstrap open information extraction. *SIGMOD Record, 37*(4), 62–68. doi:. doi:10.1145/1519103.1519113

Wilkinson, K., Sayers, C., Kuno, H. A., & Reynolds, D. (2003). Efficient RDF storage and retrieval in Jena2. In *Proceedings of SWDB,* (pp. 131–150).

Wu, F., & Weld, D. S. (2007). Autonomously semantifying Wikipedia. In *Proceedings of the Sixteenth ACM Conference on Information and Knowledge Management* (pp. 41-50). Lisbon, Portugal: ACM. doi:10.1145/1321440.1321449

Wu, F., & Weld, D. S. (2008). Automatically refining the Wikipedia infobox ontology. In *Proceeding of the 17th International Conference on World Wide Web* (pp. 635-644). Beijing, China: ACM. doi:10.1145/1367497.1367583

Yang, X., Procopiuc, C. M., & Srivastava, D. (2009). Summarizing relational databases. In *Proceedings of the 35th International Conference on Very Large Data Bases* (VLDB), (pp. 634-645). Lyon, France.

KEY TERMS AND DEFINITIONS

Business Intelligence: Business intelligence (BI) is a broad category of applications and technologies for gathering, integrating, analyzing, and providing access to data to help enterprise users make better business decisions. BI applications include the activities of decision support systems, query and reporting, online analytical processing (OLAP), statistical analysis, forecasting, and data mining.

Data Semantics: The semantics refers to the meaning of data. Such an abstraction can be formalized as a mapping between an object modeled, represented and stored in an information system and a set of agreed concepts (objects, relationships, behavior) representing a conceptualization of the real-world.

Semantic Web: The Semantic Web is an extension of the current Web that provides an easier way to find, share, reuse and combine information. It refers to the group of methods and technologies to allow machines to understand the meaning - or "semantics" - of information on the World Wide Web. The term was coined by the W3C director Tim Berners-Lee. He defines the Semantic Web as a web of data that can be processed directly and indirectly by machines. It is based on machine-readable information and builds on XML technology's capability to define customized tagging schemes and RDF's flexible approach to representing data.

About the Contributors

Marta Elena Zorrilla Pantaleón is an Assistant Professor in Computer Science at the University of Cantabria (Spain). She earned her Bachelor's degree in Telecommunication Engineering and PhD in Computer Science at the University of Cantabria in 1994 and 2001, respectively. She has participated in and managed more than 20 research projects, most of them with companies, and she is author of a database book and more than 40 works published in international journals, books, and conferences. She is an active reviewer of several international journals and conferences (DSS, IJCSA, IEEE-Education, IEEE-RITA, SCI, BEWEB, etc.). Her research interests are the design and development of Information Systems and intelligent systems for companies, and, inside the educational area, the application of data mining techniques and OLAP technologies in order to analyse and improve Web-based learning sites.

Jose-Norberto Mazón is Assistant Professor at the Department of Software and Computing Systems in the University of Alicante (Spain). He obtained his Ph.D. in Computer Science from the University of Alicante (Spain) within the Lucentia Research Group. He has published several papers about data warehouses and requirement engineering in national and international workshops and conferences, (such as DAWAK, ER, DOLAP, BNCOD, JISBD and so on) and in several journals such as Decision Support Systems (DSS), SIGMOD Record or Data and Knowledge Engineering (DKE). He has also been co-organizer of the International Workshop on Business Intelligence and the Web (BEWEB 2010) and the International Workshop on The Web and Requirements Engineering (WeRE 2010). His research interests are: business intelligence, design of data warehouses, multidimensional databases, requirement engineering, and model driven development.

Óscar Ferrández is a postdoctoral researcher in the BioMedical Informatics department at the University of Utah (USA). He got his Ph.D in Computational Linguistics at the University of Alicante (Spain) within the Natural Language Processing and Information Systems research group. He has publications in international journals (such as Information Sciences, Data and Knowledge Engineering, and Information Processing and Management) as well as communications in relevant conferences and workshops related to his research field. He has been involved in several national and European research projects together with other international research institutions. He is an active member and reviewer of several international journals and conferences. His research interests are focused on human system interaction; ontologies and Semantic Web; machine learning; knowledge discovering; and natural language processing and its application to clinical records.

Irene Garrigós is an Assistant Professor and post-doc researcher at the University of Alicante, (Spain), from which she holds a PhD and a Master's in Computer Science. She has published several papers in national and international workshops, conferences, and journals (such as ICWE, ER, WISE, APWEB, JISBD, Information and Software Technologies, Journal of Web Engineering, and so on). Dr. Garrigós has served as a Program Committee member of several workshops and conferences such as ER, JISBD, WISM, MDA, FPUML, UWA, and has served as assistant referee in several international conferences such as WWW and ICWE. She has done research stays in Belgium (Vrije Universiteit Brussel) and the Netherlands (Technische Universiteit Eindhoven). Her research interests are: Web engineering, personalization, model driven development, requirement engineering, Web and business intelligence, and adaptive systems.

Florian Daniel is a postdoctoral researcher at the Department of Information Engineering and Computer Science of the University of Trento, Italy. He has a PhD in Information Technology from Politecnico di Milano, Italy. His main research interests are mash-ups and Web/services engineering, and compliance, quality, and privacy in business intelligence applications. He is co-author of the book "Engineering Web Applications" (Springer, 2009) and has published more than 50 scientific papers in international conferences and journals. Florian is co-organizer of the international workshops ComposableWeb and BEWEB and is involved in the organization of international conferences like BPM, ICSOC, and ICWE.

Juan Trujillo is a Full-time Professor at the Department of Software and Computing Systems in the University of Alicante (Spain). His main research topics include business intelligence applications, data warehouses' development, OLAP, data mining, UML, MDA, data warehouses security and quality, etc. He has advised 9 PhD students and published more than a 120 papers in different national and international high impact conferences such as the ER, UML, ADBIS or CaiSE, and more than 30 papers in highly ranked international journals indexed by JCR such as the DKE, DSS, ISOFT, IS, or JDBM. He has also been co-editor of five special issues in different JCR journals (e.g. DKE). He has also been PC member of different events and JCR journals such as ER, DAWAK, CIKM, ICDE, DOLAP, DSS, JDM, ISOFT, and DKE, and PC Chair of DOLAP'05, DAWAK'05-'06 and FP-UML'05-'09. Further information on his main research publications can be found on: http://www.informatik.uni-trier.de/~ley/db/indices/a-tree/t/Trujillo:Juan.html.

* * *

Alberto Abelló has an MSc and a PhD in Computer Science from the Universitat Politècnica de Catalunya (Polytechnical University of Catalonia). He is an Associate Professor at the Facultat d'Informàtica de Barcelona (Computer Science School of Barcelona). He is also a member of the MPI research group (Information Processing and Modeling) at the same university, specializing in conceptual modeling and databases schema validation. His research interests are database design, datawarehousing, OLAP tools, ontologies, and reasoning. He is author of articles and papers presented and published in international conferences (e.g. CAiSE, DEXA, DaWaK, DOLAP, etc.) and journals (e.g. Information Systems, Data and Knowledge Engineering, etc.) on these subjects.

María A. Aguilar received his MS degree in Library Science and Documentation from Granada University, Granada, Spain, in 1996. She has worked as librarian at several librarians and museums (Library of Granada University, Public Library of Granada, Archaeological Museum of Granada). She is currently studying towards the Master's in Scientific Information: Treatment, Access and Evaluation at Granada University, Spain. She is the author of several papers on databases, data mining, and Information Systems. His research interests include data warehousing, extraction, transformation and loading tools from Web data sources, and the study of the quality of the libraries from the user's perspective.

María José Aramburu Cabo, Ph.D., received the BS degree in computer science from the Universidad Politécnica de Valencia in 1991 and the PhD degree from the School of Computer Science, University of Birmingham, United Kingdom, in 1998. She is Associate Professor of Computer Science at Universitat Jaume I, Spain. Dr. Aramburu Cabo is author of articles in international journals such as Information Processing & Management, Decision Support Systems, IEEE Transactions on Knowledge and Data Engineering, and numerous communications in international conferences such as ICDE, DEXA, and ECIR. Her main research interests include knowledge repositories, decision support systems, and integration of information.

Fadila Bentayeb received her PhD in computer science from the University of Orléans, France in 1998. She joined the University of Lyon 2, France in 1999 as a temporary assistant professor and became Associate Professor in 2001. She is head of the Bachelor of Computer Science and Statistics since 2003. She is a member of Complex Data Warehousing and OLAP research axis within the ERIC laboratory. Her current research interests regard database management systems, including the integration of data mining techniques into DBMSs and data warehouse design, with a special interest for schema evolution, personalization, XML and complex data warehousing, benchmarking, and optimization techniques.

Rafael Berlanga Llavori, Ph.D., is an Associate Professor of Computer Science at University Jaume I (UJI), Spain. His main research concerns the analysis and mining of semi-structured and semantic data in the context of the (Semantic) Web. He is the current leader of the Temporal Knowledge Group of the Computer Languages & Systems department (UJI). He is author of several articles in international journals of high impact, such as Decision Support Systems, BMC Bioinformatics, Information Processing & Management and Information Science, as well as more than 70 papers published in international conferences and workshops (DEXA, EDBT, ICDE, SIGMOD, etc.). He has served as PC member in several international workshops and congresses. More information of the research group is available at http://krono.act.uji.es.

Henrike Berthold joined SAP AG in 2008. She received her Ph.D. in Computer Science from Dresden University. She has been a visiting researcher at Lancaster University (UK) and at University of Alberta (Canada). After her Ph.D., she worked as a research assistant at Dresden University. Her research interests are on data management architectures, data integration, data warehousing, and approximate query answering.

Ester Boldrini is a PhD student in her 2nd year in the programme "NLP applied to specialised contexts" at the UA. She has a degree in "Translation and Interpreting" from the University of Tuscia, Italy and 2 European Masters at the UA. Her main field of interest is sentiment analysis and the creation of a solid annotation scheme for subjectivity in the new-textual genres born with the Web 2.0. and its application for the creation of a reference corpus for subjectivity. She is author of over 20 research papers and reviewer for international conferences. She also participates as a management staff and contact person in the IPeuropAware project and other European project working in the Bureau for International Project Management of UA.

Omar Boussaïd is a Full Professor in computer science at the School of Economics and Management of the University of Lyon 2, France. He received his PhD degree in computer science from the University of Lyon 1, France in 1988. Since 1995, he has been the Director of the Master Computer Science Engineering for Decision and Economic Evaluation of the University of Lyon 2. He was head of the Decision Support Databases research group within the ERIC Laboratory from 2008 to 2009. His main research subjects are data warehousing, multidimensional databases, and OLAP. His current research concerns complex data warehousing and mining, XML warehousing, combining OLAP and data mining, and the use of ontologies within complex data warehousing.

Stuart Campbell is the Chief Technical Officer of TIE. He is responsible for defining strategy, tactical planning, operational delivery, and portraying TIE's technical direction and products. Stuart has been involved in the field of e-business since 1989. Stuart has held notable positions at ICL (now Fujitsu), the Western European EDIFACT Board based within the European Commission, the European Standards, CMASS, and TIE. Stuart has produced multiple papers and regularly presents at conferences and forums such as XML Europe, eChallenges, EAN, and EU events. Stuart is chairing the SME committee in the European NESSI initiative and is Vice Chair of its Steering Committee. He also sits in the Future Internet SME group. Stuart has managed several large scale projects both internally within TIE and cooperating with external partners.

Ramón A. Carrasco received the Ph.D. degree (Sobresaliente Cum Laude) from Granada University, Granada, Spain, in 2003. Currently, he is an Associate Professor in the Department of Software Engineering at the University of Granada. He currently works at the Department of Business Intelligence (Data Warehousing, Data Mining, Balanced Scored Card, etc.) at the Spanish savings bank Caja Granada. He is the author of several papers on databases, data mining, Information Systems, and fuzzy logic. His research interests include data mining, clustering, classification, fuzzy dependencies, data mining languages, et cetera. He is a Member of the "Soft Computing and Intelligent Information Systems" Research Group and the "Evolutionary and Fuzzy Data Mining and Intelligent Systems" Laboratory.

Alessio Carenini has been working since 2007 as researcher at CEFRIEL. His research activities focus on knowledge management and Semantic Web services. He participated to the Semantic Web services research activities of the National Project *NeP4B* and to the research activities in FP6 SUPER(IST IP) related to business intelligence. He also participated to the FP6 research project TRIPCOM as responsible for the e-health use case, and to the OASIS standardization effort for the definition of a Semantic Execution Environment for Web services (SEE Technical Committee).

Erik Casagrande received a MEng in control engineering in 2003 from Padova University, visiting Lund University, and working in image processing and computer vision areas. He received an MSc in numerical modelling in 2005 from Padova University. He then completed his studies with the PhD degree from Aston University in the area of machine learning, focusing on causality, nonlinear time series, dynamical systems, and synchronisation identification analysis for biomedical data. Recent research interest has been in machine learning techniques for text analysis and technology forecasting.

Jérôme Darmont received his PhD in computer science from the University of Clermont-Ferrand II, France in 1999. He joined the University of Lyon 2, France in 1999 as an Associate Professor, and became Full Professor in 2008. He was head of the Decision Support Databases research group within the ERIC laboratory from 2000 to 2008, director of the Computer Science and Statistics Department of the Faculty of Economics and Management from 2003 to 2010, and has been in charge of the Complex Data Warehousing and OLAP research axis at ERIC since 2010. His current research interests mainly relate to handling so-called complex data in data warehouses (XML warehousing, performance optimization, auto-administration, benchmarking...), but also include data quality and security as well as medical or health-related applications.

Rodolfo Delmonte is Associate Professor of Linguistics at the University of Venice - Ca' Foscari where he teaches Corpus and Computational Linguistics. He is a specialist in experimental phonetics, speech synthesis, and computational linguistics, and he has published over 150 articles and book chapters in national and international conferences and journals. He is also the author of 7 books and editor and coeditor of another 5. His approach to research in the last years has been oriented towards the following general themes: Web, knowledge and natural language processing, analysis of spontaneous speech and the structure of dialog, semantics and pragmatics for the deep analysis of text, creation of linguistic resources like lexica and treebanks, Prosody and speech synthesis for the creation of tools for automatic language learning, and machine translation. He is co-founder and CSO of Interanalytics, a Swiss company focused on leveraging human-language technology for next generation business analytics.

Alexandra Balahur Dobrescu is research fellow at the University of Alicante. She is currently preparing to defend her PhD thesis entitled "Sentiment Analysis in Multilingual Documents of Different Text Types". She is a Computer Science graduate of the "A. I. Cuza" University of Iasi, Romania (2007). Her main fields of interest are sentiment analysis (opinion mining), emotion detection, information extraction, and textual entailment. She is the author of over 30 scientific publications, in international reviews and conference proceedings. She was a trainee for 6 months with the Europe Media Monitor action, at the European Commission's Joint Research Centre in Ispra, Italy, where she applied opinion mining to media monitoring and a trainee at the University of Saarland, Germany, where she worked on corpus development for German and opinion question answering systems. She is a member of the implementation team in different European FP6, FP7, and COST projects containing interdisciplinary research on data mining and the impact it has on economic and social phenomena.

Moez Essaidi is a Ph.D. candidate in the department of computer and information sciences at the University of Paris XIII (LIPN - UMR CNRS 7030), Villetaneuse, France. His supervisors are Pr. Céline Rouveirol and Pr. Aomar Osmani. He received a M.Sc. degree in computer science from University of

Paris I - Panthéon Sorbonne, Paris, France. His research interests are: data warehouses design, model-driven development and machine learning for engineering, and cloud-based architectures. Contact him at: moez.essaidi@lipn.univ-paris13.fr.

Lorena Etcheverry holds a Master's degree in Computer Science (2010) and an Engineer in Computer Science degree (2003) from the Computer Science Institute, Faculty of Engineering, University of the Republic. She works as a Teaching and Research Assistant at the Computer Science Institute, where she has been a member of the Information Systems Group since 2001. As such, she has been involved in the teaching of several courses, in particular, databases fundamentals and data warehousing systems design. Her research interests and activities fall in the area of Information Systems, with emphasis in data quality and data warehousing. She has also had several years of professional experience as a Systems and Applications Analyst working for several local companies.

Cécile Favre received her MSc in Knowledge Discovery from Databases in 2003, and her PhD in Computer Science in 2007, both from the University of Lyon 2, France. She has been an Associate Professor at the University of Lyon 2 since 2009. After working on integrating data mining techniques into DBMSs, her research interests now relate to data warehouse design and evolution, especially the personalization problem and the integration of users' knowledge in data warehouses. She is also interested in the domain of social networks. She is involved in various program committees of both national and international conferences.

Flavius Frasincar obtained the M.Sc. in computer science from Politehnica University Bucharest, Romania, in 1998. In 2000, he received the professional doctorate degree in software engineering from Eindhoven University of Technology, the Netherlands. He got the PhD degree in computer science from Eindhoven University of Technology, the Netherlands, in 2005. Since 2005, he is Assistant Professor in Information Systems at Erasmus University Rotterdam, the Netherlands. He has published in numerous conferences and journals in the areas of databases, Web Information Systems, personalization, and the Semantic Web. He is a member of the editorial board of the International Journal of Web Engineering and Technology.

Diego García Saiz is a student in Computer Science at the University of Cantabria (Spain) since 2005. Currently he is working in educational data mining field as a research scholar at Mathematics, Statistics and Computing department. He has also participated in Real-Time Systems projects at Real-Time Computing Department at University of Cantabria, and he is author of 2 works presented in international conferences. His research interests are software engineering, databases, and data mining.

Matteo Golfarelli received his Ph.D. for his work on autonomous agents in 1998. Since 2005 he is Associate Professor, teaching Information Systems, Database Systems, and Data Mining. He has published over 60 papers in refereed journals and international conferences in the fields of pattern recognition, mobile robotics, multi-agent systems, and business intelligence, which is now his main research field. He is co-author of a book on data warehouse design. He is co-chair of the MiproBIS Conference and member of the editorial board of the Int. Jour. of Data Mining, Modeling, and Management and of the Int. Jour. of Knowledge-Based Organizations. His current research interests include distributed and semantic data warehouse systems, what-if analysis, and business performance monitoring.

Laura González is a Teacher Assistant at the Computer Science Department, Faculty of Engineering, University of the Republic of Uruguay. She holds an Engineer in Computer Science degree, and since 2004, she has participated in research projects, consulting activities, and teaching activities at this department. She did an internship at the University of Versailles where she worked in applying service-oriented concepts in a data quality measurement tool. She is currently doing a Master's degree in Computer Science where she is addressing Enterprise Services Bus (ESB) based approaches to achieve self-adaptation in service-oriented systems. Her current research interests include middleware technologies, especially Web Services and ESB, self-adaptation in service-oriented systems, and quality of service.

Frank Goossen is currently finishing his B.Sc. degree in economics and informatics and working on his M.Sc. degree in computational economics at the Erasmus University Rotterdam, the Netherlands. The focus of his Bachelor's thesis has been on exploring the benefits of using Semantic Web technologies for recommending news items. During his Master's he continues his Bachelor research direction by proposing and evaluating more advanced forms of semantics-based recommenders.

Nouria Harbi received her PhD in computer science from the INSA Lyon, France in 1990. She was a member of ISEOR laboratory from 1985 to 2006, where she worked on Information Systems. She is currently working at the ERIC laboratory on the security of decision-support Information Systems and on modeling data warehouses. She has been the director of the MSc "Security in Information Systems" of the University of Lyon 2 since 1993.

Andreas Henschel studied Computer Science in Aarhus University, Denmark and received his M.Sc. in Computational Logic at the Technische Universitaet Dresden, Germany in 2002. He then joined Scionics Computer Innovation Ltd., where he worked for the Bioinformatics service facility of the Max Planck Institute for Cell Biology and Genetics, Dresden, Germany. In 2008 he received his Ph.D. from Technische Universitaet Dresden with summa cum laude. His main research interests are within Artificial Intelligence and Bioinformatics. He joined Masdar Institute (Abu Dhabi, UAE) as a post-doctoral researcher in April 2009, where he is working on Technology Forecasting with focus on Renewable Energy.

Frederik Hogenboom obtained the M.Sc. degree cum laude in economics and informatics from the Erasmus University Rotterdam, the Netherlands, in 2009, specializing in computational economics. During his Bachelor's and Master's programs, his research mainly focused on the Semantic Web and learning agents. Currently, he is PhD student at Erasmus University Rotterdam, the Netherlands. His PhD work focuses on methods to extract financial events from emerging news and how to employ the extracted information for algorithmic trading. This research combines techniques from various disciplines, amongst which are Semantic Web, text mining, artificial intelligence, machine learning, linguistics, and finance. Other research interests are related to applications of computer science in economic environments, agent-based systems, and applications of the Semantic Web.

Miguel J. Hornos has been a Lecturer at the University of Granada (Spain) since 1991, where he had previously received both an MSc in Computer Science and a PhD in Computing. He is currently involved in various (European, national, regional and local) Research, Development and Innovation

(R&D&I) Projects. His fields of research are specification and verification of complex software systems, software architectures for the development of collaborative applications, ubiquitous computing and intelligent environments, and Information and Communication Technologies (ICT) applied to business and education, on which he has written several textbooks as well as a series of research papers published in international journals and conferences specialized on these topics.

Wouter IJntema obtained the B.Sc. degree in economics and informatics from Erasmus University Rotterdam, the Netherlands, in 2009. Currently he is working towards his M.Sc. degree in computational economics at the Erasmus University Rotterdam, the Netherlands. The focus of his research is on methods for automatic information extracting from news. His research interests include machine learning, business intelligence, the Semantic Web foundations and applications, and Web Information Systems.

Isam Janajreh is an Associate Professor in Mechanical Engineering at Masdar Institute, received his Ph.D. (97) and Master's (92, 94) from Virginia Tech in 1998 in Engineering Science and Mechanics (ESM) and Mechanical Engineering (ME). Specialized in solid/fluid interactions, turbulence modeling, and thermomechanical coupling. He was hired at Virginia Tech as visiting Professor at ESM and Math Departments through 1998, then joined Michelin R&D as an Automotive Research Engineer in the US analyzing wet tire traction, vehicle dynamics, and rubber material modeling. In 2001 was expatriated to Michelin France heading European Project "Tire Hydroplaning: Modeling and Analysis." Dr. Janajreh joined Masdar in 2007 as visiting ME Professor at MIT conducting research on the thermochemical conversion (combustion, pyrolysis, gasification).

Wolfgang Lehner is head of the Database Technology Group at TU Dresden. He received his Master's (1995) and subsequently his Doctorate (1998) in Computer Science from the University of Erlangen-Nuremberg. After a period with the Business Intelligence group at IBM's Almaden Research Center (USA), where he was involved in projects on adding materialized view support and multiple query optimization techniques to the core engine of IBM DB2/UDB. He and his group in Erlangen-Nuremberg initiated comprehensive research on the exploitation of DB technology to support complex message-based notification systems. After a temporary professorship at the University of Halle-Wittenberg, he finished his habilitation in 2001 with a thesis on subscription systems. Since 2002, Prof. Lehner has been actively advancing research & teaching at TU Dresden. He has published several books and more than 70 reviewed research papers. His research focuses on modeling and analyzing empirically collected mass data with advanced DB technology.

Sabine Loudcher is an Associate Professor in Computer Science at the University of Lyon 2, France. She received her PhD in Computer Science from the University of Lyon 1, France in 1996. Since 2000, she has been a member of the Decision Support Databases research group within the ERIC laboratory. Her main research subjects are data mining, multidimensional databases, OLAP, and complex data. Since 2003, she has been the Assistant Director of the ERIC laboratory.

Stuart Madnick is the John Norris Maguire Professor of Information Technologies in the MIT Sloan School of Management and Professor of Engineering Systems in the MIT school of Engineering. He received his MBA and Ph.D. in Computer Science from MIT and has been on the MIT faculty since

1972 and head of IT Group more than twenty years. He is co-Director of the Productivity From Information Technology Initiative and co-Heads the Total Data Quality Management research program. He is the author/co-author of over 300 books, articles, or reports on topics such as integrating information systems, data semantics, and strategic use of IT. He was a key designer of IBM's VM/370 operating system and Lockheed's DIALOG information retrieval system and has been the co-founder of high-tech firms, including Intercomp, Mitrol, iAggregate. Dr. Madnick has been a Visiting Professor at Harvard, Nanyang Technological University, University of Newcastle, Technion, and Victoria University.

Hadj Mahboubi received his Engineering degree in computer science from the University of Tlemcen, Algeria in 2003; his MSc in computer science from the INSA Lyon, France in 2005; and his PhD in computer science from the University of Lyon 2, France in 2008. He has been a research assistant in the University of Lyon 2 from 2007 to 2009 and is currently a post-doctoral researcher at the CEMAGREF Clermont-Ferrand, France. His research interests lie in the field of data warehouse design and XML data warehouse performance evaluation and optimization.

Nora Maïz received her Engineering degree in computer science from the University of Annaba, Algeria in 2004; her MSc in computer science from the INSA Lyon, France in 2005; and her PhD in computer science from the University of Lyon 2, France in 2010. She has been temporary research assistant at the University of Lyon 2 from 2007 to 2009. Her main research subject relates to the use of ontologies in the design of complex data warehouses.

Federica Mandreoli is a Research Associate at the Department of Information Engineering of the University of Modena and Reggio Emilia, Italy. She holds a Laurea degree in Computer Science and a PhD in Electronics Engineering and Computer Science from the University of Bologna. Her scientific interests are in the field of information and knowledge management and, currently, mainly concerns data sharing in P2P networks and query processing over graph-structured data. As to those research themes, she is author of publications dealing with query processing in P2P networks, structural disambiguation for semantic-aware applications, and personalized accesses to XML and Ontologies, and she joined national and international projects.

Elena Martirena works in CRM's applications in the area of financial business. She holds a Master's degree in Computer Science where she focused her analysis in data quality measurement mechanisms. Now she is participating in research projects about quality services in the Computer Science Department, Faculty of Engineering, University of the Republic of Uruguay. Her current research interests include data quality, especially data cleaning process in databases migration processes.

Patricio Martínez-Barco has a PhD in Computer Science (2001) and a Master's in Computer Science from the University of Alicante (1994). He is Professor since 1995 at the Department of Software and Computing Science (GPLSI division), starting at this University as a Lecturer, and later becoming Head of this department in 2009. His research interests are focused on computational linguistics and natural language processing. His last projects are related to text and opinion mining, information extraction, information retrieval, and question answering. He was General Chair of the ESTAL'04 (Alicante) and SEPLN'04 (Barcelona) conferences, as well as Local Chair of the SLPLT'01 (Jaén) workshop, and

Program Chair of IBEREVAL2010 (Valencia). He has advised three PhD theses (Estela Saquete, 2005; Borja Navarro, 2007; Rafael M. Terol, 2009) related to these topics. He has edited several books, and contributed with more than 50 papers to several journals and conferences.

Adriana Marotta is Assistant Professor at the Computer Science Institute of the University of the Republic of Uruguay since 2003. She received her PhD in Computer Science from the University of the Republic of Uruguay in 2008. She did three internships at the University of Versailles, France, during her PhD studies. Her research interests and activities mainly focus on data quality and data warehouse / Web warehouse systems. She has taught multiple courses in the area of Information Systems, in particular Data Quality and Data Warehousing courses. Adriana has directed two research projects in the topic of data quality, supported by CSIC (Comisión Sectorial de Investigación Científica) of the University of the Republic, and has participated in Latin-american projects (Prosul), Ibero-american projects (CYTED), and a Microsoft- Research project in the area of bio-informatics.

Andrés Montoyo is Full Professor of Databases at the Technical School and Professor of Ontology Design in Natural Language Processing and Semantic Web at the Master Computer Science Technologies Program at the University of Alicante. He is a member of the Research Group on Natural Language Processing and Information Systems in the Department of Software and Computing Systems at the University of Alicante. He received his Master's degree in Computer Science at the Polytechnic University of Valencia, Spain and his PhD in Computer Science at the University of Alicante, Spain. He is deputy director of the Technical School at University of Alicante (2004). His research interests are information extraction, word sense disambiguation, opinion mining, ontology, and the Semantic Web. He is the author of more than 70 scientific publications on international journals and conferences on many topics such as sentiment analysis and opinion mining among others. He has been involved both in national and international research projects.

Victoria Nebot received her BSc+MSc degree in Computer Science from Universitat Jaume I, Spain, in 2008. She joined the Temporal Knowledge Bases Group (TKBG) at Universitat Jaume I as a PhD Student. Her main research is focused on analyzing and exploiting semi-structured and complex data derived mainly from the Semantic Web. In particular, she is interested in researching new techniques that exploit the rich knowledge encoded in the ontologies associated to the data in order to make it available to data mining and OLAP tools and enhance decision support tasks and knowledge discovery.

Aomar Osmani is an Associate Professor at University Paris XIII (department of computer and information sciences, LIPN - UMR CNRS 7030). His research interests are machine learning, modeling, time and space reasoning, and diagnosis of dynamic systems. Contact him at: aomar.osmani@lipn.univ-paris13.fr.

Vincenzo Pallotta is Professor of Computer Science and Research Coordinator at the Webster University, Geneva, Switzerland. He is co-founder and CTO of Interanalytics, a Swiss company focused on leveraging human-language technology for next generation business analytics. He holds a Ph.D. in Computer Science from the Swiss Federal Institute of Technology in Lausanne (EPFL), Switzerland and an M.Sc. from University of Pisa, Italy. He has been a research fellow at: ICSI and UC in Berkeley,

Stanford University, University of Venice, University of Fribourg and EPFL. His backgrounds are in artificial intelligence, human-computer interaction, computational linguistics, and ubiquitous computing. He has been involved in several national and international research projects. His research currently focuses on new man-machine interaction models and summarization of human dialogs.

Byung-Kwon Park is a Professor of Dong-A University in Korea. He graduated from Seoul National University in 1986 and received the M.S. degrees from Korea Advanced Institute of Science and Technology (KAIST) in 1988. He earned the Ph.D. degree from Korea Advanced Institute of Science and Technology (KAIST) in 1998. From 1998 to 2000, he was a Research Staff Member at the Samsung Electronics Research Center. His research interests encompass database system, text information retrieval, stream data management, business intelligence, data warehousing and OLAP. He served as a program committee member of DOLAP04, DOLAP05, DOLAP07, DOLAP08, DOLAP09, and DOLAP10.

Torben Bach Pedersen, Ph.D., is a Professor of Computer Science at Aalborg University, Denmark. His research concerns business intelligence technologies such as multidimensional databases, multidimensional data modeling, data warehousing, online analytical processing, data mining, and data integration with a focus on complex settings such as (Semantic) Web data, spatio-temporal data, and location-based services. He collaborates actively with many companies in the business intelligence industry. He is a member of the SSTD Endowment, ACM, and IEEE. He serves on the editorial boards of the International Journal of Data Warehousing and Mining, Journal of Computer Science and Engineering, and LNCS Transactions on Large-Scale Data- and Knowledge-Centered Systems. He was PC Chair for DOLAP 2007 and DaWaK 2009 and 2010, and General Chair for SSTD 2009. He has served on more than 60 program committees, including VLDB, ICDE, and EDBT.

Wilma Penzo received the MS degree in Computer Science in 1993 from the University of Bologna, Italy, and the PhD degree in Electronic and Computer Engineering from the same University in 1997. Since 1996, she has been a Research Associate at the Department of Electronics and Computer Science (DEIS), University of Bologna, and at the IEIIT Institute of Italian CNR (National Council of Research). Her main research interests include query processing in the Semantic Web, semantic peer-to-peer systems, fuzzy query languages for multimedia databases, semistructured databases, indexing and query processing in XML digital libraries. In these fields, she is author of several papers in international journals and conferences in the database area.

Bruno Rienzi got his degree in Computer Engineering from University of the Republic (Uruguay) in 2004, and has, ever since, worked at the Computer Science Department where he holds a position as lecturer, alternating teaching with research. His research interests include Geographical Information Systems, Web services, service oriented architectures, and enterprise service buses. He has also worked in the industry as software developer and consultant, and has participated in European projects (Link All, IMSATV, ELU, COTV, ALIS), either integrating or leading the development teams from French and Luxembourgish partners. He is currently taking a Master's degree in Computer Science.

Stefano Rizzi received his Ph.D. in 1996 from the University of Bologna, Italy. Since 2005 he is Full Professor at the University of Bologna, where he is the head of the Data Warehousing Laboratory and teaches Business Intelligence and Software Engineering. He has published about 100 papers in refereed journals and international conferences mainly in the fields of data warehousing, pattern recognition, and mobile robotics, and a research book on data warehouse design. He joined several research projects on the above areas and has been involved in the PANDA thematic network of the European Union concerning pattern-based management systems. He is member of the steering committee of DOLAP. His current research interests include data warehouse design and business intelligence, in particular multidimensional modeling, OLAP preferences, and what-if analysis.

Oscar Romero has an MSc and a PhD in Computer Science from the Universitat Politècnica de Catalunya (Polytechnical University of Catalonia). He is a member of the MPI research group (Modelització i Processament de la Informació) at the same university, specializing in software engineering, databases, and Information Systems. His research interests are database design, data warehousing, OLAP tools, ontologies, and reasoning. He is the author of articles and papers in national and international conferences and journals on these subjects.

Philipp Rösch is Researcher and post-doc at SAP Research Dresden since 2009. He studied Computer Science at the TU Ilmenau with focus on database technologies and received his diploma in 2005. From 2005 to 2009, he was a Research Associate at the Database Technology Group of Prof. Lehner at the Technische Universität Dresden. There, his research focus was on approximate query answering based on random samples for the analysis of large-scale datasets. In 2009, he finished his Ph.D. and joined SAP Research Dresden. Now, Philipp's research addresses the efficient management and analysis of large-scale datasets.

Raul Ruggia is Computer Engineer (University of the Republic - Uruguay) and received his Ph.D. in Computer Science from the University of Paris VI (France). He works as Professor at the Computer Science Department of the University of the Republic of Uruguay, where he lectures on Information Systems, supervises graduate students and works on data quality management, data warehousing, and middleware areas. Formerly, he worked on design tools, data warehousing and bio-informatics, participating in Ibero-American (CYTED), Microsoft Research, and European projects (UE @LIS program). He has also supervised technological projects on environmental and telecommunications domains joint with Uruguayan government agencies.

Flavia Serra is a Teacher Assistant at the Computer Science Institute of the University of the Republic of Uruguay. She holds an Engineer in Computer Science degree, and since 2004, she has participated in research projects and teaching activities at this department. She is currently doing a Master's degree in Computer Science, where she is addressing the problem of Data Quality in Data Warehousing Systems.

Alkis Simitsis is with the Intelligent Information Management Laboratory at Hewlett-Packard. He obtained his Diploma on Electrical and Computer Engineering and a PhD in Computer Science from the National Technical University of Athens (NTUA) in 2000 and 2004, respectively. In the past, he has worked as a PostDoc research fellow at the Computer Science group at the IBM Almaden Research

Center and he was a research visitor at Infolab at Stanford University. His research interests include multi-objective optimization of information integration flows, real-time business intelligence, data cleaning, query processing/optimization, and user-friendly query interfaces focusing on keyword search and NLP techniques. He has published more than 60 papers in refereed journals and international conferences in the above areas and has served in many program committees of international conferences and workshops.

Il-Yeol Song is a Professor of the iSchool of Drexel University. His research interests include conceptual modeling, object-oriented analysis & design, data warehousing, CRM, and bioinformatics. He has published over 170 peer-reviewed papers. He has won three teaching awards from Drexel University, including the prestigious Lindback Distinguished Teaching Award in 2001. He is a co-author of the ASIS Pratt-Severn Excellence in Writing Award at National ASIS meeting (1997) and the Best Paper Award of in the IEEE CIBCB 2004. He won 14 research awards from competitions of annual Drexel Research Days. He is a Co-Editor-in-Chief of the Journal of Computing Science and Engineering (JCSE). He is also an Associate Editor for the JDM, IJEBR, JDFSL, and DKE. Dr. Song is currently a steering committee chair of the ER Conference. He served as a program/general chair of 20 international conferences, including DOLAP98, CIKM99, ER03, BP-UML06, DaWaK07, DaWaK08, DESRIST09, and CIKM09.

Maik Thiele has been working as a scientific employee at the Chair of Databases of TU Dresden's Computer Science faculty since April 2005. He finished his dissertation on "Quality-Driven Data Production Controlling in Real-Time DW Systems" in May 2010 and received his doctorate with distinction. His developed solutions, concepts, and algorithms have already been published in various conference and workshop contributions as well as in scientific magazines and books. During his time as a scientific employee, Maik Thiele worked in several industry projects, e.g. with the GfK Group, Nuremberg and with the USB AG in Zurich. Currently, Maik Thiele holds a post-doc position at TU Dresden's Chair of Databases.

Elisa Turricchia received her degree in Computer Science cum laude from the University of Bologna, Italy, in March 2009, presenting a thesis about interoperability issues among heterogeneous data warehouse systems. Currently, she is a PhD student at the Department of Electrical and Computer Engineering (DEIS) of Bologna. Her research interests include data warehouse design and pervasive business intelligence. In particular, her current work focuses on the study of methods for expressing and executing OLAP preference queries and for managing distributed data warehouses.

Panos Vassiliadis received his PhD from the National Technical University of Athens in 2000 and joined the Department of Computer Science of the University of Ioannina in 2002, where he works till this day. He is the co-editor of the book "Fundamentals of Data Warehouses" by Springer-Verlag and has more than 70 publications in international journals and conferences. Prof. Vassiliadis has served as a track co-chair for ICDE 2009 and CIKM 2009, PC chair for several workshops, as well as a reviewer for various journals and as a PC member for several conferences. Prof. Vassiliadis' research in the broader area of business intelligence spans the sub-areas of metadata and quality management, OLAP, and ETL. Recently, his research is focused on the area of information ecosystem evolution, where he has proposed the technique of architecture graphs as the means for charting the components of an ecosystem and managing its evolution. More information is available at http://www.cs.uoi.gr/~pvassil

Pedro Villar was born in Granada, Spain, on August 15, 1968. He received his MS degree in Computer Science in 1991 from the University of Granada, Spain and his PhD in Computer Science in 2000 from the University of Vigo, Spain. He joined the Department of Computer Science at the University of Vigo in October 1991, as an Assistant Professor, and from May 2002 until October 2004, he was an Associate Professor in the same department. Currently, he is an Associate Professor in the Department of Software Engineering at the University of Granada. His current main research interests are genetic fuzzy systems, evolutionary algorithms, and multi-objective genetic algorithms.

Lammert Vrieling [La-mert Free-ling] (1968) worked the last 15 years as consultant, trainer/coach, and as executive. Currently he is working as strategy consultant, CEO of Interanalytics, and as Professor and Researcher at Webster University Geneva. Lammert likes to think differently, is a challenger of the status quo, and functions well as a vision caster, strategiser, and encourager. He has a cum laude PhD in business administration. Lammert is an ENTP on the Myers Briggs personality inventory and his Strengthsfinder themes are: futurist, ideation, strategic, relator, and activator.

Wei Lee Woon received a B. Eng in Electronic Engineering with first class honours from UMIST, UK in 1997, and his PhD in 2002 from the Neural Computing Research Group at Aston University, Birmingham, UK. Upon graduation he joined the Malaysia University of Science and Technology (MUST) as an Assistant Professor, where he served until 2007. He subsequently joined the faculty of the Masdar Institute. Dr. Woon has also worked as a Visiting Researcher and a Research Affiliate at the Massachusetts Institute of Technology and at the RIKEN Brain Science Institute in Tokyo. His research interests are centered around the analysis of large data sets. Recent examples include technology mining, text analysis, and EEG signal analysis.

Felix Wortmann is Research Project Manager and post-doc at the Institute of Information Management at the University of St. Gallen since 2009. He studied Information Systems at the WWU Münster, Germany, where he received his Master's in 2002. Dr. Wortmann worked as a Research Assistant at the University of St. Gallen, Institute of Information Management from 2002 to 2006. He received his Ph.D. in 2006 and transferred to SAP where he worked as an Assistant to the executive board until 2009. Since 2009 he heads the research group "Information Logistics Management" at the chair of Prof. Dr. Robert Winter. This research group focuses on business intelligence and data warehousing and works in close cooperation with several national and multinational companies.

Stefan Zöller is BI consultant with more than eight years of experience now. In 2010, Stefan joined Knauf Gips KG; before, he was responsible for all BI related topics at IBIS Prof. Thome AG. In that field, he developed content for IBIS own RBE Plus analysis methods and for BI related configuration content. In the EU IP-SUPER project, he participated in different areas reaching from business process analysis to general business process lifecycle topics. Between 2002 and 2005, Stefan worked as (senior) consultant with BearingPoint GmbH, Frankfurt am Main, in world-wide SAP implementation projects. Until 2002, he studied Business Administration at the University of Wuerzburg.

Index